Working Bibliography of the BALD EAGLE

by

Jeffrey L. Lincer
William S. Clark
and Maurice N. LeFranc, Jr.

with a Foreword

by

Dean Amadon

Published as Number 2 of the NWF Scientific/Technical Series

**Raptor Information Center
National Wildlife Federation
1412 Sixteenth Street, N. W.
Washington, D. C. 20036**

Library of Congress Cataloging in Publication Data

Lincer, Jeffrey L.   1943-
  Working bibliography of the bald eagle

(NWF scientific/technical series; no. 2)
  1. Bald eagle—Bibliography. 2. Birds—Bibliography. I. Clark, William S., 1937- joint author. II. LeFranc, Maurice N., 1951- joint author. III. Title. IV. Series: National Wildlife Federation. NWF scientific/technical series; no. 2.
Z5333.B34L56 [QL696.F32] 016.5989'1 79-3972
ISBN 0-912186-29-1

Copyright 1979, National Wildlife Federation
Library of Congress Catalog Card Number 79-3972
Cataloging in Publication Data

MAN'S PROBLEM

Dedicated by the senior author to Carolyn, Wendy and Christy for
their understanding and their love of all things bright and beautiful.

I find in me a need to write
Of what I'm not quite sure
Of birds of prey, who hunt by night
Or peregrines who hunt no more.

What is this thing we call mankind
Who acts in haste without a mind
How many times must we endure
The tragedies of man's own lore.

What makes us think that we can say
What is the best for Nature's way
Of timeless testing She can boast
To endless avarice we can toast.

The Problem should be more than clear
What man ignores year after year
Is that he like all the rest
Is but part of Nature's nest.

J. L. Lincer

National Wildlife Federation

1412 16TH ST., N.W., WASHINGTON, D.C. 20036   202—797-6800

PREFACE

The National Wildlife Federation, the world's largest nonprofit conservation education organization, has long been concerned about the reduction in numbers of our National Symbol, the bald eagle, and has been in the forefront of the efforts to understand and halt this decrease.

The Federation has purchased important tracts of bald eagle winter habitat in South Dakota, Wisconsin, California and Illinois. We set up the Raptor Information Center with primary emphasis on bald eagle projects using funds from a grant from the EXXON Corporation.

It is through the efforts of the Center that we can make available this <u>Working Bibliography of the Bald Eagle</u>, the second publication in our Scientific/Technical Series. It will be a useful companion to a <u>Working Bibliography of Owls of the World</u>, the first publication in the series.

This bibliography will be greatly helpful to researchers, wildlife managers and many others who are working with the bald eagle and it will serve as a comprehensive guide to the literature on our National Symbol. It will facilitate the incorporation of research findings into wildlife policies and decisions.

Future volumes in this series will include additional raptor bibliographies. The Raptor Information Center is preparing a bibliography on the golden eagle and other members of the genus <u>Aquila</u> and is joining with the authors of a peregrine falcon bibliography in an effort to bring that to press.

It is with great pleasure that we offer this publication.

THOMAS L. KIMBALL
Executive Vice President

March, 1979

TABLE OF CONTENTS

PAGE

FOREWORD.. ix

CHAPTER 1   INTRODUCTION..................................... 1

    HISTORICAL PERSPECTIVE.. 1
    TAXONOMY... 4
    DISTRIBUTION... 4
    LIFE HISTORY... 4
    LIMITING FACTORS AND MANAGEMENT.............................. 6
    THE BIBLIOGRAPHY AND HOW TO USE IT........................... 7
    ACKNOWLEDGEMENTS... 10
    LITERATURE CITED... 11

CHAPTER 2   THE STATUS OF THE BALD EAGLE..................... 13

    TABLE 1   BALD EAGLE NUMBERS, PRESENT vs. HISTORICAL..................... 16
    TABLE 2   CURRENT BALD EAGLE RESEARCH................................... 30

CHAPTER 3   MASTER LIST OF CITATIONS......................... 35

CHAPTER 4   PERMUTED LIST OF KEYWORDS........................ 83

APPENDIX A   DICTIONARY OF KEYWORDS.......................... A1

FOREWORD

The symbol of the United States for its two centuries of existence, the bald eagle, has also become a symbol of our country's emerging awareness of its natural heritage and the imperative need to conserve and restore that heritage. The rampant conquest of nature, as civilization pushed west across the continent, shouldered aside or destroyed wildlife, forest, and even the Indians, who saw in the shining plumes of the eagle a mark of courage and manhood. Save for farsighted individuals, such as Audubon and Thoreau, few found in the eagle anything more than a target for the Winchester rifle that accompanied the settler and cattleman.

So it was that, even by the beginning of this century, our National Symbol had been sadly reduced in numbers--often restricted to wilderness or semi-wilderness areas such as the more desolate parts of Maine or the mangrove expanses of Florida Bay. What might well have been the coup de grace for the bald eagle occurred in the 1940's with the introduction and widespread use of DDT and other chlorine-containing pesticides. A precipitous decline was soon evident in the bald eagle and other fish-eating predators such as the osprey, as well as in some other raptorial birds, notably the peregrine falcon.

Eagles and falcons are quick to detect and single out prey that is sub-par. It is for this reason that predators have had, throughout the millenia of evolution, the effect of weeding out the infirm or defective. The verve and grace of a salmon, a wild turkey, or a deer, are not accidental--they are the end product of natural selection in fleeing from predators.

With the advent of "hard" pesticides, the fish flopping helplessly at the surface, and hence attracting the eagle, is not now suffering from natural debilities--it is more often impaired by an overload of DDT or other toxic chemicals. And the eagle, by unwittingly selecting such prey, is getting more than its share--not of chemotherapy, but of "chemo-malady." Even if the eagle is not killed outright, the chlorochemicals affect its calcium metabolism and it lays thin-shelled or defective eggs that do not hatch. An example is a pair of bald eagles which for the last 15 years or more have annually nested, or one should say, attempted to nest, on the wooded slopes above a beautiful lake in western New York. A local naturalist found that this pair hatched and reared only one young in the past dozen years. This was the result of heavy spraying of the nearby forest with DDT in the 1950's. (Even though this lake is one source of the domestic water supply for the city of Rochester, New York!)

Can such dismal incidents and trends be reversed? There is some reason for hope. Quite apart from the immediate wildlife victims, it is becoming increasingly apparent that blundering, exploitative raping of the environment must stop if mankind itself is to survive.

More and more cancer is being linked to a polluted environment. Natural resources are dwindling and must be used more wisely. And then, too, the insects, far more genetically adjustable than slow reproducers like the eagle--or man--are becoming immune to the chemicals used to control them and we must perforce turn to less environmentally destructive methods of containing them, such as diversified agriculture, biological controls, and the use of sex attractants and sterilizers. The harsher pesticides have been banned in the United States and are being phased out elsewhere. The resulting improvement in the reproduction of species such as ospreys and bald eagles is already apparent.

Equally important, public and private agencies have stepped forward to man the barricades and oppose, or better, when possible, to educate, the still formidable forces that are slow to take a long-term perspective in seeking the good of our country and indeed the world.

Foremost among such agencies in the United States is the National Wildlife Federation, which sponsors and conducts many activities to instill an appreciation of nature and an awareness of the need for conservation. The present Working Bibliography of the Bald Eagle is an imaginative product of one arm of the National Wildlife Federation --the Raptor Information Center, under the guidance of Bill Clark, its present director, and Jeff Lincer who preceded him. In this bibliography, there are 2,000 references on the bald eagle. They are not merely listed, but are key-worded by subject and geographic area, so that one may easily find those references pertaining to almost any particular field of interest. For those whose research impels or requires them to dig deeper, this bibliography will save innumerable hours searching for specific references. Thus the bibliography has great intrinsic value for those interested in our National Symbol from whatever point of view. Further, it joins with the companion Working Bibliography of Owls of the World, to serve as models for other related efforts in codifying and making more available the scattered literature required by the increasingly sophisticated environmental impact studies initiated by today's conservationists.

Meanwhile, the patient pair of eagles in western New York-- apparently the only remaining resident pair in that state--have profited from the increased interest in the fate of this fine bird that has resulted in no small part from the labors of the National Wildlife Federation. In 1978 the single egg they laid in their lofty eyrie was infertile, indicating that pesticides have still not fully worked their way out of the environment. Biologists of the New York State Department of Environmental Conservation came to the rescue. They were able to obtain a bald eagle chick, which had been hatched in captivity, from the United States Fish and Wildlife Service. This was placed in the nest and for the first time since 1973 these eagles raised a youngster. It has fledged and we hope it will do its part to help in the comeback of the bald eagle in the northeast. Perhaps the time will come when visitors to Niagara Falls may, for the first time since colonial days, observe bald eagles in the gorge below the Falls, seeking their prey among the fish and wildfowl that come to grief as they are swept over the cataract. With dedicated effort, comparable opportunities to admire and study the bald eagle and other threatened wildlife can be made available throughout the length and breadth of North America.

Dean Amadon
American Museum of
    Natural History
New York, New York

CHAPTER 1.

INTRODUCTION

HISTORICAL PERSPECTIVE

From time immemorial, eagles have been admired as the kings of birds.
From ancient mythology we learn that they were held sacred even by
Jove. As early as 3500 B.C., the Sumerians, and then, three millenia
later, the Romans, made the eagle their symbol. By 800 A.D.
Charlemagne had adopted the eagle as his symbol, and later, in the
Middle Ages, the Crusades again found the eagle as a symbol of a
cause. In more recent times, many countries including France, Prussia,
Italy and Mexico have followed suit.

It was quite natural then for the United States to adopt her own
native species, the bald eagle, to adorn her standard. Nevertheless,
it took six years and three committees before the Continental Congress
decided on the bald eagle as America's National Symbol. On June 20,
1782, that declaration was made over the protests of Benjamin
Franklin, who favored the turkey. This was not the first recognition
of the beauty and power of the bald eagle in America; the American
Indians had long worshipped this eagle for these and other qualities.

During the first century as America's Symbol, our eagle fared
well. Perhaps the most famous of all bald eagles was "Old Abe,"
the war eagle who was named after Abraham Lincoln. A Chippewa Indian
chief in northern Wisconsin had traded him for a bushel of corn.
The eagle was subsequently presented to the newly formed Company 'C'
of the 8th Wisconsin Regiment to be their mascot. But that was only
the beginning for Old Abe. He was said to have inspired many a
soldier during no fewer than 25 battles and as his fame grew, so did
his worth. The showman, P. T. Barnum, was so impressed that he
offered $20,000 for Old Abe. He was not sold, however, but was
presented to the Governor of Wisconsin. Old Abe spent his remaining
years (until 1881) in the then new State House in Madison, Wisconsin,
frequently appearing at patriotic affairs and rallies. He represented
Wisconsin at the Philadelphia Centennial of 1876.

However, while Old Abe was doing well, the bald eagle population was
declining, primarily because of the activities of man. During the
late 1800's, expanding human populations began taking over and modify-
ing bald eagle nesting habitat to the exclusion of the eagles. Other
activities of man, such as egg collecting, shooting and trapping
also contributed to the decline.

Bounties, too, added incentive for the killing of bald eagles. Most
states offered bounties on eagles and other raptors until recently.
In Alaska, for instance, during the 18 years from 1923 to 1940, the
Territory paid almost $100,000 for the destruction of 103,459 bald
eagles.

It was not until June 8, 1940, when Congress enacted the Bald Eagle
Protection Act (Title 54, Stat. 256), that the National Symbol was
granted any significant legal protection. With enactment of that Act,
anyone who would "...take, possess, sell, purchase, barter, offer to
sell, purchase or barter, transport, export or import, at any time
or in any manner..." any bald eagle, whether dead or alive, would be
subject to a $500 fine and/or six months imprisonment. The Act
excluded the Alaskan bald eagle, and it was not until March 2, 1953,
that the bounty was repealed in Alaska.

By the 1950's, a growing awareness of the value of our raptors was
reflected in the enactment of total protection of these birds by
almost all states. However, despite the increased protection,
decreasing numbers of these predators, especially bald eagles,
ospreys and peregrine falcons, continued to be recorded each year.

One of the most colorful individuals associated with the bald eagle
was Charles Broley. After retiring in 1938 from the banking business
in Manitoba, Canada, Broley began banding eaglets in Florida. Before
he was done, he was to band no fewer than 1,200 eaglets, a feat
which gained him the nickname "Eagle Man." Had it not been for
Broley's work, we would not have realized that Florida-hatched eagles
flew north after fledging, sometimes as far as Nova Scotia and
Winnipeg!

Broley was one of the first to characterize the decrease in bald
eagle reproductive success. He estimated in 1957 that 80% of his
Florida birds were, in his words, "sterile." In 1946, 56 nests
which were being watched by Broley produced 103 young. In 1957,
only seven of these nests successfully raised a total of eight young.
In an incisive analysis of the situation, the total ramifications of
which he would never know, Broley linked the spraying of DDT to the
eagle's reproductive failure.

The National Audubon Society's Continental Bald Eagle Project began
in 1960 and was the first significant step toward determining the
extent of the decline and how many bald eagles were left. Not only
were initial population estimates made, but for the first time,
organized data began to be accumulated which linked man's activities
to the population decline of the National Symbol. Changes in land-
use, shooting and DDT were at the top of the list.

Federal agencies began to act to help the eagle in this, its time of
need. Some of these activities are recounted below. The first
agency to identify and protect bald eagle nests and habitat on public lands was the U.S. Forest Service, which initiated a bald eagle
management policy in 1962.

The 1966 Endangered Species Act resulted in the "southern bald eagle"
being listed by the U.S. Fish and Wildlife Service as "Endangered" in
1967. The "southern" race of the bald eagle was arbitrarily chosen
as those breeding south of the 40th parallel.

Legal mechanisms to protect habitat essential to the bald eagle have played a very important role in our saga. With the help of the then Secretary of the Interior, Stewart Udall, eagle nesting sites in all National Wildlife Refuges have been protected from disturbance since 1966.

In 1971, Congress put more teeth into the Eagle Protection Act by increasing the fine for molesting an eagle to $5,000 and/or a one-year imprisonment (double these penalties for repeat offenders). This was probably in response to the shooting of nearly 500 bald and golden eagles from helicopters over ranches in Wyoming and Colorado.

In 1972, the value of the bald eagle as a natural resource was fully recognized by the Alaska state legislature, when HB 614 was signed into law. Its purpose was to protect and preserve habitat areas that were especially crucial to the perpetuation of fish and wildlife and to restrict all other uses not compatible with that purpose. As a result, an important stretch of the Chilkat River, which supports up to 3,500 wintering bald eagles, was listed.

Similar recognition of the widespread damage of non-specific poisons finally reached the President's Office in 1973. On February 8, then President Nixon issued an Executive Order which banned the use of poisons for predator control on public lands.

The 1973 Endangered Species Act changed the criteria for listing endangered species. On February 14, 1978, the Department of the Interior officially listed the bald eagle (as a species) as "Endangered" in 43 of the 48 contiguous states and "Threatened" in the other five: Minnesota, Wisconsin, Michigan, Oregon and Washington.

Recently, many federal, state and private organizations have been censusing the bald eagles that winter in the "lower 48." Observations on these wintering birds by the U.S. Fish and Wildlife Service, state wildlife agencies, the National Wildlife Federation, the National Audubon Society and notable individuals like Elton Fawks, have provided us with some insight into the dynamics of these populations. In a continuing effort to understand this phenomenon, the National Wildlife Federation's Raptor Information Center has undertaken the job of coordinating a Midwinter Bald Eagle Census. This study, which began in January 1979 coordinates and analyzes the observations of qualified individuals, private organizations and state and federal agencies.

A reawakening to the plight of the bald eagle accompanied the Nation's Bicentennial in 1976. People began to ask piercing questions such as: "What has happened to our National Symbol?"; "How many are left?"; "What caused the decline?"; and "What can we do to help?"

In response, the National Wildlife Federation, with a grant from the Exxon Corporation, set the wheels in motion to create a bald eagle data bank. Out of that initial effort, grew the Federation's Raptor Information Center (RIC).

3

The objectives of the Raptor Information Center are to: (1) Identify and protect critical raptor habitat; (2) Increase communications among raptor scientists and managers; (3) Monitor raptor populations; and (4) Identify and encourage the support of priority raptor research. In that the very genesis of the RIC was the recognition of, and response to, a need for a bald eagle data bank, it seems particularly fitting that one of the first of many RIC working bibliographies should be on this species. The production of this computer-generated, keyworded bibliography helps the RIC to meet <u>all</u> of these goals. These bibliographies are published by the RIC as issues of the Federation's new Scientific/Technical Series.

TAXONOMY

The bald eagle is taxonomically placed in the Order Falconiformes and the Family Accipitridae. Of some historic interest is the derivation of the word "bald." It came from the Middle English and Welsh, "balde," and means "white." The bald eagle is not really bald at all, but white-headed. It has been variously called the sea eagle, the white-headed sea eagle, the American eagle, the black and brown eagle, the white-tailed eagle, the fish eagle, the Washington eagle, the gray eagle and the mottled eagle. From the taxonomic standpoint, it has over the years been assigned a myriad of scientific names, including: <u>Falco leucocephalus</u> (1776), <u>Falco pygargus</u> (1880), <u>Aquila capite</u> (1731), <u>Aquila leucocephala</u> (1807), <u>Falco ossifragus</u> (1809), <u>Falco washingtonianus</u> (1832), <u>Falco washingtonii</u> (1827), <u>Haliaeetus washingtonii</u> (1840), <u>Pandion washingtonii</u> (1856) and now <u>Haliaeetus leucocephalus</u> (1898). Each name change reflects a better understanding of the taxonomic relationship among raptors.

DISTRIBUTION

The bald eagle is the only eagle with a distribution restricted to North America. In general, this raptor, like many of the related sea eagles, is found along undisturbed sea coasts or associated with large inland lakes and rivers. It can be found from the Gulf of Mexico to the Arctic, and during migration, it is often seen along mountain ridges. After the nesting season, the more northern birds migrate south, in response to a reduced food source as the lakes freeze.

To complicate the picture, during their first summer bald eagles from Florida and other southern states demonstrate a post-fledging northward "migration" or dispersal, which takes them as far north as the Canadian Maritime Provinces.

LIFE HISTORY

Although there are exceptions, both the nesting and wintering habitats of this species are usually associated with large bodies of water which support an adequate food source. Super-canopy trees of various species are most often the bald eagle's choice for a nest platform, but smaller trees, such as mangroves in southern Florida, are used in the absence of larger trees. In fact, nesting on the ground, cliffs and seastacks has been reported from a number of locations.

Winter habitat often differs from that required for nesting and is many times less closely associated with water. Many of the northern eagles roost communally in the wintering grounds, usually in groves of trees which provide shelter from the weather and human disturbance.

Prey species vary considerably depending on location, time of year and population cycles of prey species. Without a doubt, fish are the primary prey (often representing 80-90 percent of the diet), but the bald eagle is opportunistic and will take avian, mammalian and even reptilian prey when available. Carrion, especially on the wintering grounds, will also be taken when readily available. However, since most detailed bald eagle prey studies have been conducted during the breeding season, and to a lesser extent, the winter season, very little is known about the prey of the subadults and non-breeding adults.

Hunting behavior depends on the type of prey being pursued. Usually, these predators hunt from perches close to water, but they will also hunt while in flight. Fish too heavy to be lifted from the water are dragged to shore using the wings, in a rowing motion, as "oars." On numerous occasions, two or more eagles have been observed "cooperating" in the pursuit of ducks, coots and rabbits. They take turns chasing the prey until the hapless bird or mammal becomes too exhausted to avoid the eagles' attack. Of course, no discussion of bald eagle hunting behavior, no matter how brief, would be complete without mention of the occasional fish that is stolen from ospreys and other fish-eating birds. Wintering eagles have been observed using other hunting techniques, including wading into the water to catch fish with their beaks and hunting from the edge of ice floes.

In discussing potential prey species, one has to be aware of the limited weight-lifting capacity of eagles. Innumerable "accounts" (in non-scientific literature) of eagles carrying off babies, deer and livestock could be seen in their true light if the public realized a few facts. For instance, bald eagles usually weigh between three and seven kilograms. Actual experiments with the anatomically similar golden eagle have shown that flight was strained and of very limited duration when the bird was forced to carry 1.8 kilograms. When attempting to carry 3.6 kilograms, the eagle strenuously flapped its wings, but could fly a maximum of 14 meters. (For comparison, an average deer might weigh 25 kilograms.)

The onset of the nesting season varies with latitude, beginning as early as November in Florida and as late as February and March in Alaska and Ontario. During the courtship period, the bald eagles engage in aerial somersaults and other displays which are always spectacular to watch. The pair builds, or adds to, a large stick nest and the female eagle lays one to three eggs. Incubation is shared by both parents and lasts approximately 35 days.

The newly hatched young are covered with white down, which gives way to a heavier gray down at two to three weeks. At four to five weeks, feathers appear, wing-flapping begins and by 10 to 11 weeks, the dark-colored young start to fledge. Because of the time needed to develop strong flight muscles and a fine-tuned hunting ability, young eagles continue to be dependent on the adults for many weeks after fledging.

After going through several mottled plumages, each of which identifies it as being immature, the eagle reaches sexual maturity at about five years of age. With this comes the white head and tail of the mature adult.

Unfortunately little is known about the length of time that eagles are sexually active or even how long they live. Bald eagles in captivity have lived as long as 50 years.

LIMITING FACTORS AND MANAGEMENT

Before the European settlers arrived, the factors which negatively impinged upon the bald eagle's breeding success were probably limited to severe weather, especially hurricanes, and occasional nest predators. The picture changed drastically with the progress of civilization. Now we have to add to this list the widespread impacts of environmental biocides, loss of habitat (especially from development and logging) and the needless mortality resulting from inadvertent trapping and illegal shooting. Other important, yet more often localized factors, include impact injuries (with powerlines, towers, cars and trains), electrocution, death from eating poisoned carcasses left for other predators, and disturbance at the nest site (which may lead to loss or abandonment of eggs and/or young).

To ensure that bald eagles will be seen by our children, we must intelligently manage our interactions with this endangered natural resource. Strong stands must continue to be taken against the manufacture and use of persistent biocides which affect species other than the target organisms. Critical habitat must be identified and protected from changes in land-use and from other human activities incompatible with the needs of healthy bald eagle populations. Adequate protection from wanton killing, including firm law enforcement and intensive local public education, is a must. Efforts to bolster waning populations, including the transfer of young and eggs, captive breeding and habitat improvement, should be encouraged.

Above all, the public and their elected decision-makers must be kept informed of the bald eagle's needs so that it can survive in harmony with man. Our representatives also need to understand the role that the bald eagle, other raptors and predators play, as "bioindicators" of the environment. Without this awareness, few protective laws will be passed and fewer yet funds will be made available to protect habitat or support the needed research, the platform upon which intelligent land and wildlife management is based.

THE BIBLIOGRAPHY AND HOW TO USE IT

Scope. Our intent was to include in this publication almost anything
written about the bald eagle. We found that almost all references
were written in English because of this eagle's North American distribution. Although more than 2,000 references are included in this
bibliography, it is very possible that some were missed. Because the
bibliographic data is in computer form, additions and editing can
be easily incorporated for future printings. Therefore, please do
not hesitate to let us know what we have missed. We would also
appreciate any suggestions that would improve the utility of the book.

How Bibliography was Produced. In an effort to help our readers
better utilize this bibliography, we provide this methods section.
We began this effort by extracting bald eagle citations from the
raptor bibliography compiled by the Olendorffs (1968), from an
unpublished USF&W Service Report (Tilt, W. R. - 1976) and from an
unpublished list of references compiled by Al Stumpf, Bureau of
Reclamation.

The bald eagle citations thus identified were entered onto 5" x 8"
index cards. These cards were initially catalogued by journal or
source to facilitate document acquisition. An effort was made to
locate citations to journal articles, state and federal agency reports,
theses, dissertations, unpublished reports and manuscripts and other
non-periodical literature, the so-called "underground literature."

Reprint request cards and personal letters were sent out to many
authors in an effort to acquire copies of documents, but unfortunately
the response was quite low. Advertisements requesting bald eagle
literature were placed in Raptor Research, The Eyas, and other news-
letters and journals. A computer search for bald eagle references
was conducted by the Biological Information Service of Los Angeles,
which provided a few new citations.

After approximately 1,500 citations were identified and catalogued,
acquisition of the documents began. A methodical search for these
documents included many visits to the Library of Congress, the
Smithsonian Institution's Division of Birds Library, the Department
of Interior Library, and the Agriculture Library. Every reference
found was photocopied and filed at the Raptor Information Center.
Many of the references acquired were sources of additional citations
through their literature cited sections.

During the acquisition stage, the senior author began reading and
assigning keywords to each reference. Using the procedures developed
by the Denver Public Library Service for the U.S. Fish and Wildlife
Service, a Dictionary of Keywords was developed. This is included
as Appendix A, following Chapter 4. A brief discussion of the philosophy behind keyword selection can be found later in this section.

The keywords were then included with the citation on 5" X 8" cards.
The citation cards were put into a standard format and were rechecked

against the document for accuracy. Lastly, edit marks were placed on the citation cards to be used later for printing purposes. The cards were entered onto magnetic storage media by the National Wildlife Federation Data Entry Department.

The complete data set was edited for accuracy and typographical errors using a printed listing of the citations. The corrected data were then transferred to Port City Press, the printer.

The Raptor Information Center contracted with Port City Press to computer process the data set from its original form on magnetic storage media to final printed copy. The data was first arranged alphabetically by author. This is included as Chapter 3, the Master List of Citations. Each citation was sequentially assigned a number, referred to as the Master Number of that reference. Next, a list of permuted keywords with associated Master Numbers was produced which allows the user to find citations referring to specific bald eagle subject areas. A more in-depth description of the methodology follows later in this chapter.

Organization of the Bibliography. This book is organized in a relatively simple, straightforward manner, making it easy to use for the reader, regardless of whether he is a scholar, teacher, scientist, wildlife manager or political decision-maker.

Following this Introduction, Chapter 2 presents a discussion on the status of the bald eagle. In that chapter we discuss the breeding and wintering distribution at the state and provincial level, including the latest information and indicating where information is lacking. We attempted to include any available historic information. Also presented is a summary of present bald eagle research.

Chapter 3 presents a listing of 2,000 bald eagle references. These references have been arranged alphabetically by author, using standard bibliographic guidelines. This will allow the reader to find references of any known author. In addition, these alphabetized references have been assigned sequential Master Numbers. These numbers are the connecting links between the keywords in Chapter 4 and the references in Chapter 3. The efficient use of these keywords is discussed below in the section entitled "Saving Time Using the Bibliography."

Chapter 4 is a permuted list of keyword strings, sorted alphabetically on the first keyword. These range from Account to Yukon and include geographic names such as the states, provinces, large drainage basins, national parks or refuges and well-known locations. These keywords lead the user to a reference by its associated Master Number. Each keyword is followed by an alphabetized list of all the other keywords that were assigned to that particular reference, to provide added insight into the content of that reference. The user does not have to rely solely on a single term to find the reference, however, since computerized permutation has rearranged the set of terms so that each term is presented first in the sequence. That is, if the terms: "Chippewa NF" (National Forest), "Growth," "MN" (Minnesota), and

"Nest." were assigned to an article, the list would appear in Chapter 4 under the C's, wherever "Chippewa NF" would occur in the alphabetical arrangement of the initial keywords. Next, the computer rearranged the terms in the following sequence: "MN," "Chippewa NF," "Growth," and "Nest." This sequence of terms would be found under the M's, wherever "MN" falls. Likewise for "Growth" and "Nest."

Appendix A is a dictionary of all keywords including a description of those whose meaning is not readily apparent.

Saving Time Using the Bibliography. This section might just as likely have been called, "The Use and Misuse of Keywords." As pointed out above, a reference can be identified directly by searching for the name of the first author in Chapter 3. In most cases, however, the user will not know the name of the author(s) but will know the geographic location or aspect of the bald eagle he wants to investigate. With this knowledge, the user simply looks up the keyword in Chapter 4, which lists these terms alphabetically. For instance, if you want to identify all those references which pertain to artificial nest sites, you simply look through the terms in Chapter 4 until you find the term "Art. Nest Site." On the left side of this term you will see its associated Master Number. Note that this is only the first of several references dealing with artificial nest sites. To find the actual reference, enter Chapter 3 with the Master Number and locate the reference.

Notice also that the first set of keywords beginning with "Art. Nest Site" also includes the terms: "MN", "Manage.", "Nest.", "Habit. Use", "Behav." and "Young Trans." These additional terms are presented to give you a better idea of what is contained in that particular article. Since that list of keywords has been rearranged several times, such that each term has begun the sequence once, you could just as easily have found this Master Number by looking up any of the other keywords.

But what about multiple keyword searches? For instance, what if you want to quickly identify all those references that discuss nesting surveys in California? This can be done one of two ways. You can either look up "Nest. Survey" (in Chapter 4) and then look through each set of keywords that begins with this term for the keyword "CA" or vice versa. You can be more specific by adding yet another term or you can be more general in your search by looking up only one term. The choice is yours.

Before completing this section, we include a few words concerning the philosophy behind the choice of keywords.

Often a user knows only that a certain organization carried out some work on the bald eagle. For that reason, wherever appropriate, the names of agencies and organizations (e.g. U.S. Fish and Wildlife Service, U.S. Forest Service, National Wildlife Federation, National Audubon Society, Nature Conservancy) have been assigned to references, when appropriate. These references can be identified by searching Chapter 4 by organizational keyword.

References dealing with field research and observations were assigned at least one of several levels of geographic keywords. Although very few references refer to countries outside of the United States and Canada, when they did occur, the country was used as the keyword. Whenever the reference referred to work which occurred in the United States or Canada, the state or province, respectively, was used. When more than ten of the contiguous states were involved, as with a large nesting survey, the term "Lower 48" was used. When a recognized region (like the Great Lakes Region or the Chesapeake Bay Region) was involved, the region was chosen. Since much bald eagle work has taken place among major rivers, in National Forests and in National Wildlife Refuges, their names were used wherever possible.

Keep in mind that every geographical level was not always assigned to each reference because of priorities on space and keywords. Therefore, when using this bibliography, you should try several levels of geographic identification during your search so that your efforts will be most productive.

However, there is room for ambiguity in the definition of some of the keywords. A Dictionary of Keywords (Appendix A) is included which describes the meaning of possibly confusing keywords. The user is encouraged to look up the keywords to be used for searching in Appendix A before searching through Chapter 4. A considerable amount of time might be saved. For instance, the term "Nest." as used in this bibliography, has a somewhat different meaning than the term "Nest. Survey." Similarly, "Winter. Pop." has a different meaning than does "Winter Survey." A quick check into Appendix A for the exact meanings of keywords will often result in an increase in the utility of this bibliography.

The Raptor Information Center holds copies of all the references listed in Chapter 3. Any bald eagle researcher or wildlife manager is welcome to read or look over these documents at the Center, but the Center will not be able to send out copies of these.

ACKNOWLEDGEMENTS

As always, we stand on the shoulders of those giants who go before us. We are particularly grateful to the Olendorffs for producing their bibliography on eagles and other raptors. That document saved us much effort in the identification of the bald eagle literature up to the mid-1960's.

We would also like to thank the following individuals and organizations for their help: the Fish and Wildlife Reference Service; the U.S. Fish and Wildlife Service; various state wildlife agencies too numerous to list; Jim Ruos, U.S. Fish and Wildlife Service, for coordination with the Department of the Interior Library; Kate Bailey, former NWF Librarian, for help with Inter-library loans; and the many authors who provided reprints of their articles. We want to acknowledge the considerable contribution of Keith Cline, who ferreted out numerous references and gave us assistance in many other areas and Valerie Campbell, who initiated the search for bald eagle citations. A special thanks goes to the Art Department here at the National Wildlife Federation, especially to Mary Ann Smith and Tina Bandle, who did their usual excellent job.

We thank Chuck Weigand, Gary McPherson and John Oster of Port City Press for their considerable input into the preparation of this book.

Other thanks are due to Lesley Beardow for help in coordination and manuscript preparation and to Pam Von Herbulis and Mary Ann Cubbison for their excellent job of data entry of the citations and keywords. We also thank the Library of Congress, the Main Department of Interior Library and the Smithsonian Institution Division of Birds Library for making their facilities more than just "available."

LITERATURE CITED

Olendorff, R. R. and S. E. Olendorff. 1968. An Extensive Bibliography on Falconry, Eagles, Hawks, Falcons, and Other Diurnal Birds of Prey. (Published by Authors.)

CHAPTER 2.

THE STATUS OF THE BALD EAGLE

One of the questions most frequently asked by the public about wildlife is, "How is the bald eagle doing?" The status of the bald eagle is also of much interest to the raptor biologist, birder, and the wildlife managers of our state and federal wildlife agencies, as well as many other amateurs and professionals. The symbol of the United States has a unique place among wildlife. It is more than just a species because it represents the many values and goals of the Nation. Therefore, how it is doing as a species is a matter of great concern.

Bendire, in 1892, stated:

> "The bald or American eagle, our national emblem, is pretty generally distributed over the entire United States, and breeds more or less abundantly according to food supply along the Atlantic seacoast, from northern Maine to Florida and from the Gulf of Mexico throughout the total length of the Mississippi Valley and the larger streams and lakes of the interior, as well as British North America, to the Arctic coast. It is quite abundant on the Pacific coast, and especially common at the mouth of the Columbia River, the shores of British Columbia and the Alaska mainland, as well as on all the Aleutian Islands. It appears to be equally indifferent to extreme heat or cold, but in the northern-most portions of its range it is only a summer resident, leaving these inhospitable regions and retiring to a warmer climate as soon as the rivers and lakes freeze up, which furnish it with most of its food supply."

However, as is the trend for many of our wildlife species, the number of bald eagles in the continental United States has steadily decreased from pre-colonial times to the present. Habitat destruction, shooting, trapping and egg collecting have been factors contributing to the decline. Recently, persistent pesticides have caused a severe crash in an already dwindling population within the conterminous United States. Only after mankind's recent concern about the possibility of extinction of the bald eagle has there been an optimistic outlook for the fate of this raptor.

The bald eagle is given legal protection by three separate Federal laws in the U.S.: the Bald Eagle Protection Act of 1940, the Migratory Bird Treaty Act of 1918 and the Endangered Species Act of 1966. It is also covered by State law in all states except Hawaii, where the species does not occur. In Canada, the bald eagle is protected in all provinces by Provincial law.

In 1978, the bald eagle was classified as "Endangered" in all the 48 contiguous states except five under the Endangered Species Act. In the five states, Washington, Oregon, Minnesota, Wisconsin and Michigan, it is classified as "Threatened."

Table 1 is a listing by state and province of the present and historically known status of the bald eagle. The information is further delineated by breeding and wintering numbers. The breeding and wintering range of the bald eagle is restricted to North America except for a few visitants to Europe and Asia.

Most of the data in this table concerning the present breeding and wintering status of the bald eagle were presented at a bald eagle symposium sponsored by the Raptor Information Center in conjunction with the Raptor Research Foundation's annual meeting at Allentown, Pa., on November 3, 1978.

The estimate of the number of breeding pairs of bald eagles for the lower 48 states from the data in Table 1 is between 1159 and 1170. This estimate should be considered a minimum and 1200 pairs is probably the best estimate to date.

The number of bald eagles wintering in the lower 48 states, from a composite of censuses, is a minimum of 8300 individuals (Table 1). The annual midwinter census sponsored by the Raptor Information Center should provide a more accurate measure of the wintering population. It is felt that in addition to the 1200 breeding pairs in the lower 48 states and their offspring, an additional 20,000 individuals may join them every winter from Canada and Alaska.

The historic information in Table 1 is presented to allow the reader to see the type of distributional information collected in the past. Unfortunately, this type of anecdotal and random observational data and vague reporting makes comparison with the present status almost impossible. The only thing most people agree on is that the number of bald eagles breeding in the lower 48 states has declined, in some areas rather markedly. The major causes for this decline are discussed in Chapter 1.

On the bright side, research efforts are under way in almost every state by federal and state agencies and by private or university-affiliated researchers. Table 2 is a listing by state and province of known bald eagle research efforts under way at this time. In Canada, where bald eagle numbers are greater and population decreases much less severe, research is also under way.

The special agents of the Law Enforcement Branch of the U.S. Fish and Wildlife Service are especially persistent in tracking down eagle killers. Federal, state and private rewards (including the National Wildlife Federation reward) often total $3,000 for information leading to the arrest and conviction of people who kill eagles.

The U.S. Fish and Wildlife Service, under provisions of the Endangered Species Act, has appointed regional Bald Eagle Recovery Teams to draft recovery plans for the bald eagle populations in their areas. Listed below are the five recovery teams:

- Southwest Bald Eagle Recovery Team

- Chesapeake Bay Bald Eagle Recovery Team

- Northern States Bald Eagle Recovery Team

- Southeast Bald Eagle Recovery Team

- Pacific Bald Eagle Recovery Team (being nominated)

The future of the bald eagle looks a bit brighter now than it did ten years ago. The Alaska and Canada populations are basically intact and are facing only local problems such as the potential destruction of the Chilkat Valley in southeastern Alaska. However, their wintering areas in the United States are subject to habitat destruction and they are still being shot in considerable numbers. In the lower 48 states the future looks less bright. At this time the number of breeding bald eagles has apparently stabilized and may be slowly increasing, but the pressures of a growing human population and a polluting society could reverse this at any time.

TABLE 1. BALD EAGLE NUMBERS, PRESENT vs. HISTORICAL

State or Province	Breeding Pairs		Wintering	
	Present[a]	Historical	Present[a]	Historical
Alabama	0	Holt – 1921 – Common on coast, Baldwin City Howell – 1928 – Common resident along Gulf coast, interior along Tennessee River	3[b]	
Alaska	7500 (est.)	McLenegan – 1887 – Breeding, Noatak R, northwest Grinnell – 1898 – Breeding, Sitka Chapman – 1904 – Breeding, Cook Inlet Thayer & Bays – 1914 – Breeding on Arctic coast Shortt – 1939 – Abundant, Yakutat Bay Cahn – 1947 – Very common, nesting pairs Aleutian Is. Bailey – 1948 – Common nesting	35–45,000 (est.)	
Arizona	9	Mearns – 1890 – Common in Rocky Mountain region Jenks & Stevenson – 1937 – Permanent resident in central-eastern, nests along rivers in White Mts. Woodbury & Russell – 1945 – Rare northwest Phillipps et al.– 1964 – Not uncommon resident of lakes and streams of White Mt. region, rarer near Salt River and Flagstaff	100	

a) Results, RIC Bald Eagle Population Symposium, Nov. 1978.

b) U.S. Fish and Wildlife Service Waterfowl/Eagle Inventory.

State or Province	Breeding Pairs		Wintering	
	Present[a]	Historical	Present[a]	Historical
Arkansas	0	Howell - 1911 - Rare resident Hunt - 1921 - Nesting pairs in southeast at Lake Chicot Black - 1929 - Ozarks - reported sighting 3-4 times between 1919-1929 Deaderick - 1938 - Uncommon, Hot Springs NP	122	
British Columbia	no recent data	Osgood - 1901 - Very common Queen Charlotte Islands Cumming - 1931 - Abundant, Queen Charlotte Islands Munro - 1945 - Summer visitor, breeding	no recent data	
California	42	Grinnell & Miller - 1844 - Permanent resident, scattered nesting Henshaw - 1876 - Abundant residents along coast Everman - 1886 - Ventura Cty. resident, freq. coast Blake, Jr. - 1887 - 8-9 pairs nesting on Santa Cruz Bryant - 1889 - Nesting in lower California Linton - 1908 - San Clemente - several nesting pairs Burke - 1911 - Few pairs nesting on Anacapa Is. Willett - 1912 - Breeding Orange Co. Howell - 1917 - Common resident of Santa Barbara group nesting in low numbers Grinnell & Wykee - 1927 - San Francisco Bay - very rare	500[c] (est.)	Grinnell - 1898 - Santa Catalina - common wintering

c) Siskiyou and Modoc counties only.

17

State or Province	Breeding Pairs		Wintering	
	Present[a]	Historical	Present[a]	Historical
Colorado	3	Slater – 1912 – Breeds commonly in mountains to 10,000 feet Alexander – 1937 – Rare transient near Boulder	500–600 (est.)	Slater – 1912 – on plains in winter
Connecticut	2 (no nesting)	Merriam – 1877 – Resident, breeding on Housatonic R. and suitable locations Sage & Bishop – 1913 – Rare spring and fall migrant – formerly bred in unsettled parts of the state	9–12	Merriam – 1877 – moves through in migration Sage & Bishop – 1913 – spring & fall migrant
Delaware	3	Potter – 1948 – Permanent resident in the area Abbott – 1967 – 1936–4 pr., 1962– 3 pr., 1963–4 pr., 1964–2 pr., 1965–1 pr.	1[b]	
Florida	319	Scott – 1889 – Common resident and breeds on Gulf coast Williams – 1904 – Resident in limited numbers Phelps – 1912 – Common in Caloosahatachie R. and Gulf coast islands, pair nesting on Lake Okeechobee Basanard – 1913 – Alachua – 20 pairs Phelps – 1914 – Nesting pair, Big Cypress Swamp Dangburn – 1919 – Common along coastline, 6 nests identified by author Fargo – 1926 – Common resident – breeds Tampa Bay and Gulf Shore Bent – 1927 – Common resident Greene – 1945 – Lower keys – not common, few pairs nesting	unknown	Anonymous – 1962 – 529 individuals

18

State or Province	Breeding Pairs		Wintering	
	Present[a]	Historical	Present[a]	Historical
Georgia	1 (no nesting)	Burleigh – 1895 – Common resident on coast, casual occurrence inland Erickson – 1919 – Breeding, St. Catherines Island Pearson – 1922 – Cumberland Islands nesting Green et al. – 1945 – Breeds in coastal areas, not inland	3[b]	
Idaho	4	Merrill – 1897 – Fort Merrill – few pairs breed Hand – 1941 – Rare, may be resident, ? nesting Arvey – 1947 – Uncommon resident – few breeding at Couer d'Alene Burleigh – 1972 – Scarce local summer resident, nesting in 1969.	388 (est.)	
Illinois	3–4	Nelson – 1876 – Breeds sparingly Ridgway – 1881 – Resident Woodruff – 1907 – Rare resident near Chicago Bellrose – 1915 – Last nesting record Grassett – 1926 – formerly permanent resident at north-eastern Illinois Bonnell – 1935 – Nesting	248[b]	Ridgway – 1881 – Abundant Woodruff – 1907 – Frequent along shore of Lake Michigan during fall & winter Pellett – 1927 – Wintering along Mississippi R., common Anonymous – 1963–1962, 476 wintering
Indiana	0	Butler – 1935 – Resident, common, breeding in limited numbers	5	Evermann – 1888 – Frequent winter visitor

19

State or Province	Breeding Pairs		Wintering	
	Present[a]	Historical	Present[a]	Historical
Iowa	0	Keyes – 1897 – Not as common as formerly, few breeding pairs along rivers Anderson – 1907 – No nesting records Bailey – 1918 – Approx. 32 nesting pairs DuMont – 1933 – No breeding records since 1892 Allert – 1939 – Some nesting	378[b]	Anderson – 1907 – Occasional wintering Pellett – 1927 – Along Mississippi R., common DuMont – 1933 – Migrant along rivers, wintering DuMont – 1934 – Spring-fall migrant Heuser – 1940 – Guttenberg, 25-50 individuals
Kansas	0	Gross – 1891 – Rare Lantz – 1899 – Rare resident Harris – 1919 – Kansas City region – rare in summer, formerly very common	200 (est.)	Harris – 1919 – Kansas City region – rare winter visitor Long – 1935 – Occasional wintering Goodrich – 1946 – Rare visitor
Kentucky	0	Funkhouser – 1925 – Regular visitor, not uncommon resident Barbour – 1973 – Very rare in summer	80	Barbour – 1973 – Rare to common
Louisiana	13	Beyer – 1900 – Resident Bailey – 1919 – Common along watercourses Figgins – 1923 – Breeding (Black Bayou)	3[b]	

State or Province	Breeding Pairs		Wintering	
	Present[a]	Historical	Present[a]	Historical
Maine	54	Knight – 1908 – Androscoggin summer resident, breed in Aroostock Co. – common breeding in certain regions – 50–100 pairs breeding Brewster – 1925 – No nesting L. Umbagog Anonymous – 1963–1962 – 31 nests	109	Brewster – 1925 – Autumn in L. Umbagog region
Maryland	44	Kirkwood – 1895 – Resident dispersed along Ches. Bay, Eastern Shore, shores of Potomac River. Fisher – 1899 – 8-10 pr. breed Baltimore radius Cooke – 1929 – DC permanent resident, possible breeder Anonymous – 1962 – 32 nests (Eifrig – 1904 not uncommon resident, Cumberland area, mountains near WV) Abbott – 1967 – 1936-35 pr., 1962-22 pr., 1963-18 pr., 1964-17 pr., 1965-'12 pr. Stewart & Robbins – Fairly common on eastern shore, nesting	7[b]	Stewart & Robbins – Wintering on Eastern Shore – migrants
Massachusetts	1 (no nesting)	Anonymous – 1888 – 3-4 individuals seen, Boston area Howe – 1901 – Rare resident in western state, occasionally east in all seasons Townsend – 1905 – Uncommon visitor, Essex Co. Bagg & Eliot – 1937 – Few nesting in Conn. R. Valley Hill – 1965 – Cape Cod – historically nesting – common but decreased	12-15	Howe – 1901 – Rare winter visitor & migrant Bagg & Eliot – 1937 – Occasional, wintering Griscom & Snyder – 1955 – Irregular visitor, coastal

State or Province	Breeding Pairs		Wintering	
	Present[a]	Historical	Present[a]	Historical
Massachusetts (cont.)				Hill – 1965 – Occasional immigrant, Cape Cod
Michigan	87	Cook – 1893 – Not rare Brotherton – 1894 – Returning former regions Barrows – 1912 – Commonly nesting in every county VanTyne – 1938 – Uncommon resident Haugen – 1945 – Allegan SF common summer, nesting Postupalsky – Lower peninsula – 1961-33 nests, 1962-29 nests, upper peninsula 1961-30, 1962-27	150 (est.)	VanTyne – 1938 – Few wintering & transient Haugen – 1945 – Frequent in winter, Allegan SF Wood – Rare winter resident, regular visitant late fall, winter, spring
Minnesota	154	Cantwell – 1890 – Not common, nesting reported Roberts – 1932 – Summer resident, bred throughout state – area reduced, number decreased Morrison – 1950 – Nest on L. Itasca, resident at Birch Lake	75[b]	Trippe – 1871 – Common
Mississippi	1	Trippe – 1871 – Common Stockard – 1905 – Common in western part of state along Mississippi River, nesting in swamps Burleigh – 1944 – Nests on coastal islands, rare mainland	1[b]	
Missouri	0	Coues – 1874 – Missouri region Widmann – 1907 – Once abundant, rare now	642[b]	Anonymous – 1963 – 1962, 246 birds

State or Province	Breeding Pairs		Wintering	
	Present[a]	Historical	Present[a]	Historical
Missouri (cont.)		Bennitt – 1932 – Rare permanent resident		
Montana	12	Cameron – 1907 – Occasional visitor, nested formerly, more common 1880's	116[b]	
Nebraska	0	Bruner – 1896 – Resident S. Bend Taylor & Van Vleet – 1889 – Resident, nest near Omaha Bruner – 1900 – Nesting in 2 counties	298	Haecker et al.– 1945 – Uncommon migrant, and winter visitor
Nevada	0	Austin – 1968 – Southern, none since 1959, rare in northern part of state	30–50	
Newfoundland	83[d]	Porter – 1900 – Common	75[d]	
New Hampshire	0	Allen – 1903 – Uncommon summer Comey – 1904 – Holderness region, rare	1–2	Cram – 1899 – Occasional
New Jersey	1	Stone – 1894 – Pine Barrens – pairs along coast, breeding in cedar swamps Harlow – 1918 – Not breeding, declining Potter – 1948 – Permanent resident along Delaware River, 4 nests Fables – 1955 – Permanent resident coastal plain, diminishing Anonymous – 1963 – 1962, 2 nests	12	Stone – 1937 – Many migrants, 77 sighted (1920–1937) Fables – 1955 – Regular in small numbers as migrant

d) Maritime Provinces.

State or Province	Breeding Pairs		Wintering	
	Present[a]	Historical	Present[a]	Historical
New Mexico	0	Bailey – 1928 – Nesting	350	
New York	1	Giraud – 1844 – Nest on Long Island Bull – Very rare breeder, NYC area Maxon – 1903 – Madison Co. nest Oneida Lake, less common than previous Griscom – 1933 – Uncommon visitor, may breed Dutchess Co. Spofford – 1960 – Few nests south of L. Erie and Ontario, 2 nests on St. Lawrence R., nesting population of 12–24 prs. Beardslee – 1965 – Niagara region, uncommon, no breeding U.S.D.I. – 1978 – Once 63 active nests	32	Bull – Rare wintering
North Carolina	1 (no nesting)	Cairns – 1889 – Mountains, rare resident – 1886 last nesting record Pearson – 1942 – Common along coast, breeds through coastal region	10	Pearson – 1942 – Migrants moving through
North Dakota	1	Larson – 1928 – Nested formerly, E. McKenzie Cty.	11	Larson – 1928 – Rare fall and winter E. McKenzie Cty.
Northwest Territories	unknown	Seton – 1908 – Throughout country and around Great Slave Lake Snyder & Logier – 1931 – Breeding at Long Pt. area	unknown	

State or Province	Breeding Pairs Present[a]	Breeding Pairs Historical	Wintering Present[a]	Wintering Historical
Northwest Territories (cont.)		Snyder et al. – 1941 – Nesting, numerous summer and fall occurrences		
Ohio	5	Fisher – 1907 – Breeding, Lewistown Reservoir Jones – 1909 – Cedar Point, year round residents, 4–5 nesting pairs Hicks – 1933 – Ashtabula, frequent, 1 pr. nesting (southern Ohio) Campbell – 1940 – Uncommon permanent resident, Lucas Co. Smith, Burnard, Good & Keeners – 1973 – 11 nests 1972, 1903 (Dawson) rare resident, few nests in L. Erie marsh area	4[b]	Langdon – 1879 – Migrant near Cincinnati Trautman – 1940 – Rare migrant and wintering Buckeye Lake
Oklahoma	1	Sutton – Irregular, common around large impoundments	600 (est.)	Sutton – Winter resident
Ontario	579 (est.)[e]	Bailie and Harrington – 1936 – Local in summer Dear – 1940 – Rare summer resident, Lake Superior, Thunder Bay, Jones – 1912 – nesting Pelee Is. 8–10 individuals, nest on L. Erie Island	unknown	Fleming – 1907 – Rare winter visitor
Oregon	60	Suckley – 1860 – Exceedingly abundant Merrill – 1888 – Ft. Klamath common resident, nesting	290[f]	

e) 173,900 km^2 area, northwest Ontario.

f) Klamath County only.

25

State or Province	Breeding Pairs		Wintering	
	Present[a]	Historical	Present[a]	Historical
Oregon (cont.)		Howsley – 1919 – Occasional visitor Jewett & Gabrielson – 1929 – Portland area rare, ? Columbia River		
Pennsylvania	3	Miller – 1910 – Philadelphia Co. exceedingly rare, former resident Harlow – 1918 – Some breed on Susquehanna River, declining Beck – 1924 – 1890 very common, 1924 – confined areas on Susquehanna River Sutton – 1928 – Summer resident, common around Erie Ordette – 1938 – Pymatuning, 6 resident birds, evidence of nesting	3[b]	Sutton – 1928 – Rare and irregular migrant
Rhode Island	0	Howe – 1903 – Irregular visitor, no definite breeding records	1-3[b]	
Saskatchewan	2500 (est.)		unknown	
South Carolina	14	Loomis – 1890 – Presence is an exceptional occurrence Wayne – 1910 – Permanent resident, breeds locally along coast and in less settled regions, mainland and coastal islands	9-16[b]	
South Dakota	0	Agersborg – 1885 – Rare in southwest Visher – 1909 – Western – rare resident in badlands Thomas – 1920 – Rarely nests	412[b]	Visher – 1909 – Southwest – very rare winter visitant Over & Thomas – 1920 – Frequent wintering

State or Province	Breeding Pairs		Wintering	
	Present[a]	Historical	Present[a]	Historical
South Dakota (cont.)				Anonymous – 1963 – 1962 – 273 wintering
Tennessee	0	DeLime – 1949 – Nesting on Kentucky Lake	218	
Texas	7	Dresser – 1865 – Abundant S.Texas Nehrling – 1882 – Breeding Houston, S.E. Texas Lloyd – 1887 – Tom Green and Concho Co., abundant resident and breeding Carroll – 1889 – Not very common, breeding Lacey – 1912 – Not uncommon, used to breed Guadaloupe, Frio, and Medina rivers (Kerrvile). Simmons – 1915 – Very rare resident, ? nesting	300 (est.)	
Utah	0	Woodbury and Russell – 1945 – Rare S.E. Utah	634	Behle – 1944 – May winter
Vermont	0		3–5[b]	
Virginia	37	Grey – 1950 – Southern coastal, common, some nesting Scott – 1951 – Permanent resident, fairly common Tidewater region, irregular on Piedmont, no evidence of breeding (Richmond area) Larson & Abbott – 1962 – 200 birds Chesapeake Bay Anonymous – 1963 – 1962, 32 nests Chesapeake Bay	5[b]	Grey – 1950 – 14 wintering southern

State or Province	Breeding Pairs		Wintering	
	Present[a]	Historical	Present[a]	Historical
Virginia (cont.)		Abbott – 1967 – Chesapeake Bay 1936, 18 pr., 1962 – 37 pr., 1963 – 25 pr., 1964 – 27 pr., 1965 – 37 pr.		
		Abbott – 1978 – Nesting, 1938 – 112 pr., 1940 – 47 pr. (reported), 1950 – 72 pr., 1960 – 53 pr., 1970 – 21 pr.		
Washington	100	Suckley – 1860 – Abundant	620[b]	
		Bowles – 1906 – Breeding near Tacoma		
		Dawson – 1909 – Abundant resident west of Cascades, rare east of mountains		
		Miller – 1935 – San Juan Is., common resident, nesting		
		Kitchin – 1939 – Mt. Ranier area rare, formerly bred all around		
		Kitchin – 1949 – Numerous on Olympic Peninsula, ? nesting		
West Virginia	0	Brooks – 1938 – Rare in all parts of state	0[b]	
Wisconsin	150-160	Kumlien & Hollister – 1903 – Nest in northern portion of state, along Mississippi River, inland lakes	126[b]	Kumlien & Hollister – 1923 – Fall migrant
		Jackson – 1923 – Nest regularly on Mamie L.		Barers – 1962 – Approximately 100 Christmas count
		Deusing – 1940 – Records, bred in all parts of state 1853, north forest nesting		

| | Breeding Pairs | | Wintering | |
State or Province	Present[a]	Historical	Present[a]	Historical
Wyoming	26	Kemsies – 1930 – Occasional permanent resident, Yellowstone Williams & Mattson – 1947 – Rare, not uncommon on rivers and lakes	618 (est.)	
Yukon Territory	unknown	Blackwelder – 1919 – Not very common	unknown	

Literature cited may be found in this bibliography or in Friedmann, H. 1950. The Birds of North and Middle America. Part XI. Smithsonian Institution. Bull. 50. 793 pp.

TABLE 2. CURRENT BALD EAGLE RESEARCH

State or Province	Principal Investigator(s)/ Contact(s)	Agency or Organization	Description of Research[a]
Alabama	Fred Bagley	US Fish & Wildlife Service (USF&WS)	Winter survey
Alaska	Fred Robards	USF&WS	Nesting survey
	Erwin Boeker	National Audubon Society	Winter study (Chilkat)
Arizona	Dr. Robert Ohmart	Arizona State Univ.	Nesting studies (S/Ec/B/M)
	Teryl Grubb	US Forest Service (USFS)	Nesting survey, Winter survey
Arkansas	Thurman Booth Fred Bagley	USF&WS	Winter survey
British Columbia	Wayne Campbell	BC Provincial Museum	Nesting survey
California	Dave Dunaway	USFS, CA Bald Eagle Working Team	Nesting studies (S/Ec) Winter survey
Colorado	Gerald R. Craig	CO Div. of Wildlife	Winter survey
Connecticut	-	-	-
Delaware	Lloyd Alexander	DE Div. of Fish & Wildlife	Nesting study (S/Ec/B/M)
Florida	Steve Nesbitt	FL G&FWF Comm.	Nesting survey
	Doris Mager	FL Audubon Society	
	William Robertson	USFS	
	Dave Peterson	USF&WS	

Superscripts	a) Codes:	S - Survey	Ec - Ecology
		B - Banding	Be - Behavior
		M - Marking	Mg - Management

State or Province	Principal Investigator(s)/ Contact(s)	Agency or Organization	Description of Research[a]
Georgia	Ron Odum	GA Game & Fish Div.	Nesting survey
Idaho	Lanny O. Wilson	Bureau of Land Management (BLM)	Winter survey
Illinois	Elton Fawks	National Wildlife Federation (NWF)	Winter survey
Indiana	-	-	-
Iowa	Elton Fawks	NWF	Winter survey
Kansas	-	-	-
Kentucky	John L. Mechler	Tennessee Valley Authority	Winter study (S/Mg)
	Dr. Clell Petersen	Murray St. Univ.	
Louisiana	John D. Newsom	LA Coop. Wildlife Research Unit	Nesting study (S/Ec/B/M)
	Wayne Dubuc	Private	Nesting survey
	Fred Bagley	USF&WS	Winter survey
Maine	Dr. Ray B. Owen	University of Maine	Nesting study (S/B/M), Winter survey
	Francis J. Gramlich	USF&WS	
Maritimes	Peter Austin-Smith	Nova Scotia Dept. of Lands & Forests	Nesting survey, Winter study (S/B/M)
Maryland	Gary J. Taylor	MD Wildlife Admin.	Nesting study (S/Ec/B/M)
Massachu-setts	John E. Swedberg	MA Div. of Fisheries & Game	Winter survey
Michigan	Sergej Postupalsky	University of Wisconsin	Nesting study (S/B)
Minnesota	John Mathisen	USFS	Nesting studies (S/Be/Mg/B/M)
	Dr. L. D. Frenzel	University of Minnesota	

State or Province	Principal Investigator(s)/ Contact(s)	Agency or Organization	Description of Research[a]
Mississippi	John D. Newsom	LA Coop. Wildlife Research Unit	Nesting study (Ec/B/M)
	Fred Bagley	USF&WS	Winter survey
Missouri	Elton Fawks	NWF	Winter survey
Montana	Dr. B. Riley McClelland	University of Montana	Fall migration study (B/M)
	Christopher Servheen	MT Coop. Wildlife Research Unit	Subadult plumages & molt sequences
	Lance Craighead	University of Montana	Winter study (Ec)
Nebraska	Ross Lock	NE Game & Parks Commission	Winter survey
Nevada	Gary B. Herron	NV Dept. of Game & Fish	Winter survey
New Hampshire	-	-	-
New Jersey	Paul D. McLain	NJ Dept. of Environmental Protection	Nesting survey
New Mexico	John P. Hubbard	NM Dept. of Game & Fish	Winter survey
New York	Peter E. Nye	NY Dept. of Envir. Conservation	Nesting study (Mg/Be/B/M), Winter survey
North Carolina	-	-	-
North Dakota	-	-	-
Ontario	Dr. James W. Grier	N. Dakota State University	Nesting study (S/Ec/Mg)
Ohio	Sergej Postupalsky	University of Wisconsin	Nesting study (S/B)
Oklahoma	James W. Lish	OK Coop. Wildlife Research Unit	Winter study (S/Ec)

State or Province	Principal Investigator(s)/ Contact(s)	Agency or Organization	Description of Research[a]
Oregon	Dr. Robert Anthony	Oregon State Univ.	Nesting study (S/Ec/Mg), Winter studies (S/Be/Mg)
	Ralph R. Opp	OR Dept. of Fish & Wildlife	
Pennsyl-vania	Michael Puglisi	PA Game Commission	Nesting study (S/B/M)
Rhode Island	-	-	-
Saskatche-wan	Dr. Jon Gerrard	Private	Nesting study (S/Ec/Be/B/M)
	Dr. Douglas Whitfield	University of Alberta	
South Carolina	Kenneth B. Stansell	SC Wildlife & Marine Res. Dept.	Nesting study (S/B/M), Winter survey
South Dakota	-	-	-
Tennessee	Bill Yambert	TN Wildlife Resources Agency	Winter study (S/Mg)
Texas	Dr. Keith Arnold	Texas A&M Univ.	Winter study (S/Ec)
Utah	Dr. Joseph Murphy	Brigham Young Univ.	Winter study (Ec)
	Phillip Wagner	UT Div. of Wildlife Resources	Winter survey
Vermont	-	-	-
Virginia	Dr. Mitchell Byrd	College of William & Mary	Nesting study (S/Ec/B/M)
Washington	Richard L. Knight	WA Dept. of Game	Nesting survey
	Richard Fitzner	Battelle-Northwest Inst.	Winter study (Ec)
	Walter English	Woodland Park Zoological Gardens	Study of released rehab. birds (B/M)

State or Province	Principal Investigator(s)/ Contact(s)	Agency or Organization	Description of Research[a]
West Virginia	-	-	-
Wisconsin	Charles Sindelar	Private	Nesting study (S/B)
	Terrence N. Ingram	Eagle Valley Environmentalists	Winter survey
Wyoming	Robert Oakleaf	WY Game & Fish Dept.	Winter survey
All US	Dr. Louis N. Locke	USF&WS	Autopsy of bald eagles
All US	Stanley N. Wiemeyer	USF&WS	Captive breeding Contaminant analysis

Chapter 3

Master List of Citations

Master No.   Citation

1   Abbott, J.M. *1957.* Bald eagle survey: first annual report. Atl. Nat. 12(3):118-119.

2   Abbott, J.M. *1959.* Bald eagle survey report. Atl. Nat. 14(4):252-258.

3   Abbott, J.M. *1962.* Status report on the bald eagle. Va. Wildl. 23(7):4-6.

4   Abbott, J.M. *1963.* 1963 Bald eagle nest report, Chesapeake Bay region. (Unpublished Report). 10 pp.

5   Abbott, J.M. *1963.* Bald eagle survey for Chesapeake Bay, 1962. Atl. Nat. 18(1):22-27.

6   Abbott, J.M. *1963.* 1963 Chesapeake Bay region mid-winter eagle census. (Unpublished Report). 3 pp.

7   Abbott, J.M. *1964.* 1964 bald eagle survey for the Chesapeake Bay region. (Unpublished Report). 4 pp.

8   Abbott, J.M. *1967.* Chesapeake Bay area bald eagle nesting report for 1967. (Unpublished Report). 2 pp.

9   Abbott, J.M. *1967.* The Chesapeake bald eagles: summary report - 1936 ;1955-1965. Atl. Nat. 22(1):20-25.

10   Abbott, J.M. *1968.* Chesapeake Bay area bald eagle nesting report for 1967. Atl. Nat. 23(1):19-21.

11   Abbott, J.M. *1969.* Bald eagle nesting survey, Chesapeake Bay region 1968. Atl. Nat. 24(1):18.

12   Abbott, J.M. *1969.* Bald eagle nesting survey, Chesapeake Bay region, 1969. Atl. Nat. 24(4):212.

13   Abbott, J.M. *1970.* 1970 bald eagle nest survey. Atl. Nat. 25(4):169-171.

14   Abbott, J.M. *1971.* Bald eagle nest survey 1971. Atl. Nat. 26(4):165-166.

15   Abbott, J.M. *1972.* Bald eagle nest survey 1972. Atl. Nat. 27(4):175-177.

16   Abbott, J.M. *1973.* Bald eagle nest survey 1973. Atl. Nat. 28(4):158-159.

17   Abbott, J.M. *1974.* Bald eagle nest survey 1974. Atl. Nat. 29(4):161-163.

18   Abbott, J.M. *1975.* Bald eagle nest survey 1975. Atl. Nat. 30(3):116-118.

19   Abbott, J.M. *1976.* Bald eagle nest survey 1976. Atl. Nat. 31(4):162-163.

20   Abbott, J.M. *1977.* 1977 Chesapeake Bay region eagle nest survey. Proc. of Chesapeake Bay Bald Eagles and Their Management. July 13 and 14, 1977. 7 pp.

21   Abbott, J.M. *1977.* Chesapeake Bay bald eagle survey. Annual Report, Hawk Mountain Sanctuary Association. Dec. 1977. p. 11-14.

22   Abbott, J.M. *1978.* Chesapeake Bay bald eagles. Delaware Conserv. 22(2):3-9.

23   Adkins, J. *1974.* Bald eagle nesting survey: Northwest Washington. Small Game Management Report. Washington Game Dept. p. 123-127.

24   Adkins, J. *1977.* Bald eagle research and management program: Trapping and marking program. Washington Dept. of Game. 11 pp.

25   Agersborg, G.S. *1885.* The birds of southeastern Dakota. The Auk. 2(3):276-289.

26   Alcorn, G. *1975.* Untitled? Pacific Search. 9(6):13.

27   Allan, P.F. and P.R. Sime. *1943.* A hawk census on Texas Panhandle highways. Wilson Bull. 55(1):29-39.

28   Allen, A.A. *1918.* The diurnal birds of prey - hawks, eagles, and vultures. Am. Forestry. 24(213):281-284.

29   Allen, D.L. *1960.* Big baldy. Field and Stream. 65(9):35,57-58.

30   Allen, D.L. *1961.* Emblem eagle. Boys Life. 51(7):14,23,25.

31   Allen, G.M. *1903.* A List of the Birds of New Hampshire. Proc. of the Manchester Inst. Arts and Sciences. 4:23-222.

32   Allen, G.M. *1913.* An Essex County ornithologist. The Auk. 30(1):19-21,25.

33   Allen, J.A. *1870.* What is the 'Washington Eagle'? Am. Naturalist. 4(9):524-527.

34   Allen, J.A. *1899.* Republication of descriptions of new species and subspecies of North American birds. The Auk. 16(4):338-350.

35   Allen, L.E. *1936.* Bald eagles. Oologist. 53(4):47-48.

36   Allen, R.P.and R.T. Peterson. *1936.* The hawk migrations at Cape May Point, New Jersey. The Auk. 53(4):393-404.

37   Allen, T.B. *1974.* Vanishing Wildlife of North America. Nat. Geog. Mag. 208 pp.

38   Allert, O.P. *1939.* Notes on certain raptores in Allamakee, Clayton and Dubuque Counties, Iowa. Iowa Bird Life. 9(3):34-36.

39   Allin, A.E. *1960.* The Canadian Lakehead. The Flicker. 32(3):95-98.

40   Allin, A.E. *1961.* The Canadian Lakehead. The Flicker. 33(3):79-82.

41   Allin, A.E. *1963.* The Canadian Lakehead. The Flicker. 35(3):95-98.

42   Allison, D. and H. Hothem. *1975.* An evaluation of the status of the fisheries and the status of other selected wild animals in the Maumee River Basin, Ohio. Ohio Dept. of Natural Resources. 16 pp.

43   Amadon, D. *1964.* The evolution of low reproductive rates in birds. Evolution. 18(1):105-110.

Master No. Citation

44 **Amadon, D.** *1975.* Sticky problems of hawk identification: a panel discussion. Proc. of North Am. Hawk Migration Conf., Syracuse, NY. Hawk Migration Assoc. of N. America. p. 118-136.

45 **Ambruster, J.H.** *1920.* An eagle's cunning. Nature-Study Rev. 16(9):383-384.

46 **American Ornithologists' Union.** *1902.* Bald eagle. Am. Ornithol. 2(1):2-5.

47 **American Ornithologists' Union.** *1957.* Checklist of North American Birds. The Lord Baltimore Press, Inc. Baltimore, Maryland. 691 pp.

48 **American Ornithologists' Union.** *1975.* Report of the American Ornithologists' Union Committee on Conservation, 1974-75. The Auk(Supplement). 92(4):1B-16B.

49 **American Ornithologists' Union.** *1976.* Report of the Committee on Conservation. The Auk. 93(4, Supp.):1dd-19dd.

50 **Anderson, D.W. and J.J. Hickey.** *1972.* Egg shell changes in certain North American birds. *In:* Proc. Inter. Ornithol. Congress, 15Th. The Hague. p. 514-540.

51 **Anderson, J.** *1971.* Eagle habitat requirements and forest management. *In:* Proc. of Fish and Wildlife Habitat Management Training Conference. U.S.D.A Forest Service. Region 6. Nov. 30 - Dec. 2, 1971. Eugene, OR. p. 56-69.

52 **Anderson, J.H., R.C. Erickson, D.A. Munro, W.R. Spofford, G.C. West and F.G. Evenden.** *1968.* Report of Committee on Conservation, 1967. The Auk. 85(1):117-126.

53 **Anderson, R.M.** *1907.* The Birds of Iowa. Proc. Davenport Acad. Sciences. 11:125-417.

54 **Angell, T.** *1972.* Birds of Prey on the Pacific Northwest Slope. Second Edition. Pacific Search Books. Seattle, WA. 34 pp.

55 **Anonymous.** *1851.* Eagles. Littell's Living Age. 31(385):158-164.

56 **Anonymous.** *1851.* Eagles. Zoological notes and anecdotes. Bentley's Misc. 30:115-128.

57 **Anonymous.** *1873.* A battle in the air. Forest and Stream. 1(5):71.

58 **Anonymous.** *1888.* Bald or white-headed eagle. (From Maynard's Birds of North America) Oologist. 5(1):2-4.

59 **Anonymous.** *1897.* The bald-headed eagle. Birds. 2(1):2-3,5.

60 **Anonymous.** *1898.* Townsend on a new American eagle. Ibis. 4(13):172.

61 **Anonymous.** *1899.* Nest of bald eagle. Osprey. 4(1):13.

62 **Anonymous.** *1899.* The eagle. Birds All Nature. 5(1):24-25,36.

63 **Anonymous.** *1903.* Capture of a bald eagle. J. Maine Ornithol. Soc. 5(2):34.

64 **Anonymous.** *1911.* Kills eagle attacking girls. Oologist. 28(3):52.

65 **Anonymous.** *1912.* The captive eagle. Oologist. 29(12):386-387.

66 **Anonymous.** *1920.* A renewed attempt to save the eagles. Am. Rev. of Reviews. 68(Dec.):659-660.

67 **Anonymous.** *1920.* The government exterminating our national bird. Lit. Digest. 65(2):130.

68 **Anonymous.** *1920.* The American eagle. Sat. Even. Post. 192(43):88.

69 **Anonymous.** *1923.* The American eagle in danger. Am. Rev. of Reviews. 62(Aug.1):208.

70 **Anonymous.** *1923.* Alaska's slaughter of American eagles. Lit. Digest. 79(12):40.

71 **Anonymous.** *1923.* Me-giz-ze-was, the pet eagle. Lit. Digest. 77(2):90-92.

72 **Anonymous.** *1925.* Old Abe, the war eagle of Wisconsin. Mentor. 13(5):20-21.

73 **Anonymous.** *1927.* Freedom's bird in his majesty. Lit. Digest. 93(1):74-76.

74 **Anonymous.** *1927.* Visiting day at an eagle's treetop nursery. Lit. Digest. 94(11):72,74-75.

75 **Anonymous.** *1928.* Eagles at Vermilion, Ohio. Science-Supplement. 48(1753):14.

76 **Anonymous.** *1929.* Jimmy's ride with a bald eagle. Lit. Digest. 103(6):70-71.

77 **Anonymous.** *1930.* Notes and news. The Auk. 47(2):463.

78 **Anonymous.** *1930.* Notes and news. The Auk. 47(2):310.

79 **Anonymous.** *1930.* The bald eagle, our emblem. Nature Mag. 15(3):141.

80 **Anonymous.** *1931.* The truth about our national bird. Pop. Mechanics Mag. 56(2):211-213.

81 **Anonymous.** *1932.* Pleistocene eagles. Science-Supplement. 76:10.

82 **Anonymous.** *1932.* Wrong eagle on Washington coin. Lit. Digest. 114(13):26.

83 **Anonymous.** *1933.* Nira, Chattanooga's eagle. Nature Mag. 22(6):286.

84 **Anonymous.** *1933.* The eagle in sculpture. Architecture. 67(5):293-308.

85 **Anonymous.** *1933.* The bald eagle. Science-Supplement. 77(1990):8.

86 **Anonymous.** *1934.* Pig thief revealed as American eagle. Oologist. 51(11):132.

87 **Anonymous.** *1935.* Our national bird. Penn. Game News. 6(3):13.

88 **Anonymous.** *1935.* Our national bird. Nature Mag. 26(1):25-28.

89 **Anonymous.** *1939.* Eagles did not fight when nest was invaded. Sci. News Letter. 36(24):383.

90 **Anonymous.** *1939.* Panhandle hunters mount fast autos and go eagle gunning. Nature Mag. 32(6):340.

91 **Anonymous.** *1943.* Eaglet grows up. Life. 14(25):94-97.

92 **Anonymous.** *1943.* An 18th century American carved eagle. Am. Coll. 12(5):4.

93 **Anonymous.** *1943.* Stories of vicious eagles. Nature Mag. 36(1):33.

94 **Anonymous.** *1946.* The American bald eagle; National bird wins fight for survival. Life. 21(July 1):50-54.

Master No.	Citation
95	Anonymous. *1947.* Origin and use of our national emblem. Antiques. 52(1):14,16,18.
96	Anonymous. *1949.* Miscellaneous bird notes. Maine Aud. Soc. Bull. 5(3):58-60.
97	Anonymous. *1950.* Bald eagle seriously threatened in Alaska. Audubon. 52(1):49,64.
98	Anonymous. *1950.* Bald eagle. Sci. News Letter. 58(1):14.
99	Anonymous. *1951.* Eagles nest saved. Audubon. 53(5):289.
100	Anonymous. *1951.* Bald eagle bill reintroduced. Audubon. 53(2):130.
101	Anonymous. *1951.* Bald eagle protection. Natural Hist. 60(6):242.
102	Anonymous. *1951.* Road to extinction. Newsweek. 37(21):58,60.
103	Anonymous. *1952.* Report on eagle bill. Audubon. 54(1):27.
104	Anonymous. *1952.* The bald eagle in Alaska. Natl. Parks Mag. 26(109):81,90.
105	Anonymous. *1952.* Alaska eagle bounty nullified. Audubon. 54(3):204.
106	Anonymous. *1953.* Alaska eagle bounty repealed. Audubon. 55(4):192.
107	Anonymous. *1954.* General bird list. Maine Aud. Soc. Bull. 10(2):38.
108	Anonymous. *1954.* Eagle bander. New Yorker. 30(18):19-20.
109	Anonymous. *1954.* Bald eagles. Sci. News Letter. 66(1):14.
110	Anonymous. *1955.* Miscellaneous bird notes. Maine Aud. Soc. Bull. 11(2):30-35.
111	Anonymous. *1955.* Our national emblem is endangered. Raven. 26(4):58.
112	Anonymous. *1959.* Old baldy. Holiday. 26(5):40.
113	Anonymous. *1960.* Is the eagle un-American? N.Y. Times Mag.(March 6):19,73-75.
114	Anonymous. *1960.* Freedom's big bird. True. 41(278):38-41.
115	Anonymous. *1961.* Bald eagle count. Iowa Bird Life. 31:91.
116	Anonymous. *1962.* Bald eagle film is a 33-minute treat. Audubon. 64(1):61.
117	Anonymous. *1962.* Bald eagle in danger. Sci. News Letter. 81(3):36.
118	Anonymous. *1962.* Bald eagle. Sci. News Letter. 81(4):224.
119	Anonymous. *1963.* Will the bald eagle disappear? Rod and Gun. 64(8):20.
120	Anonymous. *1963.* Protect American eagles, federal and state laws forbid hunting them. Flicker. 35(4):117.
121	Anonymous. *1966.* 1965, a rough year on eagles, osprey. Mich. Aud. Soc. Newsl. 13(5):2.
122	Anonymous. *1966.* New step to protect bald eagle. Conservationist. 20(5):40.
123	Anonymous. *1966.* Help for the eagle. Natl. Parks Mag. 40(223):21-22.
124	Anonymous. *1966.* Potomac eagle refuges. Living Wilderness. 30(94):45.
125	Anonymous. *1966.* Eagles' nest protected in safe square mile. Sci. News Letter. 89(8):119.
126	Anonymous. *1966.* Bald eagles of Jeffrey Reservoir. Nebraskaland.(March 1966):25-27.
127	Anonymous. *1967.* The bald eagle. Happy Hunt. Grounds. 23(1):18-19.
128	Anonymous. *1967.* Private power company joins fight to save the bald eagle. Raptor. Res. News. 1(3):41-42.
129	Anonymous. *1967.* Hawk and eagle numbers in decline. Natl. Parks Mag. 41(232):20-21.
130	Anonymous. *1969.* American bald eagle. Zoonooz. 42(7):13.
131	Anonymous. *1969.* Bald eagles. Neb. Bird Rev. 37(4):61-63.
132	Anonymous. *1969.* Organochlorine pesticide residues: a review of some recent findings. PANS(Pest Articles and News Summaries). 15(2):163-167.
133	Anonymous. *1970.* The bald eagle. N.J. Outdoors. 20(10):24-25.
134	Anonymous. *1970.* Bald eagles poisoned by mercury. Raptor Res. News. 4(3):70-71.
135	Anonymous. *1970.* New reports on pesticides in eagles. Raptor Res. News. 4(2):34-35.
136	Anonymous. *1970.* A wealth of eagles. Am. Home. 73(11):63-69.
137	Anonymous. *1971.* The vanishing eagle. Chemistry. 44(8):3.
138	Anonymous. *1971.* Protection for birds of prey. Biol. Conserv. 3(3):168.
139	Anonymous. *1971.* Bald eagle threatened. Conservationist. 25(5):38.
140	Anonymous. *1971.* DDT wiping out Maine eagles. Raptor Res. News. 5(1):4-5.
141	Anonymous. *1971.* They're poisoning your wildlife. Colorful Colorado. 7(1):10-16,81.
142	Anonymous. *1971.* Loss of the eagles in Wyoming: how one federal agency replied to the protests. Audubon Bull.(160):13-14.
143	Anonymous. *1972.* Hats off to Wikoff: eagles back with young. The Calif. Condor. 7(2):15.
144	Anonymous. *1972.* The symbol of America is vanishing. You can help save him. Hunt-Wesson Foods, Inc.(Advertisement). 1 p.
145	Anonymous. *1972.* Bald eagle survives shooting, information rewarded . Conserv. News. 37(10):10-11.
146	Anonymous. *1973.* Eagle protector. Ill. Aud. Bull.(164):49.
147	Anonymous. *1973.* Three records set at Hawk Mountain. Penn. Game News. 44(7):11.
148	Anonymous. *1973.* Raptor research by the Bureau of Sport Fisheries and Wildlife. Raptor Res. 7(1):17-21.
149	Anonymous. *1974.* Saving the eagle with a computer. Raptor Res. 8(3/4):84.
150	Anonymous. *1974.* Caged bald eagle. Defend. Wildl. Int. 49(5):416.
151	Anonymous. *1974.* Eagle transplant successful. Defend. Wildl. Int. 49(5):429.

Master No.	Citation

152   Anonymous. *1974.* Proposed dam on Missouri will harm national eagle refuge. Raptor Res. 8(3/4):80-83.

153   Anonymous. *1974..* A refuge for bald eagles in South Dakota. N. Dakota Outdoors. 37(4):18.

154   Anonymous. *1974..* One thousand pairs of bald eagles. N. Dakota Outdoors. 36(10):15.

155   Anonymous. *1974.* A rehabilitation and conservation program for raptorial birds in Minnesota. Defend. Wildl. News. 49(1):28-30.

156   Anonymous. *1974.* Bald eagle 'egg transplant' termed success. BioScience. 24(9):535.

157   Anonymous. *1974.* Eagle killers. Defend. Wildl. News. 49(3):250.

158   Anonymous. *1975.* America's bald eagle: A bicentennial tribute from Mutual of Omaha's Wild Kingdom. Mutual of Omaha.(Poster). 1 p.

159   Anonymous. *1975.* Bald eagles. Excellence in Western Illinois. Western Illinois University Press. 2 pp.

160   Anonymous. *1976.* Bald eagles in Ohio. The Surveyor. 5(1):1.

161   Anonymous. *1976.* People and places. BioScience. 26(1):69-70.

162   Anonymous. *1976.* National bird nested in central Ohio. Metro. Park. News. 27(7):1-2.

163   Anonymous. *1976.* Two eagles begin $10,000 DDT test. Raptor Report. 4(2):7.

164   Anonymous. *1976.* National bird given added protection. Raptor Report. 4(3):14.

165   Anonymous. *1976.* A people's history and the birds of prey. Raptor Report. 4(3):13-14.

166   Anonymous. *1976.* Bald eagles. Audubon. 78(3):132-133.

167   Anonymous. *1976.* Bald eagle killer put to work as part of sentence. Ill. Aud. Bull. 177(Summer):24.

168   Anonymous. *1976.* Skagit River bald eagle sanctuary. Nat. Conserv. News.(Spring):22.

169   Anonymous. *1977.* Winter season field notes:Dec.-Feb. 1977. N.J. Audubon. 3(5/6):77-82.

170   Anonymous. *1977.* Bald eagles for the tricentennial. Cincinnati Zoo News.(Winter 1976-77):14.

171   Anonymous. *1977.* Eagles set record. The North Woods Call. 23(8):1.

172   Anonymous. *1977.* Tomorrows dinosaurs? Senior Scolastic:Teacher's Edition. 109(16):11.

173   Anonymous. *1977.* Wanted: information on color-marked bald eagles. N. Am. Bird Band. 2(4):170.

174   Anonymous. *1977.* Color-marked bald eagles. N. Am. Bird Band. 2(4):170.

175   Anonymous. *1977.* Brainstorming nets novel idea - trapping eagles. Wildlife News. Colorado Div. Wildlife. 2(4):2-3.

176   Anonymous. *1977.* Southland's gift to the bald eagle. Southland Family.(Spring):21-23.

177   Anonymous. *1977.* Endangered birds making comeback. Valley Sportsman. 19(11):1.

178   Anonymous. *1977.* Eagles in Arkansas. Ark. Aud. News. 22(1):1.

179   Anonymous. *1978.* Eagles numerous in Jackson's Canyon. High Country News. 10(6):7.

180   Anonymous. *1978.* Eagles numerous in Jackson Canyon. High Country News. 10(6):7.

181   Anthony, E.F. *1947.* Birds at 'The Anchorage', Surry, Maine. Maine Aud. Soc. Bull. 3(3):25-27.

182   Arizona Game and Fish Dept. *1976.* Orme Dam trouble for southern bald eagles. Information Div. Wildlife Newsletter. 10(24):1-2.

183   Arizona Game and Fish Dept. *1976.* Nongame Investigations. Wildlife Surveys and Investigations. Special Performance Report. W-53-R-26. 52 pp.

184   Arizona Game and Fish Dept. *1976.* Threatened wildlife of Arizona. January, 1976. 5 pp.

185   Arizona Game and Fish Dept. *1976.* Nongame Investigations. Wildlife Surveys and Investigations. Special Performance Report. W-53-R-27. 71 pp.

186   Arizona Game and Fish Dept. *1976.* Nongame Investigations. Wildlife Surveys and Investigations. Special Performance Report. W-53-R-26. 46 pp.

187   Arrendondo, O. and S.L. Olson. *1976.* The great predatory birds of the pleistocene of Cuba. Smith. Contrib. to Paleobiology. 27:169-187.

188   Arvey, M.D. *1947.* A Check-list of the Birds of Idaho. Museum of Nat. History. Univ. of Kansas Pub. 1(10):193-216.

189   Ashworth, C.W. *1930.* 1930 collecting notes. Ventura County, Calif. Oologist. 47(10):122,124.

190   Audubon, J.J. *1828.* Notes on the bird of Washington *(Falco washingtoniana)* or great American sea eagle. Mag. of Nat. Hist. 1(2):115-120.

191   Audubon, J.J. *1834.* Ornithological Biography: Or an Account of the Habits of the Birds of the United States of America. Vol. 5. Adam & Charles Black, Edinburgh. 664 pp.

192   Audubon, J.J. *1967.* The Birds of America. (Vol.1). Dover Publications, Inc. New York. 199 pp.

193   Austin, G.T. *1968.* Additional bird records for southern Nevada. The Auk. 85(4):692.

194   Austin, O. *1961.* Birds of the World. Golden Press, New York. 316 pp.

195   Aycock, R., Jr. *1972.* Eagle and osprey progress report. (Unpublished Progress Report). 7 pp.

196   Aycock, R., Jr. *1973.* Eagle and osprey progress report, fiscal year 1973. (Unpublished Progress Report). 5 pp.

197   Aycock, R., Jr. *1978.* Bald eagle nest survey Louisiana - Mississippi, March 14, 1978. (Unpublished Progress Report). 4 pp.

198   Aymar, G. *1936.* Bird Flight. Dodd Mead. 234 pp.

199   Bagg, A.C. and S.A. Eliot, Jr. *1937.* Birds of the Connecticut Valley in Massachusetts. The Hampshire Bookshop, Northhampton, MA. 813 pp.

Master No.   **Citation**

200   Bagg, E. *1889.* A series of Florida eggs of the bald eagle. Ornithol. and Oologist. 14(5):73-74.

201   Bagley, G.E. and L.N. Locke. *1967.* The occurrence of lead in tissues of wild birds. Bull. Env. Contam. Toxic. 2(5):297-305.

202   Bagley, G.E., W.L. Reichel, and E. Cromartie. *1970.* Identification of polychlorinated biphenyls in two bald eagles by combined gas-liquid chromotography- mass spectrometry. J. Assoc. Off. Anal. Chem. 53(2):251-261.

203   Bailey, A.M. *1919.* The bald eagle in Louisiana. Wilson Bull. 31(2):52-55.

204   Bailey, A.M. *1928.* Notes on the winter birds of Chenier Au Tigre, Louisiana. The Auk. 45(3):271-282.

205   Bailey, A.M. *1948.* Birds of Arctic Alaska. Colorado Museum of Natural History. Pop. Series No. 8 317 pp.

206   Bailey, A.M. and E.G. Wright. *1931.* Birds of southern Louisiana. Wilson Bull. 43(3):190-219.

207   Bailey, A.M. and R.J. Niedrach. *1965.* Birds of Colorado Vol. 1. Denver Museum of Nat. History, Denver, CO. 895 pp.

208   Bailey, B.H. *1918.* The Raptorial Birds of Iowa. Iowa Geological Survey. Bulletin No. 6. 238 pp.

209   Bailey, F.M. *1902.* Handbook of Birds of the Western United States. Houghton Mifflin Co., Boston and New York. 514 pp.

210   Bailey, F.M. *1918.* Wild Animals of Glacier National Park. The Birds. U.S.D.I. National Park Service. 210 pp.

211   Bailey, F.M. *1928.* Birds of New Mexico. New Mexico Dept. of Game and Fish. 807 pp.

212   Bailey, H.H. *1913.* Notes from Virginia. Oologist. 30(5):85.

213   Bailey, H.H. *1914.* Eagle notes from Virginia. Oologist. 31(2):29-30.

214   Bailey, H.H. *1915.* The bald eagle. Oologist. 32(11):177,179.

215   Bailey, H.H. *1918.* The bald eagle *(Haliaeetus leucocephalus)* in Virginia. Oologist. 35(8):112-113.

216   Bailey, H.H. *1919.* How I lost that set of four bald eagles. Oologist. 36(1):2,4.

217   Bailey, H.H. *1930.* The bald eagle *(Haliaeetus leucocephalus)* in Florida. Oologist. 47(11):137-138.

218   Bailey, H.H. *1930.* Concerning the bald eagle in Florida. Oologist. 47(1):10-11.

219   Bailey, V. *1930.* Animal Life of Yellowstone National Park. Charles C. Thomas, Springfield, IL. 241 pp.

220   Baird, R.L. *1931.* A bald eagle swims. Wilson Bull. 43(4):308-309.

221   Baird, S.F., T.M. Brewer and R. Ridgway. *1905.* A History of North American Birds. Land Birds. Vol. III. Little Brown, and Co., Boston. 560 pp.

222   Baker, B.W. *1939.* A 1939 bald eagle nesting record. Jack-Pine Warb. 17(4):114.

223   Baker, J.H. *1940.* Bald eagle bill enacted. Bird-Lore. 42(4):363.

224   Baker, J.H. *1950.* Alaska pays bounties on bald eagles. Audubon. 52(2):120-121.

225   Baldwin, G.C. *1944.* Unusual records of birds from Boulder Dam area, Nevada. The Condor. 46(4):206-207.

226   Baldwin, W.P. *1940.* Bald eagle robbing marsh hawk. The Auk. 57(3):413.

227   Bangs, O. *1898.* Some new races of birds from eastern North America. The Auk. 15(2):174-183.

228   Banks, R.C. *1966.* Terrestrial vertebrates of Anacapa Island, California. Trans. of San Diego Soc. of Nat. History. 14(14):179.

229   Banks, V. *1976.* How much plucking can the bald eagle stand? Mariah. 1(1):52-53,66-68.

230   Banks, V. *1976.* Understanding our national symbol, the bald eagle. Sierra Club Bull. (Nov/Dec):42-43.

231   Barbour, R.W., C.T. Peterson, D. Rust, H.E. Shadowen, and A.L. Whitt, Jr. *1973.* Kentucky Birds, a Finding Guide. The Univ. Press of Kentucky. 306 pp.

232   Bare, O.S. *1936.* The bald eagle in Antelope County. Neb. Bird Rev. 4(4):84.

233   Barger, B.A. *1963.* Bald eagles hatched in captivity. Pass. Pigeon. 25(1):24-25.

234   Barger, N.R. (ed.). *1944.* The spring season. Pass. Pigeon. 6(3):69-71.

235   Barnes, I.R. *1951.* Persecution or freedom? Audubon. 53(5):282-289.

236   Barnes, I.R. *1951.* The bald eagle with a price on its head. Atl. Nat. 7(1):3-13.

237   Barnes, I.R. *1966.* Bald eagle-symbol of greatness or of doom. Atl. Nat. 21(4):159.

238   Barnes, R.M. *1890.* List of birds breeding in Marshall County, Ill. Ornithol. and Oologist. 15(8):113-116.

239   Barnes, R.M. *1913.* More big eagle eggs. Oologist. 30(6):97,100.

240   Barnes, R.M. *1916.* The eagle's flight. Oologist. 33(1):1.

241   Barnes, R.M. *1916.* The bald eagle. Oologist. 33(1):8.

242   Barnes, R.M. *1924.* Eagles rapidly becoming extinct. Oologist. 41(7):84-85.

243   Barnes, R.M. *1926.* Famous bald eagle nest no more. Oologist. 43(8):114.

244   Barnes, R.M. *1936.* An outrage. Oologist. 53(6):78.

245   Barnes, R.M. *1939.* Law breaking mayor kills a bald eagle. Oologist. 56(12):134-135.

246   Barnes, R.M. *1940.* Another bald eagle killer. Oologist. 57(1):8.

247   Barnes, R.M. *1940.* Scandalous! Oologist. 57(9):107.

248   Barrett, L.L. *1947.* Eagles in Minnesota. Flicker. 19(2):53-54.

249   Barrows, W.B. *1912.* Michigan Bird Life. Special Bull. Dept. of Zoology and Physiology. Michigan Agric. College. 836 pp.

250   Batchelder, C.F. *1881.* The bald eagle *(Haliaeetus leucocephalus)* as a hunter. Bull. Nuttall Ornithol. Club. 6(1):58-60.

Master No.	Citation

251   Bauers, H.A. *1962.* Winter Season. December, 1961 - February, 1962. Pass. Pigeon. 24(3):93-103.

252   Bauers, H.A. *1964.* Winter Season. December, 1963 - February, 1964. Pass. Pigeon. 26(3):143-155.

253   Bauers, H.A. *1965.* Winter Season. December 1, 1964-February 28, 1965. Pass. Pigeon. 27(4):160-171.

254   Baynard, O.E. *1913.* Breeding birds of Alachua County, Florida. The Auk. 30(2):240-247.

255   Baynard, O.E. *1916.* The bald eagle in Florida. Oologist. 33(2):17-20,21,23,25.

256   Beal, W.J. *1867.* Novel way of shooting eagles. Am. Nat. 1(8):439.

257   Beals, E. *1958.* Notes on the summer birds of the Apostle Islands. Pass. Pigeon. 20(4):151-160.

258   Beardslee, C.S. and H.D. Mitchell. *1965.* The Birds of the Niagara Frontier region. An Annotated Checklist. Bull. Buffalo Soc. of Nat. Sciences. Vol. 22. 478 pp.

259   Bebe, J. *1886.* Eagles breeding in captivity. Forest and Stream. 26(17):327.

260   Beck, H.H. *1924.* A Chapter on the Ornithology of Lancaster County, Pennsylvania. The Lewis Historical Pub. Co., Inc. New York. 39 pp.

261   Beck, H.H. *1939.* Mt. Johnson Island Eagle Sanctuary. Bird-Lore. 41(4):222-224.

262   Beck, H.H. *1958.* Sterility in Pennsylvania eagles? Audubon. 60(6):286.

263   Beckett, T.A., III. *1970.* Nesting of the bald eagle in the Charleston, S. C. region. The Chat. 34(2):48-49.

264   Beebe, C.W. *1901.* Enterprising eagles. Bird-Lore. 3(1):34.

265   Beebe, C.W. *1965.* The Bird: Its Form and Function. Dover Pub., Inc. New York. 374 pp.

266   Beebe, F.L. *1974.* Field Studies of the Falconiformes (Vultures, Eagles, Hawks, and Falcons) of British Columbia. Occasional Papers of the British Columbia Provincial Museum No. 17. 163 pp.

267   Belcher, M. *1961.* Birds of Regina. Saskatchewan Nat. Hist. Soc. Special Pub. No. 3. 76 pp.

268   Belding, L. *1890.* Land Birds of the Pacific District. Calif. Acad. of Sciences, San Francisco. 274 pp.

269   Belisle, A.A., W.L. Reichel, L.N. Locke, T.G. Lamont, B.M. Mulhern, R.M. Prouty, R.B. DeWolf, and E. Cromartie. *1972.* Residues of organochlorine pesticides, polychlorinated biphenyls, and mercury and autopsy data for bald eagles, 1969 and 1970. Pest. Monit. J. 6(3):133-138.

270   Bellrose, F.C., Jr. *1944.* Bald eagles nesting in Illinois. The Auk. 61(3):467-468.

271   Bendell, J.F. *1959.* Bony shells of musk turtles in nest of bald eagle. Can. Field-Nat. 73(2):131-132.

272   Bender, R.O. *1960.* American coot successfully escapes from a bald eagle. Wilson Bull. 72(4):404-405.

273   Bendire, C.E. *1892.* Life Histories of North American Birds. Smithsonian Institution, Special Bull. No. 1. 518 pp.

274   Bendire, C.E. *1892.* Bald eagle. Forest and Stream. 38(8):172-173.

275   Bennett, E. *1974.* Eagle transplant successful. Defend. Wildl. Int. 49(5):429.

276   Bennett, L.J. *1935.* Bald eagles and American mergansers. Iowa Bird Life. 5(1):11.

277   Bent, A.C. *1924.* Birds observed in southeastern Texas in May, 1923. Wilson Bull. 36(1):1-20.

278   Bent, A.C. and M. Copeland. *1927.* Notes on Florida birds. The Auk. 44(3):371-386.

279   Bergman, J. *1956.* About: the eagle. N.Y. Times Mag. April 22:67.

280   Berry, L.T. *1957.* May regional census: 1957. Atl. Nat. 12(5):251-254.

281   Besadny, C.D. *1954.* The early spring season. February - April 1954. Pass. Pigeon. 16(3):113-120.

282   Beshears, W.W., Jr. *1959.* Statewide waterfowl development. Alabama Div. of Game and Fish. Ala. W-034-D-06/ Wk. Pl. 01. 10 pp.

283   Beverly, R. *1975.* Osprey and eagle. Conservationist. 30(3):8.

284   Beyer, G.E., A. Allison, and H.H. Kopman. *1908.* List of the birds of Louisiana., Part V. The Auk. 25(4):439-448.

285   Bishop, L.B. *1900.* Birds of the Yukon region, with notes on other species. *In:* Results of a Biological Reconnaissance of the Yukon River Region. Osgood, W.H. (ed.) North American Fauna No. 19. 100 pp.

286   Black, C.A. *1933.* A bald eagle killed by an auto. Neb. Bird Rev. 1(2):31-32.

287   Black, J.D. *1929.* The bald eagle in Arkansas. Wilson Bull. 41(1):41.

288   Blackwelder, E. *1919.* Notes on the summer birds of the Upper Yukon region, Alaska. The Auk. 36(1):57-64.

289   Blake, E.W., Jr. *1887.* Summer birds of Santa Cruz Island, California. The Auk. 4(4):328-330.

290   Blanchan, N. *1898.* Birds That Hunt and Are Hunted. Doubleday & McClure Co., New York. 359 pp.

291   Blocher, A. *1926.* Large sets. Oologist. 43(4):49-50.

292   Blum, J.R. *1965.* Eagle versus fish. The Condor. 67(2):190.

293   Blume, I.E. *1947.* One that got away. Yellowstone Nature Notes. 21(6):70-71.

294   Blus, L.J., S.N. Wiemeyer, J.A. Kerwin, R.C. Stendell, H.M. Ohlendorf and L.F. Stickel. *1977.* Impact of estuarine pollution on birds. *In:* Proc. from a Conf. on Estuarine Pollution Control and Assessment. U.S. E.P.A. Office of Water Planning and Standards. 1:57-709

295   Bogan, E.C. *1966.* Old Abe. Audubon Bull.(137):6-8.

296   Bogan, E.C. *1969.* In company of eagles. Audubon Bull. (151):8-9.

297   Bogan, E.C. *1970.* Bald eagles, Elton Fawks, and all members - take note. Audubon Bull.(153):6.

298   Bogan, E.C. *1973.* The eagles numbered nine. Audubon Bull.(164):45.

299   Bogue, G.L. *1977.* Ishi comes home. Defend. Wildl. News. 52(1):4-9.

Master No.   Citation

300   Bolander, L.P., Jr. *1933.* Bald eagle nesting on Monterey coast. The Condor. 35(6):238.
301   Bonnell, C. *1935.* The occurrence of the American eagle along the Ohio River in Illinois. Trans. Ill. Acad. Sci. 28(2):249-250.
302   Botty, K. *1967.* How to shoot eagles. Field and Stream. 71(9):60-61.
303   Bowes, R. *1975.* Pere Marquette eagle roost. *In:* Bald Eagle Land: Preservation and Acquisition. Proc. of Bald Eagle Days, 1975, Jan. 31-Feb. 2. Ingram, T.N. (ed.). Eagle Valley Environmentalists, Inc. Apple River, IL. p. 12-14.
304   Braun, C.E. *1975.* Conservation Committee Report on Status of Eagles. Wilson Bull. 7(1):140-143.
305   Breckenridge, W.J. *1946.* Bird hawks, eagles, and vultures. Conserv. Vol. 9(50):16-22.
306   Breckenridge, W.J. *1960.* A bald eagle exploit: Dog rescues collie attacked by eagle. Flicker. 32(2):63.
307   Breninger, G.F. *1904.* San Clemente Island and its birds. The Auk. 21(2):218-223.
308   Brett, J.J. and A.C. Nagy. *1973.* Feathers in the Wind; The Mountain and the Migration. Kutztown Pub. Co., Inc. Kutztown, Pa. 69 pp.
309   Brewster, W. *1880.* Prowess of the bald eagle. Bull. Nutall Ornithol. Club. 5(1):57-58.
310   Brewster, W. *1924.* The birds of Lake Umbagog region of Maine. Bull. of the Mus. of Comp. Zoology, Harvard Univ., Cambridge, Mass. 66(Part 2):340-349.
311   Brewster, W. *1954.* St. Mary's Georgia: 1878. Hebard, F.V.(ed.). The Oriole. 19(2):13-18.
312   Bridge, D. *1959.* Maryland nest summary for 1959. Md. Birdlife. 15(4):89-96.
313   Bridge, D. *1961.* Maryland nest summary for 1960. Md. Birdlife. 17(3):73-79.
314   Bridge, D. and M. Riedel. *1962.* Maryland nest summary for 1961. Md. Birdlife. 18(3):64-70.
315   Bridge, D. and M.A. Bridge. *1964.* Maryland nest summary for 1963. Md. Birdlife. 20(2):40-47.
316   Bridge, M.A. *1963.* Maryland nest summary for 1962. Md. Birdlife. 19(2):55-62.
317   Bridgwater, D.D. *1972.* Status of rare and endangered birds in captivity with a general reference to mammals. Zoologica. 57(3):119-125.
318   Briggs, S.A. *1957.* Safer passage for hawks in Pennsylvania. Atl. Nat. 12(6):293-296.
319   Brigham, E.M., Jr. *1939.* Lazy eagles. Jack-Pine Warb. 17(3):59-63.
320   Brimley, C.S. and J.H. Grey, Jr. *1940.* The season., 135., August 15 to October 15, 1940., Carolina region. Bird-Lore. 42(6, Suppl.):573-574.
321   **British Columbia Provincial Museum.** *1904.* Catalogue of British Columbia Birds. Victoria, B.C. 69 pp.
322   Brodkorb, P. *1955.* Number of feathers and weights of various systems in a bald eagle. Wilson Bull. 67(2):142.
323   Brodkorb, P. *1972.* New discoveries of Pliocene birds in Florida. *In:* Proc. of the 15th International Ornithological Congress, The Hague. p. 634.
324   Broley, C.L. *1947.* Migration and nesting of Florida bald eagles. Wilson Bull. 59(1):3-20.
325   Broley, C.L. *1947.* Migration and nesting of Florida bald eagles. Wilson Bull. 59(1):1-68.
326   Broley, C.L. *1950.* Florida bald eagle threat growing. Aububon. 52(3):139,141.
327   Broley, C.L. *1950.* Plight of the Florida bald eagle. Audubon. 52(1):41-49.
328   Broley, C.L. *1950.* The plight of the Florida bald eagle. (Reprinted from Florida Wildlife). National Wildlife and Conservation Digest. (June):44-48.
329   Broley, C.L. *1951.* Plight of the Florida bald eagle worsens. Audubon. 53(2):72,136.
330   Broley, C.L. *1952.* Broley reports on eagles. Audubon. 54(2):71-72.
331   Broley, C.L. *1953.* The eagle and me, a retired banker's hobby. Can. Bank. 60(1):99-106.
332   Broley, C.L. *1954 - 1959.* Personal communications. (Letters to Elton Fawks). 26 pp.
333   Broley, C.L. *1957.* The bald eagle in Florida. Atl. Nat. 12(5):230-231.
334   Broley, C.L. *1957.* Bald eagle nesting failures continue. Audubon. 53(4):208.
335   Broley, C.L. *1958.* Plight of the American bald eagle. Audubon. 60(4):162-163,171.
336   Broley, M.J. *1941.* Banding eagles in Florida. Am. Forests. 47(2):70-72.
337   Broley, M.J. *1945.* How Broley bands bald eagles. Country Guide. 64(9):32,34.
338   Broley, M.J. *1952.* Broley bands 'em high. Natural Hist. 61(1):40-45.
339   Broley, M.J. *1952.* Eagle Man. Pellegrini and Cudahy, Pub., NY. 210 pp.
340   Bromley, R.G. and D.L. Trauger. *1974.* Ground nesting of bald eagles near Yellowknife, Northwest Territories. Can. Field-Nat. 88(1):73-75.
341   Brookfield, C.M. *1965.* Fourth bald eagle nesting survey in Maine, 1965. Maine Field-Nat. 21(6):3-4.
342   Brooks, A. *1922.* Notes on the abundance and habits of the bald eagle in British Columbia. The Auk. 39(4):556-559.
343   Brooks, A.B. *1931.* Bald eagle captured in a trap set for a hawk. Wilson Bull. 43(2):145.
344   Brooks, D. *1938.* Bald eagle at Spruce Knob, W. Va. Redstart. 6(2):10.
345   Brotherton, W.A. *1894.* Reappearance of bald eagles in south-east Michigan. Oologist. 11(6):214.
346   Broun, M. *1960.* Hawks Aloft: The Story of Hawk Mountain. Kutztown Pub. Co., Kutztown, Pa. 222 pp.
347   Broun, M. *1966.* What future for birds of prey? Audubon. 68(5):331-334,341-342.
348   Brown, G.W. *1967.* Bald eagles. Neb. Bird Rev. 35:45.
349   Brown, J.A.H. *1867.* Baldheaded eagle in Achill. Zoologist. 25:562-563.

Master No.   Citation

350   Brown, L.H. *1955.* Eagles. Michael Joseph, London. 274 pp.
351   Brown, L.H. *1976.* Birds of Prey: Their Biology and Ecology. Hamlyn Pub. Co. London. 256 pp.
352   Brown, L.H. *1977.* Eagles of the World. Universe Books. New York, N.Y. 244 pp.
353   Brown, L.H. and D. Amadon. *1968.* Eagles, Hawks and Falcons of the World. (Two volumes) McGraw-Hill Book Co., New York. 945 pp.
354   Brown, L.P. *1975.* The bald eagle. Conservationist. 30(3):8.
355   Brown, V., H.G. Weston and J. Buzzell. *1973.* Handbook of California Birds. Naturegraph Pub., Healdsburg. 224 pp.
356   Brown, W.H. *1975.* Winter population trends in the bald eagle. Am. Birds. 29(1):12-14.
357   Browning, M.R. *1975.* The distribution and occurrence of the birds of Jackson County, Oregon and surrounding areas. N. American Fauna No. 70. 69 pp.
358   Bruner, L. *1896.* Some Notes on Nebraska Birds. State Journal Co., Printers. Lincoln, NE. 177 pp.
359   Bruner, L. *1901.* Birds that nest in Nebraska. State Board of Agriculture. Lincoln, NE. p. 240-253.
360   Bry, E. *1975.* Young eagle dies. N. Dakota Outdoors. October:10.
361   Bry, E. *1975.* Bald eagle nest in North Dakota. North Dakota Out. 38(2):2-4.
362   Bryan, M. *1901.* A study of the birds of Santiago Canyon. The Condor. 3(3):81-82.
363   Bryant, W.E. *1889.* A catalogue of the birds of lower California, Mexico. Proc. Calif. Acad. of Sciences. 2:237-320.
364   Buchanan, B.W. *1977.* Observations of wintering bald eagles *(Haliaeetus leucocephalus alascanus)* along a portion of the Mississippi River, Nov. 10, 1976 to Feb. 23, 1977. (Unpublished Report). 7 pp.
365   Buchheister, C.W. *1961.* The bald eagle in Alaska. Audubon Mag. 63(4):224-225.
366   Buchheister, C.W. *1961.* A bill to save both eagles. Audubon. 63(5):258-259.
367   Buchheister, C.W. *1961.* Continental bald eagle project. Audubon. 63(1):18-19.
368   Buchheister, C.W. *1961.* Bald eagle study off to good start. Audubon. 63(2):95.
369   Buchheister, C.W. *1962.* Bald eagle research is urgent. Audubon. 64(1):22.
370   Buchheister, C.W. *1962.* Eagle slaughter is shameful thing. Audubon. 64(3):148.
371   Buckley, J.L. *1963.* Effects of pesticides upon wild birds and mammals. *In:* Symp. on Use and Effects of Pesticides. N.Y. State Legislative Comm. on Natural Resources. 12 pp.
372   Buckley, J.L. and J.B. Dewitt. *1963.* 1963 Progress report-Pesticide-bald eagle relationships. *In:* A Florida Notebook, National Audubon Society Annual Convention, Miami, FL. Nov. 9-13, 1963. p. 15-20.
373   Bull, J. *1964.* Birds of the New York Area. Harper and Row, Pub., New York. 540 pp.
374   Bull, W.P. *1936.* From Hummingbird to Eagle; An Account of North American Birds Which Appear or Have Appeared in the County of Peel. George J. McLeod, Ltd. Toronto. 300 pp.
375   Burdick, G.M. *1898.* Notes from Wisconsin - bald eagle. Wilson Bull. 10(19):24.
376   Burleigh, T.D. *1944.* The Bird Life of the Gulf Coast Region of Mississippi. Museum of Zoology, Louisiana State University, Occasional Papers No. 20. p. 331-490.
377   Burleigh, T.D. *1958.* Georgia Birds. Univ. of Oklahoma Press. Norman, OK. 746 pp.
378   Burleigh, T.D. *1972.* Birds of Idaho. The Caxton Printers, Ltd. Caldwell, ID. 467 pp.
379   Burns, F.L. *1929.* The vanished glory of Great Egg Harbor Bay region, New Jersey. Oologist. 46(3):33-39.
380   Burr, F.F. *1912.* Note on the bald eagle and osprey. The Auk. 29(3):393.
381   Burt, H.C. *1911.* An early spring trip to Anacapa Island. The Condor. 13(5):164-167.
382   Butler, A.W. *1897.* The Birds of Indiana. 22nd Ann. Report of Dept. of Geology and Natural Resources of Indiana, 1897.
383   Byrd, G.V., D.L. Johnson and D.D. Gibson. *1974.* The birds of Adak Island, Alaska. The Condor. 76(3):288-300.
384   Byrd, M.A., D. Prince and R.L. Moon, Jr. *1978.* The saga of the American bald eagle. Tennessee Wildlife. 1(4):19-21.
385   Bystrak, D. *1968.* Maryland nest summary for 1967. Md. Birdlife. 24(1):10-16.
386   Bystrak, D. *1969.* Maryland nest summary for 1968. Md. Birdlife. 25(2):43-50.
387   Cade, T.J., and P.R. Daque. (eds.). *1976.* Hacking bald eagles. The Peregrine Fund Newsl.(4):8-9.
388   Cahn, A.R. *1927.* Summer birds in the vicinity of Plum Lake, Vilas County, Wisconsin. Wilson Bull. 39(1):23-24.
389   Cahn, A.R. *1947.* Notes on the birds of the Dutch Harbor area of the Aleutian Islands. The Condor. 49(2):78-82.
390   Cain, S.A., J.A. Kadlec, D.L. Allen, R.A. Cooley, M.G. Hornocker, A.S. Leopold and F.H. Wagner. *1972.* Report to the Council on Environmental Quality and the Dept. of Interior. Institute for Environmental Quality. Univ. of Michigan. Ann Arbor, MI. 207 pp.
391   Cairns, J.S. *1889.* The summer birds of Buncombe County, North Carolina. Ornithol. and Oologist. 14(2):17-23.
392   Caldwell, J. *1936.* Recent eagle occurrences. Migrant. 8(2):46.
393   California Dept. of Fish and Game. *1972.* At the crossroad. Dept. of Fish and Game. 105 pp.

Master No.	Citation

394   California Dept. of Fish and Game. *1974.* Biennial report on the status of California's rare and endangered fish and wildlife. Dept. of Fish and Game. 112 pp.

395   California Dept. of Fish and Game. *1975.* California raptor survey. Nongame Wildlife Investigations, Survey and Inventory. Proj. No. W-54-R-7, Job. No. III-1.0. 14 pp.

396   Callahan, P.S. *1974.* The Magnificent Birds of Prey. Holiday House, New York. 190 pp.

397   Callison, C.H. *1971.* Massacre of eagles. Audubon. 73(4):94-95.

398   Callison, C.H. *1971.* Eagles are protected by federal law. Audubon. 73(5):109.

399   Camarena, A.M. *1976.* Environmental Analysis Report: Three Sisters Bald Eagle Wintering Area Management Unit. U.S.D.A. Forest Service, Goosenest Ranger District. 80 pp.

400   Cameron, E.S. *1907.* The birds of Custer and Dawson Counties, Montana. The Auk. 24(3):241-270.

401   Campbell, R.W. *1969.* Bald eagle swimming in ocean with prey. The Auk. 86(3):561.

402   Campbell, R.W., M.G. Shepard and R.H. Drent. *1972.* Status of birds in the Vancouver area in 1970. Syesis. 5:137-167.

403   Cantwell, G.G. *1890.* A list of the birds of Minnesota. Ornithol. and Oologist. 15(9):129-137.

404   Cantwell, G.G. *1899.* Nesting of the Alaska bald eagle. Osprey. 3(5):66-67.

405   Carleton, W. *1911.* Eagle and aeroplane. Harper's Weekly. 55(2861):32.

406   Carlson, M. *1971.* Unusual hawk migration. The Loon. 43(1):25.

407   Carolina Bird Club. *1964.* Briefs for the file. The Chat. 28(2):55.

408   Carolina Bird Club. *1965.* Briefs for the file. The Chat. 29(2):57-58.

409   Carothers, S.W. and R.R. Johnson. *1975.* Recent observations on the status and distribution of some birds of the Grand Canyon region. Plateau. 47(4):140-153.

410   Carpenter, F.S. *1933.* Bald eagle and sandhill crane at Louisville. Kentucky Warb. 9(2):4.

411   Carr, W.H. *1944.* Eagles wild and tame. Nat. History. 53(10):442-447.

412   Carroll, J.J. *1899.* Brief observations on the raptorial birds of Refugio Co., Texas. Oologist. 16(2):46-48.

413   Carroll, J.J. *1900.* Untitled. The Condor. 2(2):29.

414   Case, R.G. *1977.* Eagle watch at Montezuma. Empire Magazine, Syracuse Herald American, Nov. 13, 1977. p. 6-11.

415   Casebeer, R.L., M.J. Rognrud And S.M. Brandborg. *1950.* The Rocky Mountain goat in Montana. Wildlife Survey and Management. Montana Fish and Game Dept. Bull. No. 5. 107 pp.

416   Casillo, N.R. *1937.* A few random notes on the bald eagle Nature Mag. 30(3):171-172.

417   Catton, B. *1963.* 'Old Abe' the battle eagle. Am. Heritage. 14(6):32,33,106,107.

418   Chace, L.B. *1962.* Bald eagle portrait. Bird-Lore. 28(6):397-398.

419   Chace, L.W. *1936.* Golden bald eagle. Oologist. 53(10):134-135.

420   Chamberlain, B.R. *1966.* Briefs for the file. The Chat. 30(1):31-33.

421   Chambers, F. *1903.* The Tennessee eagles. The Independent. 55(2829):495-496.

422   Chaney, R.W. *1910.* Summer and fall birds of the Hamlin Lake region, Mason County, Michigan. The Auk. 27(3):274.

423   Chaplin, T. *1978.* Soaring over the cypress. Tenn. Conservationist. 44(1):8-10.

424   Chapman, F.M. *1895.* Handbook of Birds of Eastern North America. D. Appleton and Co., New York. 581 pp.

425   Chapman, F.M. *1906.* The North American Eagles and Their Economic Relations. (A Review of a Book by H.C. Oberholser). Bird-Lore. 8(6):213 .

426   Chapman, F.M. *1912.* Color Key to North American Birds, With Bibliographic Appendix. D. Appleton & Comp., New York. 336 pp.

427   Chapman, F.M. *1932.* Handbook of Birds of Eastern North America, With Introductory Chapters on the Study of Birds in Nature. (Second Revised Edition). D. Appleton & Comp., New York. 581 pp

428   Chapman, F.M. *1943.* Birds and Man. American Museum of Natural History. Guide Leaflet Series No. 115. 52 pp.

429   Chatham, J.H. *1919.* The bald eagle on the Susquehanna. Altoona Tribune Co. 15 pp.

430   Cheyney, E.G. *1927.* Our national bird. St. Nicholas. 54(9):717.

431   Chrest, H.R. *1964.* Nesting of the bald eagle on the Karluk Lake Drainage Kodiak Island, Alaska. M.S. Thesis. Colorado State University, Fort Collins, CO. 72 pp.

432   Chura, N.J. and P.A. Stewart. *1967.* Care, food consumption, and behavior of bald eagles used in DDT tests. Wilson Bull. 79(4):441-448.

433   Clancey, P.A. *1950.* American bald eagle in Yorkshire. Brit. Birds. 43(10):339.

434   Clark, W.E. *1975.* Endangered species of the United States. National Wildlife Federation. 6 pp.

435   Clark, W.S. *1972.* Migration trapping of hawks (and owls) at Cape May, N. J.--Fifth year. EBBA. 35(2):121-131.

436   Clark, W.S. *1973.* Cape May Point raptor banding station--1972 results. EBBA News. Aug. 1973. p. 150-165.

437   Clark, W.S. *1974.* Cape May Point raptor banding station--1973 results EBBA News. Spring. p. 51-64.

438   Clark, W.S. *1975.* Cape May Point, New Jersey. *In:* A Convocation of Hawkwatchers. North American Hawk Migration Conf., Syracuse, NY. p. 6-8.

Master No.   Citation

439   Clark, W.S. *1976.* Cape May Point raptor banding station-1974 results. N. Am. Bird Band. 1(1):5-13.

440   Clark, W.S. *1977.* Sandy Hook spring raptor banding project, Project Report March-May 1977. (Unpublished Report). 7 pp.

441   Clarke, C.H.D., I.N. Gabrielson, H.A. Hochbaum, W.B. Robertson, Jr., G.S. Wallace and V.H. Cahalane. *1964.* Report of the Committee on Bird Protection, 1963. The Auk. 81(3):417-425.

442   Clarke, C.H.D., I.N. Gabrielson, B. Kessel, W.B. Robertson, Jr., G.S. Wallace and V.H. Cahalane. *1965.* Report of the Committee on Bird Protection, 196 4. The Auk. 82(3):477-491.

443   Clarke, S.C. *1876.* Fish hawks and eagles. Forest and Stream. 7(18):276.

444   Clarke and Morgan. *1884.* The bald eagle. Ornithol. and Oologist. 9(8):104.

445   Cnare, E. *1977.* Bald eagle-osprey. U.S.D.A. Forest Service, Eastern Region Office of Information, Information Press Release. 3 pp.

446   Cofer, H.H. *1939.* Summary of information concerning the hawks, eagles, and vultures of Missouri, including a general bulletin for public use. M.A. Thesis. Univ. of Missouri, Columbia, MO. 55 pp.

447   Coffey, M.A. *1977.* Wintering populations and behavior of southern bald eagles *(Haliaeetus leucocephalus leucocephalus)* in the San Bernardino Mountains. U.S.D.A. Forest Service. San Bernadino National Forest. (Unpublished Report). 39 pp.

448   Coffin, R.P.T. *1952.* Bald eagle. Saturday Rev. 35(2):10.

449   Cohen, M. *1976.* Arizona water project threatens wildlife values. Cons. News. 41(16):2-3.

450   Cole, J.N. *1978.* It's still not safe to be an eagle. Natl. Wildl. 17(1):12-17.

451   Colorado Div. of Wildlife. *1977.* Statewide raptor populations and characteristics studies. Raptor Investigations. Proj. No. W-124-R-4. Job No. 1. p. 177-197.

452   Comey, A.C. *1904.* A partial list of the summer birds of Holderness, New Hampshire. Wilson Bull. 16(1):5-9.

453   Compton, L.V. *1938.* The pterylosis of the Falconiformes with special attention to the taxonomic position of the osprey. Univ. of California Pub. in Zoology. 42(3):173-212.

454   Comstock, H. *1943.* The eagle in Americana. Antiques. 44(1):34-35.

455   Conrad, C. *1934.* Bald eagle collected in panhandle. Redstart. 1(7):4.

456   Cook, A.J. *1893.* Birds of Michigan. Michigan Agric. Expt. Station. Bull. 94. 148 pp.

457   Cooke, F., R.K. Ross, R.K. Schmidt and A.J. Pakulak. *1975.* Birds of the tundra biome at Cape Churchill and La Perouse Bay. Can. Field-Nat. 89(4):413-422.

458   Cooke, M.T. *1929.* Birds of the Washington, D. C. region. Proc. of Biol. Soc. Washington. 42:1-80.

459   Coon, N.C., L.N. Locke, E. Cromartie and W.L. Reichel. *1970.* Causes of bald eagle mortality, 1960-1965. J. Wildl. Dis. 6(1):72-76.

460   Coon, N.C. and L.N. Locke. *1968.* Aspergillosis in a bald eagle. Bull. Wildl. Disease Assoc. 4(2):51.

461   Cooper, J. *1976.* A bicentennial salute to the bald eagle. Dakota Outdoors. 38(10):16-18.

462   Cooper, J.E. *1972.* Veterinary Aspects of Captive Birds of Prey. A.R.C. Institute for Research on Animal Diseases, Compton, England. 47 pp.

463   Cooper, J.G. *1870.* Ornithology. Land Birds. (Vol. 1). Geological Survey of California. 592 pp.

464   Cope, M.E. *1977.* 1977 Annual midwinter bald eagle survey, Land Between the Lakes. TVA, Land Between the Lakes.(Report). 1 pp.

465   Corr, P.O. *1969.* Bald eagle nest ecology. Small Game, Waterfowl, and Furbearer Investigations. Alaska Dept. of Fish and Game. W-17-1. Study Plan B. Job. No. 9. 10 pp.

466   Corr, P.O. *1974.* Bald eagle *(Haliaeetus leucocephalus alascanus)* nesting related to forestry in southeastern Alaska. M.S. Thesis. Univ. of Alaska, College, AK. 144 pp.

467   Cory, C.B. *1887.* More news of *Ardea wuerdemanni.* The Auk. 4(2):159.

468   Coues, E. *1874.* Birds of the Northwest: A Handbook of the Ornithology of the Region Drained by the Missouri River and Its Tributaries. Govt. Printing Office. 791 pp.

469   Coues, E. *1878.* Field-notes on birds observed in Dakota and Montana along the forty-ninth parallel during the seasons of 1873 and 1874. Bull. of U.S. Geol. and Geog. Survey. Territory. 4(3):545-661.

470   Cowardin, L.M. *1961.* Experimental turkey stocking. Game Population Trend and Harvest Survey. Mass. Div. of Wild life. Job Report W-35-R-3. Job. 09. 10 pp.

471   Crabb, E.D. *1903.* A note on the economic status of the bald eagle in Alaska. The Auk. 40(3):419-423.

472   Crabb, E.D. *1922.* A note on the economic status of the bald eagle in Alaska. Proc. of the Okla. Acad. of Science. 2:66-68.

473   Craig, J.R. *1973.* The eagles, hawks, and falcons of Colorado. Colorado Outdoors. 22(2):24-33.

474   Craig, J.R. *1974.* Raptor populations and characteristics studies. Colorado Div. of Wildlife. Game Research Reports 1974. (January):221-257.

475   Cram, W.E. *1899.* Winter bird notes from southern New Hampshire. Bird-Lore. 1(6):180-184.

476   Crandall, L.S. *1925.* Giant birds of prey; eagle and condor. Mentor. 13(5):1-12.

477   Crandall, L.S. *1941.* Notes on plumage changes in the bald eagle. Zoologica. 26(1):7-8.

478   Crehore, D. *1974.* Bald eagles at Prairie du Dac and Sauk City, Wisconsin. *In:* Our Eagles' Future ??? Proceedings of Bald Eagle Days, Feb. 8-9-10, 1974. Ingram, T.N. (ed.). Eagle Valley Environmentalists, Inc., Apple River, IL. p. 49-50.

Master No.   Citation

479   Crispin, W.B. *1910.* Bald eagle. Oologist. 27(4):43-44.

480   Crispin, W.B. *1913.* The lure of the wild, and the bachelor nest of the bald eagle. Oologist. 30(2):28-30.

481   Crispin, W.B. *1913.* Bald eagle. Oologist. 30(4):68-70.

482   Cromartie, E., W.L. Reichel, L.N. Locke, A.A. Belisle, T.E. Kaiser, T.G. Lamont, B.M. Mulhern, R.M. Prouty, and D.M. Swineford. *1975.* Residues of organochlorine pesticides and polychlorinated biphenyls and autopsy data for bald eagles , 1971-72. Pest. Monit. J. 9(1):11-14.

483   Crozier, B.U. *1946.* A new taenid cestode, *Cladontaenia banghami,* from a bald eagle. Trans. of Am. Micro. Soc. 65(3):222-227.

484   Cull, P. *1976.* Eagles of the Chilkat River Valley. *In:* Save the Eagles in '76. Proc. of Bald Eagle Days, 1976. Ingram, T.N. (ed.), Eagle Valley Environmentalists, Inc. Apple River, IL. p 137-138.

485   Cunningham, R.L. *1960.* The status of the bald eagle in Florida. Audubon. 62(1):24-26,41,43.

486   Cuthbert, N.L. *1963.* Michigan bird survey, spring, 1962. Jack-Pine Warb. 41(1):20-47.

487   Dadisman, A.J. *1937.* Bald eagle killed near Morgantown, W. Va. Redstart. 4(8):53.

488   Dale, F.H. *1936.* Eagle 'control' in northern California. The Condor. 38(5):208-210.

489   Dall, W.H. and H.M. Bannister. *1869.* List of the birds of Alaska, with biographical notes. Trans. of the Chicago Acad. of Science. 1:267-310.

490   Danielson, T.L. *1967.* Bald eagle swimming in the ocean with prey. The Condor. 69(3):313.

491   Dann, R.E. *1927.* American bald eagles. Oologist. 44(7):98.

492   Darlington, E.J. *1906.* *Haliaeetus leucocephalus.* Oologist. 23(7):106-107.

493   Darlington, E.J. *1908.* Hunting eagles' nests. Oologist. 25(7):107-108.

494   Darlington, E.J. *1909.* Bald eagle. Oologist. 26(5):74-75.

495   Darlington, E.J. *1912.* Bald eagles. Oologist. 29(1):206.

496   Davie, O. *1882.* Eagles in Ohio. Ornithol. and Oologist. 7(18):142.

497   Davie, O. *1886.* Egg Check List and Key to the Nests and Eggs of North American Birds. Hann & Adair, Printers., Columbus. 184 pp.

498   Davie, O. *1889.* Nests and Eggs of North American Birds. Hann & Adair, Columbus. 455 pp.

499   Davis, D.W. *1966.* Plea for conservation of the bald eagle in Saskatchewan. The Blue Jay. 24(4):160-167.

500   Davis, E. *1897.* Nesting of the bald eagle in Orange Co., Cal. Nidologist. 4(7):78-79.

501   Davis, J.C. *1958.* U.S. is losing its bald eagles; sterility suspected, DDT cited. Audubon. 60(6):275.

502   Davis, M. *1945.* The bald eagle nesting in captivity. The Auk. 62(4):634.

503   Davis, R. *1976.* Saving the eagles roost: along Washington's Skagit River, a new winter refuge. Defend. Wildl. Oct.:284-288.

504   Dawson, B. *1974.* Great horned owls go to school. Museum Talk. Santa Barbara Museum of Natural History. 48 (2):45-48.

505   Dawson, W.L. *1908.* The bird colonies of the Olympiades. The Auk. 25(2):153-166.

506   Dawson, W.L. *1923.* The Birds of California. Vol. 3. South Moulton Co., San Diego. 2121 pp.

507   Dawson, W.L. and J.H. Bowles. *1909.* The Birds of Washington. Two Volumes. Occidental Pub. Co., Seattle, WA. 997 pp.

508   Dayton, B.G. *1889.* A bald eagle's nest. Oologist. 6(5):96.

509   Deaderick, W.H. *1940.* Audubon in Tennessee. Migrant. 11(3):59-61.

510   Dean, R. *1978.* Heritage. Conservationist. Missouri Dept. of Conservation. 39(2):23.

511   Deane, J.G. *1966.* Bald eagle refuges on the Potomac. Defend Wildl. News. 41(4):339.

512   Deane, J.G. *1967.* Potomac's eagles: Interior plans a sanctuary. Defend. Wildl. News. 42(3):271.

513   Deane, J.G. *1968.* Mason Neck, wildlife refuge for bald eagles. Atl. Nat. 23(1):26.

514   Deane, R. *1899.* Oldsquaw *(Clangula hyemalis)* in Indiana. The Auk. 16(2):178-179.

515   Deane, R. *1904.* Extracts from an unpublished journal of John James Audubon. The Auk. 21(3):334-338.

516   Dekker, D. *1970.* Migrations of diurnal birds of prey in the Rocky Mountain foothills west of Cochrane, Alberta. The Blue Jay. 28(1):20-24.

517   Delime, J. *1949.* An osprey's and a bald eagle's nest at Kentucky Lake. Kentucky Warbler. 25(2):55.

518   Derleth, A. *1945.* Sac Prairie summer. Pass. Pigeon. 7(3):72-75.

519   Detrich, P.J. *1978.* Bald eagle winter habitat study Shasta, Trinity and Tehama Counties, California. U.S.D.A. Forest Service, 37 pp.

520   Deusing, M. *1940.* Bald eagle range and population study. Pass. Pigeon. 2(9):103-106.

521   Devoe, A. *1951.* Our eagle. Am. Mercury. 75(335):119-123.

522   Devoe, A. *1951.* Will we save our eagles? Read. Dig. 59(356):93-94.

523   DeGarmo, W.R. *1945.* White-winged scoters and bald eagles on Cheat Lake. Redstart. 12(4-5):23-24.

524   DeWitt, J.B. *1963.* Studies on pesticide-eagle relationships. Audubon. 65(1):30-31.

525   DeWitt, J.B. and J.L. Buckley. *1962.* Studies on pesticide-eagle relationships. Aud. Field Notes. 16(6):541.

526   Diamond, J.M. *1969.* Avifaunal equilibria and special turnover rates on the Channel Islands of California. Proc. Natl. Acad. of Sciences. 64(Sept.-Dec.):57-63.

Master No.	Citation

527   **Dieter, M.P.** *1973.* Sex determination of eagles, owls, and herons by analyzing plasma steroid hormones. U.S.D.I. Fish and Wildlife Service, Spec. Sci. Report-Wildlife, No. 167.

528   **Dieter, M.P. and S.N. Wiemeyer.** *1978.* Six different plasma enzymes in bald eagles *(Haliaeetus leucocephalus)* and their usefulness in pathological diagnosis. Comp. Biochem. Physiol. 61C:153-155.

529   **Dill, H.H.** *1960.* Bald eagle nest at Mud Lake National Wildlife Refuge. Flicker. 32(1):32.

530   **Dixon, C.** *1902.* Birds' Nests, An Introduction to the Science of Caliology. Fredrick A. Stokes, Co. 285 pp.

531   **Dixon, J.S.** *1909.* A life history of the northern bald eagle. The Condor. 11(6):187-193.

532   **Dixon, J.S. and R.M. Bond.** *1937.* Raptorial birds in the cliff areas of Lava Beds National Monument, California. The Condor. 39(32):97-102.

533   **Dixon, M.** *1944.* The eagle: eight views. N.Y. Times Mag. July 2:28-29

534   **Douglas, D.G.** *1944.* The eagle on our coins. Numismatist. 57(2):106-107.

535   **Dowhan, J.J. and R.J. Craig.** *1976.* Rare and endangered species of Connecticut and their habitats. State Geological and Natural History Survey of Connecticut. Report of Investigations No. 6. 137 pp.

536   **Downs, T.M.** *1945.* The eagle. Atl. Month. 175(5):107,109,111.

537   **Dubuc, W.** *1977.* 1975-1976 nest season. U.S.D.I. Fish and Wildlife Service. 2 pp.

538   **Dubuc, W.** *1977.* Summary, 1976-1977 nest season. U.S.D.I. Fish and Wildlife Service. 3 pp.

539   **Dubuc, W. and G.C. Payne.** *1977.* Observations of southern bald eagle nesting in southern Louisiana, 1975-1976. Nesting Survey(Unpublished). 4 pp.

540   **Duke, G.E. and P.T. Redig.** *1973.* Raptor rehabilitation program. *In:* Notes on a Bald Eagle Nest Survey Workshop, Twin Cities, MN, Aug. 15. Madsen, C.R. (ed.) U.S.D.I. Fish and Wildlife Service. p. 45-47.

541   **Duke, G.E., A. Jegers, G. Loff and O.A. Evanson.** *1975.* Gastric digestion in some raptors. Comp. Biochem. Physiol. 50(4A):649-656.

542   **Duke, G.E., O.A. Evanson and A. Egers.** *1976.* Meal to pellet intervals in 14 species of captive raptors. Comp. Biochem. and Phys. 53(1A):1-6.

543   **Dumont, P.A.** *1933.* A revised list of the birds of Iowa. The University, Iowa City. 15(5):1-171.

544   **Dumont, P.A.** *1934.* The bald eagle as an Iowa bird. Iowa Bird Life. 4(1):2-4.

545   **Dunne, P.J.** *1977.* Spring hawk movement along Racoon Ridge. Occasional Paper No. 127. New Jersey Audubon. 3(2):20-29.

546   **Dunne, P.J. and W.S. Clark** *1976.* Fall hawk movement at Cape May Point, N.J.-1976 Occasional Paper No. 130. N.J. Audubon. 3(7/8):114-124.

547   **Dunstan, T.C.** *1969.* First recovery of bald eagle banded in Minnesota. The Loon. 41(3):92.

548   **Dunstan, T.C.** *1969.* Request for information; bald eagle. Bird-Band. 40(4):355.

549   **Dunstan, T.C.** *1970.* The wintering bald eagle of South Dakota. South Dakota Conserv. Digest. 6(37):12-15.

550   **Dunstan, T.C.** *1971.* An ecosystem approach to the study of Minnesota's bald eagles. The Loon. 43(4):109-113.

551   **Dunstan, T.C.** *1973.* The biology of ospreys in Minnesota. The Loon. 5(4):108-113.

552   **Dunstan, T.C.** *1973.* Bald eagle from Minnesota recovered in Texas. The Loon. 45(4):132.

553   **Dunstan, T.C.** *1974.* Feeding activities of ospreys in Minnesota. Wilson Bull. 86(1):74-76.

554   **Dunstan, T.C.** *1974.* The status and role of bald eagle winter studies in the Midwest. *In:* Our Eagle's Future???. Proc. of Bald Eagle Days., Feb. 8,9,10, 1974. Ingram, T.N. (ed.). Eagle Valley Environmentalists, Inc. Apple River, IL. p. 62-67.

555   **Dunstan, T.C.** *1975.* Survival and food habits of nestling and fledlging bald eagles on the Chippewa National Forest, Minnesota. Final Research Report. 39 pp.

556   **Dunstan, T.C.** *1975.* Cedar Glen eagle roost. *In:* Bald Eagle Land: Preservation and Acquisition. Proc. of Bald Eagle Days, Jan. 31-Feb. 2, 1975. Ingram, T.N. (ed.). Eagle Valley Environmentalists, Inc., Apple River, IL. p. 7 -11.

557   **Dunstan, T.C.** *1978.* Our bald eagle: Freedom's symbol survives. Natl. Geog. Mag. 153(2):186-199.

558   **Dunstan, T.C., A. Griechus and J.E. Mathisen.** *1970.* Breast muscle biopsy technique and pesticide content of nestling bald eagles in Minnesota. Trans. of the 32nd Midwest Fish and Wildlife Conf. Dec. 7. 2 pp.

559   **Dunstan, T.C. and M. Borth.** *1970.* Successful reconstruction of active bald eagle nest. Wilson Bull., 82(3):326-327.

560   **Dunstan, T.C., J.E. Mathisen and J.F. Harper.** *1975.* The biology of bald eagles in Minnesota. The Loon. 47(1):5-10.

561   **Dunstan, T.C., J.F. Harper and J.E. Mathisen.** *1975.* Behavior and habitat use of fledgling bald eagles in north-central Minnesota. Proc. of the Second Joint Meeting of Cooper-Wilson Ornithological Societies. June 12, 1975. Bozeman, MT. 8 pp.

562   **Dunstan, T.C. and J.F. Harper.** *1975.* Food habits of bald eagles in north-central Minnesota. J. Wildl. Manage. 39(1):140-143.

563   **Durbin, K.** *1978.* Northwest is bald eagle stronghold. Oregon Department of Fish and Wildlife. News Release. March 16. p. 2-5.

Master No.	Citation

564 Dury, C. *1885.* Notes on food of raptorial birds. Random Notes on Natural History. 2(8):57-58.

565 Dustman, E.H. and L.F. Stickel. *1969.* The occurrence and significance of pesticide residues in wild animals. *In:* Annals of the New York Acad. of Sciences. Conf. on Biological Effects of Pesticides in Mammalian Systems, May 2-5, 1967., New York.

566 Dustman, E.H., L.F. Stickel, L.J. Blus, W.L. Reichel and S.N. Wiemeyer. *1971.* The occurence and significance of polychlorinated biphenyls in the environment. Trans. of the 36th North American Wildlife Conf., March 7,8, 9,10. Wildlife Manage. Institute. p. 118-133.

567 Dustman, E.H., W.E. Martin, R.G. Heath and W.L. Reichel. *1971.* Monitoring pesticides in wildlife. Pest. Monit. J. 5(1):50-52.

568 Dutcher, W. *1893.* Bald eagle and golden. Forest and Stream. 40(12):250.

569 Dutton, J. *1976.* Endangered species of the central Atlantic states. Atl. Nat. 31(3):96-102.

570 Duval, A.J. *1937.* Birds observed on the coast of Virginia and North Carolina. The Auk. 54(4):461-463.

571 Dwight, J., Jr. *1892.* Summer birds of the crest of the Pennsylvania Alleghanies. The Auk. 9(2):129-141.

572 E.G.&G., Environmental Consultants. *1976.* Impact of proposed Seiad Valley Airport on southern bald eagles and their habitat. Contract No. 75-12. Prep. for Div. of Aeronautics, Dept. of Transportation, State of California. 33 pp.

573 Eagle Valley Environmentalists. *1978.* Bald eagle days: learning about eagles. January 27,28,29-1978. Co-Sponsored by Eagle Valley Environmentalists, Inc. and Chicago Audubon Society. 16 pp.

574 East, B. *1928.* Sons of Sky-King. Nature Mag. 12(1):35-38.

575 East, B. *1929.* The home of Sky-King. Nature Mag. 9(3):142-146.

576 East, B. *1930.* He needs protection. Am. Forest. 36(1):14-16.

577 East, B. *1942.* Baldy of the Aleutians. Am. Forests. 48(10):444-447,480.

578 East, B. *1944.* Eagles I have known. Natural Hist. 53(1):8-15.

579 East, B. *1974.* The Last Eagle: The Story of Khan. Crown Pub., Inc., New York. 144 pp.

580 Easterla, D.A. *1962.* The bald eagle nesting in Missouri. Bluebird. 29(2):11-13.

581 Eastman, F.B. *1937.* A reminiscence. Oologist. 54(1):9-11.

582 Eastwood, S. *1925.* The season, 50; April 15 to June 15, 1925, Pittsburg region. Bird-Lore. 27(4):257-273.

583 Eaton, R.L. *1976.* Bald eagle *(Haliaeetus leucocephalus)* . *In:* Marine Shoreline Fauna of Washington, Volume II. Britell, J.D., J.M. Brown, and R.L. Eaton (eds.). Wash. Dept. of Game. Coastal Zone Environmental Studies Report No. 3. p. 119-180.

584 Eaton, S.W. (ed.). *1954.* Regional reports: Region 3 - Finger Lakes. The Kingbird. 4(1):11-12.

585 Eaton, W.F. *1935.* Eagles. (Review of a Publication by E.D. Lumley.) Bird-Lore. 37(2):136.

586 Eberhardt, R.T. *1974.* Bald eagle nest status-1974. U.S. Fish and Wildlife Service. Bemidji, MN(Report). 2 pp.

587 Eddy, G. *1940.* The season, 133; April 15-June 15, 1940, Puget Sound region. Bird-Lore. 42(4):391-392.

588 Edge, R. *1940.* Partial protection of the bald eagle. *In:* Conservation and Defense; Notes, News, and Comments. Annual Report of the Emergency Conservation Committee for the Year 1940. Publication No. 84. p. 8.

589 Edwards, N. *1950.* Broley - the eagle man. Nature Mag. 43(4):198-200.

590 Eifrig, C.W.G. *1904.* Birds of Allegheny and Garett Counties, western Maryland. The Auk. 21(2):234-250.

591 Eifrig, C.W.G. *1919.* Notes on the birds of the Chicago area and its immediate vicinity. The Auk. 36(4):513-524.

592 Einarsen, A.S. *1956.* Determination of some predator species by field signs. College Press, Oregon State College. Studies in Zoology No. 10. 34 pp.

593 Ekblaw, S.E. *1918.* A record of the bald eagle from Champaign County, Illinois. Bird-Lore. 20(6):421.

594 Eliot, W. *1892.* A day's trip for bald eagle nests in Florida. Oologist. 9(2):40.

595 Ellis, J. and J. Winship. *1973.* Eagle nest survey - Great Lakes states - objectives and progress. *In:* Notes on A Bald Eagle Nest Survey Workshop., Aug. 15, 1973. Madsen, C.R. (ed.). Twin Cities, MN. U.S.D.I. Fish and Wildlife Service. Reg. 3. p. 4-5.

596 Ellis, J.O. *1963.* Two days at Reelfoot Lake. The Migrant. 34(2):21-22.

597 Embury, L. *1940.* The odyssey of Uncle Sam's eagle. Natural Hist. 45(5):276-279.

598 Emergency Conservation Committee. *1935.* Save the Bald Eagle. Emergency Conservation Comm. Pub. No. 44. 27 pp.

599 Emlen, J.T., Jr. *1949.* Migration and nesting of Florida bald eagles. (Review of a Paper by C.L. Broley.). Bird-Band. 20(1):53.

600 Enderson, J.H. *1965.* Roadside raptor count in Colorado. Wilson Bull. 77(1):82-83.

601 Enderson, J.H., F.A. Colley and J. Stevenson. *1970.* Aerial eagle count in Colorado. The Condor. 72(1):112.

602 Engman, R.G. and A.G. Stendal. *1976.* Applied Research; Fish and Wildlife Assessment of Marshland Watershed Project Area. Wash. Game Dept. Bull. No. 9. 117 pp.

603 Erichsen, W.J. *1919.* Some summer birds of Liberty County, Georgia. The Auk. 36(3):380-393.

604 Erskine, A.J. *1968.* Encounters between bald eagles and other birds in winter. The Auk. 85(4):681-683.

605 Everett, M. *1978.* Birds of Prey. G.P. Putnam's Sons, New York. 128 pp.

Master No.	Citation

606   Evermann, B.W. *1886.* A list of the birds observed in Ventura County, California. The Auk. 3(1):86-94.

607   Evermann, B.W. *1888.* Birds of Carroll County, Indiana. The Auk. 5(4):344-351.

608   Eyre, L. and D. Paul. *1973.* Raptors of Utah. Utah Div. of Wildlife Resources. Publication No. 73-7. 76 pp.

609   Faanes, C.A. *1976.* Winter ecology of bald eagles in southeastern Minnesota. The Loon. 48(2):61-69.

610   Fables, D., Jr. *1955.* Annotated list of New Jersey birds. Urner Ornithol. Club. 95 pp.

611   Fall, B.A. *1973.* Noteworthy bird records from south Texas (Kennedy County). Southwest Nat. 18(2):244-247.

612   Fargo, W.G. *1926.* Notes on birds of Pinellas and Pasco Counties, Florida. Wilson Bull. 38(3):140-155.

613   Fawks, E. *1960.* Bald eagle study. Pass. Pigeon. 22(2):30-31.

614   Fawks, E. *1960.* Bald eagle winter survey. Audubon Bull.(115):2-3.

615   Fawks, E. *1960.* A survey of wintering bald eagles. Iowa Bird Life. 30:56-58.

616   Fawks, E. *1960.* A January bald eagle count. Audubon Bull.(113):6-7.

617   Fawks, E. *1961.* A survey of wintering bald eagles :1960-1961. Iowa Bird Life. 31(3):54-60.

618   Fawks, E. *1961.* Final report - February 19, 1961, bald eagle count. Audubon Bull.(119):21-22.

619   Fawks, E. *1962.* Bald eagle survey comparison, winters 1960-1961 and 1961-1962. Iowa Bird Life. 32(3):1.

620   Fawks, E. *1964.* Bald eagle count, February 15 or 16, 1964. Iowa Bird Life. 34(2):51.

621   Fawks, E. *1965.* One day bald eagle count, February 13 or 14, 1965. Iowa Bird Life. 35(2):56.

622   Fawks, E. *1966.* Field notes - June 1966. Audubon Bull.(138):6-8.

623   Fawks, E. *1966.* Winter birding along the Mississippi. Audubon Bull.(140):32-34.

624   Fawks, E. *1966.* One day bald eagle count on the Mississippi River - February 19 or 20, 1966. Iowa Bird Life. 36:52-53.

625   Fawks, E. *1966.* Comparison between two bald eagle counts. Audubon Bull.(138):22-23.

626   Fawks, E. *1967.* One day eagle count, February 18 or 19, 1967. Iowa Bird Life. 37(2):53.

627   Fawks, E. *1967.* Surveyors sight nearly 650 eagles in one-day winter count in state. Audubon Bull.(142):37.

628   Fawks, E. *1968.* One day eagle count, February 17 or 18, 1968. Iowa Bird Life.(38):92-93.

629   Fawks, E. *1968.* Field notes. Audubon Bull.(146):27-29.

630   Fawks, E. *1968.* Field notes. Audubon Bull.(145):14-16.

631   Fawks, E. *1969.* One day eagle count, February 15 or 16, 1969. Audubon Bull.(150):26-27.

632   Fawks, E. *1969.* One day eagle count, February 15 or 16, 1969. Iowa Bird Life. 39:46.

633   Fawks, E. *1969.* Field notes. Audubon Bull.(151):15-16.

634   Fawks, E. *1970.* One day eagle count, February 21 or 22, 1970. Iowa Bird Life. 40:52.

635   Fawks, E. *1970.* One day eagle count February 21 or 22, 1970. Audubon Bull.(154):17.

636   Fawks, E. *1971.* One day eagle count: February 20 or 21, 1971. Audubon Bull.(158):26-27.

637   Fawks, E. *1971.* One day eagle count - February 20 or 21, 1971. Bluebird. 38(2):2.

638   Fawks, E. *1972.* One day eagle count, February 19 or 20, 1972. Iowa Bird Life. 42:48-49.

639   Fawks, E. *1972.* One day eagle count: February 19 or 20, 1972. Audubon Bull.(162):21,38.

640   Fawks, E. *1972.* Field notes. Audubon Bull.(161):33-35.

641   Fawks, E. *1972.* Eagles and hawks. Audubon Bull.(161):36.

642   Fawks, E. *1973.* Field notes. Audubon Bull.(164):38-43.

643   Fawks, E. *1973.* One day bald eagle count, February 17 or 18, 1973. Iowa Bird Life. 43:49.

644   Fawks, E. *1974.* Results: the one-day bald eagle count. Ill. Aud. Bull.(169):15.

645   Fawks, E. *1974.* High counts of bald eagles - winter 1973-1974. Ill. Aud. Bull.(171):13.

646   Fawks, E. *1974.* One day bald eagle count, February 16, 1974. Iowa Bird Life. 44(2):49-50.

647   Fawks, E. *1974.* Wintering eagles. *In:* Our Eagle's Future??? Proc. of Bald Eagle Days, Feb. 8,9,10, 1974.Ingram, T.N. (ed.). Eagle Valley Environmentalists, Inc. Apple River, IL. p. 51-59.

648   Fawks, E. *1975.* Other roosting lands along the Mississippi River. *In:* Bald Eagle Land:Preservation and Acquisition. Proc. of Bald Eagle Days, Jan. 31-Feb. 2, 1975, Eagle Valley Environmentalists, Inc. Apple River, IL. p. 21-22.

649   Fawks, E. *1975.* One day eagle count - February 8, 1975. Ill. Aud. Bull.(173):14-15.

650   Fawks, E. *1975.* One day bald eagle count - February 8, 1975. Iowa Bird Life. 45(June):1.

651   Fawks, E. *1976.* Wintering eagles and roosting areas. *In:* Save the Eagle in '76. Proc. of Bald Eagle Days, 1976. Ingram, T.N. (ed.). Eagle Valley Environmentalists Inc. Apple River, IL. p. 101-103.

652   Fawks, E. *1976.* One day bald eagle count - February 14, 1976. Ill. Aud. Bull. No. 177. 1 p.

653   Fawks, E. *1976.* Bald eagle days, Madison, Wisconsin, Jan. 30, 31, and Feb. 1, 1976. (Unpublished Report). 2 pp.

654   Fawks, E. *1977.* Bald eagle days, Jan. 28-30, 1977; Winter trends and dispersals. (Unpublished Report). 2 pp.

655   Fendall-Johnston, K.M. *1935.* The war eagle. St. Nicholas. 62(2):30,51.

656   Fichter, G.S. *1971.* Birds of Florida. E.A. Seemann Pub., Inc. Miami, FL. 111 pp.

657   Fickett, S. *1977.* 1976-1977 Southern bald eagle nesting summary. (Unpublished Report). 5 pp.

658   Figgins, J.D. *1923.* The breeding birds of the vicinity of Black Bayou and Bird Island, Cameron Parish, Louisiana. The Auk. 40(4):666-677.

Master No.	Citation

659   Fimreite, N. *1974.* Mercury contamination of aquatic birds in northwestern Ontario. J. Wildl. Manage. 38(1):120-131.

660   Fink, L.C. *1974.* No bald eagle nests here? The Chat. 38(2):37.

661   Finlay, E. (ed.). *1968.* Hawks and eagles need more protection. S. Carolina Wildl. 15(2):15.

662   Finley, W.L. and I. Finley. *1923.* A war against American eagles. Nature Mag. 2(5):261-270.

663   Fisher, A.H. *1939.* Our national bird. Nature Mag. 32(6):321-324.

664   Fisher, A.K. *1893.* The Hawks and Owls of the United States in Their Relation to Agriculture. U.S.D.A. Div. of Ornithology and Mammalogy, Bull. No. 3. 210 pp.

665   Fisher, G.C. *1909.* Bald eagle's nest at Lewistown Reservoir. Wilson Bull. 19(1):13-16.

666   Fisher, W.H. *1899.* Nesting of the bald eagle in Baltimore County, Md. Osprey. 4(2):21.

667   Fleming, J.H. *1920.* The northern bald eagle a probable Californian bird. The Condor. 22(3):110.

668   Fletcher, A.J. and Mrs. A.J. Fletcher. *1958.* Maryland nest summary for 1957. Md. Birdlife. 14(1):3-9.

669   Flinn, W.L. *1957.* A guide to the eagles, hawks and falcons of Colorado. Colorado Outdoors. 6(2):14-18.

670   Florida Audubon Society (ed.). *1976.* Proc. of the Southern Bald Eagle Conference. Altamonte Springs, Florida, Dec 10,11,12,1976. 69 pp.

671   Florida Audubon Society. *1973.* Bald eagle nesting area found in Ocala forest, among nation's largest. Florida Cons. Digest. May 4(74):5.

672   Florida Audubon Society. *1974.* Three Lakes Ranch purchase approved unanimously by Cabinet. Florida Cons. Digest. Sept.12(89):3.

673   Florida Audubon Society. *1975.* Bald eagle status. Florida Cons. Digest. Dec.(101):35-36.

674   Florida Audubon Society. *1975.* Three Lakes Ranch property now protected by off-road vehicle ban during deer and turkey hunting season. Florida Cons. Digest. July(97):27.

675   Florida Audubon Society. *1976.* Bald eagle conference, Dec. 10-12, 1976. Florida Cons. Digest. Sept.(110):25-26.

676   Florida Audubon Society. *1976.* Bald eagle status. Florida Cons. Digest. Jan.(102):19-20.

677   Florida Audubon Society. *1976.* 1975-76 bald eagle survey results. Florida Cons. Digest. May(106):23-25.

678   Florida Audubon Society. *1976.* Florida Audubon Society hosts Southern Bald Eagle Conference. Florida Cons. Digest. Dec.(113):17-18.

679   Florida Audubon Society. *1976.* Bald eagle nesting in panhandle disrupted. Florida Cons. Digest. March(104):40.

680   Fluegel, F. *1919.* The eagles' nest. Overland Month. 73(4):361.

681   Fogle, W.T. *1928.* The bald eagle. Flower Grower. 15(15):226.

682   Forbis, L.A. *1975.* A habitat management plan for the bald eagle (*Haliaeetus leucocephalus l.*) , on the Klamath National Forest, Siskiyou County, California. U.S.D.A., Forest Service, California Region. 79 pp.

683   Forbis, L.A., B. Johnston, A.M. Camarena and D. McKinney. *1977.* Bald eagle-habitat management guidelines. U.S.D.A. Forest Service. 60 pp.

684   Forbush, E.H. and J.B. May. *1939.* Natural History of the Birds of Eastern and Central North America. Houghton Mifflin Co. Boston, MA. 553 pp.

685   Ford, A. (ed.). *1957.* The Bird Biographies of John James Audubon. The MacMillan Co., New York. 282 pp.

686   Ford, E.R., C.C. Sanborn and C.B. Coursen. *1934.* Birds of the Chicago region. Prog. Activities of Chicago Acad. Sci. 5(2/3):18-80.

687   Foresta Institute for Ocean and Mountain Studies. *1973.* Kills of Nevada eagles force change of policy. Nappe, L.(ed.) Wildlife and Natural Areas. 1(1):1.

688   Fortenberry, D.K. *1974.* Resources inventory, Yukon Planning Region, migratory birds, raptors, and endangered species. Resource Planning Team, Joint Federal-State Land Use Planning Commission.(Preliminary Draft). 4 pp.

689   Fortenberry, D.K. *1974.* Resources inventory, Southeastern Region, migratory birds, raptors, and endangered species. Resources Planning Team. Joint Federal-State Land Use Planning Commission.(Preliminary Draft). 2 pp.

690   Fortenberry, D.K. *1974.* Resources inventory, Southwest Planning Region, migratory birds, raptors, and endangered species. Resource Planning Team, Joint Federal-State Land Use Planning Commission.(Preliminary Draft). 3 pp.

691   Fortenberry, D.K. *1974.* Resources inventory, Arctic Planning Region, migratory birds, raptors, and endangered species. Resource Planning Team, Joint Federal-State Land Use Planning Commission.(Preliminary Draft). 1 p.

692   Fortenberry, D.K. *1974.* Resources inventory, South Central Planning Region, migratory birds, raptors, and endangered species. Resource Planning Team, Joint Federal-State Land Use Planning Commission.(Preliminary Draft). 4 pp.

693   Foster, B. *1956.* The Winter Season. December 1955 - February 1956. Pass. Pigeon. 18(2):81-93.

694   Foster, J.W. *1976.* Project Babe. N. Am. Bird Band. 1(4):179.

695   Fraser, J.D. *1976.* The effect of timber harvest and other human activities on bald eagle breeding behavior and productivity in the Deer River district of the Chippewa National Forest. (Progress Report). Univ. of Minnesota, St. Paul, MN. 3 pp.

Master No.	Citation

696   **Fraser, J.D.** *1978.* Bald eagle reproductive surveys: accuracy, precision, and timing. M.S. Thesis. Univ. of Minnesota, St. Paul, MN. 82 pp.

697   **Frenzel, L.D.** *1974.* Need for revising bald eagle nest protection regulations on U.S. Forest Service and other public lands. Trans. of 36th Midwest Fish and Wildlife Conf.(Abstract). 1 p.

698   **Frenzel, L.D.** *1975.* Protecting preserved eagle lands. *In:* Bald Eagle Land: Preservation and Acquisition. Ingram, T.N. (ed.). Proc. of Bald Eagle Days, Jan. 31-Feb. 2. Eagle Valley Environmentalists, Inc., Apple River, IL. p. 6.

699   **Frenzel, L.D., B.G. Juenemann and J.V. Kussman.** *1973.* Behavioral aspects of eagle nest surveys. *In:* Notes on A Bald Eagle Nest Survey Workshop., Aug. 15, 1973. Madsen, C.R. (ed.). Twin Cities, MN. U.S.D.I. Fish and Wildlife Service. Reg. 3. p. 33-36.

700   **Frenzel, L.D. And J.V. Kussman.** *1973.* Bald eagle-hawk interaction. The Loon. 45(3):101.

701   **Friedmann, H.** *1950.* The Birds of North and Middle America. Smithsonian Institution, U.S. National Museum. Bull. 50.(Six Volumes). 793 pp.

702   **Fries, R.F.** *1972.* Notes on acquisition and management of proposed Pickstown Eagle Roost. (Unpublished Report). 3 pp.

703   **Fries, R.F.** *1972.* Justification for proposed Fort Randall Dam Eagle Roost Refuge. (Unpublished Report). 3 pp.

704   **Frost, A. and M.S. Crosby.** *1920.* Some summer residents of Dutchess County, New York. The Auk. 37(4):597-598.

705   **Fuller, M.R., P.T. Redig and G.E. Duke.** *1974.* Raptor rehabilitation and conservation in Minnesota. Raptor Res. 8(1/2):11-19.

706   **Fullerton, G.J.** *1969.* Bald eagle captures duck. The Loon. 41(1):27.

707   **Funkhouser, W.D.** *1925.* Wildlife in Kentucky. The Kentucky Geological Survey. Frankfort, Ky.

708   **Fyfe, R.W.** *1976.* Status of Canadian raptor populations. Can. Field-Nat. 90(3):370-375.

709   **Fyfe, R.W.** *1977.* Status of Canadian raptor populations. *In:* Proc. of the World Conference on Birds of Prey. Chancellor, R.D. (ed.). International Council for Bird Preservation, October 1-3, 1975. p. 34-39.

710   **Fyfe, R.W. and R.R. Olendorff.** *1976.* Minimizing the dangers of nesting studies to raptors and other sensitive species. Canadian Wildlife Service. Occasional Paper No. 23. 17 pp.

711   **Gabrielson, I.N. and F.C. Lincoln.** *1959.* The Birds of Alaska. Stackpole Co., Harrisburg and Wildlife Manage. Institute, Wash. , D.C. 922 pp.

712   **Gabrielson, I.N., H.A. Hochbaum, R.A. McCabe, D.A. Munro, R. Pough and C. Cottam.** *1962.* Report to the American Ornithologists' Union by The Commitee on Bird Protection, 1961. The Auk. 79(3):463-478.

713   **Gabrielson, I.N. and S.G. Jewett.** *1970.* Birds of Oregon. Oregon State College, Corvallis, OR. 650 pp.

714   **Ganier, A.F.** *1931.* Facts about eagles in Tennessee. J. Tenn. Acad. Sciences. 6(2):50-57.

715   **Ganier, A.F.** *1932.* Nesting of the bald eagle. Wilson Bull. 44(1):3-9.

716   **Ganier, A.F.** *1938.* Notes from the Nashville area. Migrant. 9(2):29-30.

717   **Ganier, A.F.** *1938.* Nashville area. Migrant. 9(3):65-66.

718   **Ganier, A.F.** *1951.* Some notes on bald eagles. Migrant. 22(3):37-39.

719   **Ganier, A.F.** *1953.* Eagles at the Duck River Refuge. Migrant. 24(4):83-84.

720   **Gard, R.** *1971.* Brown bear predation on sockeye salmon at Karluk Lake, Alaska. J. Wildl. Manage. 35(2):193-204.

721   **Gault, B.T.** *1896.* Recent occurence of the turkey vulture and bald eagle in Cook County, Illinois. Wilson Ornithol. Chapter of Agassiz Assoc. Bull. No. 9. p. 3-4.

722   **George, W.G.** *1971.* Vanished and endangered birds of Illinois; a new 'black list' and 'red list'. Audubon Bull.(158):2-11.

723   **Gerberg, E.J.** *1941.* The Mallophaga occuring on the Falconiformes (vultures, kites, hawks, and eagles) of eastern North America. M.S. Thesis. Cornell University, Ithaca, N.Y. 78 pp.

724   **Gerow, J.** *1939.* Bald eagle kills black brant. Murrelet. 20(2):44.

725   **Gerrard, J.M.** *1973.* The bald eagle in Canada's northern forests. Nat. Can. 2(3):10-13.

726   **Gerrard, J.M.** *1973.* Eagle census experiences in Canada. *In:* Notes on a Bald Eagle Nest Survey Workshop., Aug. 15, 1973. Madsen, C.R. (ed.). Twin Cities, MN. U.S.D.I. Fish and Wildlife Service. Reg. 3. p. 405.

727   **Gerrard, J.M.** *1974.* Studies of bald eagle behavior in Saskatchewan. *In:* Our Eagle's Future ??? Proc. of Bald Eagle Days, Feb. 8,9,10, 1974. Ingram, T.N. (ed.). Eagle Valley Environmentalists, Inc. Apple River, IL. p. 16-34.

728   **Gerrard, J.M.** *1976.* Ecological land use planning in northern Saskatchewan. *In:* Save the Eagle in '76. Proc. of Bald Eagle Days 1976. Ingram, T.N. (ed.). Eagle Valley Environmentalists, Inc., Apple River, IL. p. 84-93.

729   **Gerrard, J.M. and D.W.A. Whitfield.** *1967.* Bald eagle banding in northern Saskatchewan. Blue Jay. 25(4):177-183.

730   **Gerrard, J.M. and D.W.A. Whitfield.** *1967.* Bald eagles in Saskatchewan. (Unpublished Report). 6 pp.

Master No.	Citation

731   Gerrard, J.M., P.N. Gerrard, D.W.A. Whitfield and W.J. Maher. *1973.* Bald eagle behavior study: Part II. Final Report to Canadian Wildlife Service on Contract 7273-43. 90 pp.

732   Gerrard, J.M., P.N. Gerrard, W.J. Maher and D.W.A. Whitfield. *1975.* Factors influencing nest site selection of bald eagles in northern Saskatchewan and Manitoba. Blue Jay. 33(3):169-176.

733   Gerrard, J.M., S. Postupalsky, D.L. Evans, J.W. Grier, J.B. Holt, Jr., A.K. Jacobsen, and C.R. Sindelar, Jr. *1975.* Migratory movements of bald eagles in interior North America. Proc. of the 93rd Meeting of the American Ornithologist's Union, Winnipeg, MB.(Abstract). 1 p.

734   Gerrard, J.M. and P.N. Gerrard. *1975.* Ecological road planning in northern Saskatchewan. Blue Jay. 33(3):131-139.

735   Gerrard, J.M., D.W.A. Whitfield and W.J. Maher. *1976.* Osprey-bald eagle relationships in Saskatchewan. Blue Jay. 34(4):240-247.

736   Gerrard, P.N., J.M. Gerrard, D.W.A. Whitfield and W.J. Maher. *1974.* Post-fledging movements of juvenile bald eagles. Blue Jay. 32(4):218-226.

737   Gianini, C.A. *1917.* Some Alaska Peninsula bird notes. The Auk. 34(4):394-402.

738   Giddings, G.W. *1915.* Bald eagles kill fawns. Calif. Fish and Game. October., 1:239.

739   Gilbertson, M. and L. Reynolds. *1974.* A summary of DDE and PCB determination in Canadian birds, 1969 to 1972. Canadian Wildlife Service, Occasional Paper No. 19. 16 pp.

740   Gilliard, E.T. *1958.* Living Birds of the World. Doubleday and Co., Inc., Garden City, N.Y. 400 pp.

741   Gilpin, J.B. *1873.* Variation in tarsal envelope of the bald eagle. Am. Nat. 7(7):429-430.

742   Giraud, J.P., Jr. *1844.* The Birds of Long Island. Wiley and Putnam, NY. 397 pp.

743   Godfrey, W.E. *1956.* Some Canadian Birds. National Museum of Canada. 44 pp.

744   Godfrey, W.E. *1958.* Birds of Cape Breton Island, Nova Scotia. Can. Field-Nat. 72(1):7-27.

745   Godfrey, W.E. *1966.* The Birds of Canada. National Museum of Canada., Bull. No. 203. Biol. Ser. No. 73. 428 pp.

746   Godfrey, W.E. *1970.* Canada's endangered birds. Can. Field-Nat. 84(1):24-26.

747   Goodrich, A.L. *1946.* Birds of Kansas. Kansas Board of Agriculture. Topeka, Kansas. 340 pp.

748   Gordon, S. *1924.* The eagle in a cage. 19th Century. 95(567):730-734.

749   Gould, J.E. *1892.* Note. Ornithol. and Oologist. 17(4):64.

750   Gove, J.G. *1946.* Birds seen and heard on Lopez Island, Washington. Murrelet. 27(2):33.

751   Graber, R.R. and J.S. Golden. *1960.* Hawks and Owls: Population Trends from Illinois Christmas Counts. Dept. of Reg. and Education. Natural History Survey Div. Biological Notes No. 14. 24 pp.

752   Graber, R.R. and J.W. Graber. *1963.* A comparative study of bird populations in Illinois, 1906-1909 and 1956-1958. Ill. Natural History Survey Bull. 28(3):383-528.

753   Graham, F., Jr. *1976.* Will the bald eagle survive to 2076? Audubon. 78(2):99-101

754   Graham, R. *1917.* Eagles. Oologist. 34(5):94.

755   Gramlich, F.J. *1975.* Maine's eagle nest sanctuary program. *In:* Bald Eagle Land. Preservation and Acquisition. Proc. of Bald Eagle Days, 1975, Jan. 31-Feb. 2. Ingram, T.N. (ed.). Eagle Valley Environmentalists, Inc., Apple River, IL. p. 31 -32.

756   Gramlich, F.J. *1976.* Bald eagle newsletter. Bald Eagle Project, Univ. of Maine, Orono. July 29, 1976. 2 pp.

757   Gramlich, F.J., R.B. Owen, Jr. and C.S. Todd *1977.* 1977 Bald Eagle Newsletter; Maine breeding bald eagle study. Bald Eagle Project. Univ. Of Maine, Orono. 2 pp.

758   Grant, M.L. *1950.* Snowy owl and bald eagle records from Black Hawk County. Iowa Bird Life. 20(1):22.

759   Grasett, F.G. *1926.* Notes on some rare birds of northeastern Illinois. The Auk. 43(4):556.

760   Grater, R.K. *1942.* Birds new to Bryce Canyon National Park. The Condor. 44(2):75.

761   Grayson, D.K. *1976.* A note on the prehistoric avifauna of the Lower Klamath Basin. The Auk. 93(4):830-833.

762   Greco, S. *1968.* 'Where the eagles fly' - Moline in January. Audubon Bull.(145):17.

763   Green, C.H. *1970.* Eagles and osprey. Wildlife in N. Carolina. 34(1):10-13.

764   Green, J. *1822.* *Falco leucocephalus* - bald eagle. Am. J. Science and Arts. 41(1):89-90.

765   Green, J.C. and J.A. Baumhofer. *1972.* The 1972 summer season. The Loon. 44(4):105-111.

766   Greene, E.R. *1946.* Birds of the lower Florida Keys. Quarterly J. Florida Acad. of Science. 8(3):222-223.

767   Gregg, M. and B.W. Read. *1961.* Alaska's bald eagles. Alaska Sportsman. 27(6):6,26-28.

768   Grenfell, W.E. *1972.* Special Wildlife Investigations: Raptor survey. Calif. Dept. of Fish and Game. and U.S. Forest Service. Proj. No. W-54-R-4., Job. No. III-6.

769   Gress, F., R.W. Riseborough and F.C. Sibley. *1971.* Shell thinning in eggs of the common murre, *(Uria aalge)* from the Farallon Islands, California. The Condor. 73(3):368-369.

770   Grewe, A.H. Jr. and L.D. Frenzel. *1976.* An overview evaluation of the influence of Orme Dam and Reservoir on the area's resident, nesting bald eagles. Report-Central Arizona Project, Bureau of Reclamation. 25 pp.

771   Grey, J.H., Jr. *1950.* Birds of the Cape Henry area. Raven. 21(7/8):38-69.

772   Grier, J.W. *1967.* Preliminary bald eagle research report. Ont. Bird Band. 3(1):1-4.

773   Grier, J.W. *1968.* Immature bald eagle with an abnormal beak. Bird-Band. 39(1):58-59.

Master No.	Citation

774   Grier, J.W. *1969.* Bald eagle behavior and productivity responses to climbing to nests. J. Wildl. Manage. 33(4):961-966.

775   Grier, J.W. *1970.* 1969 bald eagle survey: N.W. Ontario. (Unpublished Report). 3 pp.

776   Grier, J.W. *1971.* Alas, all is not well with the N.W. Ontario eagles. (Unpublished Report). 2 pp.

777   Grier, J.W. *1973.* Patterns of bald eagle productivity in northwestern Ontario, 1966-1972. *In:* Population Status of Raptors. Murphy, J.R., C.M. White, and B.E. Harrell. (eds). Proc. of the Conference on Raptor Conservation Techniques, Fort Collins, Colorado, 22-24 March 1973(Part VI). Raptor Research Foundation, Inc. Raptor Research Report, No. 3. p. 103-108.

778   Grier, J.W. *1973.* Aerial eagle census techniques as experienced in Ontario and Manitoba. *In:* Notes on A Bald Eagle Nest Survey Workshop. Aug. 15, 1973. Madsen, C.R. (ed.). U.S.D.I. Fish and Wildlife Service. Reg. 3. p. 11-20.

779   Grier, J.W. *1974.* Reproduction, organochlorines, and mercury in northwestern Ontario bald eagles. Can. Field-Nat. 88(4):469-475.

780   Grier, J.W. *1976.* Suggestions for nesting habitat management for bald eagles (and osprey) in the Lake of the Woods region of Ontario. Report for the Ontario Ministry of Natural Resources. (Unpublished). 3 pp.

781   Grier, J.W. *1976.* PCB's in bald eagle eggs. Science. 191(4233):1292.

782   Grier, J.W. *1977.* Quadrat sampling of a nesting population of bald eagles. J. Wildl. Manage. 41(3):438-443.

783   Grier, J.W. *1977.* 1977 reproduction of bald eagles in northwestern Ontario, Canada including analyses of addled eggs. Report to the Ontario Ministry of Natural Resources. 7 pp.

784   Grier, J.W. and R.W. Fyfe *1977.* Assessing the impact of research activities: Birds of prey. Canadian Wildlife Service Special Report Series. 13 pp.

785   Griffen, J. *1977.* Wintering bald eagles at Lock and Dam No. 24. (Report). 5 pp.

786   Griffin, C.R. *1978.* The ecology of bald eagles wintering at Swan Lake National Wildlife Refuge, with emphasis on eagle-waterfowl relationships. M.S. Thesis. Univ. of Missouri, Columbia, MO. 185 pp.

787   Griffin, C.R. *1978.* Successful rehabilitation and reintroduction of bald eagles. Wildl. Soc. Bull. 6(1):44-45.

788   Grimm, W.C. *1942.* The bald eagles at Pymatuning. Cardinal. 5(8):193.

789   Grinnell, G.B. *1876.* List of mammals and birds. *In:* Report of a Reconnaissance from Carroll, Montana Territory, on the Upper Missouri, to the Yellowstone National Park, and Return Made in the Summer of 1875. Ludlow, W., U.S. Army Corps of Engineers. p. 59-92.

790   Grinnell, G.B. *1929.* Eagles' prey. J. Mammalogy. 10(1):83.

791   Grinnell, J. *1898.* Land birds observed in mid-winter on Santa Catalina Island, California. The Auk. 15(3):233-236.

792   Grinnell, J., J.S. Dixon And J.M. Linsdale. *1930.* Vertebrate Natural History of a Section of Northern California Through the Lassen Peak Region. Univ. of California Press, Berkeley. 594 pp.

793   Grinnell, J. and M.W. Wythe. *1927.* Directory to the bird-life of the San Francisco Bay region. Pacific Coast Avifauna No. 18. Cooper Ornithological Club. Berkeley, CA. 160 pp.

794   Grinnell, J. and A.H. Miller. *1944.* The distribution of the birds of California. Pacific Coast Avifauna No. 27, Cooper Ornithological Club. Berkeley, CA. 608 pp.

795   Griscom, L. *1933.* The Birds of Dutchess County, New York. Trans. of the Linnaean Soc. of New York. Urner-Barry Co., N. Y. 184 pp.

796   Griscom, L. and D.E. Snyder. *1955.* The Birds of Massachusetts. Peabody Museum, Salem. 295 pp.

797   Grossman, M.L. and J. Hamlet. *1964.* Birds of Prey of the World. Bonanza Books, N.Y. 496 pp.

798   Grosvenor, G. and A. Wetmore. *1932.* The Book of Birds. Vol 1. Diving Birds, Ocean Birds, Wading Birds, Wild Fowl, Birds of Prey, Game Birds, Shore Birds. National Geographic Society. 356 pp.

799   Grubb, T.C., Jr. *1971.* Bald eagles stealing fish from common mergansers. The Auk. 88(4):928-929.

800   Grubb, T.C., Jr. and W.M. Shields. *1977.* Bald eagle interferes with an active osprey nest. The Auk. 94(1):140.

801   Grubb, T.G. *1976.* A survey and analysis of bald eagle nesting in western Washington. M.S. Thesis (unpublished). Univ. of Washington, Seattle.

802   Grubb, T.G. *1976.* Nesting bald eagle attacks researcher. The Auk. 93(4):842-843.

803   Grubb, T.G. *1976.* Majestic denizens of the skies. Wash. Wildl. 28(3):6-9.

804   Grubb, T.G. *1977.* A summary of current bald eagle research in the Southwest. U.S.D.A. Forest Service(Progress Report.) 10 pp.

805   Grubb, T.G., D.A. Manuwal and C.M. Anderson. *1975.* Nest distribution and productivity of bald eagles in western Washington. The Murrelet. 56(3):2-6.

806   Gruenhagen, R.H. *1970.* Bald facts about the bald eagle. *In:* Selected Statements from State of Washington DDT Hearings and Other Related Papers. Sobelman, M. (ed.) p. 227-228 .

807   Gruening, E. *1961.* Senator offers to share Alaska's eagles with other states. Audubon. 63(4):206-207,244.

808   Gulick, H.F. *1948.* The thrill of a lifetime. Nature Mag. 41(8):398.

809   Gurney, J.H. *1884.* A List of the Diurnal Birds of Prey. John Van Voorst, London. 187 pp.

810   Guttman, B.S. (ed.). *1956.* Minnesota nesting records, 1955. Flicker. 28(4):133-137.

Master No.	Citation

811   **Hackman, C.D. and C.J. Henny.** *1971.* Hawk migration over White Marsh, Maryland. Ches. Sci. 12(3):137-141.

812   **Hader, R.J.** *1971.* Bald eagle at Raleigh, N. C. The Chat. 35(4):108.

813   **Hadley, A.H.** *1927.* Bald eagle in Alaska. Bird-Lore. 29(2):157.

814   **Hager, D.C.** *1974.* Eagle protection and management on Lake States - National Forests. *In:* Our Eagles' Future??? Proc. of Bald Eagle Days, Feb. 8, 9, 10, 1974. Ingram, T.N. (ed.). Eagle Valley Environmentalists, Inc., Apple River, IL. p. 6-15.

815   **Hager, D.C.** *1976.* Bald eagle survey and management strategy. *In:* Save the Eagle in '76, Proc. of Bald Eagle Days, 1976. Ingram, T.N. (ed.), Eagle Valley Environmentalists, Inc., Apple River, IL. p. 118-122.

816   **Haldeman, S.S.** *1868.* The eagle a fisher. Am. Nat. 1(2):615-616.

817   **Hall, F.S.** *1933.* Studies in the history of ornithology in the state of Washington - (1792-1932) with special reference to the discovery of new species. Part II. The Murrelet. 14(3):55-75.

818   **Hall, F.S.** *1934.* Studies in the history of ornithology in the state of Washington - (1792-1932) with special reference to the discovery of new species. Part III. The Murrelet. 15(1):3-19.

819   **Hall, R.F. (ed.).** *1974.* Your questions answered. Eagles. Conservationist. 28(3):39.

820   **Hallam, F.** *1963.* Old Abe, Wisconsins Civil War Eagle was there. Audubon. 65(4):222-225.

821   **Halloran, A.F.** *1960.* Notes on the wintering populations of the bald eagle on the Wichita Mountains Wildlife Refuge. Proc. of the Okla. Acad. of Sciences. 40:120-121.

822   **Halma, R.J.** *1965.* Literature review. (Review: The Status of the Bald Eagle in New Jersey. 1964). The Lookout, Hawk Mountain Sanctuary Association, October, 1965. p. 12.

823   **Hamerstrom, F.** *1972.* Birds of Prey of Wisconsin. Wisconsin Dept. of Natural Resources, Madison, WI. 64 pp.

824   **Hamerstrom, F.** *1975.* Introducing captive-reared raptors into the wild. World Conference on Birds of Prey, Vienna, 1975. p. 348-353.

825   **Hamerstrom, F., T.Ray, C.M. White, and C.E. Braun (Chairman).** *1975.* Conservation Committee Report on status of eagles. Wilson Bull. 87(1):140-143.

826   **Hancock, D.** *1964.* Bald eagles wintering in the Southern Gulf Islands, British Columbia. Wilson Bull. 76(2):111-120.

827   **Hancock, D.** *1964.* Bald eagle population study. (Unpublished Progress Report, October, 1964). 8 pp.

828   **Hancock, D.** *1965.* Raptor Research Foundation Report. General Meeting, Madison, Wisconsin, Sept. 2, 1965. (Unpublished Report). 5 pp.

829   **Hancock, D.** *1965.* Bald eagle study. (Unpublished Progress Report, Summer 1965). 2 pp.

830   **Hancock, D.** *1965.* West coast eagle survey. Can. Audubon. 27(2):37-41.

831   **Hancock, D.** *1966.* David Hancock reports on the Bald Eagle Research Project. Can. Audubon. 28(1):88-92.

832   **Hancock, D.** *1970.* Adventure with Eagles. The Wildlife Conservation Centre, Saanichton, British Columbia, Canada. 40 pp.

833   **Hancock, D.** *1970.* Adventure with eagles; a survey flight to Barkley Sound. Calif. Condor. 5(4):1-3.

834   **Hancock, D.** *1973.* Captive propagation of bald eagles *(Haliaeetus leucocephalus)* - a review. Int. Zoo Year. 13:244-249.

835   **Hand, R.L.** *1941.* Birds of the St. Joe National Forest, Idaho. The Condor. 43(5):220-232.

836   **Hansen, A.J.** *1977.* Population dynamics and night roost requirements of bald eagles wintering in the Nooksack River Valley, Washington. Huxley College of Environmental Studies. Bellingham, WA. (Unpublished Problem Series). 26 pp.

837   **Hardy, P.A.** *1961.* The bald eagle survey. Can. Audubon. 23(4):136.

838   **Harlan, J.R.** *1943.* Bald eagles along the Mississippi River in winter. Iowa Bird Life. 13(1):13.

839   **Harlow, R.C.** *1918.* Notes on the breeding birds of Pennsylvania and New Jersey. The Auk. 35(1):18-29.

840   **Harmata, A.R. and D.W. Stahlecker.** *1977.* Trapping and colormarking wintering bald eagles in the San Luis Valley of Colorado. First Annual Report, May, 1977. 38 pp.

841   **Harper, J.F.** *1974.* Activities of fledgling bald eagles in northcentral Minnesota. M.S. Thesis. Western Illinois Univ.

842   **Harper, J.F.** *1974.* Flight activities of fledgling bald eagles. *In:* Our Eagle's Future??? Proc. of Bald Eagle Days, Feb. 8-9-10, 1974. Eagle Valley Environmentalists, Inc., Apple River, IL. p. 60-61.

843   **Harper, J.F. and T.C. Dunstan.** *1975.* Dispersal and migration of fledgling bald eagles. *In:* Proc. of the Second Joint Meeting of the Cooper and Wilson Ornithological Societies, Bozeman, MT, June 12-15, 1975.

844   **Harris, A.S., O.K. Hutchinson, W.R. Meehan, D.N. Swanston, A.E. Helmers, J.C. Hendee, and T.M. Collins.** *1974.* The forest ecosystem of southeast Alaska. 1. The setting. U.S.D.A. Forest Service. Gen. Technical Report PNW-12. 40 pp.

845   **Harris, H.** *1919.* Birds of the Kansas City region. Trans. St. Louis Acad. Sci. 23(8):213-371.

846   **Harrison, C.J.O. and C.A. Walker.** *1973.* An undescribed extinct fish eagle from Chatham Island. Ibis. 115(2):274-277.

847   **Harrod, K. (ed.).** *1976..* Florida Audubon Society hosts Southern Bald Eagle Conference. Fla. Cons. Digest. (113):12.

Master No.	Citation

848   Hatler, D.F. *1974.* Bald eagle preys upon arctic loon. The Auk. 91(41):825-827.

849   Haugen, A.O. *1945.* Bald eagle nests at Allegan. Jack-Pine Warb. 23(1):8-9.

850   Haugh, J.R. *1970.* A study of hawk migration and weather in eastern North America. Ph.D. Dissertation. Cornell University, Ithaca, NY. 240 pp.

851   Haugh, J.R. *1972.* A study of hawk migration in eastern North America. Search(Agriculture). 2(16):1-60.

852   Haughton, N. *1972.* Bald eagle study plan. Hunt-Wesson Foods, Inc. Fullerton, CA. 10 pp.

853   Hausman, L.A. *1966.* Birds of Prey of Northeastern North America. Richard R. Smith, Pub. Peterborough, NH. 164 pp.

854   Hawbecker, A.C. *1958.* Abalones eaten by bald eagles. The Condor. 60(6):407-408.

855   Hawk Mountain Sanctuary Association. *1966 - 1975.* Annual Reports of Hawk Mountain. Kempton, PA.

856   Hawkins, R.M. *1946.* Bald eagle feeding on the highway. The Auk. 63(1):85.

857   Hayman, P. *1969.* Birds of the World. Vol. 1 & 2. IPC Magazines, Ltd., London. p. 389-392.

858   Hayward, C.L. *1967.* Birds of the Upper Colorado River Basin. Brigham Young Univ., Science Bulletin. Biological Series. 9(2):1-64.

859   Hayward, J.L., Jr., W.H. Gillett, C.J. Amlaner, Jr., and J.F. Stout. *1977.* Predation on gulls by bald eagles in Washington. The Auk. 94(2):375.

860   Hebard, F.V. *1941.* Winter birds of the Okefinokee and Coleraine: A preliminary check-list of the winter birds of the interior of southeastern Georgia. Georgia Society of Naturalists, Bull. No. 3. 84 pp.

861   Hebard, F.V. *1948.* Bald eagle eating shoat on highway. Wilson Bull. 60(1):53.

862   Heddleston, K.K., T. Goodson, L. Leibovitz, and C.I. Angstrom. *1972.* Serological and biochemical characteristics of *Pasteurella multocida* from free flying birds and poultry. Avian Dis. 16(4):729-734.

863   Hehnke, M.F. *1973.* Nesting ecology and feeding behavior of bald eagles on the Alaska Peninsula. M.S. Thesis. Humboldt St. Univ., Humboldt, CA. 56 pp.

864   Heilborn, A. *1950.* A hunting bald eagle. Prothonotary. 16(2):13.

865   Heilman, G. *1926.* The Origin of Birds. H.F. & G. Witherby, London. 208 pp.

866   Heintzelman, D.S. *1975.* Autumn Hawk Flights: The Migrations in Eastern North America. Rutgers Univ. Press. New Brunswick, N.J. 398 pp.

867   Heintzelman, D.S. and R. MacClay. *1973.* The 1972 autumn hawk count at Bake Oven Knob, Pennsylvania. Cassinia.(54):3-9.

868   Heintzelman, D.S. and R. MacClay. *1975.* The 1973 and 1974 autumn hawk counts at Bake Oven Knob, Pennsylvania. Cassinia.(55):17-28.

869   Heintzelman, D.S. and R. MacClay. *1976.* The 1975 autumn hawk count at Bake Oven Knob, Pennsylvania. Cassinia.(56):15-21.

870   Heinzman, G.M. *1961.* American bald eagle. Natural Hist. 70(6):18-21.

871   Heinzman, G.M. and D. Heinzman. *1965.* Kissimmee Cooperative Bald Eagle Sanctuary: A 6-Year report. Fla. Nat. 38(4):126-127.

872   Heinzman, G.M. and D. Heinzman. *1970.* Kissimmee Cooperative Bald Eagle Sanctuary. Fla. Nat. 43(4):175.

873   Heller, E. *1901.* Notes on some little-known birds of southern California. The Condor. 3(4):100.

874   Helling, C.S., A.R. Isensee, E.A. Woolson, P.D.J. Ensor , G.E. Jones, J.R. Plimmer and P.C. Kearney. *1973.* Chlorodioxins in pesticides, soils, and plants. J. Env. Qual. 2(2):171-178.

875   Henninger, W.F. *1910.* Notes on some Ohio birds. The Auk. 27(1):66-68.

876   Henny, C.J., D.W. Anderson and C.E. Knoder. *1977.* Endangered southern bald eagle nesting in Baja, California. U.S.D.I. Fish and Wildlife Service(Unpublished Final Draft.) 5 pp.

877   Henny, C.J., D.W. Anderson, and C.E. Knoder. *1978.* Bald eagles nesting in Baja, California. The Auk. 95(2):424.

878   Hensel, R.J. and W.A. Troyer *1964.* Nesting studies of the bald eagle in Alaska. The Condor. 66(4):282-286.

879   Herrick, F.H. *1902.* The eagle's nest. St. Nicholas. 29(9):816-819.

880   Herrick, F.H. *1924.* An eagle observatory. The Auk. 41(1):89-105.

881   Herrick, F.H. *1924.* Daily life of the American eagle: Late phase. (concluded). The Auk. 41(4):517-541.

882   Herrick, F.H. *1924.* Nests and nesting habits of the American eagle. The Auk. 41(2):213-231.

883   Herrick, F.H. *1924.* The daily life of the American eagle: Late phase. The Auk. 41(3):389-422.

884   Herrick, F.H. *1929.* The eagle in action. Natl. Geog. Mag. 55(5):635-660.

885   Herrick, F.H. *1932.* Daily life of the American eagle: Early phase. The Auk. 49(4):428-435.

886   Herrick, F.H. *1932.* Daily life of the American eagle: Early phase. The Auk. 49(3):307-323.

887   Herrick, F.H. *1933.* The American Eagle. The Biological Laboratory of Western Reserve University. Cleveland, Ohio. 112 pp.

888   Herrick, F.H. *1933.* Daily life of the American eagle: Early phase. (concluded). The Auk. 50(1):35-53.

889   Herrick, F.H. *1934.* The American Eagle: A Study In Natural and Civil History. Appleton-Century, Co. New York. 267 pp.

890   Herrick, F.H. *1936.* Save the bald eagle. Bird-Lore. 38(4):274-278.

Master No.	Citation
891	Herrick, F.H. *1944.* Family life of the American eagle. Nature Mag. 4(3):132-140.
892	Heuser, E.P. *1940.* Bald eagles at Guttenberg. Iowa Bird Life. 10(2):29.
893	Hickey, J.J., P.B. Hofslund and H.F. Borchert. *1955.* Bird nests in Itasca State Park area, 1954. Flicker. 27(1):16-21.
894	Hickey, J.J., J.T. Emlen, Jr. and S.C. Kendeigh. *1965.* Early summer birdlife of Itasca State Park. The Loon. 37(1):27-39.
895	Hickey, J.J. and D.W. Anderson. *1968.* Chlorinated hydrocarbons and eggshell changes in raptorial and fish-eating birds. Science. 162(3850):271-273.
896	Hicks, L.E. *1933.* The breeding birds of Ashtabula County, Ohio. Wilson Bull. 45(4):168-195.
897	Higby, L.W. *1973.* The eagle survey in Wyoming. *In:* Population Status of Raptors. Murphy, J.R., C.M. White, and B.E. Harrell. (eds.). Proc. of the Conference on Raptor Conservation, Fort Collins, Colorado, 22-24 March 1973 (Part VI). Raptor Research Foundation, Inc., Raptor Research Report. No. 3. pp. 97-102.
898	Hill, N.P. *1965.* The Birds of Cape Cod, Massachusetts. William Morrow & Co., New York. 364 pp.
899	Hilton, J.R. *1972.* Bald eagle. Calif. Condor. 7(2):9-10.
900	Hirsch, B. *1976.* The delivery man and the eagles. Out. Ariz.(July):28.
901	Hix, G.E. *[?].* The Birds of Prey for Boy Scouts. (Pub. by Author). 32 pp.
902	Hix, G.E. *1907.* Some notes on the bald eagle in winter near New York City. Wilson Bull. 19(2):72-73.
903	Hodges, J. *1959.* The bald eagle in the upper Mississippi Valley. Iowa Bird Life. 29(4):86-91.
904	Hoefs, M. *1973.* Birds of the Kluane Game Sanctuary, Yukon Territory, and adjacent areas. Can. Field-Nat. 87(4):345-355.
905	Hofman, M.J. *1917.* Eagles in Pennsylvania Oologist. 34(1):11.
906	Hofslund, P.B. *1954.* The hawk pass at Duluth, Minnesota. Wilson Bull. 66(3):224.
907	Hofslund, P.B. *1966.* Hawk migration over the western tip of Lake Superior. Wilson Bull. 78(1):79-87.
908	Hogner, D.C. *1969.* Birds of Prey. Thomas Y. Crowell Co., New York. 132 pp.
909	Hohn, E.O. *1959.* Birds of the mouth of the Anderson River and Liverpool Bay, Northwest Territories. Can. Field-Nat. 73(1):93-113.
910	Hohn, E.O. *1959.* Eagles and thunderbirds. Can. Audubon. 21(5):146-149.
911	Holbrook, H. *1954.* Predation not serious problem on refuge. S. Carolina Wildlife. 1(3):2,21.
912	Holder, R.H. *1861.* Birds of Illinois. Trans. of the Illinois Natural History Society.(Second ed.) 1(1):1-194.
913	Holder, T. *1931.* Bald eagle. Oologist. 48(5):73.
914	Hollingsworth, J.F., Jr. *1974.* Doomsday for the bald eagle? The Chat. 38(2):37.
915	Holt, E.G. *1930.* Nesting of the sandhill crane in Florida. Wilson Bull. 42(3):163-183.
916	Honetschlager, M.A. and D. Honetschlager. *1974.* Bald eagle takes duck. The Loon. 46(2):90.
917	Hopkins, D.A. and G.S. Mersereau. (ed.). *1977.* Hawk migration, 1976 report. New England Hawk Watch. 14 pp.
918	Hopkins, E.S. *1926.* First egg of 1926. Oologist. 43(1):12.
919	Hornaday, W.T. *1920.* Alaska can save the American eagle. Natural Hist. 20(2):117-119.
920	Hornocker, M.G. *1969.* Goslings descend from aerial nest, attacked by bald eagle. The Auk. 86(4):764-765.
921	Hornung, C.P. *1941.* The American eagle. Am. Art. 5(9):10-13.
922	Horsfall, R.B. *1932.* Birds in color. Nature Mag. 19(1):34-35.
923	Horton, K.J. (ed.). *1973.* A good year for eagles. Mich. Aud. Soc. Newsl. 21(6):6.
924	Houghton, C. *1970.* Eagles and other birds near Troy, N.Y. Bird-Lore. 22(6):354-355.
925	Houston, C.S. and M.G. Street. *1959.* Birds of the Saskatchewan River, Carlton to Cumberland. Saskatchewan Nat. History Soc. Special Pub. No. 2. 210 pp.
926	Howard, H. *1930.* A census of the Pleistocene birds of Rancho La Brea from the collections of the Los Angeles Museum. The Condor. 32(2):81-88.
927	Howard, H. *1932.* Eagles and eagle-like vultures of the Pleistocene of Rancho La Brea. Carnegie Institution of Washington, D.C. Publ. 429. 82 pp.
928	Howard, H. and A.H. Miller. *1933.* Bird remains from cave deposits in New Mexico. The Condor. 35(1):15-18.
929	Howe, R.H., Jr. and G.M. Allen. *1901.* The Birds of Massachusetts. Subscription, Cambridge, MA. 154 pp.
930	Howe, R.H., Jr. and E. Sturtevant. *1903.* A Supplement to the Birds of Rhode Island. Middletown, Rhode Island. 111 pp.
931	Howell, A.B. *1917.* Birds of the islands off the coast of southern California. Pacific Coast Avifauna No. 12. Cooper Ornithological Club, California. 127 pp.
932	Howell, A.B. and A. Van Rossen. *1911.* Further notes from Santa Cruz Island. The Condor. 13(6):208-210.
933	Howell, A.H. *1911.* Birds of Arkansas. U.S.D.A. Biological Survey. Bull. No. 38. 100 pp.
934	Howell, A.H. *1928.* Birds of Alabama. (Second ed.). Birmingham Printing Co., Birmingham, AL. 384 pp.
935	Howell, J.C. *1935.* Bald eagle incubates horned owl's egg. The Auk. 52(1):79.
936	Howell, J.C. *1937.* The nesting bald eagles of southeastern Florida. The Auk. 54(3):296-299.

Master No.	Citation

937   Howell, J.C. *1941.* Comparison of 1935 and 1940 populations of nesting bald eagles in east-central Florida. The Auk. 58(3):402-403.

938   Howell, J.C. *1941.* Bald eagle killed by lightning while incubating its eggs. Wilson Bull. 53(1):42-43.

939   Howell, J.C. *1941.* Early nesting at Cape Sable, Florida. The Auk. 58(1):105-106.

940   Howell, J.C. *1948.* Observations on certain birds of the region of Kodiak, Alaska. The Auk. 65(7):352-358.

941   Howell, J.C. *1949.* Comparisons of 1935, 1940, and 1946 populations of nesting bald eagles in east-central Florida. The Auk. 66(1):84.

942   Howell, J.C. *1954.* A history of some bald eagle nest sites in east-central Florida. The Auk. 71(3):306-309.

943   Howell, J.C. *1958.* Response of Dr. Joseph C. Howell. *In:* More about Florida bald eagles. Audubon. 60(6):285-286.

944   Howell, J.C. *1958.* Further history of some bald eagle nest sites in east-central Florida. The Auk. 75(1):96-98.

945   Howell, J.C. *1958.* Comments. *In:* The Plight of the American Bald Eagle. Broley, C.L. (ed.) Audubon. 60(4):163,171.

946   Howell, J.C. *1962.* The 1961 status of some bald eagle nest sites in east-central Florida. The Auk. 79(4):716-718.

947   Howell, J.C. *1968.* The 1966 status of 24 nest sites of the bald eagle *(Haliaeetus leucocephalus)* in east-central Florida. The Auk. 85(4):680-681.

948   Howell, J.C. *1973.* The 1971 status of 24 bald eagle nest sites in east-central Florida. The Auk. 90(3):678-680.

949   Howell, J.C. and M.B. Monroe. *1958.* The birds of Knox County, Tennessee. The Migrant. 29(2):17-27.

950   Howell, J.C. and G.M. Heinzman. *1967.* Comparison of nesting sites of bald eagles in central Florida from 1930 to 1965. The Auk. 84(4):602-603.

951   Howsley, L.R. *1919.* Oregon birds. Oologist. 35(5):78-79.

952   Hoxie, W.J. *1887.* Breeding dates of birds near Frogmore, S. C., in 1886. Ornithol. and Oologist. 12(6):94.

953   Hoxie, W.J. *1888.* A bald eagle's nest. Ornithol. and Oologist. 13(4):63-64.

954   Hoxie, W.J. *1910.* Notes on the bald eagle in Georgia. The Auk. 27(4):454.

955   Hoyt, S.F. *1958.* Region 3- Finger Lakes. The Kingbird. 8(2):48-51.

956   Hoyt, S.F. *1959.* Region 3- Finger Lakes. The Kingbird. 9(3):125-128.

957   Huber, R.L. *1962.* The summer season. Flicker. 34(3):80-85.

958   Huber, R.L. *1962.* The winter season. Flicker. 34(1):22-24.

959   Huber, R.L. *1963.* The breeding season. Flicker. 35(3):85-94.

960   Huber, R.L. *1964.* The summer season. The Loon. 36(3):83-91.

961   Huber, R.L. *1966.* The summer season. The Loon. 38(1):8-21.

962   Huber, R.L. *1966.* The summer season. The Loon. 38(4):118-129.

963   Huber, R.L. *1967.* The spring season. The Loon. 39(3):86-99.

964   Huber, R.L. *1968.* The summer season. The Loon. 40(4):118-130.

965   Hulce, H. *1886.* The Toledo eaglet. Forest and Stream. 27(1):4.

966   Hulce, H. *1886.* Eagles breeding in captivity. Forest and Stream. 26(17):327.

967   Hulce, H. *1886.* The Toledo eaglet. Forest and Stream. 26(22):427.

968   Hulce, H. *1886.* Habits of the eagle. Forest and Stream. 26(19):369.

969   Hunt, C.J. *1905.* A-birding among the New Jersey Pines. Wilson Bull. 17(4):105-107.

970   Hunt, C.J. *1921.* Additional notes on Arkansas birds. The Auk. 38(4):610-611.

971   Hunt, G.L.,Jr. and M.W. Hunt. *1974.* Trophic levels and turnover rates: the avifauna of Santa Barbara Island, California. The Condor. 76(4):363-369.

972   Huser, V. *1968.* The bald eagle in Jackson Hole. Defend. Wildl. News. 43(2):148-152.

973   Imhof, T.A. *1976.* Alabama Birds. (Second Edition). Univ. of Alabama Press, University, AL. 445 pp.

974   Imler, R.H. *1934.* Bald eagles in Kansas. Nature Mag. 23(5):253.

975   Imler, R.H. *1937.* Bald eagle pellets in Kansas show rabbits as principal food. The Condor. 39(1):37-38.

976   Imler, R.H. and E.R. Kalmbach. *1955.* The bald eagle and its economic status. U.S.D.I. Fish and Wildlife Service. Circular 30. 51 pp.

977   Ingram, C. *1959.* The importance of juvenile cannibalism in the breeding biology of certain birds of prey. The Auk. 76(2):218-226.

978   Ingram, T.N. *1965.* Wintering bald eagles at Guttenberg, Iowa- Cassville, Wisconsin, 1964-1965. Iowa Bird Life. 35(3):66-78.

979   Ingram, T.N. *1966.* The bald eagle in Illinois. Audubon Bull.(138):26-28.

980   Ingram, T.N. *1975.* Eagle valley. *In:* Bald Eagle Land:Preservation and Acquisition. Proc. of Bald Eagle Days, 1975. Jan. 31-Feb.2. Ingram, T.N. (ed.). Eagle Valley Environmentalists, Inc., Apple River, IL. p. 15-20.

981   Ingram, T.N. (ed.). *1972.* Should the continental bald eagle be placed on the endangered species list? From a Hearing Conducted at 'Bald Eagle Days'. Univ. of Wisc onsin. Platteville, WI. Dec. 18, 1971. Eagle Valley Environmentalists, Inc. 33 pp.

Master No.   Citation

982   Ingram, T.N. (ed.). *1974.* Our eagle's future??? Proc. of Bald Eagle Days., Feb. 8-9-10., Eagle Valley
            Environmentalists, Inc., Apple River, IL. 82 pp.

983   Ingram, T.N. (ed.). *1975.* Bald Eagle Land: Preservation and Acquisition. Proc. of Bald Eagle Days, 1975. Jan
            31-Feb.2. Eagle Valley Environmentalists, Inc., Apple River, IL. 52 pp.

984   Ingram, T.N. (ed.). *1976.* Save the Eagle In '76. Proc. of Bald Eagle Days, 1976, Jan 30-Feb. 1. Eagle Valley
            Environmentalists, Inc. Apple River, IL. 138 pp.

985   International Union for Conservation of Nature and Natural Resources. *1966.* Red data book. Vol. 2, Aves.
            Monges, Switzerland. Sheet B/33/Halia/leu/leu.

986   Irving, L. *1960.* Birds of Anaktuvuk Pass, Kobuk, and Old Crow. A study in Arctic adaptation. United States
            National Museum Bulletin 217. Smithsonian Institution. 409 pp.

987   Irving, L. *1972.* Arctic Life of Birds and Mammals Including Man. Springer-Verlag, New York. 192 pp.

988   Isard, L. *1967.* Ohio's bald eagles - can they survive? Explorer. 9(3):4-7.

989   Isleib, M.E.P. and B. Kessel. *1973.* Birds of the North Gulf Coast Prince William Sound Region, Alaska. Univ.
            of Alaska. Biological Papers No. 14. 149 pp.

990   Ivanovs, M. *1971.* Bald eagle found nesting in Mille Lacs County. The Loon. 43(3):92.

991   Jackson, H.H.T. *1923.* Notes on summer birds of Mamie Lake Region, Wisconsin. The Auk. 40(3):478-489.

992   Jacobs, J.W. *1908.* Bald eagle *(Haliaeetus leucocephalus)* and great horned owl *(Bubo virginianus)* occupying the
            same nest. Wilson Bull. 20(2):103-104.

993   Jacobs, J.W. *1940.* A nest of the southern bald eagle and just my luck. Oologist. 57(1):2-7.

994   Jacobson, E., J.W. Carpenter and M. Novilla. *1977.* Suspected lead toxicosis in a bald eagle. J. Am. Vet.
            Medical Assoc. 171(9):952-954.

995   Jacobson, M.A. *1947.* Concentration of bald eagles in Virginia. The Auk. 64(4):619.

996   Jaffee, N.B. *1977.* A preliminary study of fledging, behavior and resource utilization of bald eagles in Virginia.
            Dept. of Biology, William and Mary College, Williamsburg, VA. (Unpublished Report).
            15 pp.

997   James, R.D., P.L. McLaren and J.C. Barlow. *1976.* Annotated Checklist of the Birds of Ontario. Life Sciences
            Miscellaneous Publications. Royal Ontario Museum, Toronto. 75 pp.

998   Jamieson, D. *1977.* The Skagit Eagle Sanctuary. View Northwest. February:53-57.

999   Janis, M. *1964.* The bald eagle. Audubon Bull. 132(Dec.):6-9.

1000   Janssen, R.B. *1972.* An eagle visits a feeder. The Loon. 44(1):21-22.

1001   Jenks, R. and J.O. Stevenson. *1937.* Bird records from central-eastern Arizona. The Condor. 39(2):87-90.

1002   Jewett, S.G. and I.N. Gabrielson. *1929.* Birds of the Portland Area, Oregon. Pacific Coast Avifauna, No. 19.
            Berkeley-Cooper Ornithological Club. 54 pp.

1003   Jewett, S.G., W.P. Taylor, W.T. Shaw and J.W. Aldrich. *1953.* Birds of Washington State. Univ. of Washington
            Press. Seattle, WA. 767 pp.

1004   Johnson, A.S. *1976.* Arizona mines it's future- by a damsite. Defend. Wildl. Int. 51(5):332-335.

1005   Johnson, D. and J.H. Enderson. *1972.* Roadside raptor census in Colorado - Winter 1971-1972. Wilson Bull.
            84(4):489-490.

1006   Johnson, D.R. and W.E. Melquist. *1973.* Unique, rare and endangered raptorial birds of northern Idaho:Nesting
            success and management recommendations. University of Idaho-U.S.D.A. Forest Service.
            R1-73-021. 42 pp.

1007   Johnson, J.C., Jr. *1961.* Winter concentration of bald eagles at Grand Lake, Oklahoma. Southwest Nat.
            6(2):107-108.

1008   Johnson, R.R. and J.W. Simpson. *1973.* The status of the bald eagle on the Verde River. J. Ariz. Acad.
            Sci.(Abstract) 8(Supp.):22.

1009   Johnston, J. *1966.* The Eagle in Fact and Fiction. Harlin Quist, Inc. 157 pp.

1010   Jollie, M.T. *1945.* Notes on raptors of the Boulder area, Colorado. The Condor. 47(1):38-39.

1011   Jonen, J.R. *1973.* The winter ecology of the bald eagle in west-central Illinois. M.S. Thesis. Western Illinois
            Univ. Macomb, IL. 84 pp.

1012   Jones, F.M. *1933.* A day with the bald eagles. Wilson Bull. 45(2):87-89.

1013   Jones, F.M. *1940.* The bald eagle. Oologist. 62(3):28-31.

1014   Jones, J. *1945.* Bald eagles along Chesapeake Bay. The Chat. 9(2):30.

1015   Jones, L. *1909.* The birds of Cedar Point and vicinity. Wilson Bull. 21(4):187-204.

1016   Jones, L. *1912.* A study of the avifauna of the Lake Erie Islands. Wilson Bull. 24(3):142-153.

1017   Jonkel, G.M. *1965.* South Dakota wintering eagle inventories. S. Dak. Bird Notes. 17(3):61-62.

1018   Juenemann, B.G. *1973.* Habitat evaluation of selected bald eagle nest sites on the Chippewa National Forest.
            M.S. Thesis. Univ. of Minnesota, Minneapolis, MN.

1019   Juenemann, B.G. and L.D. Frenzel. *1972.* Habitat evaluations of selected bald eagle nest sites on the Chippewa
            National Forest. Trans. of the 34th Annual Midwest Fish and Wildlife Conference. Dec.
            10-13, 1972. Des Moines, IA. 4 pp.

1020   Kaeding, H.B. *1905.* Birds from the west coast of lower California and adjacent islands. The Condor. 7(4):105-
            111.

Master No.	Citation
1021	**Kale, H.W., II.** *1965.* Notes on predation by the bald eagle on Sapelo Island, Georgia. Oriole. 30(1):70.
1022	**Kale, H.W., II.** *1966.* Additions to the birds of Sapelo Island and vicinity. Oriole. 31(1):1-11.
1023	**Kale, H.W., II.** *1966.* Florida's birds of prey, a valuable natural resource. Fla. Nat. 39(3):91-94,116.
1024	**Kale, H.W., II.** *1973.* The Florida bald eagle nest survey project. Fla. Aud. Soc. Ornithol. Research. 4 pp.
1025	**Kalmbach, E.R., R.H. Imler and L.W. Arnold.** *1964.* The American Eagles and Their Economic Status, 1964. U.S.D.I., Fish and Wildlife Service. 50 pp.
1026	**Kansas Academy of Science.** *1974.* Rare, endangered, and extirpated species in Kansas. (IV:Birds). Conservation Comm. Kansas Acad. of Sci. Transactions. 77(1): 1-9.
1027	**Keith, J.A. and I.M. Gruchy.** *1972.* Residue levels of chemical pollutants in North American bird life. Proc. of the International Ornithological Congress, 15th, The Hague. Voous, K.H.(ed.). p. 437-454.
1028	**Kelly, A.H.** *1972.* Michigan bird survey, winter 1971-1972. Jack-Pine Warb. 50(2):53-61.
1029	**Kelly, A.H.** *1972.* Michigan bird survey, summer 1972. Jack-Pine Warb. 50(4):119-126.
1030	**Kelly, A.H.** *1972.* Michigan bird survey, spring 1972. Jack-Pine Warb. 50(3):76-84.
1031	**Kelly, A.H.** *1974.* Michigan bird survey, fall 1973. Jack-Pine Warb. 52(1):33-43.
1032	**Kelly, A.H.** *1975.* Michigan bird survey, summer 1975. Jack-Pine Warb. 53(4):143-155.
1033	**Kelly, A.H., D.S. Middleton and W.P. Nickell.** *1963.* Birds of the Detroit - Windsor area, a ten-year survey. Cranbrook Institute of Science, Bloomfield Hills, MI. 119 pp.
1034	**Kelsey, P.** *1977.* DEC explores ways to restore bald eagles. N.Y. State Environ. 7(7):9.
1035	**Kemsies, E.** *1930.* Birds of the Yellowstone National Park, with some recent additions. Wilson Bull. 42(3):198-210.
1036	**Kenaga, E.F.** *1962.* Michigan Bird Survey, summer 1961. Jack-Pine Warb. 40(2):57-61.
1037	**Kendig, J.D.** *1946.* Island of the eagles. Am. For. 52(7):314-315.
1038	**Kennard, F.H.** *1936.* A legend corrected. Bull. Boston Soc. Nat. Hist. 79(April):18-20.
1039	**Kennedy, B.** *1977.* Annual eagle survey shows increase. Ark. Outdoors. Arkansas Game and Fish Commission. 2 pp.
1040	**Kenyon, K.W.** *1940.* An observation on the feeding of the southern bald eagle. The Condor. 42(5):265-266.
1041	**Kenyon, K.W.** *1961.* Birds of Amchitka Island, Alaska. The Auk. 78(3):316-317.
1042	**Kenyon, K.W.** *1961.* Isolation protects the bald eagle in Alaska. Audubon. 63(5):272-274.
1043	**Kenyon, K.W. and V.B. Scheffer.** *1961.* Wildlife surveys along the northwest coast of Washington. Murrelet. 42(3):29-37.
1044	**Kessel, B. and G.B. Schaller.** *1960.* Birds of the Upper Sheenjek Valley, Northern Alaska. Biological Papers of the Univ. of Alaska, Number 4. 59 pp.
1045	**Keyes, C.R.** *1897.* The Iowan raptores. Iowa Ornithol. 3(2):17-21.
1046	**Kimball, T.L.** *1976.* 7th Annual Bald Eagle Days Celebration Madison, Wisconsin. (Banquet Address). 5 pp.
1047	**Kinch, C.** *1966.* Bald eagles. Neb. Bird Rev. 34:49.
1048	**King, J.G., F.C. Robards and C.J. Lensink.** *1972.* Census of the bald eagle breeding population in southeast Alaska. J. Wildl. Manage. 36(4):1292-1295.
1049	**Kirk, D.** *1975.* Non-game Wildlife Investigations; California Raptor Survey. Project No. W-54-R-7. Job No. III-1. 10 pp.
1050	**Kirk, D.** *1976.* Nongame Wildlife Investigations, California Raptor Survey. Calif. Dept. of Fish and Game. Project. No. W-54-R-8. Job. No. III-1.0. 10 pp.
1051	**Kirkpatrick, D.** *1963.* High soars the eagle. Natl. Wildl. 1(1):28-31.
1052	**Kirkwood, F.C.** *1901.* A list of the birds of Maryland. Trans. of the Maryland Acad. of Sciences. 1:241-382.
1053	**Kitchin, E.A.** *1927.* Observations at Westport, Washington. Murrelet. 8(2):56-58.
1054	**Kitchin, E.A.** *1939.* A distributional check-list of the birds of Mount Ranier National Park. The Murrelet. 20(2):27-37.
1055	**Kitchin, E.A.** *1949.* Birds of the Olympic Peninsula. Olympic Stationers, Pt. Angeles, Washington. 262 pp.
1056	**Kleen, V.M.** *1973.* Report on the first statewide bird count. Ill. Aud. Bull.(164):16-22.
1057	**Knight, O.W.** *1896.* My '95 collecting trip in Penobscot Bay. Oologist. 13(2):9-13.
1058	**Knight, O.W.** *1908.* The Birds of Maine. Charles H. Glass and Co., Bangor, ME. 693 pp.
1059	**Knight, T.** *1977.* Watching raptors in winter. Washington Wildlife. 29(3):9-13.
1060	**Kocan, A.A. and L.N. Locke.** *1974.* Some helminth parasites of the American bald eagle. J. Wildl. Dis. 10(1):8-10.
1061	**Kochert, M.N.** *1973.* Density, food habits, and reproductive performance of raptors in the Snake River Birds of Prey Natural Area. U.S.D.I. Bureau of Land Management, Boise Dist.. Annual Prog. Rep., 1973. 54 pp.
1062	**Kopischke, E.D.** *1965.* Bald eagle attempts to kill jack rabbit. The Loon. 37(1):49.
1063	**Korowotny, S.** *1978.* Use of east Texas reservoirs by wintering bald eagles, 1977-1978. Dept. of Wildlife and Fisheries Sciences. Texas A & M University. Progress Report. 22 pp.
1064	**Krantz, W.C., B.M. Mulhern, G.E. Bagley, A. Sprunt, III, F.J. Ligas and W.B. Robertson, Jr.** *1970*. Organochlorine and heavy metal residues in bald eagle eggs. Pest. Monit. J. 4(3):136-140.

Master No.	Citation

1065 Krauss, G.D. *1977.* A report on the 1976-77 Klamath Basin bald eagle winter use area investigation. Klamath National Forest, Goosenest Ranger District., April 14, 1977. 68 pp.

1066 Krog, J. *1953.* Notes on the birds of Amchitka Island, Alaska. The Condor. 55(6):299-304.

1067 Krutch, J.W. and P.S. Eriksson. *1962.* A Treasury of Birdlore. Doubleday and Co., Garden City, New York. 390 pp.

1068 Kumlien, L. and N. Hollister. *1903.* The birds of Wisconsin. Bull. Wisc. Nat. Hist. Soc.3(1,2,3):1-143.

1069 Kumlien, L. and N. Hollister. *1949.* The birds of Wisconsin. Pass. Pigeon. 11(3):114-124.

1070 Kusser, J.D. *1912.* Note on the bald eagle, starling, and song sparrow at Bernardsville, New Jersey. Bird-Lore. 14(6):349-350.

1071 Kussman, J.V. *1977.* Post-fledging behavior of the northern bald eagle, *Haliaeetus leucocephalus alascanus* Townsend, in Chippewa National Forest, Minnesota. Phd. Dissertation, Univ. of Minnesota, St. Paul, MN.

1072 Kussman, J.V. and L.D. Frenzel. *1972.* Post-fledging activity of bald eagles on the Chippewa National Forest. Trans. of the 34th Annual Midwest Fish and Wildlife Conf., Dec. 10-13, 1972. Des Moines, IA. 3 pp.

1073 L.G.L., Ltd. *1972.* Bald eagle surveys in southern Mackenzie District and northern Alberta, May, July, August 1972. 12 pp.

1074 L.G.L., Ltd. *1972.* Surveys of terrestrial bird populations in Alaska, Yukon Territory, Northwest Territories, and Northern Alberta. Part 2. Report Prepared for Northern Engineering Services, Ltd. 372 pp.

1075 L.G.L., Ltd. *1972.* Aerial survey of proposed gas pipeline route in Alberta, Saskatchewan, and Manitoba, May, July, October, 1972. Part 2, Section 3. Report Prepared for Northern Engineering Services, Ltd. 302 pp.

1076 L.G.L., Ltd. *1972.* Surveys of terrestrial bird populations in Alaska, Yukon Territory, Northwest Territories, and Northern Alberta, Part 1. Report Prepared for Northern Engineering Services, Ltd. 171 pp.

1077 L.G.L., Ltd. *1972.* Aerial surveys of bird populations along the route of the proposed gas pipeline in the Mackenzie District, Northwest Territories, 1972. Report Prepared for Northern Engineering Services, Ltd. 156 pp.

1078 Lacey, H. *1912.* Additions to birds of Kerrville, Texas. The Auk. 29(2):254.

1079 Lahrman, F.W. *1962.* Bald eagle harries nesting canada geese. Blue Jay. 20(2):55.

1080 Langdon, F.W. *1880.* Summer birds of a northern Ohio marsh. J. Cinn. Soc. Nat. Hist. 3(3):220-232.

1081 Langowski, D.J. *1975.* Minnesota bald eagle status-1975. U.S.D.I. Fish and Wildlife Service.(Report). Bemidji, MN. 1 p.

1082 Larson, A. *1928.* Birds of eastern McKenzie County, North Dakota. Wilson Bull. 40(1):39-48.

1083 Larson, J.S. and J.M. Abbott. *1962.* Mid-winter census of American bald eagles in the Chesapeake Bay Region, 1962. Ches. Sci. 3(3):211-213.

1084 Lavine, S.A. *1974.* Wonders of the Eagle World. Dodd, Mead, & Co., N.Y. 64 pp.

1085 Laycock, G. *1973.* Autumn of the Eagle. Charles Scribner's Sons, New York. 239 pp.

1086 Laycock, G. *1973.* Saving western eagles from traps and zaps: bobcat baits and poles take heavy tolls. Audubon. 75(5):133.

1087 Laycock, G. *1974.* Bald eagles at bay. Natl. Wildl.(Aug/sept.):35-36.

1088 Laycock, G. *1975.* The eagles of Vermilion. Explorer. 17(3):13-16.

1089 Laycock, G. *1976.* Saving the bald eagle. Exxon U.S.A. 15(2):3-7.

1090 Laycock, G. *1977.* The unhuntables are finally getting attention, funds. Audubon. 79(3):128-132.

1091 Le Clear Beard, W. *1897.* Moses - a tame eagle. St. Nicholas. 24(6):444-449.

1092 Leach, H. *1971.* Who declares wildlife endangered or rare? Out. Calif. p. 24-25.

1093 Leberman, R.C. *1976.* The Birds of Ligonier Valley. Carnegie Museum of Natural History. Pittsburgh. 67 pp.

1094 Lederer, R.J. *1976.* The breeding population of piscivorous birds of Eagle Lake. Am. Birds. 30(3):771-772.

1095 Leduc, P.V. *1970.* Red-tailed hawk attacks bald eagle. The Auk. 87(3):586.

1096 Lee, F.B. *1950.* Adult bald eagles. Flicker. 22(3):109.

1097 Lewis, P.M. *1977.* Eagles arrive at Reelfoot. NEWS. Tennessee Department of Tourist Development, Nashville, Tennessee. 2 pp.

1098 LeDioyt, G., L. McDaniel, J.C.W. Bliese, G.W. Brown, G. Brown, R. Brown, L. Morris and R. Harrington. *1964.* Bald eagles. Neb. Bird Rev. 32:61.

1099 Lien, J. *1975.* Aggression between great black-backed gulls and bald eagles. The Auk. 92(3):584-585.

1100 Ligas, F.J. *1968.* Maine bald eagle survey-1968. Maine Aud. Soc. Newsl. August 1968. 1 pp.

1101 Ligon, J.S. *1961.* New Mexico Birds and Where to Find Them. Univ. of New Mexico Press. Albuquerque, NM. 360 pp.

1102 Lincer, J.L. *1975.* The potential effects of the proposed Caledon State Park on the existing bald eagle and osprey populations: final report. Eco-Analysts, Inc. Sarasota, FL. 22 pp.

Master No.	Citation

1103 Lincer, J.L. *1975.* First follow-up study on the bald eagles and ospreys of Cedar Grove Farms. Eco-Analysts, Inc. Sarasota, FL. 15 pp.

1104 Lincer, J.L. *1976.* Second follow-up study on the bald eagles and ospreys of Cedar Grove Farms. Eco-Analysts, Inc. Sarasota, FL. 18 pp.

1105 Line, L. *1961.* Bald eagle preys on white-tailed deer fawn. Jack-Pine Warb. 39(4):147.

1106 Line, L. *1966.* 1965 A rough year on eagles, ospreys. Mich. Aud. Newsl. 13(5):2.

1107 Linsdale, J.M. *1930.* Problems of bird conservation in California. Condor. 32(2):105-115.

1108 Linsley, J.H. *1843.* Catalogue of the birds of Connecticut. Am. J. Sci. Art. 43(2):249-274.

1109 Lint, J.B. *1975.* A report on the bald eagles of Wolf Lodge Bay. U.S.D.I., Bureau of Land Management, Couer D' Alene, ID. 13 pp.

1110 Linton, C.B. *1908.* Notes from San Clemente Island. Condor. 10(2):82-86.

1111 Lipps, J.H., J.W. Valentine and E. Michell. *1968.* Pleistocene paleoecology and biostratigraphy, Santa Barbara, California. J. of Paleontology. 42(2):291-307.

1112 Lish, J.W. *1973.* Status and ecology of bald eagles and nesting golden eagles in Oklahoma. M.S. Thesis. Oklahoma State University., Stillwater, OK. 99 pp.

1113 Lish, J.W. *1973.* Bald eagles wintering on the Neosho River, Oklahoma. Bull. Okla. Ornithol. Soc. 6(4):25-30.

1114 Lish, J.W. *1975.* Status and ecology of bald eagles in Oklahoma. Oklahoma Coop. Wildlife Res. Unit. Quarterly Prog. Report. 28 (1):26-32.

1115 Lish, J.W. and J.C. Lewis. *1975.* Status and ecology of bald eagles wintering in Oklahoma. Proc. of the 29th Annual Conf. of the Southeastern Assoc. of Game and Fish Commissioners. p. 415-423.

1116 Lish, J.W., J.W. Ault, III, and J.A. Bissonette. *1978.* Status update on bald eagles in Oklahoma. Oklahoma Coop. Wildl. Res. Unit, Stillwater, OK. (Unpublished Report). 4 pp.

1117 Littlewood.C. *1972.* The World's Vanishing Birds. W. Foulsham & Co., Ltd. London. 63 pp.

1118 Lloyd, G. and D. Lloyd. *[?].* Birds of Prey. Grossett and Dunlap, New York. 159 pp.

1119 Lloyd, W. *1887.* Birds of Tom Green and Concho Counties, Texas. The Auk. 4(3):181-193.

1120 Lobik, P.H. *1960.* The Christmas census - 1959. Audubon Bull.(113):14-24.

1121 Lock, R.A. *1971.* Wintering bald eagle survey. Neb. Game, and Parks Comm. Terrestrial Wildlife Div. 4 pp.

1122 Lock, R.A. *1972.* Population trends of non-game species. Neb. Game and Parks Comm. Proj. F-71, Job. F4. 7 pp.

1123 Lock, R.A. *1974.* Population surveys of raptors. Nebraska Game and Parks Comm. Proj. W-15-R-30. Job No. 02. 26 pp.

1124 Lock, R.A. *1975.* Population surveys of raptors. Population Surveys of Non-Game Species. Neb. Game and Parks Comm. Wk. Plan. 0-74, Proj. W-15-R-31. 25 pp.

1125 Lock, R.A. and J. Shuckman. *1973.* A bald eagle nest in Nebraska. Neb. Bird Rev. 41(4):76-77.

1126 Locke, L.N., N.J. Chura and P.A. Stewart. *1966.* Spermatogenesis in bald eagles experimentally fed a diet containing DDT. The Condor. 68(5):497-502.

1127 Locke, L.N., J.A. Newman and B.M. Mulhern. *1972.* Avian cholera in a bald eagle from Ohio. Ohio J. Sci. 72(5):294-296.

1128 Loftin, H. *1956.* The eagle's tribute. Sci. News Letter. 69(13):206.

1129 Loftin, H. *1959.* The bald eagle club. Sci. News Letter. 75(20):320.

1130 Loomis, L.M. *1890.* Observations on some of the summer birds of the mountain portions of Pickens County, South Carolina. The Auk. 7(1):30-39.

1131 Lound, M. and R. Lound. *1957.* Summer season, June 1 - August 15, 1957. Pass. Pigeon. 19(4):174-181.

1132 Lound, M. and R. Lound. *1957.* Spring season, March - May 1957. Pass. Pigeon. 19(3):125-141.

1133 Lound, M. and R. Lound. *1959.* Summer season, June 1 - August 15, 1958. Pass. Pigeon. 21(1):35-45.

1134 Loyster, E.L. *1942.* Possible nesting of bald eagle in Sauk county. Pass. Pigeon. 4(4,5,6):48.

1135 Lumley, E.D. *1939.* Two Eagles of North America. Emer. Cons. Comm. Pub. No. 78. 22 pp.

1136 Lund, S. *1978.* Large numbers of bald eagles winter in Casper area. Aud. Newsl. of Murie Audubon Soc. Casper. (April).

1137 Lund, S. *1978.* Eagles of Jackson's Canyon. Wy. Wildl. 42(4):29-32.

1138 Lupient, M. *1961.* Seasonal report. Flicker. 33(2):45-46.

1139 Lynch, J.F. and N.K. Johnson. *1974.* Turnover and equilibria in insular avifaunas, with special reference to the California Channel Islands. The Condor. 76(4):370-384.

1140 M'Camey, F. *1935.* An April visit to the Reelfoot crane-towns. The Migrant. 6(2):17-18.

1141 Macoun, J. and J.M. Macoun. *1909.* Catalogue of Canadian birds. Govt. Printing Office. Ottawa. 761 pp.

1142 MacAlister, P.R. *1952.* American eagle: In interior design and in decoration. Interior Design. 23(1):46-57.

1143 MacCord, H.A. *1953.* The Bintz site. Am. Ant. 18(3):239-244.

1144 MacGillivray, J. *1942.* The eagles of Oscoda. Am. Forest. 48(7):298-301,335-336.

1145 MacKenzie, J.P.S. *1977.* Birds In Peril. Houghton-Mifflin, Inc. Boston. 191 pp.

Master No.	Citation

1146   **Madsen, C.R.** *1974.* Bald eagle nest survey in the Great Lakes states. *In:* Our Eagles Future ???, Proc. of Bald Eagle Days. Feb. 8-10, 1974. Ingram, T.N. (ed.). Eagle Valley Environmentalists, Inc. Apple River, IL. p. 46-48.

1147   **Madsen, C.R. (ed.).** *1973.* Notes on a bald eagle nest survey workshop. Twin Cities, MN. Aug. 15, 1973. U.S.D.I., Fish and Wildlife Service. Region 3. 47 pp.

1148   **Maestrelli, J.R. and S.N. Wiemeyer.** *1975.* Breeding bald eagles in captivity. Wilson Bull. 87(1):45-53.

1149   **Maestrelli, J.R. and S.N. Wiemeyer.** *1976.* Breeding bald eagles in captivity. *In:* Save the Eagle in '76, Proc. of Bald Eagle Days, 1976. Ingram, T.N. (ed.). Eagle Valley Environmentalists, Inc., Apple River, IL. p. 123-129.

1150   **Magee, M.J.** *1923.* Bird notes from the north shore of Lake Superior, near Gagantua, Algoma District, Ontario. Can. Field-Nat. 37(8):145-146.

1151   **Mager, D.** *1976.* Eagle 001. The Fla. Nat.(Dec.):18-19.

1152   **Mager, D.** *1977.* Bald eagle nesting survey. U.S.D.I., Fish and Wildlife Service Endangered Species Report, June 29, 1977. 3 pp.

1153   **Mahan, H.D.** *1963.* Michigan Bird Survey, summer, 1962. Jack-Pine Warb. 41(2):75-79.

1154   **Malick, D.** *1962.* The eagles of Colorado. Colo. Out. 11(1):14-19.

1155   **Malkowski, J.M.** *1972.* De Soto National Wildlife Refuge. Nebr. Bird Rev. 40(1):23.

1156   **Mallette, R.D.** *1968.* Upland game investigations. Status of rare and endangered species, management and special survey investigations. Special Wildlife Biological, Management and Special Survey Investigations. Calif. Dept. of Fish and Game. Proj. No. W-47-R-16. Job. No. 2. 10 pp.

1157   **Mallette, R.D.** *1970.* Special Wildlife Investigations: Raptor survey. Calif. Dept. of Fish and Game and U.S. Forest Service. Proj. No. W-54-R-2. Job No. III-6. 41 pp.

1158   **Mallette, R.D.** *1973.* Special Wildlife Investigations: Raptor Survey. Calif. Dept. of Fish and Game and U.S. Forest Service. Proj. No. W-54-R-5. Job No. III-6. 19 pp.

1159   **Mallette, R.D.** *1974.* Special Wildlife Investigations; Raptor Survey. Calif. Dept. of Fish and Game. Project No. W-54-R-6. Job No. III-6. 15 pp.

1160   **Mallette, R.D. and G.I. Gould, Jr.** *1976.* Raptors of California. Calif. Dept. of Fish and Game. 85 pp.

1161   **Maniscalco, J.** *1959.* The bald eagle. Did you know? Wy. Wildl. 23(5):15.

1162   **Manley, C.H.** *1937.* Bald eagle in Allegheny County. Cardinal. 4(6):148.

1163   **Manley, C.H.** *1950.* Pelican and eagle weights. Audubon. 52(1):65-66.

1164   **Mannix, D.P.** *1941.* Hunting dragons with an eagle. Sat. Even. Post., Jan. 18:19-21,38,40-41,43.

1165   **Mannix, D.P.** *1943.* Making 'Eagle vs. Dragon'. Am. Falconer. 2(1):16-19.

1166   **Mannix, D.P.** *1943.* Making 'Eagle vs. Dragon' continued. Am. Falconer. 2(2):15-20.

1167   **Mannix, D.P.** *1946.* Our eagle catches dragons. True.(March):26-29,107-112.

1168   **Mannix, D.P.** *1949.* Speaking of pictures, a tame American eagle is trained in falconry. Life. July 4:9-10.

1169   **Mannix, D.P.** *1954.* Meet our national bird. Holiday. 16:18-19,21-22.

1170   **Mannix, D.P.** *1955.* Bird of the brave. True.(July):28-29,58-60.

1171   **Mannix, D.P.** *1965.* The Last Eagle. McGraw-Hill Book Co., N.Y. 149 pp.

1172   **Mannix, D.P.** *1970.* Did eagles really carry off babies? True.(Feb.):72-74,96-97.

1173   **Mannix, D.P.** *1971.* Reports on a bald eagle breeding project. Raptor Research News. 5(1):29-30.

1174   **Mannix, D.P.** *1973.* We're in the money. Sat. Even. Post. Jan. 16:25-25,36,39,40,42.

1175   **Mansell, W.D.** *1965.* Eagle nesting survey in the Lake of the Woods area. Can. Audubon. 27(1):18-21.

1176   **Manville, R.H.** *1949.* Bird notes from northern Michigan. Wilson Bull. 61(2):106-108.

1177   **Mapletoft, R.J. and G.J. Futter.** *1969.* Repeated Halothane anesthesia in an American bald eagle. Can. Vet. J. 10(10):274-277.

1178   **Margolis, K.** *1974.* Eagles and people on the Skagit - Is there room for both? Pacific Search. 8(4):16-17.

1179   **Maricopa Audubon Society.** *1975.* Central Arizona Project. Report to Members. 12 pp.

1180   **Marion, L.** *1935.* Why protect the bald eagle? Bird-Lore. 37(5):362-363.

1181   **Marion, W.R. and J.D. Shamis.** *1977.* An annotated bibliography of bird marking techniques. Bird-Band. 48(1):42-61.

1182   **Marler, G.D.** *1951.* Birds of the geyser basins of the Firehole. Yellowstone Nature Notes. 25(1):1-7.

1183   **Marsh, A.J.** *1941.* Bald eagle notes. The Migrant. 12(2):38.

1184   **Marshall, D.B. and P.R. Nickerson.** *1976.* The bald eagle: 1776-1976. Nat. Parks and Conserv. Mag.(July):14-19.

1185   **Marshall, W.H.** *1940.* An eagle guard developed in Idaho. The Condor. 42(3):166.

1186   **Martin, D.** *1974.* The great feather war. Defend. Wildl. Int. 49(5):371-372.

1187   **Mathematical Sciences Northwest, Inc.** *1977.* Washington Coastal Areas of Major Biological Significance. State of Washington, Dept. of Ecology. Baseline Study Program No. 11. 651 pp.

1188   **Mathisen, J.E.** *1963.* Status of the bald eagle on the Chippewa National Forest. Flicker. 35(4):114-117.

1189   **Mathisen, J.E.** *1964.* The status and management of the bald eagle on the Chippewa National Forest. Minn. Ornithol. Union. p. 1-7.

1190   **Mathisen, J.E.** *1964.* Bald eagle nesting, 1964. The Loon. 36(3):104-105.

Master No.	Citation

1191 Mathisen, J.E. *1965.* Bald eagle status report, 1965, Chippewa National Forest. The Loon. 37(3):104-105.

1192 Mathisen, J.E. *1966.* Bald eagle status report, 1966 Chippewa National Forest. The Loon. 38(4):134-136.

1193 Mathisen, J.E. *1967.* Results of bald eagle - osprey aerial nest search. The Loon. 39(3):102-103.

1194 Mathisen, J.E. *1967.* Bald eagle - osprey status report, 1967 Chippewa National Forest, Minnesota. The Loon. 39(4):121-122.

1195 Mathisen, J.E. *1968.* Effects of human disturbance on nesting of bald eagles. J. Wildl. Manage. 32(1):1-6.

1196 Mathisen, J.E. *1968.* Bald eagle - osprey status report, 1968, Chippewa National Forest, Minnesota. The Loon. 40(3):97-99.

1197 Mathisen, J.E. *1968.* Identification of bald eagle and osprey nests in Minnesota. The Loon. 40(4):113-114.

1198 Mathisen, J.E. *1969.* Bald eagle - osprey status report, 1969. The Loon. 41(3):84-87.

1199 Mathisen, J.E. *1969.* Identification of bald eagle and osprey nests in Minnesota. Inland Bird-Band. News. 41(1):21-23.

1200 Mathisen, J.E. *1969.* The bald eagle, going, going, going.... N. Dak. Outdoors. 31(10):8-11.

1201 Mathisen, J.E. *1970.* Bald eagle - osprey status report, 1970. U.S.D.A. Chippewa National Forest. 4 pp.

1202 Mathisen, J.E. *1971.* Bald eagle - osprey status report, 1971. Chippewa National Forest. 3 pp.

1203 Mathisen, J.E. *1972.* Status of ospreys on the Chippewa National Forest. North American Osprey Research Conf. Transactions, Feb. 1972. 8 pp.

1204 Mathisen, J.E. *1973.* Bald eagle - osprey status report. U.S.D.A. Forest Service. Chippewa National Forest Report. 3 pp.

1205 Mathisen, J.E. *1973.* Bald eagle - osprey status report, 1972. The Loon. 45(1):15-16.

1206 Mathisen, J.E. *1973.* The Hunt Wesson acquisition program. *In:* Notes on a Bald Eagle Nest Survey Workshop. Twin Cities, MN. Aug. 15, 1973. Madsen, C.R. (ed.). Twin Cities, MN. U.S .D.I. Fish and Wildlife Service. Reg. 3. p. 43-44.

1207 Mathisen, J.E. *1974.* Some aspects of bald eagle management and research on the Chippewa National Forest. Raptor Research Foundation, Nov. 1974. 6 pp.

1208 Mathisen, J.E. *1974.* The American bald eagle. Am. For. 80:48.

1209 Mathisen, J.E. *1974.* Bald eagle - osprey status report, 1974. U.S.D.A. Forest Service. Chippewa National Forest. 3 pp.

1210 Mathisen, J.E. *1975.* First national children's eagle nesting area. *In:* Bald Eagle Land: Preservation and Acquisition. Ingram, T.N. (ed.). Proc. of Bald Eagle Days, 1975, Jan. 31-Feb. 2. Eagle Valley Environmentalists, Inc., Apple River, IL. p. 28-30.

1211 Mathisen, J.E. *1975.* Bald eagle - osprey status report, 1975. U.S.D.A. Forest Service. Chippewa National Forest. 2 pp.

1212 Mathisen, J.E. *1975.* Kings of the avian way. Minn. Vol. 38(221):27-32.

1213 Mathisen, J.E. *1976.* Bald eagle - osprey status report, 1976. U.S.D.A. Forest Service. Chippewa National Forest. 2 pp.

1214 Mathisen, J.E. *1977.* Bald eagle - osprey status report, 1977. Chippewa National Forest. U.S.D.A. Forest Service. 2 pp.

1215 Mathisen, J.E. *1978.* Hope for our national symbol. Minn. Volunteer. (Mar.-Apr.):44-49.

1216 Mathisen, J.E. and A. Mathisen. *1968.* Species and abundance of diurnal raptors in the panhandle of Nebraska. Wilson Bull. 80(4):474-486.

1217 Mathisen, J.E. and J. Stewart. *1970.* A band for an eagle. The Loon. 42(3):84-87.

1218 Mathisen, J.E. and T.C. Dunstan. *1975.* A strategy for bald eagle management. Raptor Research Foundation, Nov. 1975. 7 pp.

1219 Mathisen, J.E., D.J. Sorenson, L.D. Frenzel and T.C. Dunstan. *1977.* Management strategy for bald eagles. Trans. of the 42nd North American Wildlife and Nat. Res. Conf. Atlanta, Ga.,(Abstract). 2 pp.

1220 Mathisen, J.E., L.D. Frenzel and T.C. Dunstan. *1977.* A management strategy for bald eagles. Trans of the 42nd North American Wildlife and Nat. Res. Conf. in Atlanta, Georgia. 16 pp.

1221 Mattsson, J.P. *1974.* Sucker Lake bald eagle study. *In:* Our Eagles Future??? Proc. of Bald Eagle Days. Feb. 8,9.10,1974. Ingram, T.N. (ed.). Eagle Valley Environmentalists', Inc. Apple River, IL. p. 35-45.

1222 Mattsson, J.P. *1974.* Interaction of a breeding pair of bald eagles with subadults at Sucker Lake, Michigan. M.A. Thesis, St. Cloud State University, St. Cloud, Minnesota. 51 pp.

1223 Mattsson, J.P. *1978.* Minnesota bald eagle status report, 1978. U.S.D.I. Fish and Wildlife Service. Report to Minneapolis Regional Office. 4 pp.

1224 Mattsson, J.P. and A.H. Grewe, Jr. *1976.* Bald eagle nesting in the Superior National Forest. U.S.D.A. Forest Service, Research Note NC-198, North Central Forest Experiment Station. 2 pp.

1225 Maxon, W.R. *1903.* Notes on the birds of Madison County, New York, with special reference to Embody's recent list. The Auk. 20(3):262-266.

1226 May, J.B. *1935.* The Hawks of North America; Their Field Identification and Feeding Habits. National Assoc. of Audubon Societies. New York. 140 pp.

Master No.   Citation

1227   McAtee, W.L. *1935.* Food Habits of Common Hawks. U.S.D.A. Circular No. 370. Wash., D.C.

1228   McClelland, B.R. *1973.* Autumn concentrations of bald eagles in Glacier National Park. The Condor. 75(1):121-123.

1229   McClelland, B.R. and D.S. Shea. *1978.* Local and long-range movements of bald eagles associated with autumn concentrations in Glacier National Park. Progress Report.(Unpublished). Univ. of Montana, Missoula, Mt. 19 pp.

1230   McClung, R.M. *1955.* Vulcan: The Story of a Bald Eagle. William Morrow and Co., Inc., New York. 64 pp.

1231   McCoy, J.J. *1963.* Lords of the Sky. Bobbs-Merrill Co., Inc. Indianapolis. 95 pp.

1232   McCreary, O. *1939.* Wyoming Bird Life. (Revised ed.) Burgess Publ. Co., Minneapolis, Minn. 124 pp.

1233   McDowell, R.T. *1948.* Pennsylvania Birds of Prey. Pennsylvania Game Commission, Harrisburg, PA.

1234   McEwan, L.C. *1977.* Nest site selection and productivity of the southern bald eagle. M.S. Thesis. Univ. of Florida, Gainesville, FL. 65 pp.

1235   McIlhenny, E.A. *1932.* The blue goose in its winter home. The Auk. 49(3):279-306.

1236   McKee, E.D. *1930.* Preliminary checklist of birds Grand Canyon. U.S.D.I. National Park Service, Grand Canyon National Park. 15 pp.

1237   McKenna, M.G. and R.W. Seabloom. *1976.* Threatened and unique wildlife of North Dakota: Initial Status Report. University of North Dakota. Inst. for Ecological Studies. Res. Report No. 13. 101 pp.

1238   McLain, R.B. *1902.* The bald eagle in Ohio County, West Virginia. The Auk. 19(3):287.

1239   McLaughlin, F.W. *1959.* Bald eagle survey in New Jersey. Interim Report 1. N.J. Nature News. 14(3):51.

1240   McLaughlin, F.W. *1961.* Bald eagle survey in New Jersey. N.J. Nature News. p. 28.

1241   McLaughlin, F.W. *1964.* Bald eagle survey in New Jersey. N.J. Nature News. 14(2):25.

1242   McLaughlin, F.W. *1964.* Status of the bald eagle in New Jersey. New Jersey Nature News. 19(2):66-75.

1243   McMillen, W. *1910.* Ohio birds. Oologist. 27(8):97.

1244   Meanley, B. and F.G. Schmid. *1960.* The bald eagle: can it survive? Md. Conserv. 37(2):5-7.

1245   Mearns, E.A. *1890.* Observations on the avifauna of portions of Arizona. The Auk. 7(1):45-55.

1246   Meinertzhagen, R. *1959.* Pirates and Predators, the Piratical and Predatory Habits of Birds. Oliver & Boyd, Edinburgh. 230 pp.

1247   Mengel, R.M. *1953.* On the name of the northern bald eagle and the identity of Audubon's gigantic 'Bird of Washington'. Wilson Bull. 65(3):145-151.

1248   Mengel, R.M. *1965.* The birds of Kentucky. American Ornithologists' Union. Ornithological Monographs No. 3. 581 pp.

1249   Merrell, T.R., Jr. *1970.* A swimming bald eagle. Wilson Bull. 82(2):220.

1250   Merriam, C.H. *1877.* A Review of the Birds of Connecticut. Tuttle, Morehouse, and Taylor, Printers.: New Haven. 165 pp.

1251   Merrill, J.C. *1888.* Notes on the birds of Fort Klamath, Oregon. The Auk. 5(2):139-146.

1252   Merrill, J.C. *1897.* Birds of Fort Sherman, Idaho. The Auk. 14(4):347-357.

1253   Milburn, E. *1977.* Summary report of the 1977 bald eagle reintroduction project at the Montezuma National Wildlife Refuge, New York. Memo. to the New York State Dept. of Environmental Conservation. 21 pp.

1254   Milburn, E. *1977.* Reintroduction of the bald eagle in New York State. Annual Report, Hawk Mountain Sanctuary Association. December 1977. p. 7-10.

1255   Milburn, E. *1977.* Reintroduction of the bald eagle in New York state. NAHO. New York State Museum. 10(2):16-19.

1256   Milburn, E. and T.J. Cade. *1976.* A report on the bald eagle reintroduction project. , June 27 - August 16, 1976. Memo. to the New York State Dept. of Environmental Conservation. 12 pp.

1257   Miller, D., E.L. Boeker, R.S. Thorsell and R.R. Olendorff. *1975.* Suggested practices for raptor protection on powerlines. Prepared by Raptor Research Foundation, Inc., for Edison Electric Institute. 19 pp.

1258   Miller, F.T. *1892.* Visiting a bald eagle's nest in Virginia. Oologist. 9(3):75-76.

1259   Miller, L.H. *1911.* A series of eagle tarsi from the pleistocene of Rancho La Brea. University of California Publication, Bull. of the Dept. of Geology. 6(12):305-316.

1260   Miller, L.H. *1929.* The fossil birds of California. Univ. of California Printing Office. 14 pp.

1261   Miller, L.H. *1957.* Bird remains from an Oregon Indian midden. The Condor. 59(1):59-63.

1262   Miller, R.C., E.D. Lumley and F.S. Hall. *1935.* Birds of the San Juan Islands, Washington. The Murrelet. 16(3):51-65.

1263   Miller, R.F. *1910.* Summer residents of Philadelphia County, Pennsylvania. Oologist. 27(10):116-119.

1264   Miller, R.F. *1926.* Pennsylvania and New Jersey, nesting dates for 1926. Oologist. 43(12):162-164.

1265   Miller, R.F. *1928.* Pennsylvania and New Jersey 1927 nesting dates. Oologist. 45(2):14-18.

1266   Miller, R.F. *1933.* Pennsylvania and New Jersey nesting dates for 1932. Oologist. 50(3):40-41.

1267   Miller, R.F. *1937.* Pennsylvania and New Jersey nesting dates for 1936. Oologist. 54(2):21-23.

Master No.	Citation

1268   Miller, R.F. *1941.* Richard F. Miller's annual report of the Pennsylvania and New Jersey nesting record for 1941. Oologist. 58(11):133-136.

1269   Miller, W.D. and C.H. Rogers. *1926.* Summer notes from the Kittatinny Mountains, N.J. The Auk. 43(4):553-554.

1270   Milligan, C.E. *1970.* Eagles, King of Birds. Exposition Press, New York. 97 pp.

1271   Mincher, B. *1977.* An eagle is flying. The Balance Wheel.(March-April):1.

1272   Minn. Dept. of Natural Resources. *1975.* Animals and Plants Which Merit Special Consideration and Management...The Uncommon Ones. Minn. Dept. of Natural Resources. 32 pp.

1273   Missouri Dept. of Conservation. *1974.* Rare and endangered species of Missouri. Missouri Dept. of Conservation, Holt, F.T., J.F. Keefe, W.H. Lewis, W.L. Pflieger and M.H. Sullivan (eds.). U.S.D.A. Soil Conserv. Service.

1274   Moffat, A.S. *1977.* Iroquois honor Cornell student for eagle restocking efforts. Press Release. Sept. 2. New York State College of Agriculture and Life Sciences, Cornell Univ. 2 pp.

1275   Moffat, A.S. *1977.* Transplanted eagle returns to New York. New York State College of Agriculture and Life Sciences, Cornell Univ.(Press Release, Sept. 31.). 2 pp.

1276   Moffat, E.E. *1932.* Duck hawk nest. Oologist. 49(8):93-94.

1277   Mogenweck, R. *1973.* Bald eagle - hawk interaction. The Loon. 45(3):101.

1278   Mondor, C. and P. Juurand. *1975.* The Churchill River: resource for conservation and recreation. Musk-Ox.(15):44-52.

1279   Monroe, B.L. and R.M. Mengel. *1941.* Bald eagle nesting in Kentucky. Wilson Bull. 53(3):196.

1280   Monson, G., J.M. Abbott, E.T. McKnight and C.W. Carlson. *1968.* 1967 Christmas bird counts. Atl. Nat. 23(1):27-34.

1281   Montagna, W. *1940.* Bald eagle in the West Virginia panhandle. The Cardinal. 5(3):68-69.

1282   Moore, G.A. and J.D. Mizelle. *1939.* Bald eagle near Stillwater, Oklahoma. Wilson Bull. 51(1):44.

1283   Morris, L. *1972.* Eagle and hawks. Neb. Bird Rev. 40(1):23.

1284   Morris, R.B. *1960.* Is the eagle un-American? N.Y. Times Mag. Feb. 14. p. 30,32,37-38,40.

1285   Morris, S. *1962.* They're killing off the eagle. Am. For. 68(8):5,51-52.

1286   Morrison, K.D. *1955.* Bird protection laws show progress. Audubon Mag. 57(5):222-225.

1287   Morrison, K.D. *1959.* Birds of Prey. National Audubon Society, Doubleday, Inc., Garden City, New York. 48 pp.

1288   Morrison, K.D. and J.D. Herz. *1950.* Where to Find Birds in Minnesota. Itasca Press. The Webb Publishing Co. Saint Paul, MN. 122 pp.

1289   Morrissey, T.J. *1968.* Notes of birds in the Davenport area. Iowa Bird Life. 38:67-80.

1290   Morzenti, A. and M. Fenn. *1975.* A new lease on life for birds of prey. Outdoor Calif. May-June:10-11.

1291   Mueller, H.C. and D.D. Berger. *1973.* The daily rhythm of hawk migration at Cedar Grove, Wisconsin. The Auk. 90(3):591-596.

1292   Mulhern, B.M., W.L. Reichel, L.N. Locke, T.G. Lamont, A.A. Belisle, E. Cromartie, G.E. Bagley and R.M. Prouty. *1970.* Organochlorine residues and autopsy data from bald eagles 1966-68. Pest. Monit. J. 4(3):141-144.

1293   Munro, J.A. *1923.* Bald eagle capturing sea-gull. Can. Field-Nat. 37(8):158-159.

1294   Munro, J.A. *1938.* The northern bald eagle in British Columbia. Wilson Bull. 50(1):28-35.

1295   Munro, R.D. *1976.* New sanctuary for an American monarch. Washington State. 4(1):10-14.

1296   Murie, O.J. *1940.* Food habits of the northern bald eagle in the Aleutian Islands, Alaska. The Condor. 42(4):198-202.

1297   Murie, O.J. *1959.* Fauna of the Aleutian Islands and Alaska Peninsula. U.S. Fish and Wildlife Service. North American Fauna No. 61. 364 pp.

1298   Murphy, J.R. *1962.* Aggressive behavior of a bald eagle. The Auk. 79(4):712-713.

1299   Murphy, J.R. *1965.* Nest site selection by the bald eagle in Yellowstone National Park. Proc. Utah Acad. Sci., Arts, and Letters. 42(2):261-264.

1300   Murphy, J.R. *1977.* Eagles and livestock-some management considerations. *In:* Proc. of the World Conference on Birds of Prey. Chancellor, R.D. (ed.). International Council for Bird Preservation, October 1-3, 1975, Vienna. p. 307-314.

1301   Murphy, J.R. *1977.* Status of eagle populations in the western United States. *In:* Proc. of the World Conference on Birds of Prey. Chancellor, R.D. (ed.). International Council for Bird Preservation, October 1-3, 1975. Vienna. p. 57-63.

1302   Murray, J.J. *1961.* The magnificent bald eagle. Va. Wildl. 22(3):10-12.

1303   Murray, J.J. (ed.). *1955.* Our national emblem is endangered. Raven. 26(4):58.

1304   Musselman, T.E. *1942.* Eagles of western Illinois. The Auk. 59(1):105-107.

1305   Musselman, T.E. *1945.* Bald eagles and woodcocks in central-western Illinois. The Auk. 62(3):458-459.

1306   Musselman, T.E. *1949.* Concentrations of bald eagles on the Mississippi River at Hamilton, Illinois. The Auk. 66(1):83.

Master No. **Citation**

1307   Nagy, A.C. *1975.* Hawk Mountain osprey project. Proc. of North American Hawk Migration Conf. Syracuse, NY. Hawk Migration Assoc. of N. America. p. 147-150.

1308   Nagy, A.C. *1977.* Population trend indices based on 40 years of autumn counts at Hawk Mountain Sanctuary in northeastern Pennsylvania. *In:* Proc. of the World Conference on Birds of Prey. Chancellor, R.D. (ed.). International Council for Bird Preservatio n, October 1-3, 1975. Vienna. p. 243-253.

1309   Nappe, L. and D.A. Klebenow. *1973.* Rare and endangered birds of Nevada. Foresta Institute for Ocean and Mountain Studies. Publication No. 24. 26 pp.

1310   National Audubon Society. *1962.* Regional reports - winter season. December 1, 1961-March 31, 1962. Southwest region. Aud. Field Notes. 16(3):353-356.

1311   National Audubon Society. *1968.* Regional reports; spring migration, April 1, 1968- May 31, 1968, Northern Rocky Mountain-Intermountain region. Aud. Field Notes. 22(4):557-560.

1312   National Audubon Society. *1968.* Regional reports. Fall Migration. Central southern region. Aug. 16 - Nov. 30, 1967. Audubon Field Notes. 22(1):50-54.

1313   National Audubon Society. *1970.* Regional reports. The fall migration. April 16, 1969-November 30, 1969. Northern Rocky Mountain-Intermountain region. Aud. Field Notes. 24(1):70-74.

1314   National Audubon Society. *1973.* The endangered bald eagle. Nat. Aud. Soc. Public Information Dept. 4 pp.

1315   National Wildlife Federation. *1971.* The NWF has announced a $500 bounty for information leading to the conviction of anyone shooting a bald eagle anywhere in the United States. News Release, Monday, Sept., 20. 2 pp.

1316   National Wildlife Federation. *1971.* NWF offers $500 bounty on eagle shooters. Outdoor Editor Service. Sept. 17, 1971. 2 pp.

1317   National Wildlife Federation. *1973.* The bald eagle. Wildlife Notes. National Wildlife Federation. 2 pp.

1318   National Wildlife Federation. *1973.* Massive 'accidental' eagle kill laid to trappers. Cons. News. 38(13):2-4.

1319   National Wildlife Federation. *1975.* List, by class, of species and subspecies found in U. S. and Puerto Rico designated by U. S. Fish and Wildlife Service as endangered. National Wildlife Federation Report. 4 pp.

1320   National Wildlife Federation. *1975.* Saving the eagle with a computer. Cons. News. 40(18):10-11.

1321   National Wildlife Federation. *1975.* Wildlife Federation launches project to help save American bald eagle. National Wildlife Federation, News Release No. 7569. 3 pp.

1322   National Wildlife Federation. *1976.* Ferry Bluff Roost located in top U. S. bald eagle nesting region. News Release 7602. Jan. 8. 1976. 2 pp.

1323   National Wildlife Federation. *1976.* Michigan farmer earns $500 reward from Wildlife Federation for aid in convicting eagle killers. News Release 7654. May 6, 1976. 2 pp.

1324   National Wildlife Federation. *1976.* Bald facts about the bald eagle. National Wildlife Federation. 5 pp.

1325   National Wildlife Federation. *1976.* Conservation group acquires sanctuary for bald eagle. News Release 7605. Jan. 8, 1976. 2 pp.

1326   National Wildlife Federation. *1976.* We can save the eagle. National Wildlife Federation. 6 pp.

1327   National Wildlife Federation. *1976.* TV stations air spectacular eagle 'spots' in effort to save national bird and symbol. National Wildlife Federation, News Release No. 7666. 3 pp.

1328   National Wildlife Federation. *1976.* Eagle project, legal victories highlight year of growth at NWF. National Wildlife Federation News Release 7621. March 20, 1976. 4 pp.

1329   National Wildlife Federation. *1976.* National poll of younsters elects bald eagle as ' Animal of the Year'. National Wildlife Federation News Release, 7687. September 20, 1976. 3 pp.

1330   National Wildlife Federation. *1976.* Conservation group acquires midwest sanctuary for threatened bald eagle. National Wildlife Federation News Release 7601. Jan. 5, 1976. 3 pp.

1331   National Wildlife Federation. *1977.* Wildlife group says eagle can be saved in 'lower 48'. National Wildlife Federation News Release. 7798. Oct. 19. 2 pp.

1332   National Wildlife Federation. *1977.* Wildlife Federation acquiring land to save two bald eagle roosting sites. National Wildlife Federation News Release No. 7762. 4 pp.

1333   National Wildlife Federation. *1977.* List, by state, of endangered and threatened animal species and subspecies of U. S., Puerto Rico, Virgin Islands, American Samoa, Guam. National Wildlife Federation Report. 12 pp.

1334   Nature Conservancy. *1976.* Skagit eagles: a management program for the Skagit River Bald Eagle Natural Area. The Nature Conservancy, Portland, OR. 73 pp.

1335   Neary, J. *1977.* Eagle doctor of Tesque. Audubon. 79(4):90-98.

1336   Nebraska Game and Parks Commission. *1977.* Wintering bald eagle survey. (Unpublished report). 3 pp.

1337   Nebraska Ornithologist's Union. *1966.* Untitled? Neb. Bird Rev. 34:14.

1338   Nebraska Ornithologist's Union. *1968.* Bald eagles. Neb. Bird Rev. 36:67.

1339   Nebraska Ornithologist's Union. *1973.* Bald eagle count. Neb. Bird Rev. 41:42.

1340   Nebraska Ornithologist's Union. *1974.* Bald eagle count. Neb. Bird Rev. 42:76-77.

1341   Nelson, M.W. and P. Nelson *1976.* Power lines and birds of prey. Idaho Wildl. Rev. 28(5):3-7.

Master No.	Citation

1342   Nelson, M.W. and P. Nelson. *1977.* Power lines and birds of prey. *In:* Proc. of the World Conference on Birds of Prey. Chancellor, R.D. (ed.). International Council for Bird Preservation, October 1-3, 1975, Vienna. p. 228-242.

1343   Nelson, R.W. *1973.* Field techniques in a study of the behavior of peregrine falcons. Raptor Research. 7(3/4):78-96.

1344   Nero, R.W. *1963.* Bald eagles of Lake Athabasca, Saskatchewan. Can. Audubon. 25(1):12-14.

1345   Nero, R.W. *1967.* Birds of northeastern Saskatchewan. Regina, Saskatchewan. 12 pp.

1346   Nesbit, R.J. *1975.* Land heritage program--National Wildlife Federation. Paper Presented at the Univ. of Wisconsin, Platteville, Wisconsin, Feb. 1, 1975.(Unpublished). 7 pp.

1347   Nesbit, R.J. *1977.* Three Sisters Bald Eagle Preserve, Siskiyou County, California. National Wildlife Federation.(Unpublished Report). 3 pp.

1348   Nesbitt, R. *1975.* Fort Randall bald eagle refuge. *In:* Bald Eagle Land: Preservation and Acquistion. Ingram, T.N. (ed.). Proc. of Bald Eagle Days, 1975, Jan. 31-Feb 2. Eagle Valley Environmentalists, Inc., Apple River, IL. p. 35-38.

1349   Nesbitt, S.A. *1976.* The bald eagle. The Fla. Nat. 49(6):14-17.

1350   Nesbitt, S.A. *1977.* Eagle production 1977. Florida Game & Fresh Water Fish Commission. 2 pp.

1351   Nesbitt, S.A., R.R. Roth and W.B. Robertson, Jr. *1975.* The status of the bald eagle in Florida, 1972-1975. Florida Cooperative Bald Eagle Survey Committee. 12 pp.

1352   Nesbitt, S.A., R.R. Roth and W.B. Robertson, Jr. *1976.* The status of the bald eagle in Florida, 1972-1975. Proc. of the Southeastern Assoc. of Game and Fish Commisioners. 24th Annual Conf. p. 424-428.

1353   New Hampshire Fish and Game. *1957.* Eagles. New Hampshire Bird News. 10(2):43.

1354   Newman, J.R., W.H. Brennan and L.M. Smith. *1977.* Twelve-year changes in nesting patterns of bald eagles *(Haliaeetus leucocephalus)* on San Juan Island, Washington. Murrelet. 58(2):37-39.

1355   Newton, I. *1976.* Population limitation in diurnal raptors. Can. Field-Nat. 90(3):274-300.

1356   Nicholson, D.J. *1911.* Untitled. Oologist. 28(3):63.

1357   Nicholson, D.J. *1952.* Little known facts about Florida bald eagles. Fla. Nat. 25(1):23-26.

1358   Nicholson, W.A. *1929.* Birds found breeding in central Florida. Oologist. 46(1):12-13.

1359   Nickerson, P.R. *1973.* Eagle nest survey objectives and progress. *In:* Notes on A Bald Eagle Nest Survey Workshop, Aug. 15, 1973. Madsen, C.R. (ed.). Twin Cities, MN. U.S.D.I. Fish and wildlife Service. Reg. 3. p. 1-3.

1360   Nickerson, P.R. *1974.* The National Bald Eagle Nesting Survey, 1973 and 1974. U.S.D.I. Fish and Wildlife Service, Div. of Technical Assistance. 7 pp.

1361   Noell, G.W. *1948.* Bald eagle captures tern. Wilson Bull. 60(1):53.

1362   Northeastern Wisconsin Audubon Society. *[?].* Last call for America's bald eagle:Our national symbol. N. Wisconsin Aud. Soc. 6 pp.

1363   Northeastern Wisconsin Audubon Society. *1975.* Distribution of 268 bald eagle nests-1975 Wisconsin survey. Northeastern Wisconsin Audubon Society. 1 pp.

1364   Norton, R.R. and H.C. Spitzer. *1965.* The 1964 Christmas bird census. Audubon Bull.(133):12-18.

1365   Norton, R.R. and H.C. Spitzer. *1966.* The 1965 Christmas bird census. Audubon Bull.(137):15-21.

1366   Nuttall, T. *1832.* A Manual of the Ornithology of the United States and of Canada. The Land Birds. Hilliard and Brown, Cambridge. 682 pp.

1367   Nuttall, T. *1903.* A Popular Handbook of the Birds of the United States and Canada. Little, Brown, and Co. Boston. 431 pp.

1368   Nye, P.E. *1977.* Ecological relationships of bald eagles on a wintering area in New York State. M.S. Thesis. College of Saint Rose, Albany, N.Y. (Unpublished). 112 pp.

1369   Nye, P.E. and L.H. Suring. *1977.* Preliminary management implications of wintering bald eagles in New York State. New York State Dept. of Environmental Conservation. (Unpublished Report). 18 pp.

1370   Oberholser, H.C. *1906.* The North American Eagles and Their Economic Relations. USDA. Biological Survey - Bull. No. 27. 32 pp.

1371   Oberholser, H.C. *1938.* The Bird Life of Louisiana. USDA. Biological Survey, Louisiana Dept. of Conservation. Bull. No. 28. 834 pp.

1372   Oberholser, H.C. *1974.* The Bird Life of Texas. Vol. 1 & 2. University of Texas Press. Austin, TX. 1068 pp.

1373   Ofelt, C.H. *1975.* Food habits of nesting bald eagles in southeast Alaska. The Condor. 77(3):337-338.

1374   Ofelt, C.H. *1976.* Unusual feeding behavior of bald eagles in British Columbia. Murrelet. 57(3):70.

1375   Ogden, J.C. *1975.* Effects of bald eagle territoriality on nesting ospreys. Wilson Bull. 87(4):496-505.

1376   Ohio Dept. of Natural Resources. *1971.* Hawks in Ohio. Div. of Wildlife. Publication No. 119. 6 pp.

1377   Olendorff, R.R. *1972.* Eagles, sheep, and powerlines. Colo. Out. 21(1):3-11.

1378   Olendorff, R.R. *1973.* Raptorial birds of the USAEC Hanford Reservation, South-central Washington. Battelle Northwest Laboratories. USAEC Rep. BNWL - 1790 US-11. 43 pp.

Master No.   Citation

1379   **Olendorff, R.R. and J.W. Stoddart, Jr.** *1974.* The potential for management of raptor populations in western grasslands. *In:* Management of Raptors. Proc. of the Conf. on Raptors Conservation Techniques, Fort Collins, CO. March 22-24, 1973 (Part 4). Hamerstrom, F.N., B.E. Harrell, and R.R. Olendorff(eds.). Raptor Research Report No. 2. p. 44-48.

1380   **Olendorff, R.R., J.E. Crawford, R.L. Means, W.A. Kennedy and J.D. Almand.** *1976.* The Bureau of Land Management Wildlife Habita t Management Program, with special emphasis on non-game bird habitats. *In:* Proc. of the Symposium on Management of Forest and Range Habitats for Non-Game Birds, USDA. Tucson, AZ., 1975. p. 305-313.

1381   **Olendorff, R.R. and M.N. Kochert.** *1977.* Land management for the conservation of birds of prey. *In:* Proc. of the World Conference on Birds of Prey. Chancellor, R.D. (ed.). International Council for Bird Preservation, October 1-3, 1975. Vienna. p. 294-306.

1382   **Olson, F.B.** *1957.* Bald eagles in Anderson County, Tenn. The Migrant. 28(1):4-6.

1383   **Omeara, D.C. and J.F. Witter.** *1971.* Aspergillosis. *In:* Infectious and Parasitic Diseases of Wild Birds. Davis, J.W., R.C. Anderson, L. Karstad, and D.O. Trainer (eds.) Iowa State Univ. Press., Ames. p. 153-162.

1384   **Oregon Fish and Wildlife.** *1976.* 1976 Annual report. Oregon Fish and Wildlife, Wildlife Division, Portland, Oregon. 166 pp.

1385   **Orr, E.** *1937.* Notes on the nesting of the bald eagle in Allamakee County, Iowa. Iowa Bird Life. 7(2):18-19.

1386   **Ott, G.** *1970.* Is the bald eagle doomed? Natl. Wildl. 8(3):4-9.

1387   **Oudette, B.L.** *1938.* Bald eagle at Pymatuning. The Cardinal. 4(8):203.

1388   **Over, W.H. and C.S. Thoms.** *1920.* Birds of S. Dakota. Geological and Natural History Survey. Series 21. Bull. No. 9. 142 pp.

1389   **Over, W.H. and C.S. Thoms.** *1946.* Birds of South Dakota. (Rev. Ed.) University of S. Dakota Museum. Natural History Studies. No. 1. 200 pp.

1390   **Owen, C.** *1977.* Plan for the protection, management, and educational uses of Mississippi's only bald eagle nest site. Mississippi Wildlife Fed.(Unpublished Report). Submitted to International Paper Comp. 11 pp.

1391   **Owen, R.B., Jr. and C.S. Todd.** *1977.* Maine wintering bald eagle study. Dept. of Wildlife Resources, University of Maine, Orono, Maine. (Unpublished Report). 3 pp.

1392   **Owen, S.P.** *1947.* Bald eagles in Wisconsin. Flicker. 19(3):81.

1393   **Pack, A.N.** *1928.* Blood money for eagles. N.Am.Rev. 226(1):22-26.

1394   **Pack, A.N.** *1936.* Eagle shooting in Alaska. Nature Mag. 28(2):106.

1395   **Pack, A.N.** *1936.* Fake eagle stories. Nature Mag. 27(2):106.

1396   **Packard, C.M.** *1955.* Field trip records. Maine Aud. Soc. Bull. 11(2):27.

1397   **Packard, F.M.** *1950.* The Birds of Rocky Mountain National Park. Rocky Mountain Nature Association, Estes Park, CO. 81 pp.

1398   **Palmer, E.L.** *1937.* Are they vermin? Cornell Rural School Leaflet, New York State College of Agriculture, Cornell Univ., Ithaca, New York. 31(2):32.

1399   **Palmer, R.S.** *1949.* Notes on birds of the upper Allagash drainage and vicinity of Maine, 1948. Maine Aud. Soc. Bull. 5(4):63-76.

1400   **Palmer, W.H.** *1914.* Our neighbor, the bald eagle. Bird-Lore. 16(4):281-282.

1401   **Pangburn, C.H.** *1919.* A three months' list of the birds of Pinellas County, Florida. The Auk. 36(3):393-405.

1402   **Pardue, S.** *1977.* Report on Reelfoot Lake Eagle Program, December 1976-March 1977. U.S.D.I. Fish and Wildlife Service.(Unpublished Report.) 6 pp.

1403   **Pardue, S.** *1977.* Wintering bald eagles of Reelfoot Lake. *In:* Proc. of Annual Bald Eagle Days. January. Ingram, T.N. (ed.). Eagle Valley Environmentalists, Inc., Apple River, IL. 4 pp.

1404   **Parkes, K.C.** *1951.* Regional reports for spring migration in New York state; Region 2, Southern Tier - Part 1. The Kingbird. 1(3):64-66.

1405   **Parmalee, P.W.** *1958.* Remains of rare and extinct birds from Illinois indian sites. The Auk. 75(2):169-176.

1406   **Parmalee, P.W.** *1977.* The avifauna from prehistoric Arikara sites in South Dakota. Plains Anthropologist. 22-77:189-222.

1407   **Parnell, J.F.** *1968.* Briefs for the files. The Chat. 32(3):79-81.

1408   **Parnell, J.F.** *1969.* Briefs for the files. The Chat. 33(4):106-107.

1409   **Patton, F.A.** *1926.* Our trip to the eagle's nest. Oologist. 43(3):30-31.

1410   **Peakall, D.B.** *1975.* Physiological effects of chlorinated hydrocarbons on avian species. *In:* Symposium on Environmental Dynamics of Pesticides. Plenum Press, NY. p. 343-360.

1411   **Pearse, T.** *1937.* Feeding habits of bald-headed eagle. Can. Field-Nat. 51(3):42-44.

1412   **Pearse, T.** *1937.* Predatores and prey--bald eagles. Murrelet. 18(1-2):31-32.

1413   **Pearse, T.** *1939.* Reactions of other birds to predators. Murrelet. 20(2):42.

1414   **Pearson, T.G.** *1901.* Stories of Bird Life. B.F. Johnson Publ. Co., Richmond, Virginia. 236 pp.

1415   **Pearson, T.G.** *1922.* Notes on the birds of Cumberland Island, Georgia. Wilson Bull. 34(2):84-90.

1416   **Pearson, T.G. (ed.).** *1915.* The bald eagle. Bird-Lore. 17(5):404-407.

Master No.	Citation
1417	**Pearson, T.G. (ed.).** *1917.* Birds of America. Garden City Pub. Comp., Garden City. 289 pp.
1418	**Pearson, T.G. (ed.).** *1919.* The eagle law of Alaska. Bird-Lore. 21(3):204.
1419	**Pearson, T.G. (ed.).** *1919.* Slaughter of American eagles. Bird-Lore. 21(1):72-73.
1420	**Pearson, T.G. (ed.).** *1920.* The dead eagles of Alaska now number 8,356! Bird-Lore. 22(4):253.
1421	**Pearson, T.G. (ed.).** *1927.* Destructive birds again. Bird-Lore. 29(1):83-85.
1422	**Pearson, T.G. (ed.).** *1928.* Eagles and the Alaska bounty. Bird-Lore. 30(1):86-90.
1423	**Pearson, T.G. (ed.).** *1930.* The eagle bill. Bird-Lore. 32(3):236-238.
1424	**Pearson, T.G. (ed.).** *1930.* Bill to protect the bald eagle. Bird-Lore. 32(1):86-87.
1425	**Pearson, T.G. (ed.).** *1930.* The bald eagle bill. Bird-Lore. 32(2):164-167.
1426	**Pearson, T.G. (ed.).** *1931.* The eagle bill. Bird-Lore. 33(2):159-160.
1427	**Pearson, T.G. (ed.).** *1933.* Bald eagle unjustly defamed. Bird-Lore. 35(1):76-77.
1428	**Pearson, T.G., C.S. Brimley and H.H. Brimley.** *1942.* Birds of North Carolina. Bynum Printing Co., Raleigh, NC. 416 pp.
1429	**Peattie, D.C.** *1946.* Uncle Sam's bird. Nature Mag. 39(1):16-18,53.
1430	**Peck, G.D.** *1924.* Reminiscences of my egging ground. Oologist. 41(6):65.
1431	**Peckham, P.** *1975.* Ferry Bluff Eagle Roost. *In:* Bald Eagle Land: Preservation and Acquisition. Ingram, T.N. (ed.). Proc. of Bald Eagle Days, 1975, Jan. 31-Feb. 2. Eagle Valley Env., Inc., Apple River, IL. p. 31-34.
1432	**Pellett, F.C.** *1927.* Bald eagles along the Mississippi River. Wilson Bull. 39(1):36.
1433	**Pemberton, J.R.** *1928.* Additions to the known avifauna of the Santa Barbara Islands. The Condor. 30(2):144-148.
1434	**Pemberton, J.R. and H.W. Carriger.** *1915.* A partial list of the summer resident land birds of Monterey County, California. The Condor. 17(5):189-201.
1435	**Pennock, J.W.** *1914.* The eagles and herons of Oneida Lake. Oologist. 31(2):26-27.
1436	**Penny, M.** *1977.* The American eagle. Wildlife. 19(9):402-407.
1437	**Perkins, S.E. III.** *1926.* The bald eagle in Indiana. Wilson Bull. 38(1):36.
1438	**Peters, J.L.** *1931.* Check-list of Birds of the World. Vol. 1. Harvard Univ. Press, Cambridge, Mass. 345 pp.
1439	**Peterson, C.T.** *1962.* Eagles in Kentucky Woodlands Wildlife Refuge. The Kentucky Warbler. 38(2):43-44.
1440	**Peterson, C.T.** *1963.* The eagles of Hematite Lake. The Kentucky Warbler. 39(3):35-45.
1441	**Peterson, C.T.** *1964.* Bald eagles in Kentucky woodlands. The Kentucky Warbler. 40(4):59-63.
1442	**Peterson, C.T.** *1976.* 1976 Annual mid-winter bald eagle survey, Land Between the Lakes. (Unpublished Report). 1 pp.
1443	**Peterson, C.T.** *1976.* Mississippi valley mid-winter bald eagle census, 1976. (Unpublished Report). 1 pp.
1444	**Peterson, C.T.** *1977.* Bald eagles in Land Between the Lakes. Tennessee Valley Authority. (Report). 5 pp.
1445	**Peterson, D.** *1976.* Summary of 1975-1976 southern bald eagle nesting in Florida. U.S.D.I., Fish and Wildlife Service.(Unpublished Report). 1 p.
1446	**Peterson, R.T.** *1937.* Snowy egret and bald eagle at Pymatuning. The Cardinal. 4(6):175-176.
1447	**Peterson, R.T.** *1947.* A Field Guide to the Birds. Houghton Mifflin, Boston. 230 pp.
1448	**Peterson, R.T.** *1948.* Eagle man. Audubon Mag. 50(1):2-11.
1449	**Peterson, R.T.** *1961.* A Field Guide to Western Birds. (Second ed.) Houghton Mifflin Co., Boston, MA. 366 pp.
1450	**Peterson, R.T.** *1964.* Birds Over America. Dodd, Mead, and Comp. New York. 342 pp.
1451	**Peterson, R.T.** *1974.* Birds. *In:* Symposium on Endangered and Threatened Species of North America. Washington, D.C. p. 159-169.
1452	**Petrow, R.** *1962.* Last chance to save the bald eagle. Pop. Sci. 181(1):99-101,192.
1453	**Pettingill, O.S., Jr.** *1963.* Wintering eagles on the Mississippi. Audubon Mag. 65(6):342-343.
1454	**Pettingill, O.S., Jr.** *1970.* Ornithology in Lab and Field. Burgess Pub. Co., Minneapolis, MN. 524 pp.
1455	**Peyton, S.B.** *1913.* A collecting trip to Anacapa Island. Oologist. 30(5):78.
1456	**Peyton, S.B.** *1931.* 1931 breeding records. Oologist. 48(11):161-163.
1457	**Phelps, F.M.** *1912.* A March birds list from the Calooshatchee River and Lake Okeechobee. Wilson Bull. 24(3):117-125.
1458	**Phelps, F.M.** *1914.* The resident bird life of the Big Cypress Swamp region. Wilson Bull. 26(2):86-101.
1459	**Phillips, A., J. Marshall and G. Monson.** *1964.* The Birds of Arizona. The University of Arizona Press. Tucson, AZ. 212 pp.
1460	**Phillips, R.E.** *1953.* Indiana hawks and owls. Indiana Dept. of Conservation. Div. of Fish and Game. 37 pp.
1461	**Phillips, R.S.** *1949.* A fair deal for our birds of prey. Audubon Mag. 51(6):376-381,392-397.
1462	**Pickering, C.F.** *1937.* A September visit to Reelfoot Lake. The Migrant. 8(3):49-50.
1463	**Pickering, C.F.** *1952.* The seasons on Reelfoot Lake. The Migrant. 23(3):39-42.
1464	**Pimental, D.** *1971.* Ecological effects of pesticides on non-target species. Executive Office of the President, Office of Science and Technology. U.S. Govt. Printing Office. 220 pp.
1465	**Pindar, L.O.** *1923.* Bald eagle in Franklin County, Kentucky. Wilson Bull. 35(2):116.
1466	**Pindar, L.O.** *1925.* Birds of Fulton County, Kentucky. Wilson Bull. 37(2):77-88.

Master No.	Citation

1467 Pinkowski, B.C. *1977.* Michigan bird survey, summer 1977. Jack-Pine Warb. 55(4):187-197.

1468 Pinkowski, B.C. *1977.* Power line and bald eagle interactions in the upper Mississippi River Valley. Report Prepared for Northern States Power Comp. 20 pp.

1469 Platt, J.B. *1972.* Desert wintering bald eagles in Utah. (Abstract of Paper Presented at 90th AOU Convention). Raptor Res. News. 6(3):108.

1470 Platt, J.B. *1976.* Bald eagles wintering in a Utah desert. Am. Birds. 30(4):783-788.

1471 Poole, E.L. *1964.* Pennsylvania Birds, An Annotated List. Livingston Pub. Comp. Narberth, PA. 94 pp.

1472 Poor, H.H. *1936.* A herring gull attacked by a bald eagle. Wilson Bull. 48(3):220-221.

1473 Postupalsky, S. *1961.* Michigan bald eagle survey. Detroit Aud. Soc. Bull. No. 2(Sept. 21). 5 pp.

1474 Postupalsky, S. *1961.* Michigan bald eagle survey. Detroit Aud. Soc. Bull. No. 1.(June 12). 3 pp.

1475 Postupalsky, S. *1962.* Michigan bald eagle survey. Detroit Aud. Soc. Bull. No. 3.(Oct 7). 2 pp.

1476 Postupalsky, S. *1963.* Michigan bald eagle survey. Detroit Aud. Soc. Bull. No. 4.(Jan. 4). 4 pp.

1477 Postupalsky, S. *1963.* Michigan bald eagle survey. Detroit Aud. Soc. Bull. No. 5.(Oct. 4). 2 pp.

1478 Postupalsky, S. *1966 - 1970.* Bald eagle and osprey survey. Michigan Bald Eagle and Osprey Project. Detroit Audubon Society. 10 pp.

1479 Postupalsky, S. *1968.* Michigan bald eagle and osprey survey. Jack-Pine Warb. 46(1):31-32.

1480 Postupalsky, S. *1971.* Bald eagle and osprey study in Ontario. (Unpublished Report) October 25, 1971. 1 p.

1481 Postupalsky, S. *1971.* Osprey gain, eagles lose, report on 1971 survey. Michigan Aud. Newsl. 19(6):1-2.

1482 Postupalsky, S. *1971.* Toxic chemicals and declining bald eagles and cormorants in Ontario. Canadian Wildlife Service. Pesticide Section. Report No. 20. 45 pp.

1483 Postupalsky, S. *1972.* Michigan bald eagle and osprey study. (Unpublished Report) March 12, 1972. 2 pp.

1484 Postupalsky, S. *1974.* The bald eagle in the Great Lakes region: Current population status, research and conservation needs. *In:* Our Eagle's Future??? Proc. of Bald Eagle Days, Feb. 8, 9, 10. Ingram, T.N. (ed.). Eagle Valley Environmentalists, Inc., Apple River, IL. p. 68-78.

1485 Postupalsky, S. *1974.* Bald eagle and osprey study. Dept. of Wildlife Ecology, University of Wisconsin. Oct. 19. (Unpublished Report). 2 pp.

1486 Postupalsky, S. *1976.* Bald eagle migration along the south shore of Lake Superior. Jack-Pine Warb. 54(3):98-104.

1487 Postupalsky, S. *1976.* Banding bald eagles in Michigan. *In:* Save the Eagle in '76., Proc. of Bald Eagle Days, 1976. Ingram, T.N. (ed.). Eagle Valley Env., Inc., Apple River, IL. p. 132-133.

1488 Postupalsky, S. *1976.* Banded northern bald eagles in Florida and other southern states. The Auk. 93(4):835-836.

1489 Postupalsky, S. *1977.* Bald eagle and osprey studies. Dept. of Wildlife Ecology, Univ. of Wisconsin, Madison, WI. (Unpublished Report). 2 pp.

1490 Postupalsky, S. and J.B. Holt, Jr. *1975.* Adoption of nestlings by breeding bald eagles. Raptor Research. 9(1/2):18-20.

1491 Potter, E.D. *1886.* The Toledo eaglet. Forest and Stream. 26(20):387.

1492 Potter, J.K. *1949.* Hawks along the Delaware. Cassinia. 37(1947-1948):13-16.

1493 Pough, R.H. *1932.* Wholesale killing of hawks in Pennsylvania. Bird-Lore. 34(6):429-430.

1494 Pough, R.H. *1936.* Audubon sanctuary for bald eagle. Bird-Lore. 38(5):356.

1495 Pough, R.H. *1939.* Federal protection for eagle. Bird-Lore. 41(2):112.

1496 Pramstaller, M.E. *1977.* Nocturnal, preroosting, and postroosting behavior of breeding adult and young of the year bald eagles *(Haliaeetus leucocephalus alascanus)* on the Chippewa National Forest. M.S. Thesis. Univ. of Minnesota. St. Paul, MN. 97 pp.

1497 Preston, J.W. *1916.* Eagle's nest at short range. Oologist. 33(1):11.

1498 Prestwich, A.A. *1955.* Records of Birds of Prey Bred in Captivity. (Published by author), London.

1499 Price, H.F. *1925.* Trapping a bald eagle. Oologist. 42(2):21.

1500 Price, H.F. *1934.* The hawks, eagles and vultures of northwestern Ohio. Oologist. 51(3):29-35.

1501 Prill, A.G. *1922.* Nesting birds of Lake County, Oregon (with special reference to Warner Valley). Wilson Bull. 34(3):131-140.

1502 Racey, K. *1939.* Bald eagle with willow grouse. Murrelet. 20(1):10-11.

1503 Radtke, R. *1973.* Eagle management guidelines on National Forests. *In:* Notes on a Bald Eagle Nest Survey Workshop. Aug. 15, 1973. Madsen, C.R. (ed.). Twin Cities, MN. U.S.D.I. Fish and Wildlife Service. Region 3. p. 37-42.

1504 Radtke, R., K. Siderits and J.E. Mathisen. *1973.* Consolidated eagle nest surveys on the National Forests. *In:* Notes on a Bald Eagle Nest Survey Workshop. Aug. 15, 1973. Madsen, C.R. (ed.). Twin Cities, MN. U.S.D.I. Fish and Wildlife Service. Region 3. p. 6-10.

1505 Raedeke, L.D., J.C. Garcia and R.D. Taber. *1977.* Wetland Surveys of Skagit and Grant Counties, Washington: Inventory, Wildlife Values, and Owner Attitudes. Part 1. Wetlands of Skagit County-Location Characteristics and Wildlife Values. State of Washington Water Res. Center. Washington State Univ. and the Univ. of Washington. 348 pp.

1506 Rand, A.L. *1971.* Birds of North America. Doubleday & Co. Inc., New York. 255 pp.

1507 Randall, D. *1974.* Will there be eagles? Defend. Wildl. Int. 49(5):431.

Master No.   Citation

1508   **Raptor Information Center.** *1977.* Approximate ages of nestling bald eagles. National Wildlife Federation.(Photographs). 1 p.

1509   **Raptor Research Foundation, Inc.** *1974.* Saving the eagle with a computer. Raptor Research. 8(3/4):84.

1510   **Rathbun, S.F.** *1916.* The Lake Crescent region, Olympic Mountains, Washington, with notes regarding its avifauna. The Auk. 33(4):357-370.

1511   **Rauber, T.C.** *1976.* Notes on a New York nest of the bald eagle. The Kingbird. Summer:122-135.

1512   **Redford, P.** *1965.* Raccoons and Eagles: Two Views of American Wildlife. E.P. Dutton and Co., Inc. New York. 254 pp.

1513   **Redig, P.T., G.E. Duke and M.R. Fuller.** *1976.* Bald eagle rehabilitation. *In:* Save the Eagle in '76, Proc. of Bald Eagle Days, 1976. Ingram, T.N. (ed.). Eagle Valley Env., Inc., Apple River, IL. pp. 104-107.

1514   **Reed, A.C.** *1941.* Bald eagle nesting in city. The Raven. 12(2/3):21.

1515   **Reed, C.A.** *1965.* North American Bird Eggs. Dover Pub., Inc., New York. 372 pp.

1516   **Reese, J.G.** *1973.* Bald eagle migration along the upper Mississippi River in Minnesota. The Loon. 45(1):22-23.

1517   **Reichel, W.L., E. Cromartie, T.G. Lamont, B.M. Mulhern and R.M. Prouty.** *1969.* Pesticide residues in eagles. Pest. Monit. J. 3(3):142-144.

1518   **Reichel, W.L., T.G. Lamont, E. Cromartie and L.N. Locke.** *1969.* Residues in two bald eagles suspected of pesticide poisoning. Bull. Environ. Contam. Toxicol. 4(1):24-30.

1519   **Reimann, E.J.** *1938.* Bald eagle takes live fish. The Auk. 55(33):524-525.

1520   **Retfalvi, L.I.** *1963.* Notes on the birds of San Juan Islands, Washington. Murrelet. 44(1):12-13.

1521   **Retfalvi, L.I.** *1965.* Breeding behavior and feeding habits of the bald eagle *(Haliaeetus leucocephalus l.)* on San Juan Island, Washington. M.F. Thesis, Univ. of British Columbia., Vancouver, B.C. 180 pp.

1522   **Retfalvi, L.I.** *1970.* Food of nesting bald eagles on San Juan Island, Washington. The Condor. 72(3):358-361.

1523   **Rett, E.Z.** *1947.* A report on the birds of San Nicolas Island. The Condor. 49(4):165-168.

1524   **Richter, C.H.** *1939.* Additions to A. J. Schoeneback's birds of Oconto County. Pass. Pigeon. 1(8):114-119.

1525   **Richter, C.H.** *1958.* Eagle nesting activity in December. Pass. Pigeon. 20(2):79.

1526   **Ridgway, R.** *1881.* A catalogue of the birds of Illinois. Illinois State Laboratory of Natural History. Bull. No. 4. p. 163-208.

1527   **Ridgway, R.** *1887.* A Manual of North American Birds. J.B. Lippincott Co. Philadelphia. 631 pp.

1528   **Rienow, R.** *1960.* The vanishing American eagle. Sci. Dig. 47(5):60-62.

1529   **Robards, F.C. and A. Taylor.** *1973.* Bald eagles in Alaska. U.S.D.I., Fish and Wildlife Service and U.S.D.A. Forest Service. Alaska Region. 12 pp.

1530   **Robards, F.C. and J.I. Hodges.** *1977.* Observations from 2,760 bald eagle nests in southeast Alaska. U.S.D.I. Fish and Wildlife Service, Eagle Management Study, Juneau, AK. Prog. Report 1969-1976. 27 pp.

1531   **Robbins, C.S.** *1960.* Status of the bald eagle, summer of 1959. U.S.D.I. Fish and Wildlife Service. Wildlife Leaflet 418. 8 pp.

1532   **Robbins, C.S.** *1962.* The season; April, May, June, 1962. Md. Birdlife. 18(3):72-81.

1533   **Robbins, C.S., B. Bruun and H.S. Zim.** *1966.* Birds of North America. Golden Press, Inc., New York. 340 pp.

1534   **Robbins, S.D., Jr.** *1947.* The 1947 nesting season. Pass. Pigeon. 9(4):133-137.

1535   **Roberts, C.G.D.** *1902.* The Lord of the Air. L.C. Page and Company, Boston, MA. 59 pp.

1536   **Roberts, N. and H. Roberts.** *1968.* Summer season, June 1-August 15, 1967. Pass. Pigeon. 30(2):92-97.

1537   **Roberts, T.S.** *1936.* The Birds of Minnesota. (Vol. 1.) University of Minnesota Press, Minneapolis. 821 pp.

1538   **Robertson, W.B., Jr. and H.B. Muller.** *1961.* Wild winds and wildlife. Audubon Mag. 63(6):308-311.

1539   **Robinson, F.B.** *1922.* Bald eagles on the Hudson. Bird-Lore. 24(3):147-148.

1540   **Robinson, P.** *1883.* The American eagle in the poets. Lippincott's Mag. 6(9):189-194.

1541   **Roever, J.M. and W. Roever.** *1973.* The North American Eagles. Steck-Vaughn Co., Austin, Texas. 30 pp.

1542   **Rogers, A.J.** *1972.* Eagles, affluence, and pesticides. Presidential Address. Mosquito News. 32(2):151-157.

1543   **Roop, L.** *1973.* Eagles today. Wy. Wildl. 37(6):14-19.

1544   **Roos, B.** *1972.* Paradox of a superstar. Natl. Wildl. 10(3):15-17.

1545   **Rosen, M.N.** *1972.* 1970-71 avian cholera epornitic's impact on certain species. J. Wildl. Dis. 8(1):75-78.

1546   **Rosen, M.N.** *1975.* Bald eagle and river otter. Can. Field-Nat. 89(4):455.

1547   **Rosier, L.** *1973.* Biography of a Bald Eagle. Putnam Son, Inc., New York. 63 pp.

1548   **Ross, F.C.** *1946.* A real American. Hobbies. 51(3):100.

1549   **Rossman, G., A. Rossman and B. Rossman.** *1971.* Bald eagles of the Chippewa National Forest. Grand Rapids Herald-Review, Grand Rapids, MN. 32 pp.

1550   **Rubink, D.M. and K. Podborny.** *1976.* The southern bald eagle in Arizona (a status report). U.S.D.I. Fish and Wildlife Service, Albuquerque, NM. Endangered Species Report No. 1. 33 pp.

1551   **Ruhl, H.D. and G.W. Brant.** *1946.* Sheep-killing eagles? Jack-Pine Warb. 24(3):105-107.

Master No.	Citation

1552   **Rusch, D. and P. Keasling.** *1973.* Eagle studies -Wisconsin. *In:* Notes on a Bald Eagle Nest Survey Workshop. Aug. 15, 1973. Madsen, C.R. (ed.). Twin Cities, MN. U.S.D.I. Fish and Wildlife Service, Region 3. p. 30-32.

1553   **Rush, W.M.** *1942.* Wildlife of Idaho. Idaho Fish and Game Commission, Boise. 299 pp.

1554   **Russell, W.L.** *1975.* Navy shares Adak with eagles. Alaska. 41(4):24-25.

1555   **Ryman, J.J.** *1904.* A season with the bald eagles. Oologist. 21(6):85-88.

1556   **Ryman, J.J.** *1905.* Bald eagle experiences in Florida (continued). Oologist. 22(1):5-8.

1557   **Sage, B.L.** *1974.* Ecological distribution of birds in the Atigun and Sagavanirktok River Valleys, Arctic Alaska. Can. Field-Nat. 88(3):281-291.

1558   **Sage, B.L.** *1975.* Recent observations in the Wrangell Mountains, Alaska. The Condor. 77(2):206-207.

1559   **Sage, J.H., L.B. Bishop and W.P. Bliss.** *1913.* Birds of Connecticut. State Geological and Natural History Survey. Bull. No. 20. Hartford. 370 pp.

1560   **Salomonsky, V.C.** *1931.* American eagle; its influence on furniture design. Good Furn. 36:(6):281-286.

1561   **Saltford, H.** *1976.* Look up! You may see a bald eagle! Yankee. 40(2):142-146.

1562   **Samuels, E.A.** *1868.* Ornithology and Oology of New England. Nichols and Noyes, Boston. 587 pp.

1563   **Sartwell, F.** *1977.* Eagle release launches island reclamation. Defend. Wildl. News Release, Feb. 2. 2 pp.

1564   **Sass, H.R.** *1925.* Ourselves and our eagle. Sat. Even. Post. 198(8):33.

1565   **Sass, H.R.** *1929.* The lord of the air. Am. Mag. 107(4):36-39,108,111,112.

1566   **Saunders, A.A.** *1921.* A distributional list of the birds of Montana with notes on the migration and nesting of the better known species. Pacific Coast Avifauna. Cooper Ornithol Club. Berkeley. 194 pp.

1567   **Saunders, W.E.** *1909.* The rapid extermination of the bald eagle. Ottawa Nat. 23(6):116-117.

1568   **Saunders, W.E.** *1918.* A protected nest of the bald eagle. Ottawa Nat. 32(1):20.

1569   **Savage, W.G.** *1917.* Bald eagles. Oologist. 34(2):31.

1570   **Savaloja, T.** *1974.* The spring season March 1 to May 31, 1974. The Loon. 46(4):143-160.

1571   **Saylor, J.P.** *1973.* Three pleas to save the bald eagle. Defend. Wildl. News. May:343.

1572   **Sayre, J.A.** *1977.* Dispute over eagle nest tree results in funding for northwest eagle survey. U.S.D.I. Fish & Wildlife Service, Region One. News Release, 77-50., July 5. 1 pp.

1573   **Sayre, R. (ed.).** *1971.* Eagle poisoners apparently haven't given up. Audubon. 73(6):110.

1574   **Sayre, R. (ed.).** *1971.* Eagle shooters are still awaiting legal action. Audubon. 73(6):110

1575   **Sayre, R. (ed.).** *1973.* The sheep rancher charged with the eagle killings in Wyoming. Audubon. 75(1):112.

1576   **Sayre, R. (ed.).** *1973.* Several hundred eagles in Nevada were caught accidentally. Audubon. 75(3):124.

1577   **Sayre, R. (ed.).** *1973.* Herman Werner, the Wyoming rancher accused in the shooting of eagles from aircraft. Audubon. 75(4):112.

1578   **Schmid, F.C.** *1967.* Number of eggs and young of bald eagles in four Middle Atlantic states. Cassinia. 50:15-17.

1579   **Schneider, F.B.** *1922.* The Season, Los Angeles region. Bird-Lore. 25(5):289-290.

1580   **Schoenback, A.J.** *1939.* The birds of Oconto County. Pass. Pigeon. 1(6):79-88.

1581   **Schweiger, N. and K.T. Barrineau.** *1974.* Bird surveys of Lake Ocklawaha. (Abstract). Paper Presented at the 35th Annual Meeting of Southern Biologists. ASB Bull. 21(2):81.

1582   **Sclater, W.L.** *1912.* A History of the Birds of Colorado. London, Witherby and Co. London. 576 pp.

1583   **Scott, C. and J. Swedberg.** *1969.* A short fracas at a carcass. Audubon. 71(2):16-19.

1584   **Scott, F.R.** *1951.* The birds of the Richmond area: Part 1. The Raven. 22(9/10):45-62.

1585   **Scott, F.R.** *1958.* The bald eagle nest survey in Virginia. The Raven. 29(3/4):22-24.

1586   **Scott, F.R.** *1963.* The bald eagle survey in Virginia: Interim status report. The Raven. 34(1):18-21.

1587   **Scott, W.E.D.** *1889.* A summary of observations on the birds of the Gulf Coast of Florida. The Auk. 6(3):245-252.

1588   **Scott, W.E.D.** *1892.* Notes on the birds of the Caloosahatchie region of Florida. The Auk. 9(3):209-218.

1589   **Scoville, S., Jr.** *1923.* The sky king. St. Nicholas. 50(9):898-905.

1590   **Sealy, S.G.** *1973.* Interspecific feeding assemblages of marine birds off British Columbia. The Auk. 90(4):796-802.

1591   **Servheen, C.W.** *1975.* Ecology of the wintering bald eagles on the Skagit River, Washington. M.S. Thesis, Univ. of Washington, Seattle, WA. 96 pp.

1592   **Servheen, C.W.** *1976.* Deck-feather molt in bald and golden eagles in relation to feather mounting of radio transmitters. Raptor Research. 10(2):58-60.

1593   **Servheen, C.W.** *1976.* Bald eagles soaring into opaque cloud. The Auk. 93(2):387.

1594   **Servheen, C.W. and W. English.** *1976.* Bald eagle rehabilitation techniques in western Washington. Raptor Research. 10(3):84-87.

1595   **Seton, E.T.** *1908.* Bird records from Great Slave Lake region. The Auk. 25(1):68-74.

1596   **Shane, T.** *1953.* Eagle man. Read. Dig. 62(371):135-138.

1597   **Sharp, D.L.** *1932.* The 'master word'. Nature Mag. 19(1):18-20.

1598   **Sharritt, G.V.** *1939.* American eagle revolutionists. Nature Mag. 32(9):528-529.

Master No.	Citation

1599   Shaver, J.M. *1931.* Nesting of the bald eagle in Tennessee. Wilson Bull. 43(1):85.

1600   Shaw, H. *1965.* Bald eagle count on the Mississippi. Audubon Bull.(133):6-7.

1601   Shea, D.S. *1973.* A management - oriented study of bald eagle concentrations in Glacier National Park. (Unpublished). M.S. Thesis, Univ. of Montana, Missoula. 78 pp.

1602   Shea, D.S. *1978.* Bald eagle concentrations in Glacier National Park. Western Birds. 9: 35-37.

1603   Shelley, L.O. *1935.* Northern bald eagle: an addition to the New Hampshire list. The Auk. 52(3):305.

1604   Sherman, E.A. *1967.* Our national emblem. Maine Fish and Game. 9(3):2-3.

1605   Sherrod, S.K., J.A. Estes and C.M. White. *1975.* Depredation of sea otter pups by bald eagles at Amchitka Island, Alaska. J. Mammalogy. 56(3):701-703.

1606   Sherrod, S.K., C.M. White and F.S.L. Williamson. *1976.* Biology of the bald eagle on Amchitka Island, Alaska. Living Bird. 15:143-182.

1607   Sherwood, L. *1946.* Old Abe, American Eagle. Charles Scribner's and Sons, Inc. N.Y. 61 pp.

1608   Shickley, G.M. *1961.* Wintering bald eagles in Nebraska, 1959-1960. Neb. Bird Rev. 29:26-31.

1609   Shultz, P.L. *1971.* Birds of prey. New Mex. Wildl. September-October:16-19.

1610   Siderits, K. *1974.* Immature bald eagle movement. The Loon. 46(4):170.

1611   Siderits, K. *1977.* Bald eagle and osprey report-1977.Superior National Forest. U.S.D.A. Forest Service.(Unpublished Report.) 2 pp.

1612   Siderits, K. *1978.* Bald eagle: osprey report, 1978. U.S.D.A. Forest Service, Superior National Forest. 2 pp.

1613   Sikken, E.A. *1921.* Untitled? Oologist. 38(4):51.

1614   Sikken, E.A. *1922.* Eagle dope. Oologist. 39(3):42.

1615   Silloway, P.M. *1901.* Summer birds of Flathead Lake. Univ. of Montana. Bull. No. 3. Biological Series No. 1. 83 pp.

1616   Simmons, G.F. *1915.* On the nesting of certain birds in Texas. The Auk. 32(3):317-331.

1617   Singer, F.J. *1974.* Status of the osprey, bald eagle and golden eagle in the Adirondacks. N.Y. Fish and Game J. 21(1):18-31.

1618   Skinner, M.P. *1924.* The Yellowstone Nature Book. A.C. McClurg and Co., Chicago. 228 pp.

1619   Skinner, M.P. *1925.* The birds of Yellowstone National Park. Roosevelt Wildlife Bull. 3(1):1-189.

1620   Skinner, M.P. *1928.* Yellowstone's winter birds. The Condor. 30(4):237-242.

1621   Smith, B.B. *1929.* The bald eagle. Flower Grower. 16(5):231.

1622   Smith, D.G. and J.R. Murphy. *1972.* Unusual causes of raptor mortality. Raptor Res. 6(1):4-5.

1623   Smith, D.R. *1954.* The Bighorn Sheep in Idaho: Its Status, Life History, and Management. Idaho Dept. of Fish and Game. Wildlife Bull. No. 1. 154 pp.

1624   Smith, E.R. *1927.* Nesting of the bald eagle in Escambia County, Florida. Oologist. 44(9):114-115.

1625   Smith, E.R. *1969.* Summary for southern Illinois area, 1968. Audubon Bull.(150):25-26.

1626   Smith, F.R. *1936.* The food and nesting habits of the bald eagle. The Auk. 53(3):301-305.

1627   Smith, H.G., R.K. Burnard, E.E. Good and J.M. Keener. *1973.* Rare and endangered vertebrates of Ohio. Ohio J. of Science. 73(5):257-271.

1628   Smith, H.I. *1924.* Eagle snaring among the Bellacoola Indians. Can. Field-Nat. 38(9):167-168.

1629   Smith, J.C. *1974.* Distribution and number of rare, endangered, and peripheral species. Texas Parks and Wildlife Dept. Special Wildlife Investigations. Proj. No. W-103-R-3. Job No. 1. 34 pp.

1630   Smith, J.C. *1975.* Distribution and number of rare and endangered and peripheral species. Texas Parks and Wildlife Dept. Special Wildlife Investigations. Proj. No. W-103-R-4. Job No. 1. 76 pp.

1631   Smith, J.C. *1975.* Bald eagle survey. Texas Parks and Wildlife Dept. Non-Game Investigations. Proj. No. W-103-R-5. Job. No. 31. 10 pp.

1632   Smith, J.C. *1976.* Bald eagle - osprey survey. Texas Parks and Wildlife Dept. Non-Game Investigations. Proj. No. W-103-R-6. Job No. 30. 41 pp.

1633   Smith, N. *1971.* The plight of the eagle. Outdoor Arizona. 43(7):10-14.

1634   Smith, N.S. *1976.* Atomics at Amchitka. Pacific Discovery. 29(4):11-17.

1635   Smith, P.A. *1918.* Bald eagle's behavior toward biplane. Oologist. 35(4):55.

1636   Smith, W.F. *1912.* An eagle story. Bird-Lore. 14(4):228.

1637   Smithwick, J.W.P. *1891.* The eagles of North America. Oologist. 8(4/5):97-99.

1638   Smylie, T.M. *1976.* 1976 bald eagle nesting survey - New Mexico. U.S.D.I. Fish and Wildlife Service. 7 pp.

1639   Smylie, T.M. *1977.* Southern bald eagle recovery team appointed for Southwest. U.S.D.I. Fish and Wildlife Service. News Release. Albuquerque, NM. 1 pp.

1640   Snow, C. *1973.* Habitat management series for endangered species. Southern bald eagle, *Haliaeetus leucocephalus leucocephalus* and *H. leucocephalus alascanus.* U.S.D.I. Bureau of Land Management. Technical Note No. 5. 58 pp.

1641   Snyder, N.F.R. and H.A. Snyder. *1976.* Raptors in range habitat. *In:* Proc. of the Symposium on Management of Forest and Range Habitats for Non-Game Birds, U.S.D.A., Tuscon, AZ, 1975. p. 190-209.

Master No.	Citation

1642   **Snyder, N.F.R. and J.W. Wiley.** *1976.* Sexual size dimorphism in hawks and owls of North America. Ornithological Monographs No. 20. The American Ornithologists' Union. 96 pp.

1643   **Snyder, W.E.** *1927.* The destruction of eagles. The Auk. 44(2):250-251.

1644   **Snyder, W.E.** *1931.* Then and now. Oologist. 48(12):172-175.

1645   **Solman, V.E.F.** *1973.* Birds and aircraft. Biol. Cons. 5(2):79-86.

1646   **Soulen, T.K.** *1961.* Spring Season-March-May 1961. Pass. Pigeon. 23(4):146-165.

1647   **Soulen, T.K.** *1965.* Spring Season-March 1-May 31, 1964. Pass. Pigeon. 27(1):24-47.

1648   **Soulen, T.K.** *1967.* Spring Season-March 1-May 31, 1966. Pass. Pigeon. 29(1):37-51.

1649   **Southern, W.E.** *1962.* Wintering bald eagles in northwestern Illinois. Audubon Bull.(124):1-6.

1650   **Southern, W.E.** *1963.* Winter populations, behavior, and seasonal dispersal of bald eagles in northwestern Illinois. Wilson Bull. 75(1):42-55.

1651   **Southern, W.E.** *1964.* Additional observations on winter bald eagle populations: including remarks on biotelemetry techniques and immature plumages. Wilson Bull. 76(2):121-137.

1652   **Southern, W.E.** *1966.* Utilization of shad as winter food by birds. The Auk. 83(2):309-311.

1653   **Southern, W.E.** *1967.* Further comments on subadult bald eagle plumages. Jack-Pine Warb. 45(3):70-80.

1654   **Sparrowe, R.D. and H.M. Wight.** *1975.* Setting priorities for the endangered species program. *In:* Trans. of the 40th North American Wildlife and Natural Resources Conf. Wildlife Management Institute. p. 142-146.

1655   **Spencer, D.A.** *1976.* Wintering of the migrant bald eagle in the lower 48 States. National Agricultural Chemicals Association. Washington, D.C. 170 pp.

1656   **Spencer, D.A.** *1978.* Habitats for symbols. Water Spectrum. 10(1):1-8.

1657   **Spinney, H.L.** *1926.* Observations on the nesting of the bald eagle. Maine Nat. 6(3):102-109.

1658   **Spitzer, E.M.** *1972.* The Christmas bird census-1971. Audubon Bull.(161):12-28.

1659   **Spitzer, H.C.** *1968.* The Christmas bird census - 1967. Audubon Bull.(145):18-30.

1660   **Spitzer, H.C.** *1970.* The Christmas bird census - 1969. Audubon Bull.(154):18-34.

1661   **Spivey, M.** *1973.* A school opens for hunting birds to learn to live. Smithsonian. April:32-38.

1662   **Splendoria, F.A.** *1973.* Observations on wintering bald eagles at Garrison Dam, North Dakota. Prairie Nat. 5(1):6.

1663   **Spofford, W.R.** *1945.* Bald eagle notes from Reelfoot Lake. The Migrant. 16(4):65.

1664   **Spofford, W.R.** *1953.* Eagles in New York. The New York State Conservationist. October-November. p. 26-27.

1665   **Spofford, W.R.** *1956.* A survey of eagles. The Kingbird. 6(2):48-49.

1666   **Spofford, W.R.** *1959.* The white-headed eagle survey. The Kingbird. 9(1):22.

1667   **Spofford, W.R.** *1960.* Immature white-headed eagle in confusing plumage. The Kingbird. 10(1):14-15.

1668   **Spofford, W.R.** *1960.* The white-headed eagle in New York State. The Kingbird. 10(4):148-152.

1669   **Spofford, W.R.** *1962.* A count of bald eagles summering along a shallow New England lake. Wilson Bull. 74(2):186-187.

1670   **Sprunt, A., IV.** *1960.* Help requested in investigation of the bald eagle. Jack-Pine Warb. 38(3):106.

1671   **Sprunt, A., IV. and R.L. Cunningham.** *1961.* Continental Bald Eagle Project. Progress Report No. 1. Paper Presented at the National Audubon Society's 57th Annual Convention. Oct. 28-Nov. 1, 1961. Atlantic City, N.J. 7 pp.

1672   **Sprunt, A., IV.** *1961.* An eagle-eyed look at our bald eagle. Audubon. 63(6):324-327.

1673   **Sprunt, A., IV., and R.L. Cunningham.** *1962.* Continental Bald Eagle Project. Progress Report No. 2. Paper Presented at the National Audubon Society's 58th Annual Convention, Nov. 10-14, 1962, Corpus Christy, TX. 11 pp.

1674   **Sprunt, A., IV. and F.J. Ligas.** *1963.* Continental Bald Eagle Project. Progress Report No. 3. *In:* A Florida Notebook. Proc. of the National Audubon Society Annual Conv., Nov. 9-13. p. 2-7.

1675   **Sprunt, A., IV.** *1963.* Bald eagles aren't producing enough young. Audubon. 65(1):32-35.

1676   **Sprunt, A., IV. and F.J. Ligas.** *1964.* The 1963 bald eagle count. Audubon. 66(1):45-46.

1677   **Sprunt, A., IV.** *1965.* Population trends of the bald eagle in North America. *In:* Peregrine Falcon Populations: Their Biology and Decline. Hickey, J.J. (ed.). Univ. of Wisconsin Press, Madison, WI. p. 347-351.

1678   **Sprunt, A., IV. and F.J. Ligas.** *1966.* Audubon bald eagle studies-1960-1966. Proc. 62nd National Audubon Society. Nov. 12, 1966. Sacramento, CA. p. 25-30.

1679   **Sprunt, A., IV.** *1969.* Status of the bald eagle. Proc. of 64th Annual Conv., Nat. Audubon Soc., St. Louis, Missouri. p. 22-24.

1680   **Sprunt, A., IV.** *1972.* The bald eagle. *In:* Proc. of Symposium on Rare and Endangered Wildlife of the Southwestern United States. New Mexico Dept. of Game and Fish, Santa Fe, New Mexico. p. 97-103.

1681   **Sprunt, A., IV., W.B. Robertson, Jr., S. Postupalsky, R.J. Hensel, C.E. Knoder, and F.J. Ligas.** *1973.* Comparative productivity of six bald eagle populations. Trans. of 38th N. American Wildlife and Natural Resources Conf. Washington, D.C. p. 96-106.

1682   **Sprunt, A., Jr.** *1935.* Do eagles steal children? Am. Forests. 41(6):263-265.

Master No.	Citation

1683   Sprunt, A., Jr. *1955.* North American Birds of Prey. Harper & Bros., New York. 227 pp.

1684   Sprunt, A., Jr. *1955.* Florida Bird Life. National Aud. Soc., Coward-McCann, Inc., N.Y. 527 pp.

1685   Sprunt, A., Jr. *1958.* More about Florida bald eagles. Audubon. 60(6):284-286.

1686   Sprunt, A. IV and R.L. Cunningham. *1962.* Wisconsin has a stake in the Continental Bald Eagle Project: A progress report. Pass. Pigeon. 24(3):63-68.

1687   Spurrell, J.A. *1917.* Annotated list of the water birds, game birds, and birds of prey of Sac County, Iowa. Wilson Bull. 29(3):141-160.

1688   Stafford, C.J., W.L. Reichel, D.M. Swineford, R.M. Prouty and M.L. Gay. *1978.* Gas-liquid chromatographic determination of kepone in field collected avian tissues and eggs. J. Assoc. Off. Anal. Chem. 61(1):8-14.

1689   Stahlecker, D.W. *1975.* Trends in wintering diurnal raptor populations from central Colorado Christmas Bird Counts. Am. Birds. 29(5):936-940.

1690   Stalmaster, M.V. and J.R. Newman. *1978.* Behavioral responses of wintering bald eagles to human activity. J. Wildl. Manage. 42(3):506-513.

1691   Stamm, A.L. *1962.* Additional data on the bald eagle winter counts, 1961-1962. The Kentucky Warbler. 38(3):44-45.

1692   Stamm, A.L. *1969.* One-day bald eagle count - 1969. The Kentucky Warbler. 45(3):57-58.

1693   Stamm, A.L. *1970.* One-day bald eagle count - 1970. The Kentucky Warbler. 46(3):52-53.

1694   Stebbins, R. *1971.* Eagles are not for killing. Am. Forests. 77(10):12-14,56-57.

1695   Steenhof, K. *1975.* The ecology of wintering bald eagles below Fort Randall Dam, South Dakota. A Preliminary Report of Data Collected during November 1974 through March 1975.(Unpublished Report). 32 pp.

1696   Steenhof, K. *1976.* The ecology of wintering bald eagles in southeastern South Dakota. M.S. Thesis. Univ. of Missouri. Columbia, MO. 146 pp.

1697   Steenhof, K. *1976.* Wintering eagles below the Fort Randall Dam. *In:* Save the Eagle in '76, Proc. of Bald Eagle Days, 1976. Ingram, T.N. (ed.). Eagle Valley Environmentalists, Inc., Apple River, IL. p. 134-136.

1698   Steenhof, K. *1977.* Management of wintering bald eagles. U.S.D.I. Fish and Wildlife Service.(Preliminary Draft). 60 pp.

1699   Steenhof, K., S.S. Berlinger and L.H. Frederickson. *1977.* Habitat use by wintering bald eagles in South Dakota. (Draft). 26 pp.

1700   Stendell, R.C. *1976.* Summary of recent information regarding effects of PCB's on birds and mammals. *In:* Proc. of the National Conference on Polychlorinated Biphenyls, Nov. 19-21, 1975. Chicago, IL. EPA. p. 262-267.

1701   Stephens, H.A. *1967.* Observations on eagles in Kansas. Kansas Ornithol. Soc. Bull. 18(1):23-25.

1702   Stevens, R.E. *1967.* Bald eagles at Santee-Cooper Reservoir. The Chat. 31(3):73-74.

1703   Stewart, C.D. *1936.* The American eagle. Atl. Month. 158(1):77-85.

1704   Stewart, P.A. *1970.* Weight changes and feeding behavior of a captive-reared bald eagle. Bird-Band. 41(2):103-110.

1705   Stewart, R.E. and C.S. Robbins. *1958.* Birds of Maryland and the District of Columbia. Washington, D.C., U.S.D.I., Fish and Wildlife Service North America Fauna No. 62. 401 pp.

1706   Stickel, L.F. *1973.* Pesticide residues in birds and mammals. *In:* Environmental Pollution by Pesticides. Edwards, C.A. (ed.). Plenum Press, N.Y.. p. 254-312.

1707   Stickel, L.F., F.C. Schmid, W.L. Reichel and P.L. Ames. *1965.* Ospreys in Connecticut and Maryland. *In:* Effects of Pesticides on Fish and Wildlife: 1964 Research Findings of the Fish and Wildlife Service. U.S.D.I. Fish and Wildlife Serv. Circ. 226:4-8.

1708   Stickel, L.F. and R.G. Heath. *1965.* Effects of pesticides on fish and wildlife; 1964 research findings of the Fish and Wildlife Service. U.S.D.I. Fish and Wildlife Service. Circular No. 226. p. 3-8.

1709   Stickel, L.F., N.J. Chura, P.A. Stewart, C.M. Menzie, R.M. Prouty and W.L. Reichel. *1966.* Bald eagle pesticide relations. Trans. of the 31st North American Wildlife and Natural Resources Conf. March 14, 15, and 16, 1966. WMI. p. 190-200.

1710   Stickel, L.F., W.H. Stickel. and R. Christiansen. *1966.* Residues of DDT in brains and bodies of birds that died on dosages and in survirors. Science. 151(March 25):1549-1551.

1711   Stickel, L.F., S.N. Wiemeyer and L.J. Blus. *1973.* Pesticide residues in eggs of wild birds: adjustment for loss of moisture and lipid. Bull. Env. Toxic. 9(4):193-196.

1712   Stickel, W.H., L.F. Stickel and F.B. Coon. *1970.* 1970 DDE and DDD residues correlated with mortality of experimental birds. *In:* Pesticides Symposia. Deichman, W.B. (ed.). Halos and Assoc., Miami, FL. p. 287-294.

1713   Stocek, R.F. and P.A. Pearce. *1978.* The bald eagle and the osprey in the Maritime Provinces. Canadian Wildlife Service, Wildlife Toxicology Div. Manuscript Reports. 64 pp.

1714   Stockard, C.R. *1905.* Nesting habits of birds in Mississippi. The Auk. 22(2):146-158.

1715   Stone, W. *1894.* Summer birds of Pine Barrens of New Jersey. The Auk. 11(2):133-140.

Master No.	Citation

1716   Stone, W. *1937.* Birds Studies at Old Cape May. Vol. 1 & 2. The Delaware Valley Ornithological Club. Philadelphia. 941 pp.

1717   Stoner, E.A. *1921.* An investigation of newspaper report that eagle kills boy. Oologist. 38(11):150.

1718   Stophlet, J.J. *1962.* The bald eagle: a fight for survival. Natl. Parks Mag. 36(180):10-14.

1719   Storer, T.I. *1920.* Bald eagle at Wawona. The Condor. 22(4):156.

1720   Stott, K., Jr. *1948.* Notes on the longevity of captive birds. The Auk. 65(3):402-405.

1721   Stout, F. *1971.* Holiday in the north. The Bluebird. 38(4):2-3.

1722   Strong, W.A. *1917.* Some facts about king eagle. Oologist. 34(2):31.

1723   Strong, W.A. *1917.* Speed cop shoots bald eagle and is arrested. Oologist. 34(6):113.

1724   Strong, W.A. *1919.* Who? Oologist. 36(3):51-52.

1725   Strong, W.A. *1919.* The power of the bald eagle. Oologist. 36(6):128.

1726   Strong, W.A. *1922.* The geese and the eagle. Oologist. 39(6):96.

1727   Strong, W.A. *1923.* Large sets. Oologist. 40(4):64-70.

1728   Struthers, D.R. *1955.* Banded bald eagle recovered in Minnesota. Flicker. 27(1):40.

1729   Stupka, A. *1963.* Notes on the Birds of the Great Smoky Mountains National Park. The Univ. of Tennessee Press. Knoxville, TN. 242 pp.

1730   Stutzman, J. *1977.* Bald eagle status report, 1977: Minnesota. U.S.D.I. Fish and Wildlife Service. 2 pp.

1731   Sumner, L. and J.S. Dixon. *1953.* Birds and Mammals of the Sierra Nevada. Univ. of California Press, Berkeley, CA. 484 pp.

1732   Suring, L.H. *1977.* Reintroduction of bald eagles into New York State. New York State Dept. of Environmental Conservation, Bureau of Wildlife.(Final Draft). 13 pp.

1733   Sutton, G.M. *1928.* An Introduction to the Birds of Pennsylvania. J. Horace McFarland Co., Harrisburg, PA. 161 pp.

1734   Sutton, G.M. *1967.* Oklahoma Birds. Univ. of Oklahoma Press, Norman, OK. 674 pp.

1735   Swann, H.K. *1920.* A Synoptical List of Accipitres (Diurnal Birds of Prey). John Weldon and Co. London. 164 pp.

1736   Swann, H.K. *1945.* A Monograph of the Birds of Prey (Order Accipitres). Vol. 1 & 2. Wheldon & Wesley, Ltd. London. 538 pp.

1737   Swarth, H.S. *1914.* A Distributional List of Birds of Arizona. Cooper Ornithological Club. Hollywood, CA. Pacific Coast Avifauna No. 10. 133 pp.

1738   Swarth, H.S. *1920.* Birds of the Papago Saguaro National Monument and the neighboring region Arizona. U.S.D.I. Govt. Printing Office. 63 pp.

1739   Swedberg, J. *1973.* To shoot an eagle. Mass. Wildl. 24(2):2-6.

1740   Swedberg, J. *1976.* Wintering eagles in Massachusetts. *In:* Save the Eagle in '76, Proc. of Bald Eagle Days, 1976. Ingram, T.N. (ed.). Eagle Valley Environmentalists, Inc., Apple River, IL. p. 130-131.

1741   Swenson, J.E. *1975.* Ecology of the bald eagle and osprey in Yellowstone National Park. M.S. Thesis.(Unpublished). Montana State Univ., Bozeman, MT. 146 pp.

1742   Swepston, D.A. and J.C. Smith. *1976.* High hopes for southern eagles. Texas Parks Wildl. 34(4):2-5.

1743   Swisher, J.F. *1964.* A roosting area of the bald eagle in northern Utah. Wilson Bull. 76(2):186-187.

1744   Takagi, N. and M. Sasaki. *1974.* A phylogenetic study of bird karyotypes. Chromosoma. 46(1):91-120.

1745   Tate, J.L., Jr. and S. Postupalsky. *1965.* Food remains at a bald eagle nest. Jack-Pine Warb. 43(3):146-147.

1746   Tate, R.C. *1923.* Some birds of the Oklahoma panhandle. Proc. Okla. Acad. of Science. 3:41-51.

1747   Taverner, P.A. *1918.* The Hawks of the Canadian Prairie Provinces in Their Relation to Agriculture. Canada Dept. of Mines. Biological Series No. 7. Museum Bull. No. 28.

1748   Taverner, P.A. *1939.* Canadian Water Birds, Game Birds: Birds of Prey. David McCay Co., Philadelphia. 291 pp.

1749   Taverner, P.A. *1947.* Birds of Canada. The Musson Book Comp., Toronto. 446 pp.

1750   Taverner, P.A. *1974.* Birds of Western Canada. Coles Pub. Co., Ltd. Toronto. 380 pp.

1751   Taylor, G. *1976.* Bald eagle study. State of Maryland. Project No. E-1, Study No. 5, Job No. 1-6. 11 pp.

1752   Taylor, G. *1976.* Resident endangered species investigations: Bald eagle study. State of Maryland. Project No. E-1. 4 pp.

1753   Taylor, J.W. *1963.* Eagles or pesticides? Md. Conserv. 40(1):2-6.

1754   Taylor, T.C., H. Woods and W.T. Fisher. *1909.* Capture of a bald eagle near Chicago, Ill. The Auk. 26(2):191.

1755   Taylor, W.E. and A.H. Van Vleet. *1889.* Notes on Nebraska birds. Ornithol. and Oologist. 14(11):163-165.

1756   Teal, J.M. *1959.* Birds of Sapelo Island and vicinity. Oriole. 24(1):1-14.

1757   Teale, E.W. *1957.* Bird of freedom. Atl. Month. 200(5):133-136.

1758   Temple, S.A. *1970.* A raptorial requiem: The decline of America's birds of prey. Explorer. 12(2):4-7.

1759   Tennessee Valley Authority. *1974.* A checklist of the birds of the Tennessee Valley. Div. of Forestry, Fisheries, and Wildlife Development. TVA. 5 pp.

Master No.	Citation

1760   Terres, J.K. *1960.* National Audubon Society requests your cooperation in obtaining information on bald eagles in Florida. Audubon. 62(1):43.

1761   Terres, J.K. *1967.* Eagles over Hawk Mountain. Audubon. 69(4):28-32.

1762   Teulings, R.P. *1970.* Briefs for the file. The Chat. 34(3):108-110.

1763   Teulings, R.P. *1971.* Briefs for the files. The Chat. 35(1):31-34.

1764   Teulings, R.P. *1973.* Briefs for the file. The Chat. 37(3):85-89.

1765   Teulings, R.P. *1975.* Briefs for the files. The Chat. 39(3):60-64.

1766   Texas Parks and Wildlife Dept. *1975.* Nongame Wildlife Investigations. Bald eagle survey. Wildlife Div. Job Performance Report. Proj. No. W-103-R-5. Job. No. 31. 10 pp.

1767   Texas Parks and Wildlife Dept. *1975.* Bald Eagle Survey. Nongame Wildlife Investigations. Job Performance Report W-103-R-5, Job No. 31. 12 pp.

1768   Texas Parks and Wildlife Dept. *1976.* Pelicans, eagles marked for study. Texas Parks and Wildlife News. Austin, Texas. 2 pp.

1769   Texas Parks and Wildlife Dept. *1976.* Nongame Wildlife Investigations. Bald eagle - osprey survey. Wildlife Division. Job Performance Report. Proj. No. W-103-R-6. Job. No. 30. 41 pp.

1770   Thacker, R. *1971.* Estimations relative to birds of prey in captivity in the United States of America. Raptor Res. News. 5(4):108-122.

1771   Thelander, C.G. *1973.* Bald eagle reproduction in California, 1972-1973. State of California Dept. of Fish and Game. Wildlife Management Branch Administrative Report No. 73-5. 17 pp.

1772   Thom, R.H. *1977.* Bald eagle roost habitat. Illinois Nature Preserves Commission,(Memorandum to Jack White). June 20, 1977. 2 pp.

1773   Thom, R.H. *1977.* Nature preserve potential of the Oak Valley Eagle Sanctuary, Rock Island County, Illinois. Illinois Nature Preserves Commission.(Unpublished Report). 4 pp.

1774   Thomas, S. *1975.* A convocation of hawk watchers: Hook Mountain, New York. Proc. of N. American Hawk Migration Conf. Syracuse, N.Y. Hawk Migration Association of North America. p. 19-20.

1775   Thomas, S. *1976.* Our trip to Florida. Raptor Report. 4(2):10-11.

1776   Thompson, F. *1961.* Scream of eagles. Sports Afield. 144(7):50-51,85,86.

1777   Thompson, R.A. *1973.* Bald eagle nesting surveys in California. U.S.D.I. Fish and Wildlife Service. 49 pp.

1778   Thomson, A.V. *1891.* Bald and golden eagles in Iowa. Oologist. 8(2):31.

1779   Thone, F. *1937.* The real eagle. Sci. News Letter. 32(847):14.

1780   Thone, F. *1941.* Hunted eagles. Sci. News Letter. 40(21):335.

1781   Thone, F. *1943.* Vanishing American. Sci. News Letter. 44(1):14.

1782   Thone, F. *1946.* On national holidays. Sci. News Letter. 49(26):410.

1783   Thone, F. *1949.* Disputed emblem. Sci. News Letter. 55(8):126.

1784   Thurber, C. *1904.* The bald eagle. Birds Nat. 16(5):232-236.

1785   Tilt, W. *1976.* The status of the bald eagle *(Haliaeetus leucocephalus)* in the United States south of Canada. (Draft, Unpublished Report). U.S.D.I. Fish and Wildlife Service. 18 pp.

1786   Time-Life Inc. *1974.* Vanishing Species. Time Life Books, N.Y. 264 pp.

1787   Tinker, A.D. *1914.* Notes on the ornithology of Clay and Palo Alto Counties, Iowa. The Auk. 31(1):70-81.

1788   Todd, R.L. *1968.* Statewide game management survey, Nongame Investigations. Arizona Game and Fish Dept. Proj. W-053-R-18 Wk. Pl. 05 Job 01. 6 pp.

1789   Todd, R.L. *1970.* Nongame Investigations. Arizona Game and Fish Dept. Progress Report. Proj. W-53-R-20. Wk. Pl. 5. Job. 01. 24 pp.

1790   Todd, R.L. *1971.* Nongame Investigations. Arizona Game and Fish Dept. Progress Report. Proj. W-53-21, Wk. Pl. 5. Job 01. July 30, 1970 - June 30, 1971. 11 pp.

1791   Todd, R.L. *1972.* Nongame Investigations. Arizona Game and Fish Dept. Progress Report. Proj. W-53-22. Wk. Pl. 5. Job 1. 20 pp.

1792   Todd, R.L. *1973.* Nongame Investigations. Arizona Game and Fish Dept. Proj. W-53-R-23. Wk. Pl. 05. Job 01. 10 pp.

1793   Todd, R.L. *1974.* Nongame Investigations. Arizona Game and Fish Dept. Performance Report. Proj. W-53-R - 24. Wk. Pl. 5. Job. 01. 6 pp.

1794   Todd, R.L. *1978.* Winter bald eagle in Arizona. Arizona Game and Fish Dept. Special Report. Proj. W-53-R. Wk. Pl. 5,Job 01. 36 pp.

1795   Todd, W.E.C. *1940.* Birds of Western Pennsylvania. Univ. of Pittsburgh Press. Pittsburgh, PA. 710 pp.

1796   Tousey, R. *1962.* Concern for the bald eagle. Atl. Nat. 17(1):4-5.

1797   Townsend, C.H. *1897.* Descriptions of a new eagle from Alaska and a new squirrel from lower California. Proc. of Biological Soc. of Washington. 11:145-146.

1798   Townsend, F.C. *1954.* Bald eagle. Maine Aud. Soc. Bull. 10(3):50.

1799   Townsend, F.C. *1957.* Banding birds of prey in Maine. Maine Field-Nat. 13(1/2):8-13.

1800   Trauger, D.L. and R.G. Bromley. *1976.* Additional bird observations on the West Mirage Islands, Great Slave Lake, Northwest Territories. Can. Field-Nat. 90(2):114-122.

Master No.	Citation

1801 Trautman, M.B. *1942.* Ducks following bald eagle. Wilson Bull. 54(2):139.

1802 Tremaine, M. *1974.* Bald eagle count. Neb. Bird Rev. 42(4):76-77.

1803 Trenholme, N.S. and R.W. Campbell. *1975.* Survey of bald eagle populations in the southern Gulf Islands, British Columbia. Syesis. 8:109-111.

1804 Troyer, W.A., and R.J. Hensel. *1965.* Nesting and productivity of bald eagles on the Kodiak National Wildlife Refuge, Alaska. The Auk. 82(4):636-638.

1805 Truslow, F.K. *1961.* Eye to eye with the eagles. Natl. Geog. Mag. 119(1):122-148.

1806 Truslow, F.K. *1965.* The eagles. *In:* Water Prey and Game Birds of North America. Wetmore, A. (ed.). National Geographic Society. p. 236-247.

1807 Truslow, F.K. *1972.* The private life of the bald eagle. Audubon. 74(6):44-51.

1808 Tufts, R.W. *1973.* The Birds of Nova Scotia. (Sec. Ed.). Nova Scotia Museum. 532 pp.

1809 Turcotte, W.H. *1975.* Successful eagle nesting on Mississippi Coast. Miss. Kite. 6:14-15.

1810 Turner, J.F. *1971.* Eagles: Vanishing Americans. Sierra Club Bull. 56(9):14-19.

1811 Turner, J.F. *1971.* The Magnificent Bald Eagle, America's National Bird. Random House, Inc. New York. 81 pp.

1812 Tyrrell, W.B. *1936.* Report of eagle survey. (Unpublished Report). Pough, R.H. (ed.). National Audubon Society. 35 pp.

1813 Tyrrell, W.B. *1946.* The bald eagle in and around Washington, D. C. Wood Thrush. 1(3):11.

1814 U.S. Congress. *1935.* Preservation of the American eagle. Report No. 899. 74th Congress. May 13, 1935. 2 pp.

1815 U.S. Congress. *1940.* Preserving from extinction the American eagle, emblem of the sovereignty of the United States of America. Report No. 1589. 76th Congress. May 14, 1940. 2 pp.

1816 U.S. Congress. *1950.* Protection of the bald eagle. Comm. on Merchant Marine and Fisheries, 81st Congress. H.R. 5507 and H.R. 5629. 34 pp.

1817 U.S. Congress. *1971.* A bill to extend to hawks, owls and certain other raptors the protection now accorded to bald and golden eagles. House of Representatives. 10482. 92nd Congress, 1st Session. August 6, 1971. 3 pp.

1818 U.S. Congress. *1971.* Hawks, owls and eagles. Comm. on Merchant Marine and Fisheries. House of Representatives. 92nd Congress. 1st Session. Serial No. 92-14. 363 pp.

1819 U.S. Congress. *1972.* Bald Eagle Protection Act. Comm. on Commerce, U.S. Senate 92nd Congress, Second Session. S. 2547, H.R. 12186 and H.R. 14731. June 29, 1972, Serial No. 92-63. 78 pp.

1820 U.S. Department of Agriculture. *1969.* Wildlife Habitat Improvement Handbook. Forest Service. Wash., D.C. Section 44.21.

1821 U.S. Department of Agriculture. *1971.* The bald eagle on the Chippewa National Forest. U.S.D.A. Forest Service.(Pamphlet). 8 pp.

1822 U.S. Department of Agriculture. *1972.* Protection of bald and golden eagles from powerlines. U.S.D.A. Rural Electrification Administration. Bull. 61-10. 8 pp.

1823 U.S. Department of Agriculture. *1973.* Forest Service Manual. Title 2600 - Wildlife Management. Amend. No. 14. p. 2633.4-2 - 2633.4-11.

1824 U.S. Department of Agriculture. *1973.* About the Children's Eagle Nesting Area. U.S.D.A., Forest Service. 2 pp.

1825 U.S. Department of Agriculture. *1977.* Bald eagle-osprey survey report, 1977. U.S.D.A. Forest Service, Eastern Region. 5 pp.

1826 U.S. Department of Agriculture. *1977.* The bald eagle on the Chippewa National Forest. (Rev.). U.S.D.A. Forest Service. 8 pp.

1827 U.S. Department of Agriculture. *1977.* Forest Service Manual Title 2600 - Wildlife Management. Amend. No. 31. U.S.D.A., Forest Service. 64 pp.

1828 U.S. Department of the Interior. *[?].* The right to exist; A report on our endangered wildlife. U.S.D.I. Fish and Wildlife Service. Res. Pub. 69. 12 pp.

1829 U.S. Department of the Interior. *1959 - 1976.* Refuge Narrative Reports. U.S.D.I. Fish and Wildlife Service, Kodiak National Wildlife Refuge.

1830 U.S. Department of the Interior. *1963.* Pesticide Wildlife Studies, A review of Fish and Wildlife Investigations during 1961 and 1962. Fish and Wildlife Service. Circular 167. 109 pp.

1831 U.S. Department of the Interior. *1963.* Effects of DDT on bald eagles. Fish and Wildlife Service Circ. 199. p. 79-80,114-115.

1832 U.S. Department of the Interior. *1966.* Rare and endangered fish and wildlife of the United States. Fish and Wildlife Service. Committee on Rare and Endangered Fish and Wildlife Species. Res. Pub. 34.

1833 U.S. Department of the Interior. *1967.* Wildlife research, problems, programs and progress, 1966. U.S.D.I. Fish and Service. Resource Pub. No. 43. p. 51-65.

1834 U.S. Department of the Interior. *1968.* Rare and endangered fish and wildlife of the United States. U.S.D.I. Fish and Wildlife Service. Committee on Rare and Endangered Wildlife Species. Res. Pub. 34.(Revised Edition).

Master No.   Citation

1835   **U.S. Department of the Interior.** *1969.* The bald eagle. U.S.D.I. Fish and Wildlife Service. Conservation Note 20. 5 pp.

1836   **U.S. Department of the Interior.** *1971.* The birds of Mason Neck National Wildlife Refuge. U.S.D.I., Fish and Wildlife Service. Refuge Leaflet 257. 6 pp.

1837   **U.S. Department of the Interior.** *1972.* Bald eagle nesting populations. Fish and Wildlife Service.(Memorandum from Region 2 Director to Director, Wash., D.C.). Dec. 6, 1972. 1 p.

1838   **U.S. Department of the Interior.** *1972.* Bald eagle nesting populations. Memorandum. Fish and Wildlife Service. Albuquerque, Nov. 13, 1972. 2 pp.

1839   **U.S. Department of the Interior.** *1972.* Status of bald eagle nesting. Fish and Wildlife Service.(Memorandum from Region 1, Director to Director, Wash., D.C., Oct. 19, 1972). 2 pp.

1840   **U.S. Department of the Interior.** *1972.* Bald eagle nesting populations. Dover, Del. Fish and Wildlife Service.(Memorandum - Sept. 1 8, 1972). 1 pp.

1841   **U.S. Department of the Interior.** *1972.* Bald eagles in Alaska. U.S.D.A. Forest Service, U.S.D.I. Fish and Wildlife Service. (Alaska Region). 12 pp.

1842   **U.S. Department of the Interior.** *1972.* Bald eagle nesting population - New Jersey. (Memorandum from USGMAIC, Trenton, N.J. to Regional Director, Boston, Mass., Sept. 18, 1972). 1 p.

1843   **U.S. Department of the Interior.** *1973.* Bald eagle nesting. Fish and Wildlife Service.(Memorandum from Reg. Director to Director, Wash., D.C., Oct. 10, 1973). 2 pp.

1844   **U.S. Department of the Interior.** *1973.* Bald eagle nesting 1973. Fish and Wildlife Service.(Memorandum from Region 1, Director to Director, Wash., D.C., Oct. 5, 1973). 2 pp.

1845   **U.S. Department of the Interior.** *1973.* Eagle nest status. (Memorandum Wildlife Services/Law Enforcement to Regional Director, Boston, Mass, Jan. 3, 1973). 2 pp.

1846   **U.S. Department of the Interior.** *1973.* Bald eagle nesting survey - osprey sightings. Denver.(Regional Director (Pa/1220:720) to Director, BSFW, Washington, D.C. Memorandum - Sept. 4, 1973). 3 pp.

1847   **U.S. Department of the Interior.** *1973.* Bald eagle nesting populations. Fish and Wildlife Service.(Memorandum - Boston, October 12, 1973). 6 pp.

1848   **U.S. Department of the Interior.** *1973.* Threatened wildlife of the United States. Fish and Wildlife Service Office of Endangered Species and International Activities. Res. Pub. 114(Rev. Resource Pub. 34). 289 pp.

1849   **U.S. Department of the Interior.** *1973.* Bald eagle nesting survey. (Denver, Acting Regional Director to Director, BSFW, Washington, D.C. Memorandum - May 29, 1973). 4 pp.

1850   **U.S. Department of the Interior.** *1974.* United States estimated to have 1,000 nesting pairs of bald eagles in lower 48 states. U.S.D.I. Fish and Wildlife Service News Release. February 20, 1974. 6 pp.

1851   **U.S. Department of the Interior.** *1974.* Eagle 'egg-plant' successful. Fish and Wildlife Service News Release. May 31, 1974. 3 pp.

1852   **U.S. Department of the Interior.** *1974.* 1974 Southern bald eagle nesting survey report-Region 2. Memorandum. Fish and Wildlife Service. Albuquerque, Sept. 24, 1974. 5 pp.

1853   **U.S. Department of the Interior.** *1974.* 1974 bald eagle nesting survey. Fish and Wildlife Service.(Memorandum from Acting Regional Director, Region 1. to Assoc. Director, Wash., D.C., Sept. 13, 1974). 2 pp.

1854   **U.S. Department of the Interior.** *1974.* Bald eagle and osprey nesting survey. Fish and Wildlife Service.(Memorandum from Fishery Mgt. Biologist to Area Manager, Billings, MT., Aug. 21, 1974). 10 pp.

1855   **U.S. Department of the Interior.** *1974.* 1974 bald eagle production survey. Fish and Wildlife Service.(Memorandum Reg. Director, Twin Cities, MN to Director, Wash., D.C., Oct. 8, 1974). 2 pp.

1856   **U.S. Department of the Interior.** *1974.* Bald eagle nesting survey-1974. (Memorandum from Area Manager, Bismarck, N. Dakota. to Regional Director, Region 6, Denver, CO. Aug. 19, 1974). 1 pp.

1857   **U.S. Department of the Interior.** *1974.* Bald eagle survey, Missouri River reservoirs in South Dakota, Nebraska area. (Memorandum from Acting Area Manager, South Dakota-Nebraska to Regional Director, Region 6, Denver, Colo. Pa/1400:6209, May 2, 1974). 6 pp.

1858   **U.S. Department of the Interior.** *1974.* Bald eagle nesting survey - 1974. (Memorandum from Acting Area Manager, Billings, MT. to Regional Director, Denver, CO., August 27, 1974). 2 pp.

1859   **U.S. Department of the Interior.** *1974.* Bald eagle nesting survey and osprey sightings - C. Y. 1974. (Memorandum to Director, USF&WS, Washington, D.C., Sept. 4, 1974). 2 pp.

1860   **U.S. Department of the Interior.** *1974.* Bald eagle nesting survey - 1974. (Memorandum from Acting Area Manager, South Dakota, Nebraska to Regional Director, USF+WS, Denver, Colo., August 12, 1974. Pa1400:620). 1 p.

1861   **U.S. Department of the Interior.** *1975.* Egg transplants helping bald eagle population. U.S.D.I. Fish and Wildlife Service News Release. May 11, 1975. 2 pp.

Master No.	Citation

1862   **U.S. Department of the Interior.** *1975.* 1975 Bald eagle nesting survey results. (Memorandum - Regional Director, Boston to Director, Washington, D.C., Dec. 29, 1975). 2 pp.

1863   **U.S. Department of the Interior.** *1975.* Endangered and threatened wildlife and plants: re-classification of American alligator and other amendments. Federal Register. 40(188):44412-44429.

1864   **U.S. Department of the Interior.** *1976.* Bicentennial eagle portrait offered for sale to the public. U.S.D.I. Fish and Wildlife Service News Release. February 20, 1976. 3 pp.

1865   **U.S. Department of the Interior.** *1976.* Bureau of Reclamation evaluation report on proposed critical habitat for the southern bald eagle. U.S.D.I. Bureau of Reclamation. 16 pp.

1866   **U.S. Department of the Interior.** *1976.* Southern bald eagle nest status. Arizona population. Memorandum. August 1976. Region 2. 1 pp.

1867   **U.S. Department of the Interior.** *1976.* Southern bald eagle nest status. Texas population. Memorandum. Region 2. 1 p.

1868   **U.S. Department of the Interior.** *1976.* 1975 bald eagle nest survey. Fish and Wildlife Service.(Memorandum from Acting Reg. Director, Region 3. To Director, Wash., D.C., Jan. 21, 1976). 1 p.

1869   **U.S. Department of the Interior.** *1976.* Public puts heat on eagle killers; DFW program called helpful. Fish and Wildlife Service News Release. Great Lakes Region News. May 11, 1976. 2 pp.

1870   **U.S. Department of the Interior.** *1976.* Endangered and threatened wildlife and plants: Re-publication of the list of species. Federal Register. 41(208):47180-47198.

1871   **U.S. Department of the Interior.** *1976.* The bald eagle transplant program - status report. U.S.D.I. Fish and Wildlife Service.(Unpublished Report.). 6 pp.

1872   **U.S. Department of the Interior.** *1976.* Raptor TV spots to be aired. U.S.D.I. Fish and Wildlife Service News. July 1976. p. 1-2.

1873   **U.S. Department of the Interior.** *1977.* Man-made disease kills two million waterfowl annually. Fish and Wildlife Service. Public Affairs Feature Release, June 20. 7 pp.

1874   **U.S. Department of the Interior.** *1977.* Bald eagle *(Haliaeetus leucocephalus)* . Fish and Wildlife Service.(Draft of Status Report) 22 pp.

1875   **U.S. Department of the Interior.** *1977.* U.S. Fish and Wildlife Service tracks American bald eagles. U.S. Fish and Wildlife Service Region 6. News Release. 77-26. April 2, 1977. 2 pp.

1876   **U.S. Department of the Interior.** *1977.* Chesapeake Bay bald eagle making strong comeback. Endang. Spec. Tech. Bull. U.S. Fish and Wildlife Service. 2(8):1-2.

1877   **U.S. Department of the Interior.** *1977.* International trade in endangered species of wild fauna and flora; Implementation of Convention. Federal Register. 42(35):10462-10488.

1878   **U.S. Department of the Interior.** *1977.* Karl E. Mundt National Wildlife Refuge: Summary Report. July 1, 1975 to December 31, 1975.(Unpublished Report). 8 pp.

1879   **U.S. Department of the Interior.** *1977.* Bald eagles of Wolf Lodge Bay. U.S.D.I. Bureau of Land Management, Couer D' Alene District. 20 pp.

1880   **U.S. Department of the Interior.** *1977.* Midwinter waterfowl and eagle survey completed. U.S.D.I. Fish and Wildlife Service News Release. 3 pp.

1881   **U.S. Department of the Interior.** *1977.* Bald eagle management guidelines, Oregon-Washington. U.S.D.I. Fish and Wildlife.(Pamphlet.) 8 pp.

1882   **U.S. Department of the Interior.** *1978.* Northern states bald eagle recovery team appointed. Endang. Spec. Tech. Bull. U.S. Fish and Wildlife Service. 3 (9):12.

1883   **U.S. Department of the Interior.** *1978.* Prime bald eagle roosting site protected from logging. Endang. Spec. Tech. Bull. U.S. Fish and Wildlife Service. 3(7):3.

1884   **U.S. Department of the Interior.** *1978.* Bald eagle's status listed for 48 states. Endang. Spec. Tech. Bull. U.S. Fish and Wildlife Service. 3(3):1,9.

1885   **U.S. Department of the Interior.** *1978.* Eagle, fox squirrel top Maryland's ES agenda. Endang. Spec. Tech. Bull. U.S. Fish and Wildlife Service. 3(2):4-6.

1886   **U.S. Nuclear Regulatory Commission.** *1976.* Final environmental statement related to construction of Douglas Point Nuclear Generating Station, Units 1 and 2. Potomac Electric Power Company. p. 2.11.

1887   **Utah State Division of Wildlife Resources.** *1977.* Utah's wintering eagles. Wildlife Report. Salt Lake City, Feb. 14. 1 pp.

1888   **Van Den Akker, J.B.** *1954.* A wintering concentration of eagles in Oklahoma. Wilson Bull. 66(2):136.

1889   **Van Kammen, I.J.** *1916.* Relative to the bald eagle in Alaska. Oologist. 33(9):156-158.

1890   **Van Name, W.G.** *1921.* Threatened extinction of the bald eagle. Ecology. 2(1):76-78.

1891   **Van Tyne, J. and A.J. Berger.** *1971.* Fundamentals of Ornithology. Dover Pub., Inc., New York. 624 pp.

1892   **Van Velzen, W.T.** *1966.* Maryland nest summary for 1965 and 10-year recapitulation. Md. Birdlife. 22(3):71-76.

1893   **Vance, J.M.** *1978.* Eagle troubles. All Outdoors. Missouri Department of Conservation. News Release. March 10. 3 pp.

1894   **Vasse, S.** *1974.* Eagle attempts capture of snow goose. Ill. Aud. Bull.(169):12.

Master No.   Citation

1895   **Vian, W.E. and J.C.W. Bliese.** *1974.* Observations on population changes and on behavior of the bald eagle in south central Nebraska. Neb. Bird Rev. 42(3):46-55.

1896   **Virginia Commission of Game and Inland Fisheries.** *1974.* Endangered vertebrates of Virginia. Virginia Wildlife. September. p. 15-18.

1897   **Visher, S.S.** *1909.* A list of the birds of western South Dakota. The Auk. 26(2):144-153.

1898   **Visher, S.S.** *1915.* A list of birds of Clay County, .southeastern South Dakota. Wilson Bull. 27(2):321-335.

1899   **Volkmar, R.S.** *1976.* A free spirit, high-soaring, courageous. Minnesota Bicentennial Commission News Release. 1976. p. 50-55.

1900   **Vosburgh, G.W.H.** *1916.* Bald eagle. Oologist. 33(1):11-12.

1901   **Wade, J.M.** *1881.* John Krider's work. Ornithol. and Oologist. 6(8):60.

1902   **Waldo, E.** *1963.* Old baldy. Louisiana Wildlife and Fisheries Commission. Wildlife Education Bulletin No. 77. 4 pp.

1903   **Walker, E.P.** *1927.* True economic status of the Alaska bald eagle. Bird Lore. 29(2):157-160.

1904   **Walker, M.J.** *1973.* How wild animals help people. Chap. 11. Our National Emblem helps too. Defend. Wildl. News. 48(5):612-614.

1905   **Walker, M.J. and J. Lowen.** *1967.* The vanishing American. Am. For. 73(10):6-9,61-63.

1906   **Walkinshaw, L.H.** *1939.* Where does the bald eagle nest in Michigan? Jack-Pine Warb. 17(3):71.

1907   **Wallace, G.J.** *1963.* An Introduction to Ornithology. (Second ed.) The MacMillan Co., New York. 491 pp.

1908   **Wallace, G.J.** *1969.* Endangered and declining species of Michigan birds. Jack-Pine Warb. 47(3):70-75.

1909   **Wampole, J.H.** *1947.* Hawk populations in Nebraska, 1945-1946. Neb. Game & Parks Comm., Terrestrial Wildlife Division. Neb. W-015-R-2. 5 pp.

1910   **Warner, D.W.** *1951.* The nesting season...1950. Flicker. 23(1/2):1-8.

1911   **Warner, E.L.** *1902.* Nest of the bald eagle. Oologist. 19(11):164.

1912   **Wayne, A.T.** *1910.* Birds of South Carolina. The Daggett Printing Co., Charleston, S.C. 254 pp.

1913   **Weakly, H.E.** *1938.* A concentration of wintering eagles along the North Platte River in Keith County. Neb. Bird Rev. 6(1):20.

1914   **Wechsler, C.A.** *1971.* The bald eagles of Chippewa. Minn. Vol. 34(197):50-58.

1915   **Weddel, J.** *1973.* The bald eagle *(Haliaeetus leucocephalus)* in southcentral Nebraska during the first quarter of 1973. Biology 630. Kearny St. College, Kearney, Nebraska. (Unpublished). 33 pp.

1916   **Weddle, F.** *1973.* Post script: the eagles are victims. Defend. of Wildl. News. 48(5):555-556.

1917   **Weddle, F.** *1973.* The eagles - victims once again. Defend. Wildl. News. 48(5):554-555.

1918   **Weeden, N.** *1973.* Bald eagle - osprey status report. U.S.D.A. Forest Service. R-9-RRE+W. 8 pp.

1919   **Weeden, N.** *1976.* Bald eagle - osprey survey report. U.S.D.A. Forest Service. Eastern Region. 3 pp.

1920   **Weekes, F.M.** *1974.* A survey of bald eagle nesting attempts in southern Ontario, 1969-1973. Can. Field-Nat. 88(4):415-419.

1921   **Weekes, F.M.** *1975.* Bald eagle nesting attempts in southern Ontario in 1974. Can. Field-Nat. 89(4):438-444.

1922   **Weekes, F.M.** *1975.* Behavior of a young bald eagle at a southern Ontario nest. Can. Field-Nat. 89(1):35-40.

1923   **Wellenkamp, J.** *1973.* A first- in baby bald eaglets. Southern Living. Sept.:36-38.

1924   **Weller, M.W., D.L. Trauger and G.L. Krapu.** *1969.* Breeding birds of the west Mirage Islands, Great Slave Lake, N. W. T. Can. Field-Nat. 83(4):344-360.

1925   **Wetmore, A.** *1933.* The eagle, king of birds, and his kin. Natl. Geog. Mag. 64(7):43-95.

1926   **Wetmore, S.P. and D.I. Gillespie.** *1976.* Osprey and bald eagle populations in Labrador and northeastern Quebec, 1969-1973. Can. Field-Nat. 90(3):330-337.

1927   **Wheeler, R.J. and L.E. Raice.** *1967.* Note on the predatory behavior of the bald eagle. The Murrelet. 48(1):20-21.

1928   **White, C.A.** *1893.* The raptores of Omaha and vicinity. Oologist. 10(5):138-140.

1929   **White, C.M.** *1974.* Current problems and techniques in raptor management and conservation. Trans. of the 39th N. American Wildlife and Natural Resources Conf. Denver, CO. p. 301-312.

1930   **White, C.M. and J.R. Haugh.** *1969.* Recent data on summer birds of the upper Yukon River, Alaska, and adjacent part of the Yukon Territory; Canada. Can. Field-Nat. 83(3):257-271.

1931   **White, C.M., W.B. Emison and F.S.L. Williamson.** *1971.* Dynamics of raptor populations on Amchitka Island, Alaska. BioScience. 21(12):623-627.

1932   **White, C.M. and S.K. Sherrod.** *1973.* Advantages and disadvantages of the use of rotor-winged aircraft in raptor surveys. Raptor Res. 7(3/4):97-104.

1933   **White, F.H., C.F. Simpson and L.E. Williams, Jr.** *1973.* Isolation of *Edwardsiella tarda* from aquatic animal species and surface waters in Florida. J. Wildl. Dis. 9(3):204-208.

1934   **White, M.C.** *1889.* Birds of Matthews County, Va. Oologist. 6(6):107-108.

1935   **White, S.E.** *1890.* Caged eagles. Oologist. 7(4):65-66.

1936   **White, S.E.** *1893.* Birds observed on Mackinac Island, Michigan, during the summers of 1889,1890, and 1891. The Auk. 10(3):221-230.

1937   **Whitehead, R.** *1968.* The First Book of Eagles. Franklin Watts, Inc. New York. 45 pp.

Master No.	Citation

1938   Whitfield, D.W.A., J.M. Gerrard, W.J. Maher and D.W. Davis. *1973.* A population study of Saskatchewan and Manitoba bald eagles. *In:* Population Status of Raptors. Murphy, J.R., C.M. White, and B.E. Harrell, (eds.) Proc. of the Conference on Raptor Conservation Techniques, Fort Collins, Colorado, 22-24 March 1973 (Part VI). Raptor Research Foundation, Inc., Raptor Research Report, No. 3. p. 109-119.

1939   Whitfield, D.W.A., J.M. Gerrard, W.J. Maher, and D.W. Davis. *1974.* Bald eagle nesting habitat, density, and reproduction in central Saskatchewan and Manitoba. Can. Field-Nat. 88(4):339-407.

1940   Wick, W.Q. *1958.* A nine year bird list from Eliza and Protection Islands, Washington. Murrelet. 39(1):1-9.

1941   Widmann, O. *1907.* A preliminary catalog of the birds of Missouri. Trans. Acad. of Science of St. Louis. 296 pp.

1942   Wiemeyer, S.N., B.M. Mulhern, F.J. Ligas, R.J. Hensel, J.E. Mathisen, F.C. Robards and S. Postupalsky. *1972.* Residues of organochlorine pesticides, polychlorinated biphenyls, and mercury in bald eagle eggs and changes in shell thickness--1969 and 1970. Pest. Monit. J. 6(1):50-55.

1943   Wiemeyer, S.N., A.A. Belisle, and F.J. Gramlich. *1978.* Organochlorine residues in potential food items of Maine bald eagles *(Haliaeetus leucocephalus)* , 1966 and 1974. Bull. Env. Contam. Toxicol. 19(1):64-72.

1944   Wiley, R.W. and E.G. Bolen. *1971.* Eagle-livestock relationships: livestock carcass cenus and wound characteristics. Southwest Nat. 16(2):151-169.

1945   Willard, B.G. *1906.* Exceptional eggs of the bald eagle. The Auk. 23(2):222.

1946   Willard, B.G. *1911.* Status of the bald eagle of New England. Oologist. 28(3):50-52.

1947   Willett, G. *1915.* Summer birds of Forrester Island, Alaska. The Auk. 32(3):32.

1948   Willett, G. *1920.* Comments upon the safety of sea birds and upon the 'probable' occurrence of the northern bald eagle in California. The Condor. 22:(6)204-205.

1949   Willett, G. *1927.* Destruction of eagles in Alaska. The Auk. 44(4):591-592.

1950   Willett, G. *1933.* A revised list of the birds of southwestern California. Pacific Coast Avifauna. No. 21 Cooper Ornithol. Club. Los Ang eles, Calif. 204 pp.

1951   Williams, G., Jr. *1971.* The winter birds of Wheeler National Refuge, 1970-1971. Alabama Acad. of Science. J. 42(3):149-150.

1952   Williams, J. *1918.* Birds about our lighthouse. Wilson Bull. 30(3):87-90.

1953   Williams, J. *1920.* Notes on the birds of Wakulla County, Florida. Wilson Bull. 32(1):5-12.

1954   Williams, R.B. and C.P. Matteson, Jr. *1947.* Wyoming hawks. Wyoming Wildlife. 11(6):9-12.

1955   Williams, R.B. and C.P. Matteson, Jr. *1973.* Wyoming hawks. Wyoming Game and Fish Dept. Bull. No. 5.(Second Edition, Reprinted from Wyoming Wildlife Mag., 1948). 84 pp.

1956   Williams, R.W., Jr. *1904.* A preliminary list of the birds of Leon County, Florida. The Auk. 21(4):449-462.

1957   Wilson, A. *1840.* Wilson's American Ornithology. Otis, Broaders, and Co., Boston. 746 pp.

1958   Wilson, A., C.L. Bonaparte and W. Jardine. *1831.* American Ornithology, or the Natural History of the Birds of the United States. (3 Vols.) London and Edinburgh. 271 pp.

1959   Wilson, C. *1973.* How the woolgrowers fleece the public. Audubon. 75(3):119-121.

1960   Wilson, E.S. *1922.* A prince of the house of eagles. Bird-Lore. 24(6):331-335.

1961   Wilson, G. *1969.* Additions to 'Birds of southcentral Kentucky.' The Kentucky Warbler. 45(2):32-39.

1962   Wilson, R.L. *1967.* The Pleistocene vertebrates of Michigan. Papers of the Michigan Acad. of Science, Arts, and Letters. 52 :197-234.

1963   Wilson, R.R. *1916.* The bald eagle. Oologist. 33(2):31.

1964   Wiswall, H. *1946.* Old nesting records from Beaufort County. The Chat. 10(4):74-75.

1965   Witzeman, R.A. *1975.* Impact of the Central Arizona Project upon riparian raptors. J. Ariz. Acad. Sci. 10:29.

1966   Witzeman, R.A. *1976.* The president's column. The Roadrunner. 24(8):6-8.

1967   Wolf, C.E. *1976.* Northeastern California bald eagle winter use area study plan (winter of 1976.) Mt. Shasta Area Audubon Society.(Unpublished Study Plan). 3 pp.

1968   Wondra, A. *1937.* The bald eagle in Gage County. Neb. Bird Rev. 5(2):32.

1969   Wood, A.A., G.M. Stirrett, and D.A. Arnott. *1941.* Observations on some interesting birds in Kent County, Ontario. Can. Field-Nat. 55(2):15.

1970   Wood, B. *1967.* More bald eagle sightings in the Lake Athabasca Region. Blue Jay. 25(1):26.

1971   Wood, J.C. *1908.* Corrections to 'A List of the Land Birds of Southeastern Michigan.' The Auk. 25(2):230-232.

1972   Wood, M. *1954.* Our bird of freedom. Coronet. 36(3):81-84.

1973   Wood, N.A. *1911.* The results of the Mershon expedition to the Charity Islands, Lake Huron: Birds. Wilson Bull. 23(2):78-112.

1974   Wood, N.A. *1923.* A Preliminary Survey of the Bird Life of North Dakota. Univ. of Michigan. Museum of Zoology, Misc. Pub. No. 10. 97 pp.

1975   Wood, N.A. *1951.* The Birds of Michigan. Univ. of Michigan. Museum of Zoology, Misc. Pub. No. 75. 559 pp.

1976   Woodruff, F.M. *1898.* Bald eagle. The Auk. 15(1):62.

1977   Woodruff, F.M. *1907.* The birds of the Chicago area. Chicago Acad. of Sciences. Natural History Survey. Bull. No. 6. 228 pp.

Master No.	Citation

1978 Woodward, B. *1949.* Birds of the Sea Islands, Georgia region. Oriole. 14(1/2):19.

1979 Woodwell, G.M. *1967.* Toxic substances and ecological cycles. Sci. Am. 216(3):24-31.

1980 Woolson, E.A., P.D.J. Ensor, W.L. Reichel and A.L. Young. *1973.* Dioxin residues in Lakeland sand and bald eagle samples. Advances in Chemistry Series, No. 120. Chlorodioxins-Origin and Fate. American Chemical Society. p. 112-118.

1981 Worthington, V. (ed.). *1976.* Power line electrocution-hazards made safer. Cons. News. 41(21):8-10.

1982 Worthington, V. (ed.). *1977.* No sympathy for the eagle slayer. Cons. News. 42(7):10-11.

1983 Wrakestraw, G.F. *1972.* 1972 Wyoming bald and golden eagle survey. Job Completion Report. Wyoming Game and Fish Commission. W-0 5-R-21. Wk. Pl. 07, Job. 31.

1984 Wrakestraw, G.F. *1973.* The 1973 Wyoming bald and golden eagle survey. Am. Birds. 27(4):716-718.

1985 Wrakestraw, G.F. *1973.* 1973 Wyoming bald and golden eagle survey. Wyoming Game and Fish Dept. Proj. W-50-R-21. Job. No. 31. 4 pp.

1986 Wright, A.H. and F. Harper. *1913.* A biological reconnaisance of Okefenokee Swamp: The birds. The Auk. 30(4):477-505.

1987 Wright, B.S. *1948.* Waterfowl investigations in eastern Canada, Newfoundland, and Labrador, 1945-1947. Trans. N. Am. Wildl. Conf. 13:356-364.

1988 Wright, B.S. *1953.* The relation of bald eagles to breeding ducks in New Brunswick. J. Wildl. Manage. 17(1):55-62.

1989 Wright, C., Jr. *1894.* Bald eagles in Missouri. Oologist. 11(2):55.

1990 Wright, G.M. and B.H. Thompson. *1935.* Fauna of the National Parks of the United States. Wildlife management in the national parks. U.S.D.I. National Park Service. Fauna Series No. 2, 142 pp.

1991 Yambert, B. *1976.* Eagles cooperate at Reelfoot Lake. Tenn. Conserv. 42(4):10.

1992 Yapp, W.B. *1970.* The Life and Organization of Birds. American Elsevier Pub. Co, Inc., New York. 246 pp.

1993 Yeager, L.E. *1950.* Bald eagles attack crippled gull. Wilson Bull. 62(4):210.

1994 Young, H. *1968.* A consideration of insecticide effects on hypothetical avian populations. Ecology. 49(5):991-994.

1995 Young, P. *1965.* Old Abe: The Eagle Hero. Prentice Hall, Englewood Cliffs, N.J. 28 pp.

1996 Youngworth, W. *1933.* Migration records of eagles and snowy owls in the upper Missouri Valley. Wilson Bull. 45(1):32-33.

1997 Zeitlin, J. *1920.* Ornithological acquaintances. Oologist. 37(4):50.

1998 Zim, H.S. and I.N. Gabrielson. *1949.* Birds. Simon and Schuster, New York. 157 pp.

1999 Zimmerman, D.A. and J. Van Tyne. *1959.* A distributional check-list of the birds of Michigan. Museum of Zoology Occasional Papers 608, University of Michigan. Ann Arbor. 63 pp.

2000 Zimmerman, W.J., L.H. Schwarte and H.E. Biester. *1956.* Incidence of trichiniasis in swine pork products and wildlife in Iowa. Am. J. of Pub. Health. 46(3):313-319.

Chapter 4

Permuted List of Keywords

Master No.	Keywords
27	Acct. · OK · Road. Census · Techniques · TX
169	Acct. · NJ · Winter. Pop.
183	Acct. · AZ · Nest. · Pub. Ed.
185	Acct. · AZ · Nest. · Pub. Ed. · Winter. Pop.
186	Acct. · AZ · Endang. Sp. · Nest. · Pub. Ed. · Winter. Pop.
210	Acct. · Glacier NP · Nest.
232	Acct. · NE
287	Acct. · AR
288	Acct. · AK
344	Acct. · WV
345	Acct. · Mortality · MI
358	Acct. · Nest. · NE
410	Acct. · Intersp. Behav. · KY
419	Acct. · PA
452	Acct. · NH · Status
505	Acct. · WA
518	Acct. · Wisconsin R · WI
523	Acct. · WV
568	Acct. · Field ID · NY
571	Acct. · PA
582	Acct. · Intersp. Behav. · PA
590	Acct. · MD · WV
591	Acct. · IL · IN
593	Acct. · IL · Shooting
602	Acct. · WA
622	Acct. · IL
633	Acct. · IL
667	Acct. · AK · CA · FL · Taxonomy · VA
691	Acct. · AK
754	Acct. · Egg Coll. · OK · Shooting
759	Acct. · IL
769	Acct. · Anacapa Is. · Channel Is. · CA · Status
789	Acct. · MO
791	Acct. · CA
793	Acct. · CA · Status
817	Acct. · History · WA
818	Acct. · History · Shooting · WA
876	Acct. · Baja · CA · Nest.
905	Acct. · PA · Susquehanna R
912	Acct. · IL
924	Acct. · NY
930	Acct. · Nest. · RI
940	Acct. · AK · Nest.
949	Acct. · AL · Nest.
964	Acct. · MN · Nest.
986	Acct. · AK · Migration
987	Acct. · AK · Migration
1001	Acct. · AZ · Habit. Use
1030	Acct. · Behav. · MI
1043	Acct. · WA
1053	Acct. · WA
1056	Acct. · IL
1070	Acct. · NJ
1074	Acct. · AB · AK · NWT · YT
1075	Acct. · AB · MB · SK
1076	Acct. · AB · AK · NWT · YT
1077	Acct. · NWT
1096	Acct. · MN
1116	Acct. · Disturb. · Nest. · OK · Status · Winter. Pop.
1122	Acct. · NE · Road. Census · Techniques · Winter. Pop.
1150	Acct. · ON
1153	Acct. · MI
1182	Acct. · Nest. · WY · Yellowstone NP
1225	Acct. · NY
1236	Acct. · AZ · Grand Canyon
1238	Acct. · Winter. Pop. · WV
1282	Acct. · OK · Winter. Pop.
1557	Acct. · AK
1558	Acct. · AK · Nest.
1570	Acct. · Migration · MN
1595	Acct. · CN · Great Slave L. · NWT
1615	Acct. · MT
1669	Acct. · Habit. Use · New England
1702	Acct. · Hunt. Behav. · Nest. · NC · Prey
1721	Acct. · AK
1729	Acct. · NC · TN · Winter. Pop.
1731	Acct. · CA · Kings Canyon NP · Sequoia NP
1738	Acct. · AZ
1759	Acct. · TN · TVA
1766	Acct. · Nest. Survey · Reprod. Succ. · TX
1767	Acct. · Nest. Survey · Reprod. Succ. · TX

Master No.	Keywords
1775	Acct. · FL · Nest.
1787	Acct. · IA · Taxonomy
1886	Acct. · Disturb. · Douglas Pt. Nuc. Plant · MD
1897	Acct. · SD
1936	Acct. · MI · Shooting
1986	Acct. · GA · Nest. · Okefinokee Swamp
959	Agassiz NWR · Chippewa NF · Itasca SP · MN · Nest. Survey · Superior NF · Tamarac NWR
55	Aggress. · Flight · Folklore · History · Hunt. Behav. · Intersp. Behav.
56	Aggress. · Flight · Folklore · History · Hunt. Behav. · Intersp. Behav.
57	Aggress. · Intrasp. Behav.
64	Aggress. · Folklore · IL
76	Aggress. · Folklore · KY
89	Aggress. · Disturb.
93	Aggress. · Econ. Import. · Folklore · Hunt. Behav.
108	Aggress. · Band. · Broley · Prey · Status · Techniques
245	Aggress. · IL · Law · Shooting
255	Aggress. · Egg Coll. · FL · Nest. · Shooting · Status
273	Aggress. · Behav. · Captivity · Distrib. · Egg Coll. · Habit. Use · Life History · Nest. · Status
274	Aggress. · Behav. · Captivity · Distrib. · Habit. Use · Life History · Nest. · Status
337	Aggress. · Band. · Broley · FL · Techniques
429	Aggress. · History · Hunt. Behav. · Life History · Nest. · Poetry · PA · Shooting · Status · Susquehanna R
578	Aggress. · Band. · Behav. · Mortality · Nest. · Photo. · Pub. Ed. · Techniques
774	Aggress. · Behav. · CN · Disturb. · ON · Reprod. Succ.
802	Aggress. · AK · Intersp. Behav.
882	Aggress. · Behav. · Disturb. · Life History · Nest. · OH · PA
932	Aggress. · CA · Nest. · Santa Cruz
967	Aggress. · Captivity · Growth
976	Aggress. · Anat. · Bounty · Distrib. · Econ. Import. · Law · Life History · Plumage · Prey · Status · Taxonomy
1025	Aggress. · Econ. Import. · Field ID · Law · Life History · Prey
1172	Aggress. · Folklore · Intersp. Behav.
1298	Aggress. · WY · Yellowstone NP
1521	Aggress. · Behav. · Disturb. · Habit. Loss · Hunt. Behav. · Nest. · Prey · San Juan Is. · Shooting · Status · Vocal. · WA
1606	Aggress. · Aleutian Is. · AK · Behav. · Depred. · Habit. Use · Life History · Mortality · Nest. Survey · Plumage · Prey · Reprod. Succ. · Status · Winter Survey
1606	Aggress. · Aleutian Is. · AK · Behav. · Depred. · Habit. Use · Life History · Mortality · Nest. Survey · Plumage · Prey · Reprod. Succ. · Status · Winter Survey
1634	Aggress. · Aleutian Is. · Amchitka Is. · AK · Disturb. · Prey
1640	Aggress. · Behav. · BLM · Disturb. · Habit. Loss · Habit. Use · Hunt. Behav. · Life History · Manage. · Nest. · Pest. · Prey · Shooting · Territory
1640	Aggress. · Behav. · BLM · Disturb. · Habit. Loss · Habit. Use · Hunt. Behav. · Life History · Manage. · Nest. · Pest. · Prey · Shooting · Territory
1776	Aggress. · Folklore
531	Aging · AK · Behav. · Hunt. Behav. · Life History · Nest. · Prey · Sexing · Techniques
1012	Aging · Behav. · Nest. · Techniques · VA
1221	Aging · Behav. · Hunt. Behav. · Impound. · Intrasp. Behav. · MI · Nest. · Ottawa NF · Techniques · Territory
1653	Aging · Molt. · Techniques
405	Aircraft · Poetry
572	Aircraft · Behav. · CA · Distrib. · Disturb. · Habit. Loss · Hunt. Behav. · Klamath R · Manage. · Nest.
696	Aircraft · Chippewa NF · Model · MN · Statistics · Techniques
1635	Aircraft · Disturb.
1825	Aircraft · Chippewa NF · Great Lakes · MI · MN · Nest. Survey · Reprod. Succ. · Status · USFS · WI
1645	Aircraft Coll.
49	Aleutian Is. · Amchitka Is. · AK · AOU · Habit. Loss · Status
383	Aleutian Is. · AK · Nest.

Master No.	Keywords
389	**Aleutian Is.** · AK · Nest. · Winter. Pop.
577	**Aleutian Is.** · AK · Bounty · Habit. Use · Nest. · Status · Symbolism
1041	**Aleutian Is.** · Amchitka Is. · AK · Nest. · Poison. · Prey
1042	**Aleutian Is.** · AK · Hunt. Behav. · Nest. · Prey · Status
1066	**Aleutian Is.** · Amchitka Is. · AK · Nest. · Prey
1296	**Aleutian Is.** · AK · Econ. Import. · Prey
1297	**Aleutian Is.** · AK · Band. · Distrib. · Econ. Import. · Nest. · Plumage · Prey · Shooting · Techniques
1554	**Aleutian Is.** · Aleutian Is. NWR · AK
1605	**Aleutian Is.** · AK · Hunt. Behav. · Prey
1606	**Aleutian Is.** · Aggress. · AK · Behav. · Depred. · Habit. Use · Life History · Mortality · Nest. Survey · Plumage · Prey · Reprod. Succ. · Status · Winter Survey
1634	**Aleutian Is.** · Aggress. · Amchitka Is. · AK · Disturb. · Prey
1554	**Aleutian Is. NWR** · Aleutian Is. · AK
849	**Allegan SF** · Kalamazoo R · MI · Nest.
49	**Amchitka Is.** · Aleutian Is. · AK · AOU · Habit. Loss · Status
1041	**Amchitka Is.** · Aleutian Is. · AK · Nest. · Poison. · Prey
1066	**Amchitka Is.** · Aleutian Is. · AK · Nest. · Prey
1634	**Amchitka Is.** · Aggress. · Aleutian Is. · AK · Disturb. · Prey
1931	**Amchitka Is.** · AK · Egg. Thin. · Habit. Use · Nest. Survey · Prey · Winter Survey
189	**Anacapa Is.** · CA · Egg Coll.
228	**Anacapa Is.** · CA · Nest. · Status
381	**Anacapa Is.** · Behav. · CA · Egg Coll. · Shooting
769	**Anacapa Is.** · Acct. · Channel Is. · CA · Status
1455	**Anacapa Is.** · CA · Nest.
202	**Anal. Tech.** · AR · Mass Spectro. · MN · PCB · Residues · Techniques
527	**Anal. Tech.** · Biochem. · Blood · Sexing · Steroids · Techniques
528	**Anal. Tech.** · Blood · Dieldrin · Heavy Metals · Pest.
33	**Anat.** · Taxonomy

Master No.	Keywords
148	**Anat.** · Autumn Conc. · FL · Glacier NP · Manage. · Merritt Is. NWR · Museum Specimen · MT · Nest. · Prey · Taxonomy
175	**Anat.** · Capture · CO · San Luis Valley · Techniques · Winter Survey
191	**Anat.** · Growth · Plumage · Taxonomy
211	**Anat.** · Distrib. · Nest. · NM · Plumage · Prey · Winter. Pop.
221	**Anat.** · Distrib. · Nest. · Plumage · Taxonomy
227	**Anat.** · Taxonomy
249	**Anat.** · Distrib. · Life History · MI · Plumage · Status
258	**Anat.** · Nest. · NY · Prey · Status · Winter. Pop.
265	**Anat.** · Eye
266	**Anat.** · Behav. · BC · Distrib. · Falconry · Field ID · Flight · Habit. Use · Migration · Nest. · Prey · Status
322	**Anat.** · FL · Plumage · Weight
353	**Anat.** · Behav. · Distrib. · Life History · Nest. · Status
426	**Anat.** · Plumage
427	**Anat.** · Distrib. · Field ID
444	**Anat.** · Folklore · Hunt. Behav. · NC · Shooting
507	**Anat.** · Behav. · Captivity · Distrib. · Nest. · WA
543	**Anat.** · IA · Migration · Nest. · Taxonomy · Winter. Pop.
664	**Anat.** · Econ. Import. · Hunt. Behav. · Life History · Prey
701	**Anat.** · Distrib. · Life History · Plumage
741	**Anat.** · Taxonomy
742	**Anat.** · NY · Shooting · Taxonomy
745	**Anat.** · CN · Distrib. · Field ID · Nest. · Taxonomy
764	**Anat.** · Behav. · Taxonomy
773	**Anat.** · CN · ON
797	**Anat.** · Behav. · Field ID · Plumage · Taxonomy
846	**Anat.** · Distrib. · Taxonomy
853	**Anat.** · Pub. Ed. · Status
865	**Anat.** · Evolution · Plumage
866	**Anat.** · Climatology · Field ID · Migration · Status
917	**Anat.** · Field ID · Plumage
927	**Anat.** · CA · FL · NE · NM · OR · Paleontology · Taxonomy

Master No.	Keywords
976	**Anat.** · Aggress. · Bounty · Distrib. · Econ. Import. · Law · Life History · Plumage · Prey · Status · Taxonomy
1084	**Anat.** · Hunt. Behav. · Life History · Migration · Nest. · Plumage
1229	**Anat.** · Autumn Conc. · Behav. · Capture · Glacier NP · Habit. Use · Manage. · Marking · Migration · MT · Techniques · Winter Survey
1247	**Anat.** · Taxonomy
1372	**Anat.** · Distrib. · Habit. Use · Nest. · Plumage · Taxonomy · TX · Winter. Pop.
1603	**Anat.** · NH · Taxonomy · Winter. Pop.
1642	**Anat.** · Dimorphism · Hunt. Behav. · Prey
1644	**Anat.**
1651	**Anat.** · Behav. · Capture · Hunt. Behav. · IL · Marking · Plumage · Prey · Techniques · Telemetry · Winter Survey
1735	**Anat.** · Field ID · Taxonomy
1797	**Anat.** · Taxonomy · WA
1899	**Anat.** · Art · Pub. Ed.
1907	**Anat.** · AK · Bounty · Nest. · Plumage · Status
1957	**Anat.** · Hunt. Behav. · Life History · Taxonomy
1988	**Anat.** · Behav. · Capture · Depred. · Econ. Import. · Intersp. Behav. · Manage. · NB · Prey · Techniques
1989	**Anat.** · Migration · MO · Shooting
1992	**Anat.** · Evolution
235	**Animal Dam.** · AK · Bounty · Law · Prey
1405	**Anthro.** · IL
1406	**Anthro.** · SD
257	**Apostle Is.** · Nest. · WI
1143	**Archaeology** · KY
1114	**Arkansas R** · Band. · Capture · Habit. Use · Intersp. Behav. · OK · Salt Plains NWR · Sequoyah NWR · Techniques · Wichita Mts. NWR · Winter Survey · Winter. Pop.
54	**Art** · Skagit R · Winter. Pop. · WA
82	**Art** · Symbolism
84	**Art** · History · Symbolism
92	**Art** · History · PA · Symbolism
94	**Art** · Broley · Field ID · Plumage · Pub. Ed.
136	**Art** · History · Symbolism

Master No.	Keywords
237	**Art** · Educ. Mat.
461	**Art** · History · Mortality · Status · Symbolism
533	**Art**
921	**Art** · History · Symbolism
1038	**Art** · Audubon
1067	**Art** · Broley · Catesby · FL · Hudson R · Winter. Pop.
1864	**Art** · History · Indian Culture · USFWS
1899	**Art** · Anat. · Pub. Ed.
1925	**Art** · Life History · Pub. Ed.
559	**Art. Nest Site** · Behav. · Habit. Use · Manage. · MN · Nest. · Techniques · Young Trans.
804	**Art. Nest Site** · AZ · Egg. Thin. · Habit. Use · Life History · Manage. · Marking · Nest. · Pest. · Research · Techniques · Telemetry · Winter. Pop.
1467	**Art. Nest Site** · Manage. · MI · Nest.
460	**Asper.** · Autopsy · Disease · MO · Rehab. · Techniques · Trapping
1383	**Asper.** · Disease
1384	**Asper.** · Nest. Survey · OR · Road. Census · Techniques · Winter Survey
190	**Audubon** · History · Shooting · Taxonomy
509	**Audubon** · Behav. · Nest. · TN
685	**Audubon** · Behav. · Life History
1038	**Audubon** · Art
269	**Autopsy** · FL · Heavy Metals · Midwest Region · MD · ME · MO · ND · Pest. · PCB
372	**Autopsy** · AK · Cont. U.S. · DDT · NB · Pest. · Residues · Toxicol.
459	**Autopsy** · AK · CN · Disease · Lower 48 · Parasites · Poison. · Shooting · Trapping
460	**Autopsy** · Asper. · Disease · MO · Rehab. · Techniques · Trapping
482	**Autopsy** · Dieldrin · Disease · Electro. · Lower 48 · Pest. · Poison. · PCB · Shooting
1112	**Autopsy** · Disturb. · Habit. Use · Hunt. Behav. · Intersp. Behav. · Manage. · Migration · OK · Prey · Salt Fork R · Shooting · Status · Taxonomy · Winter Survey

Master No.	Keywords
1112	**Autopsy** · Disturb. · Habit. Use · Hunt. Behav. · Intersp. Behav. · Manage. · Migration · OK · Prey · Salt Fork R · Shooting · Status · Taxonomy · Winter Survey
1292	**Autopsy** · Disease · Electro. · Lead Poison. · Pest. · Shooting
1518	**Autopsy** · CT · FL · Pest.
1686	**Autopsy** · Cont. B.E. Proj. · Nest. Survey · NAS · Winter Survey
1694	**Autopsy** · Poison. · WY
1712	**Autopsy** · Mortality · Pest. · Toxicol.
1831	**Autopsy** · DDT · MO · NJ · Residues · Toxicol.
148	**Autumn Conc.** · Anat. · FL · Glacier NP · Manage. · Merritt Is. NWR · Museum Specimen · MT · Nest. · Prey · Taxonomy
689	**Autumn Conc.** · AK · Nest.
767	**Autumn Conc.** · AK · Chilkat R · Hunt. Behav. · Indian Culture · Photo. · Pub. Ed.
1229	**Autumn Conc.** · Anat. · Behav. · Capture · Glacier NP · Habit. Use · Manage. · Marking · Migration · MT · Techniques · Winter Survey
1602	**Autumn Conc.** · Glacier NP · Hunt. Behav. · MT · Prey
516	**AB** · Migration
1073	**AB** · Disturb. · Nest. Survey · NWT
1074	**AB** · Acct. · AK · NWT · YT
1075	**AB** · Acct. · MB · SK
1076	**AB** · Acct. · AK · NWT · YT
26	**AK** · Depred. · Endang. Sp. · Life History · OR · WA
34	**AK** · Taxonomy
49	**AK** · Aleutian Is. · Amchitka Is. · AOU · Habit. Loss · Status
60	**AK** · Taxonomy
61	**AK** · Nest.
66	**AK** · Bounty · Pub. Ed.
67	**AK** · Bounty · Pub. Ed.
68	**AK** · Bounty · Pub. Ed.
69	**AK** · Bounty · Law · Pub. Ed. · Status
70	**AK** · Bounty · Pub. Ed.
97	**AK** · Bounty · Law
100	**AK** · Bounty · Law
101	**AK** · Bounty · Law
102	**AK** · Bounty · Law · Status
103	**AK** · Bounty · Law
104	**AK** · Bounty · Law
105	**AK** · Bounty · Law

Master No.	Keywords
106	**AK** · Bounty · Law
140	**AK** · DDT · FL · ME · Pest. · Reprod. Succ. · WI
205	**AK** · Nest. · Shooting
223	**AK** · Law
224	**AK** · Bounty · Law
229	**AK** · Pub. Ed.
235	**AK** · Animal Dam. · Bounty · Law · Prey
236	**AK** · Bounty · Law
242	**AK** · Bounty · Status
285	**AK** · Nest. · Shooting
288	**AK** · Acct.
292	**AK** · Hunt. Behav.
365	**AK** · Bounty · NAS · Shooting
372	**AK** · Autopsy · Cont. U.S. · DDT · NB · Pest. · Residues · Toxicol.
383	**AK** · Aleutian Is. · Nest.
389	**AK** · Aleutian Is. · Nest. · Winter. Pop.
404	**AK** · Egg Coll. · Nest. · Shooting
431	**AK** · Behav. · Climatology · Disease · Kodiak NWR · Life History · Marking · Nest. · Nest. Survey · Parasites · Reprod. Succ. · Techniques · Terminology
459	**AK** · Autopsy · CN · Disease · Lower 48 · Parasites · Poison. · Shooting · Trapping
465	**AK** · Disturb. · Habit. Loss · Habit. Use · Logging · Nest. · Nest. Survey · Territory
466	**AK** · Climatology · Distrib. · Disturb. · Forestry · Habit. Loss · Habit. Use · Manage. · Nest. · Nest. Survey · Reprod. Succ. · Territory
471	**AK** · Bounty · Econ. Import.
472	**AK** · Econ. Import. · Prey
484	**AK** · Chilkat R · Prey · Shooting · Winter Survey
489	**AK** · Habit. Use · Indian Culture · Prey
490	**AK** · Hunt. Behav. · Prey
531	**AK** · Aging · Behav. · Hunt. Behav. · Life History · Nest. · Prey · Sexing · Techniques
566	**AK** · FL · ME · MI · MN · PCB
577	**AK** · Aleutian Is. · Bounty · Habit. Use · Nest. · Status · Symbolism
588	**AK** · Law · Pub. Ed.
662	**AK** · Bounty · Growth · Law · Photo. · Shooting
667	**AK** · Acct. · CA · FL · Taxonomy · VA
688	**AK** · Nest.

Master No.	Keywords
689	AK · Autumn Conc. · Nest.
690	AK · Nest. · Winter. Pop.
691	AK · Acct.
692	AK · Nest. · Winter. Pop.
711	AK · Distrib. · Habit. Use · Life History · Plumage · Status
720	AK · Intersp. Behav. · Karluk L · Prey
737	AK · Depred. · Nest. · Prey · Shooting
753	AK · Lower 48 · Manage. · Status
767	AK · Autumn Conc. · Chilkat R · Hunt. Behav. · Indian Culture · Photo. · Pub. Ed.
802	AK · Aggress. · Intersp. Behav.
807	AK · Bounty · Law
813	AK · Econ. Import.
825	AK · Comm. Conserv. · CN · Lower 48 · Status · Wilson Ornithol. Soc.
844	AK · Disturb. · Econ. Import.
863	AK · Habit. Use · Hunt. Behav. · Nest. Survey · Prey · Status
878	AK · Disturb. · Habit. Use · Kodiak NWR · Life History · Nest. Fail. · Reprod. Succ. · Territory
919	AK · Bounty · Pub. Ed. · Status
940	AK · Acct. · Nest.
986	AK · Acct. · Migration
987	AK · Acct. · Migration
989	AK · Habit. Use · Migration · Nest. · Winter. Pop.
1041	AK · Aleutian Is. · Amchitka Is. · Nest. · Poison. · Prey
1042	AK · Aleutian Is. · Hunt. Behav. · Nest. · Prey · Status
1044	AK · Nest.
1048	AK · Habit. Use · Nest. Survey · Techniques
1066	AK · Aleutian Is. · Amchitka Is. · Nest. · Prey
1074	AK · Acct. · AB · NWT · YT
1076	AK · Acct. · AB · NWT · YT
1141	AK · CN · Egg Coll. · Intersp. Behav. · Nest.
1184	AK · CN · Lower 48 · Status
1296	AK · Aleutian Is. · Econ. Import. · Prey
1297	AK · Aleutian Is. · Band. · Distrib. · Econ. Import. · Nest. · Plumage · Prey · Shooting · Techniques
1359	AK · Lower 48 · Nest. Survey · USFWS
1373	AK · Hunt. Behav. · Prey
1393	AK · Bounty · Law · Pub. Ed.
1394	AK · Bounty · Shooting
1418	AK · Bounty · Law
1419	AK · Bounty · Law · NAS · Pub. Ed. · Shooting
1420	AK · Bounty · Law · Shooting
1421	AK · Bounty · Law · Shooting
1422	AK · Bounty · Law · Shooting
1424	AK · Bounty · Law · Shooting
1529	AK · Habit. Use · Hunt. Behav. · Manage. · Pub. Ed. · Status
1530	AK · Habit. Use · Manage. · Nest. Survey · Territory
1554	AK · Aleutian Is. · Aleutian Is. NWR
1557	AK · Acct.
1558	AK · Acct. · Nest.
1605	AK · Aleutian Is. · Hunt. Behav. · Prey
1606	AK · Aggress. · Aleutian Is. · Behav. · Depred. · Habit. Use · Life History · Mortality · Nest. Survey · Plumage · Prey · Reprod. Succ. · Status · Winter Survey
1634	AK · Aggress. · Aleutian Is. · Amchitka Is. · Disturb. · Prey
1643	AK · Nest. · Shooting
1708	AK · Histology · Lower 48 · Pest. · Spermato. · Techniques · Toxicol. · USFWS
1721	AK · Acct.
1780	AK · Bounty · Pub. Ed.
1804	AK · Habit. Use · Kodiak Is. · Kodiak NWR · Nest. Survey
1829	AK · Band. · Behav. · Kodiak NWR · Nest. Survey · Reprod. Succ. · Techniques
1841	AK · Life History · Manage. · Status
1850	AK · Lower 48 · Nest. Survey · Reprod. Succ. · USFWS
1889	AK · Bounty · Econ. Import. · Prey
1890	AK · Bounty · Pub. Ed. · Status
1903	AK · Econ. Import. · Prey
1907	AK · Anat. · Bounty · Nest. · Plumage · Status
1929	AK · Bounty · Logging · Manage.
1930	AK · Nest. · YT
1931	AK · Amchitka Is. · Egg. Thin. · Habit. Use · Nest. Survey · Prey · Winter Survey
1932	AK · Disturb. · Helicop. · Nest. Survey · Techniques
1942	AK · Egg. Thin. · FL · Great Lakes · Heavy Metals · ME · Pest. · PCB
1947	AK · Forrester Is. · Nest. Survey
1949	AK · Econ. Import.

Master No.	Keywords
1954	AK · Hunt. Behav. · Law · Migration · Nest. · Pub. Ed. · WY · Yellowstone NP
1955	AK · Hunt. Behav. · Law · Migration · Nest. · Pub. Ed. · WY · Yellowstone NP
282	AL · Depred. · Prey
934	AL · Nest. · Prey · Shooting · TN · Winter. Pop.
949	AL · Acct. · Nest.
973	AL · Nest. · Prey · Winter. Pop.
1951	AL · Wheeler NWR · Winter. Pop.
48	AOU · Comm. Conserv. · Endang. Sp. · Law · Status
49	AOU · Aleutian Is. · Amchitka Is. · AK · Habit. Loss · Status
52	AOU · Comm. Conserv. · Status
441	AOU · Comm. Bird Prot. · FL · Status
442	AOU · Comm. Bird Prot. · FL · Status
178	AR · Field ID · Winter Survey · Winter. Pop.
202	AR · Anal. Tech. · Mass Spectro. · MN · PCB · Residues · Techniques
287	AR · Acct.
715	AR · Habit. Use · Mississippi R · MS · Nest. · Reelfoot L · Shooting · TN
913	AR · Shooting · Taxidermy
933	AR · Habit. Use · Shooting · Winter. Pop.
970	AR · Nest.
1039	AR · Winter Survey
1488	AR · Band. · FL · GA · Manage. · Migration · MI · Techniques · TN · Young Trans.
1569	AR · Migration
173	AZ · Marking · Pub. Ed. · Techniques · Verde R
182	AZ · CAP · Falconry · Habit. Loss · Law · Orme D
183	AZ · Acct. · Nest. · Pub. Ed.
184	AZ · Endang. Sp.
185	AZ · Acct. · Nest. · Pub. Ed. · Winter. Pop.
186	AZ · Acct. · Endang. Sp. · Nest. · Pub. Ed. · Winter. Pop.
409	AZ · Grand Canyon · Nest. · Status · Winter. Pop.
449	AZ · CAP · Habit. Loss · Nest. · Orme D · Salt R · Verde R
770	AZ · CAP · Disturb. · Habit. Use · Manage. · Nest. · Orme D
804	AZ · Art. Nest Site · Egg. Thin. · Habit. Use · Life History · Manage. · Marking · Nest. · Pest. · Research · Techniques · Telemetry · Winter. Pop.
900	AZ · Nest. · Photo. · Techniques
1001	AZ · Acct. · Habit. Use
1004	AZ · CAP · Endang. Sp. · Habit. Loss · Orme D
1008	AZ · Status · Verde R
1091	AZ · Captivity · Falconry · Intersp. Behav.
1179	AZ · Habit. Loss · Nest. · Orme D
1236	AZ · Acct. · Grand Canyon
1245	AZ · Nest.
1459	AZ · Nest. · Winter. Pop.
1550	AZ · Behav. · Disturb. · Habit. Loss · Habit. Use · Hunt. Behav. · Nest. Survey · Prey · Status · Terminology · Territory
1633	AZ · Pub. Ed.
1639	AZ · CA · Endang. Sp. · NM · NV · OK · Status · TX · UT
1737	AZ · Nest. · Winter. Pop.
1738	AZ · Acct.
1788	AZ · Winter. Pop.
1789	AZ · Disturb. · Nest. Survey · Verde R
1790	AZ · Nest. · Winter. Pop.
1791	AZ · Electro. · Nest. Survey · Winter Survey
1792	AZ · Disturb. · Nest.
1793	AZ · CAP · Nest. Survey · Orme D · Salt R · Verde R
1794	AZ · Techniques · Winter Survey
1838	AZ · CO · KS · Nest. Survey · NM · OK · Salt Fork R · TX · USFWS · UT · Verde R · WY
1852	AZ · Manage. · Nest. Survey · NM · OK · Salt Fork R · TX · USFWS · Verde R
1865	AZ · BLM · CAP · Egg · Habit. Prot. · Manage. · Nest. · Orme D · Salt R · Taxonomy · Territory · Verde R
1866	AZ · Nest. Survey · USFWS
1965	AZ · CAP · Habit. Loss · Nest. · Orme D
1966	AZ · CAP · Nest. · Orme D
174	B.E. Nat. Area · Marking · Pub. Ed. · Skagit R · Techniques · WA
1816	B.E. Prot. Act · Law
1819	B.E. Prot. Act · Law

Master No.	Keywords
876	**Baja** · Acct. · CA · Nest.
877	**Baja** · CA · Nest. Survey
867	**Bake Oven Knob** · Migration · PA
868	**Bake Oven Knob** · Migration · PA
869	**Bake Oven Knob** · Migration · PA
108	**Band.** · Aggress. · Broley · Prey · Status · Techniques
324	**Band.** · FL · Life History · Migration · Nest. Fail. · Nest. Survey · Prey · Status · Techniques
327	**Band.** · FL · Habit. Loss · Intersp. Behav. · Nest. Fail. · Pub. Ed. · Shooting · Status · Techniques
332	**Band.** · FL · ON · Pest. · Pub. Ed. · Reprod. Succ. · Techniques
336	**Band.** · FL · Intersp. Behav. · Techniques
337	**Band.** · Aggress. · Broley · FL · Techniques
338	**Band.** · Broley · Dispersal · FL · Life History · Techniques
339	**Band.** · Broley · FL · Life History · Pub. Ed. · Status · Techniques
439	**Band.** · Cape May · Capture · Migration · NJ · Techniques
440	**Band.** · Capture · Migration · NJ · Sandy Hook · Techniques
547	**Band.** · IL · MN · Techniques · TX · WI
550	**Band.** · Breed. Behav. · Dieldrin · DDT · MN · Pest. · Pest. Residues · Prey · Techniques · Telemetry
552	**Band.** · Migration · MN · Techniques · Trapping · TX
554	**Band.** · Behav. · Cedar Glen Roost · IL · Migration · Mississippi R · MN · Refuge · Techniques · Telemetry · TX · Winter. Pop.
560	**Band.** · Behav. · Life History · Migration · MN · Reprod. Succ. · Techniques
574	**Band.** · Behav. · Growth · Nest. · Photo. · Pub. Ed. · Techniques
576	**Band.** · Behav. · Photo. · Pub. Ed. · Status · Techniques
578	**Band.** · Aggress. · Behav. · Mortality · Nest. · Photo. · Pub. Ed. · Techniques
589	**Band.** · Broley · FL · Techniques
729	**Band.** · Reprod. Succ. · SK · Techniques
730	**Band.** · Migration · Pub. Ed. · Status · SK · Techniques
733	**Band.** · Great Lakes · Migration · ON · Techniques
756	**Band.** · Egg Trans. · Manage. · ME · Nest. Survey · Pest. · PCB · Refuge · Techniques · Winter Survey
757	**Band.** · Disturb. · Manage. · Marking · ME · Nest. · Nest. Survey · Shooting · Techniques
772	**Band.** · Behav. · CN · ON · Reprod. Succ. · Techniques
843	**Band.** · Behav. · Chippewa NF · Dispersal · Fledging · Migration · MN · Nestling · Techniques · Telemetry
1000	**Band.** · MN · Techniques · Telemetry
1114	**Band.** · Arkansas R · Capture · Habit. Use · Intersp. Behav. · OK · Salt Plains NWR · Sequoyah NWR · Techniques · Wichita Mts. NWR · Winter Survey · Winter. Pop.
1136	**Band.** · Jackson's Canyon · Techniques · Winter Survey · WY
1137	**Band.** · Poison. · Prey · Pub. Ed. · Techniques · Winter Survey · WY
1196	**Band.** · Chippewa NF · IL · MN · Nest. Survey · Techniques · USFS · Winter. Pop.
1214	**Band.** · Chippewa NF · Marking · MN · Nest. Survey · Techniques
1217	**Band.** · Chippewa NF · MN · Nest. Survey · Status · Techniques · USFS
1223	**Band.** · Chippewa NF · MN · Nest. Survey · Reprod. Succ. · Status · Superior NF · Techniques · Terminology
1297	**Band.** · Aleutian Is. · AK · Distrib. · Econ. Import. · Nest. · Plumage · Prey · Shooting · Techniques
1448	**Band.** · FL · Migration · Prey · Techniques
1487	**Band.** · Disturb. · Great Lakes · MI · Nest. Survey · Pest. · Techniques
1488	**Band.** · AR · FL · GA · Manage. · Migration · MI · Techniques · TN · Young Trans.
1531	**Band.** · Christmas Count · Life History · Migration · Nest. · Status · USFWS · Winter Survey
1596	**Band.** · Broley · FL · Techniques
1610	**Band.** · Behav. · Dispersal · MN · Techniques · WI
1649	**Band.** · Capture · IL · Techniques · Winter. Pop.

Master No.	Keywords
1656	**Band.** · Migration · Pub. Ed. · Techniques · Winter. Pop.
1684	**Band.** · Field ID · FL · Life History · Nest. · Prey · Status · Techniques
1705	**Band.** · DC · Migration · MD · Nest. · Techniques · Winter. Pop.
1728	**Band.** · MN · Techniques · WI
1769	**Band.** · Nest. Survey · Reprod. Succ. · Techniques · TX · Winter Survey
1799	**Band.** · ME · Techniques
1829	**Band.** · AK · Behav. · Kodiak NWR · Nest. Survey · Reprod. Succ. · Techniques
827	**Barkley Sound** · Behav. · BC · Disturb. · Gulf Is. · Helicop. · Nest. Survey · Plumage · Prey
829	**Barkley Sound** · BC · Disturb. · Gulf Is. · Helicop.
1883	**Bear Valley NWR** · Habit. Prot. · OR · Refuge · USFWS
43	**Behav.** · Evolution · Reprod. Succ.
75	**Behav.** · Nest. · OH
80	**Behav.** · Life History · Nest. · OH
159	**Behav.** · Disturb. · IA · IL · MN
233	**Behav.** · Captive Breed.
266	**Behav.** · Anat. · BC · Distrib. · Falconry · Field ID · Flight · Habit. Use · Migration · Nest. · Prey · Status
273	**Behav.** · Aggress. · Captivity · Distrib. · Egg Coll. · Habit. Use · Life History · Nest. · Status
274	**Behav.** · Aggress. · Captivity · Distrib. · Habit. Use · Life History · Nest. · Status
303	**Behav.** · Illinois R · Winter. Pop.
325	**Behav.** · Dispersal · Disturb. · FL · Habit. Use · Intersp. Behav. · Migration · Mortality · Nest. · Prey
331	**Behav.** · Broley · FL
350	**Behav.** · Life History · Poetry
352	**Behav.** · Flight · Life History · Migration · Nest. · Prey · Pub. Ed. · Status · Taxonomy
353	**Behav.** · Anat. · Distrib. · Life History · Nest. · Status
361	**Behav.** · Disturb. · Nest. · ND · Photo.
381	**Behav.** · Anacapa Is. · CA · Egg Coll. · Shooting
431	**Behav.** · AK · Climatology · Disease · Kodiak NWR · Life History · Marking · Nest. · Nest. Survey · Parasites · Reprod. Succ. · Techniques · Terminology
432	**Behav.** · Captivity · DDT · Pest. · Toxicol.
447	**Behav.** · CA · Disturb. · Hunt. Behav. · Manage. · Natl. For. · Prey · San Bernardino Mts. · USFS · Winter. Pop.
497	**Behav.** · Egg · Nest. · OH · Poison. · Prey · Shooting
507	**Behav.** · Anat. · Captivity · Distrib. · Nest. · WA
509	**Behav.** · Audubon · Nest. · TN
531	**Behav.** · Aging · AK · Hunt. Behav. · Life History · Nest. · Prey · Sexing · Techniques
554	**Behav.** · Band. · Cedar Glen Roost · IL · Migration · Mississippi R · MN · Refuge · Techniques · Telemetry · TX · Winter. Pop.
555	**Behav.** · Breed. Behav. · Chippewa NF · Disturb. · Fledging · Marking · MN · Nestling · Prey · Reprod. Succ. · Techniques · Telemetry
559	**Behav.** · Art. Nest Site · Habit. Use · Manage. · MN · Nest. · Techniques · Young Trans.
560	**Behav.** · Band. · Life History · Migration · MN · Reprod. Succ. · Techniques
561	**Behav.** · Fledging · Habit. Use · Marking · MN · Parent. Behav. · Techniques · Telemetry
572	**Behav.** · Aircraft · CA · Distrib. · Disturb. · Habit. Loss · Hunt. Behav. · Klamath R · Manage. · Nest.
574	**Behav.** · Band. · Growth · Nest. · Photo. · Pub. Ed. · Techniques
575	**Behav.** · Growth · Nest. · Photo. · Prey · Pub. Ed.
576	**Behav.** · Band. · Photo. · Pub. Ed. · Status · Techniques
578	**Behav.** · Aggress. · Band. · Mortality · Nest. · Photo. · Pub. Ed. · Techniques
579	**Behav.** · Nest. · Pub. Ed. · Status
599	**Behav.** · Disturb. · FL · Migration · Nest. · Nest. Fail.

Master No.	Keywords
609	Behav. · Habit. Use · Mississippi R · MN · Pest. Residues · Prey · Winter Survey
683	Behav. · CA · Distrib. · Disturb. · Field ID · Flight · Hunt. Behav. · Life History · Manage. · Mortality · Nest. · Winter. Pop.
685	Behav. · Audubon · Life History
695	Behav. · Chippewa NF · Disturb. · Logging · MN · Nest. · Reprod. Succ.
699	Behav. · Chippewa NF · Fledging · Nestling · Techniques · Telemetry
727	Behav. · Nestling · Parent. Behav. · SK
731	Behav. · Disturb. · Nestling · Parent. Behav. · SK
764	Behav. · Anat. · Taxonomy
772	Behav. · Band. · CN · ON · Reprod. Succ. · Techniques
774	Behav. · Aggress. · CN · Disturb. · ON · Reprod. Succ.
786	Behav. · Distrib. · Hunt. Behav. · Manage. · Marking · Migration · Mortality · MO · Nest. · Pest. · Prey · Swan Lake NWR · Techniques · Telemetry
786	Behav. · Distrib. · Hunt. Behav. · Manage. · Marking · Migration · Mortality · MO · Nest. · Pest. · Prey · Swan Lake NWR · Techniques · Telemetry
792	Behav. · CA · Habit. Use · Intersp. Behav. · Nest. · Winter. Pop.
797	Behav. · Anat. · Field ID · Plumage · Taxonomy
808	Behav. · Flight · Poetry
827	Behav. · Barkley Sound · BC · Disturb. · Gulf Is. · Helicop. · Nest. Survey · Plumage · Prey
836	Behav. · Disturb. · Habit. Loss · Habit. Use · Hunt. Behav. · Logging · · Manage. · Prey · Winter Survey · WA
840	Behav. · Capture · CO · Habit. Use · Marking · Migration · Techniques · Winter Survey
841	Behav. · Chippewa NF · Dispersal · Disturb. · Fledging · MN · Nestling · Techniques · Telemetry
842	Behav. · Chippewa NF · Dispersal · Fledging · Hunt. Behav. · MN · Nestling · Techniques · Telemetry
843	Behav. · Band. · Chippewa NF · Dispersal · Fledging · Migration · MN · Nestling · Techniques · Telemetry
851	Behav. · Great Lakes · Migration
880	Behav. · Life History · Nest. · Nestling · OH · Parent. Behav. · Photo. · Techniques
881	Behav. · Fledging · Life History · Nest. · Nestling · OH
882	Behav. · Aggress. · Disturb. · Life History · Nest. · OH · PA
883	Behav. · Fledging · Hunt. Behav. · Life History · Nest. · OH · Prey
884	Behav. · History · Nest. · OH · Photo. · Techniques
885	Behav. · Captive Breed. · Intrasp. Behav. · Nestling · OH
887	Behav. · Life History · Nest. · OH · Photo. · Techniques
888	Behav. · Fledging · Intersp. Behav. · Life History · Nest. · OH · Parent. Behav. · Photo. · Prey
889	Behav. · Life History · Nest. · OH · Photo. · Techniques
891	Behav. · Life History · Nest. · OH · Prey
953	Behav. · Nest. · SC
968	Behav. · Growth · Habit. Use
972	Behav. · Disturb. · Habit. Use · Nest. · Snake R · WY
977	Behav. · Cannibal. · Nestling
995	Behav. · Fledging · VA · Winter. Pop.
1011	Behav. · Climatology · Habit. Use · Hunt. Behav. · Intersp. Behav. · Intrasp. Behav. · IA · IL · Mississippi R · MO · Prey · Winter Survey
1012	Behav. · Aging · Nest. · Techniques · VA
1030	Behav. · Acct. · MI
1063	Behav. · Disturb. · Habit. Loss · Habit. Use · Manage. · Prey · Research · TX · Winter Survey
1065	Behav. · CA · Disturb. · Habit. Use · Klamath · Lower Klamath Lake NWR · Manage. · OR · Prey · Tule Lake NWR · Winter Survey
1071	Behav. · Chippewa NF · Fledging · Intrasp. Behav. · Marking · Mortality · MN · Nest. · Techniques · Telemetry · Vocal.
1072	Behav. · Chippewa NF · Fledging · Marking · MN · Techniques

Master No.	Keywords
1102	**Behav.** · Caledon SP · Disturb. · Habit. Loss · Habit. Use · Manage. · Nest. · Prey · VA
1104	**Behav.** · Caledon SP · Disturb. · Habit. Loss · Habit. Use · Manage. · VA
1109	**Behav.** · Habit. Loss · Habit. Use · Intersp. Behav. · Intrasp. Behav. · ID · Manage. · Prey · Winter Survey · Wolf Lodge Bay
1118	**Behav.** · Taxonomy
1121	**Behav.** · Manage. · NE · Prey · Status · Winter Survey
1144	**Behav.** · Captivity
1149	**Behav.** · Captive Breed. · Taxonomy
1171	**Behav.** · Captivity
1221	**Behav.** · Aging · Hunt. Behav. · Impound. · Intrasp. Behav. · MI · Nest. · Ottawa NF · Techniques · Territory
1222	**Behav.** · Fledging · Hunt. Behav. · Intersp. Behav. · Intrasp. Behav. · Marking · MI · Ottawa NF · Techniques · Territory
1229	**Behav.** · Anat. · Autumn Conc. · Capture · Glacier NP · Habit. Use · Manage. · Marking · Migration · MT · Techniques · Winter Survey
1253	**Behav.** · Hacking · Heavy Metals · Intrasp. Behav. · Marking · Montezuma NWR · MI · MN · NY · Pest. · Techniques · Telemetry · Young Trans.
1256	**Behav.** · Hacking · Manage. · NY · Pest. · Prey · PCB · Techniques · Young Trans.
1336	**Behav.** · Manage. · NE · Prey · Status · Winter Survey
1342	**Behav.** · Electro. · Manage.
1368	**Behav.** · Climatology · Disturb. · Habit. Use · Hunt. Behav. · Intersp. Behav. · Intrasp. Behav. · Manage. · NY · Prey · Winter Survey
1369	**Behav.** · Habit. Use · Heavy Metals · Hunt. Behav. · Intersp. Behav. · Intrasp. Behav. · Manage. · NY · Pest. · Prey · PCB · Winter Survey
1375	**Behav.** · FL · Intersp. Behav.
1440	**Behav.** · Habit. Loss · Habit. Use · Kentucky Wood. NWR · KY · Winter Survey
1470	**Behav.** · Habit. Use · Hunt. Behav. · Prey · UT · Winter Survey
1496	**Behav.** · Chippewa NF · Fledging · Manage. · MN · Nest. · Nocturnal Behav.
1511	**Behav.** · Habit. Use · Heavy Metals · Nest. · NY · Pest. · PCB
1521	**Behav.** · Aggress. · Disturb. · Habit. Loss · Hunt. Behav. · Nest. · Prey · San Juan Is. · Shooting · Status · Vocal. · WA
1550	**Behav.** · AZ · Disturb. · Habit. Loss · Habit. Use · Hunt. Behav. · Nest. Survey · Prey · Status · Terminology · Territory
1591	**Behav.** · Climatology · Disturb. · Habit. Use · Intrasp. Behav. · Plumage · Prey · Skagit R · Winter Survey · WA
1593	**Behav.** · Migration · WA
1601	**Behav.** · Capture · Glacier NP · Hunt. Behav. · Intersp. Behav. · Intrasp. Behav. · Manage. · MT · Techniques · Winter Survey
1606	**Behav.** · Aggress. · Aleutian Is. · AK · Depred. · Habit. Use · Life History · Mortality · Nest. Survey · Plumage · Prey · Reprod. Succ. · Status · Winter Survey
1610	**Behav.** · Band. · Dispersal · MN · Techniques · WI
1640	**Behav.** · Aggress. · BLM · Disturb. · Habit. Loss · Habit. Use · Hunt. Behav. · Life History · Manage. · Nest. · Pest. · Prey · Shooting · Territory
1651	**Behav.** · Anat. · Capture · Hunt. Behav. · IL · Marking · Plumage · Prey · Techniques · Telemetry · Winter Survey
1690	**Behav.** · Disturb. · Manage. · Winter. Pop. · WA
1695	**Behav.** · Ft. Randall D · Habit. Use · Hunt. Behav. · Karl Mundt NWR · L Andes NWR · SD · Winter Survey
1699	**Behav.** · Disturb. · Ft. Randall D · Habit. Use · Manage. · Missouri R · SD · Winter Survey
1795	**Behav.** · Habit. Use · Life History · Nest. · Pub. Ed. · PA · Taxonomy
1805	**Behav.** · FL · History · Photo. · Status
1806	**Behav.** · Everglades NP · Nest. · Photo.
1807	**Behav.** · FL · Intersp. Behav. · Life History · Photo.

Master No.	Keywords
1811	**Behav.** · Habit. Loss · Pub. Ed.
1829	**Behav.** · AK · Band. · Kodiak NWR · Nest. Survey · Reprod. Succ. · Techniques
1879	**Behav.** · Hunt. Behav. · Intersp. Behav. · ID · L Couer D' Alene · Manage. · Winter Survey
1895	**Behav.** · Habit. Use · Hunt. Behav. · Intrasp. Behav. · Migration · NE · Platte R · Winter Survey
1914	**Behav.** · Chippewa NF · Disturb. · Manage. · MN · USFS
1915	**Behav.** · Migration · NE · Platte R · Prey · Winter Survey
1922	**Behav.** · Disturb. · Fledging · ON
1988	**Behav.** · Anat. · Capture · Depred. · Econ. Import. · Intersp. Behav. · Manage. · NB · Prey · Techniques
1458	**Big Cypress Swamp** · FL · Nest.
527	**Biochem.** · Anal. Tech. · Blood · Sexing · Steroids · Techniques
541	**Biochem.** · Digest. · Pellets · Prey
862	**Biochem.** · Blood · Disease · Fowl Cholera
558	**Biopsy** · MN · Pest. Residues · PCB · Techniques
527	**Blood** · Anal. Tech. · Biochem. · Sexing · Steroids · Techniques
528	**Blood** · Anal. Tech. · Dieldrin · Heavy Metals · Pest.
862	**Blood** · Biochem. · Disease · Fowl Cholera
22	**Bombay Hook NWR** · Distrib. · DE · Endang. Sp. · Field ID · Life History · Nest. · Nest. Survey · Pub. Ed. · Status
225	**Boulder D** · NV · Winter. Pop.
66	**Bounty** · AK · Pub. Ed.
67	**Bounty** · AK · Pub. Ed.
68	**Bounty** · AK · Pub. Ed.
69	**Bounty** · AK · Law · Pub. Ed. · Status
70	**Bounty** · AK · Pub. Ed.
79	**Bounty** · History · Status · Symbolism
97	**Bounty** · AK · Law
100	**Bounty** · AK · Law
101	**Bounty** · AK · Law
102	**Bounty** · AK · Law · Status
103	**Bounty** · AK · Law
104	**Bounty** · AK · Law
105	**Bounty** · AK · Law
106	**Bounty** · AK · Law
224	**Bounty** · AK · Law

Master No.	Keywords
235	**Bounty** · Animal Dam. · AK · Law · Prey
236	**Bounty** · AK · Law
242	**Bounty** · AK · Status
247	**Bounty** · CN · Depred. · Law
347	**Bounty** · Hawk Mt. · Pub. Ed. · PA · Status
365	**Bounty** · AK · NAS · Shooting
471	**Bounty** · AK · Econ. Import.
521	**Bounty** · Law · Pub. Ed. · Symbolism
522	**Bounty** · Pub. Ed. · Status
577	**Bounty** · Aleutian Is. · AK · Habit. Use · Nest. · Status · Symbolism
662	**Bounty** · AK · Growth · Law · Photo. · Shooting
807	**Bounty** · AK · Law
919	**Bounty** · AK · Pub. Ed. · Status
976	**Bounty** · Aggress. · Anat. · Distrib. · Econ. Import. · Law · Life History · Plumage · Prey · Status · Taxonomy
1393	**Bounty** · AK · Law · Pub. Ed.
1394	**Bounty** · AK · Shooting
1418	**Bounty** · AK · Law
1419	**Bounty** · AK · Law · NAS · Pub. Ed. · Shooting
1420	**Bounty** · AK · Law · Shooting
1421	**Bounty** · AK · Law · Shooting
1422	**Bounty** · AK · Law · Shooting
1424	**Bounty** · AK · Law · Shooting
1780	**Bounty** · AK · Pub. Ed.
1889	**Bounty** · AK · Econ. Import. · Prey
1890	**Bounty** · AK · Pub. Ed. · Status
1907	**Bounty** · Anat. · AK · Nest. · Plumage · Status
1929	**Bounty** · AK · Logging · Manage.
264	**Breed. Behav.** · Captive Breed. · Intersp. Behav.
550	**Breed. Behav.** · Band. · Dieldrin · DDT · MN · Pest. · Pest. Residues · Prey · Techniques · Telemetry
555	**Breed. Behav.** · Behav. · Chippewa NF · Disturb. · Fledging · Marking · MN · Nestling · Prey · Reprod. Succ. · Techniques · Telemetry
886	**Breed. Behav.** · Intersp. Behav. · Life History · Nest. · OH · Parent. Behav. · Prey
1148	**Breed. Behav.** · Captive Breed. · Intrasp. Behav. · USFWS
94	**Broley** · Art · Field ID · Plumage · Pub. Ed.

Master No.	Keywords
108	**Broley** · Aggress. · Band. · Prey · Status · Techniques
331	**Broley** · Behav. · FL
337	**Broley** · Aggress. · Band. · FL · Techniques
338	**Broley** · Band. · Dispersal · FL · Life History · Techniques
339	**Broley** · Band. · FL · Life History · Pub. Ed. · Status · Techniques
589	**Broley** · Band. · FL · Techniques
1067	**Broley** · Art · Catesby · FL · Hudson R · Winter. Pop.
1450	**Broley** · FL
1596	**Broley** · Band. · FL · Techniques
266	**BC** · Anat. · Behav. · Distrib. · Falconry · Field ID · Flight · Habit. Use · Migration · Nest. · Prey · Status
268	**BC** · CA · Nest. · OR · Status · Winter. Pop. · WA
321	**BC** · Nest.
342	**BC** · Econ. Import. · Hunt. Behav. · Prey · Shooting
401	**BC** · Hunt. Behav. · Intersp. Behav. · Prey
402	**BC** · Nest. · Winter. Pop.
826	**BC** · Gulf Is. · Habit. Use · Migration · Nest. Survey · Prey · San Juan Is. · Techniques · Winter Survey · WA
827	**BC** · Barkley Sound · Behav. · Disturb. · Gulf Is. · Helicop. · Nest. Survey · Plumage · Prey
829	**BC** · Barkley Sound · Disturb. · Gulf Is. · Helicop.
830	**BC** · Helicop. · Nest. Survey · Techniques
831	**BC** · Disturb. · Helicop. · Nest. Survey · Pest. · Refuge
832	**BC** · Intrasp. Behav. · Marking · Nest. Survey · Pub. Ed. · Techniques · Territory
833	**BC** · Hunt. Behav. · Intersp. Behav. · Intrasp. Behav. · Nest. Survey · Prey · Territory
910	**BC** · History · Indian Culture
1293	**BC** · Hunt. Behav.
1294	**BC** · Hunt. Behav. · Intersp. Behav. · Nest. · Prey
1374	**BC** · Hunt. Behav. · Intersp. Behav.
1411	**BC** · Hunt. Behav. · Nest. · Vancouver Is.
1412	**BC** · Hunt. Behav. · Intersp. Behav.
1413	**BC** · Hunt. Behav. · Intersp. Behav.
1502	**BC** · Intersp. Behav. · Prey
1590	**BC** · Hunt. Behav. · Intersp. Behav.
1803	**BC** · Gulf Is. · Nest. Survey · Winter Survey
1380	**BLM** · Endang. Sp. · Manage. · Pub. Ed.
1640	**BLM** · Aggress. · Behav. · Disturb. · Habit. Loss · Habit. Use · Hunt. Behav. · Life History · Manage. · Nest. · Pest. · Prey · Shooting · Territory
1865	**BLM** · AZ · CAP · Egg · Habit. Prot. · Manage. · Nest. · Orme D · Salt R · Taxonomy · Territory · Verde R
1102	**Caledon SP** · Behav. · Disturb. · Habit. Loss · Habit. Use · Manage. · Nest. · Prey · VA
1103	**Caledon SP** · Disturb. · Habit. Loss · Manage. · Nest. · VA
1104	**Caledon SP** · Behav. · Disturb. · Habit. Loss · Habit. Use · Manage. · VA
977	**Cannibal.** · Behav. · Nestling
36	**Cape May** · Migration · NJ
435	**Cape May** · Capture · Migration · NJ · Techniques
436	**Cape May** · Migration · NJ
437	**Cape May** · Migration · NJ
438	**Cape May** · Migration · NJ · Status
439	**Cape May** · Band. · Capture · Migration · NJ · Techniques
546	**Cape May** · Migration · NJ
1446	**Cape May** · Migration · NJ · Pymatuning · PA · Winter. Pop.
1716	**Cape May** · Migration · Nest. · NJ
130	**Captive Breed.** · Life History · Pub. Ed. · Status
150	**Captive Breed.** · Rehab. · Techniques
170	**Captive Breed.** · Manage. · Pub. Ed.
233	**Captive Breed.** · Behav.
259	**Captive Breed.** · OH
264	**Captive Breed.** · Breed. Behav. · Intersp. Behav.
502	**Captive Breed.**
694	**Captive Breed.** · Rehab. · Techniques · Telemetry
828	**Captive Breed.**
834	**Captive Breed.** · Captivity · Manage.
847	**Captive Breed.** · Disease · FAS · FL · Rehab. · Techniques
885	**Captive Breed.** · Behav. · Intrasp. Behav. · Nestling · \OH
965	**Captive Breed.** · Growth

Master No.	Keywords
966	**Captive Breed.** · Plumage
1148	**Captive Breed.** · Breed. Behav. · Intrasp. Behav. · USFWS
1149	**Captive Breed.** · Behav. · Taxonomy
1173	**Captive Breed.**
1491	**Captive Breed.** · OH
1498	**Captive Breed.**
1923	**Captive Breed.** · FL · Rehab.
45	**Captivity** · Capture · CO · Techniques
65	**Captivity** · Poetry
71	**Captivity** · Capture · MI · Techniques
72	**Captivity** · History · Old Abe · WI
273	**Captivity** · Aggress. · Behav. · Distrib. · Egg Coll. · Habit. Use · Life History · Nest. · Status
274	**Captivity** · Aggress. · Behav. · Distrib. · Habit. Use · Life History · Nest. · Status
317	**Captivity** · Endang. Sp. · Taxonomy
343	**Captivity** · Depred. · Trapping · Winter. Pop. · WV
411	**Captivity** · Hunt. Behav. · NY · Winter. Pop.
432	**Captivity** · Behav. · DDT · Pest. · Toxicol.
506	**Captivity** · CA · Depred. · Distrib. · Habit. Use · Life History · Nest. · Santa Barbara Is.
507	**Captivity** · Anat. · Behav. · Distrib. · Nest. · WA
536	**Captivity** · Rehab. · Techniques
663	**Captivity** · DC · History · Pub. Ed.
748	**Captivity** · Poetry
834	**Captivity** · Captive Breed. · Manage.
967	**Captivity** · Aggress. · Growth
974	**Captivity** · KS · Prey · Winter. Pop.
984	**Captivity** · Egg Trans. · Heavy Metals · Law · Manage. · Migration · Nest. Survey · Pest. · Pub. Ed. · Status · Techniques · Territory · Young Trans.
1091	**Captivity** · AZ · Falconry · Intersp. Behav.
1144	**Captivity** · Behav.
1171	**Captivity** · Behav.
1250	**Captivity** · CT · Nest.
1512	**Captivity** · Pub. Ed. · Status
1704	**Captivity** · Growth
1770	**Captivity**
1935	**Captivity** · Capture · Techniques
24	**Capture** · Manage. · Marking · Skagit R · Techniques · WA
45	**Capture** · Captivity · CO · Techniques
63	**Capture** · ME · Techniques
71	**Capture** · Captivity · MI · Techniques
175	**Capture** · Anat. · CO · San Luis Valley · Techniques · Winter Survey
421	**Capture** · Folklore · Nest. · Prey · Techniques · TN
435	**Capture** · Cape May · Migration · NJ · Techniques
439	**Capture** · Band. · Cape May · Migration · NJ · Techniques
440	**Capture** · Band. · Migration · NJ · Sandy Hook · Techniques
840	**Capture** · Behav. · CO · Habit. Use · Marking · Migration · Techniques · Winter Survey
978	**Capture** · Intrasp. Behav. · IA · Mississippi R · Techniques · Upper Miss. NWR · Winter Survey · WI
1114	**Capture** · Arkansas R · Band. · Habit. Use · Intersp. Behav. · OK · Salt Plains NWR · Sequoyah NWR · Techniques · Wichita Mts. NWR · Winter Survey · Winter. Pop.
1229	**Capture** · Anat. · Autumn Conc. · Behav. · Glacier NP · Habit. Use · Manage. · Marking · Migration · MT · Techniques · Winter Survey
1499	**Capture** · OH · Techniques · Trapping · Winter. Pop.
1601	**Capture** · Behav. · Glacier NP · Hunt. Behav. · Intersp. Behav. · Intrasp. Behav. · Manage. · MT · Techniques · Winter Survey
1628	**Capture** · Indian Culture · Techniques · Trapping
1649	**Capture** · Band. · IL · Techniques · Winter. Pop.
1650	**Capture** · Habit. Use · Hunt. Behav. · Intersp. Behav. · IL · Marking · Mississippi R · Prey · Techniques · Winter Survey
1651	**Capture** · Anat. · Behav. · Hunt. Behav. · IL · Marking · Plumage · Prey · Techniques · Telemetry · Winter Survey
1935	**Capture** · Captivity · Techniques
1988	**Capture** · Anat. · Behav. · Depred. · Econ. Import. · Intersp. Behav. · Manage. · NB · Prey · Techniques
1067	**Catesby** · Art · Broley · FL · Hudson R · Winter. Pop.

Master No.	Keywords
554	**Cedar Glen Roost** · Band. · Behav. · IL · Migration · Mississippi R · MN · Refuge · Techniques · Telemetry · TX · Winter. Pop.
556	**Cedar Glen Roost** · Habit. Prot. · Habit. Use · IL · Manage. · Prey · Refuge
1291	**Cedar Grove** · Migration · WI
526	**Channel Is.** · CA · Pest.
769	**Channel Is.** · Acct. · Anacapa Is. · CA · Status
1139	**Channel Is.** · CA · Disturb. · Egg Coll. · Poison. · Pop. Turnover · Shooting
1523	**Channel Is.** · CA · Nest.
1563	**Channel Is.** · CA · Rehab. · Techniques · Telemetry
1993	**Chautauqua NWR** · Hunt. Behav. · IL · Winter. Pop.
1	**Ches. Bay** · Nest. Survey
2	**Ches. Bay** · Nest. Survey
3	**Ches. Bay** · Nest. Survey
4	**Ches. Bay** · Nest. Survey
5	**Ches. Bay** · Nest. Survey · Winter Survey
6	**Ches. Bay** · Winter Survey
7	**Ches. Bay** · Nest. Survey · Winter Survey
8	**Ches. Bay** · Nest. Survey
9	**Ches. Bay** · Nest. Survey · Status · Winter Survey
10	**Ches. Bay** · Nest. Survey · Status
11	**Ches. Bay** · Nest. Survey
12	**Ches. Bay** · Nest. Survey
13	**Ches. Bay** · Nest. Survey · Status
14	**Ches. Bay** · Nest. Survey
15	**Ches. Bay** · Nest. Survey
16	**Ches. Bay** · Nest. Survey · Status
17	**Ches. Bay** · Nest. Survey · Status
18	**Ches. Bay** · Nest. Survey · Status
19	**Ches. Bay** · Nest. Survey
20	**Ches. Bay** · Nest. Survey · Status
21	**Ches. Bay** · Mason Neck NWR · Nest. Survey · Reprod. Succ.
124	**Ches. Bay** · Manage. · Mason Neck NWR · Refuge · VA
334	**Ches. Bay** · FL · Hurricane · Nest. Fail. · ON
479	**Ches. Bay** · Egg Coll. · Habit. Use
480	**Ches. Bay** · Disturb. · Egg Coll. · GA · NC
511	**Ches. Bay** · Endang. Sp. · Manage. · Refuge · VA
512	**Ches. Bay** · Manage. · Mason Neck NWR · Refuge · VA
513	**Ches. Bay** · DC · Manage. · Mason Neck NWR · Refuge · VA
569	**Ches. Bay** · Endang. Sp. · Manage. · Status
1014	**Ches. Bay** · Nest.
1083	**Ches. Bay** · Techniques · Winter Survey
1244	**Ches. Bay** · Distrib. · Habit. Use · MD · Pub. Ed.
1688	**Ches. Bay** · Kepone · Pest. · Techniques
1796	**Ches. Bay** · Nest. Survey · Winter Survey
1812	**Ches. Bay** · DE · Econ. Import. · Habit. Use · Life History · MD · Nest. Survey · NC · NJ · Prey · PA · VA
1813	**Ches. Bay** · DC · Life History · Nest.
1847	**Ches. Bay** · Nest. Survey · New England · USFWS
1862	**Ches. Bay** · Nest. Survey · New England · USFWS
1876	**Ches. Bay** · Nest. Survey
1885	**Ches. Bay** · Endang. Sp. · Reprod. Succ. · Status
1210	**Child. Eagle Area** · Hunt-Wesson · Pub. Ed. · Refuge · USFS
1824	**Child. Eagle Area** · Chippewa NF · Hunt-Wesson · Manage. · MN · Pub. Ed. · Refuge · USFS
1230	**Children's Story** · Pub. Ed.
484	**Chilkat R** · AK · Prey · Shooting · Winter Survey
767	**Chilkat R** · Autumn Conc. · AK · Hunt. Behav. · Indian Culture · Photo. · Pub. Ed.
120	**Chippewa NF** · Manage. · Mississippi R · MN
551	**Chippewa NF** · Disturb. · Intersp. Behav. · USFS
555	**Chippewa NF** · Behav. · Breed. Behav. · Disturb. · Fledging · Marking · MN · Nestling · Prey · Reprod. Succ. · Techniques · Telemetry
557	**Chippewa NF** · Disturb. · Life History · Migration · Nest. · Photo. · Pub. Ed. · Status · Techniques · Telemetry · Winter. Pop.
695	**Chippewa NF** · Behav. · Disturb. · Logging · MN · Nest. · Reprod. Succ.
696	**Chippewa NF** · Aircraft · Model · MN · Statistics · Techniques
698	**Chippewa NF** · Manage. · MN · Nest.

Master No.	Keywords
699	**Chippewa NF** · Behav. · Fledging · Nestling · Techniques · Telemetry
700	**Chippewa NF** · Intersp. Behav.
815	**Chippewa NF** · Great Lakes · Manage. · Nest. Survey · USFS
841	**Chippewa NF** · Behav. · Dispersal · Disturb. · Fledging · MN · Nestling · Techniques · Telemetry
842	**Chippewa NF** · Behav. · Dispersal · Fledging · Hunt. Behav. · MN · Nestling · Techniques · Telemetry
843	**Chippewa NF** · Band. · Behav. · Dispersal · Fledging · Migration · MN · Nestling · Techniques · Telemetry
959	**Chippewa NF** · Agassiz NWR · Itasca SP · MN · Nest. Survey · Superior NF · Tamarac NWR
960	**Chippewa NF** · MN · Nest. Survey
1018	**Chippewa NF** · Disturb. · Habit. Use · Manage. · MN · Nest. · Prey · Reprod. Succ.
1019	**Chippewa NF** · Disturb. · Habit. Use · Manage.
1071	**Chippewa NF** · Behav. · Fledging · Intrasp. Behav. · Marking · Mortality · MN · Nest. · Techniques · Telemetry · Vocal.
1072	**Chippewa NF** · Behav. · Fledging · Marking · MN · Techniques
1188	**Chippewa NF** · Habit. Use · Manage. · MN · Nest. Survey · Status · USFS
1189	**Chippewa NF** · Habit. Use · Manage. · MN · Nest. Survey · USFS
1190	**Chippewa NF** · MN · Nest. Survey · USFS
1191	**Chippewa NF** · MN · Nest. Survey · USFS
1192	**Chippewa NF** · MN · Nest. Survey · USFS
1193	**Chippewa NF** · MN · Nest. Survey · USFS
1194	**Chippewa NF** · MN · Nest. Survey · USFS
1195	**Chippewa NF** · Disturb. · Habit. Loss · MN · USFS
1196	**Chippewa NF** · Band. · IL · MN · Nest. Survey · Techniques · USFS · Winter. Pop.
1197	**Chippewa NF** · Field ID · Habit. Use · MN · Nest. · USFS
1198	**Chippewa NF** · MN · Nest. Survey · USFS
1199	**Chippewa NF** · Field ID · MN · Nest.
1200	**Chippewa NF** · Disturb. · MN · ND · Poison. · Pub. Ed. · Shooting · Status · USFS
1201	**Chippewa NF** · MN · Nest. Survey · Status · USFS
1202	**Chippewa NF** · MN · Nest. Survey · Status · USFS
1203	**Chippewa NF** · MN · Nest. Survey · USFS
1204	**Chippewa NF** · MN · Nest. Survey · USFS
1205	**Chippewa NF** · MN · Nest. Survey · USFS
1206	**Chippewa NF** · Habit. Prot. · Hunt-Wesson · MN · Pub. Ed. · USFS
1207	**Chippewa NF** · Manage. · MN · Nest. Survey · Status · USFS
1209	**Chippewa NF** · MN · Nest. Survey · Status · USFS
1211	**Chippewa NF** · MN · Nest. Survey · Status · USFS
1213	**Chippewa NF** · MN · Nest. Survey · Status · USFS
1214	**Chippewa NF** · Band. · Marking · MN · Nest. Survey · Techniques
1215	**Chippewa NF** · Manage. · MN · Nest. Survey · Refuge · USFS
1217	**Chippewa NF** · Band. · MN · Nest. Survey · Status · Techniques · USFS
1218	**Chippewa NF** · Manage. · MN · USFS
1219	**Chippewa NF** · Manage. · MN · USFS
1220	**Chippewa NF** · Manage. · MN · USFS
1223	**Chippewa NF** · Band. · MN · Nest. Survey · Reprod. Succ. · Status · Superior NF · Techniques · Terminology
1496	**Chippewa NF** · Behav. · Fledging · Manage. · MN · Nest. · Nocturnal Behav.
1549	**Chippewa NF** · Field ID · Life History · MN · Pub. Ed.
1821	**Chippewa NF** · Manage. · MN · Pub. Ed. · USFS
1824	**Chippewa NF** · Child. Eagle Area · Hunt-Wesson · Manage. · MN · Pub. Ed. · Refuge · USFS
1825	**Chippewa NF** · Aircraft · Great Lakes · MI · MN · Nest. Survey · Reprod. Succ. · Status · USFS · WI
1826	**Chippewa NF** · Pub. Ed. · USFS

Master No.	Keywords
1914	**Chippewa NF** · Behav. · Disturb. · Manage. · MN · USFS
356	**Christmas Count** · Status · Winter Survey
751	**Christmas Count** · IL · Mississippi R · Status · Techniques · Winter Survey
903	**Christmas Count** · IA · Mississippi R · Nest. · Status · Winter Survey
1280	**Christmas Count** · DC
1364	**Christmas Count** · IL · Winter Survey
1365	**Christmas Count** · IL · Winter Survey
1531	**Christmas Count** · Band. · Life History · Migration · Nest. · Status · USFWS · Winter Survey
1655	**Christmas Count** · Lower 48 · Migration · Prey · Refuge · Winter. Pop.
1658	**Christmas Count** · IL · Winter. Pop.
1659	**Christmas Count** · IL · Winter. Pop.
1660	**Christmas Count** · IL · Winter. Pop.
1278	**Churchill R** · Nest. · SK
431	**Climatology** · AK · Behav. · Disease · Kodiak NWR · Life History · Marking · Nest. · Nest. Survey · Parasites · Reprod. Succ. · Techniques · Terminology
466	**Climatology** · AK · Distrib. · Disturb. · Forestry · Habit. Loss · Habit. Use · Manage. · Nest. · Nest. Survey · Reprod. Succ. · Territory
496	**Climatology** · Migration · OH · Poison. · Shooting · Winter Survey
866	**Climatology** · Anat. · Field ID · Migration · Status
1011	**Climatology** · Behav. · Habit. Use · Hunt. Behav. · Intersp. Behav. · Intrasp. Behav. · IA · IL · Mississippi R · MO · Prey · Winter Survey
1368	**Climatology** · Behav. · Disturb. · Habit. Use · Hunt. Behav. · Intersp. Behav. · Intrasp. Behav. · Manage. · NY · Prey · Winter Survey
1591	**Climatology** · Behav. · Disturb. · Habit. Use · Intrasp. Behav. · Plumage · Prey · Skagit R · Winter Survey · WA
1696	**Climatology** · Ft. Randall D · Habit. Use · Hunt. Behav. · Karl Mundt NWR · L Andes NWR · Manage. · Prey · SD · Winter Survey
1698	**Climatology** · Disturb. · Electro. · Habit. Use · Manage. · Prey · Winter Survey
1774	**Climatology** · Hook Mt. · Migration · NY
441	**Comm. Bird Prot.** · AOU · FL · Status
442	**Comm. Bird Prot.** · AOU · FL · Status
48	**Comm. Conserv.** · AOU · Endang. Sp. · Law · Status
52	**Comm. Conserv.** · AOU · Status
825	**Comm. Conserv.** · AK · CN · Lower 48 · Status · Wilson Ornithol. Soc.
367	**Cont. B.E. Proj.** · Nest. Survey · NAS
368	**Cont. B.E. Proj.** · Nest. Survey · NAS
837	**Cont. B.E. Proj.** · CAS · CN
1670	**Cont. B.E. Proj.** · Nest. Survey · NAS · Status
1671	**Cont. B.E. Proj.** · Migration · Nest. Survey · NAS · Status · Winter Survey
1672	**Cont. B.E. Proj.** · Hurricane · Nest. Survey · NAS · Status · Winter Survey
1673	**Cont. B.E. Proj.** · Manage. · Migration · Nest. Survey · NAS · Status · Winter Survey
1674	**Cont. B.E. Proj.** · Manage. · Nest. Survey · NAS · Refuge · Status · Winter Survey
1675	**Cont. B.E. Proj.** · Nest. Survey · NAS · Status · Winter Survey
1676	**Cont. B.E. Proj.** · Nest. Survey · NAS · Status · Winter Survey
1678	**Cont. B.E. Proj.** · Manage. · Nest. Survey · NAS · Status · Winter Survey
1681	**Cont. B.E. Proj.** · Nest. Survey · NAS · Status · Terminology
1686	**Cont. B.E. Proj.** · Autopsy · Nest. Survey · NAS · Winter Survey
1691	**Cont. B.E. Proj.** · KY · Winter Survey
372	**Cont. U.S.** · Autopsy · AK · DDT · NB · Pest. · Residues · Toxicol.
152	**Corps** · Habit. Loss · Karl Mundt NWR · Missouri R · NE · NWF · SD
81	**CA** · Paleontology
189	**CA** · Anacapa Is. · Egg Coll.
228	**CA** · Anacapa Is. · Nest. · Status
244	**CA** · Depred. · Shooting
268	**CA** · BC · Nest. · OR · Status · Winter. Pop. · WA
289	**CA** · Nest.
299	**CA** · Rehab. · San Clemente Is. · Techniques
300	**CA** · Habit. Loss · Nest.

Master No.	Keywords
307	CA · Intersp. Behav. · Nest. · San Clemente Is. · Shooting
355	CA · Habit. Use
362	CA · Shooting
363	CA · Nest.
381	CA · Anacapa Is. · Behav. · Egg Coll. · Shooting
393	CA · Endang. Sp. · Manage. · Status
394	CA · Endang. Sp. · Manage. · Status
395	CA · Nest. Survey · Winter Survey
399	CA · Manage. · Refuge · Three Sisters B.E. Pres. · USFS · Winter Survey
447	CA · Behav. · Disturb. · Hunt. Behav. · Manage. · Natl. For. · Prey · San Bernardino Mts. · USFS · Winter. Pop.
488	CA · Depred. · Shooting
500	CA · Egg Coll. · Habit. Use · Nest.
504	CA · Hacking · Rehab. · Techniques
506	CA · Captivity · Depred. · Distrib. · Habit. Use · Life History · Nest. · Santa Barbara Is.
519	CA · Depred. · Habit. Use · Manage. · Mortality · Nest. · Prey · Shasta-Trinity NF · Winter Survey
526	CA · Channel Is. · Pest.
532	CA · Lava Beds NM · Nest.
563	CA · Nest. · OR · Winter. Pop.
572	CA · Aircraft · Behav. · Distrib. · Disturb. · Habit. Loss · Hunt. Behav. · Klamath R · Manage. · Nest.
606	CA · Nest.
667	CA · Acct. · AK · FL · Taxonomy · VA
682	CA · Disturb. · Klamath NF · Manage. · Nest. · Prey · Status · Winter. Pop.
683	CA · Behav. · Distrib. · Disturb. · Field ID · Flight · Hunt. Behav. · Life History · Manage. · Mortality · Nest. · Winter. Pop.
738	CA · Depred. · Hunt. Behav. · Prey
761	CA · Klamath · OR · Paleontology
768	CA · Nest. Survey · Techniques · Winter Survey
769	CA · Acct. · Anacapa Is. · Channel Is. · Status
791	CA · Acct.
792	CA · Behav. · Habit. Use · Intersp. Behav. · Nest. · Winter. Pop.
793	CA · Acct. · Status
794	CA · Distrib. · Habit. Use · Winter. Pop.
873	CA · Nest.
876	CA · Acct. · Baja · Nest.
877	CA · Baja · Nest. Survey
926	CA · Paleontology · Status
927	CA · Anat. · FL · NE · NM · OR · Paleontology · Taxonomy
931	CA · Depred. · Nest.
932	CA · Aggress. · Nest. · Santa Cruz
971	CA · Habit. Loss · Nest. · Santa Barbara Is.
1020	CA · Nest.
1040	CA · Hunt. Behav. · Prey · San Bernardino Mts.
1049	CA · Nest. Survey · Road. Census · Techniques · Winter Survey
1050	CA · Nest. Survey · Winter Survey
1065	CA · Behav. · Disturb. · Habit. Use · Klamath · Lower Klamath Lake NWR · Manage. · OR · Prey · Tule Lake NWR · Winter Survey
1092	CA · Endang. Sp.
1094	CA · Disturb. · Nest.
1107	CA · Shooting · Status
1110	CA · Depred. · Habit. Use · Prey · San Clemente Is.
1111	CA · Paleontology · Santa Barbara Is.
1139	CA · Channel Is. · Disturb. · Egg Coll. · Poison. · Pop. Turnover · Shooting
1156	CA · Distrib. · Endang. Sp. · Field ID
1157	CA · Distrib. · Endang. Sp.
1158	CA · Distrib. · Endang. Sp.
1159	CA · Nest. Survey · Road. Census · Techniques · Winter Survey
1160	CA · Distrib. · Life History · Nest. · Prey · Pub. Ed. · Winter. Pop.
1259	CA · Evolution · Paleontology · Taxonomy
1260	CA · Evolution · Paleontology · Taxonomy
1290	CA · Rehab. · Techniques
1310	CA · Migration · Winter. Pop.
1332	CA · Habit. Prot. · IL · NWF · RIC
1347	CA · Three Sisters B.E. Pres.
1433	CA · Nest. · Santa Barbara Is.
1434	CA · Winter. Pop.
1455	CA · Anacapa Is. · Nest.
1456	CA · Nest.
1523	CA · Channel Is. · Nest.
1545	CA · Fowl Cholera · Winter. Pop.
1563	CA · Channel Is. · Rehab. · Techniques · Telemetry

Master No.	Keywords
1579	CA · Nest.
1639	CA · AZ · Endang. Sp. · NM · NV · OK · Status · TX · UT
1661	CA · Falconry · Rehab. · Techniques
1719	CA · Shooting · Taxonomy
1726	CA · Intersp. Behav.
1731	CA · Acct. · Kings Canyon NP · Sequoia NP
1771	CA · Disturb. · Habit. Loss · Habit. Use · Manage. · Nest. Survey · Prey · Shooting · Territory · Trapping
1777	CA · Habit. Use · Manage. · Nest. Survey · Status · Territory
1839	CA · ID · MT · Nest. Survey · NV · OR · USFWS · WA
1844	CA · ID · Nest. Survey · NV · OR · USFWS · WA
1853	CA · ID · Nest. Survey · NV · OR · USFWS · WA
1927	CA · Hunt. Behav.
1948	CA · Taxonomy
1950	CA · Egg Coll. · Nest.
1967	CA · Disturb. · Habit. Use · Lower Klamath Lake NWR · Modoc NWR · Tule Lake NWR · Winter Survey
182	CAP · AZ · Falconry · Habit. Loss · Law · Orme D
449	CAP · AZ · Habit. Loss · Nest. · Orme D · Salt R · Verde R
770	CAP · AZ · Disturb. · Habit. Use · Manage. · Nest. · Orme D
1004	CAP · AZ · Endang. Sp. · Habit. Loss · Orme D
1793	CAP · AZ · Nest. Survey · Orme D · Salt R · Verde R
1865	CAP · AZ · BLM · Egg · Habit. Prot. · Manage. · Nest. · Orme D · Salt R · Taxonomy · Territory · Verde R
1965	CAP · AZ · Habit. Loss · Nest. · Orme D
1966	CAP · AZ · Nest. · Orme D
837	CAS · Cont. B.E. Proj. · CN
39	CN · Nest.
40	CN · Nest.
41	CN · Nest.
247	CN · Bounty · Depred. · Law
459	CN · Autopsy · AK · Disease · Lower 48 · Parasites · Poison. · Shooting · Trapping
708	CN · Status

Master No.	Keywords
709	CN · Pest. · Status
739	CN · DDT · ON · PCB · SK
743	CN · Flight
745	CN · Anat. · Distrib. · Field ID · Nest. · Taxonomy
746	CN · Endang. Sp. · Status
772	CN · Band. · Behav. · ON · Reprod. Succ. · Techniques
773	CN · Anat. · ON
774	CN · Aggress. · Behav. · Disturb. · ON · Reprod. Succ.
777	CN · Habit. Use · ON · Reprod. Succ. · Status · Techniques · Territory
780	CN · Disturb. · Habit. Use · Lake of The Woods · Manage. · ON
825	CN · AK · Comm. Conserv. · Lower 48 · Status · Wilson Ornithol. Soc.
837	CN · Cont. B.E. Proj. · CAS
1141	CN · AK · Egg Coll. · Intersp. Behav. · Nest.
1184	CN · AK · Lower 48 · Status
1595	CN · Acct. · Great Slave L. · NWT
1747	CN · Econ. Import.
1748	CN · Field ID
1749	CN · Econ. Import. · Field ID · Prey
1750	CN · Econ. Import. · Field ID · Life History · Prey
1958	CN · Distrib. · Hunt. Behav. · NY · Prey
45	CO · Captivity · Capture · Techniques
175	CO · Anat. · Capture · San Luis Valley · Techniques · Winter Survey
207	CO · Distrib. · Nest. · Winter. Pop.
451	CO · Habit. Use · Nest. · San Luis Valley · Status · Winter Survey
473	CO · Disturb. · Field ID · Habit. Loss · Manage. · Nest. · Pest. · Pub. Ed. · Winter. Pop.
474	CO · Habit. Use · Nest. · San Luis Valley · Status · Winter Survey
600	CO · Road. Census · Techniques · Winter. Pop.
601	CO · Prey · Winter. Pop.
669	CO · Field ID · Pub. Ed.
712	CO · Hawk Mt. · Migration · PA · Status
840	CO · Behav. · Capture · Habit. Use · Marking · Migration · Techniques · Winter Survey
858	CO · Nest. · UT · Winter. Pop.
1005	CO · Road. Census · Techniques · Winter. Pop.
1010	CO · Intersp. Behav. · Winter. Pop.

Master No.	Keywords
1086	CO · Electro. · Manage. · NV · Trapping · TX · UT
1119	CO · Nest.
1154	CO · Pub. Ed.
1397	CO · Field ID · Winter. Pop.
1573	CO · Poison. · Pub. Ed. · Shooting · WY
1574	CO · Poison. · Pub. Ed. · Shooting · WY
1575	CO · Law · Shooting · WY
1582	CO · Life History · Nest. · Status · Winter. Pop.
1689	CO · Status · Winter Survey
1838	CO · AZ · KS · Nest. Survey · NM · OK · Salt Fork R · TX · USFWS · UT · Verde R · WY
1846	CO · IA · KS · MO · MT · Nest. Survey · ND · NE · SD · USFWS · UT · WY
1849	CO · IA · KS · MO · MT · Nest. Survey · ND · NE · SD · USFWS · UT · WY
1854	CO · Glacier NP · Manage. · Missouri R · MT · Nest. Survey · SD · USFWS
1981	CO · Electro. · ID · Manage. · NV · UT · WY
535	CT · Egg Coll. · Endang. Sp. · Habit. Loss · Nest. · Pest. · PCB · Shooting · Status
1108	CT · Nest. · Status
1250	CT · Captivity · Nest.
1276	CT · Nest.
1518	CT · Autopsy · FL · Pest.
1559	CT · Migration · Nest. · Shooting · Taxonomy · Winter. Pop.
1636	CT · Folklore · Prey
1900	CT · Distrib.
187	CU · Paleontology
1823	Data Coll. · Manage. · USFS
26	Depred. · AK · Endang. Sp. · Life History · OR · WA
86	Depred. · Folklore · Hunt. Behav.
217	Depred. · Egg Coll. · FL · Nest.
218	Depred. · Egg Coll. · FL · Nest.
244	Depred. · CA · Shooting
247	Depred. · Bounty · CN · Law
282	Depred. · AL · Prey
343	Depred. · Captivity · Trapping · Winter. Pop. · WV
415	Depred. · Hunt. Behav. · MT
416	Depred. · Folklore · Prey · Pub. Ed.
455	Depred. · Ohio R · Shooting · WV
470	Depred. · MA · Prey
487	Depred. · Plumage · Shooting · WV
488	Depred. · CA · Shooting
506	Depred. · Captivity · CA · Distrib. · Habit. Use · Life History · Nest. · Santa Barbara Is.
519	Depred. · CA · Habit. Use · Manage. · Mortality · Nest. · Prey · Shasta-Trinity NF · Winter Survey
737	Depred. · AK · Nest. · Prey · Shooting
738	Depred. · CA · Hunt. Behav. · Prey
931	Depred. · CA · Nest.
1110	Depred. · CA · Habit. Use · Prey · San Clemente Is.
1300	Depred. · Manage. · Pred. Cont. · Prey
1377	Depred. · Electro.
1543	Depred. · Law · Poison. · Shooting · WY
1551	Depred. · Pub. Ed.
1568	Depred. · Nest. · ON · Prey · Shooting
1606	Depred. · Aggress. · Aleutian Is. · AK · Behav. · Habit. Use · Life History · Mortality · Nest. Survey · Plumage · Prey · Reprod. Succ. · Status · Winter Survey
1623	Depred. · ID
1810	Depred. · Pub. Ed. · Status
1944	Depred. · Hunt. Behav. · NM · TX
1988	Depred. · Anat. · Behav. · Capture · Econ. Import. · Intersp. Behav. · Manage. · NB · Prey · Techniques
850	Derby Hill · Great Lakes · Hawk Mt. · Migration · NY
482	Dieldrin · Autopsy · Disease · Electro. · Lower 48 · Pest. · Poison. · PCB · Shooting
528	Dieldrin · Anal. Tech. · Blood · Heavy Metals · Pest.
550	Dieldrin · Band. · Breed. Behav. · DDT · MN · Pest. · Pest. Residues · Prey · Techniques · Telemetry
1943	Dieldrin · ME · Pest. · Prey · PCB
541	Digest. · Biochem. · Pellets · Prey
542	Digest. · Prey
1642	Dimorphism · Anat. · Hunt. Behav. · Prey
874	Dioxins · Pest.
431	Disease · AK · Behav. · Climatology · Kodiak NWR · Life History · Marking · Nest. · Nest. Survey · Parasites · Reprod. Succ. · Techniques · Terminology

Master No.	Keywords
459	**Disease** · Autopsy · AK · CN · Lower 48 · Parasites · Poison. · Shooting · Trapping
460	**Disease** · Asper. · Autopsy · MO · Rehab. · Techniques · Trapping
482	**Disease** · Autopsy · Dieldrin · Electro. · Lower 48 · Pest. · Poison. · PCB · Shooting
705	**Disease** · Rehab. · Shooting · Techniques · Trapping
847	**Disease** · Captive Breed. · FAS · FL · Rehab. · Techniques
862	**Disease** · Biochem. · Blood · Fowl Cholera
994	**Disease** · Heavy Metals · Histology · Lead Poison. · MD · Techniques
1060	**Disease** · Parasites
1127	**Disease** · Fowl Cholera · Heavy Metals · OH · Pest.
1292	**Disease** · Autopsy · Electro. · Lead Poison. · Pest. · Shooting
1383	**Disease** · Asper.
1513	**Disease** · MN · Rehab. · Shooting · Techniques · Trapping
1933	**Disease** · FL · L Apopka
2000	**Disease**
325	**Dispersal** · Behav. · Disturb. · FL · Habit. Use · Intersp. Behav. · Migration · Mortality · Nest. · Prey
338	**Dispersal** · Band. · Broley · FL · Life History · Techniques
841	**Dispersal** · Behav. · Chippewa NF · Disturb. · Fledging · MN · Nestling · Techniques · Telemetry
842	**Dispersal** · Behav. · Chippewa NF · Fledging · Hunt. Behav. · MN · Nestling · Techniques · Telemetry
843	**Dispersal** · Band. · Behav. · Chippewa NF · Fledging · Migration · MN · Nestling · Techniques · Telemetry
1275	**Dispersal** · NY · Techniques · Young Trans.
1349	**Dispersal** · FL · Life History · Migration · NAS · Pub. Ed. · Status
1610	**Dispersal** · Band. · Behav. · MN · Techniques · WI
1666	**Dispersal** · Nest. Survey · NY · Winter. Pop.
1891	**Dispersal** · Migration · Plumage

Master No.	Keywords
22	**Distrib.** · Bombay Hook NWR · DE · Endang. Sp. · Field ID · Life History · Nest. · Nest. Survey · Pub. Ed. · Status
31	**Distrib.** · Nest. · NH · Winter. Pop.
47	**Distrib.** · Life History · Taxonomy
53	**Distrib.** · IA · Nest. · Status · Winter. Pop.
195	**Distrib.** · LA · Nest. Survey · Winter Survey
196	**Distrib.** · LA · Migration · Mortality · Nest. Survey · Reprod. Succ. · Shooting · Status · Winter Survey
207	**Distrib.** · CO · Nest. · Winter. Pop.
209	**Distrib.** · Life History
211	**Distrib.** · Anat. · Nest. · NM · Plumage · Prey · Winter. Pop.
221	**Distrib.** · Anat. · Nest. · Plumage · Taxonomy
249	**Distrib.** · Anat. · Life History · MI · Plumage · Status
266	**Distrib.** · Anat. · Behav. · BC · Falconry · Field ID · Flight · Habit. Use · Migration · Nest. · Prey · Status
273	**Distrib.** · Aggress. · Behav. · Captivity · Egg Coll. · Habit. Use · Life History · Nest. · Status
274	**Distrib.** · Aggress. · Behav. · Captivity · Habit. Use · Life History · Nest. · Status
349	**Distrib.** · Ireland · Shooting
353	**Distrib.** · Anat. · Behav. · Life History · Nest. · Status
377	**Distrib.** · GA · Habit. Use · Life History · Migration · Nest. · Status
382	**Distrib.** · Egg Coll. · IN · Life History · Nest. · Status
396	**Distrib.** · Evolution
424	**Distrib.** · Field ID · Life History
427	**Distrib.** · Anat. · Field ID
433	**Distrib.** · England · Taxonomy
466	**Distrib.** · AK · Climatology · Disturb. · Forestry · Habit. Loss · Habit. Use · Manage. · Nest. · Nest. Survey · Reprod. Succ. · Territory
498	**Distrib.** · Egg · Nest. · Plumage
506	**Distrib.** · Captivity · CA · Depred. · Habit. Use · Life History · Nest. · Santa Barbara Is.
507	**Distrib.** · Anat. · Behav. · Captivity · Nest. · WA

Master No.	Keywords
520	**Distrib.** · Habit. Use · Migration · Nest. Survey · Status · Winter Survey · WI
537	**Distrib.** · LA · Nest. Survey · Reprod. Succ.
538	**Distrib.** · LA · Nest. Survey · Reprod. Succ.
572	**Distrib.** · Aircraft · Behav. · CA · Disturb. · Habit. Loss · Hunt. Behav. · Klamath R · Manage. · Nest.
608	**Distrib.** · Electro. · Field ID · Life History · Prey · UT · Winter. Pop.
683	**Distrib.** · Behav. · CA · Disturb. · Field ID · Flight · Hunt. Behav. · Life History · Manage. · Mortality · Nest. · Winter. Pop.
684	**Distrib.** · Life History
701	**Distrib.** · Anat. · Life History · Plumage
711	**Distrib.** · AK · Habit. Use · Life History · Plumage · Status
714	**Distrib.** · Habit. Use · Nest. · Plumage · Shooting · Taxonomy · TN · Winter. Pop.
721	**Distrib.** · IL
745	**Distrib.** · Anat. · CN · Field ID · Nest. · Taxonomy
786	**Distrib.** · Behav. · Hunt. Behav. · Manage. · Marking · Migration · Mortality · MO · Nest. · Pest. · Prey · Swan Lake NWR · Techniques · Telemetry
794	**Distrib.** · CA · Habit. Use · Winter. Pop.
846	**Distrib.** · Anat. · Taxonomy
976	**Distrib.** · Aggress. · Anat. · Bounty · Econ. Import. · Law · Life History · Plumage · Prey · Status · Taxonomy
1156	**Distrib.** · CA · Endang. Sp. · Field ID
1157	**Distrib.** · CA · Endang. Sp.
1158	**Distrib.** · CA · Endang. Sp.
1160	**Distrib.** · CA · Life History · Nest. · Prey · Pub. Ed. · Winter. Pop.
1237	**Distrib.** · Endang. Sp. · Habit. Use · Migration · Nest. · ND · Status · Winter. Pop.
1244	**Distrib.** · Ches. Bay · Habit. Use · MD · Pub. Ed.
1297	**Distrib.** · Aleutian Is. · AK · Band. · Econ. Import. · Nest. · Plumage · Prey · Shooting · Techniques
1372	**Distrib.** · Anat. · Habit. Use · Nest. · Plumage · Taxonomy · TX · Winter. Pop.
1438	**Distrib.** · Taxonomy
1449	**Distrib.** · Field ID
1629	**Distrib.** · Endang. Sp. · Nest. Survey · TX · Winter Survey
1630	**Distrib.** · Endang. Sp. · Nest. Survey · TX · Winter Survey
1631	**Distrib.** · Nest. Survey · Reprod. Succ. · Status · TX · Winter Survey
1632	**Distrib.** · Habit. Use · Nest. Survey · Status · TX · Winter Survey
1733	**Distrib.** · Life History · PA
1874	**Distrib.** · Endang. Sp. · Law · Life History · Manage. · Status · Taxonomy · USFWS
1900	**Distrib.** · CT
1901	**Distrib.** · DE · Life History · NJ · Prey · VA
1909	**Distrib.** · NE
1928	**Distrib.** · NE
1958	**Distrib.** · CN · Hunt. Behav. · NY · Prey
51	**Disturb.** · Habit. Use · Manage. · Nest. · OR · USFS
89	**Disturb.** · Aggress.
122	**Disturb.** · Law · Logging · Manage. · Refuge
123	**Disturb.** · Logging · Manage. · Nest.
125	**Disturb.** · Law · Logging · Manage. · Nest. · Territory
159	**Disturb.** · Behav. · IA · IL · MN
301	**Disturb.** · Habit. Use · IL · Nest. · Ohio R · Rehab. · Shooting · Techniques · Winter. Pop.
310	**Disturb.** · Migration · ME · Nest. · Shooting · Winter. Pop.
325	**Disturb.** · Behav. · Dispersal · FL · Habit. Use · Intersp. Behav. · Migration · Mortality · Nest. · Prey
361	**Disturb.** · Behav. · Nest. · ND · Photo.
447	**Disturb.** · Behav. · CA · Hunt. Behav. · Manage. · Natl. For. · Prey · San Bernardino Mts. · USFS · Winter. Pop.
465	**Disturb.** · AK · Habit. Loss · Habit. Use · Logging · Nest. · Nest. Survey · Territory

Master No.	Keywords
466	**Disturb.** · AK · Climatology · Distrib. · Forestry · Habit. Loss · Habit. Use · Manage. · Nest. · Nest. Survey · Reprod. Succ. · Territory
473	**Disturb.** · CO · Field ID · Habit. Loss · Manage. · Nest. · Pest. · Pub. Ed. · Winter. Pop.
480	**Disturb.** · Ches. Bay · Egg Coll. · GA · NC
481	**Disturb.** · Egg Coll. · NJ
485	**Disturb.** · FL · Habit. Loss · Status
551	**Disturb.** · Chippewa NF · Intersp. Behav. · USFS
555	**Disturb.** · Behav. · Breed. Behav. · Chippewa NF · Fledging · Marking · MN · Nestling · Prey · Reprod. Succ. · Techniques · Telemetry
557	**Disturb.** · Chippewa NF · Life History · Migration · Nest. · Photo. · Pub. Ed. · Status · Techniques · Telemetry · Winter. Pop.
572	**Disturb.** · Aircraft · Behav. · CA · Distrib. · Habit. Loss · Hunt. Behav. · Klamath R · Manage. · Nest.
580	**Disturb.** · MO · Nest.
599	**Disturb.** · Behav. · FL · Migration · Nest. · Nest. Fail.
682	**Disturb.** · CA · Klamath NF · Manage. · Nest. · Prey · Status · Winter. Pop.
683	**Disturb.** · Behav. · CA · Distrib. · Field ID · Flight · Hunt. Behav. · Life History · Manage. · Mortality · Nest. · Winter. Pop.
695	**Disturb.** · Behav. · Chippewa NF · Logging · MN · Nest. · Reprod. Succ.
697	**Disturb.** · Law · USFS
710	**Disturb.** · Helicop. · Pub. Ed.
731	**Disturb.** · Behav. · Nestling · Parent. Behav. · SK
732	**Disturb.** · Habit. Use · MB · Nest. · SK · Territory
735	**Disturb.** · Habit. Use · Intersp. Behav. · SK
755	**Disturb.** · Manage. · ME · Nest. Survey · Pub. Ed. · Shooting · Winter. Pop.
757	**Disturb.** · Band. · Manage. · Marking · ME · Nest. · Nest. Survey · Shooting · Techniques
770	**Disturb.** · AZ · CAP · Habit. Use · Manage. · Nest. · Orme D
774	**Disturb.** · Aggress. · Behav. · CN · ON · Reprod. Succ.
778	**Disturb.** · MB · Nest. Survey · ON · Reprod. Succ. · Techniques
780	**Disturb.** · CN · Habit. Use · Lake of The Woods · Manage. · ON
782	**Disturb.** · MB · Nest. Survey · ON · Status · Techniques
783	**Disturb.** · Egg. Thin. · Heavy Metals · Nest. Survey · ON · Pest. · PCB · Reprod. Succ. · Status
784	**Disturb.** · Research
801	**Disturb.** · Nest. · Nest. Survey · Reprod. Succ. · Statistics · Territory · WA
814	**Disturb.** · Great Lakes · Manage. · Nest. Survey · Pub. Ed. · Status · USFS
827	**Disturb.** · Barkley Sound · Behav. · BC · Gulf Is. · Helicop. · Nest. Survey · Plumage · Prey
829	**Disturb.** · Barkley Sound · BC · Gulf Is. · Helicop.
831	**Disturb.** · BC · Helicop. · Nest. Survey · Pest. · Refuge
836	**Disturb.** · Behav. · Habit. Loss · Habit. Use · Hunt. Behav. · Logging · Manage. · Prey · Winter Survey · WA
841	**Disturb.** · Behav. · Chippewa NF · Dispersal · Fledging · MN · Nestling · Techniques · Telemetry
844	**Disturb.** · AK · Econ. Import.
870	**Disturb.** · Life History · Pub. Ed.
871	**Disturb.** · FL · Habit. Use · Kissimee B.E. Sanct. · Nest. Survey · Refuge · Reprod. Succ.
872	**Disturb.** · FL · Habit. Use · Kissimee B.E. Sanct. · Nest. Survey · Refuge · Reprod. Succ.
878	**Disturb.** · AK · Habit. Use · Kodiak NWR · Life History · Nest. Fail. · Reprod. Succ. · Territory
882	**Disturb.** · Aggress. · Behav. · Life History · Nest. · OH · PA
945	**Disturb.** · FL · Habit. Loss · Nest. Fail. · Nest. Survey · Reprod. Succ.
946	**Disturb.** · FL · Habit. Loss · Nest. Survey · Status
972	**Disturb.** · Behav. · Habit. Use · Nest. · Snake R · WY
996	**Disturb.** · Fledging · Habit. Use · Intersp. Behav. · Intrasp. Behav. · VA

Master No.	Keywords
1018	**Disturb.** · Chippewa NF · Habit. Use · Manage. · MN · Nest. · Prey · Reprod. Succ.
1019	**Disturb.** · Chippewa NF · Habit. Use · Manage.
1063	**Disturb.** · Behav. · Habit. Loss · Habit. Use · Manage. · Prey · Research · TX · Winter Survey
1065	**Disturb.** · Behav. · CA · Habit. Use · Klamath · Lower Klamath Lake NWR · Manage. · OR · Prey · Tule Lake NWR · Winter Survey
1073	**Disturb.** · AB · Nest. Survey · NWT
1085	**Disturb.** · Habit. Loss · Nest. · OH · Status
1094	**Disturb.** · CA · Nest.
1102	**Disturb.** · Behav. · Caledon SP · Habit. Loss · Habit. Use · Manage. · Nest. · Prey · VA
1103	**Disturb.** · Caledon SP · Habit. Loss · Manage. · Nest. · VA
1104	**Disturb.** · Behav. · Caledon SP · Habit. Loss · Habit. Use · Manage. · VA
1112	**Disturb.** · Autopsy · Habit. Use · Hunt. Behav. · Intersp. Behav. · Manage. · Migration · OK · Prey · Salt Fork R · Shooting · Status · Taxonomy · Winter Survey
1115	**Disturb.** · Habit. Use · Manage. · Migration · OK · Prey · Salt Fork R · Salt Plains NWR · Sequoyah NWR · Shooting · Status · Taxonomy · Wichita Mts. NWR · Winter Survey
1115	**Disturb.** · Habit. Use · Manage. · Migration · OK · Prey · Salt Fork R · Salt Plains NWR · Sequoyah NWR · Shooting · Status · Taxonomy · Wichita Mts. NWR · Winter Survey
1116	**Disturb.** · Acct. · Nest. · OK · Status · Winter. Pop.
1139	**Disturb.** · Channel Is. · CA · Egg Coll. · Poison. · Pop. Turnover · Shooting
1178	**Disturb.** · Pub. Ed. · Skagit R · WA
1195	**Disturb.** · Chippewa NF · Habit. Loss · MN · USFS
1200	**Disturb.** · Chippewa NF · MN · ND · Poison. · Pub. Ed. · Shooting · Status · USFS
1354	**Disturb.** · Nest. Survey · San Juan Is. · Status · WA
1368	**Disturb.** · Behav. · Climatology · Habit. Use · Hunt. Behav. · Intersp. Behav. · Intrasp. Behav. · Manage. · NY · Prey · Winter Survey
1430	**Disturb.** · Egg Coll. · Nest. · OR
1484	**Disturb.** · Great Lakes · Manage. · Nest. Survey · ON · Research · Status · Techniques
1487	**Disturb.** · Band. · Great Lakes · MI · Nest. Survey · Pest. · Techniques
1497	**Disturb.** · Habit. Use · Nest.
1521	**Disturb.** · Aggress. · Behav. · Habit. Loss · Hunt. Behav. · Nest. · Prey · San Juan Is. · Shooting · Status · Vocal. · WA
1550	**Disturb.** · AZ · Behav. · Habit. Loss · Habit. Use · Hunt. Behav. · Nest. Survey · Prey · Status · Terminology · Territory
1591	**Disturb.** · Behav. · Climatology · Habit. Use · Intrasp. Behav. · Plumage · Prey · Skagit R · Winter Survey · WA
1624	**Disturb.** · Egg Coll. · FL · Nest.
1634	**Disturb.** · Aggress. · Aleutian Is. · Amchitka Is. · AK · Prey
1635	**Disturb.** · Aircraft
1640	**Disturb.** · Aggress. · Behav. · BLM · Habit. Loss · Habit. Use · Hunt. Behav. · Life History · Manage. · Nest. · Pest. · Prey · Shooting · Territory
1690	**Disturb.** · Behav. · Manage. · Winter. Pop. · WA
1698	**Disturb.** · Climatology · Electro. · Habit. Use · Manage. · Prey · Winter Survey
1699	**Disturb.** · Behav. · Ft. Randall D · Habit. Use · Manage. · Missouri R · SD · Winter Survey
1741	**Disturb.** · Habit. Use · Manage. · MT · Nest. Survey · Pop. Turnover · Reprod. Succ. · Status · Territory · Yellowstone NP
1771	**Disturb.** · CA · Habit. Loss · Habit. Use · Manage. · Nest. Survey · Prey · Shooting · Territory · Trapping
1789	**Disturb.** · AZ · Nest. Survey · Verde R
1792	**Disturb.** · AZ · Nest.
1886	**Disturb.** · Acct. · Douglas Pt. Nuc. Plant · MD
1914	**Disturb.** · Behav. · Chippewa NF · Manage. · MN · USFS

Master No.	Keywords
1920	**Disturb.** · Habit. Loss · Manage. · Nest. Survey · ON · Status
1922	**Disturb.** · Behav. · Fledging · ON
1932	**Disturb.** · AK · Helicop. · Nest. Survey · Techniques
1967	**Disturb.** · CA · Habit. Use · Lower Klamath Lake NWR · Modoc NWR · Tule Lake NWR · Winter Survey
1886	**Douglas Pt. Nuc. Plant** · Acct. · Disturb. · MD
907	**Duluth Fly.** · Great Lakes · L Superior · Migration · MN
458	**DC** · Nest.
513	**DC** · Ches. Bay · Manage. · Mason Neck NWR · Refuge · VA
663	**DC** · Captivity · History · Pub. Ed.
1280	**DC** · Christmas Count
1705	**DC** · Band. · Migration · MD · Nest. · Techniques · Winter. Pop.
1813	**DC** · Ches. Bay · Life History · Nest.
140	**DDT** · AK · FL · ME · Pest. · Reprod. Succ. · WI
333	**DDT** · FL · Nest. Fail. · Pest. · Red Tide
335	**DDT** · FL · Nest. Fail. · Pest. · Status
372	**DDT** · Autopsy · AK · Cont. U.S. · NB · Pest. · Residues · Toxicol.
432	**DDT** · Behav. · Captivity · Pest. · Toxicol.
501	**DDT** · Pest. · Status
524	**DDT** · Pest. · Toxicol. · USFWS
525	**DDT** · Pest. · Toxicol. · USFWS
550	**DDT** · Band. · Breed. Behav. · Dieldrin · MN · Pest. · Pest. Residues · Prey · Techniques · Telemetry
739	**DDT** · CN · ON · PCB · SK
806	**DDT** · Law · Pest.
1126	**DDT** · Histology · Pest. · Phys. · Spermato. · Techniques
1830	**DDT** · Pest. · Toxicol.
1831	**DDT** · Autopsy · MO · NJ · Residues · Toxicol.
22	**DE** · Bombay Hook NWR · Distrib. · Endang. Sp. · Field ID · Life History · Nest. · Nest. Survey · Pub. Ed. · Status
492	**DE** · Egg · Egg Coll. · MD · Nest. · NJ
493	**DE** · Egg Coll. · Nest.
494	**DE** · Egg · Egg Coll. · MD · Nest. · VA
495	**DE** · Egg · Egg Coll. · MD

Master No.	Keywords
581	**DE** · Egg Coll. · Habit. Use · MD · Nest.
1268	**DE** · Nest.
1492	**DE** · Nest. · Winter. Pop.
1578	**DE** · Great Lakes · MD · Nest. Survey · NJ · PA · Status
1589	**DE** · Egg Coll. · Nest.
1812	**DE** · Ches. Bay · Econ. Import. · Habit. Use · Life History · MD · Nest. Survey · NC · NJ · Prey · PA · VA
1840	**DE** · Nest. Survey · USFWS
1901	**DE** · Distrib. · Life History · NJ · Prey · VA
980	**Eagle Valley Refuge**
29	**Econ. Import.** · Life History · Pub. Ed.
93	**Econ. Import.** · Aggress. · Folklore · Hunt. Behav.
342	**Econ. Import.** · BC · Hunt. Behav. · Prey · Shooting
425	**Econ. Import.** · Prey
446	**Econ. Import.** · Law · Life History · Manage. · MO · Nest. · Prey · Pub. Ed. · Shooting
471	**Econ. Import.** · AK · Bounty
472	**Econ. Import.** · AK · Prey
664	**Econ. Import.** · Anat. · Hunt. Behav. · Life History · Prey
813	**Econ. Import.** · AK
844	**Econ. Import.** · AK · Disturb.
976	**Econ. Import.** · Aggress. · Anat. · Bounty · Distrib. · Law · Life History · Plumage · Prey · Status · Taxonomy
1025	**Econ. Import.** · Aggress. · Field ID · Law · Life History · Prey
1226	**Econ. Import.** · Life History · Prey · Pub. Ed. · Status
1296	**Econ. Import.** · Aleutian Is. · AK · Prey
1297	**Econ. Import.** · Aleutian Is. · AK · Band. · Distrib. · Nest. · Plumage · Prey · Shooting · Techniques
1370	**Econ. Import.** · Life History · Prey · Shooting
1747	**Econ. Import.** · CN
1749	**Econ. Import.** · CN · Field ID · Prey
1750	**Econ. Import.** · CN · Field ID · Life History · Prey
1812	**Econ. Import.** · Ches. Bay · DE · Habit. Use · Life History · MD · Nest. Survey · NC · NJ · Prey · PA · VA

Master No.	Keywords
1889	**Econ. Import.** · AK · Bounty · Prey
1903	**Econ. Import.** · AK · Prey
1949	**Econ. Import.** · AK
1987	**Econ. Import.** · LB · Maritime Prov. · · NF · Prey
1988	**Econ. Import.** · Anat. · Behav. · Capture · Depred. · Intersp. Behav. · Manage. · NB · Prey · Techniques
37	**Educ. Mat.**
116	**Educ. Mat.**
158	**Educ. Mat.**
172	**Educ. Mat.**
237	**Educ. Mat.** · Art
308	**Educ. Mat.** · Field ID · Hawk Mt. · Migration · Pub. Ed. · PA · Shooting
434	**Educ. Mat.** · Endang. Sp. · Manage. · NWF
1835	**Educ. Mat.** · USFWS
1872	**Educ. Mat.**
200	**Egg** · Egg Coll. · FL
492	**Egg** · DE · Egg Coll. · MD · Nest. · NJ
494	**Egg** · DE · Egg Coll. · MD · Nest. · VA
495	**Egg** · DE · Egg Coll. · MD
497	**Egg** · Behav. · Nest. · OH · Poison. · Prey · Shooting
498	**Egg** · Distrib. · Nest. · Plumage
508	**Egg** · Egg Coll. · FL · Nest.
1515	**Egg** · Life History
1711	**Egg** · Pest. · Techniques
1724	**Egg** · Egg Coll. · MI
1727	**Egg** · Egg Coll. · MI · VA
1865	**Egg** · AZ · BLM · CAP · Habit. Prot. · Manage. · Nest. · Orme D · Salt R · Taxonomy · Territory · Verde R
1945	**Egg** · Egg Coll. · ME · Nest.
1946	**Egg** · New England · Status · Taxonomy
35	**Egg Coll.** · LA · MN · MS · Status · WI
189	**Egg Coll.** · Anacapa Is. · CA
200	**Egg Coll.** · Egg · FL
212	**Egg Coll.** · Nest. · VA
213	**Egg Coll.** · Nest. · VA
214	**Egg Coll.** · Nest. · Prey · VA
215	**Egg Coll.** · Habit. Use · Nest. · Photo. · VA
216	**Egg Coll.** · Nest. · VA
217	**Egg Coll.** · Depred. · FL · Nest.
218	**Egg Coll.** · Depred. · FL · Nest.
239	**Egg Coll.**

Master No.	Keywords
255	**Egg Coll.** · Aggress. · FL · Nest. · Shooting · Status
273	**Egg Coll.** · Aggress. · Behav. · Captivity · Distrib. · Habit. Use · Life History · Nest. · Status
291	**Egg Coll.** · LA
379	**Egg Coll.** · Habit. Loss · Nest. · NJ
381	**Egg Coll.** · Anacapa Is. · Behav. · CA · Shooting
382	**Egg Coll.** · Distrib. · IN · Life History · Nest. · Status
404	**Egg Coll.** · AK · Nest. · Shooting
413	**Egg Coll.** · Nest. · TX
467	**Egg Coll.** · FL · Nest.
476	**Egg Coll.** · Flight · Life History · Shooting · Status
479	**Egg Coll.** · Ches. Bay · Habit. Use
480	**Egg Coll.** · Ches. Bay · Disturb. · GA · NC
481	**Egg Coll.** · Disturb. · NJ
491	**Egg Coll.** · FL · L Apopka · Nest.
492	**Egg Coll.** · DE · Egg · MD · Nest. · NJ
493	**Egg Coll.** · DE · Nest.
494	**Egg Coll.** · DE · Egg · MD · Nest. · VA
495	**Egg Coll.** · DE · Egg · MD
500	**Egg Coll.** · CA · Habit. Use · Nest.
508	**Egg Coll.** · Egg · FL · Nest.
535	**Egg Coll.** · CT · Endang. Sp. · Habit. Loss · Nest. · Pest. · PCB · Shooting · Status
581	**Egg Coll.** · DE · Habit. Use · MD · Nest.
594	**Egg Coll.** · FL · Nest.
666	**Egg Coll.** · MD · Nest.
749	**Egg Coll.** · Habit. Use · IN · Nest.
754	**Egg Coll.** · Acct. · OK · Shooting
954	**Egg Coll.** · GA · Nest. · PA
992	**Egg Coll.** · FL · Intersp. Behav.
993	**Egg Coll.** · FL · Nest.
1013	**Egg Coll.** · Nest. · VA
1052	**Egg Coll.** · MD · Nest.
1139	**Egg Coll.** · Channel Is. · CA · Disturb. · Poison. · Pop. Turnover · Shooting
1141	**Egg Coll.** · AK · CN · Intersp. Behav. · Nest.
1251	**Egg Coll.** · Nest. · OR
1258	**Egg Coll.** · Nest. · VA
1356	**Egg Coll.** · FL · Nest.
1414	**Egg Coll.** · FL · Pub. Ed. · Shooting
1430	**Egg Coll.** · Disturb. · Nest. · OR
1524	**Egg Coll.** · Migration · Nest. · WI

Master No.	Keywords
1555	Egg Coll. · FL · Habit. Use · Nest. · Shooting
1556	Egg Coll. · Habit. Use · Nest.
1589	Egg Coll. · DE · Nest.
1614	Egg Coll. · MD · Nest. · VA
1624	Egg Coll. · Disturb. · FL · Nest.
1657	Egg Coll. · Habit. Use · Logging · ME · Nest.
1724	Egg Coll. · Egg · MI
1727	Egg Coll. · Egg · MI · VA
1778	Egg Coll. · IA · Nest.
1911	Egg Coll. · FL · Nest.
1945	Egg Coll. · Egg · ME · Nest.
1950	Egg Coll. · CA · Nest.
1956	Egg Coll. · FL · Nest.
1997	Egg Coll. · Nest. · TX
151	Egg Trans. · Manage.
156	Egg Trans. · Manage. · ME · MN · USFWS
275	Egg Trans. · Manage. · ME · MN
756	Egg Trans. · Band. · Manage. · ME · Nest. Survey · Pest. · PCB · Refuge · Techniques · Winter Survey
824	Egg Trans. · Techniques · Young Trans.
983	Egg Trans. · Habit. Prot. · Nest. · Pub. Ed. · Winter. Pop.
984	Egg Trans. · Captivity · Heavy Metals · Law · Manage. · Migration · Nest. Survey · Pest. · Pub. Ed. · Status · Techniques · Territory · Young Trans.
1851	Egg Trans. · Manage. · ME · MN · USFWS
1861	Egg Trans. · Manage. · ME · MN · USFWS · WI
1871	Egg Trans. · Hacking · Manage. · ME · MN · NY · Pest. · PCB · Techniques · WI · Young Trans.
50	Egg. Thin. · FL · LA · Pest. · Status · TX
132	Egg. Thin. · FL · Status
294	Egg. Thin. · Pest. · PCB
779	Egg. Thin. · Heavy Metals · ON · Pest. · PCB · Reprod. Succ. · Status
783	Egg. Thin. · Disturb. · Heavy Metals · Nest. Survey · ON · Pest. · PCB · Reprod. Succ. · Status
804	Egg. Thin. · Art. Nest Site · AZ · Habit. Use · Life History · Manage. · Marking · Nest. · Pest. · Research · Techniques · Telemetry · Winter. Pop.
895	Egg. Thin. · FL
1234	Egg. Thin. · FL · Habit. Use · Nest. Survey · Ocala NF · Prey · Reprod. Succ.
1410	Egg. Thin. · Pest.
1464	Egg. Thin. · Pest.
1482	Egg. Thin. · Heavy Metals · ON · Pest. · PCB
1679	Egg. Thin. · Pest. · Status
1732	Egg. Thin. · Hacking · NY · Techniques · Telemetry · Young Trans.
1751	Egg. Thin. · Habit. Use · Manage. · MD · Nest. Survey · Pest.
1752	Egg. Thin. · Habit. Use · Manage. · MD · Nest. Survey · Pest. · Techniques
1931	Egg. Thin. · Amchitka Is. · AK · Habit. Use · Nest. Survey · Prey · Winter Survey
1942	Egg. Thin. · AK · FL · Great Lakes · Heavy Metals · ME · Pest. · PCB
482	Electro. · Autopsy · Dieldrin · Disease · Lower 48 · Pest. · Poison. · PCB · Shooting
608	Electro. · Distrib. · Field ID · Life History · Prey · UT · Winter. Pop.
1086	Electro. · CO · Manage. · NV · Trapping · TX · UT
1185	Electro. · ID · Manage. · Winter. Pop.
1257	Electro. · Manage.
1292	Electro. · Autopsy · Disease · Lead Poison. · Pest. · Shooting
1314	Electro. · Law · NAS · Pest. · Poison. · Pub. Ed. · Shooting · Status
1341	Electro. · ID · Manage.
1342	Electro. · Behav. · Manage.
1377	Electro. · Depred.
1468	Electro. · Mississippi R
1622	Electro. · UT
1698	Electro. · Climatology · Disturb. · Habit. Use · Manage. · Prey · Winter Survey
1791	Electro. · AZ · Nest. Survey · Winter Survey
1822	Electro. · Manage.
1981	Electro. · CO · ID · Manage. · NV · UT · WY

Master No.	Keywords
22	**Endang. Sp.** · Bombay Hook NWR · Distrib. · DE · Field ID · Life History · Nest. · Nest. Survey · Pub. Ed. · Status
26	**Endang. Sp.** · AK · Depred. · Life History · OR · WA
48	**Endang. Sp.** · AOU · Comm. Conserv. · Law · Status
111	**Endang. Sp.** · NAS · Status
184	**Endang. Sp.** · AZ
186	**Endang. Sp.** · Acct. · AZ · Nest. · Pub. Ed. · Winter. Pop.
317	**Endang. Sp.** · Captivity · Taxonomy
390	**Endang. Sp.** · Poison. · Pred. Cont. · Status
393	**Endang. Sp.** · CA · Manage. · Status
394	**Endang. Sp.** · CA · Manage. · Status
434	**Endang. Sp.** · Educ. Mat. · Manage. · NWF
511	**Endang. Sp.** · Ches. Bay · Manage. · Refuge · VA
535	**Endang. Sp.** · CT · Egg Coll. · Habit. Loss · Nest. · Pest. · PCB · Shooting · Status
569	**Endang. Sp.** · Ches. Bay · Manage. · Status
722	**Endang. Sp.** · IL
746	**Endang. Sp.** · CN · Status
981	**Endang. Sp.** · Great Lakes · Nest. Survey · Pub. Ed. · Status · USFS
985	**Endang. Sp.** · IUCN · Status
1004	**Endang. Sp.** · AZ · CAP · Habit. Loss · Orme D
1026	**Endang. Sp.** · KS · Winter. Pop.
1092	**Endang. Sp.** · CA
1145	**Endang. Sp.** · Life History · Status
1156	**Endang. Sp.** · CA · Distrib. · Field ID
1157	**Endang. Sp.** · CA · Distrib.
1158	**Endang. Sp.** · CA · Distrib.
1237	**Endang. Sp.** · Distrib. · Habit. Use · Migration · Nest. · ND · Status · Winter. Pop.
1272	**Endang. Sp.** · Habit. Use · Manage. · MN · Status
1273	**Endang. Sp.** · MO · Nest. · Winter. Pop.
1309	**Endang. Sp.** · Manage. · Nest. · NV · Status
1319	**Endang. Sp.** · USFWS
1333	**Endang. Sp.** · USFWS
1380	**Endang. Sp.** · BLM · Manage. · Pub. Ed.
1451	**Endang. Sp.** · Manage. · Status
1627	**Endang. Sp.** · Nest. · OH · Pest. · Status
1629	**Endang. Sp.** · Distrib. · Nest. Survey · TX · Winter Survey
1630	**Endang. Sp.** · Distrib. · Nest. Survey · TX · Winter Survey
1639	**Endang. Sp.** · AZ · CA · NM · NV · OK · Status · TX · UT
1654	**Endang. Sp.** · Manage. · Techniques
1680	**Endang. Sp.** · Manage. · Status · Taxonomy
1785	**Endang. Sp.** · Lower 48 · Nest. Survey · Status
1786	**Endang. Sp.**
1818	**Endang. Sp.** · Law
1828	**Endang. Sp.** · Habit. Prot. · Manage. · MN
1832	**Endang. Sp.** · Field ID · Manage. · Status · USFWS
1834	**Endang. Sp.** · Field ID · Manage. · Status · USFWS
1848	**Endang. Sp.** · Field ID · Manage. · Status · USFWS
1863	**Endang. Sp.** · Law
1870	**Endang. Sp.** · Law
1874	**Endang. Sp.** · Distrib. · Law · Life History · Manage. · Status · Taxonomy · USFWS
1877	**Endang. Sp.** · Law
1882	**Endang. Sp.** · Recovery Team
1884	**Endang. Sp.** · Law · Taxonomy
1885	**Endang. Sp.** · Ches. Bay · Reprod. Succ. · Status
1896	**Endang. Sp.** · Status · VA
1908	**Endang. Sp.** · MI · Nest.
433	**England** · Distrib. · Taxonomy
1806	**Everglades NP** · Behav. · Nest. · Photo.
43	**Evolution** · Behav. · Reprod. Succ.
396	**Evolution** · Distrib.
865	**Evolution** · Anat. · Plumage
1259	**Evolution** · CA · Paleontology · Taxonomy
1260	**Evolution** · CA · Paleontology · Taxonomy
1992	**Evolution** · Anat.
265	**Eye** · Anat.
182	**Falconry** · AZ · CAP · Habit. Loss · Law · Orme D
266	**Falconry** · Anat. · Behav. · BC · Distrib. · Field ID · Flight · Habit. Use · Migration · Nest. · Prey · Status
540	**Falconry** · MN · Rehab. · Techniques
1091	**Falconry** · AZ · Captivity · Intersp. Behav.

Master No.	Keywords
1164	Falconry
1165	Falconry
1166	Falconry
1167	Falconry
1168	Falconry
1169	Falconry
1170	Falconry
1174	Falconry
1270	Falconry · Folklore · History
1661	Falconry · CA · Rehab. · Techniques
1960	Falconry · Plumage
1186	Feather War · History · Indian Culture · Law
1322	Ferry Bluff Sanct. · NWF · Refuge · WI
1325	Ferry Bluff Sanct. · NWF · Refuge · WI
1330	Ferry Bluff Sanct. · Habit. Prot. · NWF · Refuge · Winter. Pop. · Wisconsin R · WI
1431	Ferry Bluff Sanct. · Habit. Prot. · Refuge · WI
22	Field ID · Bombay Hook NWR · Distrib. · DE · Endang. Sp. · Life History · Nest. · Nest. Survey · Pub. Ed. · Status
44	Field ID
94	Field ID · Art · Broley · Plumage · Pub. Ed.
178	Field ID · AR · Winter Survey · Winter. Pop.
266	Field ID · Anat. · Behav. · BC · Distrib. · Falconry · Flight · Habit. Use · Migration · Nest. · Prey · Status
308	Field ID · Educ. Mat. · Hawk Mt. · Migration · Pub. Ed. · PA · Shooting
424	Field ID · Distrib. · Life History
427	Field ID · Anat. · Distrib.
473	Field ID · CO · Disturb. · Habit. Loss · Manage. · Nest. · Pest. · Pub. Ed. · Winter. Pop.
568	Field ID · Acct. · NY
592	Field ID · Hunt. Behav. · OR · Prey
608	Field ID · Distrib. · Electro. · Life History · Prey · UT · Winter. Pop.
669	Field ID · CO · Pub. Ed.
683	Field ID · Behav. · CA · Distrib. · Disturb. · Flight · Hunt. Behav. · Life History · Manage. · Mortality · Nest. · Winter. Pop.
745	Field ID · Anat. · CN · Distrib. · Nest. · Taxonomy
797	Field ID · Anat. · Behav. · Plumage · Taxonomy
823	Field ID · Winter. Pop. · WI
866	Field ID · Anat. · Climatology · Migration · Status
917	Field ID · Anat. · Plumage
1025	Field ID · Aggress. · Econ. Import. · Law · Life History · Prey
1156	Field ID · CA · Distrib. · Endang. Sp.
1197	Field ID · Chippewa NF · Habit. Use · MN · Nest. · USFS
1199	Field ID · Chippewa NF · MN · Nest.
1212	Field ID · Life History · MN
1227	Field ID · Life History · Prey
1232	Field ID · Life History · Nest. · WY · Yellowstone NP
1233	Field ID · Hawk Mt. · Mt. Johnson Is. Sanct. · PA
1353	Field ID · Life History · NH
1376	Field ID · Nest. · OH · Pub. Ed. · Status
1397	Field ID · CO · Winter. Pop.
1398	Field ID · Life History · Pub. Ed.
1447	Field ID
1449	Field ID · Distrib.
1508	Field ID · Nest. Survey · NWF · RIC · USFS
1533	Field ID
1549	Field ID · Chippewa NF · Life History · MN · Pub. Ed.
1667	Field ID · Montezuma NWR · NY
1683	Field ID · Pub. Ed. · Taxonomy
1684	Field ID · Band. · FL · Life History · Nest. · Prey · Status · Techniques
1735	Field ID · Anat. · Taxonomy
1748	Field ID · CN
1749	Field ID · CN · Econ. Import. · Prey
1750	Field ID · CN · Econ. Import. · Life History · Prey
1808	Field ID · Life History · Nest. · NS · Poetry
1832	Field ID · Endang. Sp. · Manage. · Status · USFWS
1834	Field ID · Endang. Sp. · Manage. · Status · USFWS
1848	Field ID · Endang. Sp. · Manage. · Status · USFWS
1998	Field ID · Pub. Ed.
955	Finger Lakes · Montezuma NWR · Nest. · NY
956	Finger Lakes · Montezuma NWR · Nest. · NY

Master No.	Keywords
670	**Fla. B.E. Sur. Comm.** · FL · Great Lakes · Rehab. · Reprod. Succ. · Status · Techniques · WI
1352	**Fla. B.E. Sur. Comm.** · FL · Habit. Use · Nest. Survey · Status
555	**Fledging** · Behav. · Breed. Behav. · Chippewa NF · Disturb. · Marking · MN · Nestling · Prey · Reprod. Succ. · Techniques · Telemetry
561	**Fledging** · Behav. · Habit. Use · Marking · MN · Parent. Behav. · Techniques · Telemetry
699	**Fledging** · Behav. · Chippewa NF · Nestling · Techniques · Telemetry
841	**Fledging** · Behav. · Chippewa NF · Dispersal · Disturb. · MN · Nestling · Techniques · Telemetry
842	**Fledging** · Behav. · Chippewa NF · Dispersal · Hunt. Behav. · MN · Nestling · Techniques · Telemetry
843	**Fledging** · Band. · Behav. · Chippewa NF · Dispersal · Migration · MN · Nestling · Techniques · Telemetry
881	**Fledging** · Behav. · Life History · Nest. · Nestling · OH
883	**Fledging** · Behav. · Hunt. Behav. · Life History · Nest. · OH · Prey
888	**Fledging** · Behav. · Intersp. Behav. · Life History · Nest. · OH · Parent. Behav. · Photo. · Prey
995	**Fledging** · Behav. · VA · Winter. Pop.
996	**Fledging** · Disturb. · Habit. Use · Intersp. Behav. · Intrasp. Behav. · VA
1071	**Fledging** · Behav. · Chippewa NF · Intrasp. Behav. · Marking · Mortality · MN · Nest. · Techniques · Telemetry · Vocal.
1072	**Fledging** · Behav. · Chippewa NF · Marking · MN · Techniques
1222	**Fledging** · Behav. · Hunt. Behav. · Intersp. Behav. · Intrasp. Behav. · Marking · MI · Ottawa NF · Techniques · Territory
1496	**Fledging** · Behav. · Chippewa NF · Manage. · MN · Nest. · Nocturnal Behav.
1922	**Fledging** · Behav. · Disturb. · ON
55	**Flight** · Aggress. · Folklore · History · Hunt. Behav. · Intersp. Behav.
56	**Flight** · Aggress. · Folklore · History · Hunt. Behav. · Intersp. Behav.
90	**Flight** · Shooting · TX
198	**Flight** · Photo.
266	**Flight** · Anat. · Behav. · BC · Distrib. · Falconry · Field ID · Habit. Use · Migration · Nest. · Prey · Status
352	**Flight** · Behav. · Life History · Migration · Nest. · Prey · Pub. Ed. · Status · Taxonomy
476	**Flight** · Egg Coll. · Life History · Shooting · Status
683	**Flight** · Behav. · CA · Distrib. · Disturb. · Field ID · Hunt. Behav. · Life History · Manage. · Mortality · Nest. · Winter. Pop.
743	**Flight** · CN
808	**Flight** · Behav. · Poetry
55	**Folklore** · Aggress. · Flight · History · Hunt. Behav. · Intersp. Behav.
56	**Folklore** · Aggress. · Flight · History · Hunt. Behav. · Intersp. Behav.
59	**Folklore** · Life History · Old Abe · Pub. Ed.
62	**Folklore** · Growth · Hunt. Behav. · Indian Culture · Life History · Plumage
64	**Folklore** · Aggress. · IL
76	**Folklore** · Aggress. · KY
86	**Folklore** · Depred. · Hunt. Behav.
93	**Folklore** · Aggress. · Econ. Import. · Hunt. Behav.
260	**Folklore** · Prey · PA · Status · Taxonomy
416	**Folklore** · Depred. · Prey · Pub. Ed.
421	**Folklore** · Capture · Nest. · Prey · Techniques · TN
444	**Folklore** · Anat. · Hunt. Behav. · NC · Shooting
1009	**Folklore** · History · Pub. Ed.
1051	**Folklore** · Life History · Pub. Ed. · Status
1172	**Folklore** · Aggress. · Intersp. Behav.
1270	**Folklore** · Falconry · History
1366	**Folklore** · Life History
1395	**Folklore** · Prey
1452	**Folklore** · Pub. Ed.
1636	**Folklore** · CT · Prey
1637	**Folklore** · FL · Intrasp. Behav. · Taxonomy
1682	**Folklore** · Prey
1717	**Folklore** · Prey
1725	**Folklore** · Prey
1776	**Folklore** · Aggress.

Master No.	Keywords
466	Forestry · AK · Climatology · Distrib. · Disturb. · Habit. Loss · Habit. Use · Manage. · Nest. · Nest. Survey · Reprod. Succ. · Territory
1947	Forrester Is. · AK · Nest. Survey
862	Fowl Cholera · Biochem. · Blood · Disease
1127	Fowl Cholera · Disease · Heavy Metals · OH · Pest.
1545	Fowl Cholera · CA · Winter. Pop.
1695	Ft. Randall D · Behav. · Habit. Use · Hunt. Behav. · Karl Mundt NWR · L Andes NWR · SD · Winter Survey
1696	Ft. Randall D · Climatology · Habit. Use · Hunt. Behav. · Karl Mundt NWR · L Andes NWR · Manage. · Prey · SD · Winter Survey
1697	Ft. Randall D · Habit. Loss · Habit. Use · Hunt. Behav. · Migration · Prey · SD · Winter Survey
1699	Ft. Randall D · Behav. · Disturb. · Habit. Use · Manage. · Missouri R · SD · Winter Survey
847	FAS · Captive Breed. · Disease · FL · Rehab. · Techniques
50	FL · Egg. Thin. · LA · Pest. · Status · TX
132	FL · Egg. Thin. · Status
140	FL · AK · DDT · ME · Pest. · Reprod. Succ. · WI
143	FL · Manage. · Pub. Ed. · Refuge
148	FL · Anat. · Autumn Conc. · Glacier NP · Manage. · Merritt Is. NWR · Museum Specimen · MT · Nest. · Prey · Taxonomy
200	FL · Egg · Egg Coll.
217	FL · Depred. · Egg Coll. · Nest.
218	FL · Depred. · Egg Coll. · Nest.
241	FL · Nest.
250	FL · Hunt. Behav. · Intersp. Behav. · Prey · Shooting
254	FL · Nest. · Shooting
255	FL · Aggress. · Egg Coll. · Nest. · Shooting · Status
269	FL · Autopsy · Heavy Metals · Midwest Region · MD · ME · MO · ND · Pest. · PCB
278	FL · Gulf of Mex. · Nest.
322	FL · Anat. · Plumage · Weight
323	FL · Paleontology
324	FL · Band. · Life History · Migration · Nest. Fail. · Nest. Survey · Prey · Status · Techniques
325	FL · Behav. · Dispersal · Disturb. · Habit. Use · Intersp. Behav. · Migration · Mortality · Nest. · Prey
326	FL · Habit. Loss · Intersp. Behav. · Nest. Fail.
327	FL · Band. · Habit. Loss · Intersp. Behav. · Nest. Fail. · Pub. Ed. · Shooting · Status · Techniques
328	FL · Habit. Loss · Intersp. Behav. · Manage. · Nest. Fail.
329	FL · Habit. Loss · Hurricane · Nest. Fail. · Status
330	FL · Nest. Fail.
331	FL · Behav. · Broley
332	FL · Band. · ON · Pest. · Pub. Ed. · Reprod. Succ. · Techniques
333	FL · DDT · Nest. Fail. · Pest. · Red Tide
334	FL · Ches. Bay · Hurricane · Nest. Fail. · ON
335	FL · DDT · Nest. Fail. · Pest. · Status
336	FL · Band. · Intersp. Behav. · Techniques
337	FL · Aggress. · Band. · Broley · Techniques
338	FL · Band. · Broley · Dispersal · Life History · Techniques
339	FL · Band. · Broley · Life History · Pub. Ed. · Status · Techniques
441	FL · AOU · Comm. Bird Prot. · Status
442	FL · AOU · Comm. Bird Prot. · Status
467	FL · Egg Coll. · Nest.
485	FL · Disturb. · Habit. Loss · Status
491	FL · Egg Coll. · L Apopka · Nest.
508	FL · Egg · Egg Coll. · Nest.
565	FL · ME · NJ · Pest. · Toxicol.
566	FL · AK · ME · MI · MN · PCB
589	FL · Band. · Broley · Techniques
594	FL · Egg Coll. · Nest.
599	FL · Behav. · Disturb. · Migration · Nest. · Nest. Fail.
612	FL · Nest. · Prey
656	FL · Pub. Ed.
657	FL · Nest. Survey · Reprod. Succ.
667	FL · Acct. · AK · CA · Taxonomy · VA
670	FL · Fla. B.E. Sur. Comm. · Great Lakes · Rehab. · Reprod. Succ. · Status · Techniques · WI
671	FL · Nest. · Ocala NF · USFS

Master No.	Keywords
672	FL · Habit. Prot. · Refuge · Three Lakes Ranch
673	FL · Habit. Use · Nest. Survey · Reprod. Succ.
674	FL · Habit. Prot. · Refuge · Three Lakes Ranch
675	FL · Pub. Ed.
676	FL · Nest. Survey · Reprod. Succ.
677	FL · Nest. Survey · Reprod. Succ.
678	FL · Pub. Ed.
679	FL · Shooting
766	FL · Nest.
800	FL · Intersp. Behav.
847	FL · Captive Breed. · Disease · FAS · Rehab. · Techniques
871	FL · Disturb. · Habit. Use · Kissimee B.E. Sanct. · Nest. Survey · Refuge · Reprod. Succ.
872	FL · Disturb. · Habit. Use · Kissimee B.E. Sanct. · Nest. Survey · Refuge · Reprod. Succ.
895	FL · Egg. Thin.
915	FL · Nest.
927	FL · Anat. · CA · NE · NM · OR · Paleontology · Taxonomy
935	FL · Intersp. Behav. · Nest.
936	FL · Nest. Fail. · Nest. Survey · Status
937	FL · Nest. · Nest. Fail. · Status
938	FL · Nest. · Nest. Fail.
939	FL · Nest.
941	FL · Nest. · Status
942	FL · Nest. · Nest. Fail. · Status
943	FL · Nest. Fail. · Status · Techniques
944	FL · Habit. Loss · Nest. Fail. · Nest. Survey · Status
945	FL · Disturb. · Habit. Loss · Nest. Fail. · Nest. Survey · Reprod. Succ.
946	FL · Disturb. · Habit. Loss · Nest. Survey · Status
947	FL · Nest. Survey
948	FL · Merritt Is. NWR · Nest. Survey
950	FL · Nest. Survey · Status
992	FL · Egg Coll. · Intersp. Behav.
993	FL · Egg Coll. · Nest.
1023	FL · Pub. Ed.
1024	FL · Nest. Survey · Techniques · Territory
1064	FL · Heavy Metals · ME · Nest. · Pest. · PCB · Reprod. Succ. · WI
1067	FL · Art · Broley · Catesby · Hudson R · Winter. Pop.
1128	FL · Intersp. Behav.
1151	FL · Rehab. · Techniques
1152	FL · Nest. Survey · Rehab. · Techniques
1234	FL · Egg. Thin. · Habit. Use · Nest. Survey · Ocala NF · Prey · Reprod. Succ.
1312	FL · LA · Migration
1349	FL · Dispersal · Life History · Migration · NAS · Pub. Ed. · Status
1350	FL · Nest. Survey
1351	FL · Habit. Use · Nest. Survey
1352	FL · Fla. B.E. Sur. Comm. · Habit. Use · Nest. Survey · Status
1356	FL · Egg Coll. · Nest.
1357	FL · Habit. Use · Life History · Nest. · Status
1358	FL · Nest.
1361	FL · Hunt. Behav. · Prey
1375	FL · Behav. · Intersp. Behav.
1401	FL · Nest.
1414	FL · Egg Coll. · Pub. Ed. · Shooting
1416	FL · Hunt. Behav. · Life History · Nest. · Prey
1445	FL · Nest. Survey
1448	FL · Band. · Migration · Prey · Techniques
1450	FL · Broley
1457	FL · Nest.
1458	FL · Big Cypress Swamp · Nest.
1488	FL · AR · Band. · GA · Manage. · Migration · MI · Techniques · TN · Young Trans.
1518	FL · Autopsy · CT · Pest.
1519	FL · Hunt. Behav.
1538	FL · Hurricane · Nest.
1555	FL · Egg Coll. · Habit. Use · Nest. · Shooting
1581	FL · L Ocklawaha · Nest. · Rodman Reservoir
1587	FL · Nest.
1588	FL · Nest.
1596	FL · Band. · Broley · Techniques
1624	FL · Disturb. · Egg Coll. · Nest.
1637	FL · Folklore · Intrasp. Behav. · Taxonomy
1684	FL · Band. · Field ID · Life History · Nest. · Prey · Status · Techniques
1685	FL · Pub. Ed. · Status
1709	FL · ME · MO · NJ · Pest. · Toxicol. · USFWS
1760	FL · Habit. Loss · NAS · Status
1775	FL · Acct. · Nest.

Master No.	Keywords
1805	FL · Behav. · History · Photo. · Status
1807	FL · Behav. · Intersp. Behav. · Life History · Photo.
1911	FL · Egg Coll. · Nest.
1923	FL · Captive Breed. · Rehab.
1933	FL · Disease · L Apopka
1942	FL · AK · Egg. Thin. · Great Lakes · Heavy Metals · ME · Pest. · PCB
1952	FL · Nest. · Winter. Pop.
1953	FL · Nest.
1956	FL · Egg Coll. · Nest.
148	Glacier NP · Anat. · Autumn Conc. · FL · Manage. · Merritt Is. NWR · Museum Specimen · MT · Nest. · Prey · Taxonomy
210	Glacier NP · Acct. · Nest.
1228	Glacier NP · Hunt. Behav. · Intersp. Behav. · MN · Prey · Winter Survey
1229	Glacier NP · Anat. · Autumn Conc. · Behav. · Capture · Habit. Use · Manage. · Marking · Migration · MT · Techniques · Winter Survey
1313	Glacier NP · MT · Winter. Pop. · WA
1601	Glacier NP · Behav. · Capture · Hunt. Behav. · Intersp. Behav. · Intrasp. Behav. · Manage. · MT · Techniques · Winter Survey
1602	Glacier NP · Autumn Conc. · Hunt. Behav. · MT · Prey
1854	Glacier NP · CO · Manage. · Missouri R · MT · Nest. Survey · SD · USFWS
409	Grand Canyon · AZ · Nest. · Status · Winter. Pop.
1236	Grand Canyon · Acct. · AZ
445	Great Lakes · Manage. · MI · MN · Natl. For. · Nest. Survey · USFS · WI
595	Great Lakes · MN · Nest. Survey · Techniques
670	Great Lakes · Fla. B.E. Sur. Comm. · FL · Rehab. · Reprod. Succ. · Status · Techniques · WI
733	Great Lakes · Band. · Migration · ON · Techniques
814	Great Lakes · Disturb. · Manage. · Nest. Survey · Pub. Ed. · Status · USFS
815	Great Lakes · Chippewa NF · Manage. · Nest. Survey · USFS
850	Great Lakes · Derby Hill · Hawk Mt. · Migration · NY

Master No.	Keywords
851	Great Lakes · Behav. · Migration
890	Great Lakes · L Erie · Prey · Pub. Ed. · Status
907	Great Lakes · Duluth Fly. · L Superior · Migration · MN
923	Great Lakes · MI · Nest. Survey
981	Great Lakes · Endang. Sp. · Nest. Survey · Pub. Ed. · Status · USFS
988	Great Lakes · L Erie · Manage. · Nest. Survey · OH · Winter Survey
1146	Great Lakes · Nest. Survey · USFWS
1147	Great Lakes · Habit. Prot. · Manage. · MB · Nest. Survey · ON · Rehab. · Techniques · Techniques
1484	Great Lakes · Disturb. · Manage. · Nest. Survey · ON · Research · Status · Techniques
1486	Great Lakes · Migration · MI · WI
1487	Great Lakes · Band. · Disturb. · MI · Nest. Survey · Pest. · Techniques
1503	Great Lakes · Manage. · USFS
1504	Great Lakes · Nest. Survey · USFS
1578	Great Lakes · DE · MD · Nest. Survey · NJ · PA · Status
1825	Great Lakes · Aircraft · Chippewa NF · MI · MN · Nest. Survey · Reprod. Succ. · Status · USFS · WI
1918	Great Lakes · Nest. Survey · USFS
1919	Great Lakes · Nest. Survey · USFS
1942	Great Lakes · AK · Egg. Thin. · FL · Heavy Metals · ME · Pest. · PCB
1973	Great Lakes · MI · Nest.
1595	Great Slave L. · Acct. · CN · NWT
1924	Great Slave L. · Nest. · NWT
160	Ground Nest. · Law · Nest. · OH
319	Ground Nest. · MI · Nest.
340	Ground Nest. · Nest. · NWT
1598	Ground Nest. · MI · Prey
1800	Ground Nest. · Nest. · NWT
62	Growth · Folklore · Hunt. Behav. · Indian Culture · Life History · Plumage
88	Growth · MD · Nest. · Photo. · Plumage
91	Growth · Photo. · Plumage
191	Growth · Anat. · Plumage · Taxonomy
453	Growth · Plumage
477	Growth · GA · Molt. · Plumage
574	Growth · Band. · Behav. · Nest. · Photo. · Pub. Ed. · Techniques
575	Growth · Behav. · Nest. · Photo. · Prey · Pub. Ed.

Master No.	Keywords
662	**Growth** · AK · Bounty · Law · Photo. · Shooting
965	**Growth** · Captive Breed.
967	**Growth** · Aggress. · Captivity
968	**Growth** · Behav. · Habit. Use
1704	**Growth** · Captivity
204	**Gulf of Mex.** · LA · Winter. Pop.
278	**Gulf of Mex.** · FL · Nest.
284	**Gulf of Mex.** · LA · Nest.
826	**Gulf Is.** · BC · Habit. Use · Migration · Nest. Survey · Prey · San Juan Is. · Techniques · Winter Survey · WA
827	**Gulf Is.** · Barkley Sound · Behav. · BC · Disturb. · Helicop. · Nest. Survey · Plumage · Prey
829	**Gulf Is.** · Barkley Sound · BC · Disturb. · Helicop.
1803	**Gulf Is.** · BC · Nest. Survey · Winter Survey
311	**GA** · Nest.
377	**GA** · Distrib. · Habit. Use · Life History · Migration · Nest. · Status
477	**GA** · Growth · Molt. · Plumage
480	**GA** · Ches. Bay · Disturb. · Egg Coll. · NC
603	**GA** · Nest.
860	**GA** · Nest. · Okefinokee Swamp · Prey
861	**GA** · Hunt. Behav. · Prey
954	**GA** · Egg Coll. · Nest. · PA
1021	**GA** · Hunt. Behav. · Prey · Sapelo Is.
1022	**GA** · Nest. · Sapelo Is.
1415	**GA** · Nest.
1488	**GA** · AR · Band. · FL · Manage. · Migration · MI · Techniques · TN · Young Trans.
1756	**GA** · Nest. · Winter. Pop.
1978	**GA** · Nest.
1986	**GA** · Acct. · Nest. · Okefinokee Swamp
49	**Habit. Loss** · Aleutian Is. · Amchitka Is. · AK · AOU · Status
152	**Habit. Loss** · Corps · Karl Mundt NWR · Missouri R · NE · NWF · SD
182	**Habit. Loss** · AZ · CAP · Falconry · Law · Orme D
300	**Habit. Loss** · CA · Nest.
326	**Habit. Loss** · FL · Intersp. Behav. · Nest. Fail.
327	**Habit. Loss** · Band. · FL · Intersp. Behav. · Nest. Fail. · Pub. Ed. · Shooting · Status · Techniques
328	**Habit. Loss** · FL · Intersp. Behav. · Manage. · Nest. Fail.
329	**Habit. Loss** · FL · Hurricane · Nest. Fail. · Status
379	**Habit. Loss** · Egg Coll. · Nest. · NJ
449	**Habit. Loss** · AZ · CAP · Nest. · Orme D · Salt R · Verde R
465	**Habit. Loss** · AK · Disturb. · Habit. Use · Logging · Nest. · Nest. Survey · Territory
466	**Habit. Loss** · AK · Climatology · Distrib. · Disturb. · Forestry · Habit. Use · Manage. · Nest. · Nest. Survey · Reprod. Succ. · Territory
473	**Habit. Loss** · CO · Disturb. · Field ID · Manage. · Nest. · Pest. · Pub. Ed. · Winter. Pop.
485	**Habit. Loss** · Disturb. · FL · Status
535	**Habit. Loss** · CT · Egg Coll. · Endang. Sp. · Nest. · Pest. · PCB · Shooting · Status
572	**Habit. Loss** · Aircraft · Behav. · CA · Distrib. · Disturb. · Hunt. Behav. · Klamath R · Manage. · Nest.
660	**Habit. Loss** · Nest. Survey · NC · SC
728	**Habit. Loss** · Habit. Use · Manage. · McHargian Overlay · Nest. · Reprod. Succ. · SK · Techniques
734	**Habit. Loss** · Habit. Use · Road Plan. · SK · Techniques
836	**Habit. Loss** · Behav. · Disturb. · Habit. Use · Hunt. Behav. · Logging · Manage. · Prey · Winter Survey · WA
944	**Habit. Loss** · FL · Nest. Fail. · Nest. Survey · Status
945	**Habit. Loss** · Disturb. · FL · Nest. Fail. · Nest. Survey · Reprod. Succ.
946	**Habit. Loss** · Disturb. · FL · Nest. Survey · Status
971	**Habit. Loss** · CA · Nest. · Santa Barbara Is.
1002	**Habit. Loss** · OR · Shooting
1004	**Habit. Loss** · AZ · CAP · Endang. Sp. · Orme D
1063	**Habit. Loss** · Behav. · Disturb. · Habit. Use · Manage. · Prey · Research · TX · Winter Survey
1068	**Habit. Loss** · Habit. Use · Nest. · WI
1069	**Habit. Loss** · Habit. Use · Nest. · WI
1085	**Habit. Loss** · Disturb. · Nest. · OH · Status

116

Master No.	Keywords
1102	**Habit. Loss** · Behav. · Caledon SP · Disturb. · Habit. Use · Manage. · Nest. · Prey · VA
1103	**Habit. Loss** · Caledon SP · Disturb. · Manage. · Nest. · VA
1104	**Habit. Loss** · Behav. · Caledon SP · Disturb. · Habit. Use · Manage. · VA
1109	**Habit. Loss** · Behav. · Habit. Use · Intersp. Behav. · Intrasp. Behav. · ID · Manage. · Prey · Winter Survey · Wolf Lodge Bay
1179	**Habit. Loss** · AZ · Nest. · Orme D
1195	**Habit. Loss** · Chippewa NF · Disturb. · MN · USFS
1360	**Habit. Loss** · Nest. Survey · Pest. · Shooting · Techniques · Terminology · USFWS
1440	**Habit. Loss** · Behav. · Habit. Use · Kentucky Wood. NWR · KY · Winter Survey
1441	**Habit. Loss** · Kentucky Wood. NWR · KY · Status · Winter Survey
1500	**Habit. Loss** · Nest. · OH
1521	**Habit. Loss** · Aggress. · Behav. · Disturb. · Hunt. Behav. · Nest. · Prey · San Juan Is. · Shooting · Status · Vocal. · WA
1550	**Habit. Loss** · AZ · Behav. · Disturb. · Habit. Use · Hunt. Behav. · Nest. Survey · Prey · Status · Terminology · Territory
1572	**Habit. Loss** · OR · USFWS · WA
1640	**Habit. Loss** · Aggress. · Behav. · BLM · Disturb. · Habit. Use · Hunt. Behav. · Life History · Manage. · Nest. · Pest. · Prey · Shooting · Territory
1697	**Habit. Loss** · Ft. Randall D · Habit. Use · Hunt. Behav. · Migration · Prey · SD · Winter Survey
1760	**Habit. Loss** · FL · NAS · Status
1771	**Habit. Loss** · CA · Disturb. · Habit. Use · Manage. · Nest. Survey · Prey · Shooting · Territory · Trapping
1811	**Habit. Loss** · Behav. · Pub. Ed.
1920	**Habit. Loss** · Disturb. · Manage. · Nest. Survey · ON · Status
1965	**Habit. Loss** · AZ · CAP · Nest. · Orme D
99	**Habit. Prot.** · VA
128	**Habit. Prot.** · Indian Culture · Manage. · MN · Refuge · St. Croix R · WI
144	**Habit. Prot.**
153	**Habit. Prot.** · Missouri R · NWF · SD · Winter. Pop.
168	**Habit. Prot.** · Manage. · Nat. Conserv. · Skagit R · Wash. Dept. Game · Winter. Pop. · WA
176	**Habit. Prot.** · NWF · Refuge · Southland · SD
450	**Habit. Prot.** · ME · Nest. Survey · Pub. Ed. · RIC · Shooting · Status
503	**Habit. Prot.** · Nat. Conserv. · Prey · Refuge · Skagit R Nat. Area · WA
556	**Habit. Prot.** · Cedar Glen Roost · Habit. Use · IL · Manage. · Prey · Refuge
573	**Habit. Prot.** · Marking · Nest. · Pub. Ed. · Techniques · Winter. Pop.
648	**Habit. Prot.** · IA · IL · Mississippi R · MO · Winter Survey
672	**Habit. Prot.** · FL · Refuge · Three Lakes Ranch
674	**Habit. Prot.** · FL · Refuge · Three Lakes Ranch
702	**Habit. Prot.** · Karl Mundt NWR · L Andes NWR · Manage. · Missouri R · NWF · Refuge · SD · Winter. Pop.
703	**Habit. Prot.** · Karl Mundt NWR · Missouri R · Refuge · SD · Winter. Pop.
983	**Habit. Prot.** · Egg Trans. · Nest. · Pub. Ed. · Winter. Pop.
998	**Habit. Prot.** · Refuge · Skagit R Nat. Area · Winter. Pop. · WA
1087	**Habit. Prot.** · Manage. · NWF · Pub. Ed. · SD · Techniques · Winter. Pop. · Young Trans.
1147	**Habit. Prot.** · Great Lakes · Manage. · MB · Nest. Survey · ON · Rehab. · Techniques · Techniques
1206	**Habit. Prot.** · Chippewa NF · Hunt-Wesson · MN · Pub. Ed. · USFS
1295	**Habit. Prot.** · Manage. · Nat. Conserv. · WA
1328	**Habit. Prot.** · NWF · Pub. Ed. · Research · RIC
1330	**Habit. Prot.** · Ferry Bluff Sanct. · NWF · Refuge · Winter. Pop. · Wisconsin R · WI
1332	**Habit. Prot.** · CA · IL · NWF · RIC
1334	**Habit. Prot.** · Manage. · Nat. Conserv. · Refuge · Skagit R Nat. Area · Winter Survey · WA

Master No.	Keywords
1346	**Habit. Prot.** · Manage. · NWF · Pub. Ed. · Reward
1348	**Habit. Prot.** · Karl Mundt NWR · Manage. · NWF
1381	**Habit. Prot.** · Manage. · Pub. Ed.
1431	**Habit. Prot.** · Ferry Bluff Sanct. · Refuge · WI
1772	**Habit. Prot.** · IL · Winter Survey
1773	**Habit. Prot.** · IL · Oak V. Eagle Sanct. · Refuge
1820	**Habit. Prot.** · Manage. · Nest. · USFS · Winter Survey
1828	**Habit. Prot.** · Endang. Sp. · Manage. · MN
1865	**Habit. Prot.** · AZ · BLM · CAP · Egg · Manage. · Nest. · Orme D · Salt R · Taxonomy · Territory · Verde R
1883	**Habit. Prot.** · Bear Valley NWR · OR · Refuge · USFWS
51	**Habit. Use** · Disturb. · Manage. · Nest. · OR · USFS
197	**Habit. Use** · LA · MS · Nest. Survey
215	**Habit. Use** · Egg Coll. · Nest. · Photo. · VA
266	**Habit. Use** · Anat. · Behav. · BC · Distrib. · Falconry · Field ID · Flight · Migration · Nest. · Prey · Status
273	**Habit. Use** · Aggress. · Behav. · Captivity · Distrib. · Egg Coll. · Life History · Nest. · Status
274	**Habit. Use** · Aggress. · Behav. · Captivity · Distrib. · Life History · Nest. · Status
301	**Habit. Use** · Disturb. · IL · Nest. · Ohio R · Rehab. · Shooting · Techniques · Winter. Pop.
325	**Habit. Use** · Behav. · Dispersal · Disturb. · FL · Intersp. Behav. · Migration · Mortality · Nest. · Prey
355	**Habit. Use** · CA
376	**Habit. Use** · LA · Nest. · Winter. Pop.
377	**Habit. Use** · Distrib. · GA · Life History · Migration · Nest. · Status
451	**Habit. Use** · CO · Nest. · San Luis Valley · Status · Winter Survey
465	**Habit. Use** · AK · Disturb. · Habit. Loss · Logging · Nest. · Nest. Survey · Territory
466	**Habit. Use** · AK · Climatology · Distrib. · Disturb. · Forestry · Habit. Loss · Manage. · Nest. · Nest. Survey · Reprod. Succ. · Territory
474	**Habit. Use** · CO · Nest. · San Luis Valley · Status · Winter Survey
479	**Habit. Use** · Ches. Bay · Egg Coll.
489	**Habit. Use** · AK · Indian Culture · Prey
500	**Habit. Use** · CA · Egg Coll. · Nest.
506	**Habit. Use** · Captivity · CA · Depred. · Distrib. · Life History · Nest. · Santa Barbara Is.
519	**Habit. Use** · CA · Depred. · Manage. · Mortality · Nest. · Prey · Shasta-Trinity NF · Winter Survey
520	**Habit. Use** · Distrib. · Migration · Nest. Survey · Status · Winter Survey · WI
556	**Habit. Use** · Cedar Glen Roost · Habit. Prot. · IL · Manage. · Prey · Refuge
559	**Habit. Use** · Art. Nest Site · Behav. · Manage. · MN · Nest. · Techniques · Young Trans.
561	**Habit. Use** · Behav. · Fledging · Marking · MN · Parent. Behav. · Techniques · Telemetry
577	**Habit. Use** · Aleutian Is. · AK · Bounty · Nest. · Status · Symbolism
581	**Habit. Use** · DE · Egg Coll. · MD · Nest.
583	**Habit. Use** · Manage. · Nest. Survey · OR · Poison. · Prey · San Juan Is. · Shooting · Status · Winter Survey · WA
609	**Habit. Use** · Behav. · Mississippi R · MN · Pest. Residues · Prey · Winter Survey
665	**Habit. Use** · Nest. · OH
673	**Habit. Use** · FL · Nest. Survey · Reprod. Succ.
711	**Habit. Use** · AK · Distrib. · Life History · Plumage · Status
713	**Habit. Use** · Life History · OR
714	**Habit. Use** · Distrib. · Nest. · Plumage · Shooting · Taxonomy · TN · Winter. Pop.
715	**Habit. Use** · AR · Mississippi R · MS · Nest. · Reelfoot L · Shooting · TN
726	**Habit. Use** · MB · Reprod. Succ. · Status · SK · Techniques

Master No.	Keywords
728	**Habit. Use** · Habit. Loss · Manage. · McHargian Overlay · Nest. · Reprod. Succ. · SK · Techniques
732	**Habit. Use** · Disturb. · MB · Nest. · SK · Territory
734	**Habit. Use** · Habit. Loss · Road Plan. · SK · Techniques
735	**Habit. Use** · Disturb. · Intersp. Behav. · SK
736	**Habit. Use** · Marking · Migration · MO · ND · SD · SK · Techniques · WY
749	**Habit. Use** · Egg Coll. · IN · Nest.
770	**Habit. Use** · AZ · CAP · Disturb. · Manage. · Nest. · Orme D
777	**Habit. Use** · CN · ON · Reprod. Succ. · Status · Techniques · Territory
780	**Habit. Use** · CN · Disturb. · Lake of The Woods · Manage. · ON
792	**Habit. Use** · Behav. · CA · Intersp. Behav. · Nest. · Winter. Pop.
794	**Habit. Use** · CA · Distrib. · Winter. Pop.
803	**Habit. Use** · Life History · Nest. · Photo. · Pub. Ed. · Winter. Pop. · WA
804	**Habit. Use** · Art. Nest Site · AZ · Egg. Thin. · Life History · Manage. · Marking · Nest. · Pest. · Research · Techniques · Telemetry · Winter. Pop.
805	**Habit. Use** · Nest. Survey · Reprod. Succ. · San Juan Is. · WA
821	**Habit. Use** · OK · Status · Winter Survey
826	**Habit. Use** · BC · Gulf Is. · Migration · Nest. Survey · Prey · San Juan Is. · Techniques · Winter Survey · WA
836	**Habit. Use** · Behav. · Disturb. · Habit. Loss · Hunt. Behav. · Logging · Manage. · Prey · Winter Survey · WA
840	**Habit. Use** · Behav. · Capture · CO · Marking · Migration · Techniques · Winter Survey
863	**Habit. Use** · AK · Hunt. Behav. · Nest. Survey · Prey · Status
871	**Habit. Use** · Disturb. · FL · Kissimee B.E. Sanct. · Nest. Survey · Refuge · Reprod. Succ.
872	**Habit. Use** · Disturb. · FL · Kissimee B.E. Sanct. · Nest. Survey · Refuge · Reprod. Succ.
878	**Habit. Use** · AK · Disturb. · Kodiak NWR · Life History · Nest. Fail. · Reprod. Succ. · Territory
933	**Habit. Use** · AR · Shooting · Winter. Pop.
968	**Habit. Use** · Behav. · Growth
972	**Habit. Use** · Behav. · Disturb. · Nest. · Snake R · WY
989	**Habit. Use** · AK · Migration · Nest. · Winter. Pop.
996	**Habit. Use** · Disturb. · Fledging · Intersp. Behav. · Intrasp. Behav. · VA
1001	**Habit. Use** · Acct. · AZ
1011	**Habit. Use** · Behav. · Climatology · Hunt. Behav. · Intersp. Behav. · Intrasp. Behav. · IA · IL · Mississippi R · MO · Prey · Winter Survey
1018	**Habit. Use** · Chippewa NF · Disturb. · Manage. · MN · Nest. · Prey · Reprod. Succ.
1019	**Habit. Use** · Chippewa NF · Disturb. · Manage.
1048	**Habit. Use** · AK · Nest. Survey · Techniques
1058	**Habit. Use** · Intersp. Behav. · Life History · ME · Nest. · Status
1063	**Habit. Use** · Behav. · Disturb. · Habit. Loss · Manage. · Prey · Research · TX · Winter Survey
1065	**Habit. Use** · Behav. · CA · Disturb. · Klamath · Lower Klamath Lake NWR · Manage. · OR · Prey · Tule Lake NWR · Winter Survey
1068	**Habit. Use** · Habit. Loss · Nest. · WI
1069	**Habit. Use** · Habit. Loss · Nest. · WI
1102	**Habit. Use** · Behav. · Caledon SP · Disturb. · Habit. Loss · Manage. · Nest. · Prey · VA
1104	**Habit. Use** · Behav. · Caledon SP · Disturb. · Habit. Loss · Manage. · VA
1109	**Habit. Use** · Behav. · Habit. Loss · Intersp. Behav. · Intrasp. Behav. · ID · Manage. · Prey · Winter Survey · Wolf Lodge Bay
1110	**Habit. Use** · CA · Depred. · Prey · San Clemente Is.
1112	**Habit. Use** · Autopsy · Disturb. · Hunt. Behav. · Intersp. Behav. · Manage. · Migration · OK · Prey · Salt Fork R · Shooting · Status · Taxonomy · Winter Survey

Master No.	Keywords
1114	**Habit. Use** · Arkansas R · Band. · Capture · Intersp. Behav. · OK · Salt Plains NWR · Sequoyah NWR · Techniques · Wichita Mts. NWR · Winter Survey · Winter. Pop.
1115	**Habit. Use** · Disturb. · Manage. · Migration · OK · Prey · Salt Fork R · Salt Plains NWR · Sequoyah NWR · Shooting · Status · Taxonomy · Wichita Mts. NWR · Winter Survey
1187	**Habit. Use** · Life History · Nest. Survey · Prey · Winter Survey · WA
1188	**Habit. Use** · Chippewa NF · Manage. · MN · Nest. Survey · Status · USFS
1189	**Habit. Use** · Chippewa NF · Manage. · MN · Nest. Survey · USFS
1197	**Habit. Use** · Chippewa NF · Field ID · MN · Nest. · USFS
1224	**Habit. Use** · Nest. Survey · Superior NF · USFS
1229	**Habit. Use** · Anat. · Autumn Conc. · Behav. · Capture · Glacier NP · Manage. · Marking · Migration · MT · Techniques · Winter Survey
1234	**Habit. Use** · Egg. Thin. · FL · Nest. Survey · Ocala NF · Prey · Reprod. Succ.
1237	**Habit. Use** · Distrib. · Endang. Sp. · Migration · Nest. · ND · Status · Winter. Pop.
1244	**Habit. Use** · Ches. Bay · Distrib. · MD · Pub. Ed.
1272	**Habit. Use** · Endang. Sp. · Manage. · MN · Status
1299	**Habit. Use** · Intersp. Behav. · Nest. Survey · Territory · Yellowstone NP
1351	**Habit. Use** · FL · Nest. Survey
1352	**Habit. Use** · Fla. B.E. Sur. Comm. · FL · Nest. Survey · Status
1357	**Habit. Use** · FL · Life History · Nest. · Status
1363	**Habit. Use** · Nest. Survey · WI
1368	**Habit. Use** · Behav. · Climatology · Disturb. · Hunt. Behav. · Intersp. Behav. · Intrasp. Behav. · Manage. · NY · Prey · Winter Survey
1369	**Habit. Use** · Behav. · Heavy Metals · Hunt. Behav. · Intersp. Behav. · Intrasp. Behav. · Manage. · NY · Pest. · Prey · PCB · Winter Survey
1372	**Habit. Use** · Anat. · Distrib. · Nest. · Plumage · Taxonomy · TX · Winter. Pop.
1440	**Habit. Use** · Behav. · Habit. Loss · Kentucky Wood. NWR · KY · Winter Survey
1470	**Habit. Use** · Behav. · Hunt. Behav. · Prey · UT · Winter Survey
1497	**Habit. Use** · Disturb. · Nest.
1505	**Habit. Use** · Nest. · Winter. Pop. · WA
1511	**Habit. Use** · Behav. · Heavy Metals · Nest. · NY · Pest. · PCB
1529	**Habit. Use** · AK · Hunt. Behav. · Manage. · Pub. Ed. · Status
1530	**Habit. Use** · AK · Manage. · Nest. Survey · Territory
1550	**Habit. Use** · AZ · Behav. · Disturb. · Habit. Loss · Hunt. Behav. · Nest. Survey · Prey · Status · Terminology · Territory
1555	**Habit. Use** · Egg Coll. · FL · Nest. · Shooting
1556	**Habit. Use** · Egg Coll. · Nest.
1591	**Habit. Use** · Behav. · Climatology · Disturb. · Intrasp. Behav. · Plumage · Prey · Skagit R · Winter Survey · WA
1606	**Habit. Use** · Aggress. · Aleutian Is. · AK · Behav. · Depred. · Life History · Mortality · Nest. Survey · Plumage · Prey · Reprod. Succ. · Status · Winter Survey
1608	**Habit. Use** · NE · Platte R · Winter Survey
1632	**Habit. Use** · Distrib. · Nest. Survey · Status · TX · Winter Survey
1640	**Habit. Use** · Aggress. · Behav. · BLM · Disturb. · Habit. Loss · Hunt. Behav. · Life History · Manage. · Nest. · Pest. · Prey · Shooting · Territory
1650	**Habit. Use** · Capture · Hunt. Behav. · Intersp. Behav. · IL · Marking · Mississippi R · Prey · Techniques · Winter Survey
1657	**Habit. Use** · Egg Coll. · Logging · ME · Nest.
1669	**Habit. Use** · Acct. · New England

Master No.	Keywords
1695	**Habit. Use** · Behav. · Ft. Randall D · Hunt. Behav. · Karl Mundt NWR · L Andes NWR · SD · Winter Survey
1696	**Habit. Use** · Climatology · Ft. Randall D · Hunt. Behav. · Karl Mundt NWR · L Andes NWR · Manage. · Prey · SD · Winter Survey
1697	**Habit. Use** · Ft. Randall D · Habit. Loss · Hunt. Behav. · Migration · Prey · SD · Winter Survey
1698	**Habit. Use** · Climatology · Disturb. · Electro. · Manage. · Prey · Winter Survey
1699	**Habit. Use** · Behav. · Disturb. · Ft. Randall D · Manage. · Missouri R · SD · Winter Survey
1734	**Habit. Use** · Nest. · OK · Prey · Winter. Pop.
1741	**Habit. Use** · Disturb. · Manage. · MT · Nest. Survey · Pop. Turnover · Reprod. Succ. · Status · Territory · Yellowstone NP
1742	**Habit. Use** · Nest. Survey · TX
1743	**Habit. Use** · Prey · UT · Winter. Pop.
1751	**Habit. Use** · Egg. Thin. · Manage. · MD · Nest. Survey · Pest.
1752	**Habit. Use** · Egg. Thin. · Manage. · MD · Nest. Survey · Pest. · Techniques
1771	**Habit. Use** · CA · Disturb. · Habit. Loss · Manage. · Nest. Survey · Prey · Shooting · Territory · Trapping
1777	**Habit. Use** · CA · Manage. · Nest. Survey · Status · Territory
1795	**Habit. Use** · Behav. · Life History · Nest. · Pub. Ed. · PA · Taxonomy
1804	**Habit. Use** · AK · Kodiak Is. · Kodiak NWR · Nest. Survey
1812	**Habit. Use** · Ches. Bay · DE · Econ. Import. · Life History · MD · Nest. Survey · NC · NJ · Prey · PA · VA
1895	**Habit. Use** · Behav. · Hunt. Behav. · Intrasp. Behav. · Migration · NE · Platte R · Winter Survey
1931	**Habit. Use** · Amchitka Is. · AK · Egg. Thin. · Nest. Survey · Prey · Winter Survey
1939	**Habit. Use** · MB · Nest. Survey · SK · Terminology
1967	**Habit. Use** · CA · Disturb. · Lower Klamath Lake NWR · Modoc NWR · Tule Lake NWR · Winter Survey
1984	**Habit. Use** · Platte R · Snake R · Winter Survey · WY
1985	**Habit. Use** · Platte R · Snake R · Winter Survey · WY
166	**Hacking** · Manage. · NY · Techniques · Young Trans.
387	**Hacking** · Manage. · Montezuma NWR · NY · Techniques · WI · Young Trans.
414	**Hacking** · Montezuma NWR · NY · Techniques · Telemetry · Young Trans.
504	**Hacking** · CA · Rehab. · Techniques
1034	**Hacking** · Manage. · NY · Photo. · Techniques
1253	**Hacking** · Behav. · Heavy Metals · Intrasp. Behav. · Marking · Montezuma NWR · MI · MN · NY · Pest. · Techniques · Telemetry · Young Trans.
1254	**Hacking** · NY · Pub. Ed. · Techniques · Young Trans.
1255	**Hacking** · Manage. · NY · Techniques · Young Trans.
1256	**Hacking** · Behav. · Manage. · NY · Pest. · Prey · PCB · Techniques · Young Trans.
1732	**Hacking** · Egg. Thin. · NY · Techniques · Telemetry · Young Trans.
1871	**Hacking** · Egg Trans. · Manage. · ME · MN · NY · Pest. · PCB · Techniques · WI · Young Trans.
147	**Hawk Mt.** · Migration · PA
308	**Hawk Mt.** · Educ. Mat. · Field ID · Migration · Pub. Ed. · PA · Shooting
318	**Hawk Mt.** · Migration · PA
346	**Hawk Mt.** · Migration · PA
347	**Hawk Mt.** · Bounty · Pub. Ed. · PA · Status
712	**Hawk Mt.** · CO · Migration · PA · Status
850	**Hawk Mt.** · Derby Hill · Great Lakes · Migration · NY
855	**Hawk Mt.** · Migration · Pub. Ed. · PA
1233	**Hawk Mt.** · Field ID · Mt. Johnson Is. Sanct. · PA
1307	**Hawk Mt.** · Migration · NJ
1308	**Hawk Mt.** · Migration · PA · Status

Master No.	Keywords
134	**Heavy Metals** · Mortality · MN
139	**Heavy Metals** · Mortality · MN
201	**Heavy Metals** · Lead Poison.
269	**Heavy Metals** · Autopsy · FL · Midwest Region · MD · ME · MO · ND · Pest. · PCB
528	**Heavy Metals** · Anal. Tech. · Blood · Dieldrin · Pest.
659	**Heavy Metals** · ON
779	**Heavy Metals** · Egg. Thin. · ON · Pest. · PCB · Reprod. Succ. · Status
783	**Heavy Metals** · Disturb. · Egg. Thin. · Nest. Survey · ON · Pest. · PCB · Reprod. Succ. · Status
984	**Heavy Metals** · Captivity · Egg Trans. · Law · Manage. · Migration · Nest. Survey · Pest. · Pub. Ed. · Status · Techniques · Territory · Young Trans.
994	**Heavy Metals** · Disease · Histology · Lead Poison. · MD · Techniques
1064	**Heavy Metals** · FL · ME · Nest. · Pest. · PCB · Reprod. Succ. · WI
1127	**Heavy Metals** · Disease · Fowl Cholera · OH · Pest.
1253	**Heavy Metals** · Behav. · Hacking · Intrasp. Behav. · Marking · Montezuma NWR · MI · MN · NY · Pest. · Techniques · Telemetry · Young Trans.
1367	**Heavy Metals** · Life History · Taxonomy · Toxicol.
1369	**Heavy Metals** · Behav. · Habit. Use · Hunt. Behav. · Intersp. Behav. · Intrasp. Behav. · Manage. · NY · Pest. · Prey · PCB · Winter Survey
1482	**Heavy Metals** · Egg. Thin. · ON · Pest. · PCB
1511	**Heavy Metals** · Behav. · Habit. Use · Nest. · NY · Pest. · PCB
1873	**Heavy Metals** · IL · Lead Poison. · Poison.
1942	**Heavy Metals** · AK · Egg. Thin. · FL · Great Lakes · ME · Pest. · PCB
710	**Helicop.** · Disturb. · Pub. Ed.
827	**Helicop.** · Barkley Sound · Behav. · BC · Disturb. · Gulf Is. · Nest. Survey · Plumage · Prey
829	**Helicop.** · Barkley Sound · BC · Disturb. · Gulf Is.
830	**Helicop.** · BC · Nest. Survey · Techniques
831	**Helicop.** · BC · Disturb. · Nest. Survey · Pest. · Refuge

Master No.	Keywords
1932	**Helicop.** · AK · Disturb. · Nest. Survey · Techniques
994	**Histology** · Disease · Heavy Metals · Lead Poison. · MD · Techniques
1126	**Histology** · DDT · Pest. · Phys. · Spermato. · Techniques
1708	**Histology** · AK · Lower 48 · Pest. · Spermato. · Techniques · Toxicol. · USFWS
55	**History** · Aggress. · Flight · Folklore · Hunt. Behav. · Intersp. Behav.
56	**History** · Aggress. · Flight · Folklore · Hunt. Behav. · Intersp. Behav.
72	**History** · Captivity · Old Abe · WI
73	**History** · Pub. Ed. · Status · Symbolism
79	**History** · Bounty · Status · Symbolism
83	**History** · Pub. Ed. · Status · Symbolism
84	**History** · Art · Symbolism
85	**History** · Pub. Ed. · Status
92	**History** · Art · PA · Symbolism
95	**History** · Symbolism
98	**History** · Hunt. Behav. · Symbolism
109	**History** · Hunt. Behav. · Symbolism
112	**History** · Life History · Pub. Ed. · Symbolism
113	**History** · Symbolism
114	**History** · Symbolism
118	**History** · Pub. Ed. · Symbolism
136	**History** · Art · Symbolism
162	**History** · OH
165	**History** · Pub. Ed. · Status
190	**History** · Audubon · Shooting · Taxonomy
279	**History** · Symbolism
295	**History** · Old Abe · WI
384	**History** · Law · Life History · Pub. Ed.
417	**History** · Old Abe · WI
428	**History** · Indian Culture · Symbolism
429	**History** · Aggress. · Hunt. Behav. · Life History · Nest. · Poetry · PA · Shooting · Status · Susquehanna R
430	**History** · Life History · Nest.
448	**History** · Poetry
454	**History** · Symbolism
461	**History** · Art · Mortality · Status · Symbolism
534	**History** · Symbolism
597	**History** · Indian Culture · Symbolism
655	**History** · Old Abe
663	**History** · Captivity · DC · Pub. Ed.
817	**History** · Acct. · WA

Master No.	Keywords
818	**History** · Acct. · Shooting · WA
820	**History** · Old Abe
884	**History** · Behav. · Nest. · OH · Photo. · Techniques
910	**History** · BC · Indian Culture
921	**History** · Art · Symbolism
1009	**History** · Folklore · Pub. Ed.
1142	**History** · Symbolism
1186	**History** · Feather War · Indian Culture · Law
1242	**History** · Nest. Survey · NJ · Pest. · Status
1261	**History** · Indian Culture · OR
1270	**History** · Falconry · Folklore
1284	**History** · Symbolism
1388	**History** · Nest. · Pub. Ed. · SD · Winter. Pop.
1429	**History** · Life History · Pub. Ed.
1461	**History** · Law
1542	**History** · Pest. · Pub. Ed.
1544	**History** · Pub. Ed. · Status · Symbolism
1548	**History** · Symbolism
1560	**History** · Symbolism
1561	**History** · Pub. Ed. · Status
1564	**History** · Pub. Ed. · Symbolism
1565	**History** · Hunt. Behav. · Prey
1607	**History** · Old Abe
1703	**History** · Pub. Ed.
1722	**History** · Life History
1739	**History** · MA · Photo. · Winter. Pop.
1805	**History** · Behav. · FL · Photo. · Status
1864	**History** · Art · Indian Culture · USFWS
1905	**History** · Life History · Pub. Ed. · Status
1937	**History** · Life History · Pub. Ed.
1972	**History** · Life History · Pub. Ed.
1995	**History** · Old Abe
1774	**Hook Mt.** · Climatology · Migration · NY
457	**Hudson Bay** · Intersp. Behav. · MB · Nest. · Prey
1067	**Hudson R** · Art · Broley · Catesby · FL · Winter. Pop.
1539	**Hudson R** · NY · Winter. Pop.
55	**Hunt. Behav.** · Aggress. · Flight · Folklore · History · Intersp. Behav.
56	**Hunt. Behav.** · Aggress. · Flight · Folklore · History · Intersp. Behav.
62	**Hunt. Behav.** · Folklore · Growth · Indian Culture · Life History · Plumage
86	**Hunt. Behav.** · Depred. · Folklore
93	**Hunt. Behav.** · Aggress. · Econ. Import. · Folklore
98	**Hunt. Behav.** · History · Symbolism
109	**Hunt. Behav.** · History · Symbolism
192	**Hunt. Behav.** · Intersp. Behav. · Life History · Prey
220	**Hunt. Behav.** · OH · Winter. Pop.
250	**Hunt. Behav.** · FL · Intersp. Behav. · Prey · Shooting
272	**Hunt. Behav.** · NJ
283	**Hunt. Behav.** · Intersp. Behav.
292	**Hunt. Behav.** · AK
293	**Hunt. Behav.** · Intersp. Behav. · Yellowstone NP
309	**Hunt. Behav.** · Prey · Shooting · VA · Winter. Pop.
342	**Hunt. Behav.** · BC · Econ. Import. · Prey · Shooting
364	**Hunt. Behav.** · IL · Mississippi R · MO · Winter Survey
401	**Hunt. Behav.** · BC · Intersp. Behav. · Prey
411	**Hunt. Behav.** · Captivity · NY · Winter. Pop.
415	**Hunt. Behav.** · Depred. · MT
429	**Hunt. Behav.** · Aggress. · History · Life History · Nest. · Poetry · PA · Shooting · Status · Susquehanna R
444	**Hunt. Behav.** · Anat. · Folklore · NC · Shooting
447	**Hunt. Behav.** · Behav. · CA · Disturb. · Manage. · Natl. For. · Prey · San Bernardino Mts. · USFS · Winter. Pop.
463	**Hunt. Behav.** · Life History · Prey
478	**Hunt. Behav.** · Prey · Winter. Pop. · WI
490	**Hunt. Behav.** · AK · Prey
514	**Hunt. Behav.** · IN · Nest. · Prey
531	**Hunt. Behav.** · Aging · AK · Behav. · Life History · Nest. · Prey · Sexing · Techniques
572	**Hunt. Behav.** · Aircraft · Behav. · CA · Distrib. · Disturb. · Habit. Loss · Klamath R · Manage. · Nest.
592	**Hunt. Behav.** · Field ID · OR · Prey
605	**Hunt. Behav.** · Taxonomy
664	**Hunt. Behav.** · Anat. · Econ. Import. · Life History · Prey
683	**Hunt. Behav.** · Behav. · CA · Distrib. · Disturb. · Field ID · Flight · Life History · Manage. · Mortality · Nest. · Winter. Pop.

Master No.	Keywords
706	**Hunt. Behav.** · MN · Prey · Winter. Pop.
724	**Hunt. Behav.** · OR
738	**Hunt. Behav.** · CA · Depred. · Prey
744	**Hunt. Behav.** · Nest. · NS · Prey
767	**Hunt. Behav.** · Autumn Conc. · AK · Chilkat R · Indian Culture · Photo. · Pub. Ed.
786	**Hunt. Behav.** · Behav. · Distrib. · Manage. · Marking · Migration · Mortality · MO · Nest. · Pest. · Prey · Swan Lake NWR · Techniques · Telemetry
796	**Hunt. Behav.** · MA · Nest. · Prey · Winter. Pop.
799	**Hunt. Behav.** · Intersp. Behav. · Winter. Pop. · WI
816	**Hunt. Behav.** · Nest. · PA · Terminology
833	**Hunt. Behav.** · BC · Intersp. Behav. · Intrasp. Behav. · Nest. Survey · Prey · Territory
836	**Hunt. Behav.** · Behav. · Disturb. · Habit. Loss · Habit. Use · Logging · Manage. · Prey · Winter Survey · WA
838	**Hunt. Behav.** · IA · Mississippi R · Prey · Winter. Pop.
842	**Hunt. Behav.** · Behav. · Chippewa NF · Dispersal · Fledging · MN · Nestling · Techniques · Telemetry
848	**Hunt. Behav.** · Prey
856	**Hunt. Behav.** · Prey
859	**Hunt. Behav.** · Intersp. Behav. · Prey · WA
861	**Hunt. Behav.** · GA · Prey
863	**Hunt. Behav.** · AK · Habit. Use · Nest. Survey · Prey · Status
864	**Hunt. Behav.**
883	**Hunt. Behav.** · Behav. · Fledging · Life History · Nest. · OH · Prey
892	**Hunt. Behav.** · IA · Mississippi R · Prey · Winter. Pop.
916	**Hunt. Behav.** · MN · Prey
920	**Hunt. Behav.** · MT · Prey
1011	**Hunt. Behav.** · Behav. · Climatology · Habit. Use · Intersp. Behav. · Intrasp. Behav. · IA · IL · Mississippi R · MO · Prey · Winter Survey
1015	**Hunt. Behav.** · Nest. · OH · Winter. Pop.
1021	**Hunt. Behav.** · GA · Prey · Sapelo Is.
1040	**Hunt. Behav.** · CA · Prey · San Bernardino Mts.

Master No.	Keywords
1042	**Hunt. Behav.** · Aleutian Is. · AK · Nest. · Prey · Status
1062	**Hunt. Behav.** · MN · Prey
1084	**Hunt. Behav.** · Anat. · Life History · Migration · Nest. · Plumage
1112	**Hunt. Behav.** · Autopsy · Disturb. · Habit. Use · Intersp. Behav. · Manage. · Migration · OK · Prey · Salt Fork R · Shooting · Status · Taxonomy · Winter Survey
1113	**Hunt. Behav.** · Intrasp. Behav. · Migration · Neosho R · OK · Prey · Winter Survey
1221	**Hunt. Behav.** · Aging · Behav. · Impound. · Intrasp. Behav. · MI · Nest. · Ottawa NF · Techniques · Territory
1222	**Hunt. Behav.** · Behav. · Fledging · Intersp. Behav. · Intrasp. Behav. · Marking · MI · Ottawa NF · Techniques · Territory
1228	**Hunt. Behav.** · Glacier NP · Intersp. Behav. · MN · Prey · Winter Survey
1235	**Hunt. Behav.** · Intrasp. Behav. · LA · Nest. · Prey · Winter. Pop.
1249	**Hunt. Behav.** · Swimming
1293	**Hunt. Behav.** · BC
1294	**Hunt. Behav.** · BC · Intersp. Behav. · Nest. · Prey
1355	**Hunt. Behav.** · Prey · Territory · Winter. Pop.
1361	**Hunt. Behav.** · FL · Prey
1368	**Hunt. Behav.** · Behav. · Climatology · Disturb. · Habit. Use · Intersp. Behav. · Intrasp. Behav. · Manage. · NY · Prey · Winter Survey
1369	**Hunt. Behav.** · Behav. · Habit. Use · Heavy Metals · Intersp. Behav. · Intrasp. Behav. · Manage. · NY · Pest. · Prey · PCB · Winter Survey
1371	**Hunt. Behav.** · Life History · LA · Pub. Ed. · Taxonomy
1373	**Hunt. Behav.** · AK · Prey
1374	**Hunt. Behav.** · BC · Intersp. Behav.
1391	**Hunt. Behav.** · Migration · ME · Prey · Winter Survey
1403	**Hunt. Behav.** · TN · Winter Survey
1411	**Hunt. Behav.** · BC · Nest. · Vancouver Is.
1412	**Hunt. Behav.** · BC · Intersp. Behav.
1413	**Hunt. Behav.** · BC · Intersp. Behav.

Master No.	Keywords
1416	**Hunt. Behav.** · FL · Life History · Nest. · Prey
1453	**Hunt. Behav.** · IA · IL · Mississippi R · Winter. Pop.
1470	**Hunt. Behav.** · Behav. · Habit. Use · Prey · UT · Winter Survey
1472	**Hunt. Behav.** · Prey
1476	**Hunt. Behav.** · MI · Prey · Winter Survey
1519	**Hunt. Behav.** · FL
1521	**Hunt. Behav.** · Aggress. · Behav. · Disturb. · Habit. Loss · Nest. · Prey · San Juan Is. · Shooting · Status · Vocal. · WA
1529	**Hunt. Behav.** · AK · Habit. Use · Manage. · Pub. Ed. · Status
1537	**Hunt. Behav.** · Life History · Migration · MN · Nest. · Prey · Shooting · Status · Winter. Pop.
1550	**Hunt. Behav.** · AZ · Behav. · Disturb. · Habit. Loss · Habit. Use · Nest. Survey · Prey · Status · Terminology · Territory
1565	**Hunt. Behav.** · History · Prey
1583	**Hunt. Behav.** · Intrasp. Behav. · MA · Prey · Winter. Pop.
1590	**Hunt. Behav.** · BC · Intersp. Behav.
1601	**Hunt. Behav.** · Behav. · Capture · Glacier NP · Intersp. Behav. · Intrasp. Behav. · Manage. · MT · Techniques · Winter Survey
1602	**Hunt. Behav.** · Autumn Conc. · Glacier NP · MT · Prey
1605	**Hunt. Behav.** · Aleutian Is. · AK · Prey
1626	**Hunt. Behav.** · Hurricane · MD · Nest. · Prey
1640	**Hunt. Behav.** · Aggress. · Behav. · BLM · Disturb. · Habit. Loss · Habit. Use · Life History · Manage. · Nest. · Pest. · Prey · Shooting · Territory
1642	**Hunt. Behav.** · Anat. · Dimorphism · Prey
1650	**Hunt. Behav.** · Capture · Habit. Use · Intersp. Behav. · IL · Marking · Mississippi R · Prey · Techniques · Winter Survey
1651	**Hunt. Behav.** · Anat. · Behav. · Capture · IL · Marking · Plumage · Prey · Techniques · Telemetry · Winter Survey
1695	**Hunt. Behav.** · Behav. · Ft. Randall D · Habit. Use · Karl Mundt NWR · L Andes NWR · SD · Winter Survey
1696	**Hunt. Behav.** · Climatology · Ft. Randall D · Habit. Use · Karl Mundt NWR · L Andes NWR · Manage. · Prey · SD · Winter Survey
1697	**Hunt. Behav.** · Ft. Randall D · Habit. Loss · Habit. Use · Migration · Prey · SD · Winter Survey
1702	**Hunt. Behav.** · Acct. · Nest. · NC · Prey
1879	**Hunt. Behav.** · Behav. · Intersp. Behav. · ID · L Couer D' Alene · Manage. · Winter Survey
1881	**Hunt. Behav.** · Manage. · Nest. · OR · Winter. Pop. · WA
1894	**Hunt. Behav.** · IL · Winter. Pop.
1895	**Hunt. Behav.** · Behav. · Habit. Use · Intrasp. Behav. · Migration · NE · Platte R · Winter Survey
1927	**Hunt. Behav.** · CA
1944	**Hunt. Behav.** · Depred. · NM · TX
1954	**Hunt. Behav.** · AK · Law · Migration · Nest. · Pub. Ed. · WY · Yellowstone NP
1955	**Hunt. Behav.** · AK · Law · Migration · Nest. · Pub. Ed. · WY · Yellowstone NP
1957	**Hunt. Behav.** · Anat. · Life History · Taxonomy
1958	**Hunt. Behav.** · CN · Distrib. · NY · Prey
1990	**Hunt. Behav.** · Intersp. Behav.
1993	**Hunt. Behav.** · Chautauqua NWR · IL · Winter. Pop.
852	**Hunt-Wesson** · Pub. Ed.
1206	**Hunt-Wesson** · Chippewa NF · Habit. Prot. · MN · Pub. Ed. · USFS
1210	**Hunt-Wesson** · Child. Eagle Area · Pub. Ed. · Refuge · USFS
1824	**Hunt-Wesson** · Child. Eagle Area · Chippewa NF · Manage. · MN · Pub. Ed. · Refuge · USFS
329	**Hurricane** · FL · Habit. Loss · Nest. Fail. · Status
334	**Hurricane** · Ches. Bay · FL · Nest. Fail. · ON
1538	**Hurricane** · FL · Nest.
1616	**Hurricane** · Nest. · TX
1626	**Hurricane** · Hunt. Behav. · MD · Nest. · Prey

Master No.	Keywords
1672	**Hurricane** · Cont. B.E. Proj. · Nest. Survey · NAS · Status · Winter Survey
303	**Illinois R** · Behav. · Winter. Pop.
620	**Illinois R** · IA · IL · Mississippi R · Winter Survey · WI
621	**Illinois R** · IL · KY · Mississippi R · NE · Winter Survey
624	**Illinois R** · IA · IL · KY · Mississippi R · NE · Winter Survey
626	**Illinois R** · IA · IL · Mississippi R · MO · Winter Survey
628	**Illinois R** · IA · IL · KY · Mississippi R · MO · Winter Survey
631	**Illinois R** · IA · IL · KY · Mississippi R · Winter Survey
632	**Illinois R** · IA · IL · KY · Mississippi R · Winter Survey
634	**Illinois R** · IA · IL · KY · Mississippi R · MO · NE · Winter Survey
635	**Illinois R** · IA · IL · KY · Mississippi R · Missouri R · MO · NE · Winter Survey · Wisconsin R
636	**Illinois R** · IA · IL · KY · Mississippi R · Missouri R · MO · NE · Winter Survey · Wisconsin R
637	**Illinois R** · IA · IL · KY · Mississippi R · Missouri R · MO · NE · Winter Survey · Wisconsin R
638	**Illinois R** · IA · IL · KY · Mississippi R · MO · NE · Winter Survey
639	**Illinois R** · IA · IL · KY · Mississippi R · MO · NE · Winter Survey
643	**Illinois R** · IL · KY · Mississippi R · MO · NE · Winter Survey
644	**Illinois R** · IL · KY · Mississippi R · MO · NE · Winter Survey
646	**Illinois R** · IL · KY · Mississippi R · MO · NE · Winter Survey
647	**Illinois R** · Lower 48 · Mississippi R · Winter Survey
649	**Illinois R** · IL · KY · Mississippi R · TN · Winter Survey
650	**Illinois R** · IL · KY · Mississippi R · TN · Winter Survey
651	**Illinois R** · IA · IL · KY · Mississippi R · MO · NE · TN · Winter Survey
652	**Illinois R** · IA · KY · Mississippi R · MO · NE · TN · Winter Survey
1692	**Illinois R** · KY · Mississippi R · Ohio R · Winter Survey

Master No.	Keywords
1221	**Impound.** · Aging · Behav. · Hunt. Behav. · Intrasp. Behav. · MI · Nest. · Ottawa NF · Techniques · Territory
62	**Indian Culture** · Folklore · Growth · Hunt. Behav. · Life History · Plumage
128	**Indian Culture** · Habit. Prot. · Manage. · MN · Refuge · St. Croix R · WI
428	**Indian Culture** · History · Symbolism
489	**Indian Culture** · AK · Habit. Use · Prey
597	**Indian Culture** · History · Symbolism
767	**Indian Culture** · Autumn Conc. · AK · Chilkat R · Hunt. Behav. · Photo. · Pub. Ed.
910	**Indian Culture** · BC · History
1186	**Indian Culture** · Feather War · History · Law
1261	**Indian Culture** · History · OR
1628	**Indian Culture** · Capture · Techniques · Trapping
1864	**Indian Culture** · Art · History · USFWS
55	**Intersp. Behav.** · Aggress. · Flight · Folklore · History · Hunt. Behav.
56	**Intersp. Behav.** · Aggress. · Flight · Folklore · History · Hunt. Behav.
192	**Intersp. Behav.** · Hunt. Behav. · Life History · Prey
226	**Intersp. Behav.** · Prey · SC
250	**Intersp. Behav.** · FL · Hunt. Behav. · Prey · Shooting
263	**Intersp. Behav.** · Manage. · Nest. · SC
264	**Intersp. Behav.** · Breed. Behav. · Captive Breed.
283	**Intersp. Behav.** · Hunt. Behav.
293	**Intersp. Behav.** · Hunt. Behav. · Yellowstone NP
306	**Intersp. Behav.** · MN · Prey
307	**Intersp. Behav.** · CA · Nest. · San Clemente Is. · Shooting
325	**Intersp. Behav.** · Behav. · Dispersal · Disturb. · FL · Habit. Use · Migration · Mortality · Nest. · Prey
326	**Intersp. Behav.** · FL · Habit. Loss · Nest. Fail.
327	**Intersp. Behav.** · Band. · FL · Habit. Loss · Nest. Fail. · Pub. Ed. · Shooting · Status · Techniques
328	**Intersp. Behav.** · FL · Habit. Loss · Manage. · Nest. Fail.
336	**Intersp. Behav.** · Band. · FL · Techniques

Master No.	Keywords
380	**Intersp. Behav.** · ME
401	**Intersp. Behav.** · BC · Hunt. Behav. · Prey
410	**Intersp. Behav.** · Acct. · KY
443	**Intersp. Behav.** · Intrasp. Behav.
457	**Intersp. Behav.** · Hudson Bay · MB · Nest. · Prey
551	**Intersp. Behav.** · Chippewa NF · Disturb. · USFS
553	**Intersp. Behav.** · MN
582	**Intersp. Behav.** · Acct. · PA
604	**Intersp. Behav.** · NS · Prey · Winter. Pop.
700	**Intersp. Behav.** · Chippewa NF
720	**Intersp. Behav.** · AK · Karluk L · Prey
735	**Intersp. Behav.** · Disturb. · Habit. Use · SK
792	**Intersp. Behav.** · Behav. · CA · Habit. Use · Nest. · Winter. Pop.
799	**Intersp. Behav.** · Hunt. Behav. · Winter. Pop. · WI
800	**Intersp. Behav.** · FL
802	**Intersp. Behav.** · Aggress. · AK
833	**Intersp. Behav.** · BC · Hunt. Behav. · Intrasp. Behav. · Nest. Survey · Prey · Territory
859	**Intersp. Behav.** · Hunt. Behav. · Prey · WA
879	**Intersp. Behav.** · Nest. · OH · Photo.
886	**Intersp. Behav.** · Breed. Behav. · Life History · Nest. · OH · Parent. Behav. · Prey
888	**Intersp. Behav.** · Behav. · Fledging · Life History · Nest. · OH · Parent. Behav. · Photo. · Prey
902	**Intersp. Behav.** · NY · Winter. Pop.
935	**Intersp. Behav.** · FL · Nest.
992	**Intersp. Behav.** · Egg Coll. · FL
996	**Intersp. Behav.** · Disturb. · Fledging · Habit. Use · Intrasp. Behav. · VA
1010	**Intersp. Behav.** · CO · Winter. Pop.
1011	**Intersp. Behav.** · Behav. · Climatology · Habit. Use · Hunt. Behav. · Intrasp. Behav. · IA · IL · Mississippi R · MO · Prey · Winter Survey
1058	**Intersp. Behav.** · Habit. Use · Life History · ME · Nest. · Status
1079	**Intersp. Behav.**
1091	**Intersp. Behav.** · AZ · Captivity · Falconry
1095	**Intersp. Behav.** · MN
1099	**Intersp. Behav.** · NF
1109	**Intersp. Behav.** · Behav. · Habit. Loss · Habit. Use · Intrasp. Behav. · ID · Manage. · Prey · Winter Survey · Wolf Lodge Bay
1112	**Intersp. Behav.** · Autopsy · Disturb. · Habit. Use · Hunt. Behav. · Manage. · Migration · OK · Prey · Salt Fork R · Shooting · Status · Taxonomy · Winter Survey
1114	**Intersp. Behav.** · Arkansas R · Band. · Capture · Habit. Use · OK · Salt Plains NWR · Sequoyah NWR · Techniques · Wichita Mts. NWR · Winter Survey · Winter. Pop.
1128	**Intersp. Behav.** · FL
1141	**Intersp. Behav.** · AK · CN · Egg Coll. · Nest.
1172	**Intersp. Behav.** · Aggress. · Folklore
1222	**Intersp. Behav.** · Behav. · Fledging · Hunt. Behav. · Intrasp. Behav. · Marking · MI · Ottawa NF · Techniques · Territory
1228	**Intersp. Behav.** · Glacier NP · Hunt. Behav. · MN · Prey · Winter Survey
1277	**Intersp. Behav.** · WI
1294	**Intersp. Behav.** · BC · Hunt. Behav. · Nest. · Prey
1299	**Intersp. Behav.** · Habit. Use · Nest. Survey · Territory · Yellowstone NP
1343	**Intersp. Behav.** · Photo. · Techniques
1368	**Intersp. Behav.** · Behav. · Climatology · Disturb. · Habit. Use · Hunt. Behav. · Intrasp. Behav. · Manage. · NY · Prey · Winter Survey
1369	**Intersp. Behav.** · Behav. · Habit. Use · Heavy Metals · Hunt. Behav. · Intrasp. Behav. · Manage. · NY · Pest. · Prey · PCB · Winter Survey
1374	**Intersp. Behav.** · BC · Hunt. Behav.
1375	**Intersp. Behav.** · Behav. · FL
1412	**Intersp. Behav.** · BC · Hunt. Behav.
1413	**Intersp. Behav.** · BC · Hunt. Behav.
1502	**Intersp. Behav.** · BC · Prey
1546	**Intersp. Behav.** · NF · Terra Nova NP · Winter. Pop.
1590	**Intersp. Behav.** · BC · Hunt. Behav.
1601	**Intersp. Behav.** · Behav. · Capture · Glacier NP · Hunt. Behav. · Intrasp. Behav. · Manage. · MT · Techniques · Winter Survey

Master No.	Keywords
1650	**Intersp. Behav.** · Capture · Habit. Use · Hunt. Behav. · IL · Marking · Mississippi R · Prey · Techniques · Winter Survey
1726	**Intersp. Behav.** · CA
1801	**Intersp. Behav.** · OH · Winter. Pop.
1807	**Intersp. Behav.** · Behav. · FL · Life History · Photo.
1879	**Intersp. Behav.** · Behav. · Hunt. Behav. · ID · L Couer D' Alene · Manage. · Winter Survey
1988	**Intersp. Behav.** · Anat. · Behav. · Capture · Depred. · Econ. Import. · Manage. · NB · Prey · Techniques
1990	**Intersp. Behav.** · Hunt. Behav.
57	**Intrasp. Behav.** · Aggress.
443	**Intrasp. Behav.** · Intersp. Behav.
832	**Intrasp. Behav.** · BC · Marking · Nest. Survey · Pub. Ed. · Techniques · Territory
833	**Intrasp. Behav.** · BC · Hunt. Behav. · Intersp. Behav. · Nest. Survey · Prey · Territory
885	**Intrasp. Behav.** · Behav. · Captive Breed. · Nestling · OH
978	**Intrasp. Behav.** · Capture · IA · Mississippi R · Techniques · Upper Miss. NWR · Winter Survey · WI
996	**Intrasp. Behav.** · Disturb. · Fledging · Habit. Use · Intersp. Behav. · VA
1011	**Intrasp. Behav.** · Behav. · Climatology · Habit. Use · Hunt. Behav. · Intersp. Behav. · IA · IL · Mississippi R · MO · Prey · Winter Survey
1071	**Intrasp. Behav.** · Behav. · Chippewa NF · Fledging · Marking · Mortality · MN · Nest. · Techniques · Telemetry · Vocal.
1109	**Intrasp. Behav.** · Behav. · Habit. Loss · Habit. Use · Intersp. Behav. · ID · Manage. · Prey · Winter Survey · Wolf Lodge Bay
1113	**Intrasp. Behav.** · Hunt. Behav. · Migration · Neosho R · OK · Prey · Winter Survey
1148	**Intrasp. Behav.** · Breed. Behav. · Captive Breed. · USFWS
1221	**Intrasp. Behav.** · Aging · Behav. · Hunt. Behav. · Impound. · MI · Nest. · Ottawa NF · Techniques · Territory

Master No.	Keywords
1222	**Intrasp. Behav.** · Behav. · Fledging · Hunt. Behav. · Intersp. Behav. · Marking · MI · Ottawa NF · Techniques · Territory
1235	**Intrasp. Behav.** · Hunt. Behav. · LA · Nest. · Prey · Winter. Pop.
1253	**Intrasp. Behav.** · Behav. · Hacking · Heavy Metals · Marking · Montezuma NWR · MI · MN · NY · Pest. · Techniques · Telemetry · Young Trans.
1368	**Intrasp. Behav.** · Behav. · Climatology · Disturb. · Habit. Use · Hunt. Behav. · Intersp. Behav. · Manage. · NY · Prey · Winter Survey
1369	**Intrasp. Behav.** · Behav. · Habit. Use · Heavy Metals · Hunt. Behav. · Intersp. Behav. · Manage. · NY · Pest. · Prey · PCB · Winter Survey
1583	**Intrasp. Behav.** · Hunt. Behav. · MA · Prey · Winter. Pop.
1591	**Intrasp. Behav.** · Behav. · Climatology · Disturb. · Habit. Use · Plumage · Prey · Skagit R · Winter Survey · WA
1601	**Intrasp. Behav.** · Behav. · Capture · Glacier NP · Hunt. Behav. · Intersp. Behav. · Manage. · MT · Techniques · Winter Survey
1637	**Intrasp. Behav.** · Folklore · FL · Taxonomy
1895	**Intrasp. Behav.** · Behav. · Habit. Use · Hunt. Behav. · Migration · NE · Platte R · Winter Survey
349	**Ireland** · Distrib. · Shooting
893	**Itasca SP** · MN · Nest.
894	**Itasca SP** · MN · Nest.
957	**Itasca SP** · Migration · MN · Nest.
959	**Itasca SP** · Agassiz NWR · Chippewa NF · MN · Nest. Survey · Superior NF · Tamarac NWR
38	**IA** · Mississippi R · Nest. · Winter. Pop.
53	**IA** · Distrib. · Nest. · Status · Winter. Pop.
115	**IA** · Winter Survey
159	**IA** · Behav. · Disturb. · IL · MN
208	**IA** · Nest. · Prey · Winter. Pop.
276	**IA** · Mississippi R · Winter. Pop.
543	**IA** · Anat. · Migration · Nest. · Taxonomy · Winter. Pop.
544	**IA** · Migration · Nest. · Shooting · Winter. Pop.

Master No.	Keywords
614	IA · IL · Mississippi R · NE · Winter Survey · WI
615	IA · IL · Mississippi R · NE · Winter Survey
620	IA · Illinois R · IL · Mississippi R · Winter Survey · WI
624	IA · Illinois R · IL · KY · Mississippi R · NE · Winter Survey
626	IA · Illinois R · IL · Mississippi R · MO · Winter Survey
628	IA · Illinois R · IL · KY · Mississippi R · MO · Winter Survey
631	IA · Illinois R · IL · KY · Mississippi R · Winter Survey
632	IA · Illinois R · IL · KY · Mississippi R · Winter Survey
634	IA · Illinois R · IL · KY · Mississippi R · MO · NE · Winter Survey
635	IA · Illinois R · IL · KY · Mississippi R · Missouri R · MO · NE · Winter Survey · Wisconsin R
636	IA · Illinois R · IL · KY · Mississippi R · Missouri R · MO · NE · Winter Survey · Wisconsin R
637	IA · Illinois R · IL · KY · Mississippi R · Missouri R · MO · NE · Winter Survey · Wisconsin R
638	IA · Illinois R · IL · KY · Mississippi R · MO · NE · Winter Survey
639	IA · Illinois R · IL · KY · Mississippi R · MO · NE · Winter Survey
645	IA · IL · Mississippi R · MN · MO · NE · WI
648	IA · Habit. Prot. · IL · Mississippi R · MO · Winter Survey
651	IA · Illinois R · IL · KY · Mississippi R · MO · NE · TN · Winter Survey
652	IA · Illinois R · KY · Mississippi R · MO · NE · TN · Winter Survey
758	IA · Mortality · Winter. Pop.
838	IA · Hunt. Behav. · Mississippi R · Prey · Winter. Pop.
892	IA · Hunt. Behav. · Mississippi R · Prey · Winter. Pop.
903	IA · Christmas Count · Mississippi R · Nest. · Status · Winter Survey
978	IA · Capture · Intrasp. Behav. · Mississippi R · Techniques · Upper Miss. NWR · Winter Survey · WI
979	IA · IL · Mississippi R · Winter. Pop.
1011	IA · Behav. · Climatology · Habit. Use · Hunt. Behav. · Intersp. Behav. · Intrasp. Behav. · IL · Mississippi R · MO · Prey · Winter Survey
1045	IA · Migration · Nest. · Status
1155	IA · Winter. Pop.
1289	IA · Mississippi R · Winter. Pop.
1385	IA · Nest.
1432	IA · IL · Mississippi R · Winter. Pop.
1453	IA · Hunt. Behav. · IL · Mississippi R · Winter. Pop.
1687	IA · Nest. · Winter. Pop.
1778	IA · Egg Coll. · Nest.
1787	IA · Acct. · Taxonomy
1846	IA · CO · KS · MO · MT · Nest. Survey · ND · NE · SD · USFWS · UT · WY
1849	IA · CO · KS · MO · MT · Nest. Survey · ND · NE · SD · USFWS · UT · WY
1859	IA · KS · Missouri R · MO · Nest. Survey · ND · NE · Rocky Mt. Region · SD · USFWS · Winter. Pop.
157	ID · Shooting
188	ID · Nest.
378	ID · Life History · Nest. · Status
835	ID · Nest. · Winter. Pop.
1006	ID · Manage. · Status
1061	ID · Winter. Pop.
1109	ID · Behav. · Habit. Loss · Habit. Use · Intersp. Behav. · Intrasp. Behav. · Manage. · Prey · Winter Survey · Wolf Lodge Bay
1185	ID · Electro. · Manage. · Winter. Pop.
1252	ID · Nest.
1341	ID · Electro. · Manage.
1553	ID · Pub. Ed.
1623	ID · Depred.
1839	ID · CA · MT · Nest. Survey · NV · OR · USFWS · WA
1843	ID · Nest. Survey · OR · USFWS · WA
1844	ID · CA · Nest. Survey · NV · OR · USFWS · WA
1853	ID · CA · Nest. Survey · NV · OR · USFWS · WA
1879	ID · Behav. · Hunt. Behav. · Intersp. Behav. · L Couer D' Alene · Manage. · Winter Survey
1981	ID · CO · Electro. · Manage. · NV · UT · WY
64	IL · Aggress. · Folklore

Master No.	Keywords
159	IL · Behav. · Disturb. · IA · MN
167	IL · Law · Shooting
238	IL · Nest.
245	IL · Aggress. · Law · Shooting
270	IL · Nest.
296	IL · Winter. Pop.
297	IL · Pub. Ed. · Winter. Pop.
298	IL · Winter. Pop.
301	IL · Disturb. · Habit. Use · Nest. · Ohio R · Rehab. · Shooting · Techniques · Winter. Pop.
364	IL · Hunt. Behav. · Mississippi R · MO · Winter Survey
547	IL · Band. · MN · Techniques · TX · WI
554	IL · Band. · Behav. · Cedar Glen Roost · Migration · Mississippi R · MN · Refuge · Techniques · Telemetry · TX · Winter. Pop.
556	IL · Cedar Glen Roost · Habit. Prot. · Habit. Use · Manage. · Prey · Refuge
591	IL · Acct. · IN
593	IL · Acct. · Shooting
614	IL · IA · Mississippi R · NE · Winter Survey · WI
615	IL · IA · Mississippi R · NE · Winter Survey
620	IL · Illinois R · IA · Mississippi R · Winter Survey · WI
621	IL · Illinois R · KY · Mississippi R · NE · Winter Survey
622	IL · Acct.
624	IL · Illinois R · IA · KY · Mississippi R · NE · Winter Survey
626	IL · Illinois R · IA · Mississippi R · MO · Winter Survey
628	IL · Illinois R · IA · KY · Mississippi R · MO · Winter Survey
629	IL · Winter. Pop.
630	IL · Winter. Pop.
631	IL · Illinois R · IA · KY · Mississippi R · Winter Survey
632	IL · Illinois R · IA · KY · Mississippi R · Winter Survey
633	IL · Acct.
634	IL · Illinois R · IA · KY · Mississippi R · MO · NE · Winter Survey
635	IL · Illinois R · IA · KY · Mississippi R · Missouri R · MO · NE · Winter Survey · Wisconsin R
636	IL · Illinois R · IA · KY · Mississippi R · Missouri R · MO · NE · Winter Survey · Wisconsin R
637	IL · Illinois R · IA · KY · Mississippi R · Missouri R · MO · NE · Winter Survey · Wisconsin R
638	IL · Illinois R · IA · KY · Mississippi R · MO · NE · Winter Survey
639	IL · Illinois R · IA · KY · Mississippi R · MO · NE · Winter Survey
640	IL · Winter. Pop.
641	IL · Winter Survey · WI
642	IL · Winter. Pop.
643	IL · Illinois R · KY · Mississippi R · MO · NE · Winter Survey
644	IL · Illinois R · KY · Mississippi R · MO · NE · Winter Survey
645	IL · IA · Mississippi R · MN · MO · NE · WI
646	IL · Illinois R · KY · Mississippi R · MO · NE · Winter Survey
648	IL · Habit. Prot. · IA · Mississippi R · MO · Winter Survey
649	IL · Illinois R · KY · Mississippi R · TN · Winter Survey
650	IL · Illinois R · KY · Mississippi R · TN · Winter Survey
651	IL · Illinois R · IA · KY · Mississippi R · MO · NE · TN · Winter Survey
686	IL · Nest. · Terminology · Winter. Pop.
721	IL · Distrib.
722	IL · Endang. Sp.
751	IL · Christmas Count · Mississippi R · Status · Techniques · Winter Survey
752	IL · Migration · Nest. · Status · Winter. Pop.
759	IL · Acct.
762	IL · Pub. Ed. · Winter. Pop.
785	IL · Mississippi R · Winter. Pop.
912	IL · Acct.
979	IL · IA · Mississippi R · Winter. Pop.
1011	IL · Behav. · Climatology · Habit. Use · Hunt. Behav. · Intersp. Behav. · Intrasp. Behav. · IA · Mississippi R · MO · Prey · Winter Survey
1033	IL · Migration · Nest. · Winter. Pop.
1056	IL · Acct.
1120	IL · Winter. Pop.
1196	IL · Band. · Chippewa NF · MN · Nest. Survey · Techniques · USFS · Winter. Pop.

Master No.	Keywords
1304	IL · Prey · Shooting · Winter Survey
1305	IL · Mississippi R · Winter. Pop.
1306	IL · Mississippi R · Winter. Pop.
1332	IL · CA · Habit. Prot. · NWF · RIC
1364	IL · Christmas Count · Winter Survey
1365	IL · Christmas Count · Winter Survey
1405	IL · Anthro.
1432	IL · IA · Mississippi R · Winter. Pop.
1453	IL · Hunt. Behav. · IA · Mississippi R · Winter. Pop.
1526	IL · Nest. · Winter. Pop.
1625	IL · Mississippi R · Winter Survey
1649	IL · Band. · Capture · Techniques · Winter. Pop.
1650	IL · Capture · Habit. Use · Hunt. Behav. · Intersp. Behav. · Marking · Mississippi R · Prey · Techniques · Winter Survey
1651	IL · Anat. · Behav. · Capture · Hunt. Behav. · Marking · Plumage · Prey · Techniques · Telemetry · Winter Survey
1652	IL · Mississippi R · Prey · Winter. Pop.
1658	IL · Christmas Count · Winter. Pop.
1659	IL · Christmas Count · Winter. Pop.
1660	IL · Christmas Count · Winter. Pop.
1754	IL · Shooting · Winter. Pop.
1772	IL · Habit. Prot. · Winter Survey
1773	IL · Habit. Prot. · Oak V. Eagle Sanct. · Refuge
1855	IL · IN · MI · MN · Nest. Survey · OH · Terminology · USFWS · WI
1873	IL · Heavy Metals · Lead Poison. · Poison.
1894	IL · Hunt. Behav. · Winter. Pop.
1977	IL · IN · Nest. · Shooting
1993	IL · Chautauqua NWR · Hunt. Behav. · Winter. Pop.
382	IN · Distrib. · Egg Coll. · Life History · Nest. · Status
514	IN · Hunt. Behav. · Nest. · Prey
591	IN · Acct. · IL
607	IN · Nest. · Winter. Pop.
749	IN · Egg Coll. · Habit. Use · Nest.
1437	IN · Nest. · Winter. Pop.
1460	IN · Nest. · Winter. Pop.
1855	IN · IL · MI · MN · Nest. Survey · OH · Terminology · USFWS · WI
1977	IN · IL · Nest. · Shooting
985	IUCN · Endang. Sp. · Status
141	Jackson's Canyon · Poison. · WY

Master No.	Keywords
179	Jackson's Canyon · Winter Survey · WY
180	Jackson's Canyon · Winter Survey · WY
397	Jackson's Canyon · Law · NAS · Poison. · WY
398	Jackson's Canyon · Law · Poison. · Shooting · WY
1136	Jackson's Canyon · Band. · Techniques · Winter Survey · WY
849	Kalamazoo R · Allegan SF · MI · Nest.
152	Karl Mundt NWR · Corps · Habit. Loss · Missouri R · NE · NWF · SD
702	Karl Mundt NWR · Habit. Prot. · L Andes NWR · Manage. · Missouri R · NWF · Refuge · SD · Winter. Pop.
703	Karl Mundt NWR · Habit. Prot. · Missouri R · Refuge · SD · Winter. Pop.
1348	Karl Mundt NWR · Habit. Prot. · Manage. · NWF
1695	Karl Mundt NWR · Behav. · Ft. Randall D · Habit. Use · Hunt. Behav. · L Andes NWR · SD · Winter Survey
1696	Karl Mundt NWR · Climatology · Ft. Randall D · Habit. Use · Hunt. Behav. · L Andes NWR · Manage. · Prey · SD · Winter Survey
1878	Karl Mundt NWR · SD · Winter Survey
720	Karluk L · AK · Intersp. Behav. · Prey
1744	Karyotype
1439	Kentucky Wood. NWR · KY · Winter Survey
1440	Kentucky Wood. NWR · Behav. · Habit. Loss · Habit. Use · KY · Winter Survey
1441	Kentucky Wood. NWR · Habit. Loss · KY · Status · Winter Survey
1688	Kepone · Ches. Bay · Pest. · Techniques
1731	Kings Canyon NP · Acct. · CA · Sequoia NP
871	Kissimee B.E. Sanct. · Disturb. · FL · Habit. Use · Nest. Survey · Refuge · Reprod. Succ.
872	Kissimee B.E. Sanct. · Disturb. · FL · Habit. Use · Nest. Survey · Refuge · Reprod. Succ.
761	Klamath · CA · OR · Paleontology
1065	Klamath · Behav. · CA · Disturb. · Habit. Use · Lower Klamath Lake NWR · Manage. · OR · Prey · Tule Lake NWR · Winter Survey

Master No.	Keywords
682	**Klamath NF** · CA · Disturb. · Manage. · Nest. · Prey · Status · Winter. Pop.
572	**Klamath R** · Aircraft · Behav. · CA · Distrib. · Disturb. · Habit. Loss · Hunt. Behav. · Manage. · Nest.
904	**Kluane Game Sanct.** · Nest. · YT
1804	**Kodiak Is.** · AK · Habit. Use · Kodiak NWR · Nest. Survey
431	**Kodiak NWR** · AK · Behav. · Climatology · Disease · Life History · Marking · Nest. · Nest. Survey · Parasites · Reprod. Succ. · Techniques · Terminology
878	**Kodiak NWR** · AK · Disturb. · Habit. Use · Life History · Nest. Fail. · Reprod. Succ. · Territory
1804	**Kodiak NWR** · AK · Habit. Use · Kodiak Is. · Nest. Survey
1829	**Kodiak NWR** · AK · Band. · Behav. · Nest. Survey · Reprod. Succ. · Techniques
747	**KS** · Nest. · Winter. Pop.
845	**KS** · Missouri R · Nest. · Prey · Winter. Pop.
974	**KS** · Captivity · Prey · Winter. Pop.
975	**KS** · Prey · Winter. Pop.
1026	**KS** · Endang. Sp. · Winter. Pop.
1701	**KS** · Nest. · Winter. Pop.
1838	**KS** · AZ · CO · Nest. Survey · NM · OK · Salt Fork R · TX · USFWS · UT · Verde R · WY
1846	**KS** · CO · IA · MO · MT · Nest. Survey · ND · NE · SD · USFWS · UT · WY
1849	**KS** · CO · IA · MO · MT · Nest. Survey · ND · NE · SD · USFWS · UT · WY
1859	**KS** · IA · Missouri R · MO · Nest. Survey · ND · NE · Rocky Mt. Region · SD · USFWS · Winter. Pop.
76	**KY** · Aggress. · Folklore
231	**KY** · Nest. · Winter. Pop.
410	**KY** · Acct. · Intersp. Behav.
464	**KY** · Land Between the Lakes · Winter Survey
621	**KY** · Illinois R · IL · Mississippi R · NE · Winter Survey
624	**KY** · Illinois R · IA · IL · Mississippi R · NE · Winter Survey
628	**KY** · Illinois R · IA · IL · Mississippi R · MO · Winter Survey
631	**KY** · Illinois R · IA · IL · Mississippi R · Winter Survey
632	**KY** · Illinois R · IA · IL · Mississippi R · Winter Survey
634	**KY** · Illinois R · IA · IL · Mississippi R · MO · NE · Winter Survey
635	**KY** · Illinois R · IA · IL · Mississippi R · Missouri R · MO · NE · Winter Survey · Wisconsin R
636	**KY** · Illinois R · IA · IL · Mississippi R · Missouri R · MO · NE · Winter Survey · Wisconsin R
637	**KY** · Illinois R · IA · IL · Mississippi R · Missouri R · MO · NE · Winter Survey · Wisconsin R
638	**KY** · Illinois R · IA · IL · Mississippi R · MO · NE · Winter Survey
639	**KY** · Illinois R · IA · IL · Mississippi R · MO · NE · Winter Survey
643	**KY** · Illinois R · IL · Mississippi R · MO · NE · Winter Survey
644	**KY** · Illinois R · IL · Mississippi R · MO · NE · Winter Survey
646	**KY** · Illinois R · IL · Mississippi R · MO · NE · Winter Survey
649	**KY** · Illinois R · IL · Mississippi R · TN · Winter Survey
650	**KY** · Illinois R · IL · Mississippi R · TN · Winter Survey
651	**KY** · Illinois R · IA · IL · Mississippi R · MO · NE · TN · Winter Survey
652	**KY** · Illinois R · IA · Mississippi R · MO · NE · TN · Winter Survey
707	**KY** · Nest. · Winter. Pop.
1143	**KY** · Archaeology
1248	**KY** · Nest. · Winter. Pop.
1279	**KY** · Nest.
1439	**KY** · Kentucky Wood. NWR · Winter Survey
1440	**KY** · Behav. · Habit. Loss · Habit. Use · Kentucky Wood. NWR · Winter Survey
1441	**KY** · Habit. Loss · Kentucky Wood. NWR · Status · Winter Survey
1442	**KY** · Land Between the Lakes · Winter Survey
1444	**KY** · Land Between the Lakes · Pub. Ed. · TVA · Winter. Pop.
1465	**KY** · Nest. · Shooting
1466	**KY** · Nest.
1691	**KY** · Cont. B.E. Proj. · Winter Survey

Master No.	Keywords
1692	KY · Illinois R · Mississippi R · Ohio R · Winter Survey
1693	KY · Mississippi R · Ohio R · Winter Survey
1961	KY · Winter. Pop.
702	L Andes NWR · Habit. Prot. · Karl Mundt NWR · Manage. · Missouri R · NWF · Refuge · SD · Winter. Pop.
1017	L Andes NWR · Missouri R · NAS · Status · SD · Winter Survey
1695	L Andes NWR · Behav. · Ft. Randall D · Habit. Use · Hunt. Behav. · Karl Mundt NWR · SD · Winter Survey
1696	L Andes NWR · Climatology · Ft. Randall D · Habit. Use · Hunt. Behav. · Karl Mundt NWR · Manage. · Prey · SD · Winter Survey
491	L Apopka · Egg Coll. · FL · Nest.
1933	L Apopka · Disease · FL
1879	L Couer D' Alene · Behav. · Hunt. Behav. · Intersp. Behav. · ID · Manage. · Winter Survey
890	L Erie · Great Lakes · Prey · Pub. Ed. · Status
988	L Erie · Great Lakes · Manage. · Nest. Survey · OH · Winter Survey
1581	L Ocklawaha · FL · Nest. · Rodman Reservoir
907	L Superior · Duluth Fly. · Great Lakes · Migration · MN
1344	L. Athabasca · Nest. · SK
780	Lake of The Woods · CN · Disturb. · Habit. Use · Manage. · ON
464	Land Between the Lakes · KY · Winter Survey
1442	Land Between the Lakes · KY · Winter Survey
1444	Land Between the Lakes · KY · Pub. Ed. · TVA · Winter. Pop.
532	Lava Beds NM · CA · Nest.
48	Law · AOU · Comm. Conserv. · Endang. Sp. · Status
69	Law · AK · Bounty · Pub. Ed. · Status
77	Law
78	Law
87	Law · Status
97	Law · AK · Bounty
100	Law · AK · Bounty
101	Law · AK · Bounty
102	Law · AK · Bounty · Status
103	Law · AK · Bounty
104	Law · AK · Bounty
105	Law · AK · Bounty
106	Law · AK · Bounty
117	Law · Status
122	Law · Disturb. · Logging · Manage. · Refuge
125	Law · Disturb. · Logging · Manage. · Nest. · Territory
137	Law · Poison. · Pred. Cont.
160	Law · Ground Nest. · Nest. · OH
164	Law · Manage. · Pub. Ed.
167	Law · IL · Shooting
182	Law · AZ · CAP · Falconry · Habit. Loss · Orme D
223	Law · AK
224	Law · AK · Bounty
235	Law · Animal Dam. · AK · Bounty · Prey
236	Law · AK · Bounty
245	Law · Aggress. · IL · Shooting
247	Law · Bounty · CN · Depred.
366	Law · Shooting
369	Law · MI · Nest. Survey · NJ · Winter Survey
370	Law · Shooting
384	Law · History · Life History · Pub. Ed.
397	Law · Jackson's Canyon · NAS · Poison. · WY
398	Law · Jackson's Canyon · Poison. · Shooting · WY
446	Law · Econ. Import. · Life History · Manage. · MO · Nest. · Prey · Pub. Ed. · Shooting
499	Law · Manage. · Nest. · Poison. · Pub. Ed. · Shooting · SK · Trapping
521	Law · Bounty · Pub. Ed. · Symbolism
588	Law · AK · Pub. Ed.
662	Law · AK · Bounty · Growth · Photo. · Shooting
687	Law · NV · Shooting
697	Law · Disturb. · USFS
806	Law · DDT · Pest.
807	Law · AK · Bounty
976	Law · Aggress. · Anat. · Bounty · Distrib. · Econ. Import. · Life History · Plumage · Prey · Status · Taxonomy

Master No.	Keywords
984	**Law** · Captivity · Egg Trans. · Heavy Metals · Manage. · Migration · Nest. Survey · Pest. · Pub. Ed. · Status · Techniques · Territory · Young Trans.
1025	**Law** · Aggress. · Econ. Import. · Field ID · Life History · Prey
1090	**Law** · Manage. · Nongame Sp.
1135	**Law** · Life History · Pub. Ed.
1186	**Law** · Feather War · History · Indian Culture
1285	**Law** · Pub. Ed. · Shooting
1286	**Law** · Status
1314	**Law** · Electro. · NAS · Pest. · Poison. · Pub. Ed. · Shooting · Status
1317	**Law** · Life History · NWF · Pest. · Pub. Ed. · Status
1393	**Law** · AK · Bounty · Pub. Ed.
1418	**Law** · AK · Bounty
1419	**Law** · AK · Bounty · NAS · Pub. Ed. · Shooting
1420	**Law** · AK · Bounty · Shooting
1421	**Law** · AK · Bounty · Shooting
1422	**Law** · AK · Bounty · Shooting
1423	**Law**
1424	**Law** · AK · Bounty · Shooting
1425	**Law**
1426	**Law**
1427	**Law** · Pub. Ed.
1461	**Law** · History
1495	**Law**
1543	**Law** · Depred. · Poison. · Shooting · WY
1575	**Law** · CO · Shooting · WY
1577	**Law** · Pub. Ed. · Shooting · WY
1723	**Law** · OR · Shooting
1814	**Law**
1815	**Law**
1816	**Law** · B.E. Prot. Act
1817	**Law**
1818	**Law** · Endang. Sp.
1819	**Law** · B.E. Prot. Act
1863	**Law** · Endang. Sp.
1869	**Law** · Shooting · USFWS
1870	**Law** · Endang. Sp.
1874	**Law** · Distrib. · Endang. Sp. · Life History · Manage. · Status · Taxonomy · USFWS
1877	**Law** · Endang. Sp.
1884	**Law** · Endang. Sp. · Taxonomy
1954	**Law** · AK · Hunt. Behav. · Migration · Nest. · Pub. Ed. · WY · Yellowstone NP
1955	**Law** · AK · Hunt. Behav. · Migration · Nest. · Pub. Ed. · WY · Yellowstone NP
1982	**Law** · MS · Shooting
201	**Lead Poison.** · Heavy Metals
994	**Lead Poison.** · Disease · Heavy Metals · Histology · MD · Techniques
1292	**Lead Poison.** · Autopsy · Disease · Electro. · Pest. · Shooting
1873	**Lead Poison.** · Heavy Metals · IL · Poison.
22	**Life History** · Bombay Hook NWR · Distrib. · DE · Endang. Sp. · Field ID · Nest. · Nest. Survey · Pub. Ed. · Status
26	**Life History** · AK · Depred. · Endang. Sp. · OR · WA
28	**Life History** · Pub. Ed. · Taxonomy
29	**Life History** · Econ. Import. · Pub. Ed.
46	**Life History**
47	**Life History** · Distrib. · Taxonomy
58	**Life History**
59	**Life History** · Folklore · Old Abe · Pub. Ed.
62	**Life History** · Folklore · Growth · Hunt. Behav. · Indian Culture · Plumage
74	**Life History** · Pub. Ed.
80	**Life History** · Behav. · Nest. · OH
112	**Life History** · History · Pub. Ed. · Symbolism
130	**Life History** · Captive Breed. · Pub. Ed. · Status
133	**Life History** · Nest. · NJ · Pub. Ed. · Winter. Pop.
192	**Life History** · Hunt. Behav. · Intersp. Behav. · Prey
194	**Life History** · Pub. Ed. · Status
209	**Life History** · Distrib.
249	**Life History** · Anat. · Distrib. · MI · Plumage · Status
273	**Life History** · Aggress. · Behav. · Captivity · Distrib. · Egg Coll. · Habit. Use · Nest. · Status
274	**Life History** · Aggress. · Behav. · Captivity · Distrib. · Habit. Use · Nest. · Status
290	**Life History** · Pub. Ed.
305	**Life History** · MN

Master No.	Keywords
324	**Life History** · Band. · FL · Migration · Nest. Fail. · Nest. Survey · Prey · Status · Techniques
338	**Life History** · Band. · Broley · Dispersal · FL · Techniques
339	**Life History** · Band. · Broley · FL · Pub. Ed. · Status · Techniques
350	**Life History** · Behav. · Poetry
352	**Life History** · Behav. · Flight · Migration · Nest. · Prey · Pub. Ed. · Status · Taxonomy
353	**Life History** · Anat. · Behav. · Distrib. · Nest. · Status
377	**Life History** · Distrib. · GA · Habit. Use · Migration · Nest. · Status
378	**Life History** · ID · Nest. · Status
382	**Life History** · Distrib. · Egg Coll. · IN · Nest. · Status
384	**Life History** · History · Law · Pub. Ed.
424	**Life History** · Distrib. · Field ID
429	**Life History** · Aggress. · History · Hunt. Behav. · Nest. · Poetry · PA · Shooting · Status · Susquehanna R
430	**Life History** · History · Nest.
431	**Life History** · AK · Behav. · Climatology · Disease · Kodiak NWR · Marking · Nest. · Nest. Survey · Parasites · Reprod. Succ. · Techniques · Terminology
446	**Life History** · Econ. Import. · Law · Manage. · MO · Nest. · Prey · Pub. Ed. · Shooting
463	**Life History** · Hunt. Behav. · Prey
468	**Life History** · Missouri R · Plumage · Taxonomy
476	**Life History** · Egg Coll. · Flight · Shooting · Status
506	**Life History** · Captivity · CA · Depred. · Distrib. · Habit. Use · Nest. · Santa Barbara Is.
531	**Life History** · Aging · AK · Behav. · Hunt. Behav. · Nest. · Prey · Sexing · Techniques
549	**Life History** · Missouri R · Pub. Ed. · SD · Winter Survey
557	**Life History** · Chippewa NF · Disturb. · Migration · Nest. · Photo. · Pub. Ed. · Status · Techniques · Telemetry · Winter. Pop.
560	**Life History** · Band. · Behav. · Migration · MN · Reprod. Succ. · Techniques
608	**Life History** · Distrib. · Electro. · Field ID · Prey · UT · Winter. Pop.
664	**Life History** · Anat. · Econ. Import. · Hunt. Behav. · Prey
683	**Life History** · Behav. · CA · Distrib. · Disturb. · Field ID · Flight · Hunt. Behav. · Manage. · Mortality · Nest. · Winter. Pop.
684	**Life History** · Distrib.
685	**Life History** · Audubon · Behav.
701	**Life History** · Anat. · Distrib. · Plumage
711	**Life History** · AK · Distrib. · Habit. Use · Plumage · Status
713	**Life History** · Habit. Use · OR
725	**Life History** · Status · SK
740	**Life History** · Plumage
763	**Life History** · NC · Pub. Ed. · Status
798	**Life History** · Pub. Ed. · Trapping
803	**Life History** · Habit. Use · Nest. · Photo. · Pub. Ed. · Winter. Pop. · WA
804	**Life History** · Art. Nest Site · AZ · Egg. Thin. · Habit. Use · Manage. · Marking · Nest. · Pest. · Research · Techniques · Telemetry · Winter. Pop.
857	**Life History** · Pub. Ed. · Status
870	**Life History** · Disturb. · Pub. Ed.
878	**Life History** · AK · Disturb. · Habit. Use · Kodiak NWR · Nest. Fail. · Reprod. Succ. · Territory
880	**Life History** · Behav. · Nest. · Nestling · OH · Parent. Behav. · Photo. · Techniques
881	**Life History** · Behav. · Fledging · Nest. · Nestling · OH
882	**Life History** · Aggress. · Behav. · Disturb. · Nest. · OH · PA
883	**Life History** · Behav. · Fledging · Hunt. Behav. · Nest. · OH · Prey
886	**Life History** · Breed. Behav. · Intersp. Behav. · Nest. · OH · Parent. Behav. · Prey
887	**Life History** · Behav. · Nest. · OH · Photo. · Techniques
888	**Life History** · Behav. · Fledging · Intersp. Behav. · Nest. · OH · Parent. Behav. · Photo. · Prey
889	**Life History** · Behav. · Nest. · OH · Photo. · Techniques
891	**Life History** · Behav. · Nest. · OH · Prey
908	**Life History** · Pub. Ed.
922	**Life History** · Pub. Ed.

Master No.	Keywords
976	Life History · Aggress. · Anat. · Bounty · Distrib. · Econ. Import. · Law · Plumage · Prey · Status · Taxonomy
997	Life History · Nest. · ON · Winter. Pop.
1003	Life History · Nest. · WA
1025	Life History · Aggress. · Econ. Import. · Field ID · Law · Prey
1051	Life History · Folklore · Pub. Ed. · Status
1058	Life History · Habit. Use · Intersp. Behav. · ME · Nest. · Status
1084	Life History · Anat. · Hunt. Behav. · Migration · Nest. · Plumage
1088	Life History · Photo.
1135	Life History · Law · Pub. Ed.
1145	Life History · Endang. Sp. · Status
1160	Life History · CA · Distrib. · Nest. · Prey · Pub. Ed. · Winter. Pop.
1161	Life History · Pub. Ed.
1187	Life History · Habit. Use · Nest. Survey · Prey · Winter Survey · WA
1212	Life History · Field ID · MN
1226	Life History · Econ. Import. · Prey · Pub. Ed. · Status
1227	Life History · Field ID · Prey
1232	Life History · Field ID · Nest. · WY · Yellowstone NP
1246	Life History
1302	Life History · Pub. Ed.
1317	Life History · Law · NWF · Pest. · Pub. Ed. · Status
1349	Life History · Dispersal · FL · Migration · NAS · Pub. Ed. · Status
1353	Life History · Field ID · NH
1357	Life History · FL · Habit. Use · Nest. · Status
1366	Life History · Folklore
1367	Life History · Heavy Metals · Taxonomy · Toxicol.
1370	Life History · Econ. Import. · Prey · Shooting
1371	Life History · Hunt. Behav. · LA · Pub. Ed. · Taxonomy
1398	Life History · Field ID · Pub. Ed.
1416	Life History · FL · Hunt. Behav. · Nest. · Prey
1417	Life History · Poetry
1428	Life History · Nest. · NC
1429	Life History · History · Pub. Ed.
1506	Life History · Pub. Ed.
1515	Life History · Egg

Master No.	Keywords
1527	Life History · Plumage
1531	Life History · Band. · Christmas Count · Migration · Nest. · Status · USFWS · Winter Survey
1535	Life History · Pub. Ed.
1537	Life History · Hunt. Behav. · Migration · MN · Nest. · Prey · Shooting · Status · Winter. Pop.
1541	Life History · Pub. Ed.
1547	Life History · Pub. Ed.
1549	Life History · Chippewa NF · Field ID · MN · Pub. Ed.
1562	Life History · New England
1582	Life History · CO · Nest. · Status · Winter. Pop.
1606	Life History · Aggress. · Aleutian Is. · AK · Behav. · Depred. · Habit. Use · Mortality · Nest. Survey · Plumage · Prey · Reprod. Succ. · Status · Winter Survey
1621	Life History · Pub. Ed.
1640	Life History · Aggress. · Behav. · BLM · Disturb. · Habit. Loss · Habit. Use · Hunt. Behav. · Manage. · Nest. · Pest. · Prey · Shooting · Territory
1684	Life History · Band. · Field ID · FL · Nest. · Prey · Status · Techniques
1722	Life History · History
1733	Life History · Distrib. · PA
1736	Life History · Plumage · Taxonomy
1750	Life History · CN · Econ. Import. · Field ID · Prey
1757	Life History · Pub. Ed.
1784	Life History · Poetry
1795	Life History · Behav. · Habit. Use · Nest. · Pub. Ed. · PA · Taxonomy
1807	Life History · Behav. · FL · Intersp. Behav. · Photo.
1808	Life History · Field ID · Nest. · NS · Poetry
1812	Life History · Ches. Bay · DE · Econ. Import. · Habit. Use · MD · Nest. Survey · NC · NJ · Prey · PA · VA
1813	Life History · Ches. Bay · DC · Nest.
1841	Life History · AK · Manage. · Status
1874	Life History · Distrib. · Endang. Sp. · Law · Manage. · Status · Taxonomy · USFWS
1901	Life History · Distrib. · DE · NJ · Prey · VA

Master No.	Keywords
1905	**Life History** · History · Pub. Ed. · Status
1912	**Life History** · Nest. · SC
1925	**Life History** · Art · Pub. Ed.
1937	**Life History** · History · Pub. Ed.
1957	**Life History** · Anat. · Hunt. Behav. · Taxonomy
1964	**Life History** · Nest. · NC
1972	**Life History** · History · Pub. Ed.
149	**Literature** · Manage. · NWF · RIC · Status
161	**Literature** · Manage. · NWF · RIC · Status
122	**Logging** · Disturb. · Law · Manage. · Refuge
123	**Logging** · Disturb. · Manage. · Nest.
125	**Logging** · Disturb. · Law · Manage. · Nest. · Territory
465	**Logging** · AK · Disturb. · Habit. Loss · Habit. Use · Nest. · Nest. Survey · Territory
695	**Logging** · Behav. · Chippewa NF · Disturb. · MN · Nest. · Reprod. Succ.
836	**Logging** · Behav. · Disturb. · Habit. Loss · Habit. Use · Hunt. Behav. · Manage. · Prey · Winter Survey · WA
1657	**Logging** · Egg Coll. · Habit. Use · ME · Nest.
1929	**Logging** · AK · Bounty · Manage.
1065	**Lower Klamath Lake NWR** · Behav. · CA · Disturb. · Habit. Use · Klamath · Manage. · OR · Prey · Tule Lake NWR · Winter Survey
1967	**Lower Klamath Lake NWR** · CA · Disturb. · Habit. Use · Modoc NWR · Tule Lake NWR · Winter Survey
154	**Lower 48** · Manage. · Nest. Survey · Status · USFWS
459	**Lower 48** · Autopsy · AK · CN · Disease · Parasites · Poison. · Shooting · Trapping
482	**Lower 48** · Autopsy · Dieldrin · Disease · Electro. · Pest. · Poison. · PCB · Shooting
617	**Lower 48** · Migration · Mississippi R · Winter Survey
618	**Lower 48** · Mississippi R · Winter Survey
647	**Lower 48** · Illinois R · Mississippi R · Winter Survey
753	**Lower 48** · AK · Manage. · Status

Master No.	Keywords
825	**Lower 48** · AK · Comm. Conserv. · CN · Status · Wilson Ornithol. Soc.
1184	**Lower 48** · AK · CN · Status
1359	**Lower 48** · AK · Nest. Survey · USFWS
1655	**Lower 48** · Christmas Count · Migration · Prey · Refuge · Winter. Pop.
1708	**Lower 48** · AK · Histology · Pest. · Spermato. · Techniques · Toxicol. · USFWS
1785	**Lower 48** · Endang. Sp. · Nest. Survey · Status
1850	**Lower 48** · AK · Nest. Survey · Reprod. Succ. · USFWS
35	**LA** · Egg Coll. · MN · MS · Status · WI
50	**LA** · Egg. Thin. · FL · Pest. · Status · TX
195	**LA** · Distrib. · Nest. Survey · Winter Survey
196	**LA** · Distrib. · Migration · Mortality · Nest. Survey · Reprod. Succ. · Shooting · Status · Winter Survey
197	**LA** · Habit. Use · MS · Nest. Survey
203	**LA** · Nest.
204	**LA** · Gulf of Mex. · Winter. Pop.
206	**LA** · Nest. · Status
284	**LA** · Gulf of Mex. · Nest.
291	**LA** · Egg Coll.
376	**LA** · Habit. Use · Nest. · Winter. Pop.
515	**LA** · Nest.
537	**LA** · Distrib. · Nest. Survey · Reprod. Succ.
538	**LA** · Distrib. · Nest. Survey · Reprod. Succ.
539	**LA** · Nest. Survey · Prey
658	**LA** · Nest. · Winter. Pop.
918	**LA** · Nest.
1235	**LA** · Hunt. Behav. · Intrasp. Behav. · Nest. · Prey · Winter. Pop.
1312	**LA** · FL · Migration
1371	**LA** · Hunt. Behav. · Life History · Pub. Ed. · Taxonomy
1902	**LA** · Nest.
1926	**LB** · Nest. Survey · QU · Status
1987	**LB** · Econ. Import. · Maritime Prov. · NF · Prey
24	**Manage.** · Capture · Marking · Skagit R · Techniques · WA
51	**Manage.** · Disturb. · Habit. Use · Nest. · OR · USFS
120	**Manage.** · Chippewa NF · Mississippi R · MN

Master No.	Keywords
122	**Manage.** · Disturb. · Law · Logging · Refuge
123	**Manage.** · Disturb. · Logging · Nest.
124	**Manage.** · Ches. Bay · Mason Neck NWR · Refuge · VA
125	**Manage.** · Disturb. · Law · Logging · Nest. · Territory
127	**Manage.** · Pub. Ed. · Symbolism
128	**Manage.** · Habit. Prot. · Indian Culture · MN · Refuge · St. Croix R · WI
129	**Manage.** · NAS · Status
138	**Manage.**
143	**Manage.** · FL · Pub. Ed. · Refuge
145	**Manage.** · NWF · Reward · Shooting · WI
146	**Manage.** · NWF · Reward
148	**Manage.** · Anat. · Autumn Conc. · FL · Glacier NP · Merritt Is. NWR · Museum Specimen · MT · Nest. · Prey · Taxonomy
149	**Manage.** · Literature · NWF · RIC · Status
151	**Manage.** · Egg Trans.
154	**Manage.** · Lower 48 · Nest. Survey · Status · USFWS
156	**Manage.** · Egg Trans. · ME · MN · USFWS
161	**Manage.** · Literature · NWF · RIC · Status
163	**Manage.** · NY · Techniques · Young Trans.
164	**Manage.** · Law · Pub. Ed.
166	**Manage.** · Hacking · NY · Techniques · Young Trans.
168	**Manage.** · Habit. Prot. · Nat. Conserv. · Skagit R · Wash. Dept. Game · Winter. Pop. · WA
170	**Manage.** · Captive Breed. · Pub. Ed.
261	**Manage.** · Mt. Johnson Is. Sanct. · Nest. · PA · Refuge · Shooting
263	**Manage.** · Intersp. Behav. · Nest. · SC
275	**Manage.** · Egg Trans. · ME · MN
304	**Manage.** · Status
328	**Manage.** · FL · Habit. Loss · Intersp. Behav. · Nest. Fail.
354	**Manage.** · NY · Pub. Ed.
387	**Manage.** · Hacking · Montezuma NWR · NY · Techniques · WI · Young Trans.
393	**Manage.** · CA · Endang. Sp. · Status
394	**Manage.** · CA · Endang. Sp. · Status
399	**Manage.** · CA · Refuge · Three Sisters B.E. Pres. · USFS · Winter Survey
434	**Manage.** · Educ. Mat. · Endang. Sp. · NWF
445	**Manage.** · Great Lakes · MI · MN · Natl. For. · Nest. Survey · USFS · WI
446	**Manage.** · Econ. Import. · Law · Life History · MO · Nest. · Prey · Pub. Ed. · Shooting
447	**Manage.** · Behav. · CA · Disturb. · Hunt. Behav. · Natl. For. · Prey · San Bernardino Mts. · USFS · Winter. Pop.
466	**Manage.** · AK · Climatology · Distrib. · Disturb. · Forestry · Habit. Loss · Habit. Use · Nest. · Nest. Survey · Reprod. Succ. · Territory
473	**Manage.** · CO · Disturb. · Field ID · Habit. Loss · Nest. · Pest. · Pub. Ed. · Winter. Pop.
499	**Manage.** · Law · Nest. · Poison. · Pub. Ed. · Shooting · SK · Trapping
511	**Manage.** · Ches. Bay · Endang. Sp. · Refuge · VA
512	**Manage.** · Ches. Bay · Mason Neck NWR · Refuge · VA
513	**Manage.** · Ches. Bay · DC · Mason Neck NWR · Refuge · VA
519	**Manage.** · CA · Depred. · Habit. Use · Mortality · Nest. · Prey · Shasta-Trinity NF · Winter Survey
556	**Manage.** · Cedar Glen Roost · Habit. Prot. · Habit. Use · IL · Prey · Refuge
559	**Manage.** · Art. Nest Site · Behav. · Habit. Use · MN · Nest. · Techniques · Young Trans.
569	**Manage.** · Ches. Bay · Endang. Sp. · Status
572	**Manage.** · Aircraft · Behav. · CA · Distrib. · Disturb. · Habit. Loss · Hunt. Behav. · Klamath R · Nest.
583	**Manage.** · Habit. Use · Nest. Survey · OR · Poison. · Prey · San Juan Is. · Shooting · Status · Winter Survey · WA
598	**Manage.** · Pub. Ed. · Shooting · Status
661	**Manage.** · Nest. · NAS · Pub. Ed.
682	**Manage.** · CA · Disturb. · Klamath NF · Nest. · Prey · Status · Winter. Pop.

Master No.	Keywords
683	**Manage.** · Behav. · CA · Distrib. · Disturb. · Field ID · Flight · Hunt. Behav. · Life History · Mortality · Nest. · Winter. Pop.
698	**Manage.** · Chippewa NF · MN · Nest.
702	**Manage.** · Habit. Prot. · Karl Mundt NWR · L Andes NWR · Missouri R · NWF · Refuge · SD · Winter. Pop.
728	**Manage.** · Habit. Loss · Habit. Use · McHargian Overlay · Nest. · Reprod. Succ. · SK · Techniques
753	**Manage.** · AK · Lower 48 · Status
755	**Manage.** · Disturb. · ME · Nest. Survey · Pub. Ed. · Shooting · Winter. Pop.
756	**Manage.** · Band. · Egg Trans. · ME · Nest. Survey · Pest. · PCB · Refuge · Techniques · Winter Survey
757	**Manage.** · Band. · Disturb. · Marking · ME · Nest. · Nest. Survey · Shooting · Techniques
770	**Manage.** · AZ · CAP · Disturb. · Habit. Use · Nest. · Orme D
780	**Manage.** · CN · Disturb. · Habit. Use · Lake of The Woods · ON
786	**Manage.** · Behav. · Distrib. · Hunt. Behav. · Marking · Migration · Mortality · MO · Nest. · Pest. · Prey · Swan Lake NWR · Techniques · Telemetry
804	**Manage.** · Art. Nest Site · AZ · Egg. Thin. · Habit. Use · Life History · Marking · Nest. · Pest. · Research · Techniques · Telemetry · Winter. Pop.
814	**Manage.** · Disturb. · Great Lakes · Nest. Survey · Pub. Ed. · Status · USFS
815	**Manage.** · Chippewa NF · Great Lakes · Nest. Survey · USFS
834	**Manage.** · Captive Breed. · Captivity
836	**Manage.** · Behav. · Disturb. · Habit. Loss · Habit. Use · Hunt. Behav. · Logging · Prey · Winter Survey · WA
984	**Manage.** · Captivity · Egg Trans. · Heavy Metals · Law · Migration · Nest. Survey · Pest. · Pub. Ed. · Status · Techniques · Territory · Young Trans.
988	**Manage.** · Great Lakes · L Erie · Nest. Survey · OH · Winter Survey
1006	**Manage.** · ID · Status
1018	**Manage.** · Chippewa NF · Disturb. · Habit. Use · MN · Nest. · Prey · Reprod. Succ.
1019	**Manage.** · Chippewa NF · Disturb. · Habit. Use
1034	**Manage.** · Hacking · NY· Photo. · Techniques
1063	**Manage.** · Behav. · Disturb. · Habit. Loss · Habit. Use · Prey · Research · TX · Winter Survey
1065	**Manage.** · Behav. · CA · Disturb. · Habit. Use · Klamath · Lower Klamath Lake NWR · OR · Prey · Tule Lake NWR · Winter Survey
1086	**Manage.** · CO · Electro. · NV · Trapping · TX · UT
1087	**Manage.** · Habit. Prot. · NWF · Pub. Ed. · SD · Techniques · Winter. Pop. · Young Trans.
1090	**Manage.** · Law · Nongame Sp.
1102	**Manage.** · Behav. · Caledon SP · Disturb. · Habit. Loss · Habit. Use · Nest. · Prey · VA
1103	**Manage.** · Caledon SP · Disturb. · Habit. Loss · Nest. · VA
1104	**Manage.** · Behav. · Caledon SP · Disturb. · Habit. Loss · Habit. Use · VA
1109	**Manage.** · Behav. · Habit. Loss · Habit. Use · Intersp. Behav. · Intrasp. Behav. · ID · Prey · Winter Survey · Wolf Lodge Bay
1112	**Manage.** · Autopsy · Disturb. · Habit. Use · Hunt. Behav. · Intersp. Behav. · Migration · OK · Prey · Salt Fork R · Shooting · Status · Taxonomy · Winter Survey
1115	**Manage.** · Disturb. · Habit. Use · Migration · OK · Prey · Salt Fork R · Salt Plains NWR · Sequoyah NWR · Shooting · Status · Taxonomy · Wichita Mts. NWR · Winter Survey
1121	**Manage.** · Behav. · NE · Prey · Status · Winter Survey
1147	**Manage.** · Great Lakes · Habit. Prot. · MB · Nest. Survey · ON · Rehab. · Techniques · Techniques
1185	**Manage.** · Electro. · ID · Winter. Pop.
1188	**Manage.** · Chippewa NF · Habit. Use · MN · Nest. Survey · Status · USFS

Master No.	Keywords
1189	**Manage.** · Chippewa NF · Habit. Use · MN · Nest. Survey · USFS
1207	**Manage.** · Chippewa NF · MN · Nest. Survey · Status · USFS
1215	**Manage.** · Chippewa NF · MN · Nest. Survey · Refuge · USFS
1218	**Manage.** · Chippewa NF · MN · USFS
1219	**Manage.** · Chippewa NF · MN · USFS
1220	**Manage.** · Chippewa NF · MN · USFS
1229	**Manage.** · Anat. · Autumn Conc. · Behav. · Capture · Glacier NP · Habit. Use · Marking · Migration · MT · Techniques · Winter Survey
1255	**Manage.** · Hacking · NY · Techniques · Young Trans.
1256	**Manage.** · Behav. · Hacking · NY · Pest. · Prey · PCB · Techniques · Young Trans.
1257	**Manage.** · Electro.
1272	**Manage.** · Endang. Sp. · Habit. Use · MN · Status
1274	**Manage.** · NY · Techniques · Young Trans.
1295	**Manage.** · Habit. Prot. · Nat. Conserv. · WA
1300	**Manage.** · Depred. · Pred. Cont. · Prey
1309	**Manage.** · Endang. Sp. · Nest. · NV · Status
1316	**Manage.** · NWF · Reward · Shooting
1321	**Manage.** · NWF · RIC
1334	**Manage.** · Habit. Prot. · Nat. Conserv. · Refuge · Skagit R Nat. Area · Winter Survey · WA
1336	**Manage.** · Behav. · NE · Prey · Status · Winter Survey
1341	**Manage.** · Electro. · ID
1342	**Manage.** · Behav. · Electro.
1346	**Manage.** · Habit. Prot. · NWF · Pub. Ed. · Reward
1348	**Manage.** · Habit. Prot. · Karl Mundt NWR · NWF
1362	**Manage.** · Pub. Ed. · WI
1368	**Manage.** · Behav. · Climatology · Disturb. · Habit. Use · Hunt. Behav. · Intersp. Behav. · Intrasp. Behav. · NY · Prey · Winter Survey
1369	**Manage.** · Behav. · Habit. Use · Heavy Metals · Hunt. Behav. · Intersp. Behav. · Intrasp. Behav. · NY · Pest. · Prey · PCB · Winter Survey
1378	**Manage.**
1379	**Manage.**
1380	**Manage.** · BLM · Endang. Sp. · Pub. Ed.
1381	**Manage.** · Habit. Prot. · Pub. Ed.
1390	**Manage.** · MS · Nest.
1451	**Manage.** · Endang. Sp. · Status
1467	**Manage.** · Art. Nest Site · MI · Nest.
1484	**Manage.** · Disturb. · Great Lakes · Nest. Survey · ON · Research · Status · Techniques
1488	**Manage.** · AR · Band. · FL · GA · Migration · MI · Techniques · TN · Young Trans.
1490	**Manage.** · MI · Techniques · Young Trans.
1496	**Manage.** · Behav. · Chippewa NF · Fledging · MN · Nest. · Nocturnal Behav.
1503	**Manage.** · Great Lakes · USFS
1528	**Manage.** · Pub. Ed. · Status
1529	**Manage.** · AK · Habit. Use · Hunt. Behav. · Pub. Ed. · Status
1530	**Manage.** · AK · Habit. Use · Nest. Survey · Territory
1601	**Manage.** · Behav. · Capture · Glacier NP · Hunt. Behav. · Intersp. Behav. · Intrasp. Behav. · MT · Techniques · Winter Survey
1640	**Manage.** · Aggress. · Behav. · BLM · Disturb. · Habit. Loss · Habit. Use · Hunt. Behav. · Life History · Nest. · Pest. · Prey · Shooting · Territory
1641	**Manage.**
1654	**Manage.** · Endang. Sp. · Techniques
1673	**Manage.** · Cont. B.E. Proj. · Migration · Nest. Survey · NAS · Status · Winter Survey
1674	**Manage.** · Cont. B.E. Proj. · Nest. Survey · NAS · Refuge · Status · Winter Survey
1678	**Manage.** · Cont. B.E. Proj. · Nest. Survey · NAS · Status · Winter Survey
1680	**Manage.** · Endang. Sp. · Status · Taxonomy
1690	**Manage.** · Behav. · Disturb. · Winter. Pop. · WA
1696	**Manage.** · Climatology · Ft. Randall D · Habit. Use · Hunt. Behav. · Karl Mundt NWR · L Andes NWR · Prey · SD · Winter Survey
1698	**Manage.** · Climatology · Disturb. · Electro. · Habit. Use · Prey · Winter Survey

Master No.	Keywords
1699	**Manage.** · Behav. · Disturb. · Ft. Randall D · Habit. Use · Missouri R · SD · Winter Survey
1730	**Manage.** · MN · Nest. Survey
1741	**Manage.** · Disturb. · Habit. Use · MT · Nest. Survey · Pop. Turnover · Reprod. Succ. · Status · Territory · Yellowstone NP
1751	**Manage.** · Egg. Thin. · Habit. Use · MD · Nest. Survey · Pest.
1752	**Manage.** · Egg. Thin. · Habit. Use · MD · Nest. Survey · Pest. · Techniques
1771	**Manage.** · CA · Disturb. · Habit. Loss · Habit. Use · Nest. Survey · Prey · Shooting · Territory · Trapping
1777	**Manage.** · CA · Habit. Use · Nest. Survey · Status · Territory
1820	**Manage.** · Habit. Prot. · Nest. · USFS · Winter Survey
1821	**Manage.** · Chippewa NF · MN · Pub. Ed. · USFS
1822	**Manage.** · Electro.
1823	**Manage.** · Data Coll. · USFS
1824	**Manage.** · Child. Eagle Area · Chippewa NF · Hunt-Wesson · MN · Pub. Ed. · Refuge · USFS
1827	**Manage.** · USFS
1828	**Manage.** · Endang. Sp. · Habit. Prot. · MN
1832	**Manage.** · Endang. Sp. · Field ID · Status · USFWS
1834	**Manage.** · Endang. Sp. · Field ID · Status · USFWS
1841	**Manage.** · AK · Life History · Status
1848	**Manage.** · Endang. Sp. · Field ID · Status · USFWS
1851	**Manage.** · Egg Trans. · ME · MN · USFWS
1852	**Manage.** · AZ · Nest. Survey · NM · OK · Salt Fork R · TX · USFWS · Verde R
1854	**Manage.** · CO · Glacier NP · Missouri R · MT · Nest. Survey · SD · USFWS
1861	**Manage.** · Egg Trans. · ME · MN · USFWS · WI
1865	**Manage.** · AZ · BLM · CAP · Egg · Habit. Prot. · Nest. · Orme D · Salt R · Taxonomy · Territory · Verde R
1871	**Manage.** · Egg Trans. · Hacking · ME · MN · NY · Pest. · PCB · Techniques · WI · Young Trans.
1874	**Manage.** · Distrib. · Endang. Sp. · Law · Life History · Status · Taxonomy · USFWS
1879	**Manage.** · Behav. · Hunt. Behav. · Intersp. Behav. · ID · L Couer D' Alene · Winter Survey
1881	**Manage.** · Hunt. Behav. · Nest. · OR · Winter. Pop. · WA
1914	**Manage.** · Behav. · Chippewa NF · Disturb. · MN · USFS
1920	**Manage.** · Disturb. · Habit. Loss · Nest. Survey · ON · Status
1929	**Manage.** · AK · Bounty · Logging
1981	**Manage.** · CO · Electro. · ID · NV · UT · WY
1988	**Manage.** · Anat. · Behav. · Capture · Depred. · Econ. Import. · Intersp. Behav. · NB · Prey · Techniques
1987	**Maritime Prov.** · Econ. Import. · LB · NF · Prey
24	**Marking** · Capture · Manage. · Skagit R · Techniques · WA
173	**Marking** · AZ · Pub. Ed. · Techniques · Verde R
174	**Marking** · B.E. Nat. Area · Pub. Ed. · Skagit R · Techniques · WA
431	**Marking** · AK · Behav. · Climatology · Disease · Kodiak NWR · Life History · Nest. · Nest. Survey · Parasites · Reprod. Succ. · Techniques · Terminology
548	**Marking** · MN · SD · Techniques
555	**Marking** · Behav. · Breed. Behav. · Chippewa NF · Disturb. · Fledging · MN · Nestling · Prey · Reprod. Succ. · Techniques · Telemetry
561	**Marking** · Behav. · Fledging · Habit. Use · MN · Parent. Behav. · Techniques · Telemetry
573	**Marking** · Habit. Prot. · Nest. · Pub. Ed. · Techniques · Winter. Pop.
586	**Marking** · MN · Nest. Survey · Techniques · USFWS
736	**Marking** · Habit. Use · Migration · MO · ND · SD · SK · Techniques · WY
757	**Marking** · Band. · Disturb. · Manage. · ME · Nest. · Nest. Survey · Shooting · Techniques

Master No.	Keywords
786	**Marking** · Behav. · Distrib. · Hunt. Behav. · Manage. · Migration · Mortality · MO · Nest. · Pest. · Prey · Swan Lake NWR · Techniques · Telemetry
804	**Marking** · Art. Nest Site · AZ · Egg. Thin. · Habit. Use · Life History · Manage. · Nest. · Pest. · Research · Techniques · Telemetry · Winter. Pop.
832	**Marking** · BC · Intrasp. Behav. · Nest. Survey · Pub. Ed. · Techniques · Territory
840	**Marking** · Behav. · Capture · CO · Habit. Use · Migration · Techniques · Winter Survey
1071	**Marking** · Behav. · Chippewa NF · Fledging · Intrasp. Behav. · Mortality · MN · Nest. · Techniques · Telemetry · Vocal.
1072	**Marking** · Behav. · Chippewa NF · Fledging · MN · Techniques
1181	**Marking** · Techniques
1214	**Marking** · Band. · Chippewa NF · MN · Nest. Survey · Techniques
1222	**Marking** · Behav. · Fledging · Hunt. Behav. · Intersp. Behav. · Intrasp. Behav. · MI · Ottawa NF · Techniques · Territory
1229	**Marking** · Anat. · Autumn Conc. · Behav. · Capture · Glacier NP · Habit. Use · Manage. · Migration · MT · Techniques · Winter Survey
1253	**Marking** · Behav. · Hacking · Heavy Metals · Intrasp. Behav. · Montezuma NWR · MI · MN · NY · Pest. · Techniques · Telemetry · Young Trans.
1592	**Marking** · Molt. · Techniques · Telemetry
1650	**Marking** · Capture · Habit. Use · Hunt. Behav. · Intersp. Behav. · IL · Mississippi R · Prey · Techniques · Winter Survey
1651	**Marking** · Anat. · Behav. · Capture · Hunt. Behav. · IL · Plumage · Prey · Techniques · Telemetry · Winter Survey
1768	**Marking** · Migration · MN · Techniques
1875	**Marking** · Pub. Ed. · Techniques · USFWS
21	**Mason Neck NWR** · Ches. Bay · Nest. Survey · Reprod. Succ.
124	**Mason Neck NWR** · Ches. Bay · Manage. · Refuge · VA
512	**Mason Neck NWR** · Ches. Bay · Manage. · Refuge · VA
513	**Mason Neck NWR** · Ches. Bay · DC · Manage. · Refuge · VA
1836	**Mason Neck NWR** · Refuge · VA
202	**Mass Spectro.** · Anal. Tech. · AR · MN · PCB · Residues · Techniques
1763	**Mattamuskett NWR** · Nest. · NC · Savannah NWR · SC
728	**McHargian Overlay** · Habit. Loss · Habit. Use · Manage. · Nest. · Reprod. Succ. · SK · Techniques
148	**Merritt Is. NWR** · Anat. · Autumn Conc. · FL · Glacier NP · Manage. · Museum Specimen · MT · Nest. · Prey · Taxonomy
948	**Merritt Is. NWR** · FL · Nest. Survey
269	**Midwest Region** · Autopsy · FL · Heavy Metals · MD · ME · MO · ND · Pest. · PCB
36	**Migration** · Cape May · NJ
147	**Migration** · Hawk Mt. · PA
196	**Migration** · Distrib. · LA · Mortality · Nest. Survey · Reprod. Succ. · Shooting · Status · Winter Survey
253	**Migration** · Winter. Pop. · WI
266	**Migration** · Anat. · Behav. · BC · Distrib. · Falconry · Field ID · Flight · Habit. Use · Nest. · Prey · Status
267	**Migration** · SK
308	**Migration** · Educ. Mat. · Field ID · Hawk Mt. · Pub. Ed. · PA · Shooting
310	**Migration** · Disturb. · ME · Nest. · Shooting · Winter. Pop.
318	**Migration** · Hawk Mt. · PA
324	**Migration** · Band. · FL · Life History · Nest. Fail. · Nest. Survey · Prey · Status · Techniques
325	**Migration** · Behav. · Dispersal · Disturb. · FL · Habit. Use · Intersp. Behav. · Mortality · Nest. · Prey
346	**Migration** · Hawk Mt. · PA
351	**Migration** · Nest. · Prey · Reprod. Succ. · Status
352	**Migration** · Behav. · Flight · Life History · Nest. · Prey · Pub. Ed. · Status · Taxonomy
377	**Migration** · Distrib. · GA · Habit. Use · Life History · Nest. · Status

Master No.	Keywords
406	**Migration** · MN
435	**Migration** · Cape May · Capture · NJ · Techniques
436	**Migration** · Cape May · NJ
437	**Migration** · Cape May · NJ
438	**Migration** · Cape May · NJ · Status
439	**Migration** · Band. · Cape May · Capture · NJ · Techniques
440	**Migration** · Band. · Capture · NJ · Sandy Hook · Techniques
496	**Migration** · Climatology · OH · Poison. · Shooting · Winter Survey
516	**Migration** · AB
520	**Migration** · Distrib. · Habit. Use · Nest. Survey · Status · Winter Survey · WI
543	**Migration** · Anat. · IA · Nest. · Taxonomy · Winter. Pop.
544	**Migration** · IA · Nest. · Shooting · Winter. Pop.
545	**Migration** · NJ · Racoon Ridge
546	**Migration** · Cape May · NJ
552	**Migration** · Band. · MN · Techniques · Trapping · TX
554	**Migration** · Band. · Behav. · Cedar Glen Roost · IL · Mississippi R · MN · Refuge · Techniques · Telemetry · TX · Winter. Pop.
557	**Migration** · Chippewa NF · Disturb. · Life History · Nest. · Photo. · Pub. Ed. · Status · Techniques · Telemetry · Winter. Pop.
560	**Migration** · Band. · Behav. · Life History · MN · Reprod. Succ. · Techniques
599	**Migration** · Behav. · Disturb. · FL · Nest. · Nest. Fail.
610	**Migration** · Nest. · NJ
617	**Migration** · Lower 48 · Mississippi R · Winter Survey
654	**Migration** · Mississippi R · Winter Survey
712	**Migration** · CO · Hawk Mt. · PA · Status
730	**Migration** · Band. · Pub. Ed. · Status · SK · Techniques
733	**Migration** · Band. · Great Lakes · ON · Techniques
736	**Migration** · Habit. Use · Marking · MO · ND · SD · SK · Techniques · WY
752	**Migration** · IL · Nest. · Status · Winter. Pop.
786	**Migration** · Behav. · Distrib. · Hunt. Behav. · Manage. · Marking · Mortality · MO · Nest. · Pest. · Prey · Swan Lake NWR · Techniques · Telemetry
811	**Migration** · MD · Status
826	**Migration** · BC · Gulf Is. · Habit. Use · Nest. Survey · Prey · San Juan Is. · Techniques · Winter Survey · WA
840	**Migration** · Behav. · Capture · CO · Habit. Use · Marking · Techniques · Winter Survey
843	**Migration** · Band. · Behav. · Chippewa NF · Dispersal · Fledging · MN · Nestling · Techniques · Telemetry
850	**Migration** · Derby Hill · Great Lakes · Hawk Mt. · NY
851	**Migration** · Behav. · Great Lakes
855	**Migration** · Hawk Mt. · Pub. Ed. · PA
866	**Migration** · Anat. · Climatology · Field ID · Status
867	**Migration** · Bake Oven Knob · PA
868	**Migration** · Bake Oven Knob · PA
869	**Migration** · Bake Oven Knob · PA
906	**Migration** · MN
907	**Migration** · Duluth Fly. · Great Lakes · L Superior · MN
957	**Migration** · Itasca SP · MN · Nest.
984	**Migration** · Captivity · Egg Trans. · Heavy Metals · Law · Manage. · Nest. Survey · Pest. · Pub. Ed. · Status · Techniques · Territory · Young Trans.
986	**Migration** · Acct. · AK
987	**Migration** · Acct. · AK
989	**Migration** · AK · Habit. Use · Nest. · Winter. Pop.
1033	**Migration** · IL · Nest. · Winter. Pop.
1045	**Migration** · IA · Nest. · Status
1055	**Migration** · Nest. · Winter. Pop. · WA
1084	**Migration** · Anat. · Hunt. Behav. · Life History · Nest. · Plumage
1093	**Migration** · PA
1112	**Migration** · Autopsy · Disturb. · Habit. Use · Hunt. Behav. · Intersp. Behav. · Manage. · OK · Prey · Salt Fork R · Shooting · Status · Taxonomy · Winter Survey
1113	**Migration** · Hunt. Behav. · Intrasp. Behav. · Neosho R · OK · Prey · Winter Survey

Master No.	Keywords
1115	**Migration** · Disturb. · Habit. Use · Manage. · OK · Prey · Salt Fork R · Salt Plains NWR · Sequoyah NWR · Shooting · Status · Taxonomy · Wichita Mts. NWR · Winter Survey
1229	**Migration** · Anat. · Autumn Conc. · Behav. · Capture · Glacier NP · Habit. Use · Manage. · Marking · MT · Techniques · Winter Survey
1237	**Migration** · Distrib. · Endang. Sp. · Habit. Use · Nest. · ND · Status · Winter. Pop.
1291	**Migration** · Cedar Grove · WI
1301	**Migration** · Nest. · Status · Winter. Pop.
1307	**Migration** · Hawk Mt. · NJ
1308	**Migration** · Hawk Mt. · PA · Status
1310	**Migration** · CA · Winter. Pop.
1312	**Migration** · FL · LA
1349	**Migration** · Dispersal · FL · Life History · NAS · Pub. Ed. · Status
1391	**Migration** · Hunt. Behav. · ME · Prey · Winter Survey
1446	**Migration** · Cape May · NJ · Pymatuning · PA · Winter. Pop.
1448	**Migration** · Band. · FL · Prey · Techniques
1471	**Migration** · Nest. · PA
1486	**Migration** · Great Lakes · MI · WI
1488	**Migration** · AR · Band. · FL · GA · Manage. · MI · Techniques · TN · Young Trans.
1516	**Migration** · Mississippi R · MN
1524	**Migration** · Egg Coll. · Nest. · WI
1531	**Migration** · Band. · Christmas Count · Life History · Nest. · Status · USFWS · Winter Survey
1537	**Migration** · Hunt. Behav. · Life History · MN · Nest. · Prey · Shooting · Status · Winter. Pop.
1559	**Migration** · CT · Nest. · Shooting · Taxonomy · Winter. Pop.
1566	**Migration** · MT · Nest. · Winter. Pop.
1569	**Migration** · AR
1570	**Migration** · Acct. · MN
1593	**Migration** · Behav. · WA
1655	**Migration** · Christmas Count · Lower 48 · Prey · Refuge · Winter. Pop.
1656	**Migration** · Band. · Pub. Ed. · Techniques · Winter. Pop.
1671	**Migration** · Cont. B.E. Proj. · Nest. Survey · NAS · Status · Winter Survey
1673	**Migration** · Cont. B.E. Proj. · Manage. · Nest. Survey · NAS · Status · Winter Survey
1697	**Migration** · Ft. Randall D · Habit. Loss · Habit. Use · Hunt. Behav. · Prey · SD · Winter Survey
1705	**Migration** · Band. · DC · MD · Nest. · Techniques · Winter. Pop.
1716	**Migration** · Cape May · Nest. · NJ
1761	**Migration** · PA
1768	**Migration** · Marking · MN · Techniques
1774	**Migration** · Climatology · Hook Mt. · NY
1891	**Migration** · Dispersal · Plumage
1895	**Migration** · Behav. · Habit. Use · Hunt. Behav. · Intrasp. Behav. · NE · Platte R · Winter Survey
1915	**Migration** · Behav. · NE · Platte R · Prey · Winter Survey
1954	**Migration** · AK · Hunt. Behav. · Law · Nest. · Pub. Ed. · WY · Yellowstone NP
1955	**Migration** · AK · Hunt. Behav. · Law · Nest. · Pub. Ed. · WY · Yellowstone NP
1968	**Migration** · NE
1975	**Migration** · MI · Nest. · Winter. Pop.
1989	**Migration** · Anat. · MO · Shooting
1996	**Migration** · Missouri R · MN · NE · Shooting
38	**Mississippi R** · IA · Nest. · Winter. Pop.
120	**Mississippi R** · Chippewa NF · Manage. · MN
248	**Mississippi R** · MN · Winter. Pop.
276	**Mississippi R** · IA · Winter. Pop.
364	**Mississippi R** · Hunt. Behav. · IL · MO · Winter Survey
423	**Mississippi R** · Nest. · Pub. Ed. · Reelfoot L · Shooting · Status · TN · Winter. Pop.
554	**Mississippi R** · Band. · Behav. · Cedar Glen Roost · IL · Migration · MN · Refuge · Techniques · Telemetry · TX · Winter. Pop.
609	**Mississippi R** · Behav. · Habit. Use · MN · Pest. Residues · Prey · Winter Survey
613	**Mississippi R** · Techniques · Winter Survey

Master No.	Keywords
614	**Mississippi R** · IA · IL · NE · Winter Survey · WI
615	**Mississippi R** · IA · IL · NE · Winter Survey
616	**Mississippi R** · Winter Survey
617	**Mississippi R** · Lower 48 · Migration · Winter Survey
618	**Mississippi R** · Lower 48 · Winter Survey
619	**Mississippi R** · Winter Survey
620	**Mississippi R** · Illinois R · IA · IL · Winter Survey · WI
621	**Mississippi R** · Illinois R · IL · KY · NE · Winter Survey
623	**Mississippi R** · Winter. Pop.
624	**Mississippi R** · Illinois R · IA · IL · KY · NE · Winter Survey
625	**Mississippi R** · Winter Survey
626	**Mississippi R** · Illinois R · IA · IL · MO · Winter Survey
627	**Mississippi R** · Winter Survey
628	**Mississippi R** · Illinois R · IA · IL · KY · MO · Winter Survey
631	**Mississippi R** · Illinois R · IA · IL · KY · Winter Survey
632	**Mississippi R** · Illinois R · IA · IL · KY · Winter Survey
634	**Mississippi R** · Illinois R · IA · IL · KY · MO · NE · Winter Survey
635	**Mississippi R** · Illinois R · IA · IL · KY · Missouri R · MO · NE · Winter Survey · Wisconsin R
636	**Mississippi R** · Illinois R · IA · IL · KY · Missouri R · MO · NE · Winter Survey · Wisconsin R
637	**Mississippi R** · Illinois R · IA · IL · KY · Missouri R · MO · NE · Winter Survey · Wisconsin R
638	**Mississippi R** · Illinois R · IA · IL · KY · MO · NE · Winter Survey
639	**Mississippi R** · Illinois R · IA · IL · KY · MO · NE · Winter Survey
643	**Mississippi R** · Illinois R · IL · KY · MO · NE · Winter Survey
644	**Mississippi R** · Illinois R · IL · KY · MO · NE · Winter Survey
645	**Mississippi R** · IA · IL · MN · MO · NE · WI
646	**Mississippi R** · Illinois R · IL · KY · MO · NE · Winter Survey
647	**Mississippi R** · Illinois R · Lower 48 · Winter Survey
648	**Mississippi R** · Habit. Prot. · IA · IL · MO · Winter Survey
649	**Mississippi R** · Illinois R · IL · KY · TN · Winter Survey
650	**Mississippi R** · Illinois R · IL · KY · TN · Winter Survey
651	**Mississippi R** · Illinois R · IA · IL · KY · MO · NE · TN · Winter Survey
652	**Mississippi R** · Illinois R · IA · KY · MO · NE · TN · Winter Survey
653	**Mississippi R** · Winter Survey
654	**Mississippi R** · Migration · Winter Survey
715	**Mississippi R** · AR · Habit. Use · MS · Nest. · Reelfoot L · Shooting · TN
751	**Mississippi R** · Christmas Count · IL · Status · Techniques · Winter Survey
785	**Mississippi R** · IL · Winter. Pop.
838	**Mississippi R** · Hunt. Behav. · IA · Prey · Winter. Pop.
892	**Mississippi R** · Hunt. Behav. · IA · Prey · Winter. Pop.
903	**Mississippi R** · Christmas Count · IA · Nest. · Status · Winter Survey
978	**Mississippi R** · Capture · Intrasp. Behav. · IA · Techniques · Upper Miss. NWR · Winter Survey · WI
979	**Mississippi R** · IA · IL · Winter. Pop.
1011	**Mississippi R** · Behav. · Climatology · Habit. Use · Hunt. Behav. · Intersp. Behav. · Intrasp. Behav. · IA · IL · MO · Prey · Winter Survey
1289	**Mississippi R** · IA · Winter. Pop.
1305	**Mississippi R** · IL · Winter. Pop.
1306	**Mississippi R** · IL · Winter. Pop.
1432	**Mississippi R** · IA · IL · Winter. Pop.
1453	**Mississippi R** · Hunt. Behav. · IA · IL · Winter. Pop.
1468	**Mississippi R** · Electro.
1516	**Mississippi R** · Migration · MN
1600	**Mississippi R** · Winter Survey
1625	**Mississippi R** · IL · Winter Survey
1650	**Mississippi R** · Capture · Habit. Use · Hunt. Behav. · Intersp. Behav. · IL · Marking · Prey · Techniques · Winter Survey
1652	**Mississippi R** · IL · Prey · Winter. Pop.
1692	**Mississippi R** · Illinois R · KY · Ohio R · Winter Survey

Master No.	Keywords
1693	**Mississippi R** · KY · Ohio R · Winter Survey
1714	**Mississippi R** · MS · Nest.
1893	**Mississippi R** · MO · Nest. · Squaw Creek NWR · Winter Survey
152	**Missouri R** · Corps · Habit. Loss · Karl Mundt NWR · NE · NWF · SD
153	**Missouri R** · Habit. Prot. · NWF · SD · Winter. Pop.
468	**Missouri R** · Life History · Plumage · Taxonomy
549	**Missouri R** · Life History · Pub. Ed. · SD · Winter Survey
635	**Missouri R** · Illinois R · IA · IL · KY · Mississippi R · MO · NE · Winter Survey · Wisconsin R
636	**Missouri R** · Illinois R · IA · IL · KY · Mississippi R · MO · NE · Winter Survey · Wisconsin R
637	**Missouri R** · Illinois R · IA · IL · KY · Mississippi R · MO · NE · Winter Survey · Wisconsin R
702	**Missouri R** · Habit. Prot. · Karl Mundt NWR · L Andes NWR · Manage. · NWF · Refuge · SD · Winter. Pop.
703	**Missouri R** · Habit. Prot. · Karl Mundt NWR · Refuge · SD · Winter. Pop.
790	**Missouri R** · Nest.
845	**Missouri R** · KS · Nest. · Prey · Winter. Pop.
1017	**Missouri R** · L Andes NWR · NAS · Status · SD · Winter Survey
1699	**Missouri R** · Behav. · Disturb. · Ft. Randall D · Habit. Use · Manage. · SD · Winter Survey
1854	**Missouri R** · CO · Glacier NP · Manage. · MT · Nest. Survey · SD · USFWS
1857	**Missouri R** · Nest. Survey · SD · USFWS
1859	**Missouri R** · IA · KS · MO · Nest. Survey · ND · NE · Rocky Mt. Region · SD · USFWS · Winter. Pop.
1860	**Missouri R** · Nest. Survey · NE · SD · USFWS · Winter. Pop.
1880	**Missouri R** · SD · Winter. Pop.
1963	**Missouri R** · Winter. Pop.
1996	**Missouri R** · Migration · MN · NE · Shooting
696	**Model** · Aircraft · Chippewa NF · MN · Statistics · Techniques
1994	**Model** · Status · Techniques
1967	**Modoc NWR** · CA · Disturb. · Habit. Use · Lower Klamath Lake NWR · Tule Lake NWR · Winter Survey
477	**Molt.** · Growth · GA · Plumage
1592	**Molt.** · Marking · Techniques · Telemetry
1653	**Molt.** · Aging · Techniques
387	**Montezuma NWR** · Hacking · Manage. · NY · Techniques · WI · Young Trans.
414	**Montezuma NWR** · Hacking · NY · Techniques · Telemetry · Young Trans.
955	**Montezuma NWR** · Finger Lakes · Nest. · NY
956	**Montezuma NWR** · Finger Lakes · Nest. · NY
1253	**Montezuma NWR** · Behav. · Hacking · Heavy Metals · Intrasp. Behav. · Marking · MI · MN · NY · Pest. · Techniques · Telemetry · Young Trans.
1404	**Montezuma NWR** · Nest. · NY
1667	**Montezuma NWR** · Field ID · NY
1668	**Montezuma NWR** · Nest. Survey · NY · Status
134	**Mortality** · Heavy Metals · MN
139	**Mortality** · Heavy Metals · MN
196	**Mortality** · Distrib. · LA · Migration · Nest. Survey · Reprod. Succ. · Shooting · Status · Winter Survey
230	**Mortality** · Pub. Ed. · Status
243	**Mortality** · Nest. · OH
286	**Mortality** · NE · Winter. Pop.
325	**Mortality** · Behav. · Dispersal · Disturb. · FL · Habit. Use · Intersp. Behav. · Migration · Nest. · Prey
345	**Mortality** · Acct. · MI
360	**Mortality** · Nest. · ND
461	**Mortality** · Art · History · Status · Symbolism
519	**Mortality** · CA · Depred. · Habit. Use · Manage. · Nest. · Prey · Shasta-Trinity NF · Winter Survey
578	**Mortality** · Aggress. · Band. · Behav. · Nest. · Photo. · Pub. Ed. · Techniques

Master No.	Keywords
683	**Mortality** · Behav. · CA · Distrib. · Disturb. · Field ID · Flight · Hunt. Behav. · Life History · Manage. · Nest. · Winter. Pop.
758	**Mortality** · IA · Winter. Pop.
786	**Mortality** · Behav. · Distrib. · Hunt. Behav. · Manage. · Marking · Migration · MO · Nest. · Pest. · Prey · Swan Lake NWR · Techniques · Telemetry
1071	**Mortality** · Behav. · Chippewa NF · Fledging · Intrasp. Behav. · Marking · MN · Nest. · Techniques · Telemetry · Vocal.
1606	**Mortality** · Aggress. · Aleutian Is. · AK · Behav. · Depred. · Habit. Use · Life History · Nest. Survey · Plumage · Prey · Reprod. Succ. · Status · Winter Survey
1710	**Mortality** · Pest. · Toxicol.
1712	**Mortality** · Autopsy · Pest. · Toxicol.
1720	**Mortality**
261	**Mt. Johnson Is. Sanct.** · Manage. · Nest. · PA · Refuge · Shooting
262	**Mt. Johnson Is. Sanct.** · Nest. · PA
1037	**Mt. Johnson Is. Sanct.** · PA · Refuge
1233	**Mt. Johnson Is. Sanct.** · Field ID · Hawk Mt. · PA
1494	**Mt. Johnson Is. Sanct.** · Nest. · PA · Refuge
1054	**Mt. Ranier NP** · Nest. · Status · WA
529	**Mud Lake NWR** · MN · Nest.
148	**Museum Specimen** · Anat. · Autumn Conc. · FL · Glacier NP · Manage. · Merritt Is. NWR · MT · Nest. · Prey · Taxonomy
809	**Museum Specimen** · Taxonomy
32	**MA** · NH · Winter. Pop.
199	**MA** · Nest. · Winter. Pop.
302	**MA** · Photo. · Winter. Pop.
470	**MA** · Depred. · Prey
796	**MA** · Hunt. Behav. · Nest. · Prey · Winter. Pop.
898	**MA** · Nest. · Status · Winter. Pop.
929	**MA** · Nest. · Winter. Pop.
1583	**MA** · Hunt. Behav. · Intrasp. Behav. · Prey · Winter. Pop.
1739	**MA** · History · Photo. · Winter. Pop.
1740	**MA** · Photo. · Winter. Pop.
457	**MB** · Hudson Bay · Intersp. Behav. · Nest. · Prey
726	**MB** · Habit. Use · Reprod. Succ. · Status · SK · Techniques
732	**MB** · Disturb. · Habit. Use · Nest. · SK · Territory
778	**MB** · Disturb. · Nest. Survey · ON · Reprod. Succ. · Techniques
782	**MB** · Disturb. · Nest. Survey · ON · Status · Techniques
1075	**MB** · Acct. · AB · SK
1147	**MB** · Great Lakes · Habit. Prot. · Manage. · Nest. Survey · ON · Rehab. · Techniques · Techniques
1938	**MB** · Nest. Survey · Reprod. Succ. · SK
1939	**MB** · Habit. Use · Nest. Survey · SK · Terminology
88	**MD** · Growth · Nest. · Photo. · Plumage
269	**MD** · Autopsy · FL · Heavy Metals · Midwest Region · ME · MO · ND · Pest. · PCB
280	**MD** · Nest. Survey · VA
312	**MD** · Nest. Survey
313	**MD** · Nest. Survey
314	**MD** · Nest. Survey
315	**MD** · Nest. Survey
316	**MD** · Nest. Survey
385	**MD** · Nest.
386	**MD** · Nest.
492	**MD** · DE · Egg · Egg Coll. · Nest. · NJ
494	**MD** · DE · Egg · Egg Coll. · Nest. · VA
495	**MD** · DE · Egg · Egg Coll.
581	**MD** · DE · Egg Coll. · Habit. Use · Nest.
590	**MD** · Acct. · WV
666	**MD** · Egg Coll. · Nest.
668	**MD** · Nest.
811	**MD** · Migration · Status
994	**MD** · Disease · Heavy Metals · Histology · Lead Poison. · Techniques
1052	**MD** · Egg Coll. · Nest.
1244	**MD** · Ches. Bay · Distrib. · Habit. Use · Pub. Ed.
1532	**MD** · Nest.
1578	**MD** · DE · Great Lakes · Nest. Survey · NJ · PA · Status
1614	**MD** · Egg Coll. · Nest. · VA
1626	**MD** · Hunt. Behav. · Hurricane · Nest. · Prey
1705	**MD** · Band. · DC · Migration · Nest. · Techniques · Winter. Pop.
1751	**MD** · Egg. Thin. · Habit. Use · Manage. · Nest. Survey · Pest.

Master No.	Keywords
1752	MD · Egg. Thin. · Habit. Use · Manage. · Nest. Survey · Pest. · Techniques
1812	MD · Ches. Bay · DE · Econ. Import. · Habit. Use · Life History · Nest. Survey · NC · NJ · Prey · PA · VA
1886	MD · Acct. · Disturb. · Douglas Pt. Nuc. Plant
1892	MD · Nest.
63	ME · Capture · Techniques
96	ME · Nest.
107	ME · Nest.
110	ME · Nest.
140	ME · AK · DDT · FL · Pest. · Reprod. Succ. · WI
156	ME · Egg Trans. · Manage. · MN · USFWS
181	ME · Nest. · Prey · Winter. Pop.
269	ME · Autopsy · FL · Heavy Metals · Midwest Region · MD · MO · ND · Pest. · PCB
275	ME · Egg Trans. · Manage. · MN
310	ME · Disturb. · Migration · Nest. · Shooting · Winter. Pop.
341	ME · Nest. Survey · Pest. · Reprod. Succ.
380	ME · Intersp. Behav.
418	ME · Photo.
450	ME · Habit. Prot. · Nest. Survey · Pub. Ed. · RIC · Shooting · Status
565	ME · FL · NJ · Pest. · Toxicol.
566	ME · AK · FL · MI · MN · PCB
755	ME · Disturb. · Manage. · Nest. Survey · Pub. Ed. · Shooting · Winter. Pop.
756	ME · Band. · Egg Trans. · Manage. · Nest. Survey · Pest. · PCB · Refuge · Techniques · Winter Survey
757	ME · Band. · Disturb. · Manage. · Marking · Nest. · Nest. Survey · Shooting · Techniques
1057	ME · Nest.
1058	ME · Habit. Use · Intersp. Behav. · Life History · Nest. · Status
1064	ME · FL · Heavy Metals · Nest. · Pest. · PCB · Reprod. Succ. · WI
1100	ME · Nest. Survey
1271	ME · Pub. Ed. · Young Trans.
1391	ME · Hunt. Behav. · Migration · Prey · Winter Survey
1396	ME · Nest.

Master No.	Keywords
1399	ME · Nest.
1400	ME · Nest.
1604	ME · Nest. · Status
1657	ME · Egg Coll. · Habit. Use · Logging · Nest.
1709	ME · FL · MO · NJ · Pest. · Toxicol. · USFWS
1798	ME · Nest.
1799	ME · Band. · Techniques
1845	ME · Nest. Survey · USFWS
1851	ME · Egg Trans. · Manage. · MN · USFWS
1861	ME · Egg Trans. · Manage. · MN · USFWS · WI
1871	ME · Egg Trans. · Hacking · Manage. · MN · NY · Pest. · PCB · Techniques · WI · Young Trans.
1942	ME · AK · Egg. Thin. · FL · Great Lakes · Heavy Metals · Pest. · PCB
1943	ME · Dieldrin · Pest. · Prey · PCB
1945	ME · Egg · Egg Coll. · Nest.
71	MI · Captivity · Capture · Techniques
121	MI · Nest. Survey
171	MI · Nest. Survey
222	MI · Nest.
249	MI · Anat. · Distrib. · Life History · Plumage · Status
319	MI · Ground Nest. · Nest.
345	MI · Acct. · Mortality
369	MI · Law · Nest. Survey · NJ · Winter Survey
422	MI · Nest. · Winter. Pop.
445	MI · Great Lakes · Manage. · MN · Natl. For. · Nest. Survey · USFS · WI
456	MI · Nest. · Status · Trapping · Winter. Pop.
486	MI · Nest. Survey
566	MI · AK · FL · ME · MN · PCB
787	MI · MO · Rehab. · Reintroduction · Shooting · Swan Lake NWR · WI
849	MI · Allegan SF · Kalamazoo R · Nest.
923	MI · Great Lakes · Nest. Survey
1028	MI · Winter. Pop.
1029	MI · Nest.
1030	MI · Acct. · Behav.
1031	MI · Nest. Survey · Reprod. Succ.
1032	MI · Nest. Survey · Reprod. Succ.
1036	MI · Nest.
1105	MI · Prey

Master No.	Keywords
1106	MI · Nest. Survey · Reprod. Succ. · Status
1153	MI · Acct.
1176	MI · Nest.
1221	MI · Aging · Behav. · Hunt. Behav. · Impound. · Intrasp. Behav. · Nest. · Ottawa NF · Techniques · Territory
1222	MI · Behav. · Fledging · Hunt. Behav. · Intersp. Behav. · Intrasp. Behav. · Marking · Ottawa NF · Techniques · Territory
1253	MI · Behav. · Hacking · Heavy Metals · Intrasp. Behav. · Marking · Montezuma NWR · MN · NY · Pest. · Techniques · Telemetry · Young Trans.
1323	MI · Reward · Shooting
1467	MI · Art. Nest Site · Manage. · Nest.
1473	MI · Nest. Survey · ON · Terminology
1474	MI · Status · Winter Survey
1475	MI · Nest. Survey · ON · Terminology
1476	MI · Hunt. Behav. · Prey · Winter Survey
1477	MI · Winter Survey
1478	MI · Nest. Survey
1479	MI · Nest. Survey
1481	MI · Nest. Survey
1483	MI · Nest. Survey
1485	MI · Nest. Survey
1486	MI · Great Lakes · Migration · WI
1487	MI · Band. · Disturb. · Great Lakes · Nest. Survey · Pest. · Techniques
1488	MI · AR · Band. · FL · GA · Manage. · Migration · Techniques · TN · Young Trans.
1489	MI · Nest. Survey
1490	MI · Manage. · Techniques · Young Trans.
1598	MI · Ground Nest. · Prey
1724	MI · Egg · Egg Coll.
1727	MI · Egg · Egg Coll. · VA
1745	MI · Nest. · Prey · Seney NWR
1825	MI · Aircraft · Chippewa NF · Great Lakes · MN · Nest. Survey · Reprod. Succ. · Status · USFS · WI
1855	MI · IL · IN · MN · Nest. Survey · OH · Terminology · USFWS · WI
1868	MI · MN · Nest. Survey · OH · USFWS · WI
1906	MI · Nest.
1908	MI · Endang. Sp. · Nest.
1936	MI · Acct. · Shooting
1962	MI · Paleontology
1971	MI · Nest.
1973	MI · Great Lakes · Nest.
1975	MI · Migration · Nest. · Winter. Pop.
1976	MI · Nest.
1999	MI · Nest. · Winter. Pop.
35	MN · Egg Coll. · LA · MS · Status · WI
120	MN · Chippewa NF · Manage. · Mississippi R
128	MN · Habit. Prot. · Indian Culture · Manage. · Refuge · St. Croix R · WI
134	MN · Heavy Metals · Mortality
139	MN · Heavy Metals · Mortality
155	MN · Pub. Ed. · Rehab. · Techniques
156	MN · Egg Trans. · Manage. · ME · USFWS
159	MN · Behav. · Disturb. · IA · IL
202	MN · Anal. Tech. · AR · Mass Spectro. · PCB · Residues · Techniques
248	MN · Mississippi R · Winter. Pop.
275	MN · Egg Trans. · Manage. · ME
305	MN · Life History
306	MN · Intersp. Behav. · Prey
403	MN · Nest.
406	MN · Migration
445	MN · Great Lakes · Manage. · MI · Natl. For. · Nest. Survey · USFS · WI
529	MN · Mud Lake NWR · Nest.
540	MN · Falconry · Rehab. · Techniques
547	MN · Band. · IL · Techniques · TX · WI
548	MN · Marking · SD · Techniques
550	MN · Band. · Breed. Behav. · Dieldrin · DDT · Pest. · Pest. Residues · Prey · Techniques · Telemetry
552	MN · Band. · Migration · Techniques · Trapping · TX
553	MN · Intersp. Behav.
554	MN · Band. · Behav. · Cedar Glen Roost · IL · Migration · Mississippi R · Refuge · Techniques · Telemetry · TX · Winter. Pop.
555	MN · Behav. · Breed. Behav. · Chippewa NF · Disturb. · Fledging · Marking · Nestling · Prey · Reprod. Succ. · Techniques · Telemetry
558	MN · Biopsy · Pest. Residues · PCB · Techniques

Master No.	Keywords
559	MN · Art. Nest Site · Behav. · Habit. Use · Manage. · Nest. · Techniques · Young Trans.
560	MN · Band. · Behav. · Life History · Migration · Reprod. Succ. · Techniques
561	MN · Behav. · Fledging · Habit. Use · Marking · Parent. Behav. · Techniques · Telemetry
562	MN · Prey
566	MN · AK · FL · ME · MI · PCB
586	MN · Marking · Nest. Survey · Techniques · USFWS
595	MN · Great Lakes · Nest. Survey · Techniques
609	MN · Behav. · Habit. Use · Mississippi R · Pest. Residues · Prey · Winter Survey
645	MN · IA · IL · Mississippi R · MO · NE · WI
695	MN · Behav. · Chippewa NF · Disturb. · Logging · Nest. · Reprod. Succ.
696	MN · Aircraft · Chippewa NF · Model · Statistics · Techniques
698	MN · Chippewa NF · Manage. · Nest.
706	MN · Hunt. Behav. · Prey · Winter. Pop.
765	MN · Nest.
810	MN · Nest.
841	MN · Behav. · Chippewa NF · Dispersal · Disturb. · Fledging · Nestling · Techniques · Telemetry
842	MN · Behav. · Chippewa NF · Dispersal · Fledging · Hunt. Behav. · Nestling · Techniques · Telemetry
843	MN · Band. · Behav. · Chippewa NF · Dispersal · Fledging · Migration · Nestling · Techniques · Telemetry
893	MN · Itasca SP · Nest.
894	MN · Itasca SP · Nest.
906	MN · Migration
907	MN · Duluth Fly. · Great Lakes · L Superior · Migration
916	MN · Hunt. Behav. · Prey
957	MN · Itasca SP · Migration · Nest.
958	MN · Winter. Pop.
959	MN · Agassiz NWR · Chippewa NF · Itasca SP · Nest. Survey · Superior NF · Tamarac NWR
960	MN · Chippewa NF · Nest. Survey
961	MN · Nest.
962	MN · Nest.
963	MN · Winter. Pop.

Master No.	Keywords
964	MN · Acct. · Nest.
990	MN · Nest.
1000	MN · Band. · Techniques · Telemetry
1018	MN · Chippewa NF · Disturb. · Habit. Use · Manage. · Nest. · Prey · Reprod. Succ.
1062	MN · Hunt. Behav. · Prey
1071	MN · Behav. · Chippewa NF · Fledging · Intrasp. Behav. · Marking · Mortality · Nest. · Techniques · Telemetry · Vocal.
1072	MN · Behav. · Chippewa NF · Fledging · Marking · Techniques
1081	MN · Nest. Survey · USFWS
1095	MN · Intersp. Behav.
1096	MN · Acct.
1138	MN · Winter. Pop.
1188	MN · Chippewa NF · Habit. Use · Manage. · Nest. Survey · Status · USFS
1189	MN · Chippewa NF · Habit. Use · Manage. · Nest. Survey · USFS
1190	MN · Chippewa NF · Nest. Survey · USFS
1191	MN · Chippewa NF · Nest. Survey · USFS
1192	MN · Chippewa NF · Nest. Survey · USFS
1193	MN · Chippewa NF · Nest. Survey · USFS
1194	MN · Chippewa NF · Nest. Survey · USFS
1195	MN · Chippewa NF · Disturb. · Habit. Loss · USFS
1196	MN · Band. · Chippewa NF · IL · Nest. Survey · Techniques · USFS · Winter. Pop.
1197	MN · Chippewa NF · Field ID · Habit. Use · Nest. · USFS
1198	MN · Chippewa NF · Nest. Survey · USFS
1199	MN · Chippewa NF · Field ID · Nest.
1200	MN · Chippewa NF · Disturb. · ND · Poison. · Pub. Ed. · Shooting · Status · USFS
1201	MN · Chippewa NF · Nest. Survey · Status · USFS
1202	MN · Chippewa NF · Nest. Survey · Status · USFS
1203	MN · Chippewa NF · Nest. Survey · USFS

Master No.	Keywords
1204	MN · Chippewa NF · Nest. Survey · USFS
1205	MN · Chippewa NF · Nest. Survey · USFS
1206	MN · Chippewa NF · Habit. Prot. · Hunt-Wesson · Pub. Ed. · USFS
1207	MN · Chippewa NF · Manage. · Nest. Survey · Status · USFS
1209	MN · Chippewa NF · Nest. Survey · Status · USFS
1211	MN · Chippewa NF · Nest. Survey · Status · USFS
1212	MN · Field ID · Life History
1213	MN · Chippewa NF · Nest. Survey · Status · USFS
1214	MN · Band. · Chippewa NF · Marking · Nest. Survey · Techniques
1215	MN · Chippewa NF · Manage. · Nest. Survey · Refuge · USFS
1217	MN · Band. · Chippewa NF · Nest. Survey · Status · Techniques · USFS
1218	MN · Chippewa NF · Manage. · USFS
1219	MN · Chippewa NF · Manage. · USFS
1220	MN · Chippewa NF · Manage. · USFS
1223	MN · Band. · Chippewa NF · Nest. Survey · Reprod. Succ. · Status · Superior NF · Techniques · Terminology
1228	MN · Glacier NP · Hunt. Behav. · Intersp. Behav. · Prey · Winter Survey
1253	MN · Behav. · Hacking · Heavy Metals · Intrasp. Behav. · Marking · Montezuma NWR · MI · NY · Pest. · Techniques · Telemetry · Young Trans.
1272	MN · Endang. Sp. · Habit. Use · Manage. · Status
1288	MN · Nest.
1496	MN · Behav. · Chippewa NF · Fledging · Manage. · Nest. · Nocturnal Behav.
1513	MN · Disease · Rehab. · Shooting · Techniques · Trapping
1516	MN · Migration · Mississippi R
1537	MN · Hunt. Behav. · Life History · Migration · Nest. · Prey · Shooting · Status · Winter. Pop.
1549	MN · Chippewa NF · Field ID · Life History · Pub. Ed.
1570	MN · Acct. · Migration

Master No.	Keywords
1610	MN · Band. · Behav. · Dispersal · Techniques · WI
1612	MN · Nest. Survey · Reprod. Succ. · Superior NF
1728	MN · Band. · Techniques · WI
1730	MN · Manage. · Nest. Survey
1768	MN · Marking · Migration · Techniques
1821	MN · Chippewa NF · Manage. · Pub. Ed. · USFS
1824	MN · Child. Eagle Area · Chippewa NF · Hunt-Wesson · Manage. · Pub. Ed. · Refuge · USFS
1825	MN · Aircraft · Chippewa NF · Great Lakes · MI · Nest. Survey · Reprod. Succ. · Status · USFS · WI
1828	MN · Endang. Sp. · Habit. Prot. · Manage.
1851	MN · Egg Trans. · Manage. · ME · USFWS
1855	MN · IL · IN · MI · Nest. Survey · OH · Terminology · USFWS · WI
1861	MN · Egg Trans. · Manage. · ME · USFWS · WI
1868	MN · MI · Nest. Survey · OH · USFWS · WI
1871	MN · Egg Trans. · Hacking · Manage. · ME · NY · Pest. · PCB · Techniques · WI · Young Trans.
1910	MN · Nest.
1914	MN · Behav. · Chippewa NF · Disturb. · Manage. · USFS
1996	MN · Migration · Missouri R · NE · Shooting
269	MO · Autopsy · FL · Heavy Metals · Midwest Region · MD · ME · ND · Pest. · PCB
364	MO · Hunt. Behav. · IL · Mississippi R · Winter Survey
446	MO · Econ. Import. · Law · Life History · Manage. · Nest. · Prey · Pub. Ed. · Shooting
460	MO · Asper. · Autopsy · Disease · Rehab. · Techniques · Trapping
510	MO · Squaw Creek NWR · Winter. Pop.
580	MO · Disturb. · Nest.
626	MO · Illinois R · IA · IL · Mississippi R · Winter Survey
628	MO · Illinois R · IA · IL · KY · Mississippi R · Winter Survey

Master No.	Keywords
634	MO · Illinois R · IA · IL · KY · Mississippi R · NE · Winter Survey
635	MO · Illinois R · IA · IL · KY · Mississippi R · Missouri R · NE · Winter Survey · Wisconsin R
636	MO · Illinois R · IA · IL · KY · Mississippi R · Missouri R · NE · Winter Survey · Wisconsin R
637	MO · Illinois R · IA · IL · KY · Mississippi R · Missouri R · NE · Winter Survey · Wisconsin R
638	MO · Illinois R · IA · IL · KY · Mississippi R · NE · Winter Survey
639	MO · Illinois R · IA · IL · KY · Mississippi R · NE · Winter Survey
643	MO · Illinois R · IL · KY · Mississippi R · NE · Winter Survey
644	MO · Illinois R · IL · KY · Mississippi R · NE · Winter Survey
645	MO · IA · IL · Mississippi R · MN · NE · WI
646	MO · Illinois R · IL · KY · Mississippi R · NE · Winter Survey
648	MO · Habit. Prot. · IA · IL · Mississippi R · Winter Survey
651	MO · Illinois R · IA · IL · KY · Mississippi R · NE · TN · Winter Survey
652	MO · Illinois R · IA · KY · Mississippi R · NE · TN · Winter Survey
736	MO · Habit. Use · Marking · Migration · ND · SD · SK · Techniques · WY
786	MO · Behav. · Distrib. · Hunt. Behav. · Manage. · Marking · Migration · Mortality · Nest. · Pest. · Prey · Swan Lake NWR · Techniques · Telemetry
787	MO · MI · Rehab. · Reintroduction · Shooting · Swan Lake NWR · WI
789	MO · Acct.
1011	MO · Behav. · Climatology · Habit. Use · Hunt. Behav. · Intersp. Behav. · Intrasp. Behav. · IA · IL · Mississippi R · Prey · Winter Survey
1273	MO · Endang. Sp. · Nest. · Winter. Pop.
1709	MO · FL · ME · NJ · Pest. · Toxicol. · USFWS
1831	MO · Autopsy · DDT · NJ · Residues · Toxicol.
1846	MO · CO · IA · KS · MT · Nest. Survey · ND · NE · SD · USFWS · UT · WY
1849	MO · CO · IA · KS · MT · Nest. Survey · ND · NE · SD · USFWS · UT · WY
1859	MO · IA · KS · Missouri R · Nest. Survey · ND · NE · Rocky Mt. Region · SD · USFWS · Winter. Pop.
1893	MO · Mississippi R · Nest. · Squaw Creek NWR · Winter Survey
1941	MO · Nest. · Status · Trapping
1989	MO · Anat. · Migration · Shooting
35	MS · Egg Coll. · LA · MN · Status · WI
197	MS · Habit. Use · LA · Nest. Survey
715	MS · AR · Habit. Use · Mississippi R · Nest. · Reelfoot L · Shooting · TN
1390	MS · Manage. · Nest.
1714	MS · Mississippi R · Nest.
1809	MS · Nest.
1982	MS · Law · Shooting
148	MT · Anat. · Autumn Conc. · FL · Glacier NP · Manage. · Merritt Is. NWR · Museum Specimen · Nest. · Prey · Taxonomy
400	MT · Nest. · Poison. · Shooting
415	MT · Depred. · Hunt. Behav.
469	MT · Nest. · ND
920	MT · Hunt. Behav. · Prey
1229	MT · Anat. · Autumn Conc. · Behav. · Capture · Glacier NP · Habit. Use · Manage. · Marking · Migration · Techniques · Winter Survey
1311	MT · OR
1313	MT · Glacier NP · Winter. Pop. · WA
1566	MT · Migration · Nest. · Winter. Pop.
1601	MT · Behav. · Capture · Glacier NP · Hunt. Behav. · Intersp. Behav. · Intrasp. Behav. · Manage. · Techniques · Winter Survey
1602	MT · Autumn Conc. · Glacier NP · Hunt. Behav. · Prey
1615	MT · Acct.
1741	MT · Disturb. · Habit. Use · Manage. Nest. Survey · Pop. Turnover · Reprod. Succ. · Status · Territory · Yellowstone NP
1839	MT · CA · ID · Nest. Survey · NV · OR · USFWS · WA

Master No.	Keywords
1846	MT · CO · IA · KS · MO · Nest. Survey · ND · NE · SD · USFWS · UT · WY
1849	MT · CO · IA · KS · MO · Nest. Survey · ND · NE · SD · USFWS · UT · WY
1854	MT · CO · Glacier NP · Manage. · Missouri R · Nest. Survey · SD · USFWS
1858	MT · Nest. Survey · USFWS · WY
168	Nat. Conserv. · Habit. Prot. · Manage. · Skagit R · Wash. Dept. Game · Winter. Pop. · WA
503	Nat. Conserv. · Habit. Prot. · Prey · Refuge · Skagit R Nat. Area · WA
1295	Nat. Conserv. · Habit. Prot. · Manage. · WA
1334	Nat. Conserv. · Habit. Prot. · Manage. · Refuge · Skagit R Nat. Area · Winter Survey · WA
445	Natl. For. · Great Lakes · Manage. · MI · MN · Nest. Survey · USFS · WI
447	Natl. For. · Behav. · CA · Disturb. · Hunt. Behav. · Manage. · Prey · San Bernardino Mts. · USFS · Winter. Pop.
1113	Neosho R · Hunt. Behav. · Intrasp. Behav. · Migration · OK · Prey · Winter Survey
22	Nest. · Bombay Hook NWR · Distrib. · DE · Endang. Sp. · Field ID · Life History · Nest. Survey · Pub. Ed. · Status
25	Nest. · SD
31	Nest. · Distrib. · NH · Winter. Pop.
38	Nest. · IA · Mississippi R · Winter. Pop.
39	Nest. · CN
40	Nest. · CN
41	Nest. · CN
42	Nest. · OH · Status · Winter. Pop.
51	Nest. · Disturb. · Habit. Use · Manage. · OR · USFS
53	Nest. · Distrib. · IA · Status · Winter. Pop.
61	Nest. · AK
75	Nest. · Behav. · OH
80	Nest. · Behav. · Life History · OH
88	Nest. · Growth · MD · Photo. · Plumage
96	Nest. · ME
107	Nest. · ME
110	Nest. · ME

Master No.	Keywords
123	Nest. · Disturb. · Logging · Manage.
125	Nest. · Disturb. · Law · Logging · Manage. · Territory
133	Nest. · Life History · NJ · Pub. Ed. · Winter. Pop.
148	Nest. · Anat. · Autumn Conc. · FL · Glacier NP · Manage. · Merritt Is. NWR · Museum Specimen · MT · Prey · Taxonomy
160	Nest. · Ground Nest. · Law · OH
181	Nest. · ME · Prey · Winter. Pop.
183	Nest. · Acct. · AZ · Pub. Ed.
185	Nest. · Acct. · AZ · Pub. Ed. · Winter. Pop.
186	Nest. · Acct. · AZ · Endang. Sp. · Pub. Ed. · Winter. Pop.
188	Nest. · ID
199	Nest. · MA · Winter. Pop.
203	Nest. · LA
205	Nest. · AK · Shooting
206	Nest. · LA · Status
207	Nest. · CO · Distrib. · Winter. Pop.
208	Nest. · IA · Prey · Winter. Pop.
210	Nest. · Acct. · Glacier NP
211	Nest. · Anat. · Distrib. · NM · Plumage · Prey · Winter. Pop.
212	Nest. · Egg Coll. · VA
213	Nest. · Egg Coll. · VA
214	Nest. · Egg Coll. · Prey · VA
215	Nest. · Egg Coll. · Habit. Use · Photo. · VA
216	Nest. · Egg Coll. · VA
217	Nest. · Depred. · Egg Coll. · FL
218	Nest. · Depred. · Egg Coll. · FL
219	Nest. · Winter. Pop. · Yellowstone NP
221	Nest. · Anat. · Distrib. · Plumage · Taxonomy
222	Nest. · MI
228	Nest. · Anacapa Is. · CA · Status
231	Nest. · KY · Winter. Pop.
234	Nest. · WI
238	Nest. · IL
241	Nest. · FL
243	Nest. · Mortality · OH
254	Nest. · FL · Shooting
255	Nest. · Aggress. · Egg Coll. · FL · Shooting · Status
257	Nest. · Apostle Is. · WI
258	Nest. · Anat. · NY · Prey · Status · Winter. Pop.

Master No.	Keywords
261	**Nest.** · Manage. · Mt. Johnson Is. Sanct. · PA · Refuge · Shooting
262	**Nest.** · Mt. Johnson Is. Sanct. · PA
263	**Nest.** · Intersp. Behav. · Manage. · SC
266	**Nest.** · Anat. · Behav. · BC · Distrib. · Falconry · Field ID · Flight · Habit. Use · Migration · Prey · Status
268	**Nest.** · BC · CA · OR · Status · Winter. Pop. · WA
270	**Nest.** · IL
271	**Nest.** · ON · Prey
273	**Nest.** · Aggress. · Behav. · Captivity · Distrib. · Egg Coll. · Habit. Use · Life History · Status
274	**Nest.** · Aggress. · Behav. · Captivity · Distrib. · Habit. Use · Life History · Status
277	**Nest.** · TX
278	**Nest.** · FL · Gulf of Mex.
281	**Nest.** · Status · WI
284	**Nest.** · Gulf of Mex. · LA
285	**Nest.** · AK · Shooting
289	**Nest.** · CA
300	**Nest.** · CA · Habit. Loss
301	**Nest.** · Disturb. · Habit. Use · IL · Ohio R · Rehab. · Shooting · Techniques · Winter. Pop.
307	**Nest.** · CA · Intersp. Behav. · San Clemente Is. · Shooting
310	**Nest.** · Disturb. · Migration · ME · Shooting · Winter. Pop.
311	**Nest.** · GA
319	**Nest.** · Ground Nest. · MI
320	**Nest.** · SC
321	**Nest.** · BC
325	**Nest.** · Behav. · Dispersal · Disturb. · FL · Habit. Use · Intersp. Behav. · Migration · Mortality · Prey
340	**Nest.** · Ground Nest. · NWT
351	**Nest.** · Migration · Prey · Reprod. Succ. · Status
352	**Nest.** · Behav. · Flight · Life History · Migration · Prey · Pub. Ed. · Status · Taxonomy
353	**Nest.** · Anat. · Behav. · Distrib. · Life History · Status
357	**Nest.** · OR
358	**Nest.** · Acct. · NE
359	**Nest.** · NE
360	**Nest.** · Mortality · ND
361	**Nest.** · Behav. · Disturb. · ND · Photo.
363	**Nest.** · CA
373	**Nest.** · NY · Status · Taxonomy · Winter. Pop.
374	**Nest.** · ON · Winter. Pop.
376	**Nest.** · Habit. Use · LA · Winter. Pop.
377	**Nest.** · Distrib. · GA · Habit. Use · Life History · Migration · Status
378	**Nest.** · ID · Life History · Status
379	**Nest.** · Egg Coll. · Habit. Loss · NJ
382	**Nest.** · Distrib. · Egg Coll. · IN · Life History · Status
383	**Nest.** · Aleutian Is. · AK
385	**Nest.** · MD
386	**Nest.** · MD
388	**Nest.** · WI
389	**Nest.** · Aleutian Is. · AK · Winter. Pop.
391	**Nest.** · NC
400	**Nest.** · MT · Poison. · Shooting
402	**Nest.** · BC · Winter. Pop.
403	**Nest.** · MN
404	**Nest.** · AK · Egg Coll. · Shooting
407	**Nest.** · NC · SC
408	**Nest.** · NC · SC
409	**Nest.** · AZ · Grand Canyon · Status · Winter. Pop.
412	**Nest.** · TX · Winter. Pop.
413	**Nest.** · Egg Coll. · TX
420	**Nest.** · NC · SC · Winter. Pop.
421	**Nest.** · Capture · Folklore · Prey · Techniques · TN
422	**Nest.** · MI · Winter. Pop.
423	**Nest.** · Mississippi R · Pub. Ed. · Reelfoot L · Shooting · Status · TN · Winter. Pop.
429	**Nest.** · Aggress. · History · Hunt. Behav. · Life History · Poetry · PA · Shooting · Status · Susquehanna R
430	**Nest.** · History · Life History
431	**Nest.** · AK · Behav. · Climatology · Disease · Kodiak NWR · Life History · Marking · Nest. Survey · Parasites · Reprod. Succ. · Techniques · Terminology
446	**Nest.** · Econ. Import. · Law · Life History · Manage. · MO · Prey · Pub. Ed. · Shooting
449	**Nest.** · AZ · CAP · Habit. Loss · Orme D · Salt R · Verde R
451	**Nest.** · CO · Habit. Use · San Luis Valley · Status · Winter Survey
456	**Nest.** · MI · Status · Trapping · Winter. Pop.

Master No.	Keywords
457	Nest. · Hudson Bay · Intersp. Behav. · MB · Prey
458	Nest. · DC
465	Nest. · AK · Disturb. · Habit. Loss · Habit. Use · Logging · Nest. Survey · Territory
466	Nest. · AK · Climatology · Distrib. · Disturb. · Forestry · Habit. Loss · Habit. Use · Manage. · Nest. Survey · Reprod. Succ. · Territory
467	Nest. · Egg Coll. · FL
469	Nest. · MT · ND
473	Nest. · CO · Disturb. · Field ID · Habit. Loss · Manage. · Pest. · Pub. Ed. · Winter. Pop.
474	Nest. · CO · Habit. Use · San Luis Valley · Status · Winter Survey
491	Nest. · Egg Coll. · FL · L Apopka
492	Nest. · DE · Egg · Egg Coll. · MD · NJ
493	Nest. · DE · Egg Coll.
494	Nest. · DE · Egg · Egg Coll. · MD · VA
497	Nest. · Behav. · Egg · OH · Poison. · Prey · Shooting
498	Nest. · Distrib. · Egg · Plumage
499	Nest. · Law · Manage. · Poison. · Pub. Ed. · Shooting · SK · Trapping
500	Nest. · CA · Egg Coll. · Habit. Use
506	Nest. · Captivity · CA · Depred. · Distrib. · Habit. Use · Life History · Santa Barbara Is.
507	Nest. · Anat. · Behav. · Captivity · Distrib. · WA
508	Nest. · Egg · Egg Coll. · FL
509	Nest. · Audubon · Behav. · TN
514	Nest. · Hunt. Behav. · IN · Prey
515	Nest. · LA
517	Nest. · TN
519	Nest. · CA · Depred. · Habit. Use · Manage. · Mortality · Prey · Shasta-Trinity NF · Winter Survey
529	Nest. · Mud Lake NWR · MN
530	Nest.
531	Nest. · Aging · AK · Behav. · Hunt. Behav. · Life History · Prey · Sexing · Techniques
532	Nest. · CA · Lava Beds NM
535	Nest. · CT · Egg Coll. · Endang. Sp. · Habit. Loss · Pest. · PCB · Shooting · Status
543	Nest. · Anat. · IA · Migration · Taxonomy · Winter. Pop.
544	Nest. · IA · Migration · Shooting · Winter. Pop.
557	Nest. · Chippewa NF · Disturb. · Life History · Migration · Photo. · Pub. Ed. · Status · Techniques · Telemetry · Winter. Pop.
559	Nest. · Art. Nest Site ·· Behav. · Habit. Use · Manage. · MN · Techniques · Young Trans.
563	Nest. · CA · OR · Winter. Pop.
570	Nest. · NC
572	Nest. · Aircraft · Behav. · CA · Distrib. · Disturb. · Habit. Loss · Hunt. Behav. · Klamath R · Manage.
573	Nest. · Habit. Prot. · Marking · Pub. Ed. · Techniques · Winter. Pop.
574	Nest. · Band. · Behav. · Growth · Photo. · Pub. Ed. · Techniques
575	Nest. · Behav. · Growth · Photo. · Prey · Pub. Ed.
577	Nest. · Aleutian Is. · AK · Bounty · Habit. Use · Status · Symbolism
578	Nest. · Aggress. · Band. · Behav. · Mortality · Photo. · Pub. Ed. · Techniques
579	Nest. · Behav. · Pub. Ed. · Status
580	Nest. · Disturb. · MO
581	Nest. · DE · Egg Coll. · Habit. Use · MD
594	Nest. · Egg Coll. · FL
596	Nest. · Reelfoot L · TN
599	Nest. · Behav. · Disturb. · FL · Migration · Nest. Fail.
603	Nest. · GA
606	Nest. · CA
607	Nest. · IN · Winter. Pop.
610	Nest. · Migration · NJ
612	Nest. · FL · Prey
658	Nest. · LA · Winter. Pop.
661	Nest. · Manage. · NAS · Pub. Ed.
665	Nest. · Habit. Use · OH
666	Nest. · Egg Coll. · MD
668	Nest. · MD
671	Nest. · FL · Ocala NF · USFS
680	Nest. · Poetry
682	Nest. · CA · Disturb. · Klamath NF · Manage. · Prey · Status · Winter. Pop.
683	Nest. · Behav. · CA · Distrib. · Disturb. · Field ID · Flight · Hunt. Behav. · Life History · Manage. · Mortality · Winter. Pop.

Master No.	Keywords
686	Nest. · IL · Terminology · Winter. Pop.
688	Nest. · AK
689	Nest. · Autumn Conc. · AK
690	Nest. · AK · Winter. Pop.
692	Nest. · AK · Winter. Pop.
695	Nest. · Behav. · Chippewa NF · Disturb. · Logging · MN · Reprod. Succ.
698	Nest. · Chippewa NF · Manage. · MN
704	Nest. · NY
707	Nest. · KY · Winter. Pop.
714	Nest. · Distrib. · Habit. Use · Plumage · Shooting · Taxonomy · TN · Winter. Pop.
715	Nest. · AR · Habit. Use · Mississippi R · MS · Reelfoot L · Shooting · TN
716	Nest. · TN
717	Nest. · TN
718	Nest. · Prey · TN · Winter. Pop.
728	Nest. · Habit. Loss · Habit. Use · Manage. · McHargian Overlay · Reprod. Succ. · SK · Techniques
732	Nest. · Disturb. · Habit. Use · MB · SK · Territory
737	Nest. · AK · Depred. · Prey · Shooting
744	Nest. · Hunt. Behav. · NS · Prey
745	Nest. · Anat. · CN · Distrib. · Field ID · Taxonomy ·
747	Nest. · KS · Winter. Pop.
749	Nest. · Egg Coll. · Habit. Use · IN
752	Nest. · IL · Migration · Status · Winter. Pop.
757	Nest. · Band. · Disturb. · Manage. · Marking · ME · Nest. Survey · Shooting · Techniques
765	Nest. · MN
766	Nest. · FL
770	Nest. · AZ · CAP · Disturb. · Habit. Use · Manage. · Orme D
771	Nest. · VA · Winter. Pop.
786	Nest. · Behav. · Distrib. · Hunt. Behav. · Manage. · Marking · Migration · Mortality · MO · Pest. · Prey · Swan Lake NWR · Techniques · Telemetry
788	Nest. · Pymatuning · PA · Winter. Pop.
790	Nest. · Missouri R
792	Nest. · Behav. · CA · Habit. Use · Intersp. Behav. · Winter. Pop.
795	Nest. · NY · Winter. Pop.
796	Nest. · Hunt. Behav. · MA · Prey · Winter. Pop.
801	Nest. · Disturb. · Nest. Survey · Reprod. Succ. · Statistics · Territory · WA
803	Nest. · Habit. Use · Life History · Photo. · Pub. Ed. · Winter. Pop. · WA
804	Nest. · Art. Nest Site · AZ · Egg. Thin. · Habit. Use · Life History · Manage. · Marking · Pest. · Research · Techniques · Telemetry · Winter. Pop.
810	Nest. · MN
816	Nest. · Hunt. Behav. · PA · Terminology
819	Nest. · NY · Winter. Pop.
835	Nest. · ID · Winter. Pop.
839	Nest. · PA
845	Nest. · KS · Missouri R · Prey · Winter. Pop.
849	Nest. · Allegan SF · Kalamazoo R · MI
858	Nest. · CO · UT · Winter. Pop.
860	Nest. · GA · Okefinokee Swamp · Prey
873	Nest. · CA
875	Nest. · OH
876	Nest. · Acct. · Baja · CA
879	Nest. · Intersp. Behav. · OH · Photo.
880	Nest. · Behav. · Life History · Nestling · OH · Parent. Behav. · Photo. · Techniques
881	Nest. · Behav. · Fledging · Life History · Nestling · OH
882	Nest. · Aggress. · Behav. · Disturb. · Life History · OH · PA
883	Nest. · Behav. · Fledging · Hunt. Behav. · Life History · OH · Prey
884	Nest. · Behav. · History · OH · Photo. · Techniques
886	Nest. · Breed. Behav. · Intersp. Behav. · Life History · OH · Parent. Behav. · Prey
887	Nest. · Behav. · Life History · OH · Photo. · Techniques
888	Nest. · Behav. · Fledging · Intersp. Behav. · Life History · OH · Parent. Behav. · Photo. · Prey
889	Nest. · Behav. · Life History · OH · Photo. · Techniques
891	Nest. · Behav. · Life History · OH · Prey
893	Nest. · Itasca SP · MN
894	Nest. · Itasca SP · MN
896	Nest. · OH
898	Nest. · MA · Status · Winter. Pop.
900	Nest. · AZ · Photo. · Techniques

Master No.	Keywords
903	Nest. · Christmas Count · IA · Mississippi R · Status · Winter Survey
904	Nest. · Kluane Game Sanct. · YT
909	Nest. · NWT
914	Nest. · NC · Photo.
915	Nest. · FL
918	Nest. · LA
925	Nest. · SK
929	Nest. · MA · Winter. Pop.
930	Nest. · Acct. · RI
931	Nest. · CA · Depred.
932	Nest. · Aggress. · CA · Santa Cruz
934	Nest. · AL · Prey · Shooting · TN · Winter. Pop.
935	Nest. · FL · Intersp. Behav.
937	Nest. · FL · Nest. Fail. · Status
938	Nest. · FL · Nest. Fail.
939	Nest. · FL
940	Nest. · Acct. · AK
941	Nest. · FL · Status
942	Nest. · FL · Nest. Fail. · Status
949	Nest. · Acct. · AL
951	Nest. · OR
952	Nest. · SC
953	Nest. · Behav. · SC
954	Nest. · Egg Coll. · GA · PA
955	Nest. · Finger Lakes · Montezuma NWR · NY
956	Nest. · Finger Lakes · Montezuma NWR · NY
957	Nest. · Itasca SP · Migration · MN
961	Nest. · MN
962	Nest. · MN
964	Nest. · Acct. · MN
969	Nest. · NJ
970	Nest. · AR
971	Nest. · CA · Habit. Loss · Santa Barbara Is.
972	Nest. · Behav. · Disturb. · Habit. Use · Snake R · WY
973	Nest. · AL · Prey · Winter. Pop.
983	Nest. · Egg Trans. · Habit. Prot. · Pub. Ed. · Winter. Pop.
989	Nest. · AK · Habit. Use · Migration · Winter. Pop.
990	Nest. · MN
991	Nest. · WI
993	Nest. · Egg Coll. · FL
997	Nest. · Life History · ON · Winter. Pop.
1003	Nest. · Life History · WA
1012	Nest. · Aging · Behav. · Techniques · VA
1013	Nest. · Egg Coll. · VA
1014	Nest. · Ches. Bay
1015	Nest. · Hunt. Behav. · OH · Winter. Pop.
1016	Nest. · ON · Shooting
1018	Nest. · Chippewa NF · Disturb. · Habit. Use · Manage. · MN · Prey · Reprod. Succ.
1020	Nest. · CA
1022	Nest. · GA · Sapelo Is.
1029	Nest. · MI
1033	Nest. · IL · Migration · Winter. Pop.
1035	Nest. · WY · Yellowstone NP
1036	Nest. · MI
1041	Nest. · Aleutian Is. · Amchitka Is. · AK · Poison. · Prey
1042	Nest. · Aleutian Is. · AK · Hunt. Behav. · Prey · Status
1044	Nest. · AK
1045	Nest. · IA · Migration · Status
1052	Nest. · Egg Coll. · MD
1054	Nest. · Mt. Ranier NP · Status · WA
1055	Nest. · Migration · Winter. Pop. · WA
1057	Nest. · ME
1058	Nest. · Habit. Use · Intersp. Behav. · Life History · ME · Status
1059	Nest. · Pub. Ed. · Winter. Pop. · WA
1064	Nest. · FL · Heavy Metals · ME · Pest. · PCB · Reprod. Succ. · WI
1066	Nest. · Aleutian Is. · Amchitka Is. · AK · Prey
1068	Nest. · Habit. Loss · Habit. Use · WI
1069	Nest. · Habit. Loss · Habit. Use · WI
1071	Nest. · Behav. · Chippewa NF · Fledging · Intrasp. Behav. · Marking · Mortality · MN · Techniques · Telemetry · Vocal.
1078	Nest. · TX
1080	Nest. · OH
1082	Nest. · ND · Winter. Pop.
1084	Nest. · Anat. · Hunt. Behav. · Life History · Migration · Plumage
1085	Nest. · Disturb. · Habit. Loss · OH · Status
1089	Nest. · NWF · Pub. Ed. · Status · Winter. Pop.
1094	Nest. · CA · Disturb.
1101	Nest. · NM · Status · Winter. Pop.
1102	Nest. · Behav. · Caledon SP · Disturb. · Habit. Loss · Habit. Use · Manage. · Prey · VA

Master No.	Keywords
1103	Nest. · Caledon SP · Disturb. · Habit. Loss · Manage. · VA
1108	Nest. · CT · Status
1116	Nest. · Acct. · Disturb. · OK · Status · Winter. Pop.
1119	Nest. · CO
1125	Nest. · NE · Winter. Pop.
1130	Nest. · SC
1131	Nest. · Winter. Pop. · WI
1132	Nest. · WI
1133	Nest. · WI
1134	Nest. · WI
1140	Nest. · TN
1141	Nest. · AK · CN · Egg Coll. · Intersp. Behav.
1160	Nest. · CA · Distrib. · Life History · Prey · Pub. Ed. · Winter. Pop.
1162	Nest. · PA
1176	Nest. · MI
1179	Nest. · AZ · Habit. Loss · Orme D
1182	Nest. · Acct. · WY · Yellowstone NP
1197	Nest. · Chippewa NF · Field ID · Habit. Use · MN · USFS
1199	Nest. · Chippewa NF · Field ID · MN
1221	Nest. · Aging · Behav. · Hunt. Behav. · Impound. · Intrasp. Behav. · MI · Ottawa NF · Techniques · Territory
1232	Nest. · Field ID · Life History · WY · Yellowstone NP
1235	Nest. · Hunt. Behav. · Intrasp. Behav. · LA · Prey · Winter. Pop.
1237	Nest. · Distrib. · Endang. Sp. · Habit. Use · Migration · ND · Status · Winter. Pop.
1243	Nest. · OH
1245	Nest. · AZ
1248	Nest. · KY · Winter. Pop.
1250	Nest. · Captivity · CT
1251	Nest. · Egg Coll. · OR
1252	Nest. · ID
1258	Nest. · Egg Coll. · VA
1262	Nest. · San Juan Is. · WA
1263	Nest. · PA
1264	Nest. · NJ
1265	Nest. · NJ
1266	Nest. · NJ
1267	Nest. · NJ
1268	Nest. · DE
1269	Nest. · NJ
1273	Nest. · Endang. Sp. · MO · Winter. Pop.
1276	Nest. · CT
1278	Nest. · Churchill R · SK
1279	Nest. · KY
1288	Nest. · MN
1294	Nest. · BC · Hunt. Behav. · Intersp. Behav. · Prey
1297	Nest. · Aleutian Is. · AK · Band. · Distrib. · Econ. Import. · Plumage · Prey · Shooting · Techniques
1301	Nest. · Migration · Status · Winter. Pop.
1309	Nest. · Endang. Sp. · Manage. · NV · Status
1344	Nest. · L. Athabasca · SK
1345	Nest. · SK
1356	Nest. · Egg Coll. · FL
1357	Nest. · FL · Habit. Use · Life History · Status
1358	Nest. · FL
1372	Nest. · Anat. · Distrib. · Habit. Use · Plumage · Taxonomy · TX · Winter. Pop.
1376	Nest. · Field ID · OH · Pub. Ed. · Status
1385	Nest. · IA
1387	Nest. · Pymatuning · PA
1388	Nest. · History · Pub. Ed. · SD · Winter. Pop.
1389	Nest. · Pub. Ed. · SD · Winter. Pop.
1390	Nest. · Manage. · MS
1396	Nest. · ME
1399	Nest. · ME
1400	Nest. · ME
1401	Nest. · FL
1404	Nest. · Montezuma NWR · NY
1407	Nest. · SC
1408	Nest. · NC
1409	Nest. · Shooting · SD
1411	Nest. · BC · Hunt. Behav. · Vancouver Is.
1415	Nest. · GA
1416	Nest. · FL · Hunt. Behav. · Life History · Prey
1428	Nest. · Life History · NC
1430	Nest. · Disturb. · Egg Coll. · OR
1433	Nest. · CA · Santa Barbara Is.
1437	Nest. · IN · Winter. Pop.
1454	Nest. · Nestling · Territory
1455	Nest. · Anacapa Is. · CA
1456	Nest. · CA
1457	Nest. · FL
1458	Nest. · Big Cypress Swamp · FL
1459	Nest. · AZ · Winter. Pop.

Master No.	Keywords
1460	Nest. · IN · Winter. Pop.
1462	Nest. · Reelfoot L · TN
1463	Nest. · Reelfoot L · TN · Winter. Pop.
1465	Nest. · KY · Shooting
1466	Nest. · KY
1467	Nest. · Art. Nest Site · Manage. · MI
1471	Nest. · Migration · PA
1492	Nest. · DE · Winter. Pop.
1494	Nest. · Mt. Johnson Is. Sanct. · PA · Refuge
1496	Nest. · Behav. · Chippewa NF · Fledging · Manage. · MN · Nocturnal Behav.
1497	Nest. · Disturb. · Habit. Use
1500	Nest. · Habit. Loss · OH
1501	Nest. · OR
1505	Nest. · Habit. Use · Winter. Pop. · WA
1510	Nest. · WA
1511	Nest. · Behav. · Habit. Use · Heavy Metals · NY · Pest. · PCB
1514	Nest. · VA
1520	Nest. · San Juan Is. · WA
1521	Nest. · Aggress. · Behav. · Disturb. · Habit. Loss · Hunt. Behav. · Prey · San Juan Is. · Shooting · Status · Vocal. · WA
1523	Nest. · Channel Is. · CA
1524	Nest. · Egg Coll. · Migration · WI
1525	Nest. · WI
1526	Nest. · IL · Winter. Pop.
1531	Nest. · Band. · Christmas Count · Life History · Migration · Status · USFWS · Winter Survey
1532	Nest. · MD
1534	Nest. · WI
1537	Nest. · Hunt. Behav. · Life History · Migration · MN · Prey · Shooting · Status · Winter. Pop.
1538	Nest. · FL · Hurricane
1555	Nest. · Egg Coll. · FL · Habit. Use · Shooting
1556	Nest. · Egg Coll. · Habit. Use
1558	Nest. · Acct. · AK
1559	Nest. · CT · Migration · Shooting · Taxonomy · Winter. Pop.
1566	Nest. · Migration · MT · Winter. Pop.
1568	Nest. · Depred. · ON · Prey · Shooting
1579	Nest. · CA
1580	Nest. · WI
1581	Nest. · FL · L Ocklawaha · Rodman Reservoir
1582	Nest. · CO · Life History · Status · Winter. Pop.
1584	Nest. · VA
1587	Nest. · FL
1588	Nest. · FL
1589	Nest. · DE · Egg Coll.
1597	Nest. · OH
1599	Nest. · Reelfoot L · TN
1604	Nest. · ME · Status
1613	Nest. · VA
1614	Nest. · Egg Coll. · MD · VA
1616	Nest. · Hurricane · TX
1619	Nest. · WY · Yellowstone NP
1624	Nest. · Disturb. · Egg Coll. · FL
1626	Nest. · Hunt. Behav. · Hurricane · MD · Prey
1627	Nest. · Endang. Sp. · OH · Pest. · Status
1640	Nest. · Aggress. · Behav. · BLM · Disturb. · Habit. Loss · Habit. Use · Hunt. Behav. · Life History · Manage. · Pest. · Prey · Shooting · Territory
1643	Nest. · AK · Shooting
1646	Nest. · Winter. Pop. · WI
1647	Nest. · WI
1648	Nest. · Winter. Pop.
1657	Nest. · Egg Coll. · Habit. Use · Logging · ME
1663	Nest. · Prey · Reelfoot L · TN
1664	Nest. · NY · Winter. Pop.
1684	Nest. · Band. · Field ID · FL · Life History · Prey · Status · Techniques
1687	Nest. · IA · Winter. Pop.
1701	Nest. · KS · Winter. Pop.
1702	Nest. · Acct. · Hunt. Behav. · NC · Prey
1705	Nest. · Band. · DC · Migration · MD · Techniques · Winter. Pop.
1714	Nest. · Mississippi R · MS
1715	Nest. · NJ · Winter. Pop.
1716	Nest. · Cape May · Migration · NJ
1734	Nest. · Habit. Use · OK · Prey · Winter. Pop.
1737	Nest. · AZ · Winter. Pop.
1745	Nest. · MI · Prey · Seney NWR
1746	Nest. · OK · Status · Trapping
1755	Nest. · NE
1756	Nest. · GA · Winter. Pop.
1762	Nest. · NC · SC
1763	Nest. · Mattamuskett NWR · NC · Savannah NWR · SC

Master No.	Keywords
1764	Nest. · NC · SC
1765	Nest. · NC · SC · Winter. Pop.
1775	Nest. · Acct. · FL
1778	Nest. · Egg Coll. · IA
1790	Nest. · AZ · Winter. Pop.
1792	Nest. · AZ · Disturb.
1795	Nest. · Behav. · Habit. Use · Life History · Pub. Ed. · PA · Taxonomy
1798	Nest. · ME
1800	Nest. · Ground Nest. · NWT
1806	Nest. · Behav. · Everglades NP · Photo.
1808	Nest. · Field ID · Life History · NS · Poetry
1809	Nest. · MS
1813	Nest. · Ches. Bay · DC · Life History
1820	Nest. · Habit. Prot. · Manage. · USFS · Winter Survey
1865	Nest. · AZ · BLM · CAP · Egg · Habit. Prot. · Manage. · Orme D · Salt R · Taxonomy · Territory · Verde R
1881	Nest. · Hunt. Behav. · Manage. · OR · Winter. Pop. · WA
1892	Nest. · MD
1893	Nest. · Mississippi R · MO · Squaw Creek NWR · Winter Survey
1902	Nest. · LA
1906	Nest. · MI
1907	Nest. · Anat. · AK · Bounty · Plumage · Status
1908	Nest. · Endang. Sp. · MI
1910	Nest. · MN
1911	Nest. · Egg Coll. · FL
1912	Nest. · Life History · SC
1924	Nest. · Great Slave L. · NWT
1930	Nest. · AK · YT
1934	Nest. · VA
1940	Nest. · WA
1941	Nest. · MO · Status · Trapping
1945	Nest. · Egg · Egg Coll. · ME
1950	Nest. · CA · Egg Coll.
1952	Nest. · FL · Winter. Pop.
1953	Nest. · FL
1954	Nest. · AK · Hunt. Behav. · Law · Migration · Pub. Ed. · WY · Yellowstone NP
1955	Nest. · AK · Hunt. Behav. · Law · Migration · Pub. Ed. · WY · Yellowstone NP
1956	Nest. · Egg Coll. · FL
1964	Nest. · Life History · NC
1965	Nest. · AZ · CAP · Habit. Loss · Orme D
1966	Nest. · AZ · CAP · Orme D
1969	Nest. · ON
1970	Nest. · SK
1971	Nest. · MI
1973	Nest. · Great Lakes · MI
1974	Nest. · ND · Shooting
1975	Nest. · Migration · MI · Winter. Pop.
1976	Nest. · MI
1977	Nest. · IL · IN · Shooting
1978	Nest. · GA
1986	Nest. · Acct. · GA · Okefinokee Swamp
1997	Nest. · Egg Coll. · TX
1999	Nest. · MI · Winter. Pop.
324	Nest. Fail. · Band. · FL · Life History · Migration · Nest. Survey · Prey · Status · Techniques
326	Nest. Fail. · FL · Habit. Loss · Intersp. Behav.
327	Nest. Fail. · Band. · FL · Habit. Loss · Intersp. Behav. · Pub. Ed. · Shooting · Status · Techniques
328	Nest. Fail. · FL · Habit. Loss · Intersp. Behav. · Manage.
329	Nest. Fail. · FL · Habit. Loss · Hurricane · Status
330	Nest. Fail. · FL
333	Nest. Fail. · DDT · FL · Pest. · Red Tide
334	Nest. Fail. · Ches. Bay · FL · Hurricane · ON
335	Nest. Fail. · DDT · FL · Pest. · Status
599	Nest. Fail. · Behav. · Disturb. · FL · Migration · Nest.
878	Nest. Fail. · AK · Disturb. · Habit. Use · Kodiak NWR · Life History · Reprod. Succ. · Territory
936	Nest. Fail. · FL · Nest. Survey · Status
937	Nest. Fail. · FL · Nest. · Status
938	Nest. Fail. · FL · Nest.
942	Nest. Fail. · FL · Nest. · Status
943	Nest. Fail. · FL · Status · Techniques
944	Nest. Fail. · FL · Habit. Loss · Nest. Survey · Status
945	Nest. Fail. · Disturb. · FL · Habit. Loss · Nest. Survey · Reprod. Succ.
1921	Nest. Fail. · Nest. Survey · ON
1	Nest. Survey · Ches. Bay
2	Nest. Survey · Ches. Bay
3	Nest. Survey · Ches. Bay
4	Nest. Survey · Ches. Bay

Master No.	Keywords
5	Nest. **Survey** · Ches. Bay · Winter Survey
7	Nest. **Survey** · Ches. Bay · Winter Survey
8	Nest. **Survey** · Ches. Bay
9	Nest. **Survey** · Ches. Bay · Status · Winter Survey
10	Nest. **Survey** · Ches. Bay · Status
11	Nest. **Survey** · Ches. Bay
12	Nest. **Survey** · Ches. Bay
13	Nest. **Survey** · Ches. Bay · Status
14	Nest. **Survey** · Ches. Bay
15	Nest. **Survey** · Ches. Bay
16	Nest. **Survey** · Ches. Bay · Status
17	Nest. **Survey** · Ches. Bay · Status
18	Nest. **Survey** · Ches. Bay · Status
19	Nest. **Survey** · Ches. Bay
20	Nest. **Survey** · Ches. Bay · Status
21	Nest. **Survey** · Ches. Bay · Mason Neck NWR · Reprod. Succ.
22	Nest. **Survey** · Bombay Hook NWR · Distrib. · DE · Endang. Sp. · Field ID · Life History · Nest. · Pub. Ed. · Status
23	Nest. **Survey** · Reprod. Succ. · San Juan Is. · WA
119	Nest. **Survey** · NAS · Pub. Ed. · Status · Winter Survey
121	Nest. **Survey** · MI
154	Nest. **Survey** · Lower 48 · Manage. · Status · USFWS
171	Nest. **Survey** · MI
177	Nest. **Survey** · TX · Winter Survey · Winter. Pop.
195	Nest. **Survey** · Distrib. · LA · Winter Survey
196	Nest. **Survey** · Distrib. · LA · Migration · Mortality · Reprod. Succ. · Shooting · Status · Winter Survey
197	Nest. **Survey** · Habit. Use · LA · MS
280	Nest. **Survey** · MD · VA
312	Nest. **Survey** · MD
313	Nest. **Survey** · MD
314	Nest. **Survey** · MD
315	Nest. **Survey** · MD
316	Nest. **Survey** · MD
324	Nest. **Survey** · Band. · FL · Life History · Migration · Nest. Fail. · Prey · Status · Techniques
341	Nest. **Survey** · ME · Pest. · Reprod. Succ.
367	Nest. **Survey** · Cont. B.E. Proj. · NAS
368	Nest. **Survey** · Cont. B.E. Proj. · NAS
369	Nest. **Survey** · Law · MI · NJ · Winter Survey
395	Nest. **Survey** · CA · Winter Survey
431	Nest. **Survey** · AK · Behav. · Climatology · Disease · Kodiak NWR · Life History · Marking · Nest. · Parasites · Reprod. Succ. · Techniques · Terminology
445	Nest. **Survey** · Great Lakes · Manage. · MI · MN · Natl. For. · USFS · WI
450	Nest. **Survey** · Habit. Prot. · ME · Pub. Ed. · RIC · Shooting · Status
465	Nest. **Survey** · AK · Disturb. · Habit. Loss · Habit. Use · Logging · Nest. · Territory
466	Nest. **Survey** · AK · Climatology · Distrib. · Disturb. · Forestry · Habit. Loss · Habit. Use · Manage. · Nest. · Reprod. Succ. · Territory
486	Nest. **Survey** · MI
520	Nest. **Survey** · Distrib. · Habit. Use · Migration · Status · Winter Survey · WI
537	Nest. **Survey** · Distrib. · LA · Reprod. Succ.
538	Nest. **Survey** · Distrib. · LA · Reprod. Succ.
539	Nest. **Survey** · LA · Prey
583	Nest. **Survey** · Habit. Use · Manage. · OR · Poison. · Prey · San Juan Is. · Shooting · Status · Winter Survey · WA
586	Nest. **Survey** · Marking · MN · Techniques · USFWS
595	Nest. **Survey** · Great Lakes · MN · Techniques
657	Nest. **Survey** · FL · Reprod. Succ.
660	Nest. **Survey** · Habit. Loss · NC · SC
673	Nest. **Survey** · FL · Habit. Use · Reprod. Succ.
676	Nest. **Survey** · FL · Reprod. Succ.
677	Nest. **Survey** · FL · Reprod. Succ.
755	Nest. **Survey** · Disturb. · Manage. · ME · Pub. Ed. · Shooting · Winter. Pop.
756	Nest. **Survey** · Band. · Egg Trans. · Manage. · ME · Pest. · PCB · Refuge · Techniques · Winter Survey

Master No.	Keywords
757	**Nest. Survey** · Band. · Disturb. · Manage. · Marking · ME · Nest. · Shooting · Techniques
768	**Nest. Survey** · CA · Techniques · Winter Survey
775	**Nest. Survey** · ON · Reprod. Succ. · Status · Territory
776	**Nest. Survey** · ON · Reprod. Succ. · Status · Territory
778	**Nest. Survey** · Disturb. · MB · ON · Reprod. Succ. · Techniques
782	**Nest. Survey** · Disturb. · MB · ON · Status · Techniques
783	**Nest. Survey** · Disturb. · Egg. Thin. · Heavy Metals · ON · Pest. · PCB · Reprod. Succ. · Status
801	**Nest. Survey** · Disturb. · Nest. · Reprod. Succ. · Statistics · Territory · WA
805	**Nest. Survey** · Habit. Use · Reprod. Succ. · San Juan Is. · WA
814	**Nest. Survey** · Disturb. · Great Lakes · Manage. · Pub. Ed. · Status · USFS
815	**Nest. Survey** · Chippewa NF · Great Lakes · Manage. · USFS
826	**Nest. Survey** · BC · Gulf Is. · Habit. Use · Migration · Prey · San Juan Is. · Techniques · Winter Survey · WA
827	**Nest. Survey** · Barkley Sound · Behav. · BC · Disturb. · Gulf Is. · Helicop. · Plumage · Prey
830	**Nest. Survey** · BC · Helicop. · Techniques
831	**Nest. Survey** · BC · Disturb. · Helicop. · Pest. · Refuge
832	**Nest. Survey** · BC · Intrasp. Behav. · Marking · Pub. Ed. · Techniques · Territory
833	**Nest. Survey** · BC · Hunt. Behav. · Intersp. Behav. · Intrasp. Behav. · Prey · Territory
863	**Nest. Survey** · AK · Habit. Use · Hunt. Behav. · Prey · Status
871	**Nest. Survey** · Disturb. · FL · Habit. Use · Kissimee B.E. Sanct. · Refuge · Reprod. Succ.
872	**Nest. Survey** · Disturb. · FL · Habit. Use · Kissimee B.E. Sanct. · Refuge · Reprod. Succ.
877	**Nest. Survey** · Baja · CA
923	**Nest. Survey** · Great Lakes · MI
936	**Nest. Survey** · FL · Nest. Fail. · Status
944	**Nest. Survey** · FL · Habit. Loss · Nest. Fail. · Status
945	**Nest. Survey** · Disturb. · FL · Habit. Loss · Nest. Fail. · Reprod. Succ.
946	**Nest. Survey** · Disturb. · FL · Habit. Loss · Status
947	**Nest. Survey** · FL
948	**Nest. Survey** · FL · Merritt Is. NWR
950	**Nest. Survey** · FL · Status
959	**Nest. Survey** · Agassiz NWR · Chippewa NF · Itasca SP · MN · Superior NF · Tamarac NWR
960	**Nest. Survey** · Chippewa NF · MN
981	**Nest. Survey** · Endang. Sp. · Great Lakes · Pub. Ed. · Status · USFS
984	**Nest. Survey** · Captivity · Egg Trans. · Heavy Metals · Law · Manage. · Migration · Pest. · Pub. Ed. · Status · Techniques · Territory · Young Trans.
988	**Nest. Survey** · Great Lakes · L Erie · Manage. · OH · Winter Survey
1024	**Nest. Survey** · FL · Techniques · Territory
1031	**Nest. Survey** · MI · Reprod. Succ.
1032	**Nest. Survey** · MI · Reprod. Succ.
1048	**Nest. Survey** · AK · Habit. Use · Techniques
1049	**Nest. Survey** · CA · Road. Census · Techniques · Winter Survey
1050	**Nest. Survey** · CA · Winter Survey
1073	**Nest. Survey** · AB · Disturb. · NWT
1081	**Nest. Survey** · MN · USFWS
1100	**Nest. Survey** · ME
1106	**Nest. Survey** · MI · Reprod. Succ. · Status
1146	**Nest. Survey** · Great Lakes · USFWS
1147	**Nest. Survey** · Great Lakes · Habit. Prot. · Manage. · MB · ON · Rehab. · Techniques · Techniques
1152	**Nest. Survey** · FL · Rehab. · Techniques
1159	**Nest. Survey** · CA · Road. Census · Techniques · Winter Survey
1175	**Nest. Survey** · ON
1187	**Nest. Survey** · Habit. Use · Life History · Prey · Winter Survey · WA
1188	**Nest. Survey** · Chippewa NF · Habit. Use · Manage. · MN · Status · USFS
1189	**Nest. Survey** · Chippewa NF · Habit. Use · Manage. · MN · USFS

Master No.	Keywords
1190	Nest. **Survey** · Chippewa NF · MN · USFS
1191	Nest. **Survey** · Chippewa NF · MN · USFS
1192	Nest. **Survey** · Chippewa NF · MN · USFS
1193	Nest. **Survey** · Chippewa NF · MN · USFS
1194	Nest. **Survey** · Chippewa NF · MN · USFS
1196	Nest. **Survey** · Band. · Chippewa NF · IL · MN · Techniques · USFS · Winter. Pop.
1198	Nest. **Survey** · Chippewa NF · MN · USFS
1201	Nest. **Survey** · Chippewa NF · MN · Status · USFS
1202	Nest. **Survey** · Chippewa NF · MN · Status · USFS
1203	Nest. **Survey** · Chippewa NF · MN · USFS
1204	Nest. **Survey** · Chippewa NF · MN · USFS
1205	Nest. **Survey** · Chippewa NF · MN · USFS
1207	Nest. **Survey** · Chippewa NF · Manage. · MN · Status · USFS
1209	Nest. **Survey** · Chippewa NF · MN · Status · USFS
1211	Nest. **Survey** · Chippewa NF · MN · Status · USFS
1213	Nest. **Survey** · Chippewa NF · MN · Status · USFS
1214	Nest. **Survey** · Band. · Chippewa NF · Marking · MN · Techniques
1215	Nest. **Survey** · Chippewa NF · Manage. · MN · Refuge · USFS
1217	Nest. **Survey** · Band. · Chippewa NF · MN · Status · Techniques · USFS
1223	Nest. **Survey** · Band. · Chippewa NF · MN · Reprod. Succ. · Status · Superior NF · Techniques · Terminology
1224	Nest. **Survey** · Habit. Use · Superior NF · USFS
1234	Nest. **Survey** · Egg. Thin. · FL · Habit. Use · Ocala NF · Prey · Reprod. Succ.
1239	Nest. **Survey** · NJ
1240	Nest. **Survey** · NJ
1241	Nest. **Survey** · NJ
1242	Nest. **Survey** · History · NJ · Pest. · Status
1299	Nest. **Survey** · Habit. Use · Intersp. Behav. · Territory · Yellowstone NP
1350	Nest. **Survey** · FL
1351	Nest. **Survey** · FL · Habit. Use
1352	Nest. **Survey** · Fla. B.E. Sur. Comm. · FL · Habit. Use · Status
1354	Nest. **Survey** · Disturb. · San Juan Is. · Status · WA
1359	Nest. **Survey** · AK · Lower 48 · USFWS
1360	Nest. **Survey** · Habit. Loss · Pest. · Shooting · Techniques · Terminology · USFWS
1363	Nest. **Survey** · Habit. Use · WI
1384	Nest. **Survey** · Asper. · OR · Road. Census · Techniques · Winter Survey
1445	Nest. **Survey** · FL
1473	Nest. **Survey** · MI · ON · Terminology
1475	Nest. **Survey** · MI · ON · Terminology
1478	Nest. **Survey** · MI
1479	Nest. **Survey** · MI
1480	Nest. **Survey** · ON
1481	Nest. **Survey** · MI
1483	Nest. **Survey** · MI
1484	Nest. **Survey** · Disturb. · Great Lakes · Manage. · ON · Research · Status · Techniques
1485	Nest. **Survey** · MI
1487	Nest. **Survey** · Band. · Disturb. · Great Lakes · MI · Pest. · Techniques
1489	Nest. **Survey** · MI
1504	Nest. **Survey** · Great Lakes · USFS
1508	Nest. **Survey** · Field ID · NWF · RIC · USFS
1530	Nest. **Survey** · AK · Habit. Use · Manage. · Territory
1550	Nest. **Survey** · AZ · Behav. · Disturb. · Habit. Loss · Habit. Use · Hunt. Behav. · Prey · Status · Terminology · Territory
1578	Nest. **Survey** · DE · Great Lakes · MD · NJ · PA · Status
1585	Nest. **Survey** · Techniques · VA
1586	Nest. **Survey** · VA
1606	Nest. **Survey** · Aggress. · Aleutian Is. · AK · Behav. · Depred. · Habit. Use · Life History · Mortality · Plumage · Prey · Reprod. Succ. · Status · Winter Survey

Master No.	Keywords
1611	Nest. **Survey** · Superior NF
1612	Nest. **Survey** · MN · Reprod. Succ. · Superior NF
1617	Nest. **Survey** · NY · Status
1629	Nest. **Survey** · Distrib. · Endang. Sp. · TX · Winter Survey
1630	Nest. **Survey** · Distrib. · Endang. Sp. · TX · Winter Survey
1631	Nest. **Survey** · Distrib. · Reprod. Succ. · Status · TX · Winter Survey
1632	Nest. **Survey** · Distrib. · Habit. Use · Status · TX · Winter Survey
1638	Nest. **Survey** · NM · Winter. Pop.
1665	Nest. **Survey** · NY
1666	Nest. **Survey** · Dispersal · NY · Winter. Pop.
1668	Nest. **Survey** · Montezuma NWR · NY · Status
1670	Nest. **Survey** · Cont. B.E. Proj. · NAS · Status
1671	Nest. **Survey** · Cont. B.E. Proj. · Migration · NAS · Status · Winter Survey
1672	Nest. **Survey** · Cont. B.E. Proj. · Hurricane · NAS · Status · Winter Survey
1673	Nest. **Survey** · Cont, B.E. Proj. · Manage. · Migration · NAS · Status · Winter Survey
1674	Nest. **Survey** · Cont. B.E. Proj. · Manage. · NAS · Refuge · Status · Winter Survey
1675	Nest. **Survey** · Cont. B.E. Proj. · NAS · Status · Winter Survey
1676	Nest. **Survey** · Cont. B.E. Proj. · NAS · Status · Winter Survey
1677	Nest. **Survey** · NAS · Status
1678	Nest. **Survey** · Cont. B.E. Proj. · Manage. · NAS · Status · Winter Survey
1681	Nest. **Survey** · Cont. B.E. Proj. · NAS · Status · Terminology
1686	Nest. **Survey** · Autopsy · Cont. B.E. Proj. · NAS · Winter Survey
1713	Nest. **Survey** · NB · NS · PE · Reprod. Succ. · Winter Survey
1730	Nest. **Survey** · Manage. · MN
1741	Nest. **Survey** · Disturb. · Habit. Use · Manage. · MT · Pop. Turnover · Reprod. Succ. · Status · Territory · Yellowstone NP
1742	Nest. **Survey** · Habit. Use · TX
1751	Nest. **Survey** · Egg. Thin. · Habit. Use · Manage. · MD · Pest.
1752	Nest. **Survey** · Egg. Thin. · Habit. Use · Manage. · MD · Pest. · Techniques
1766	Nest. **Survey** · Acct. · Reprod. Succ. · TX
1767	Nest. **Survey** · Acct. · Reprod. Succ. · TX
1769	Nest. **Survey** · Band. · Reprod. Succ. · Techniques · TX · Winter Survey
1771	Nest. **Survey** · CA · Disturb. · Habit. Loss · Habit. Use · Manage. · Prey · Shooting · Territory · Trapping
1777	Nest. **Survey** · CA · Habit. Use · Manage. · Status · Territory
1785	Nest. **Survey** · Endang. Sp. · Lower 48 · Status
1789	Nest. **Survey** · AZ · Disturb. · Verde R
1791	Nest. **Survey** · AZ · Electro. · Winter Survey
1793	Nest. **Survey** · AZ · CAP · Orme D · Salt R · Verde R
1796	Nest. **Survey** · Ches. Bay · Winter Survey
1803	Nest. **Survey** · BC · Gulf Is. · Winter Survey
1804	Nest. **Survey** · AK · Habit. Use · Kodiak Is. · Kodiak NWR
1812	Nest. **Survey** · Ches. Bay · DE · Econ. Import. · Habit. Use · Life History · MD · NC · NJ · Prey · PA · VA
1825	Nest. **Survey** · Aircraft · Chippewa NF · Great Lakes · MI · MN · Reprod. Succ. · Status · USFS · WI
1829	Nest. **Survey** · AK · Band. · Behav. · Kodiak NWR · Reprod. Succ. · Techniques
1837	Nest. **Survey** · NM · USFWS
1838	Nest. **Survey** · AZ · CO · KS · NM · OK · Salt Fork R · TX · USFWS · UT · Verde R · WY
1839	Nest. **Survey** · CA · ID · MT · NV · OR · USFWS · WA
1840	Nest. **Survey** · DE · USFWS
1842	Nest. **Survey** · NJ · USFWS
1843	Nest. **Survey** · ID · OR · USFWS · WA
1844	Nest. **Survey** · CA · ID · NV · OR · USFWS · WA
1845	Nest. **Survey** · ME · USFWS
1846	Nest. **Survey** · CO · IA · KS · MO · MT · ND · NE · SD · USFWS · UT · WY

Master No.	Keywords
1847	**Nest. Survey** · Ches. Bay · New England · USFWS
1849	**Nest. Survey** · CO · IA · KS · MO · MT · ND · NE · SD · USFWS · UT · WY
1850	**Nest. Survey** · AK · Lower 48 · Reprod. Succ. · USFWS
1852	**Nest. Survey** · AZ · Manage. · NM · OK · Salt Fork R · TX · USFWS · Verde R
1853	**Nest. Survey** · CA · ID · NV · OR · USFWS · WA
1854	**Nest. Survey** · CO · Glacier NP · Manage. · Missouri R · MT · SD · USFWS
1855	**Nest. Survey** · IL · IN · MI · MN · OH · Terminology · USFWS · WI
1856	**Nest. Survey** · ND · USFWS
1857	**Nest. Survey** · Missouri R · SD · USFWS
1858	**Nest. Survey** · MT · USFWS · WY
1859	**Nest. Survey** · IA · KS · Missouri R · MO · ND · NE · Rocky Mt. Region · SD · USFWS · Winter. Pop.
1860	**Nest. Survey** · Missouri R · NE · SD · USFWS · Winter. Pop.
1862	**Nest. Survey** · Ches. Bay · New England · USFWS
1866	**Nest. Survey** · AZ · USFWS
1867	**Nest. Survey** · TX · USFWS
1868	**Nest. Survey** · MI · MN · OH · USFWS · WI
1876	**Nest. Survey** · Ches. Bay
1918	**Nest. Survey** · Great Lakes · USFS
1919	**Nest. Survey** · Great Lakes · USFS
1920	**Nest. Survey** · Disturb. · Habit. Loss · Manage. · ON · Status
1921	**Nest. Survey** · Nest. Fail. · ON
1926	**Nest. Survey** · LB · QU · Status
1931	**Nest. Survey** · Amchitka Is. · AK · Egg. Thin. · Habit. Use · Prey · Winter Survey
1932	**Nest. Survey** · AK · Disturb. · Helicop. · Techniques
1938	**Nest. Survey** · MB · Reprod. Succ. · SK
1939	**Nest. Survey** · Habit. Use · MB · SK · Terminology
1947	**Nest. Survey** · AK · Forrester Is.

Master No.	Keywords
555	**Nestling** · Behav. · Breed. Behav. · Chippewa NF · Disturb. · Fledging · Marking · MN · Prey · Reprod. Succ. · Techniques · Telemetry
699	**Nestling** · Behav. · Chippewa NF · Fledging · Techniques · Telemetry
727	**Nestling** · Behav. · Parent. Behav. · SK
731	**Nestling** · Behav. · Disturb. · Parent. Behav. · SK
841	**Nestling** · Behav. · Chippewa NF · Dispersal · Disturb. · Fledging · MN · Techniques · Telemetry
842	**Nestling** · Behav. · Chippewa NF · Dispersal · Fledging · Hunt. Behav. · MN · Techniques · Telemetry
843	**Nestling** · Band. · Behav. · Chippewa NF · Dispersal · Fledging · Migration · MN · Techniques · Telemetry
880	**Nestling** · Behav. · Life History · Nest. · OH · Parent. Behav. · Photo. · Techniques
881	**Nestling** · Behav. · Fledging · Life History · Nest. · OH
885	**Nestling** · Behav. · Captive Breed. · Intrasp. Behav. · OH
977	**Nestling** · Behav. · Cannibal.
1454	**Nestling** · Nest. · Territory
1562	**New England** · Life History
1669	**New England** · Acct. · Habit. Use
1847	**New England** · Ches. Bay · Nest. Survey · USFWS
1862	**New England** · Ches. Bay · Nest. Survey · USFWS
1946	**New England** · Egg · Status · Taxonomy
1496	**Nocturnal Behav.** · Behav. · Chippewa NF · Fledging · Manage. · MN · Nest.
1090	**Nongame Sp.** · Law · Manage.
111	**NAS** · Endang. Sp. · Status
119	**NAS** · Nest. Survey · Pub. Ed. · Status · Winter Survey
129	**NAS** · Manage. · Status
365	**NAS** · AK · Bounty · Shooting
367	**NAS** · Cont. B.E. Proj. · Nest. Survey
368	**NAS** · Cont. B.E. Proj. · Nest. Survey
397	**NAS** · Jackson's Canyon · Law · Poison. · WY
661	**NAS** · Manage. · Nest. · Pub. Ed.
1017	**NAS** · L Andes NWR · Missouri R · Status · SD · Winter Survey

Master No.	Keywords
1314	NAS · Electro. · Law · Pest. · Poison. · Pub. Ed. · Shooting · Status
1349	NAS · Dispersal · FL · Life History · Migration · Pub. Ed. · Status
1419	NAS · AK · Bounty · Law · Pub. Ed. · Shooting
1670	NAS · Cont. B.E. Proj. · Nest. Survey · Status
1671	NAS · Cont. B.E. Proj. · Migration · Nest. Survey · Status · Winter Survey
1672	NAS · Cont. B.E. Proj. · Hurricane · Nest. Survey · Status · Winter Survey
1673	NAS · Cont. B.E. Proj. · Manage. · Migration · Nest. Survey · Status · Winter Survey
1674	NAS · Cont. B.E. Proj. · Manage. · Nest. Survey · Refuge · Status · Winter Survey
1675	NAS · Cont. B.E. Proj. · Nest. Survey · Status · Winter Survey
1676	NAS · Cont. B.E. Proj. · Nest. Survey · Status · Winter Survey
1677	NAS · Nest. Survey · Status
1678	NAS · Cont. B.E. Proj. · Manage. · Nest. Survey · Status · Winter Survey
1681	NAS · Cont. B.E. Proj. · Nest. Survey · Status · Terminology
1686	NAS · Autopsy · Cont. B.E. Proj. · Nest. Survey · Winter Survey
1760	NAS · FL · Habit. Loss · Status
372	NB · Autopsy · AK · Cont. U.S. · DDT · Pest. · Residues · Toxicol.
1713	NB · Nest. Survey · NS · PE · Reprod. Succ. · Winter Survey
1988	NB · Anat. · Behav. · Capture · Depred. · Econ. Import. · Intersp. Behav. · Manage. · Prey · Techniques
391	NC · Nest.
407	NC · Nest. · SC
408	NC · Nest. · SC
420	NC · Nest. · SC · Winter. Pop.
444	NC · Anat. · Folklore · Hunt. Behav. · Shooting
480	NC · Ches. Bay · Disturb. · Egg Coll. · GA
570	NC · Nest.
660	NC · Habit. Loss · Nest. Survey · SC
763	NC · Life History · Pub. Ed. · Status
812	NC · Winter. Pop.
914	NC · Nest. · Photo.

Master No.	Keywords
1408	NC · Nest.
1428	NC · Life History · Nest.
1702	NC · Acct. · Hunt. Behav. · Nest. · Prey
1729	NC · Acct. · TN · Winter. Pop.
1762	NC · Nest. · SC
1763	NC · Mattamuskett NWR · Nest. · Savannah NWR · SC
1764	NC · Nest. · SC
1765	NC · Nest. · SC · Winter. Pop.
1812	NC · Ches. Bay · DE · Econ. Import. · Habit. Use · Life History · MD · Nest. Survey · NJ · Prey · PA · VA
1964	NC · Life History · Nest.
269	ND · Autopsy · FL · Heavy Metals · Midwest Region · MD · ME · MO · Pest. · PCB
360	ND · Mortality · Nest.
361	ND · Behav. · Disturb. · Nest. · Photo.
469	ND · MT · Nest.
736	ND · Habit. Use · Marking · Migration · MO · SD · SK · Techniques · WY
1082	ND · Nest. · Winter. Pop.
1200	ND · Chippewa NF · Disturb. · MN · Poison. · Pub. Ed. · Shooting · Status · USFS
1237	ND · Distrib. · Endang. Sp. · Habit. Use · Migration · Nest. · Status · Winter. Pop.
1662	ND · Winter. Pop.
1846	ND · CO · IA · KS · MO · MT · Nest. Survey · NE · SD · USFWS · UT · WY
1849	ND · CO · IA · KS · MO · MT · Nest. Survey · NE · SD · USFWS · UT · WY
1856	ND · Nest. Survey · USFWS
1859	ND · IA · KS · Missouri R · MO · Nest. Survey · NE · Rocky Mt. Region · SD · USFWS · Winter. Pop.
1974	ND · Nest. · Shooting
126	NE · Winter. Pop.
131	NE · Platte R · Winter Survey
152	NE · Corps · Habit. Loss · Karl Mundt NWR · Missouri R · NWF · SD
232	NE · Acct.
286	NE · Mortality · Winter. Pop.
348	NE · Platte R · Winter Survey
358	NE · Acct. · Nest.
359	NE · Nest.
614	NE · IA · IL · Mississippi R · Winter Survey · WI

Master No.	Keywords
615	NE · IA · IL · Mississippi R · Winter Survey
621	NE · Illinois R · IL · KY · Mississippi R · Winter Survey
624	NE · Illinois R · IA · IL · KY · Mississippi R · Winter Survey
634	NE · Illinois R · IA · IL · KY · Mississippi R · MO · Winter Survey
635	NE · Illinois R · IA · IL · KY · Mississippi R · Missouri R · MO · Winter Survey · Wisconsin R
636	NE · Illinois R · IA · IL · KY · Mississippi R · Missouri R · MO · Winter Survey · Wisconsin R
637	NE · Illinois R · IA · IL · KY · Mississippi R · Missouri R · MO · Winter Survey · Wisconsin R
638	NE · Illinois R · IA · IL · KY · Mississippi R · MO · Winter Survey
639	NE · Illinois R · IA · IL · KY · Mississippi R · MO · Winter Survey
643	NE · Illinois R · IL · KY · Mississippi R · MO · Winter Survey
644	NE · Illinois R · IL · KY · Mississippi R · MO · Winter Survey
645	NE · IA · IL · Mississippi R · MN · MO · WI
646	NE · Illinois R · IL · KY · Mississippi R · MO · Winter Survey
651	NE · Illinois R · IA · IL · KY · Mississippi R · MO · TN · Winter Survey
652	NE · Illinois R · IA · KY · Mississippi R · MO · TN · Winter Survey
927	NE · Anat. · CA · FL · NM · OR · Paleontology · Taxonomy
1047	NE · Platte R · Winter. Pop.
1098	NE · Winter. Pop.
1121	NE · Behav. · Manage. · Prey · Status · Winter Survey
1122	NE · Acct. · Road. Census · Techniques · Winter. Pop.
1123	NE · Road. Census · Techniques · Winter. Pop.
1124	NE · Rehab. · Techniques
1125	NE · Nest. · Winter. Pop.
1216	NE · Road. Census · Techniques
1283	NE · Winter. Pop.

Master No.	Keywords
1336	NE · Behav. · Manage. · Prey · Status · Winter Survey
1337	NE · Road. Census · Techniques · Winter. Pop.
1338	NE · Platte R · Winter Survey
1339	NE · Platte R · Winter Survey
1340	NE · Platte R · Winter Survey
1608	NE · Habit. Use · Platte R · Winter Survey
1755	NE · Nest.
1802	NE · Platte R · Winter Survey
1846	NE · CO · IA · KS · MO · MT · Nest. Survey · ND · SD · USFWS · UT · WY
1849	NE · CO · IA · KS · MO · MT · Nest. Survey · ND · SD · USFWS · UT · WY
1859	NE · IA · KS · Missouri R · MO · Nest. Survey · ND · Rocky Mt. Region · SD · USFWS · Winter. Pop.
1860	NE · Missouri R · Nest. Survey · SD · USFWS · Winter. Pop.
1895	NE · Behav. · Habit. Use · Hunt. Behav. · Intrasp. Behav. · Migration · Platte R · Winter Survey
1909	NE · Distrib.
1913	NE · Platte R · Winter. Pop.
1915	NE · Behav. · Migration · Platte R · Prey · Winter Survey
1928	NE · Distrib.
1968	NE · Migration
1996	NE · Migration · Missouri R · MN · Shooting
1099	NF · Intersp. Behav.
1546	NF · Intersp. Behav. · Terra Nova NP · Winter. Pop.
1987	NF · Econ. Import. · LB · Maritime Prov. · Prey
31	NH · Distrib. · Nest. · Winter. Pop.
32	NH · MA · Winter. Pop.
452	NH · Acct. · Status
475	NH · Winter. Pop.
1353	NH · Field ID · Life History
1603	NH · Anat. · Taxonomy · Winter. Pop.
36	NJ · Cape May · Migration
133	NJ · Life History · Nest. · Pub. Ed. · Winter. Pop.
169	NJ · Acct. · Winter. Pop.
272	NJ · Hunt. Behav.
369	NJ · Law · MI · Nest. Survey · Winter Survey
379	NJ · Egg Coll. · Habit. Loss · Nest.

Master No.	Keywords
435	NJ · Cape May · Capture · Migration · Techniques
436	NJ · Cape May · Migration
437	NJ · Cape May · Migration
438	NJ · Cape May · Migration · Status
439	NJ · Band. · Cape May · Capture · Migration · Techniques
440	NJ · Band. · Capture · Migration · Sandy Hook · Techniques
481	NJ · Disturb. · Egg Coll.
492	NJ · DE · Egg · Egg Coll. · MD · Nest.
545	NJ · Migration · Racoon Ridge
546	NJ · Cape May · Migration
565	NJ · FL · ME · Pest. · Toxicol.
610	NJ · Migration · Nest.
822	NJ · Status
969	NJ · Nest.
1070	NJ · Acct.
1239	NJ · Nest. Survey
1240	NJ · Nest. Survey
1241	NJ · Nest. Survey
1242	NJ · History · Nest. Survey · Pest. · Status
1264	NJ · Nest.
1265	NJ · Nest.
1266	NJ · Nest.
1267	NJ · Nest.
1269	NJ · Nest.
1307	NJ · Hawk Mt. · Migration
1446	NJ · Cape May · Migration · Pymatuning · PA · Winter. Pop.
1578	NJ · DE · Great Lakes · MD · Nest. Survey · PA · Status
1709	NJ · FL · ME · MO · Pest. · Toxicol. · USFWS
1715	NJ · Nest. · Winter. Pop.
1716	NJ · Cape May · Migration · Nest.
1812	NJ · Ches. Bay · DE · Econ. Import. · Habit. Use · Life History · MD · Nest. Survey · NC · Prey · PA · VA
1831	NJ · Autopsy · DDT · MO · Residues · Toxicol.
1842	NJ · Nest. Survey · USFWS
1901	NJ · Distrib. · DE · Life History · Prey · VA
211	NM · Anat. · Distrib. · Nest. · Plumage · Prey · Winter. Pop.
927	NM · Anat. · CA · FL · NE · OR · Paleontology · Taxonomy
928	NM · Paleontology
1101	NM · Nest. · Status · Winter. Pop.
1335	NM · Rehab. · Techniques
1609	NM · Pub. Ed. · Winter. Pop.
1638	NM · Nest. Survey · Winter. Pop.
1639	NM · AZ · CA · Endang. Sp. · NV · OK · Status · TX · UT
1837	NM · Nest. Survey · USFWS
1838	NM · AZ · CO · KS · Nest. Survey · OK · Salt Fork R · TX · USFWS · UT · Verde R · WY
1852	NM · AZ · Manage. · Nest. Survey · OK · Salt Fork R · TX · USFWS · Verde R
1944	NM · Depred. · Hunt. Behav. · TX
604	NS · Intersp. Behav. · Prey · Winter. Pop.
744	NS · Hunt. Behav. · Nest. · Prey
1713	NS · Nest. Survey · NB · PE · Reprod. Succ. · Winter Survey
1808	NS · Field ID · Life History · Nest. · Poetry
193	NV · Winter. Pop.
225	NV · Boulder D · Winter. Pop.
687	NV · Law · Shooting
1086	NV · CO · Electro. · Manage. · Trapping · TX · UT
1309	NV · Endang. Sp. · Manage. · Nest. · Status
1318	NV · Trapping
1576	NV · Pub. Ed. · Trapping
1639	NV · AZ · CA · Endang. Sp. · NM · OK · Status · TX · UT
1839	NV · CA · ID · MT · Nest. Survey · OR · USFWS · WA
1844	NV · CA · ID · Nest. Survey · OR · USFWS · WA
1853	NV · CA · ID · Nest. Survey · OR · USFWS · WA
1981	NV · CO · Electro. · ID · Manage. · UT · WY
145	NWF · Manage. · Reward · Shooting · WI
146	NWF · Manage. · Reward
149	NWF · Literature · Manage. · RIC · Status
152	NWF · Corps · Habit. Loss · Karl Mundt NWR · Missouri R · NE · SD
153	NWF · Habit. Prot. · Missouri R · SD · Winter. Pop.
161	NWF · Literature · Manage. · RIC · Status

Master No.	Keywords
176	NWF · Habit. Prot. · Refuge · Southland · SD
434	NWF · Educ. Mat. · Endang. Sp. · Manage.
702	NWF · Habit. Prot. · Karl Mundt NWR · L Andes NWR · Manage. · Missouri R · Refuge · SD · Winter. Pop.
1046	NWF · Pub. Ed. · Status
1087	NWF · Habit. Prot. · Manage. · Pub. Ed. · SD · Techniques · Winter. Pop. · Young Trans.
1089	NWF · Nest. · Pub. Ed. · Status · Winter. Pop.
1315	NWF · Reward · Shooting
1316	NWF · Manage. · Reward · Shooting
1317	NWF · Law · Life History · Pest. · Pub. Ed. · Status
1320	NWF · RIC
1321	NWF · Manage. · RIC
1322	NWF · Ferry Bluff Sanct. · Refuge · WI
1324	NWF · Pub. Ed.
1325	NWF · Ferry Bluff Sanct. · Refuge · WI
1326	NWF · Pub. Ed.
1327	NWF · Pub. Ed.
1328	NWF · Habit. Prot. · Pub. Ed. · Research · RIC
1329	NWF · Pub. Ed.
1330	NWF · Ferry Bluff Sanct. · Habit. Prot. · Refuge · Winter. Pop. · Wisconsin R · WI
1331	NWF · Pub. Ed.
1332	NWF · CA · Habit. Prot. · IL · RIC
1346	NWF · Habit. Prot. · Manage. · Pub. Ed. · Reward
1348	NWF · Habit. Prot. · Karl Mundt NWR · Manage.
1508	NWF · Field ID · Nest. Survey · RIC · USFS
340	NWT · Ground Nest. · Nest.
909	NWT · Nest.
1073	NWT · AB · Disturb. · Nest. Survey
1074	NWT · Acct. · AB · AK · YT
1076	NWT · Acct. · AB · AK · YT
1077	NWT · Acct.
1595	NWT · Acct. · CN · Great Slave L.
1800	NWT · Ground Nest. · Nest.
1924	NWT · Great Slave L. · Nest.
163	NY · Manage. · Techniques · Young Trans.
166	NY · Hacking · Manage. · Techniques · Young Trans.
256	NY · Shooting · Winter. Pop.
258	NY · Anat. · Nest. · Prey · Status · Winter. Pop.
354	NY · Manage. · Pub. Ed.
373	NY · Nest. · Status · Taxonomy · Winter. Pop.
387	NY · Hacking · Manage. · Montezuma NWR · Techniques · WI · Young Trans.
411	NY · Captivity · Hunt. Behav. · Winter. Pop.
414	NY · Hacking · Montezuma NWR · Techniques · Telemetry · Young Trans.
568	NY · Acct. · Field ID
584	NY · Winter. Pop.
704	NY · Nest.
742	NY · Anat. · Shooting · Taxonomy
795	NY · Nest. · Winter. Pop.
819	NY · Nest. · Winter. Pop.
850	NY · Derby Hill · Great Lakes · Hawk Mt. · Migration
902	NY · Intersp. Behav. · Winter. Pop.
924	NY · Acct.
955	NY · Finger Lakes · Montezuma NWR · Nest.
956	NY · Finger Lakes · Montezuma NWR · Nest.
1034	NY · Hacking · Manage. · Photo. · Techniques
1225	NY · Acct.
1253	NY · Behav. · Hacking · Heavy Metals · Intrasp. Behav. · Marking · Montezuma NWR · MI · MN · Pest. · Techniques · Telemetry · Young Trans.
1254	NY · Hacking · Pub. Ed. · Techniques · Young Trans.
1255	NY · Hacking · Manage. · Techniques · Young Trans.
1256	NY · Behav. · Hacking · Manage. · Pest. · Prey · PCB · Techniques · Young Trans.
1274	NY · Manage. · Techniques · Young Trans.
1275	NY · Dispersal · Techniques · Young Trans.
1368	NY · Behav. · Climatology · Disturb. · Habit. Use · Hunt. Behav. · Intersp. Behav. · Intrasp. Behav. · Manage. · Prey · Winter Survey

Master No.	Keywords
1369	NY · Behav. · Habit. Use · Heavy Metals · Hunt. Behav. · Intersp. Behav. · Intrasp. Behav. · Manage. · Pest. · Prey · PCB · Winter Survey
1404	NY · Montezuma NWR · Nest.
1435	NY · Oneida L
1511	NY · Behav. · Habit. Use · Heavy Metals · Nest. · Pest. · PCB
1539	NY · Hudson R · Winter. Pop.
1617	NY · Nest. Survey · Status
1664	NY · Nest. · Winter. Pop.
1665	NY · Nest. Survey
1666	NY · Dispersal · Nest. Survey · Winter. Pop.
1667	NY · Field ID · Montezuma NWR
1668	NY · Montezuma NWR · Nest. Survey · Status
1732	NY · Egg. Thin. · Hacking · Techniques · Telemetry · Young Trans.
1774	NY · Climatology · Hook Mt. · Migration
1871	NY · Egg Trans. · Hacking · Manage. · ME · MN · Pest. · PCB · Techniques · WI · Young Trans.
1958	NY · CN · Distrib. · Hunt. Behav. · Prey
1773	Oak V. Eagle Sanct. · Habit. Prot. · IL · Refuge
671	Ocala NF · FL · Nest. · USFS
1234	Ocala NF · Egg. Thin. · FL · Habit. Use · Nest. Survey · Prey · Reprod. Succ.
301	Ohio R · Disturb. · Habit. Use · IL · Nest. · Rehab. · Shooting · Techniques · Winter. Pop.
455	Ohio R · Depred. · Shooting · WV
1692	Ohio R · Illinois R · KY · Mississippi R · Winter Survey
1693	Ohio R · KY · Mississippi R · Winter Survey
860	Okefinokee Swamp · GA · Nest. · Prey
1986	Okefinokee Swamp · Acct. · GA · Nest.
59	Old Abe · Folklore · Life History · Pub. Ed.
72	Old Abe · Captivity · History · WI
295	Old Abe · History · WI
417	Old Abe · History · WI
655	Old Abe · History
820	Old Abe · History
1607	Old Abe · History
1995	Old Abe · History
1435	Oneida L · NY
182	Orme D · AZ · CAP · Falconry · Habit. Loss · Law

Master No.	Keywords
449	Orme D · AZ · CAP · Habit. Loss · Nest. · Salt R · Verde R
770	Orme D · AZ · CAP · Disturb. · Habit. Use · Manage. · Nest.
1004	Orme D · AZ · CAP · Endang. Sp. · Habit. Loss
1179	Orme D · AZ · Habit. Loss · Nest.
1793	Orme D · AZ · CAP · Nest. Survey · Salt R · Verde R
1865	Orme D · AZ · BLM · CAP · Egg · Habit. Prot. · Manage. · Nest. · Salt R · Taxonomy · Territory · Verde R
1965	Orme D · AZ · CAP · Habit. Loss · Nest.
1966	Orme D · AZ · CAP · Nest.
1221	Ottawa NF · Aging · Behav. · Hunt. Behav. · Impound. · Intrasp. Behav. · MI · Nest. · Techniques · Territory
1222	Ottawa NF · Behav. · Fledging · Hunt. Behav. · Intersp. Behav. · Intrasp. Behav. · Marking · MI · Techniques · Territory
42	OH · Nest. · Status · Winter. Pop.
75	OH · Behav. · Nest.
80	OH · Behav. · Life History · Nest.
160	OH · Ground Nest. · Law · Nest.
162	OH · History
220	OH · Hunt. Behav. · Winter. Pop.
243	OH · Mortality · Nest.
259	OH · Captive Breed.
496	OH · Climatology · Migration · Poison. · Shooting · Winter Survey
497	OH · Behav. · Egg · Nest. · Poison. · Prey · Shooting
665	OH · Habit. Use · Nest.
875	OH · Nest.
879	OH · Intersp. Behav. · Nest. · Photo.
880	OH · Behav. · Life History · Nest. · Nestling · Parent. Behav. · Photo. · Techniques
881	OH · Behav. · Fledging · Life History · Nest. · Nestling
882	OH · Aggress. · Behav. · Disturb. · Life History · Nest. · PA
883	OH · Behav. · Fledging · Hunt. Behav. · Life History · Nest. · Prey
884	OH · Behav. · History · Nest. · Photo. · Techniques
885	OH · Behav. · Captive Breed. · Intrasp. Behav. · Nestling

Master No.	Keywords
886	OH · Breed. Behav. · Intersp. Behav. · Life History · Nest. · Parent. Behav. · Prey
887	OH · Behav. · Life History · Nest. · Photo. · Techniques
888	OH · Behav. · Fledging · Intersp. Behav. · Life History · Nest. · Parent. Behav. · Photo. · Prey
889	OH · Behav. · Life History · Nest. · Photo. · Techniques
891	OH · Behav. · Life History · Nest. · Prey
896	OH · Nest.
988	OH · Great Lakes · L Erie · Manage. · Nest. Survey · Winter Survey
1015	OH · Hunt. Behav. · Nest. · Winter. Pop.
1080	OH · Nest.
1085	OH · Disturb. · Habit. Loss · Nest. · Status
1127	OH · Disease · Fowl Cholera · Heavy Metals · Pest.
1243	OH · Nest.
1376	OH · Field ID · Nest. · Pub. Ed. · Status
1491	OH · Captive Breed.
1499	OH · Capture · Techniques · Trapping · Winter. Pop.
1500	OH · Habit. Loss · Nest.
1597	OH · Nest.
1627	OH · Endang. Sp. · Nest. · Pest. · Status
1801	OH · Intersp. Behav. · Winter. Pop.
1855	OH · IL · IN · MI · MN · Nest. Survey · Terminology · USFWS · WI
1868	OH · MI · MN · Nest. Survey · USFWS · WI
27	OK · Acct. · Road. Census · Techniques · TX
754	OK · Acct. · Egg Coll. · Shooting
821	OK · Habit. Use · Status · Winter Survey
1007	OK · Winter. Pop.
1112	OK · Autopsy · Disturb. · Habit. Use · Hunt. Behav. · Intersp. Behav. · Manage. · Migration · Prey · Salt Fork R · Shooting · Status · Taxonomy · Winter Survey
1113	OK · Hunt. Behav. · Intrasp. Behav. · Migration · Neosho R · Prey · Winter Survey
1114	OK · Arkansas R · Band. · Capture · Habit. Use · Intersp. Behav. · Salt Plains NWR · Sequoyah NWR · Techniques · Wichita Mts. NWR · Winter Survey · Winter. Pop.
1115	OK · Disturb. · Habit. Use · Manage. · Migration · Prey · Salt Fork R · Salt Plains NWR · Sequoyah NWR · Shooting · Status · Taxonomy · Wichita Mts. NWR · Winter Survey
1116	OK · Acct. · Disturb. · Nest. · Status · Winter. Pop.
1282	OK · Acct. · Winter. Pop.
1639	OK · AZ · CA · Endang. Sp. · NM · NV · Status · TX · UT
1734	OK · Habit. Use · Nest. · Prey · Winter. Pop.
1746	OK · Nest. · Status · Trapping
1838	OK · AZ · CO · KS · Nest. Survey · NM · Salt Fork R · TX · USFWS · UT · Verde R · WY
1852	OK · AZ · Manage. · Nest. Survey · NM · Salt Fork R · TX · USFWS · Verde R
1888	OK · Winter. Pop.
271	ON · Nest. · Prey
332	ON · Band. · FL · Pest. · Pub. Ed. · Reprod. Succ. · Techniques
334	ON · Ches. Bay · FL · Hurricane · Nest. Fail.
374	ON · Nest. · Winter. Pop.
659	ON · Heavy Metals
733	ON · Band. · Great Lakes · Migration · Techniques
739	ON · CN · DDT · PCB · SK
772	ON · Band. · Behav. · CN · Reprod. Succ. · Techniques
773	ON · Anat. · CN
774	ON · Aggress. · Behav. · CN · Disturb. · Reprod. Succ.
775	ON · Nest. Survey · Reprod. Succ. · Status · Territory
776	ON · Nest. Survey · Reprod. Succ. · Status · Territory
777	ON · CN · Habit. Use · Reprod. Succ. · Status · Techniques · Territory
778	ON · Disturb. · MB · Nest. Survey · Reprod. Succ. · Techniques
779	ON · Egg. Thin. · Heavy Metals · Pest. · PCB · Reprod. Succ. · Status
780	ON · CN · Disturb. · Habit. Use · Lake of The Woods · Manage.
781	ON · PCB
782	ON · Disturb. · MB · Nest. Survey · Status · Techniques

Master No.	Keywords
783	ON · Disturb. · Egg. Thin. · Heavy Metals · Nest. Survey · Pest. · PCB · Reprod. Succ. · Status
997	ON · Life History · Nest. · Winter. Pop.
1016	ON · Nest. · Shooting
1147	ON · Great Lakes · Habit. Prot. · Manage. · MB · Nest. Survey · Rehab. · Techniques · Techniques
1150	ON · Acct.
1175	ON · Nest. Survey
1473	ON · MI · Nest. Survey · Terminology
1475	ON · MI · Nest. Survey · Terminology
1480	ON · Nest. Survey
1482	ON · Egg. Thin. · Heavy Metals · Pest. · PCB
1484	ON · Disturb. · Great Lakes · Manage. · Nest. Survey · Research · Status · Techniques
1567	ON · Pub. Ed. · Shooting · Status
1568	ON · Depred. · Nest. · Prey · Shooting
1920	ON · Disturb. · Habit. Loss · Manage. · Nest. Survey · Status
1921	ON · Nest. Fail. · Nest. Survey
1922	ON · Behav. · Disturb. · Fledging
1969	ON · Nest.
26	OR · AK · Depred. · Endang. Sp. · Life History · WA
51	OR · Disturb. · Habit. Use · Manage. · Nest. · USFS
268	OR · BC · CA · Nest. · Status · Winter. Pop. · WA
357	OR · Nest.
563	OR · CA · Nest. · Winter. Pop.
583	OR · Habit. Use · Manage. · Nest. Survey · Poison. · Prey · San Juan Is. · Shooting · Status · Winter Survey · WA
592	OR · Field ID · Hunt. Behav. · Prey
713	OR · Habit. Use · Life History
724	OR · Hunt. Behav.
761	OR · CA · Klamath · Paleontology
927	OR · Anat. · CA · FL · NE · NM · · Paleontology · Taxonomy
951	OR · Nest.
1002	OR · Habit. Loss · Shooting
1065	OR · Behav. · CA · Disturb. · Habit. Use · Klamath · Lower Klamath Lake NWR · Manage. · Prey · Tule Lake NWR · Winter Survey
1251	OR · Egg. Coll. · Nest.
1261	OR · History · Indian Culture
1311	OR · MT

Master No.	Keywords
1384	OR · Asper. · Nest. Survey · Road. Census · Techniques · Winter Survey
1430	OR · Disturb. · Egg Coll. · Nest.
1501	OR · Nest.
1572	OR · Habit. Loss · USFWS · WA
1723	OR · Law · Shooting
1839	OR · CA · ID · MT · Nest. Survey · NV · USFWS · WA
1843	OR · ID · Nest. Survey · USFWS · WA
1844	OR · CA · ID · Nest. Survey · NV · USFWS · WA
1853	OR · CA · ID · Nest. Survey · NV · USFWS · WA
1881	OR · Hunt. Behav. · Manage. · Nest. · Winter. Pop. · WA
1883	OR · Bear Valley NWR · Habit. Prot. · Refuge · USFWS
81	Paleontology · CA
187	Paleontology · CU
323	Paleontology · FL
761	Paleontology · CA · Klamath · OR
926	Paleontology · CA · Status
927	Paleontology · Anat. · CA · FL · NE · NM · OR · Taxonomy
928	Paleontology · NM
1111	Paleontology · CA · Santa Barbara Is.
1259	Paleontology · CA · Evolution · Taxonomy
1260	Paleontology · CA · Evolution · Taxonomy
1962	Paleontology · MI
431	Parasites · AK · Behav. · Climatology · Disease · Kodiak NWR · Life History · Marking · Nest. · Nest. Survey · Reprod. Succ. · Techniques · Terminology
459	Parasites · Autopsy · AK · CN · Disease · Lower 48 · Poison. · Shooting · Trapping
483	Parasites
723	Parasites
1060	Parasites · Disease
561	Parent. Behav. · Behav. · Fledging · Habit. Use · Marking · MN · Techniques · Telemetry
727	Parent. Behav. · Behav. · Nestling · SK
731	Parent. Behav. · Behav. · Disturb. · Nestling · SK
880	Parent. Behav. · Behav. · Life History · Nest. · Nestling · OH · Photo. · Techniques

Master No.	Keywords
886	**Parent. Behav.** · Breed. Behav. · Intersp. Behav. · Life History · Nest. · OH · Prey
888	**Parent. Behav.** · Behav. · Fledging · Intersp. Behav. · Life History · Nest. · OH · Photo. · Prey
541	**Pellets** · Biochem. · Digest. · Prey
50	**Pest.** · Egg. Thin. · FL · LA · Status · TX
135	**Pest.** · PCB
140	**Pest.** · AK · DDT · FL · ME · Reprod. Succ. · WI
269	**Pest.** · Autopsy · FL · Heavy Metals · Midwest Region · MD · ME · MO · ND · PCB
294	**Pest.** · Egg. Thin. · PCB
332	**Pest.** · Band. · FL · ON · Pub. Ed. · Reprod. Succ. · Techniques
333	**Pest.** · DDT · FL · Nest. Fail. · Red Tide
335	**Pest.** · DDT · FL · Nest. Fail. · Status
341	**Pest.** · ME · Nest. Survey · Reprod. Succ.
371	**Pest.** · Reprod. Succ.
372	**Pest.** · Autopsy · AK · Cont. U.S. · DDT · NB · Residues · Toxicol.
432	**Pest.** · Behav. · Captivity · DDT · Toxicol.
473	**Pest.** · CO · Disturb. · Field ID · Habit. Loss · Manage. · Nest. · Pub. Ed. · Winter. Pop.
482	**Pest.** · Autopsy · Dieldrin · Disease · Electro. · Lower 48 · Poison. · PCB · Shooting
501	**Pest.** · DDT · Status
524	**Pest.** · DDT · Toxicol. · USFWS
525	**Pest.** · DDT · Toxicol. · USFWS
526	**Pest.** · Channel Is. · CA
528	**Pest.** · Anal. Tech. · Blood · Dieldrin · Heavy Metals
535	**Pest.** · CT · Egg Coll. · Endang. Sp. · Habit. Loss · Nest. · PCB · Shooting · Status
550	**Pest.** · Band. · Breed. Behav. · Dieldrin · DDT · MN · Pest. Residues · Prey · Techniques · Telemetry
565	**Pest.** · FL · ME · NJ · Toxicol.
567	**Pest.** · PCB · USFWS
709	**Pest.** · CN · Status
756	**Pest.** · Band. · Egg Trans. · Manage. · ME · Nest. Survey · PCB · Refuge · Techniques · Winter Survey
779	**Pest.** · Egg. Thin. · Heavy Metals · ON · PCB · Reprod. Succ. · Status
783	**Pest.** · Disturb. · Egg. Thin. · Heavy Metals · Nest. Survey · ON · PCB · Reprod. Succ. · Status
786	**Pest.** · Behav. · Distrib. · Hunt. Behav. · Manage. · Marking · Migration Mortality · MO · Nest. · Prey · Swan Lake NWR · Techniques · Telemetry
804	**Pest.** · Art. Nest Site · AZ · Egg. Thin. · Habit. Use · Life History · Manage. · Marking · Nest. · Research · Techniques · Telemetry · Winter. Pop.
806	**Pest.** · DDT · Law
831	**Pest.** · BC · Disturb. · Helicop. · Nest. Survey · Refuge
874	**Pest.** · Dioxins
984	**Pest.** · Captivity · Egg Trans. · Heavy Metals · Law · Manage. · Migration · Nest. Survey · Pub. Ed. · Status · Techniques · Territory · Young Trans.
1027	**Pest.**
1064	**Pest.** · FL · Heavy Metals · ME · Nest. · PCB · Reprod. Succ. · WI
1126	**Pest.** · DDT · Histology · Phys. · Spermato. · Techniques
1127	**Pest.** · Disease · Fowl Cholera · Heavy Metals · OH
1242	**Pest.** · History · Nest. Survey · NJ · Status
1253	**Pest.** · Behav. · Hacking · Heavy Metals · Intrasp. Behav. · Marking · Montezuma NWR · MI · MN · NY · Techniques · Telemetry · Young Trans.
1256	**Pest.** · Behav. · Hacking · Manage. · NY · Prey · PCB · Techniques · Young Trans.
1292	**Pest.** · Autopsy · Disease · Electro. · Lead Poison. · Shooting
1314	**Pest.** · Electro. · Law · NAS · Poison. · Pub. Ed. · Shooting · Status
1317	**Pest.** · Law · Life History · NWF · Pub. Ed. · Status
1360	**Pest.** · Habit. Loss · Nest. Survey · Shooting · Techniques · Terminology · USFWS

Master No.	Keywords
1369	**Pest.** · Behav. · Habit. Use · Heavy Metals · Hunt. Behav. · Intersp. Behav. · Intrasp. Behav. · Manage. · NY · Prey · PCB · Winter Survey
1410	**Pest.** · Egg. Thin.
1464	**Pest.** · Egg. Thin.
1482	**Pest.** · Egg. Thin. · Heavy Metals · ON · PCB
1487	**Pest.** · Band. · Disturb. · Great Lakes · MI · Nest. Survey · Techniques
1511	**Pest.** · Behav. · Habit. Use · Heavy Metals · Nest. · NY · PCB
1517	**Pest.** · PCB · USFWS
1518	**Pest.** · Autopsy · CT · FL
1542	**Pest.** · History · Pub. Ed.
1627	**Pest.** · Endang. Sp. · Nest. · OH · Status
1640	**Pest.** · Aggress. · Behav. · BLM · Disturb. · Habit. Loss · Habit. Use · Hunt. Behav. · Life History · Manage. · Nest. · Prey · Shooting · Territory
1679	**Pest.** · Egg. Thin. · Status
1688	**Pest.** · Ches. Bay · Kepone · Techniques
1706	**Pest.**
1707	**Pest.** · Spermato. · Toxicol.
1708	**Pest.** · AK · Histology · Lower 48 · Spermato. · Techniques · Toxicol. · USFWS
1709	**Pest.** · FL · ME · MO · NJ · Toxicol. · USFWS
1710	**Pest.** · Mortality · Toxicol.
1711	**Pest.** · Egg · Techniques
1712	**Pest.** · Autopsy · Mortality · Toxicol.
1751	**Pest.** · Egg. Thin. · Habit. Use · Manage. · MD · Nest. Survey
1752	**Pest.** · Egg. Thin. · Habit. Use · Manage. · MD · Nest. Survey · Techniques
1753	**Pest.**
1830	**Pest.** · DDT · Toxicol.
1833	**Pest.** · USFWS
1871	**Pest.** · Egg Trans. · Hacking · Manage. · ME · MN · NY · PCB · Techniques · WI · Young Trans.
1942	**Pest.** · AK · Egg. Thin. · FL · Great Lakes · Heavy Metals · ME · PCB
1943	**Pest.** · Dieldrin · ME · Prey · PCB
1979	**Pest.**
1980	**Pest.**
550	**Pest. Residues** · Band. · Breed. Behav. · Dieldrin · DDT · MN · Pest. · Prey · Techniques · Telemetry
558	**Pest. Residues** · Biopsy · MN · PCB · Techniques
609	**Pest. Residues** · Behav. · Habit. Use · Mississippi R · MN · Prey · Winter Survey
88	**Photo.** · Growth · MD · Nest. · Plumage
91	**Photo.** · Growth · Plumage
198	**Photo.** · Flight
215	**Photo.** · Egg Coll. · Habit. Use · Nest. · VA
302	**Photo.** · MA · Winter. Pop.
361	**Photo.** · Behav. · Disturb. · Nest. · ND
418	**Photo.** · ME
557	**Photo.** · Chippewa NF · Disturb. · Life History · Migration · Nest. · Pub. Ed. · Status · Techniques · Telemetry · Winter. Pop.
574	**Photo.** · Band. · Behav. · Growth · Nest. · Pub. Ed. · Techniques
575	**Photo.** · Behav. · Growth · Nest. · Prey · Pub. Ed.
576	**Photo.** · Band. · Behav. · Pub. Ed. · Status · Techniques
578	**Photo.** · Aggress. · Band. · Behav. · Mortality · Nest. · Pub. Ed. · Techniques
662	**Photo.** · AK · Bounty · Growth · Law · Shooting
767	**Photo.** · Autumn Conc. · AK · Chilkat R · Hunt. Behav. · Indian Culture · Pub. Ed.
803	**Photo.** · Habit. Use · Life History · Nest. · Pub. Ed. · Winter. Pop. · WA
879	**Photo.** · Intersp. Behav. · Nest. · OH
880	**Photo.** · Behav. · Life History · Nest. · Nestling · OH · Parent. Behav. · Techniques
884	**Photo.** · Behav. · History · Nest. · OH · Techniques
887	**Photo.** · Behav. · Life History · Nest. · OH · Techniques
888	**Photo.** · Behav. · Fledging · Intersp. Behav. · Life History · Nest. · OH · Parent. Behav. · Prey
889	**Photo.** · Behav. · Life History · Nest. · OH · Techniques
900	**Photo.** · AZ · Nest. · Techniques
914	**Photo.** · Nest. · NC
1034	**Photo.** · Hacking · Manage. · NY · Techniques
1088	**Photo.** · Life History
1343	**Photo.** · Intersp. Behav. · Techniques

Master No.	Keywords
1739	**Photo.** · History · MA · Winter. Pop.
1740	**Photo.** · MA · Winter. Pop.
1805	**Photo.** · Behav. · FL · History · Status
1806	**Photo.** · Behav. · Everglades NP · Nest.
1807	**Photo.** · Behav. · FL · Intersp. Behav. · Life History
1126	**Phys.** · DDT · Histology · Pest. · Spermato. · Techniques
131	**Platte R** · NE · Winter Survey
348	**Platte R** · NE · Winter Survey
1047	**Platte R** · NE · Winter. Pop.
1338	**Platte R** · NE · Winter Survey
1339	**Platte R** · NE · Winter Survey
1340	**Platte R** · NE · Winter Survey
1608	**Platte R** · Habit. Use · NE · Winter Survey
1802	**Platte R** · NE · Winter Survey
1895	**Platte R** · Behav. · Habit. Use · Hunt. Behav. · Intrasp. Behav. · Migration · NE · Winter Survey
1913	**Platte R** · NE · Winter. Pop.
1915	**Platte R** · Behav. · Migration · NE · Prey · Winter Survey
1984	**Platte R** · Habit. Use · Snake R · Winter Survey · WY
1985	**Platte R** · Habit. Use · Snake R · Winter Survey · WY
62	**Plumage** · Folklore · Growth · Hunt. Behav. · Indian Culture · Life History
88	**Plumage** · Growth · MD · Nest. · Photo.
91	**Plumage** · Growth · Photo.
94	**Plumage** · Art · Broley · Field ID · Pub. Ed.
191	**Plumage** · Anat. · Growth · Taxonomy
211	**Plumage** · Anat. · Distrib. · Nest. · NM · Prey · Winter. Pop.
221	**Plumage** · Anat. · Distrib. · Nest. · Taxonomy
249	**Plumage** · Anat. · Distrib. · Life History · MI · Status
322	**Plumage** · Anat. · FL · Weight
426	**Plumage** · Anat.
453	**Plumage** · Growth
468	**Plumage** · Life History · Missouri R · Taxonomy
477	**Plumage** · Growth · GA · Molt.
487	**Plumage** · Depred. · Shooting · WV
498	**Plumage** · Distrib. · Egg · Nest.
701	**Plumage** · Anat. · Distrib. · Life History
711	**Plumage** · AK · Distrib. · Habit. Use · Life History · Status
714	**Plumage** · Distrib. · Habit. Use · Nest. · Shooting · Taxonomy · TN · Winter. Pop.
740	**Plumage** · Life History
797	**Plumage** · Anat. · Behav. · Field ID · Taxonomy
827	**Plumage** · Barkley Sound · Behav. · BC · Disturb. · Gulf Is. · Helicop. · Nest. Survey · Prey
865	**Plumage** · Anat. · Evolution
917	**Plumage** · Anat. · Field ID
966	**Plumage** · Captive Breed.
976	**Plumage** · Aggress. · Anat. · Bounty · Distrib. · Econ. Import. · Law · Life History · Prey · Status · Taxonomy
1084	**Plumage** · Anat. · Hunt. Behav. · Life History · Migration · Nest.
1297	**Plumage** · Aleutian Is. · AK · Band. · Distrib. · Econ. Import. · Nest. · Prey · Shooting · Techniques
1372	**Plumage** · Anat. · Distrib. · Habit. Use · Nest. · Taxonomy · TX · Winter. Pop.
1527	**Plumage** · Life History
1591	**Plumage** · Behav. · Climatology · Disturb. · Habit. Use · Intrasp. Behav. · Prey · Skagit R · Winter Survey · WA
1606	**Plumage** · Aggress. · Aleutian Is. · AK · Behav. · Depred. · Habit. Use · Life History · Mortality · Nest. Survey · Prey · Reprod. Succ. · Status · Winter Survey
1651	**Plumage** · Anat. · Behav. · Capture · Hunt. Behav. · IL · Marking · Prey · Techniques · Telemetry · Winter Survey
1736	**Plumage** · Life History · Taxonomy
1891	**Plumage** · Dispersal · Migration
1907	**Plumage** · Anat. · AK · Bounty · Nest. · Status
1960	**Plumage** · Falconry
65	**Poetry** · Captivity
240	**Poetry**
350	**Poetry** · Behav. · Life History
405	**Poetry** · Aircraft
429	**Poetry** · Aggress. · History · Hunt. Behav. · Life History · Nest. · PA · Shooting · Status · Susquehanna R
448	**Poetry** · History

Master No.	Keywords
680	**Poetry** · Nest.
748	**Poetry** · Captivity
808	**Poetry** · Behav. · Flight
1417	**Poetry** · Life History
1540	**Poetry**
1784	**Poetry** · Life History
1808	**Poetry** · Field ID · Life History · Nest. · NS
137	**Poison.** · Law · Pred. Cont.
141	**Poison.** · Jackson's Canyon · WY
142	**Poison.** · Shooting · Winter. Pop. · WY
390	**Poison.** · Endang. Sp. · Pred. Cont. · Status
397	**Poison.** · Jackson's Canyon · Law · NAS · WY
398	**Poison.** · Jackson's Canyon · Law · Shooting · WY
400	**Poison.** · MT · Nest. · Shooting
459	**Poison.** · Autopsy · AK · CN · Disease · Lower 48 · Parasites · Shooting · Trapping
482	**Poison.** · Autopsy · Dieldrin · Disease · Electro. · Lower 48 · Pest. · PCB · Shooting
496	**Poison.** · Climatology · Migration · OH · Shooting · Winter Survey
497	**Poison.** · Behav. · Egg · Nest. · OH · Prey · Shooting
499	**Poison.** · Law · Manage. · Nest. · Pub. Ed. · Shooting · SK · Trapping
583	**Poison.** · Habit. Use · Manage. · Nest. Survey · OR · Prey · San Juan Is. · Shooting · Status · Winter Survey · WA
1041	**Poison.** · Aleutian Is. · Amchitka Is. · AK · Nest. · Prey
1137	**Poison.** · Band. · Prey · Pub. Ed. · Techniques · Winter Survey · WY
1139	**Poison.** · Channel Is. · CA · Disturb. · Egg Coll. · Pop. Turnover · · Shooting
1200	**Poison.** · Chippewa NF · Disturb. · MN · ND · Pub. Ed. · Shooting · Status · USFS
1314	**Poison.** · Electro. · Law · NAS · Pest. · Pub. Ed. · Shooting · Status
1543	**Poison.** · Depred. · Law · Shooting · WY
1573	**Poison.** · CO · Pub. Ed. · Shooting · WY
1574	**Poison.** · CO · Pub. Ed. · Shooting · WY
1694	**Poison.** · Autopsy · WY
1873	**Poison.** · Heavy Metals · IL · Lead Poison.

Master No.	Keywords
1139	**Pop. Turnover** · Channel Is. · CA · Disturb. · Egg Coll. · Poison. · Shooting
1741	**Pop. Turnover** · Disturb. · Habit. Use · Manage. · MT · Nest. Survey · Reprod. Succ. · Status · Territory · Yellowstone NP
137	**Pred. Cont.** · Law · Poison.
390	**Pred. Cont.** · Endang. Sp. · Poison. · Status
1300	**Pred. Cont.** · Depred. · Manage. · Prey
108	**Prey** · Aggress. · Band. · Broley · Status · Techniques
148	**Prey** · Anat. · Autumn Conc. · FL · Glacier NP · Manage. · Merritt Is. NWR · Museum Specimen · MT · Nest. · Taxonomy
181	**Prey** · ME · Nest. · Winter. Pop.
192	**Prey** · Hunt. Behav. · Intersp. Behav. · Life History
208	**Prey** · IA · Nest. · Winter. Pop.
211	**Prey** · Anat. · Distrib. · Nest. · NM · Plumage · Winter. Pop.
214	**Prey** · Egg Coll. · Nest. · VA
226	**Prey** · Intersp. Behav. · SC
235	**Prey** · Animal Dam. · AK · Bounty · Law
250	**Prey** · FL · Hunt. Behav. · Intersp. Behav. · Shooting
258	**Prey** · Anat. · Nest. · NY · Status · Winter. Pop.
260	**Prey** · Folklore · PA · Status · Taxonomy
266	**Prey** · Anat. · Behav. · BC · Distrib. · Falconry · Field ID · Flight · Habit. Use · Migration · Nest. · Status
271	**Prey** · Nest. · ON
282	**Prey** · AL · Depred.
306	**Prey** · Intersp. Behav. · MN
309	**Prey** · Hunt. Behav. · Shooting · VA · Winter. Pop.
324	**Prey** · Band. · FL · Life History · Migration · Nest. Fail. · Nest. Survey · Status · Techniques
325	**Prey** · Behav. · Dispersal · Disturb. · FL · Habit. Use · Intersp. Behav. · Migration · Mortality · Nest.
342	**Prey** · BC · Econ. Import. · Hunt. Behav. · Shooting
351	**Prey** · Migration · Nest. · Reprod. Succ. · Status

Master No.	Keywords
352	**Prey** · Behav. · Flight · Life History · Migration · Nest. · Pub. Ed. · Status · Taxonomy
401	**Prey** · BC · Hunt. Behav. · Intersp. Behav.
416	**Prey** · Depred. · Folklore · Pub. Ed.
421	**Prey** · Capture · Folklore · Nest. · Techniques · TN
425	**Prey** · Econ. Import.
446	**Prey** · Econ. Import. · Law · Life History · Manage. · MO · Nest. · Pub. Ed. · Shooting
447	**Prey** · Behav. · CA · Disturb. · Hunt. Behav. · Manage. · Natl. For. · San Bernardino Mts. · USFS · Winter. Pop.
457	**Prey** · Hudson Bay · Intersp. Behav. · MB · Nest.
463	**Prey** · Hunt. Behav. · Life History
470	**Prey** · Depred. · MA
472	**Prey** · AK · Econ. Import.
478	**Prey** · Hunt. Behav. · Winter. Pop. · WI
484	**Prey** · AK · Chilkat R · Shooting · Winter Survey
489	**Prey** · AK · Habit. Use · Indian Culture
490	**Prey** · AK · Hunt. Behav.
497	**Prey** · Behav. · Egg · Nest. · OH · Poison. · Shooting
503	**Prey** · Habit. Prot. · Nat. Conserv. · Refuge · Skagit R Nat. Area · WA
514	**Prey** · Hunt. Behav. · IN · Nest.
519	**Prey** · CA · Depred. · Habit. Use · Manage. · Mortality · Nest. · Shasta-Trinity NF · Winter Survey
531	**Prey** · Aging · AK · Behav. · Hunt. Behav. · Life History · Nest. · Sexing · Techniques
539	**Prey** · LA · Nest. Survey
541	**Prey** · Biochem. · Digest. · Pellets
542	**Prey** · Digest.
550	**Prey** · Band. · Breed. Behav. · Dieldrin · DDT · MN · Pest. · Pest. Residues · Techniques · Telemetry
555	**Prey** · Behav. · Breed. Behav. · Chippewa NF · Disturb. · Fledging · Marking · MN · Nestling · Reprod. Succ. · Techniques · Telemetry
556	**Prey** · Cedar Glen Roost · Habit. Prot. · Habit. Use · IL · Manage. · Refuge
562	**Prey** · MN
564	**Prey** · RI · Winter. Pop.
575	**Prey** · Behav. · Growth · Nest. · Photo. · Pub. Ed.
583	**Prey** · Habit. Use · Manage. · Nest. Survey · OR · Poison. · San Juan Is. · Shooting · Status · Winter Survey · WA
592	**Prey** · Field ID · Hunt. Behav. · OR
601	**Prey** · CO · Winter. Pop.
604	**Prey** · Intersp. Behav. · NS · Winter. Pop.
608	**Prey** · Distrib. · Electro. · Field ID · Life History · UT · Winter. Pop.
609	**Prey** · Behav. · Habit. Use · Mississippi R · MN · Pest. Residues · Winter Survey
612	**Prey** · FL · Nest.
664	**Prey** · Anat. · Econ. Import. · Hunt. Behav. · Life History
682	**Prey** · CA · Disturb. · Klamath NF · Manage. · Nest. · Status · Winter. Pop.
706	**Prey** · Hunt. Behav. · MN · Winter. Pop.
718	**Prey** · Nest. · TN · Winter. Pop.
719	**Prey** · Tennessee NWR · Winter Survey
720	**Prey** · AK · Intersp. Behav. · Karluk L
737	**Prey** · AK · Depred. · Nest. · Shooting
738	**Prey** · CA · Depred. · Hunt. Behav.
744	**Prey** · Hunt. Behav. · Nest. · NS
786	**Prey** · Behav. · Distrib. · Hunt. Behav. · Manage. · Marking · Migration · Mortality · MO · Nest. · Pest. · Swan Lake NWR · Techniques · Telemetry
796	**Prey** · Hunt. Behav. · MA · Nest. · Winter. Pop.
826	**Prey** · BC · Gulf Is. · Habit. Use · Migration · Nest. Survey · San Juan Is. · Techniques · Winter Survey · WA
827	**Prey** · Barkley Sound · Behav. · BC · Disturb. · Gulf Is. · Helicop. · Nest. Survey · Plumage
833	**Prey** · BC · Hunt. Behav. · Intersp. Behav. · Intrasp. Behav. · Nest. Survey · Territory
836	**Prey** · Behav. · Disturb. · Habit. Loss · Habit. Use · Hunt. Behav. · Logging · Manage. · Winter Survey · WA
838	**Prey** · Hunt. Behav. · IA · Mississippi R · Winter. Pop.

Master No.	Keywords
845	Prey · KS · Missouri R · Nest. · Winter. Pop.
848	Prey · Hunt. Behav.
854	Prey
856	Prey · Hunt. Behav.
859	Prey · Hunt. Behav. · Intersp. Behav. · WA
860	Prey · GA · Nest. · Okefinokee Swamp
861	Prey · GA · Hunt. Behav.
863	Prey · AK · Habit. Use · Hunt. Behav. · Nest. Survey · Status
883	Prey · Behav. · Fledging · Hunt. Behav. · Life History · Nest. · OH
886	Prey · Breed. Behav. · Intersp. Behav. · Life History · Nest. · OH · Parent. Behav.
888	Prey · Behav. · Fledging · Intersp. Behav. · Life History · Nest. · OH · Parent. Behav. · Photo.
890	Prey · Great Lakes · L Erie · Pub. Ed. · Status
891	Prey · Behav. · Life History · Nest. · OH
892	Prey · Hunt. Behav. · IA · Mississippi R · Winter. Pop.
911	Prey · SC
916	Prey · Hunt. Behav. · MN
920	Prey · Hunt. Behav. · MT
934	Prey · AL · Nest. · Shooting · TN · Winter. Pop.
973	Prey · AL · Nest. · Winter. Pop.
974	Prey · Captivity · KS · Winter. Pop.
975	Prey · KS · Winter. Pop.
976	Prey · Aggress. · Anat. · Bounty · Distrib. · Econ. Import. · Law · Life History · Plumage · Status · Taxonomy
1011	Prey · Behav. · Climatology · Habit. Use · Hunt. Behav. · Intersp. Behav. · Intrasp. Behav. · IA · IL · Mississippi R · MO · Winter Survey
1018	Prey · Chippewa NF · Disturb. · Habit. Use · Manage. · MN · Nest. · Reprod. Succ.
1021	Prey · GA · Hunt. Behav. · Sapelo Is.
1025	Prey · Aggress. · Econ. Import. · Field ID · Law · Life History
1040	Prey · CA · Hunt. Behav. · San Bernardino Mts.
1041	Prey · Aleutian Is. · Amchitka Is. · AK · Nest. · Poison.
1042	Prey · Aleutian Is. · AK · Hunt. Behav. · Nest. · Status
1062	Prey · Hunt. Behav. · MN
1063	Prey · Behav. · Disturb. · Habit. Loss · Habit. Use · Manage. · Research · TX · Winter Survey
1065	Prey · Behav. · CA · Disturb. · Habit. Use · Klamath · Lower Klamath Lake NWR · Manage. · OR · Tule Lake NWR · Winter Survey
1066	Prey · Aleutian Is. · Amchitka Is. · AK · Nest.
1102	Prey · Behav. · Caledon SP · Disturb. · Habit. Loss · Habit. Use · Manage. · Nest. · VA
1105	Prey · MI
1109	Prey · Behav. · Habit. Loss · Habit. Use · Intersp. Behav. · Intrasp. Behav. · ID · Manage. · Winter Survey · Wolf Lodge Bay
1110	Prey · CA · Depred. · Habit. Use · San Clemente Is.
1112	Prey · Autopsy · Disturb. · Habit. Use · Hunt. Behav. · Intersp. Behav. · Manage. · Migration · OK · Salt Fork R · Shooting · Status · Taxonomy · Winter Survey
1113	Prey · Hunt. Behav. · Intrasp. Behav. · Migration · Neosho R · OK · Winter Survey
1115	Prey · Disturb. · Habit. Use · Manage. · Migration · OK · Salt Fork R · Salt Plains NWR · Sequoyah NWR · Shooting · Status · Taxonomy · Wichita Mts. NWR · Winter Survey
1121	Prey · Behav. · Manage. · NE · Status · Winter Survey
1137	Prey · Band. · Poison. · Pub. Ed. · Techniques · Winter Survey · WY
1160	Prey · CA · Distrib. · Life History · Nest. · Pub. Ed. · Winter. Pop.
1187	Prey · Habit. Use · Life History · Nest. Survey · Winter Survey · WA
1226	Prey · Econ. Import. · Life History · Pub. Ed. · Status
1227	Prey · Field ID · Life History
1228	Prey · Glacier NP · Hunt. Behav. · Intersp. Behav. · MN · Winter Survey
1234	Prey · Egg. Thin. · FL · Habit. Use · Nest. Survey · Ocala NF · Reprod. Succ.

Master No.	Keywords
1235	**Prey** · Hunt. Behav. · Intrasp. Behav. · LA · Nest. · Winter. Pop.
1256	**Prey** · Behav. · Hacking · Manage. · NY · Pest. · PCB · Techniques · Young Trans.
1294	**Prey** · BC · Hunt. Behav. · Intersp. Behav. · Nest.
1296	**Prey** · Aleutian Is. · AK · Econ. Import.
1297	**Prey** · Aleutian Is. · AK · Band. · Distrib. · Econ. Import. · Nest. · Plumage · Shooting · Techniques
1300	**Prey** · Depred. · Manage. · Pred. Cont.
1304	**Prey** · IL · Shooting · Winter Survey
1336	**Prey** · Behav. · Manage. · NE · Status · Winter Survey
1355	**Prey** · Hunt. Behav. · Territory · Winter. Pop.
1361	**Prey** · FL · Hunt. Behav.
1368	**Prey** · Behav. · Climatology · Disturb. · Habit. Use · Hunt. Behav. · Intersp. Behav. · Intrasp. Behav. · Manage. · NY · Winter Survey
1369	**Prey** · Behav. · Habit. Use · Heavy Metals · Hunt. Behav. · Intersp. Behav. · Intrasp. Behav. · Manage. · NY · Pest. · PCB · Winter Survey
1370	**Prey** · Econ. Import. · Life History · Shooting
1373	**Prey** · AK · Hunt. Behav.
1391	**Prey** · Hunt. Behav. · Migration · ME · Winter Survey
1395	**Prey** · Folklore
1416	**Prey** · FL · Hunt. Behav. · Life History · Nest.
1448	**Prey** · Band. · FL · Migration · Techniques
1469	**Prey** · UT · Winter Survey
1470	**Prey** · Behav. · Habit. Use · Hunt. Behav. · UT · Winter Survey
1472	**Prey** · Hunt. Behav.
1476	**Prey** · Hunt. Behav. · MI · Winter Survey
1502	**Prey** · BC · Intersp. Behav.
1521	**Prey** · Aggress. · Behav. · Disturb. · Habit. Loss · Hunt. Behav. · Nest. · San Juan Is. · Shooting · Status · Vocal. · WA
1522	**Prey** · San Juan Is. · WA
1537	**Prey** · Hunt. Behav. · Life History · Migration · MN · Nest. · Shooting · Status · Winter. Pop.
1550	**Prey** · AZ · Behav. · Disturb. · Habit. Loss · Habit. Use · Hunt. Behav. · Nest. Survey · Status · Terminology · Territory
1565	**Prey** · History · Hunt. Behav.
1568	**Prey** · Depred. · Nest. · ON · Shooting
1583	**Prey** · Hunt. Behav. · Intrasp. Behav. · MA · Winter. Pop.
1591	**Prey** · Behav. · Climatology · Disturb. · Habit. Use · Intrasp. Behav. · Plumage · Skagit R · Winter Survey · WA
1598	**Prey** · Ground Nest. · MI
1602	**Prey** · Autumn Conc. · Glacier NP · Hunt. Behav. · MT
1605	**Prey** · Aleutian Is. · AK · Hunt. Behav.
1606	**Prey** · Aggress. · Aleutian Is. · AK · Behav. · Depred. · Habit. Use · Life History · Mortality · Nest. Survey · Plumage · Reprod. Succ. · Status · Winter Survey
1626	**Prey** · Hunt. Behav. · Hurricane · MD · Nest.
1634	**Prey** · Aggress. · Aleutian Is. · Amchitka Is. · AK · Disturb.
1636	**Prey** · CT · Folklore
1640	**Prey** · Aggress. · Behav. · BLM · Disturb. · Habit. Loss · Habit. Use · Hunt. Behav. · Life History · Manage. · Nest. · Pest. · Shooting · Territory
1642	**Prey** · Anat. · Dimorphism · Hunt. Behav.
1650	**Prey** · Capture · Habit. Use · Hunt. Behav. · Intersp. Behav. · IL · Marking · Mississippi R · Techniques · Winter Survey
1651	**Prey** · Anat. · Behav. · Capture · Hunt. Behav. · IL · Marking · Plumage · Techniques · Telemetry · Winter Survey
1652	**Prey** · IL · Mississippi R · Winter. Pop.
1655	**Prey** · Christmas Count · Lower 48 · Migration · Refuge · Winter. Pop.
1663	**Prey** · Nest. · Reelfoot L · TN
1682	**Prey** · Folklore
1684	**Prey** · Band. · Field ID · FL · Life History · Nest. · Status · Techniques
1696	**Prey** · Climatology · Ft. Randall D · Habit. Use · Hunt. Behav. · Karl Mundt NWR · L Andes NWR · Manage. · SD · Winter Survey

Master No.	Keywords
1697	**Prey** · Ft. Randall D · Habit. Loss · Habit. Use · Hunt. Behav. · Migration · SD · Winter Survey
1698	**Prey** · Climatology · Disturb. · Electro. · Habit. Use · Manage. · Winter Survey
1702	**Prey** · Acct. · Hunt. Behav. · Nest. · NC
1717	**Prey** · Folklore
1725	**Prey** · Folklore
1734	**Prey** · Habit. Use · Nest. · OK · Winter. Pop.
1743	**Prey** · Habit. Use · UT · Winter. Pop.
1745	**Prey** · MI · Nest. · Seney NWR
1749	**Prey** · CN · Econ. Import. · Field ID
1750	**Prey** · CN · Econ. Import. · Field ID · Life History
1771	**Prey** · CA · Disturb. · Habit. Loss · Habit. Use · Manage. · Nest. Survey · Shooting · Territory · Trapping
1812	**Prey** · Ches. Bay · DE · Econ. Import. · Habit. Use · Life History · MD · Nest. Survey · NC · NJ · PA · VA
1889	**Prey** · AK · Bounty · Econ. Import.
1901	**Prey** · Distrib. · DE · Life History · NJ · VA
1903	**Prey** · AK · Econ. Import.
1915	**Prey** · Behav. · Migration · NE · Platte R · Winter Survey
1931	**Prey** · Amchitka Is. · AK · Egg. Thin. · Habit. Use · Nest. Survey · Winter Survey
1943	**Prey** · Dieldrin · ME · Pest. · PCB
1958	**Prey** · CN · Distrib. · Hunt. Behav. · NY
1987	**Prey** · Econ. Import. · LB · Maritime Prov. · NF
1988	**Prey** · Anat. · Behav. · Capture · Depred. · Econ. Import. · Intersp. Behav. · Manage. · NB · Techniques
22	**Pub. Ed.** · Bombay Hook NWR · Distrib. · DE · Endang. Sp. · Field ID · Life History · Nest. · Nest. Survey · Status
28	**Pub. Ed.** · Life History · Taxonomy
29	**Pub. Ed.** · Econ. Import. · Life History
30	**Pub. Ed.** · Status
59	**Pub. Ed.** · Folklore · Life History · Old Abe
66	**Pub. Ed.** · AK · Bounty
67	**Pub. Ed.** · AK · Bounty
68	**Pub. Ed.** · AK · Bounty
69	**Pub. Ed.** · AK · Bounty · Law · Status
70	**Pub. Ed.** · AK · Bounty
73	**Pub. Ed.** · History · Status · Symbolism
74	**Pub. Ed.** · Life History
83	**Pub. Ed.** · History · Status · Symbolism
85	**Pub. Ed.** · History · Status
94	**Pub. Ed.** · Art · Broley · Field ID · Plumage
112	**Pub. Ed.** · History · Life History · Symbolism
118	**Pub. Ed.** · History · Symbolism
119	**Pub. Ed.** · Nest. Survey · NAS · Status · Winter Survey
127	**Pub. Ed.** · Manage. · Symbolism
130	**Pub. Ed.** · Captive Breed. · Life History · Status
133	**Pub. Ed.** · Life History · Nest. · NJ · Winter. Pop.
143	**Pub. Ed.** · FL · Manage. · Refuge
155	**Pub. Ed.** · MN · Rehab. · Techniques
164	**Pub. Ed.** · Law · Manage.
165	**Pub. Ed.** · History · Status
170	**Pub. Ed.** · Captive Breed. · Manage.
173	**Pub. Ed.** · AZ · Marking · Techniques · Verde R
174	**Pub. Ed.** · B.E. Nat. Area · Marking · Skagit R · Techniques · WA
183	**Pub. Ed.** · Acct. · AZ · Nest.
185	**Pub. Ed.** · Acct. · AZ · Nest. · Winter. Pop.
186	**Pub. Ed.** · Acct. · AZ · Endang. Sp. · Nest. · Winter. Pop.
194	**Pub. Ed.** · Life History · Status
229	**Pub. Ed.** · AK
230	**Pub. Ed.** · Mortality · Status
290	**Pub. Ed.** · Life History
297	**Pub. Ed.** · IL · Winter. Pop.
308	**Pub. Ed.** · Educ. Mat. · Field ID · Hawk Mt. · Migration · PA · Shooting
327	**Pub. Ed.** · Band. · FL · Habit. Loss · Intersp. Behav. · Nest. Fail. · Shooting · Status · Techniques
332	**Pub. Ed.** · Band. · FL · ON · Pest. · Reprod. Succ. · Techniques
339	**Pub. Ed.** · Band. · Broley · FL · Life History · Status · Techniques
347	**Pub. Ed.** · Bounty · Hawk Mt. · PA · Status
352	**Pub. Ed.** · Behav. · Flight · Life History · Migration · Nest. · Prey · Status · Taxonomy
354	**Pub. Ed.** · Manage. · NY

Master No.	Keywords
384	**Pub. Ed.** · History · Law · Life History
416	**Pub. Ed.** · Depred. · Folklore · Prey
423	**Pub. Ed.** · Mississippi R · Nest. · Reelfoot L · Shooting · Status · TN · Winter. Pop.
446	**Pub. Ed.** · Econ. Import. · Law · Life History · Manage. · MO · Nest. · Prey · Shooting
450	**Pub. Ed.** · Habit. Prot. · ME · Nest. Survey · RIC · Shooting · Status
473	**Pub. Ed.** · CO · Disturb. · Field ID · Habit. Loss · Manage. · Nest. · Pest. · Winter. Pop.
499	**Pub. Ed.** · Law · Manage. · Nest. · Poison. · Shooting · SK · Trapping
521	**Pub. Ed.** · Bounty · Law · Symbolism
522	**Pub. Ed.** · Bounty · Status
549	**Pub. Ed.** · Life History · Missouri R · SD · Winter Survey
557	**Pub. Ed.** · Chippewa NF · Disturb. · Life History · Migration · Nest. · Photo. · Status · Techniques · Telemetry · Winter. Pop.
573	**Pub. Ed.** · Habit. Prot. · Marking · Nest. · Techniques · Winter. Pop.
574	**Pub. Ed.** · Band. · Behav. · Growth · Nest. · Photo. · Techniques
575	**Pub. Ed.** · Behav. · Growth · Nest. · Photo. · Prey
576	**Pub. Ed.** · Band. · Behav. · Photo. · Status · Techniques
578	**Pub. Ed.** · Aggress. · Band. · Behav. · Mortality · Nest. · Photo. · Techniques
579	**Pub. Ed.** · Behav. · Nest. · Status
585	**Pub. Ed.**
588	**Pub. Ed.** · AK · Law
598	**Pub. Ed.** · Manage. · Shooting · Status
656	**Pub. Ed.** · FL
661	**Pub. Ed.** · Manage. · Nest. · NAS
663	**Pub. Ed.** · Captivity · DC · History
669	**Pub. Ed.** · CO · Field ID
675	**Pub. Ed.** · FL
678	**Pub. Ed.** · FL
681	**Pub. Ed.**
710	**Pub. Ed.** · Disturb. · Helicop.
730	**Pub. Ed.** · Band. · Migration · Status · SK · Techniques
755	**Pub. Ed.** · Disturb. · Manage. · ME · Nest. Survey · Shooting · Winter. Pop.
762	**Pub. Ed.** · IL · Winter. Pop.
763	**Pub. Ed.** · Life History · NC · Status
767	**Pub. Ed.** · Autumn Conc. · AK · Chilkat R · Hunt. Behav. · Indian Culture · Photo.
798	**Pub. Ed.** · Life History · Trapping
803	**Pub. Ed.** · Habit. Use · Life History · Nest. · Photo. · Winter. Pop. · WA
814	**Pub. Ed.** · Disturb. · Great Lakes · Manage. · Nest. Survey · Status · USFS
832	**Pub. Ed.** · BC · Intrasp. Behav. · Marking · Nest. Survey · Techniques · Territory
852	**Pub. Ed.** · Hunt-Wesson
853	**Pub. Ed.** · Anat. · Status
855	**Pub. Ed.** · Hawk Mt. · Migration · PA
857	**Pub. Ed.** · Life History · Status
870	**Pub. Ed.** · Disturb. · Life History
890	**Pub. Ed.** · Great Lakes · L Erie · Prey · Status
899	**Pub. Ed.** · Status
901	**Pub. Ed.**
908	**Pub. Ed.** · Life History
919	**Pub. Ed.** · AK · Bounty · Status
922	**Pub. Ed.** · Life History
981	**Pub. Ed.** · Endang. Sp. · Great Lakes · Nest. Survey · Status · USFS
982	**Pub. Ed.**
983	**Pub. Ed.** · Egg Trans. · Habit. Prot. · Nest. · Winter. Pop.
984	**Pub. Ed.** · Captivity · Egg Trans. · Heavy Metals · Law · Manage. · Migration · Nest. Survey · Pest. · Status · Techniques · Territory · Young Trans.
999	**Pub. Ed.** · Status
1009	**Pub. Ed.** · Folklore · History
1023	**Pub. Ed.** · FL
1046	**Pub. Ed.** · NWF · Status
1051	**Pub. Ed.** · Folklore · Life History · Status
1059	**Pub. Ed.** · Nest. · Winter. Pop. · WA
1087	**Pub. Ed.** · Habit. Prot. · Manage. · NWF · SD · Techniques · Winter. Pop. · Young Trans.
1089	**Pub. Ed.** · Nest. · NWF · Status · Winter. Pop.
1117	**Pub. Ed.** · Status
1129	**Pub. Ed.**
1135	**Pub. Ed.** · Law · Life History

Master No.	Keywords
1137	**Pub. Ed.** · Band. · Poison. · Prey · Techniques · Winter Survey · WY
1154	**Pub. Ed.** · CO
1160	**Pub. Ed.** · CA · Distrib. · Life History · Nest. · Prey · Winter. Pop.
1161	**Pub. Ed.** · Life History
1178	**Pub. Ed.** · Disturb. · Skagit R · WA
1180	**Pub. Ed.**
1200	**Pub. Ed.** · Chippewa NF · Disturb. · MN · ND · Poison. · Shooting · Status · USFS
1206	**Pub. Ed.** · Chippewa NF · Habit. Prot. · Hunt-Wesson · MN · USFS
1208	**Pub. Ed.** · Status
1210	**Pub. Ed.** · Child. Eagle Area · Hunt-Wesson · Refuge · USFS
1226	**Pub. Ed.** · Econ. Import. · Life History · Prey · Status
1230	**Pub. Ed.** · Children's Story
1231	**Pub. Ed.** · Status
1244	**Pub. Ed.** · Ches. Bay · Distrib. · Habit. Use · MD
1254	**Pub. Ed.** · Hacking · NY · Techniques · Young Trans.
1271	**Pub. Ed.** · ME · Young Trans.
1285	**Pub. Ed.** · Law · Shooting
1287	**Pub. Ed.**
1302	**Pub. Ed.** · Life History
1303	**Pub. Ed.** · Status
1314	**Pub. Ed.** · Electro. · Law · NAS · Pest. · Poison. · Shooting · Status
1317	**Pub. Ed.** · Law · Life History · NWF · Pest. · Status
1324	**Pub. Ed.** · NWF
1326	**Pub. Ed.** · NWF
1327	**Pub. Ed.** · NWF
1328	**Pub. Ed.** · Habit. Prot. · NWF · Research · RIC
1329	**Pub. Ed.** · NWF
1331	**Pub. Ed.** · NWF
1346	**Pub. Ed.** · Habit. Prot. · Manage. · NWF · Reward
1349	**Pub. Ed.** · Dispersal · FL · Life History · Migration · NAS · Status
1362	**Pub. Ed.** · Manage. · WI
1371	**Pub. Ed.** · Hunt. Behav. · Life History · LA · Taxonomy
1376	**Pub. Ed.** · Field ID · Nest. · OH · Status
1380	**Pub. Ed.** · BLM · Endang. Sp. · Manage.
1381	**Pub. Ed.** · Habit. Prot. · Manage.
1386	**Pub. Ed.** · Status
1388	**Pub. Ed.** · History · Nest. · SD · Winter. Pop.
1389	**Pub. Ed.** · Nest. · SD · Winter. Pop.
1393	**Pub. Ed.** · AK · Bounty · Law
1398	**Pub. Ed.** · Field ID · Life History
1402	**Pub. Ed.** · Reelfoot L · TN · Winter. Pop.
1414	**Pub. Ed.** · Egg Coll. · FL · Shooting
1419	**Pub. Ed.** · AK · Bounty · Law · NAS · Shooting
1427	**Pub. Ed.** · Law
1429	**Pub. Ed.** · History · Life History
1436	**Pub. Ed.** · Status
1444	**Pub. Ed.** · KY · Land Between the Lakes · TVA · Winter. Pop.
1452	**Pub. Ed.** · Folklore
1506	**Pub. Ed.** · Life History
1507	**Pub. Ed.**
1509	**Pub. Ed.** · RIC
1512	**Pub. Ed.** · Captivity · Status
1528	**Pub. Ed.** · Manage. · Status
1529	**Pub. Ed.** · AK · Habit. Use · Hunt. Behav. · Manage. · Status
1535	**Pub. Ed.** · Life History
1541	**Pub. Ed.** · Life History
1542	**Pub. Ed.** · History · Pest.
1544	**Pub. Ed.** · History · Status · Symbolism
1547	**Pub. Ed.** · Life History
1549	**Pub. Ed.** · Chippewa NF · Field ID · Life History · MN
1551	**Pub. Ed.** · Depred.
1553	**Pub. Ed.** · ID
1561	**Pub. Ed.** · History · Status
1564	**Pub. Ed.** · History · Symbolism
1567	**Pub. Ed.** · ON · Shooting · Status
1571	**Pub. Ed.** · Status
1573	**Pub. Ed.** · CO · Poison. · Shooting · WY
1574	**Pub. Ed.** · CO · Poison. · Shooting · WY
1576	**Pub. Ed.** · NV · Trapping
1577	**Pub. Ed.** · Law · Shooting · WY
1609	**Pub. Ed.** · NM · Winter. Pop.
1618	**Pub. Ed.** · Trapping · WY · Yellowstone NP
1621	**Pub. Ed.** · Life History
1633	**Pub. Ed.** · AZ
1656	**Pub. Ed.** · Band. · Migration · Techniques · Winter. Pop.
1683	**Pub. Ed.** · Field ID · Taxonomy
1685	**Pub. Ed.** · FL · Status
1703	**Pub. Ed.** · History
1718	**Pub. Ed.** · Status

Master No.	Keywords
1757	**Pub. Ed.** · Life History
1758	**Pub. Ed.** · Status
1779	**Pub. Ed.**
1780	**Pub. Ed.** · AK · Bounty
1781	**Pub. Ed.** · Status
1782	**Pub. Ed.** · Status
1783	**Pub. Ed.** · Status
1795	**Pub. Ed.** · Behav. · Habit. Use · Life History · Nest. · PA · Taxonomy
1810	**Pub. Ed.** · Depred. · Status
1811	**Pub. Ed.** · Behav. · Habit. Loss
1821	**Pub. Ed.** · Chippewa NF · Manage. · MN · USFS
1824	**Pub. Ed.** · Child. Eagle Area · Chippewa NF · Hunt-Wesson · Manage. · MN · Refuge · USFS
1826	**Pub. Ed.** · Chippewa NF · USFS
1875	**Pub. Ed.** · Marking · Techniques · USFWS
1890	**Pub. Ed.** · AK · Bounty · Status
1899	**Pub. Ed.** · Anat. · Art
1904	**Pub. Ed.** · Status
1905	**Pub. Ed.** · History · Life History · Status
1916	**Pub. Ed.** · Shooting
1917	**Pub. Ed.**
1925	**Pub. Ed.** · Art · Life History
1937	**Pub. Ed.** · History · Life History
1954	**Pub. Ed.** · AK · Hunt. Behav. · Law · Migration · Nest. · WY · Yellowstone NP
1955	**Pub. Ed.** · AK · Hunt. Behav. · Law · Migration · Nest. · WY · Yellowstone NP
1972	**Pub. Ed.** · History · Life History
1991	**Pub. Ed.** · TN · Winter Survey
1998	**Pub. Ed.** · Field ID
788	**Pymatuning** · Nest. · PA · Winter. Pop.
1387	**Pymatuning** · Nest. · PA
1446	**Pymatuning** · Cape May · Migration · NJ · PA · Winter. Pop.
92	**PA** · Art · History · Symbolism
147	**PA** · Hawk Mt. · Migration
260	**PA** · Folklore · Prey · Status · Taxonomy
261	**PA** · Manage. · Mt. Johnson Is. Sanct. · Nest. · Refuge · Shooting
262	**PA** · Mt. Johnson Is. Sanct. · Nest.
308	**PA** · Educ. Mat. · Field ID · Hawk Mt. · Migration · Pub. Ed. · Shooting
318	**PA** · Hawk Mt. · Migration
346	**PA** · Hawk Mt. · Migration

Master No.	Keywords
347	**PA** · Bounty · Hawk Mt. · Pub. Ed. · Status
419	**PA** · Acct.
429	**PA** · Aggress. · History · Hunt. Behav. · Life History · Nest. · Poetry · Shooting · Status · Susquehanna R
571	**PA** · Acct.
582	**PA** · Acct. · Intersp. Behav.
712	**PA** · CO · Hawk Mt. · Migration · Status
788	**PA** · Nest. · Pymatuning · Winter. Pop.
816	**PA** · Hunt. Behav. · Nest. · Terminology
839	**PA** · Nest.
855	**PA** · Hawk Mt. · Migration · Pub. Ed.
867	**PA** · Bake Oven Knob · Migration
868	**PA** · Bake Oven Knob · Migration
869	**PA** · Bake Oven Knob · Migration
882	**PA** · Aggress. · Behav. · Disturb. · Life History · Nest. · OH
905	**PA** · Acct. · Susquehanna R
954	**PA** · Egg Coll. · GA · Nest.
1037	**PA** · Mt. Johnson Is. Sanct. · Refuge
1093	**PA** · Migration
1162	**PA** · Nest.
1233	**PA** · Field ID · Hawk Mt. · Mt. Johnson Is. Sanct.
1263	**PA** · Nest.
1308	**PA** · Hawk Mt. · Migration · Status
1387	**PA** · Nest. · Pymatuning
1446	**PA** · Cape May · Migration · NJ · Pymatuning · Winter. Pop.
1471	**PA** · Migration · Nest.
1493	**PA** · Shooting
1494	**PA** · Mt. Johnson Is. Sanct. · Nest. · Refuge
1578	**PA** · DE · Great Lakes · MD · Nest. Survey · NJ · Status
1733	**PA** · Distrib. · Life History
1761	**PA** · Migration
1795	**PA** · Behav. · Habit. Use · Life History · Nest. · Pub. Ed. · Taxonomy
1812	**PA** · Ches. Bay · DE · Econ. Import. · Habit. Use · Life History · MD · Nest. Survey · NC · NJ · Prey · VA
135	**PCB** · Pest.
202	**PCB** · Anal. Tech. · AR · Mass Spectro. · MN · Residues · Techniques
269	**PCB** · Autopsy · FL · Heavy Metals · Midwest Region · MD · ME · MO · ND · Pest.
294	**PCB** · Egg. Thin. · Pest.

Master No.	Keywords
482	PCB · Autopsy · Dieldrin · Disease · Electro. · Lower 48 · Pest. · Poison. · Shooting
535	PCB · CT · Egg Coll. · Endang. Sp. · Habit. Loss · Nest. · Pest. · Shooting · Status
558	PCB · Biopsy · MN · Pest. Residues · Techniques
566	PCB · AK · FL · ME · MI · MN
567	PCB · Pest. · USFWS
739	PCB · CN · DDT · ON · SK
756	PCB · Band. · Egg Trans. · Manage. · ME · Nest. Survey · Pest. · Refuge · Techniques · Winter Survey
779	PCB · Egg. Thin. · Heavy Metals · ON · Pest. · Reprod. Succ. · Status
781	PCB · ON
783	PCB · Disturb. · Egg. Thin. · Heavy Metals · Nest. Survey · ON · Pest. · Reprod. Succ. · Status
1064	PCB · FL · Heavy Metals · ME · Nest. · Pest. · Reprod. Succ. · WI
1256	PCB · Behav. · Hacking · Manage. · NY · Pest. · Prey · Techniques · Young Trans.
1369	PCB · Behav. · Habit. Use · Heavy Metals · Hunt. Behav. · Intersp. Behav. · Intrasp. Behav. · Manage. · NY · Pest. · Prey · Winter Survey
1482	PCB · Egg. Thin. · Heavy Metals · ON · Pest.
1511	PCB · Behav. · Habit. Use · Heavy Metals · Nest. · NY · Pest.
1517	PCB · Pest. · USFWS
1700	PCB
1871	PCB · Egg Trans. · Hacking · Manage. · ME · MN · NY · Pest. · Techniques · WI · Young Trans.
1942	PCB · AK · Egg. Thin. · FL · Great Lakes · Heavy Metals · ME · Pest.
1943	PCB · Dieldrin · ME · Pest. · Prey
1713	PE · Nest. Survey · NB · NS · Reprod. Succ. · Winter Survey
1926	QU · LB · Nest. Survey · Status
545	Racoon Ridge · Migration · NJ
1882	Recovery Team · Endang. Sp.
333	Red Tide · DDT · FL · Nest. Fail. · Pest.
423	Reelfoot L · Mississippi R · Nest. · Pub. Ed. · Shooting · Status · TN · Winter. Pop.

Master No.	Keywords
596	Reelfoot L · Nest. · TN
715	Reelfoot L · AR · Habit. Use · Mississippi R · MS · Nest. · Shooting · TN
1097	Reelfoot L · TN · Winter Survey
1183	Reelfoot L · TN · Winter. Pop.
1402	Reelfoot L · Pub. Ed. · TN · Winter. Pop.
1462	Reelfoot L · Nest. · TN
1463	Reelfoot L · Nest. · TN · Winter. Pop.
1599	Reelfoot L · Nest. · TN
1663	Reelfoot L · Nest. · Prey · TN
122	Refuge · Disturb. · Law · Logging · Manage.
124	Refuge · Ches. Bay · Manage. · Mason Neck NWR · VA
128	Refuge · Habit. Prot. · Indian Culture · Manage. · MN · St. Croix R · WI
143	Refuge · FL · Manage. · Pub. Ed.
176	Refuge · Habit. Prot. · NWF · Southland · SD
261	Refuge · Manage. · Mt. Johnson Is. Sanct. · Nest. · PA · Shooting
399	Refuge · CA · Manage. · Three Sisters B.E. Pres. · USFS · Winter Survey
503	Refuge · Habit. Prot. · Nat. Conserv. · Prey · Skagit R Nat. Area · WA
511	Refuge · Ches. Bay · Endang. Sp. · Manage. · VA
512	Refuge · Ches. Bay · Manage. · Mason Neck NWR · VA
513	Refuge · Ches. Bay · DC · Manage. · Mason Neck NWR · VA
554	Refuge · Band. · Behav. · Cedar Glen Roost · IL · Migration · Mississippi R · MN · Techniques · Telemetry · TX · Winter. Pop.
556	Refuge · Cedar Glen Roost · Habit. Prot. · Habit. Use · IL · Manage. · Prey
672	Refuge · FL · Habit. Prot. · Three Lakes Ranch
674	Refuge · FL · Habit. Prot. · Three Lakes Ranch
702	Refuge · Habit. Prot. · Karl Mundt NWR · L Andes NWR · Manage. · Missouri R · NWF · SD · Winter. Pop.
703	Refuge · Habit. Prot. · Karl Mundt NWR · Missouri R · SD · Winter. Pop.

Master No.	Keywords
756	**Refuge** · Band. · Egg Trans. · Manage. · ME · Nest. Survey · Pest. · PCB · Techniques · Winter Survey
831	**Refuge** · BC · Disturb. · Helicop. · Nest. Survey · Pest.
871	**Refuge** · Disturb. · FL · Habit. Use · Kissimee B.E. Sanct. · Nest. Survey · Reprod. Succ.
872	**Refuge** · Disturb. · FL · Habit. Use · Kissimee B.E. Sanct. · Nest. Survey · Reprod. Succ.
998	**Refuge** · Habit. Prot. · Skagit R Nat. Area · Winter. Pop. · WA
1037	**Refuge** · Mt. Johnson Is. Sanct. · PA
1210	**Refuge** · Child. Eagle Area · Hunt-Wesson · Pub. Ed. · USFS
1215	**Refuge** · Chippewa NF · Manage. · MN · Nest. Survey · USFS
1322	**Refuge** · Ferry Bluff Sanct. · NWF · WI
1325	**Refuge** · Ferry Bluff Sanct. · NWF · WI
1330	**Refuge** · Ferry Bluff Sanct. · Habit. Prot. · NWF · Winter. Pop. · Wisconsin R · WI
1334	**Refuge** · Habit. Prot. · Manage. · Nat. Conserv. · Skagit R Nat. Area · Winter Survey · WA
1431	**Refuge** · Ferry Bluff Sanct. · Habit. Prot. · WI
1494	**Refuge** · Mt. Johnson Is. Sanct. · Nest. · PA
1655	**Refuge** · Christmas Count · Lower 48 · Migration · Prey · Winter. Pop.
1674	**Refuge** · Cont. B.E. Proj. · Manage. · Nest. Survey · NAS · Status · Winter Survey
1773	**Refuge** · Habit. Prot. · IL · Oak V. Eagle Sanct.
1824	**Refuge** · Child. Eagle Area · Chippewa NF · Hunt-Wesson · Manage. · MN · Pub. Ed. · USFS
1836	**Refuge** · Mason Neck NWR · VA
1883	**Refuge** · Bear Valley NWR · Habit. Prot. · OR · USFWS
150	**Rehab.** · Captive Breed. · Techniques
155	**Rehab.** · MN · Pub. Ed. · Techniques
299	**Rehab.** · CA · San Clemente Is. · Techniques
301	**Rehab.** · Disturb. · Habit. Use · IL · Nest. · Ohio R · Shooting · Techniques · Winter. Pop.
460	**Rehab.** · Asper. · Autopsy · Disease · MO · Techniques · Trapping
462	**Rehab.** · Techniques
504	**Rehab.** · CA · Hacking · Techniques
536	**Rehab.** · Captivity · Techniques
540	**Rehab.** · Falconry · MN · Techniques
670	**Rehab.** · Fla. B.E. Sur. Comm. · FL · Great Lakes · Reprod. Succ. · Status · Techniques · WI
694	**Rehab.** · Captive Breed. · Techniques · Telemetry
705	**Rehab.** · Disease · Shooting · Techniques · Trapping
787	**Rehab.** · MI · MO · Reintroduction Shooting · Swan Lake NWR · WI
847	**Rehab.** · Captive Breed. · Disease · FAS · FL · Techniques
1124	**Rehab.** · NE · Techniques
1147	**Rehab.** · Great Lakes · Habit. Prot. · Manage. · MB · Nest. Survey · ON · Techniques · Techniques
1151	**Rehab.** · FL · Techniques
1152	**Rehab.** · FL · Nest. Survey · Techniques
1177	**Rehab.** · SK · Techniques
1290	**Rehab.** · CA · Techniques
1335	**Rehab.** · NM · Techniques
1513	**Rehab.** · Disease · MN · Shooting · Techniques · Trapping
1563	**Rehab.** · Channel Is. · CA · Techniques · Telemetry
1594	**Rehab.** · Techniques · WA
1661	**Rehab.** · CA · Falconry · Techniques
1923	**Rehab.** · Captive Breed. · FL
787	**Reintroduction** · MI · MO · Rehab. · Shooting · Swan Lake NWR · WI
21	**Reprod. Succ.** · Ches. Bay · Mason Neck NWR · Nest. Survey
23	**Reprod. Succ.** · Nest. Survey · San Juan Is. · WA
43	**Reprod. Succ.** · Behav. · Evolution
140	**Reprod. Succ.** · AK · DDT · FL · ME · Pest. · WI
196	**Reprod. Succ.** · Distrib. · LA · Migration · Mortality · Nest. Survey · Shooting · Status · Winter Survey
332	**Reprod. Succ.** · Band. · FL · ON · Pest. · Pub. Ed. · Techniques
341	**Reprod. Succ.** · ME · Nest. Survey · Pest.
351	**Reprod. Succ.** · Migration · Nest. · Prey · Status
371	**Reprod. Succ.** · Pest.

Master No.	Keywords
431	**Reprod. Succ.** · AK · Behav. · Climatology · Disease · Kodiak NWR · Life History · Marking · Nest. · Nest. Survey · Parasites · Techniques · Terminology
466	**Reprod. Succ.** · AK · Climatology · Distrib. · Disturb. · Forestry · Habit. Loss · Habit. Use · Manage. · Nest. · Nest. Survey · Territory
537	**Reprod. Succ.** · Distrib. · LA · Nest. Survey
538	**Reprod. Succ.** · Distrib. · LA · Nest. Survey
555	**Reprod. Succ.** · Behav. · Breed. Behav. · Chippewa NF · Disturb. · Fledging · Marking · MN · Nestling · Prey · Techniques · Telemetry
560	**Reprod. Succ.** · Band. · Behav. · Life History · Migration · MN · Techniques
657	**Reprod. Succ.** · FL · Nest. Survey
670	**Reprod. Succ.** · Fla. B.E. Sur. Comm. · FL · Great Lakes · Rehab. · Status · Techniques · WI
673	**Reprod. Succ.** · FL · Habit. Use · Nest. Survey
676	**Reprod. Succ.** · FL · Nest. Survey
677	**Reprod. Succ.** · FL · Nest. Survey
695	**Reprod. Succ.** · Behav. · Chippewa NF · Disturb. · Logging · MN · Nest.
726	**Reprod. Succ.** · Habit. Use · MB · Status · SK · Techniques
728	**Reprod. Succ.** · Habit. Loss · Habit. Use · Manage. · McHargian Overlay · Nest. · SK · Techniques
729	**Reprod. Succ.** · Band. · SK · Techniques
772	**Reprod. Succ.** · Band. · Behav. · CN · ON · Techniques
774	**Reprod. Succ.** · Aggress. · Behav. · CN · Disturb. · ON
775	**Reprod. Succ.** · Nest. Survey · ON · Status · Territory
776	**Reprod. Succ.** · Nest. Survey · ON · Status · Territory
777	**Reprod. Succ.** · CN · Habit. Use · ON · Status · Techniques · Territory
778	**Reprod. Succ.** · Disturb. · MB · Nest. Survey · ON · Techniques
779	**Reprod. Succ.** · Egg. Thin. · Heavy Metals · ON · Pest. · PCB · Status
783	**Reprod. Succ.** · Disturb. · Egg. Thin. · Heavy Metals · Nest. Survey · ON · Pest. · PCB · Status
801	**Reprod. Succ.** · Disturb. · Nest. · Nest. Survey · Statistics · Territory · WA
805	**Reprod. Succ.** · Habit. Use · Nest. Survey · San Juan Is. · WA
871	**Reprod. Succ.** · Disturb. · FL · Habit. Use · Kissimee B.E. Sanct. · Nest. Survey · Refuge
872	**Reprod. Succ.** · Disturb. · FL · Habit. Use · Kissimee B.E. Sanct. · Nest. Survey · Refuge
878	**Reprod. Succ.** · AK · Disturb. · Habit. Use · Kodiak NWR · Life History · Nest. Fail. · Territory
945	**Reprod. Succ.** · Disturb. · FL · Habit. Loss · Nest. Fail. · Nest. Survey
1018	**Reprod. Succ.** · Chippewa NF · Disturb. · Habit. Use · Manage. · MN · Nest. · Prey
1031	**Reprod. Succ.** · MI · Nest. Survey
1032	**Reprod. Succ.** · MI · Nest. Survey
1064	**Reprod. Succ.** · FL · Heavy Metals · ME · Nest. · Pest. · PCB · WI
1106	**Reprod. Succ.** · MI · Nest. Survey · Status
1223	**Reprod. Succ.** · Band. · Chippewa NF · MN · Nest. Survey · Status · Superior NF · Techniques · Terminology
1234	**Reprod. Succ.** · Egg. Thin. · FL · Habit. Use · Nest. Survey · Ocala NF · Prey
1606	**Reprod. Succ.** · Aggress. · Aleutian Is. · AK · Behav. · Depred. · Habit. Use · Life History · Mortality · Nest. Survey · Plumage · Prey · Status · Winter Survey
1612	**Reprod. Succ.** · MN · Nest. Survey · Superior NF
1631	**Reprod. Succ.** · Distrib. · Nest. Survey · Status · TX · Winter Survey
1713	**Reprod. Succ.** · Nest. Survey · NB · NS · PE · Winter Survey
1741	**Reprod. Succ.** · Disturb. · Habit. Use · Manage. · MT · Nest. Survey · Pop. Turnover · Status · Territory · Yellowstone NP
1766	**Reprod. Succ.** · Acct. · Nest. Survey · TX
1767	**Reprod. Succ.** · Acct. · Nest. Survey · TX

Master No.	Keywords
1769	**Reprod. Succ.** · Band. · Nest. Survey · Techniques · TX · Winter Survey
1825	**Reprod. Succ.** · Aircraft · Chippewa NF · Great Lakes · MI · MN · Nest. Survey · Status · USFS · WI
1829	**Reprod. Succ.** · AK · Band. · Behav. · Kodiak NWR · Nest. Survey · Techniques
1850	**Reprod. Succ.** · AK · Lower 48 · Nest. Survey · USFWS
1885	**Reprod. Succ.** · Ches. Bay · Endang. Sp. · Status
1938	**Reprod. Succ.** · MB · Nest. Survey · SK
784	**Research** · Disturb.
804	**Research** · Art. Nest Site · AZ · Egg. Thin. · Habit. Use · Life History · Manage. · Marking · Nest. · Pest. · Techniques · Telemetry · Winter. Pop.
1063	**Research** · Behav. · Disturb. · Habit. Loss · Habit. Use · Manage. · Prey · TX · Winter Survey
1328	**Research** · Habit. Prot. · NWF · Pub. Ed. · RIC
1484	**Research** · Disturb. · Great Lakes · Manage. · Nest. Survey · ON · Status · Techniques
1552	**Research** · WI
202	**Residues** · Anal. Tech. · AR · Mass Spectro. · MN · PCB · Techniques
372	**Residues** · Autopsy · AK · Cont. U.S. · DDT · NB · Pest. · Toxicol.
1831	**Residues** · Autopsy · DDT · MO · NJ · Toxicol.
145	**Reward** · Manage. · NWF · Shooting · WI
146	**Reward** · Manage. · NWF
1315	**Reward** · NWF · Shooting
1316	**Reward** · Manage. · NWF · Shooting
1323	**Reward** · MI · Shooting
1346	**Reward** · Habit. Prot. · Manage. · NWF · Pub. Ed.
734	**Road Plan.** · Habit. Loss · Habit. Use · SK · Techniques
27	**Road. Census** · Acct. · OK · Techniques · TX
600	**Road. Census** · CO · Techniques · Winter. Pop.
1005	**Road. Census** · CO · Techniques · Winter. Pop.
1049	**Road. Census** · CA · Nest. Survey · Techniques · Winter Survey
1122	**Road. Census** · Acct. · NE · Techniques · Winter. Pop.
1123	**Road. Census** · NE · Techniques · Winter. Pop.
1159	**Road. Census** · CA · Nest. Survey · Techniques · Winter Survey
1216	**Road. Census** · NE · Techniques
1337	**Road. Census** · NE · Techniques · Winter. Pop.
1384	**Road. Census** · Asper. · Nest. Survey · OR · Techniques · Winter Survey
1859	**Rocky Mt. Region** · IA · KS · Missouri R · MO · Nest. Survey · ND · NE · SD · USFWS · Winter. Pop.
1581	**Rodman Reservoir** · FL · L Ocklawaha · Nest.
564	**RI** · Prey · Winter. Pop.
930	**RI** · Acct. · Nest.
149	**RIC** · Literature · Manage. · NWF · Status
161	**RIC** · Literature · Manage. · NWF · Status
450	**RIC** · Habit. Prot. · ME · Nest. Survey · Pub. Ed. · Shooting · Status
1320	**RIC** · NWF
1321	**RIC** · Manage. · NWF
1328	**RIC** · Habit. Prot. · NWF · Pub. Ed. · Research
1332	**RIC** · CA · Habit. Prot. · IL · NWF
1508	**RIC** · Field ID · Nest. Survey · NWF · USFS
1509	**RIC** · Pub. Ed.
1112	**Salt Fork R** · Autopsy · Disturb. · Habit. Use · Hunt. Behav. · Intersp. Behav. · Manage. · Migration · OK · Prey · Shooting · Status · Taxonomy · Winter Survey
1115	**Salt Fork R** · Disturb. · Habit. Use · Manage. · Migration · OK · Prey · Salt Plains NWR · Sequoyah NWR · Shooting · Status · Taxonomy · Wichita Mts. NWR · Winter Survey
1838	**Salt Fork R** · AZ · CO · KS · Nest. Survey · NM · OK · TX · USFWS · UT · Verde R · WY
1852	**Salt Fork R** · AZ · Manage. · Nest. Survey · NM · OK · TX · USFWS · Verde R

187

Master No.	Keywords
1114	**Salt Plains NWR** · Arkansas R · Band. · Capture · Habit. Use · Intersp. Behav. · OK · Sequoyah NWR · Techniques · Wichita Mts. NWR · Winter Survey · Winter. Pop.
1115	**Salt Plains NWR** · Disturb. · Habit. Use · Manage. · Migration · OK · Prey · Salt Fork R · Sequoyah NWR · Shooting · Status · Taxonomy · Wichita Mts. NWR · Winter Survey
449	**Salt R** · AZ · CAP · Habit. Loss · Nest. · Orme D · Verde R
1793	**Salt R** · AZ · CAP · Nest. Survey · Orme D · Verde R
1865	**Salt R** · AZ · BLM · CAP · Egg · Habit. Prot. · Manage. · Nest. · Orme D · Taxonomy · Territory · Verde R
447	**San Bernardino Mts.** · Behav. · CA · Disturb. · Hunt. Behav. · Manage. · Natl. For. · Prey · USFS · Winter. Pop.
1040	**San Bernardino Mts.** · CA · Hunt. Behav. · Prey
299	**San Clemente Is.** · CA · Rehab. · Techniques
307	**San Clemente Is.** · CA · Intersp. Behav. · Nest. · Shooting
1110	**San Clemente Is.** · CA · Depred. · Habit. Use · Prey
23	**San Juan Is.** · Nest. Survey · Reprod. Succ. · WA
583	**San Juan Is.** · Habit. Use · Manage. · Nest. Survey · OR · Poison. · Prey · Shooting · Status · Winter Survey · WA
587	**San Juan Is.** · Status · WA
750	**San Juan Is.** · WA
805	**San Juan Is.** · Habit. Use · Nest. Survey · Reprod. Succ. · WA
826	**San Juan Is.** · BC · Gulf Is. · Habit. Use · Migration · Nest. Survey · Prey · Techniques · Winter Survey · WA
1262	**San Juan Is.** · Nest. · WA
1354	**San Juan Is.** · Disturb. · Nest. Survey · Status · WA
1520	**San Juan Is.** · Nest. · WA
1521	**San Juan Is.** · Aggress. · Behav. · Disturb. · Habit. Loss · Hunt. Behav. · Nest. · Prey · Shooting · Status · Vocal. · WA
1522	**San Juan Is.** · Prey · WA

Master No.	Keywords
175	**San Luis Valley** · Anat. · Capture · CO · Techniques · Winter Survey
451	**San Luis Valley** · CO · Habit. Use · Nest. · Status · Winter Survey
474	**San Luis Valley** · CO · Habit. Use · Nest. · Status · Winter Survey
440	**Sandy Hook** · Band. · Capture · Migration · NJ · Techniques
506	**Santa Barbara Is.** · Captivity · CA · Depred. · Distrib. · Habit. Use · Life History · Nest.
971	**Santa Barbara Is.** · CA · Habit. Loss · Nest.
1111	**Santa Barbara Is.** · CA · Paleontology
1433	**Santa Barbara Is.** · CA · Nest.
932	**Santa Cruz** · Aggress. · CA · Nest.
1021	**Sapelo Is.** · GA · Hunt. Behav. · Prey
1022	**Sapelo Is.** · GA · Nest.
1763	**Savannah NWR** · Mattamuskett NWR · Nest. · NC · SC
1745	**Seney NWR** · MI · Nest. · Prey
1731	**Sequoia NP** · Acct. · CA · Kings Canyon NP
1114	**Sequoyah NWR** · Arkansas R · Band. · Capture · Habit. Use · Intersp. Behav. · OK · Salt Plains NWR · Techniques · Wichita Mts. NWR · Winter Survey · Winter. Pop.
1115	**Sequoyah NWR** · Disturb. · Habit. Use · Manage. · Migration · OK · Prey · Salt Fork R · Salt Plains NWR · Shooting · Status · Taxonomy · Wichita Mts. NWR · Winter Survey
527	**Sexing** · Anal. Tech. · Biochem. · Blood · Steroids · Techniques
531	**Sexing** · Aging · AK · Behav. · Hunt. Behav. · Life History · Nest. · Prey · Techniques
519	**Shasta-Trinity NF** · CA · Depred. · Habit. Use · Manage. · Mortality · Nest. · Prey · Winter Survey
90	**Shooting** · Flight · TX
142	**Shooting** · Poison. · Winter. Pop. · WY
145	**Shooting** · Manage. · NWF · Reward · WI
157	**Shooting** · ID
167	**Shooting** · IL · Law
190	**Shooting** · Audubon · History · Taxonomy

Master No.	Keywords
196	**Shooting** · Distrib. · LA · Migration · Mortality · Nest. Survey · Reprod. Succ. · Status · Winter Survey
205	**Shooting** · AK · Nest.
244	**Shooting** · CA · Depred.
245	**Shooting** · Aggress. · IL · Law
246	**Shooting**
250	**Shooting** · FL · Hunt. Behav. · Intersp. Behav. · Prey
254	**Shooting** · FL · Nest.
255	**Shooting** · Aggress. · Egg Coll. · FL · Nest. · Status
256	**Shooting** · NY · Winter. Pop.
261	**Shooting** · Manage. · Mt. Johnson Is. Sanct. · Nest. · PA · Refuge
285	**Shooting** · AK · Nest.
301	**Shooting** · Disturb. · Habit. Use · IL · Nest. · Ohio R · Rehab. · Techniques · Winter. Pop.
307	**Shooting** · CA · Intersp. Behav. · Nest. · San Clemente Is.
308	**Shooting** · Educ. Mat. · Field ID · Hawk Mt. · Migration · Pub. Ed. · PA
309	**Shooting** · Hunt. Behav. · Prey · VA · Winter. Pop.
310	**Shooting** · Disturb. · Migration · ME · Nest. · Winter. Pop.
327	**Shooting** · Band. · FL · Habit. Loss · Intersp. Behav. · Nest. Fail. · Pub. Ed. · Status · Techniques
342	**Shooting** · BC · Econ. Import. · Hunt. Behav. · Prey
349	**Shooting** · Distrib. · Ireland
362	**Shooting** · CA
365	**Shooting** · AK · Bounty · NAS
366	**Shooting** · Law
370	**Shooting** · Law
381	**Shooting** · Anacapa Is. · Behav. · CA · Egg Coll.
392	**Shooting** · TN · Winter. Pop.
398	**Shooting** · Jackson's Canyon · Law · Poison. · WY
400	**Shooting** · MT · Nest. · Poison.
404	**Shooting** · AK · Egg Coll. · Nest.
423	**Shooting** · Mississippi R · Nest. · Pub. Ed. · Reelfoot L · Status · TN · Winter. Pop.
429	**Shooting** · Aggress. · History · Hunt. Behav. · Life History · Nest. · Poetry · PA · Status · Susquehanna R
444	**Shooting** · Anat. · Folklore · Hunt. Behav. · NC
446	**Shooting** · Econ. Import. · Law · Life History · Manage. · MO · Nest. · Prey · Pub. Ed.
450	**Shooting** · Habit. Prot. · ME · Nest. Survey · Pub. Ed. · RIC · Status
455	**Shooting** · Depred. · Ohio R · WV
459	**Shooting** · Autopsy · AK · CN · Disease · Lower 48 · Parasites · Poison. · Trapping
476	**Shooting** · Egg Coll. · Flight · Life History · Status
482	**Shooting** · Autopsy · Dieldrin · Disease · Electro. · Lower 48 · Pest. · Poison. · PCB
484	**Shooting** · AK · Chilkat R · Prey · Winter Survey
487	**Shooting** · Depred. · Plumage · WV
488	**Shooting** · CA · Depred.
496	**Shooting** · Climatology · Migration · OH · Poison. · Winter Survey
497	**Shooting** · Behav. · Egg · Nest. · OH · Poison. · Prey
499	**Shooting** · Law · Manage. · Nest. · Poison. · Pub. Ed. · SK · Trapping
535	**Shooting** · CT · Egg Coll. · Endang. Sp. · Habit. Loss · Nest. · Pest. · PCB · Status
544	**Shooting** · IA · Migration · Nest. · Winter. Pop.
583	**Shooting** · Habit. Use · Manage. · Nest. Survey · OR · Poison. · Prey · San Juan Is. · Status · Winter Survey · WA
593	**Shooting** · Acct. · IL
598	**Shooting** · Manage. · Pub. Ed. · Status
662	**Shooting** · AK · Bounty · Growth · Law · Photo.
679	**Shooting** · FL
687	**Shooting** · Law · NV
705	**Shooting** · Disease · Rehab. · Techniques · Trapping
714	**Shooting** · Distrib. · Habit. Use · Nest. · Plumage · Taxonomy · TN · Winter. Pop.
715	**Shooting** · AR · Habit. Use · Mississippi R · MS · Nest. · Reelfoot L · TN
737	**Shooting** · AK · Depred. · Nest. · Prey
742	**Shooting** · Anat. · NY · Taxonomy
754	**Shooting** · Acct. · Egg Coll. · OK

Master No.	Keywords
755	**Shooting** · Disturb. · Manage. · ME · Nest. Survey · Pub. Ed. · Winter. Pop.
757	**Shooting** · Band. · Disturb. · Manage. · Marking · ME · Nest. · Nest. Survey · Techniques
787	**Shooting** · MI · MO · Rehab. · Reintroduction · Swan Lake NWR · WI
818	**Shooting** · Acct. · History · WA
913	**Shooting** · AR · Taxidermy
933	**Shooting** · AR · Habit. Use · Winter. Pop.
934	**Shooting** · AL · Nest. · Prey · TN · Winter. Pop.
1002	**Shooting** · Habit. Loss · OR
1016	**Shooting** · Nest. · ON
1107	**Shooting** · CA · Status
1112	**Shooting** · Autopsy · Disturb. · Habit. Use · Hunt. Behav. · Intersp. Behav. · Manage. · Migration · OK · Prey · Salt Fork R · Status · Taxonomy · Winter Survey
1115	**Shooting** · Disturb. · Habit. Use · Manage. · Migration · OK · Prey · Salt Fork R · Salt Plains NWR · Sequoyah NWR · Status · Taxonomy · Wichita Mts. NWR · Winter Survey
1139	**Shooting** · Channel Is. · CA · Disturb. · Egg Coll. · Poison. · Pop. Turnover
1200	**Shooting** · Chippewa NF · Disturb. · MN · ND · Poison. · Pub. Ed. · Status · USFS
1281	**Shooting** · WV
1285	**Shooting** · Law · Pub. Ed.
1292	**Shooting** · Autopsy · Disease · Electro. · Lead Poison. · Pest.
1297	**Shooting** · Aleutian Is. · AK · Band. · Distrib. · Econ. Import. · Nest. · Plumage · Prey · Techniques
1304	**Shooting** · IL · Prey · Winter Survey
1314	**Shooting** · Electro. · Law · NAS · Pest. · Poison. · Pub. Ed. · Status
1315	**Shooting** · NWF · Reward
1316	**Shooting** · Manage. · NWF · Reward
1323	**Shooting** · MI · Reward
1360	**Shooting** · Habit. Loss · Nest. Survey · Pest. · Techniques · Terminology · USFWS
1370	**Shooting** · Econ. Import. · Life History · Prey

Master No.	Keywords
1394	**Shooting** · AK · Bounty
1409	**Shooting** · Nest. · SD
1414	**Shooting** · Egg Coll. · FL · Pub. Ed.
1419	**Shooting** · AK · Bounty · Law · NAS · Pub. Ed.
1420	**Shooting** · AK · Bounty · Law
1421	**Shooting** · AK · Bounty · Law
1422	**Shooting** · AK · Bounty · Law
1424	**Shooting** · AK · Bounty · Law
1465	**Shooting** · KY · Nest.
1493	**Shooting** · PA
1513	**Shooting** · Disease · MN · Rehab. · Techniques · Trapping
1521	**Shooting** · Aggress. · Behav. · Disturb. · Habit. Loss · Hunt. Behav. · Nest. · Prey · San Juan Is. · Status · Vocal. · WA
1537	**Shooting** · Hunt. Behav. · Life History · Migration · MN · Nest. · Prey · Status · Winter. Pop.
1543	**Shooting** · Depred. · Law · Poison. · WY
1555	**Shooting** · Egg Coll. · FL · Habit. Use · Nest.
1559	**Shooting** · CT · Migration · Nest. · Taxonomy · Winter. Pop.
1567	**Shooting** · ON · Pub. Ed. · Status
1568	**Shooting** · Depred. · Nest. · ON · Prey
1573	**Shooting** · CO · Poison. · Pub. Ed. · WY
1574	**Shooting** · CO · Poison. · Pub. Ed. · WY
1575	**Shooting** · CO · Law · WY
1577	**Shooting** · Law · Pub. Ed. · WY
1640	**Shooting** · Aggress. · Behav. · BLM · Disturb. · Habit. Loss · Habit. Use · Hunt. Behav. · Life History · Manage. · Nest. · Pest. · Prey · Territory
1643	**Shooting** · AK · Nest.
1719	**Shooting** · CA · Taxonomy
1723	**Shooting** · Law · OR
1754	**Shooting** · IL · Winter. Pop.
1771	**Shooting** · CA · Disturb. · Habit. Loss · Habit. Use · Manage. · Nest. Survey · Prey · Territory · Trapping
1869	**Shooting** · Law · USFWS
1916	**Shooting** · Pub. Ed.
1936	**Shooting** · Acct. · MI
1959	**Shooting** · WY
1974	**Shooting** · Nest. · ND
1977	**Shooting** · IL · IN · Nest.
1982	**Shooting** · Law · MS
1989	**Shooting** · Anat. · Migration · MO

Master No.	Keywords
1996	**Shooting** · Migration · Missouri R · MN · NE
24	**Skagit R** · Capture · Manage. · Marking · Techniques · WA
54	**Skagit R** · Art · Winter. Pop. · WA
168	**Skagit R** · Habit. Prot. · Manage. · Nat. Conserv. · Wash. Dept. Game · Winter. Pop. · WA
174	**Skagit R** · B.E. Nat. Area · Marking · Pub. Ed. · Techniques · WA
1178	**Skagit R** · Disturb. · Pub. Ed. · WA
1591	**Skagit R** · Behav. · Climatology · Disturb. · Habit. Use · Intrasp. Behav. · Plumage · Prey · Winter Survey · WA
503	**Skagit R Nat. Area** · Habit. Prot. · Nat. Conserv. · Prey · Refuge · WA
998	**Skagit R Nat. Area** · Habit. Prot. · Refuge · Winter. Pop. · WA
1334	**Skagit R Nat. Area** · Habit. Prot. · Manage. · Nat. Conserv. · Refuge · Winter Survey · WA
972	**Snake R** · Behav. · Disturb. · Habit. Use · Nest. · WY
1984	**Snake R** · Habit. Use · Platte R · Winter Survey · WY
1985	**Snake R** · Habit. Use · Platte R · Winter Survey · WY
176	**Southland** · Habit. Prot. · NWF · Refuge · SD
1126	**Spermato.** · DDT · Histology · Pest. · Phys. · Techniques
1707	**Spermato.** · Pest. · Toxicol.
1708	**Spermato.** · AK · Histology · Lower 48 · Pest. · Techniques · Toxicol. · USFWS
510	**Squaw Creek NWR** · MO · Winter. Pop.
1893	**Squaw Creek NWR** · Mississippi R · MO · Nest. · Winter Survey
128	**St. Croix R** · Habit. Prot. · Indian Culture · Manage. · MN · Refuge · WI
696	**Statistics** · Aircraft · Chippewa NF · Model · MN · Techniques
801	**Statistics** · Disturb. · Nest. · Nest. Survey · Reprod. Succ. · Territory · WA
9	**Status** · Ches. Bay · Nest. Survey · Winter Survey
10	**Status** · Ches. Bay · Nest. Survey
13	**Status** · Ches. Bay · Nest. Survey
16	**Status** · Ches. Bay · Nest. Survey
17	**Status** · Ches. Bay · Nest. Survey
18	**Status** · Ches. Bay · Nest. Survey
20	**Status** · Ches. Bay · Nest. Survey
22	**Status** · Bombay Hook NWR · Distrib. · DE · Endang. Sp. · Field ID · Life History · Nest. · Nest. Survey · Pub. Ed.
30	**Status** · Pub. Ed.
35	**Status** · Egg Coll. · LA · MN · MS · WI
42	**Status** · Nest. · OH · Winter. Pop.
48	**Status** · AOU · Comm. Conserv. · Endang. Sp. · Law
49	**Status** · Aleutian Is. · Amchitka Is. · AK · AOU · Habit. Loss
50	**Status** · Egg. Thin. · FL · LA · Pest. · TX
52	**Status** · AOU · Comm. Conserv.
53	**Status** · Distrib. · IA · Nest. · Winter. Pop.
69	**Status** · AK · Bounty · Law · Pub. Ed.
73	**Status** · History · Pub. Ed. · Symbolism
79	**Status** · Bounty · History · Symbolism
83	**Status** · History · Pub. Ed. · Symbolism
85	**Status** · History · Pub. Ed.
87	**Status** · Law
102	**Status** · AK · Bounty · Law
108	**Status** · Aggress. · Band. · Broley · Prey · Techniques
111	**Status** · Endang. Sp. · NAS
117	**Status** · Law
119	**Status** · Nest. Survey · NAS · Pub. Ed. · Winter Survey
129	**Status** · Manage. · NAS
130	**Status** · Captive Breed. · Life History · Pub. Ed.
132	**Status** · Egg. Thin. · FL
149	**Status** · Literature · Manage. · NWF · RIC
154	**Status** · Lower 48 · Manage. · Nest. Survey · USFWS
161	**Status** · Literature · Manage. · NWF · RIC
165	**Status** · History · Pub. Ed.
194	**Status** · Life History · Pub. Ed.
196	**Status** · Distrib. · LA · Migration · Mortality · Nest. Survey · Reprod. Succ. · Shooting · Winter Survey
206	**Status** · LA · Nest.
228	**Status** · Anacapa Is. · CA · Nest.
230	**Status** · Mortality · Pub. Ed.
242	**Status** · AK · Bounty
249	**Status** · Anat. · Distrib. · Life History · MI · Plumage

Master No.	Keywords
255	**Status** · Aggress. · Egg Coll. · FL · Nest. · Shooting
258	**Status** · Anat. · Nest. · NY · Prey · Winter. Pop.
260	**Status** · Folklore · Prey · PA · Taxonomy
266	**Status** · Anat. · Behav. · BC · Distrib. · Falconry · Field ID · Flight · Habit. Use · Migration · Nest. · Prey
268	**Status** · BC · CA · Nest. · OR · Winter. Pop. · WA
273	**Status** · Aggress. · Behav. · Captivity · Distrib. · Egg Coll. · Habit. Use · Life History · Nest.
274	**Status** · Aggress. · Behav. · Captivity · Distrib. · Habit. Use · Life History · Nest.
281	**Status** · Nest. · WI
304	**Status** · Manage.
324	**Status** · Band. · FL · Life History · Migration · Nest. Fail. · Nest. Survey · Prey · Techniques
327	**Status** · Band. · FL · Habit. Loss · Intersp. Behav. · Nest. Fail. · Pub. Ed. · Shooting · Techniques
329	**Status** · FL · Habit. Loss · Hurricane · Nest. Fail.
335	**Status** · DDT · FL · Nest. Fail. · Pest.
339	**Status** · Band. · Broley · FL · Life History · Pub. Ed. · Techniques
347	**Status** · Bounty · Hawk Mt. · Pub. Ed. · PA
351	**Status** · Migration · Nest. · Prey · Reprod. Succ.
352	**Status** · Behav. · Flight · Life History · Migration · Nest. · Prey · Pub. Ed. · Taxonomy
353	**Status** · Anat. · Behav. · Distrib. · Life History · Nest.
356	**Status** · Christmas Count · Winter Survey
373	**Status** · Nest. · NY · Taxonomy · Winter. Pop.
377	**Status** · Distrib. · GA · Habit. Use · Life History · Migration · Nest.
378	**Status** · ID · Life History · Nest.
382	**Status** · Distrib. · Egg Coll. · IN · Life History · Nest.
390	**Status** · Endang. Sp. · Poison. · Pred. Cont.
393	**Status** · CA · Endang. Sp. · Manage.
394	**Status** · CA · Endang. Sp. · Manage.
409	**Status** · AZ · Grand Canyon · Nest. · Winter. Pop.
423	**Status** · Mississippi R · Nest. · Pub. Ed. · Reelfoot L · Shooting · TN · Winter. Pop.
429	**Status** · Aggress. · History · Hunt. Behav. · Life History · Nest. · Poetry · PA · Shooting · Susquehanna R
438	**Status** · Cape May · Migration · NJ
441	**Status** · AOU · Comm. Bird Prot. · FL
442	**Status** · AOU · Comm. Bird Prot. · FL
450	**Status** · Habit. Prot. · ME · Nest. Survey · Pub. Ed. · RIC · Shooting
451	**Status** · CO · Habit. Use · Nest. · San Luis Valley · Winter Survey
452	**Status** · Acct. · NH
456	**Status** · MI · Nest. · Trapping · Winter. Pop.
461	**Status** · Art · History · Mortality · Symbolism
474	**Status** · CO · Habit. Use · Nest. · San Luis Valley · Winter Survey
476	**Status** · Egg Coll. · Flight · Life History · Shooting
485	**Status** · Disturb. · FL · Habit. Loss
501	**Status** · DDT · Pest.
520	**Status** · Distrib. · Habit. Use · Migration · Nest. Survey · Winter Survey · WI
522	**Status** · Bounty · Pub. Ed.
535	**Status** · CT · Egg Coll. · Endang. Sp. · Habit. Loss · Nest. · Pest. · PCB · Shooting
557	**Status** · Chippewa NF · Disturb. · Life History · Migration · Nest. · Photo. · Pub. Ed. · Techniques · Telemetry · Winter. Pop.
569	**Status** · Ches. Bay · Endang. Sp. · Manage.
576	**Status** · Band. · Behav. · Photo. · Pub. Ed. · Techniques
577	**Status** · Aleutian Is. · AK · Bounty · Habit. Use · Nest. · Symbolism
579	**Status** · Behav. · Nest. · Pub. Ed.
583	**Status** · Habit. Use · Manage. · Nest. Survey · OR · Poison. · Prey · San Juan Is. · Shooting · Winter Survey · WA
587	**Status** · San Juan Is. · WA
598	**Status** · Manage. · Pub. Ed. · Shooting

Master No.	Keywords
670	**Status** · Fla. B.E. Sur. Comm. · FL · Great Lakes · Rehab. · Reprod. Succ. · Techniques · WI
682	**Status** · CA · Disturb. · Klamath NF · Manage. · Nest. · Prey · Winter. Pop.
708	**Status** · CN
709	**Status** · CN · Pest.
711	**Status** · AK · Distrib. · Habit. Use · Life History · Plumage
712	**Status** · CO · Hawk Mt. · Migration · PA
725	**Status** · Life History · SK
726	**Status** · Habit. Use · MB · Reprod. Succ. · SK · Techniques
730	**Status** · Band. · Migration · Pub. Ed. · SK · Techniques
746	**Status** · CN · Endang. Sp.
751	**Status** · Christmas Count · IL · Mississippi R · Techniques · Winter Survey
752	**Status** · IL · Migration · Nest. · Winter. Pop.
753	**Status** · AK · Lower 48 · Manage.
763	**Status** · Life History · NC · Pub. Ed.
769	**Status** · Acct. · Anacapa Is. · Channel Is. · CA
775	**Status** · Nest. Survey · ON · Reprod. Succ. · Territory
776	**Status** · Nest. Survey · ON · Reprod. Succ. · Territory
777	**Status** · CN · Habit. Use · ON · Reprod. Succ. · Techniques · Territory
779	**Status** · Egg. Thin. · Heavy Metals · ON · Pest. · PCB · Reprod. Succ.
782	**Status** · Disturb. · MB · Nest. Survey · ON · Techniques
783	**Status** · Disturb. · Egg. Thin. · Heavy Metals · Nest. Survey · ON · Pest. · PCB · Reprod. Succ.
793	**Status** · Acct. · CA
811	**Status** · Migration · MD
814	**Status** · Disturb. · Great Lakes · Manage. · Nest. Survey · Pub. Ed. · USFS
821	**Status** · Habit. Use · OK · Winter Survey
822	**Status** · NJ
825	**Status** · AK · Comm. Conserv. · CN · Lower 48 · Wilson Ornithol. Soc.
853	**Status** · Anat. · Pub. Ed.
857	**Status** · Life History · Pub. Ed.
863	**Status** · AK · Habit. Use · Hunt. Behav. · Nest. Survey · Prey
866	**Status** · Anat. · Climatology · Field ID · Migration
890	**Status** · Great Lakes · L Erie · Prey · Pub. Ed.
898	**Status** · MA · Nest. · Winter. Pop.
899	**Status** · Pub. Ed.
903	**Status** · Christmas Count · IA · Mississippi R · Nest. · Winter Survey
919	**Status** · AK · Bounty · Pub. Ed.
926	**Status** · CA · Paleontology
936	**Status** · FL · Nest. Fail. · Nest. Survey
937	**Status** · FL · Nest. · Nest. Fail.
941	**Status** · FL · Nest.
942	**Status** · FL · Nest. · Nest. Fail.
943	**Status** · FL · Nest. Fail. · Techniques
944	**Status** · FL · Habit. Loss · Nest. Fail. · Nest. Survey
946	**Status** · Disturb. · FL · Habit. Loss · Nest. Survey
950	**Status** · FL · Nest. Survey
976	**Status** · Aggress. · Anat. · Bounty · Distrib. · Econ. Import. · Law · Life History · Plumage · Prey · Taxonomy
981	**Status** · Endang. Sp. · Great Lakes · Nest. Survey · Pub. Ed. · USFS
984	**Status** · Captivity · Egg Trans. · Heavy Metals · Law · Manage. · Migration · Nest. Survey · Pest. · Pub. Ed. · Techniques · Territory · Young Trans.
985	**Status** · Endang. Sp. · IUCN
999	**Status** · Pub. Ed.
1006	**Status** · ID · Manage.
1008	**Status** · AZ · Verde R
1017	**Status** · L Andes NWR · Missouri R · NAS · SD · Winter Survey
1042	**Status** · Aleutian Is. · AK · Hunt. Behav. · Nest. · Prey
1045	**Status** · IA · Migration · Nest.
1046	**Status** · NWF · Pub. Ed.
1051	**Status** · Folklore · Life History · Pub. Ed.
1054	**Status** · Mt. Ranier NP · Nest. · WA
1058	**Status** · Habit. Use · Intersp. Behav. · Life History · ME · Nest.
1085	**Status** · Disturb. · Habit. Loss · Nest. · OH

Master No.	Keywords
1089	**Status** · Nest. · NWF · Pub. Ed. · Winter. Pop.
1101	**Status** · Nest. · NM · Winter. Pop.
1106	**Status** · MI · Nest. Survey · Reprod. Succ.
1107	**Status** · CA · Shooting
1108	**Status** · CT · Nest.
1112	**Status** · Autopsy · Disturb. · Habit. Use · Hunt. Behav. · Intersp. Behav. · Manage. · Migration · OK · Prey · Salt Fork R · Shooting · Taxonomy · Winter Survey
1115	**Status** · Disturb. · Habit. Use · Manage. · Migration · OK · Prey · Salt Fork R · Salt Plains NWR · Sequoyah NWR · Shooting · Taxonomy · Wichita Mts. NWR · Winter Survey
1116	**Status** · Acct. · Disturb. · Nest. · OK · Winter. Pop.
1117	**Status** · Pub. Ed.
1121	**Status** · Behav. · Manage. · NE · Prey · Winter Survey
1145	**Status** · Endang. Sp. · Life History
1184	**Status** · AK · CN · Lower 48
1188	**Status** · Chippewa NF · Habit. Use · Manage. · MN · Nest. Survey · USFS
1200	**Status** · Chippewa NF · Disturb. · MN · ND · Poison. · Pub. Ed. · Shooting · USFS
1201	**Status** · Chippewa NF · MN · Nest. Survey · USFS
1202	**Status** · Chippewa NF · MN · Nest. Survey · USFS
1207	**Status** · Chippewa NF · Manage. · MN · Nest. Survey · USFS
1208	**Status** · Pub. Ed.
1209	**Status** · Chippewa NF · MN · Nest. Survey · USFS
1211	**Status** · Chippewa NF · MN · Nest. Survey · USFS
1213	**Status** · Chippewa NF · MN · Nest. Survey · USFS
1217	**Status** · Band. · Chippewa NF · MN · Nest. Survey · Techniques · USFS
1223	**Status** · Band. · Chippewa NF · MN · Nest. Survey · Reprod. Succ. · Superior NF · Techniques · Terminology
1226	**Status** · Econ. Import. · Life History · Prey · Pub. Ed.
1231	**Status** · Pub. Ed.
1237	**Status** · Distrib. · Endang. Sp. · Habit. Use · Migration · Nest. · ND · Winter. Pop.
1242	**Status** · History · Nest. Survey · NJ · Pest.
1272	**Status** · Endang. Sp. · Habit. Use · Manage. · MN
1286	**Status** · Law
1301	**Status** · Migration · Nest. · Winter. Pop.
1303	**Status** · Pub. Ed.
1308	**Status** · Hawk Mt. · Migration · PA
1309	**Status** · Endang. Sp. · Manage. · Nest. · NV
1314	**Status** · Electro. · Law · NAS · Pest. · Poison. · Pub. Ed. · Shooting
1317	**Status** · Law · Life History · NWF · Pest. · Pub. Ed.
1336	**Status** · Behav. · Manage. · NE · Prey · Winter Survey
1349	**Status** · Dispersal · FL · Life History · Migration · NAS · Pub. Ed.
1352	**Status** · Fla. B.E. Sur. Comm. · FL · Habit. Use · Nest. Survey
1354	**Status** · Disturb. · Nest. Survey · San Juan Is. · WA
1357	**Status** · FL · Habit. Use · Life History · Nest.
1376	**Status** · Field ID · Nest. · OH · Pub. Ed.
1386	**Status** · Pub. Ed.
1436	**Status** · Pub. Ed.
1441	**Status** · Habit. Loss · Kentucky Wood. NWR · KY · Winter Survey
1451	**Status** · Endang. Sp. · Manage.
1474	**Status** · MI · Winter Survey
1484	**Status** · Disturb. · Great Lakes · Manage. · Nest. Survey · ON · Research Techniques
1512	**Status** · Captivity · Pub. Ed.
1521	**Status** · Aggress. · Behav. · Disturb. · Habit. Loss · Hunt. Behav. · Nest. · Prey · San Juan Is. · Shooting · Vocal. · WA
1528	**Status** · Manage. · Pub. Ed.
1529	**Status** · AK · Habit. Use · Hunt. Behav. · Manage. · Pub. Ed.
1531	**Status** · Band. · Christmas Count · Life History · Migration · Nest. · USFWS · Winter Survey
1537	**Status** · Hunt. Behav. · Life History · Migration · MN · Nest. · Prey · Shooting · Winter. Pop.

Master No.	Keywords
1544	**Status** · History · Pub. Ed. · Symbolism
1550	**Status** · AZ · Behav. · Disturb. · Habit. Loss · Habit. Use · Hunt. Behav. · Nest. Survey · Prey · Terminology · Territory
1561	**Status** · History · Pub. Ed.
1567	**Status** · ON · Pub. Ed. · Shooting
1571	**Status** · Pub. Ed.
1578	**Status** · DE · Great Lakes · MD · Nest. Survey · NJ · PA
1582	**Status** · CO · Life History · Nest. · Winter. Pop.
1604	**Status** · ME · Nest.
1606	**Status** · Aggress. · Aleutian Is. · AK · Behav. · Depred. · Habit. Use · Life History · Mortality · Nest. Survey · Plumage · Prey · Reprod. Succ. · Winter Survey
1617	**Status** · Nest. Survey · NY
1627	**Status** · Endang. Sp. · Nest. · OH · Pest.
1631	**Status** · Distrib. · Nest. Survey · Reprod. Succ. · TX · Winter Survey
1632	**Status** · Distrib. · Habit. Use · Nest. Survey · TX · Winter Survey
1639	**Status** · AZ · CA · Endang. Sp. · NM · NV · OK · TX · UT
1668	**Status** · Montezuma NWR · Nest. Survey · NY
1670	**Status** · Cont. B.E. Proj. · Nest. Survey · NAS
1671	**Status** · Cont. B.E. Proj. · Migration · Nest. Survey · NAS · Winter Survey
1672	**Status** · Cont. B.E. Proj. · Hurricane · Nest. Survey · NAS · Winter Survey
1673	**Status** · Cont. B.E. Proj. · Manage. · Migration · Nest. Survey · NAS · Winter Survey
1674	**Status** · Cont. B.E. Proj. · Manage. · Nest. Survey · NAS · Refuge · Winter Survey
1675	**Status** · Cont. B.E. Proj. · Nest. Survey · NAS · Winter Survey
1676	**Status** · Cont. B.E. Proj. · Nest. Survey · NAS · Winter Survey
1677	**Status** · Nest. Survey · NAS
1678	**Status** · Cont. B.E. Proj. · Manage. · Nest. Survey · NAS · Winter Survey
1679	**Status** · Egg. Thin. · Pest.
1680	**Status** · Endang. Sp. · Manage. · Taxonomy
1681	**Status** · Cont. B.E. Proj. · Nest. Survey · NAS · Terminology
1684	**Status** · Band. · Field ID · FL · Life History · Nest. · Prey · Techniques
1685	**Status** · FL · Pub. Ed.
1689	**Status** · CO · Winter Survey
1718	**Status** · Pub. Ed.
1741	**Status** · Disturb. · Habit. Use · Manage. · MT · Nest. Survey · Pop. Turnover · Reprod. Succ. · Territory · Yellowstone NP
1746	**Status** · Nest. · OK · Trapping
1758	**Status** · Pub. Ed.
1760	**Status** · FL · Habit. Loss · NAS
1777	**Status** · CA · Habit. Use · Manage. · Nest. Survey · Territory
1781	**Status** · Pub. Ed.
1782	**Status** · Pub. Ed.
1783	**Status** · Pub. Ed.
1785	**Status** · Endang. Sp. · Lower 48 · Nest. Survey
1805	**Status** · Behav. · FL · History · Photo.
1810	**Status** · Depred. · Pub. Ed.
1825	**Status** · Aircraft · Chippewa NF · Great Lakes · MI · MN · Nest. Survey · Reprod. Succ. · USFS · WI
1832	**Status** · Endang. Sp. · Field ID · Manage. · USFWS
1834	**Status** · Endang. Sp. · Field ID · Manage. · USFWS
1841	**Status** · AK · Life History · Manage.
1848	**Status** · Endang. Sp. · Field ID · Manage. · USFWS
1874	**Status** · Distrib. · Endang. Sp. · Law · Life History · Manage. · Taxonomy · USFWS
1885	**Status** · Ches. Bay · Endang. Sp. · Reprod. Succ.
1890	**Status** · AK · Bounty · Pub. Ed.
1896	**Status** · Endang. Sp. · VA
1904	**Status** · Pub. Ed.
1905	**Status** · History · Life History · Pub. Ed.
1907	**Status** · Anat. · AK · Bounty · Nest. · Plumage
1920	**Status** · Disturb. · Habit. Loss · Manage. · Nest. Survey · ON
1926	**Status** · LB · Nest. Survey · QU
1941	**Status** · MO · Nest. · Trapping
1946	**Status** · Egg · New England · Taxonomy
1994	**Status** · Model · Techniques

Master No.	Keywords
527	**Steroids** · Anal. Tech. · Biochem. · Blood · Sexing · Techniques
959	**Superior NF** · Agassiz NWR · Chippewa NF · Itasca SP · MN · Nest. Survey · Tamarac NWR
1223	**Superior NF** · Band. · Chippewa NF · MN · Nest. Survey · Reprod. Succ. · Status · Techniques · Terminology
1224	**Superior NF** · Habit. Use · Nest. Survey · USFS
1611	**Superior NF** · Nest. Survey
1612	**Superior NF** · MN · Nest. Survey · Reprod. Succ.
429	**Susquehanna R** · Aggress. · History · Hunt. Behav. · Life History · Nest. · Poetry · PA · Shooting · Status
905	**Susquehanna R** · Acct. · PA
786	**Swan Lake NWR** · Behav. · Distrib. · Hunt. Behav. · Manage. · Marking · Migration · Mortality · MO · Nest. · Pest. · Prey · Techniques · Telemetry
787	**Swan Lake NWR** · MI · MO · Rehab. · Reintroduction · Shooting · WI
1249	**Swimming** · Hunt. Behav.
73	**Symbolism** · History · Pub. Ed. · Status
79	**Symbolism** · Bounty · History · Status
82	**Symbolism** · Art
83	**Symbolism** · History · Pub. Ed. · Status
84	**Symbolism** · Art · History
92	**Symbolism** · Art · History · PA
95	**Symbolism** · History
98	**Symbolism** · History · Hunt. Behav.
109	**Symbolism** · History · Hunt. Behav.
112	**Symbolism** · History · Life History · Pub. Ed.
113	**Symbolism** · History
114	**Symbolism** · History
118	**Symbolism** · History · Pub. Ed.
127	**Symbolism** · Manage. · Pub. Ed.
136	**Symbolism** · Art · History
279	**Symbolism** · History
428	**Symbolism** · History · Indian Culture
454	**Symbolism** · History
461	**Symbolism** · Art · History · Mortality · Status
521	**Symbolism** · Bounty · Law · Pub. Ed.
534	**Symbolism** · History
577	**Symbolism** · Aleutian Is. · AK · Bounty · Habit. Use · Nest. · Status
597	**Symbolism** · History · Indian Culture
921	**Symbolism** · Art · History
1142	**Symbolism** · History
1284	**Symbolism** · History
1544	**Symbolism** · History · Pub. Ed. · Status
1548	**Symbolism** · History
1560	**Symbolism** · History
1564	**Symbolism** · History · Pub. Ed.
226	**SC** · Intersp. Behav. · Prey
263	**SC** · Intersp. Behav. · Manage. · Nest.
320	**SC** · Nest.
407	**SC** · Nest. · NC
408	**SC** · Nest. · NC
420	**SC** · Nest. · NC · Winter. Pop.
660	**SC** · Habit. Loss · Nest. Survey · NC
911	**SC** · Prey
952	**SC** · Nest.
953	**SC** · Behav. · Nest.
1130	**SC** · Nest.
1407	**SC** · Nest.
1762	**SC** · Nest. · NC
1763	**SC** · Mattamuskett NWR · Nest. · NC · Savannah NWR
1764	**SC** · Nest. · NC
1765	**SC** · Nest. · NC · Winter. Pop.
1912	**SC** · Life History · Nest.
25	**SD** · Nest.
152	**SD** · Corps · Habit. Loss · Karl Mundt NWR · Missouri R · NE · NWF
153	**SD** · Habit. Prot. · Missouri R · NWF · Winter. Pop.
176	**SD** · Habit. Prot. · NWF · Refuge · Southland
548	**SD** · Marking · MN · Techniques
549	**SD** · Life History · Missouri R · Pub. Ed. · Winter Survey
702	**SD** · Habit. Prot. · Karl Mundt NWR · L Andes NWR · Manage. · Missouri R · NWF · Refuge · Winter. Pop.
703	**SD** · Habit. Prot. · Karl Mundt NWR · Missouri R · Refuge · Winter. Pop.
736	**SD** · Habit. Use · Marking · Migration · MO · ND · SK · Techniques · WY
1017	**SD** · L Andes NWR · Missouri R · NAS · Status · Winter Survey
1087	**SD** · Habit. Prot. · Manage. · NWF · Pub. Ed. · Techniques · Winter. Pop. · Young Trans.
1388	**SD** · History · Nest. · Pub. Ed. · Winter. Pop.

Master No.	Keywords
1389	SD · Nest. · Pub. Ed. · Winter. Pop.
1406	SD · Anthro.
1409	SD · Nest. · Shooting
1695	SD · Behav. · Ft. Randall D · Habit. Use · Hunt. Behav. · Karl Mundt NWR · L Andes NWR · Winter Survey
1696	SD · Climatology · Ft. Randall D · Habit. Use · Hunt. Behav. · Karl Mundt NWR · L Andes NWR · Manage. · Prey · Winter Survey
1697	SD · Ft. Randall D · Habit. Loss · Habit. Use · Hunt. Behav. · Migration · Prey · Winter Survey
1699	SD · Behav. · Disturb. · Ft. Randall D · Habit. Use · Manage. · Missouri R · Winter Survey
1846	SD · CO · IA · KS · MO · MT · Nest. Survey · ND · NE · USFWS · UT · WY
1849	SD · CO · IA · KS · MO · MT · Nest. Survey · ND · NE · USFWS · UT · WY
1854	SD · CO · Glacier NP · Manage. · Missouri R · MT · Nest. Survey · USFWS
1857	SD · Missouri R · Nest. Survey · USFWS
1859	SD · IA · KS · Missouri R · MO · Nest. Survey · ND · NE · Rocky Mt. Region · USFWS · Winter. Pop.
1860	SD · Missouri R · Nest. Survey · NE · USFWS · Winter. Pop.
1878	SD · Karl Mundt NWR · Winter Survey
1880	SD · Missouri R · Winter. Pop.
1897	SD · Acct.
1898	SD · Winter. Pop.
267	SK · Migration
499	SK · Law · Manage. · Nest. · Poison. · Pub. Ed. · Shooting · Trapping
725	SK · Life History · Status
726	SK · Habit. Use · MB · Reprod. Succ. · Status · Techniques
727	SK · Behav. · Nestling · Parent. Behav.
728	SK · Habit. Loss · Habit. Use · Manage. · McHargian Overlay · Nest. · Reprod. Succ. · Techniques
729	SK · Band. · Reprod. Succ. · Techniques
730	SK · Band. · Migration · Pub. Ed. · Status · Techniques
731	SK · Behav. · Disturb. · Nestling · Parent. Behav.

Master No.	Keywords
732	SK · Disturb. · Habit. Use · MB · Nest. · Territory
734	SK · Habit. Loss · Habit. Use · Road Plan. · Techniques
735	SK · Disturb. · Habit. Use · Intersp. Behav.
736	SK · Habit. Use · Marking · Migration · MO · ND · SD · Techniques · WY
739	SK · CN · DDT · ON · PCB
925	SK · Nest.
1075	SK · Acct. · AB · MB
1177	SK · Rehab. · Techniques
1278	SK · Churchill R · Nest.
1344	SK · L. Athabasca · Nest.
1345	SK · Nest.
1938	SK · MB · Nest. Survey · Reprod. Succ.
1939	SK · Habit. Use · MB · Nest. Survey · Terminology
1970	SK · Nest.
959	**Tamarac NWR** · Agassiz NWR · Chippewa NF · Itasca SP · MN · Nest. Survey · Superior NF
913	**Taxidermy** · AR · Shooting
28	**Taxonomy** · Life History · Pub. Ed.
33	**Taxonomy** · Anat.
34	**Taxonomy** · AK
47	**Taxonomy** · Distrib. · Life History
60	**Taxonomy** · AK
148	**Taxonomy** · Anat. · Autumn Conc. · FL · Glacier NP · Manage. · Merritt Is. NWR · Museum Specimen · MT · Nest. · Prey
190	**Taxonomy** · Audubon · History · Shooting
191	**Taxonomy** · Anat. · Growth · Plumage
221	**Taxonomy** · Anat. · Distrib. · Nest. · Plumage
227	**Taxonomy** · Anat.
260	**Taxonomy** · Folklore · Prey · PA · Status
317	**Taxonomy** · Captivity · Endang. Sp.
352	**Taxonomy** · Behav. · Flight · Life History · Migration · Nest. · Prey · Pub. Ed. · Status
373	**Taxonomy** · Nest. · NY · Status · Winter. Pop.
433	**Taxonomy** · Distrib. · England
468	**Taxonomy** · Life History · Missouri R · Plumage
543	**Taxonomy** · Anat. · IA · Migration · Nest. · Winter. Pop.
605	**Taxonomy** · Hunt. Behav.
667	**Taxonomy** · Acct. · AK · CA · FL · VA

Master No.	Keywords
714	**Taxonomy** · Distrib. · Habit. Use · Nest. · Plumage · Shooting · TN · Winter. Pop.
741	**Taxonomy** · Anat.
742	**Taxonomy** · Anat. · NY · Shooting
745	**Taxonomy** · Anat. · CN · Distrib. · Field ID · Nest.
764	**Taxonomy** · Anat. · Behav.
797	**Taxonomy** · Anat. · Behav. · Field ID · Plumage
809	**Taxonomy** · Museum Specimen
846	**Taxonomy** · Anat. · Distrib.
927	**Taxonomy** · Anat. · CA · FL · NE · NM · OR · Paleontology
976	**Taxonomy** · Aggress. · Anat. · Bounty · Distrib. · Econ. Import. · Law · Life History · Plumage · Prey · Status
1112	**Taxonomy** · Autopsy · Disturb. · Habit. Use · Hunt. Behav. · Intersp. Behav. · Manage. · Migration · OK · Prey · Salt Fork R · Shooting · Status · Winter Survey
1115	**Taxonomy** · Disturb. · Habit. Use · Manage. · Migration · OK · Prey · Salt Fork R · Salt Plains NWR · Sequoyah NWR · Shooting · Status · Wichita Mts. NWR · Winter Survey
1118	**Taxonomy** · Behav.
1149	**Taxonomy** · Behav. · Captive Breed.
1247	**Taxonomy** · Anat.
1259	**Taxonomy** · CA · Evolution · Paleontology
1260	**Taxonomy** · CA · Evolution · Paleontology
1367	**Taxonomy** · Heavy Metals · Life History · Toxicol.
1371	**Taxonomy** · Hunt. Behav. · Life History · LA · Pub. Ed.
1372	**Taxonomy** · Anat. · Distrib. · Habit. Use · Nest. · Plumage · TX · Winter. Pop.
1438	**Taxonomy** · Distrib.
1559	**Taxonomy** · CT · Migration · Nest. · Shooting · Winter. Pop.
1603	**Taxonomy** · Anat. · NH · Winter. Pop.
1637	**Taxonomy** · Folklore · FL · Intrasp. Behav.
1680	**Taxonomy** · Endang. Sp. · Manage. · Status
1683	**Taxonomy** · Field ID · Pub. Ed.
1719	**Taxonomy** · CA · Shooting
1735	**Taxonomy** · Anat. · Field ID
1736	**Taxonomy** · Life History · Plumage
1787	**Taxonomy** · Acct. · IA
1795	**Taxonomy** · Behav. · Habit. Use · Life History · Nest. · Pub. Ed. · PA
1797	**Taxonomy** · Anat. · WA
1865	**Taxonomy** · AZ · BLM · CAP · Egg · Habit. Prot. · Manage. · Nest. · Orme D · Salt R · Territory · Verde R
1874	**Taxonomy** · Distrib. · Endang. Sp. · Law · Life History · Manage. · Status · USFWS
1884	**Taxonomy** · Endang. Sp. · Law
1946	**Taxonomy** · Egg · New England · Status
1948	**Taxonomy** · CA
1957	**Taxonomy** · Anat. · Hunt. Behav. · Life History
24	**Techniques** · Capture · Manage. · Marking · Skagit R · WA
27	**Techniques** · Acct. · OK · Road. Census · TX
45	**Techniques** · Captivity · Capture · CO
63	**Techniques** · Capture · ME
71	**Techniques** · Captivity · Capture · MI
108	**Techniques** · Aggress. · Band. · Broley · Prey · Status
150	**Techniques** · Captive Breed. · Rehab.
155	**Techniques** · MN · Pub. Ed. · Rehab.
163	**Techniques** · Manage. · NY · Young Trans.
166	**Techniques** · Hacking · Manage. · NY · Young Trans.
173	**Techniques** · AZ · Marking · Pub. Ed. · Verde R
174	**Techniques** · B.E. Nat. Area · Marking · Pub. Ed. · Skagit R · WA
175	**Techniques** · Anat. · Capture · CO · San Luis Valley · Winter Survey
202	**Techniques** · Anal. Tech. · AR · Mass Spectro. · MN · PCB · Residues
299	**Techniques** · CA · Rehab. · San Clemente Is.
301	**Techniques** · Disturb. · Habit. Use · IL · Nest. · Ohio R · Rehab. · Shooting · Winter. Pop.
324	**Techniques** · Band. · FL · Life History · Migration · Nest. Fail. · Nest. Survey · Prey · Status

Master No.	Keywords
327	**Techniques** · Band. · FL · Habit. Loss · Intersp. Behav. · Nest. Fail. · Pub. Ed. · Shooting · Status
332	**Techniques** · Band. · FL · ON · Pest. · Pub. Ed. · Reprod. Succ.
336	**Techniques** · Band. · FL · Intersp. Behav.
337	**Techniques** · Aggress. · Band. · Broley · FL
338	**Techniques** · Band. · Broley · Dispersal · FL · Life History
339	**Techniques** · Band. · Broley · FL · Life History · Pub. Ed. · Status
387	**Techniques** · Hacking · Manage. · Montezuma NWR · NY · WI · Young Trans.
414	**Techniques** · Hacking · Montezuma NWR · NY · Telemetry · Young Trans.
421	**Techniques** · Capture · Folklore · Nest. · Prey · TN
431	**Techniques** · AK · Behav. · Climatology · Disease · Kodiak NWR · Life History · Marking · Nest. · Nest. Survey · Parasites · Reprod. Succ. · Terminology
435	**Techniques** · Cape May · Capture · Migration · NJ
439	**Techniques** · Band. · Cape May · Capture · Migration · NJ
440	**Techniques** · Band. · Capture · Migration · NJ · Sandy Hook
460	**Techniques** · Asper. · Autopsy · Disease · MO · Rehab. · Trapping
462	**Techniques** · Rehab.
504	**Techniques** · CA · Hacking · Rehab.
527	**Techniques** · Anal. Tech. · Biochem. · Blood · Sexing · Steroids
531	**Techniques** · Aging · AK · Behav. · Hunt. Behav. · Life History · Nest. · Prey · Sexing
536	**Techniques** · Captivity · Rehab.
540	**Techniques** · Falconry · MN · Rehab.
547	**Techniques** · Band. · IL · MN · TX · WI
548	**Techniques** · Marking · MN · SD
550	**Techniques** · Band. · Breed. Behav. · Dieldrin · DDT · MN · Pest. · Pest. Residues · Prey · Telemetry
552	**Techniques** · Band. · Migration · MN · Trapping · TX
554	**Techniques** · Band. · Behav. · Cedar Glen Roost · IL · Migration · Mississippi R · MN · Refuge · Telemetry · TX · Winter. Pop.
555	**Techniques** · Behav. · Breed. Behav. · Chippewa NF · Disturb. · Fledging · Marking · MN · Nestling · Prey · Reprod. Succ. · Telemetry
557	**Techniques** · Chippewa NF · Disturb. · Life History · Migration · Nest. · Photo. · Pub. Ed. · Status · Telemetry · Winter. Pop.
558	**Techniques** · Biopsy · MN · Pest. Residues · PCB
559	**Techniques** · Art. Nest Site · Behav. · Habit. Use · Manage. · MN · Nest. · Young Trans.
560	**Techniques** · Band. · Behav. · Life History · Migration · MN · Reprod. Succ.
561	**Techniques** · Behav. · Fledging · Habit. Use · Marking · MN · Parent. Behav. · Telemetry
573	**Techniques** · Habit. Prot. · Marking · Nest. · Pub. Ed. · Winter. Pop.
574	**Techniques** · Band. · Behav. · Growth · Nest. · Photo. · Pub. Ed.
576	**Techniques** · Band. · Behav. · Photo. · Pub. Ed. · Status
578	**Techniques** · Aggress. · Band. · Behav. · Mortality · Nest. · Photo. · Pub. Ed.
586	**Techniques** · Marking · MN · Nest. Survey · USFWS
589	**Techniques** · Band. · Broley · FL
595	**Techniques** · Great Lakes · MN · Nest. Survey
600	**Techniques** · CO · Road. Census · Winter. Pop.
613	**Techniques** · Mississippi R · Winter. Survey
670	**Techniques** · Fla. B.E. Sur. Comm. · FL · Great Lakes · Rehab. · Reprod. Succ. · Status · WI
694	**Techniques** · Captive Breed. · Rehab. · Telemetry
696	**Techniques** · Aircraft · Chippewa NF · Model · MN · Statistics
699	**Techniques** · Behav. · Chippewa NF · Fledging · Nestling · Telemetry
705	**Techniques** · Disease · Rehab. · Shooting · Trapping
726	**Techniques** · Habit. Use · MB · Reprod. Succ. · Status · SK
728	**Techniques** · Habit. Loss · Habit. Use · Manage. · McHargian Overlay · Nest. · Reprod. Succ. · SK

Master No.	Keywords
729	**Techniques** · Band. · Reprod. Succ. · SK
730	**Techniques** · Band. · Migration · Pub. Ed. · Status · SK
733	**Techniques** · Band. · Great Lakes · Migration · ON
734	**Techniques** · Habit. Loss · Habit. Use · Road Plan. · SK
736	**Techniques** · Habit. Use · Marking · Migration · MO · ND · SD · SK · WY
751	**Techniques** · Christmas Count · IL · Mississippi R · Status · Winter Survey
756	**Techniques** · Band. · Egg Trans. · Manage. · ME · Nest. Survey · Pest. · PCB · Refuge · Winter Survey
757	**Techniques** · Band. · Disturb. · Manage. · Marking · ME · Nest. · Nest. Survey · Shooting
768	**Techniques** · CA · Nest. Survey · Winter Survey
772	**Techniques** · Band. · Behav. · CN · ON · Reprod. Succ.
777	**Techniques** · CN · Habit. Use · ON · Reprod. Succ. · Status · Territory
778	**Techniques** · Disturb. · MB · Nest. Survey · ON · Reprod. Succ.
782	**Techniques** · Disturb. · MB · Nest. Survey · ON · Status
786	**Techniques** · Behav. · Distrib. · Hunt. Behav. · Manage. · Marking · Migration · Mortality · MO · Nest. · Pest. · Prey · Swan Lake NWR · Telemetry
804	**Techniques** · Art. Nest Site · AZ · Egg. Thin. · Habit. Use · Life History · Manage. · Marking · Nest. · Pest. · Research · Telemetry · Winter. Pop.
824	**Techniques** · Egg Trans. · Young Trans.
826	**Techniques** · BC · Gulf Is. · Habit. Use · Migration · Nest. Survey · Prey · San Juan Is. · Winter Survey · WA
830	**Techniques** · BC · Helicop. · Nest. Survey
832	**Techniques** · BC · Intrasp. Behav. · Marking · Nest. Survey · Pub. Ed. · Territory
840	**Techniques** · Behav. · Capture · CO · Habit. Use · Marking · Migration · Winter Survey
841	**Techniques** · Behav. · Chippewa NF · Dispersal · Disturb. · Fledging · MN · Nestling · Telemetry
842	**Techniques** · Behav. · Chippewa NF · Dispersal · Fledging · Hunt. Behav. · MN · Nestling · Telemetry
843	**Techniques** · Band. · Behav. · Chippewa NF · Dispersal · Fledging · Migration · MN · Nestling · Telemetry
847	**Techniques** · Captive Breed. · Disease · FAS · FL · Rehab.
880	**Techniques** · Behav. · Life History · Nest. · Nestling · OH · Parent. Behav. · Photo.
884	**Techniques** · Behav. · History · Nest. · OH · Photo.
887	**Techniques** · Behav. · Life History · Nest. · OH · Photo.
889	**Techniques** · Behav. · Life History · Nest. · OH · Photo.
897	**Techniques** · Winter Survey · WY
900	**Techniques** · AZ · Nest. · Photo.
943	**Techniques** · FL · Nest. Fail. · Status
978	**Techniques** · Capture · Intrasp. Behav. · IA · Mississippi R · Upper Miss. NWR · Winter Survey · WI
984	**Techniques** · Captivity · Egg Trans. · Heavy Metals · Law · Manage. · Migration · Nest. Survey · Pest. · Pub. Ed. · Status · Territory · Young Trans.
994	**Techniques** · Disease · Heavy Metals · Histology · Lead Poison. · MD
1000	**Techniques** · Band. · MN · Telemetry
1005	**Techniques** · CO · Road. Census · Winter. Pop.
1012	**Techniques** · Aging · Behav. · Nest. · VA
1024	**Techniques** · FL · Nest. Survey · Territory
1034	**Techniques** · Hacking · Manage. · NY · Photo.
1048	**Techniques** · AK · Habit. Use · Nest. Survey
1049	**Techniques** · CA · Nest. Survey · Road. Census · Winter Survey
1071	**Techniques** · Behav. · Chippewa NF · Fledging · Intrasp. Behav. · Marking · Mortality · MN · Nest. · Telemetry · Vocal.
1072	**Techniques** · Behav. · Chippewa NF · Fledging · Marking · MN

Master No.	Keywords
1083	**Techniques** · Ches. Bay · Winter Survey
1087	**Techniques** · Habit. Prot. · Manage. · NWF · Pub. Ed. · SD · Winter. Pop. · Young Trans.
1114	**Techniques** · Arkansas R · Band. · Capture · Habit. Use · Intersp. Behav. · OK · Salt Plains NWR · Sequoyah NWR · Wichita Mts. NWR · Winter Survey · Winter. Pop.
1122	**Techniques** · Acct. · NE · Road. Census · Winter. Pop.
1123	**Techniques** · NE · Road. Census · Winter. Pop.
1124	**Techniques** · NE · Rehab.
1126	**Techniques** · DDT · Histology · Pest. · Phys. · Spermato.
1136	**Techniques** · Band. · Jackson's Canyon · Winter Survey · WY
1137	**Techniques** · Band. · Poison. · Prey · Pub. Ed. · Winter Survey · WY
1147	**Techniques** · Great Lakes · Habit. Prot. · Manage. · MB · Nest. Survey · ON · Rehab. · Techniques
1147	**Techniques** · Great Lakes · Habit. Prot. · Manage. · MB · Nest. Survey · ON · Rehab. · Techniques
1151	**Techniques** · FL · Rehab.
1152	**Techniques** · FL · Nest. Survey · Rehab.
1159	**Techniques** · CA · Nest. Survey · Road. Census · Winter Survey
1177	**Techniques** · Rehab. · SK
1181	**Techniques** · Marking
1196	**Techniques** · Band. · Chippewa NF · IL · MN · Nest. Survey · USFS · Winter. Pop.
1214	**Techniques** · Band. · Chippewa NF · Marking · MN · Nest. Survey
1216	**Techniques** · NE · Road. Census
1217	**Techniques** · Band. · Chippewa NF · MN · Nest. Survey · Status · USFS
1221	**Techniques** · Aging · Behav. · Hunt. Behav. · Impound. · Intrasp. Behav. · MI · Nest. · Ottawa NF · Territory
1222	**Techniques** · Behav. · Fledging · Hunt. Behav. · Intersp. Behav. · Intrasp. Behav. · Marking · MI · Ottawa NF · Territory
1223	**Techniques** · Band. · Chippewa NF · MN · Nest. Survey · Reprod. Succ. · Status · Superior NF · Terminology
1229	**Techniques** · Anat. · Autumn Conc. · Behav. · Capture · Glacier NP · Habit. Use · Manage. · Marking · Migration · MT · Winter Survey
1253	**Techniques** · Behav. · Hacking · Heavy Metals · Intrasp. Behav. · Marking · Montezuma NWR · MI · MN · NY · Pest. · Telemetry · Young Trans.
1254	**Techniques** · Hacking · NY · Pub. Ed. · Young Trans.
1255	**Techniques** · Hacking · Manage. · NY · Young Trans.
1256	**Techniques** · Behav. · Hacking · Manage. · NY · Pest. · Prey · PCB · Young Trans.
1274	**Techniques** · Manage. · NY · Young Trans.
1275	**Techniques** · Dispersal · NY · Young Trans.
1290	**Techniques** · CA · Rehab.
1297	**Techniques** · Aleutian Is. · AK · Band. · Distrib. · Econ. Import. · Nest. · Plumage · Prey · Shooting
1335	**Techniques** · NM · Rehab.
1337	**Techniques** · NE · Road. Census · Winter. Pop.
1343	**Techniques** · Intersp. Behav. · Photo.
1360	**Techniques** · Habit. Loss · Nest. Survey · Pest. · Shooting · Terminology · USFWS
1384	**Techniques** · Asper. · Nest. Survey · OR · Road. Census · Winter Survey
1448	**Techniques** · Band. · FL · Migration · Prey
1484	**Techniques** · Disturb. · Great Lakes · Manage. · Nest. Survey · ON · Research · Status
1487	**Techniques** · Band. · Disturb. · Great Lakes · MI · Nest. Survey · Pest.
1488	**Techniques** · AR · Band. · FL · GA · Manage. · Migration · MI · TN · Young Trans.
1490	**Techniques** · Manage. · MI · Young Trans.
1499	**Techniques** · Capture · OH · Trapping · Winter. Pop.
1513	**Techniques** · Disease · MN · Rehab. · Shooting · Trapping
1563	**Techniques** · Channel Is. · CA · Rehab. · Telemetry
1585	**Techniques** · Nest. Survey · VA
1592	**Techniques** · Marking · Molt. · Telemetry

Master No.	Keywords
1594	**Techniques** · Rehab. · WA
1596	**Techniques** · Band. · Broley · FL
1601	**Techniques** · Behav. · Capture · Glacier NP · Hunt. Behav. · Intersp. Behav. · Intrasp. Behav. · Manage. · MT · Winter Survey
1610	**Techniques** · Band. · Behav. · Dispersal · MN · WI
1628	**Techniques** · Capture · Indian Culture · Trapping
1649	**Techniques** · Band. · Capture · IL · Winter. Pop.
1650	**Techniques** · Capture · Habit. Use · Hunt. Behav. · Intersp. Behav. · IL · Marking · Mississippi R · Prey · Winter Survey
1651	**Techniques** · Anat. · Behav. · Capture · Hunt. Behav. · IL · Marking · Plumage · Prey · Telemetry · Winter Survey
1653	**Techniques** · Aging · Molt.
1654	**Techniques** · Endang. Sp. · Manage.
1656	**Techniques** · Band. · Migration · Pub. Ed. · Winter. Pop.
1661	**Techniques** · CA · Falconry · Rehab.
1684	**Techniques** · Band. · Field ID · FL · Life History · Nest. · Prey · Status
1688	**Techniques** · Ches. Bay · Kepone · Pest.
1705	**Techniques** · Band. · DC · Migration · MD · Nest. · Winter. Pop.
1708	**Techniques** · AK · Histology · Lower 48 · Pest. · Spermato. · Toxicol. · USFWS
1711	**Techniques** · Egg · Pest.
1728	**Techniques** · Band. · MN · WI
1732	**Techniques** · Egg. Thin. · Hacking · NY · Telemetry · Young Trans.
1752	**Techniques** · Egg. Thin. · Habit. Use · Manage. · MD · Nest. Survey · Pest.
1768	**Techniques** · Marking · Migration · MN
1769	**Techniques** · Band. · Nest. Survey · Reprod. Succ. · TX · Winter Survey
1794	**Techniques** · AZ · Winter Survey
1799	**Techniques** · Band. · ME
1829	**Techniques** · AK · Band. · Behav. · Kodiak NWR · Nest. Survey · Reprod. Succ.
1871	**Techniques** · Egg Trans. · Hacking · Manage. · ME · MN · NY · Pest. · PCB · WI · Young Trans.

Master No.	Keywords
1875	**Techniques** · Marking · Pub. Ed. · USFWS
1932	**Techniques** · AK · Disturb. · Helicop. · Nest. Survey
1935	**Techniques** · Captivity · Capture
1988	**Techniques** · Anat. · Behav. · Capture · Depred. · Econ. Import. · Intersp. Behav. · Manage. · NB · Prey
1994	**Techniques** · Model · Status
414	**Telemetry** · Hacking · Montezuma NWR · NY · Techniques · Young Trans.
550	**Telemetry** · Band. · Breed. Behav. · Dieldrin · DDT · MN · Pest. · Pest. Residues · Prey · Techniques
554	**Telemetry** · Band. · Behav. · Cedar Glen Roost · IL · Migration · Mississippi R · MN · Refuge · Techniques · TX · Winter. Pop.
555	**Telemetry** · Behav. · Breed. Behav. · Chippewa NF · Disturb. · Fledging · Marking · MN · Nestling · Prey · Reprod. Succ. · Techniques
557	**Telemetry** · Chippewa NF · Disturb. · Life History · Migration · Nest. · Photo. · Pub. Ed. · Status · Techniques · Winter. Pop.
561	**Telemetry** · Behav. · Fledging · Habit. Use · Marking · MN · Parent. Behav. · Techniques
694	**Telemetry** · Captive Breed. · Rehab. · Techniques
699	**Telemetry** · Behav. · Chippewa NF · Fledging · Nestling · Techniques
786	**Telemetry** · Behav. · Distrib. · Hunt. Behav. · Manage. · Marking · Migration · Mortality · MO · Nest. · Pest. · Prey · Swan Lake NWR · Techniques
804	**Telemetry** · Art. Nest Site · AZ · Egg. Thin. · Habit. Use · Life History · Manage. · Marking · Nest. · Pest. · Research · Techniques · Winter. Pop.
841	**Telemetry** · Behav. · Chippewa NF · Dispersal · Disturb. · Fledging · MN · Nestling · Techniques
842	**Telemetry** · Behav. · Chippewa NF · Dispersal · Fledging · Hunt. Behav. · MN · Nestling · Techniques

Master No.	Keywords
843	**Telemetry** · Band. · Behav. · Chippewa NF · Dispersal · Fledging · Migration · MN · Nestling · Techniques
1000	**Telemetry** · Band. · MN · Techniques
1071	**Telemetry** · Behav. · Chippewa NF · Fledging · Intrasp. Behav. · Marking · Mortality · MN · Nest. · Techniques · Vocal.
1253	**Telemetry** · Behav. · Hacking · Heavy Metals · Intrasp. Behav. · Marking · Montezuma NWR · MI · MN · NY · Pest. · Techniques · Young Trans.
1563	**Telemetry** · Channel Is. · CA · Rehab. · Techniques
1592	**Telemetry** · Marking · Molt. · Techniques
1651	**Telemetry** · Anat. · Behav. · Capture · Hunt. Behav. · IL · Marking · Plumage · Prey · Techniques · Winter Survey
1732	**Telemetry** · Egg. Thin. · Hacking · NY · Techniques · Young Trans.
719	**Tennessee NWR** · Prey · Winter Survey
431	**Terminology** · AK · Behav. · Climatology · Disease · Kodiak NWR · Life History · Marking · Nest. · Nest. Survey · Parasites · Reprod. Succ. · Techniques
686	**Terminology** · IL · Nest. · Winter. Pop.
816	**Terminology** · Hunt. Behav. · Nest. · PA
1223	**Terminology** · Band. · Chippewa NF · MN · Nest. Survey · Reprod. Succ. · Status · Superior NF · Techniques
1360	**Terminology** · Habit. Loss · Nest. Survey · Pest. · Shooting · Techniques · USFWS
1473	**Terminology** · MI · Nest. Survey · ON
1475	**Terminology** · MI · Nest. Survey · ON
1550	**Terminology** · AZ · Behav. · Disturb. · Habit. Loss · Habit. Use · Hunt. Behav. · Nest. Survey · Prey · Status · Territory
1681	**Terminology** · Cont. B.E. Proj. · Nest. Survey · NAS · Status
1855	**Terminology** · IL · IN · MI · MN · Nest. Survey · OH · USFWS · WI
1939	**Terminology** · Habit. Use · MB · Nest. Survey · SK
1546	**Terra Nova NP** · Intersp. Behav. · NF · Winter. Pop.
125	**Territory** · Disturb. · Law · Logging · Manage. · Nest.
465	**Territory** · AK · Disturb. · Habit. Loss · Habit. Use · Logging · Nest. · Nest. Survey
466	**Territory** · AK · Climatology · Distrib. · Disturb. · Forestry · Habit. Loss · Habit. Use · Manage. · Nest. · Nest. Survey · Reprod. Succ.
732	**Territory** · Disturb. · Habit. Use · MB · Nest. · SK
775	**Territory** · Nest. Survey · ON · Reprod. Succ. · Status
776	**Territory** · Nest. Survey · ON · Reprod. Succ. · Status
777	**Territory** · CN · Habit. Use · ON · Reprod. Succ. · Status · Techniques
801	**Territory** · Disturb. · Nest. · Nest. Survey · Reprod. Succ. · Statistics · WA
832	**Territory** · BC · Intrasp. Behav. · Marking · Nest. Survey · Pub. Ed. · Techniques
833	**Territory** · BC · Hunt. Behav. · Intersp. Behav. · Intrasp. Behav. · Nest. Survey · Prey
878	**Territory** · AK · Disturb. · Habit. Use · Kodiak NWR · Life History · Nest. Fail. · Reprod. Succ.
984	**Territory** · Captivity · Egg Trans. · Heavy Metals · Law · Manage. · Migration · Nest. Survey · Pest. · Pub. Ed. · Status · Techniques · Young Trans.
1024	**Territory** · FL · Nest. Survey · Techniques
1221	**Territory** · Aging · Behav. · Hunt. Behav. · Impound. · Intrasp. Behav. · MI · Nest. · Ottawa NF · Techniques
1222	**Territory** · Behav. · Fledging · Hunt. Behav. · Intersp. Behav. · Intrasp. Behav. · Marking · MI · Ottawa NF · Techniques
1299	**Territory** · Habit. Use · Intersp. Behav. · Nest. Survey · Yellowstone NP
1355	**Territory** · Hunt. Behav. · Prey · Winter. Pop.
1454	**Territory** · Nest. · Nestling
1530	**Territory** · AK · Habit. Use · Manage. · Nest. Survey

Master No.	Keywords
1550	**Territory** · AZ · Behav. · Disturb. · Habit. Loss · Habit. Use · Hunt. Behav. · Nest. Survey · Prey · Status · Terminology
1640	**Territory** · Aggress. · Behav. · BLM · Disturb. · Habit. Loss · Habit. Use · Hunt. Behav. · Life History · Manage. · Nest. · Pest. · Prey · Shooting
1741	**Territory** · Disturb. · Habit. Use · Manage. · MT · Nest. Survey · Pop. Turnover · Reprod. Succ. · Status · Yellowstone NP
1771	**Territory** · CA · Disturb. · Habit. Loss · Habit. Use · Manage. · Nest. Survey · Prey · Shooting · Trapping
1777	**Territory** · CA · Habit. Use · Manage. · Nest. Survey · Status
1865	**Territory** · AZ · BLM · CAP · Egg · Habit. Prot. · Manage. · Nest. · Orme D · Salt R · Taxonomy · Verde R
672	**Three Lakes Ranch** · FL · Habit. Prot. · Refuge
674	**Three Lakes Ranch** · FL · Habit. Prot. · Refuge
399	**Three Sisters B.E. Pres.** · CA · Manage. · Refuge · USFS · Winter Survey
1347	**Three Sisters B.E. Pres.** · CA
372	**Toxicol.** · Autopsy · AK · Cont. U.S. · DDT · NB · Pest. · Residues
432	**Toxicol.** · Behav. · Captivity · DDT · Pest.
524	**Toxicol.** · DDT · Pest. · USFWS
525	**Toxicol.** · DDT · Pest. · USFWS
565	**Toxicol.** · FL · ME · NJ · Pest.
1367	**Toxicol.** · Heavy Metals · Life History · Taxonomy
1707	**Toxicol.** · Pest. · Spermato.
1708	**Toxicol.** · AK · Histology · Lower 48 · Pest. · Spermato. · Techniques · USFWS
1709	**Toxicol.** · FL · ME · MO · NJ · Pest. · USFWS
1710	**Toxicol.** · Mortality · Pest.
1712	**Toxicol.** · Autopsy · Mortality · Pest.
1830	**Toxicol.** · DDT · Pest.
1831	**Toxicol.** · Autopsy · DDT · MO · NJ · Residues
343	**Trapping** · Captivity · Depred. · Winter. Pop. · WV
456	**Trapping** · MI · Nest. · Status · Winter. Pop.
459	**Trapping** · Autopsy · AK · CN · Disease · Lower 48 · Parasites · Poison. · Shooting
460	**Trapping** · Asper. · Autopsy · Disease · MO · Rehab. · Techniques
499	**Trapping** · Law · Manage. · Nest. · Poison. · Pub. Ed. · Shooting · SK
552	**Trapping** · Band. · Migration · MN · Techniques · TX
705	**Trapping** · Disease · Rehab. · Shooting · Techniques
798	**Trapping** · Life History · Pub. Ed.
1086	**Trapping** · CO · Electro. · Manage. · NV · TX · UT
1318	**Trapping** · NV
1499	**Trapping** · Capture · OH · Techniques · Winter. Pop.
1513	**Trapping** · Disease · MN · Rehab. · Shooting · Techniques
1576	**Trapping** · NV · Pub. Ed.
1618	**Trapping** · Pub. Ed. · WY · Yellowstone NP
1628	**Trapping** · Capture · Indian Culture · Techniques
1746	**Trapping** · Nest. · OK · Status
1771	**Trapping** · CA · Disturb. · Habit. Loss · Habit. Use · Manage. · Nest. Survey · Prey · Shooting · Territory
1941	**Trapping** · MO · Nest. · Status
1065	**Tule Lake NWR** · Behav. · CA · Disturb. · Habit. Use · Klamath Lower Klamath Lake NWR · Manage. · OR · Prey · Winter Survey
1967	**Tule Lake NWR** · CA · Disturb. · Habit. Use · Lower Klamath Lake NWR · Modoc NWR · Winter Survey
392	**TN** · Shooting · Winter. Pop.
421	**TN** · Capture · Folklore · Nest. · Prey · Techniques
423	**TN** · Mississippi R · Nest. · Pub. Ed. · Reelfoot L · Shooting · Status · Winter. Pop.
509	**TN** · Audubon · Behav. · Nest.
517	**TN** · Nest.
596	**TN** · Nest. · Reelfoot L
649	**TN** · Illinois R · IL · KY · Mississippi R · Winter Survey

Master No.	Keywords
650	TN · Illinois R · IL · KY · Mississippi R · Winter Survey
651	TN · Illinois R · IA · IL · KY · Mississippi R · MO · NE · Winter Survey
652	TN · Illinois R · IA · KY · Mississippi R · MO · NE · Winter Survey
714	TN · Distrib. · Habit. Use · Nest. · Plumage · Shooting · Taxonomy · Winter. Pop.
715	TN · AR · Habit. Use · Mississippi R · MS · Nest. · Reelfoot L · Shooting
716	TN · Nest.
717	TN · Nest.
718	TN · Nest. · Prey · Winter. Pop.
934	TN · AL · Nest. · Prey · Shooting · Winter. Pop.
1097	TN · Reelfoot L · Winter Survey
1140	TN · Nest.
1183	TN · Reelfoot L · Winter. Pop.
1382	TN · TVA · Winter. Pop.
1402	TN · Pub. Ed. · Reelfoot L · Winter. Pop.
1403	TN · Hunt. Behav. · Winter Survey
1462	TN · Nest. · Reelfoot L
1463	TN · Nest. · Reelfoot L · Winter. Pop.
1488	TN · AR · Band. · FL · GA · Manage. · Migration · MI · Techniques · Young Trans.
1599	TN · Nest. · Reelfoot L
1663	TN · Nest. · Prey · Reelfoot L
1729	TN · Acct. · NC · Winter. Pop.
1759	TN · Acct. · TVA
1991	TN · Pub. Ed. · Winter Survey
1382	TVA · TN · Winter. Pop.
1444	TVA · KY · Land Between the Lakes · Pub. Ed. · Winter. Pop.
1759	TVA · Acct. · TN
27	TX · Acct. · OK · Road. Census · Techniques
50	TX · Egg. Thin. · FL · LA · Pest. · Status
90	TX · Flight · Shooting
177	TX · Nest. Survey · Winter Survey · Winter. Pop.
277	TX · Nest.
412	TX · Nest. · Winter. Pop.
413	TX · Egg Coll. · Nest.
547	TX · Band. · IL · MN · Techniques · WI
552	TX · Band. · Migration · MN · Techniques · Trapping

Master No.	Keywords
554	TX · Band. · Behav. · Cedar Glen Roost · IL · Migration · Mississippi R · MN · Refuge · Techniques · Telemetry · Winter. Pop.
611	TX · Winter. Pop.
1063	TX · Behav. · Disturb. · Habit. Loss · Habit. Use · Manage. · Prey · Research · Winter Survey
1078	TX · Nest.
1086	TX · CO · Electro. · Manage. · NV · Trapping · UT
1372	TX · Anat. · Distrib. · Habit. Use · Nest. · Plumage · Taxonomy · Winter. Pop.
1616	TX · Hurricane · Nest.
1629	TX · Distrib. · Endang. Sp. · Nest. Survey · Winter Survey
1630	TX · Distrib. · Endang. Sp. · Nest. Survey · Winter Survey
1631	TX · Distrib. · Nest. Survey · Reprod. Succ. · Status · Winter Survey
1632	TX · Distrib. · Habit. Use · Nest. Survey · Status · Winter Survey
1639	TX · AZ · CA · Endang. Sp. · NM · NV · OK · Status · UT
1742	TX · Habit. Use · Nest. Survey
1766	TX · Acct. · Nest. Survey · Reprod. Succ.
1767	TX · Acct. · Nest. Survey · Reprod. Succ.
1769	TX · Band. · Nest. Survey · Reprod. Succ. · Techniques · Winter Survey
1838	TX · AZ · CO · KS · Nest. Survey · NM · OK · Salt Fork R · USFWS · UT · Verde R · WY
1852	TX · AZ · Manage. · Nest. Survey · NM · OK · Salt Fork R · USFWS · Verde R
1867	TX · Nest. Survey · USFWS
1944	TX · Depred. · Hunt. Behav. · NM
1997	TX · Egg Coll. · Nest.
1443	Upper Miss. · Winter Survey
978	Upper Miss. NWR · Capture · Intrasp. Behav. · IA · Mississippi R · Techniques · Winter Survey · WI
154	USFWS · Lower 48 · Manage. · Nest. Survey · Status
156	USFWS · Egg Trans. · Manage. · ME · MN
524	USFWS · DDT · Pest. · Toxicol.
525	USFWS · DDT · Pest. · Toxicol.
567	USFWS · Pest. · PCB

Master No.	Keywords
586	USFWS · Marking · MN · Nest. Survey · Techniques
1081	USFWS · MN · Nest. Survey
1146	USFWS · Great Lakes · Nest. Survey
1148	USFWS · Breed. Behav. · Captive Breed. · Intrasp. Behav.
1319	USFWS · Endang. Sp.
1333	USFWS · Endang. Sp.
1359	USFWS · AK · Lower 48 · Nest. Survey
1360	USFWS · Habit. Loss · Nest. Survey · Pest. · Shooting · Techniques · Terminology
1517	USFWS · Pest. · PCB
1531	USFWS · Band. · Christmas Count · Life History · Migration · Nest. · Status · Winter Survey
1572	USFWS · Habit. Loss · OR · WA
1708	USFWS · AK · Histology · Lower 48 · Pest. · Spermato. · Techniques · Toxicol.
1709	USFWS · FL · ME · MO · NJ · Pest. · Toxicol.
1832	USFWS · Endang. Sp. · Field ID · Manage. · Status
1833	USFWS · Pest.
1834	USFWS · Endang. Sp. · Field ID · Manage. · Status
1835	USFWS · Educ. Mat.
1837	USFWS · Nest. Survey · NM
1838	USFWS · AZ · CO · KS · Nest. Survey · NM · OK · Salt Fork R · TX · UT · Verde R · WY
1839	USFWS · CA · ID · MT · Nest. Survey · NV · OR · WA
1840	USFWS · DE · Nest. Survey
1842	USFWS · Nest. Survey · NJ
1843	USFWS · ID · Nest. Survey · OR · WA
1844	USFWS · CA · ID · Nest. Survey · NV · OR · WA
1845	USFWS · ME · Nest. Survey
1846	USFWS · CO · IA · KS · MO · MT · Nest. Survey · ND · NE · SD · UT · WY
1847	USFWS · Ches. Bay · Nest. Survey · New England
1848	USFWS · Endang. Sp. · Field ID · Manage. · Status
1849	USFWS · CO · IA · KS · MO · MT · Nest. Survey · ND · NE · SD · UT · WY
1850	USFWS · AK · Lower 48 · Nest. Survey · Reprod. Succ.
1851	USFWS · Egg Trans. · Manage. · ME · MN
1852	USFWS · AZ · Manage. · Nest. Survey · NM · OK · Salt Fork R · TX · Verde R
1853	USFWS · CA · ID · Nest. Survey · NV · OR · WA
1854	USFWS · CO · Glacier NP · Manage. · Missouri R · MT · Nest. Survey · SD
1855	USFWS · IL · IN · MI · MN · Nest. Survey · OH · Terminology · WI
1856	USFWS · Nest. Survey · ND
1857	USFWS · Missouri R · Nest. Survey · SD
1858	USFWS · MT · Nest. Survey · WY
1859	USFWS · IA · KS · Missouri R · MO · Nest. Survey · ND · NE · Rocky Mt. Region · SD · Winter. Pop.
1860	USFWS · Missouri R · Nest. Survey · NE · SD · Winter. Pop.
1861	USFWS · Egg Trans. · Manage. · ME · MN · WI
1862	USFWS · Ches. Bay · Nest. Survey · New England
1864	USFWS · Art · History · Indian Culture
1866	USFWS · AZ · Nest. Survey
1867	USFWS · Nest. Survey · TX
1868	USFWS · MI · MN · Nest. Survey · OH · WI
1869	USFWS · Law · Shooting
1874	USFWS · Distrib. · Endang. Sp. · Law · Life History · Manage. · Status · Taxonomy
1875	USFWS · Marking · Pub. Ed. · Techniques
1883	USFWS · Bear Valley NWR · Habit. Prot. · OR · Refuge
51	USFS · Disturb. · Habit. Use · Manage. · Nest. · OR
399	USFS · CA · Manage. · Refuge · Three Sisters B.E. Pres. · Winter Survey
445	USFS · Great Lakes · Manage. · MI · MN · Natl. For. · Nest. Survey · WI
447	USFS · Behav. · CA · Disturb. · Hunt. Behav. · Manage. · Natl. For. · Prey · San Bernardino Mts. · Winter. Pop.
551	USFS · Chippewa NF · Disturb. · Intersp. Behav.
671	USFS · FL · Nest. · Ocala NF

Master No.	Keywords
697	USFS · Disturb. · Law
814	USFS · Disturb. · Great Lakes · Manage. · Nest. Survey · Pub. Ed. · Status
815	USFS · Chippewa NF · Great Lakes · Manage. · Nest. Survey
981	USFS · Endang. Sp. · Great Lakes · Nest. Survey · Pub. Ed. · Status
1188	USFS · Chippewa NF · Habit. Use · Manage. · MN · Nest. Survey · Status
1189	USFS · Chippewa NF · Habit. Use · Manage. · MN · Nest. Survey
1190	USFS · Chippewa NF · MN · Nest. Survey
1191	USFS · Chippewa NF · MN · Nest. Survey
1192	USFS · Chippewa NF · MN · Nest. Survey
1193	USFS · Chippewa NF · MN · Nest. Survey
1194	USFS · Chippewa NF · MN · Nest. Survey
1195	USFS · Chippewa NF · Disturb. · Habit. Loss · MN
1196	USFS · Band. · Chippewa NF · IL · MN · Nest. Survey · Techniques · Winter. Pop.
1197	USFS · Chippewa NF · Field ID · Habit. Use · MN · Nest.
1198	USFS · Chippewa NF · MN · Nest. Survey
1200	USFS · Chippewa NF · Disturb. · MN · ND · Poison. · Pub. Ed. · Shooting · Status
1201	USFS · Chippewa NF · MN · Nest. Survey · Status
1202	USFS · Chippewa NF · MN · Nest. Survey · Status
1203	USFS · Chippewa NF · MN · Nest. Survey
1204	USFS · Chippewa NF · MN · Nest. Survey
1205	USFS · Chippewa NF · MN · Nest. Survey
1206	USFS · Chippewa NF · Habit. Prot. · Hunt-Wesson · MN · Pub. Ed.
1207	USFS · Chippewa NF · Manage. · MN · Nest. Survey · Status
1209	USFS · Chippewa NF · MN · Nest. Survey · Status
1210	USFS · Child. Eagle Area · Hunt-Wesson · Pub. Ed. · Refuge
1211	USFS · Chippewa NF · MN · Nest. Survey · Status
1213	USFS · Chippewa NF · MN · Nest. Survey · Status
1215	USFS · Chippewa NF · Manage. · MN · Nest. Survey · Refuge
1217	USFS · Band. · Chippewa NF · MN · Nest. Survey · Status · Techniques
1218	USFS · Chippewa NF · Manage. · MN
1219	USFS · Chippewa NF · Manage. · MN
1220	USFS · Chippewa NF · Manage. · MN
1224	USFS · Habit. Use · Nest. Survey · Superior NF
1503	USFS · Great Lakes · Manage.
1504	USFS · Great Lakes · Nest. Survey
1508	USFS · Field ID · Nest. Survey · NWF · RIC
1820	USFS · Habit. Prot. · Manage. · Nest. · Winter Survey
1821	USFS · Chippewa NF · Manage. · MN · Pub. Ed.
1823	USFS · Data Coll. · Manage.
1824	USFS · Child. Eagle Area · Chippewa NF · Hunt-Wesson · Manage. · MN · Pub. Ed. · Refuge
1825	USFS · Aircraft · Chippewa NF · Great Lakes · MI · MN · Nest. Survey · Reprod. Succ. · Status · WI
1826	USFS · Chippewa NF · Pub. Ed.
1827	USFS · Manage.
1914	USFS · Behav. · Chippewa NF · Disturb. · Manage. · MN
1918	USFS · Great Lakes · Nest. Survey
1919	USFS · Great Lakes · Nest. Survey
608	UT · Distrib. · Electro. · Field ID · Life History · Prey · Winter. Pop.
760	UT · Winter. Pop.
858	UT · CO · Nest. · Winter. Pop.
1086	UT · CO · Electro. · Manage. · NV · Trapping · TX
1469	UT · Prey · Winter Survey
1470	UT · Behav. · Habit. Use · Hunt. Behav. · Prey · Winter Survey
1622	UT · Electro.
1639	UT · AZ · CA · Endang. Sp. · NM · NV · OK · Status · TX
1743	UT · Habit. Use · Prey · Winter. Pop.
1838	UT · AZ · CO · KS · Nest. Survey · NM · OK · Salt Fork R · TX · USFWS · Verde R · WY

Master No.	Keywords
1846	UT · CO · IA · KS · MO · MT · Nest. Survey · ND · NE · SD · USFWS · WY
1849	UT · CO · IA · KS · MO · MT · Nest. Survey · ND · NE · SD · USFWS · WY
1887	UT · Winter. Pop.
1981	UT · CO · Electro. · ID · Manage. · NV · WY
1411	Vancouver Is. · BC · Hunt. Behav. · Nest.
173	Verde R · AZ · Marking · Pub. Ed. · Techniques
449	Verde R · AZ · CAP · Habit. Loss · Nest. · Orme D · Salt R
1008	Verde R · AZ · Status
1789	Verde R · AZ · Disturb. · Nest. Survey
1793	Verde R · AZ · CAP · Nest. Survey · Orme D · Salt R
1838	Verde R · AZ · CO · KS · Nest. Survey · NM · OK · Salt Fork R · TX · USFWS · UT · WY
1852	Verde R · AZ · Manage. · Nest. Survey · NM · OK · Salt Fork R · TX · USFWS
1865	Verde R · AZ · BLM · CAP · Egg · Habit. Prot. · Manage. · Nest. · Orme D · Salt R · Taxonomy · Territory
1071	Vocal. · Behav. · Chippewa NF · Fledging · Intrasp. Behav. · Marking · Mortality · MN · Nest. · Techniques · Telemetry
1521	Vocal. · Aggress. · Behav. · Disturb. · Habit. Loss · Hunt. Behav. · Nest. · Prey · San Juan Is. · Shooting · Status · WA
99	VA · Habit. Prot.
124	VA · Ches. Bay · Manage. · Mason Neck NWR · Refuge
212	VA · Egg Coll. · Nest.
213	VA · Egg Coll. · Nest.
214	VA · Egg Coll. · Nest. · Prey
215	VA · Egg Coll. · Habit. Use · Nest. · Photo.
216	VA · Egg Coll. · Nest.
280	VA · MD · Nest. Survey
309	VA · Hunt. Behav. · Prey · Shooting · Winter. Pop.
494	VA · DE · Egg · Egg Coll. · MD · Nest.
511	VA · Ches. Bay · Endang. Sp. · Manage. · Refuge
512	VA · Ches. Bay · Manage. · Mason Neck NWR · Refuge
513	VA · Ches. Bay · DC · Manage. · Mason Neck NWR · Refuge
667	VA · Acct. · AK · CA · FL · Taxonomy
771	VA · Nest. · Winter. Pop.
995	VA · Behav. · Fledging · Winter. Pop.
996	VA · Disturb. · Fledging · Habit. Use · Intersp. Behav. · Intrasp. Behav.
1012	VA · Aging · Behav. · Nest. · Techniques
1013	VA · Egg Coll. · Nest.
1102	VA · Behav. · Caledon SP · Disturb. · Habit. Loss · Habit. Use · Manage. · Nest. · Prey
1103	VA · Caledon SP · Disturb. · Habit. Loss · Manage. · Nest.
1104	VA · Behav. · Caledon SP · Disturb. · Habit. Loss · Habit. Use · Manage.
1258	VA · Egg Coll. · Nest.
1514	VA · Nest.
1584	VA · Nest.
1585	VA · Nest. Survey · Techniques
1586	VA · Nest. Survey
1613	VA · Nest.
1614	VA · Egg Coll. · MD · Nest.
1727	VA · Egg · Egg Coll. · MI
1812	VA · Ches. Bay · DE · Econ. Import. · Habit. Use · Life History · MD · Nest. Survey · NC · NJ · Prey · PA
1836	VA · Mason Neck NWR · Refuge
1896	VA · Endang. Sp. · Status
1901	VA · Distrib. · DE · Life History · NJ · Prey
1934	VA · Nest.
168	Wash. Dept. Game · Habit. Prot. · Manage. · Nat. Conserv. · Skagit R · Winter. Pop. · WA
322	Weight · Anat. · FL · Plumage
1163	Weight
1951	Wheeler NWR · AL · Winter. Pop.
1114	Wichita Mts. NWR · Arkansas R · Band. · Capture · Habit. Use · Intersp. Behav. · OK · Salt Plains NWR · Sequoyah NWR · Techniques · Winter Survey · Winter. Pop.

Master No.	Keywords
1115	**Wichita Mts. NWR** · Disturb. · Habit. Use · Manage. · Migration · OK · Prey · Salt Fork R · Salt Plains NWR · Sequoyah NWR · Shooting · Status · Taxonomy · Winter Survey
825	**Wilson Ornithol. Soc.** · AK · Comm. Conserv. · CN · Lower 48 · Status
5	**Winter Survey** · Ches. Bay · Nest. Survey
6	**Winter Survey** · Ches. Bay
7	**Winter Survey** · Ches. Bay · Nest. Survey
9	**Winter Survey** · Ches. Bay · Nest. Survey · Status
115	**Winter Survey** · IA
119	**Winter Survey** · Nest. Survey · NAS · Pub. Ed. · Status
131	**Winter Survey** · NE · Platte R
175	**Winter Survey** · Anat. · Capture · CO · San Luis Valley · Techniques
177	**Winter Survey** · Nest. Survey · TX · Winter. Pop.
178	**Winter Survey** · AR · Field ID · Winter. Pop.
179	**Winter Survey** · Jackson's Canyon · WY
180	**Winter Survey** · Jackson's Canyon · WY
195	**Winter Survey** · Distrib. · LA · Nest. Survey
196	**Winter Survey** · Distrib. · LA · Migration · Mortality · Nest. Survey · Reprod. Succ. · Shooting · Status
348	**Winter Survey** · NE · Platte R
356	**Winter Survey** · Christmas Count · Status
364	**Winter Survey** · Hunt. Behav. · IL · Mississippi R · MO
369	**Winter Survey** · Law · MI · Nest. Survey · NJ
395	**Winter Survey** · CA · Nest. Survey
399	**Winter Survey** · CA · Manage. · Refuge · Three Sisters B.E. Pres. · USFS
451	**Winter Survey** · CO · Habit. Use · Nest. · San Luis Valley · Status
464	**Winter Survey** · KY · Land Between the Lakes
474	**Winter Survey** · CO · Habit. Use · Nest. · San Luis Valley · Status
484	**Winter Survey** · AK · Chilkat R · Prey · Shooting

Master No.	Keywords
496	**Winter Survey** · Climatology · Migration · OH · Poison. · Shooting
519	**Winter Survey** · CA · Depred. · Habit. Use · Manage. · Mortality · Nest. · Prey · Shasta-Trinity NF
520	**Winter Survey** · Distrib. · Habit. Use · Migration · Nest. Survey · Status · WI
549	**Winter Survey** · Life History · Missouri R · Pub. Ed. · SD
583	**Winter Survey** · Habit. Use · Manage. · Nest. Survey · OR · Poison. · Prey · San Juan Is. · Shooting · Status · WA
609	**Winter Survey** · Behav. · Habit. Use · Mississippi R · MN · Pest. Residues · Prey
613	**Winter Survey** · Mississippi R · Techniques
614	**Winter Survey** · IA · IL · Mississippi R · NE · WI
615	**Winter Survey** · IA · IL · Mississippi R · NE
616	**Winter Survey** · Mississippi R
617	**Winter Survey** · Lower 48 · Migration · Mississippi R
618	**Winter Survey** · Lower 48 · Mississippi R
619	**Winter Survey** · Mississippi R
620	**Winter Survey** · Illinois R · IA · IL · Mississippi R · WI
621	**Winter Survey** · Illinois R · IL · KY · Mississippi R · NE
624	**Winter Survey** · Illinois R · IA · IL · KY · Mississippi R · NE
625	**Winter Survey** · Mississippi R
626	**Winter Survey** · Illinois R · IA · IL · Mississippi R · MO
627	**Winter Survey** · Mississippi R
628	**Winter Survey** · Illinois R · IA · IL · KY · Mississippi R · MO
631	**Winter Survey** · Illinois R · IA · IL · KY · Mississippi R
632	**Winter Survey** · Illinois R · IA · IL · KY · Mississippi R
634	**Winter Survey** · Illinois R · IA · IL · KY · Mississippi R · MO · NE
635	**Winter Survey** · Illinois R · IA · IL · KY · Mississippi R · Missouri R · MO · NE · Wisconsin R
636	**Winter Survey** · Illinois R · IA · IL · KY · Mississippi R · Missouri R · MO · NE · Wisconsin R

Master No.	Keywords
637	**Winter Survey** · Illinois R · IA · IL · KY · Mississippi R · Missouri R · MO · NE · Wisconsin R
638	**Winter Survey** · Illinois R · IA · IL · KY · Mississippi R · MO · NE
639	**Winter Survey** · Illinois R · IA · IL · KY · Mississippi R · MO · NE
641	**Winter Survey** · IL · WI
643	**Winter Survey** · Illinois R · IL · KY · Mississippi R · MO · NE
644	**Winter Survey** · Illinois R · IL · KY · Mississippi R · MO · NE
646	**Winter Survey** · Illinois R · IL · KY · Mississippi R · MO · NE
647	**Winter Survey** · Illinois R · Lower 48 · Mississippi R
648	**Winter Survey** · Habit. Prot. · IA · IL · Mississippi R · MO
649	**Winter Survey** · Illinois R · IL · KY · Mississippi R · TN
650	**Winter Survey** · Illinois R · IL · KY · Mississippi R · TN
651	**Winter Survey** · Illinois R · IA · IL · KY · Mississippi R · MO · NE · TN
652	**Winter Survey** · Illinois R · IA · KY · Mississippi R · MO · NE · TN
653	**Winter Survey** · Mississippi R
654	**Winter Survey** · Migration · Mississippi R
693	**Winter Survey** · Wisconsin R · WI
719	**Winter Survey** · Prey · Tennessee NWR
751	**Winter Survey** · Christmas Count · IL · Mississippi R · Status · Techniques
756	**Winter Survey** · Band. · Egg Trans. · Manage. · ME · Nest. Survey · Pest. · PCB · Refuge · Techniques
768	**Winter Survey** · CA · Nest. Survey · Techniques
821	**Winter Survey** · Habit. Use · OK · Status
826	**Winter Survey** · BC · Gulf Is. · Habit. Use · Migration · Nest. Survey · Prey · San Juan Is. · Techniques · WA
836	**Winter Survey** · Behav. · Disturb. · Habit. Loss · Habit. Use · Hunt. Behav. · Logging · Manage. · Prey · WA
840	**Winter Survey** · Behav. · Capture · CO · Habit. Use · Marking · Migration · Techniques
897	**Winter Survey** · Techniques · WY
903	**Winter Survey** · Christmas Count · IA · Mississippi R · Nest. · Status
978	**Winter Survey** · Capture · Intrasp. Behav. · IA · Mississippi R · Techniques · Upper Miss. NWR · WI
988	**Winter Survey** · Great Lakes · L Erie · Manage. · Nest. Survey · OH
1011	**Winter Survey** · Behav. · Climatology · Habit. Use · Hunt. Behav. · Intersp. Behav. · Intrasp. Behav. · IA · IL · Mississippi R · MO · Prey
1017	**Winter Survey** · L Andes NWR · Missouri R · NAS · Status · SD
1039	**Winter Survey** · AR
1049	**Winter Survey** · CA · Nest. Survey · Road. Census · Techniques
1050	**Winter Survey** · CA · Nest. Survey
1063	**Winter Survey** · Behav. · Disturb. · Habit. Loss · Habit. Use · Manage. · Prey · Research · TX
1065	**Winter Survey** · Behav. · CA · Disturb. · Habit. Use · Klamath · Lower Klamath Lake NWR · Manage. · OR · Prey · Tule Lake NWR
1083	**Winter Survey** · Ches. Bay · Techniques
1097	**Winter Survey** · Reelfoot L · TN
1109	**Winter Survey** · Behav. · Habit. Loss · Habit. Use · Intersp. Behav. · Intrasp. Behav. · ID · Manage. · Prey · Wolf Lodge Bay
1112	**Winter Survey** · Autopsy · Disturb. · Habit. Use · Hunt. Behav. · Intersp. Behav. · Manage. · Migration · OK · Prey · Salt Fork R · Shooting · Status · Taxonomy
1113	**Winter Survey** · Hunt. Behav. · Intrasp. Behav. · Migration · Neosho R · OK · Prey
1114	**Winter Survey** · Arkansas R · Band. · Capture · Habit. Use · Intersp. Behav. · OK · Salt Plains NWR · Sequoyah NWR · Techniques · Wichita Mts. NWR · Winter. Pop.
1115	**Winter Survey** · Disturb. · Habit. Use · Manage. · Migration · OK · Prey · Salt Fork R · Salt Plains NWR · Sequoyah NWR · Shooting · Status · Taxonomy · Wichita Mts. NWR
1121	**Winter Survey** · Behav. · Manage. · NE · Prey · Status

Master No.	Keywords
1136	**Winter Survey** · Band. · Jackson's Canyon · Techniques · WY
1137	**Winter Survey** · Band. · Poison. · Prey · Pub. Ed. · Techniques · WY
1159	**Winter Survey** · CA · Nest. Survey · Road. Census · Techniques
1187	**Winter Survey** · Habit. Use · Life History · Nest. Survey · Prey · WA
1228	**Winter Survey** · Glacier NP · Hunt. Behav. · Intersp. Behav. · MN · Prey
1229	**Winter Survey** · Anat. · Autumn Conc. · Behav. · Capture · Glacier NP · Habit. Use · Manage. · Marking · Migration · MT · Techniques
1304	**Winter Survey** · IL · Prey · Shooting
1334	**Winter Survey** · Habit. Prot. · Manage. · Nat. Conserv. · Refuge · Skagit R Nat. Area · WA
1336	**Winter Survey** · Behav. · Manage. · NE · Prey · Status
1338	**Winter Survey** · NE · Platte R
1339	**Winter Survey** · NE · Platte R
1340	**Winter Survey** · NE · Platte R
1364	**Winter Survey** · Christmas Count · IL
1365	**Winter Survey** · Christmas Count · IL
1368	**Winter Survey** · Behav. · Climatology · Disturb. · Habit. Use · Hunt. Behav. · Intersp. Behav. · Intrasp. Behav. · Manage. · NY · Prey
1369	**Winter Survey** · Behav. · Habit. Use · Heavy Metals · Hunt. Behav. · Intersp. Behav. · Intrasp. Behav. · Manage. · NY · Pest. · Prey · PCB
1384	**Winter Survey** · Asper. · Nest. Survey · OR · Road. Census · Techniques
1391	**Winter Survey** · Hunt. Behav. · Migration · ME · Prey
1403	**Winter Survey** · Hunt. Behav. · TN
1439	**Winter Survey** · Kentucky Wood. NWR · KY
1440	**Winter Survey** · Behav. · Habit. Loss · Habit. Use · Kentucky Wood. NWR · KY
1441	**Winter Survey** · Habit. Loss · Kentucky Wood. NWR · KY · Status
1442	**Winter Survey** · KY · Land Between the Lakes
1443	**Winter Survey** · Upper Miss.
1469	**Winter Survey** · Prey · UT
1470	**Winter Survey** · Behav. · Habit. Use · Hunt. Behav. · Prey · UT
1474	**Winter Survey** · MI · Status
1476	**Winter Survey** · Hunt. Behav. · MI · Prey
1477	**Winter Survey** · MI
1531	**Winter Survey** · Band. · Christmas Count · Life History · Migration · Nest. · Status · USFWS
1591	**Winter Survey** · Behav. · Climatology · Disturb. · Habit. Use · Intrasp. Behav. · Plumage · Prey · Skagit R · WA
1600	**Winter Survey** · Mississippi R
1601	**Winter Survey** · Behav. · Capture · Glacier NP · Hunt. Behav. · Intersp. Behav. · Intrasp. Behav. · Manage. · MT · Techniques
1606	**Winter Survey** · Aggress. · Aleutian Is. · AK · Behav. · Depred. · Habit. Use · Life History · Mortality · Nest. Survey · Plumage · Prey · Reprod. Succ. · Status
1608	**Winter Survey** · Habit. Use · NE · Platte R
1625	**Winter Survey** · IL · Mississippi R
1629	**Winter Survey** · Distrib. · Endang. Sp. · Nest. Survey · TX
1630	**Winter Survey** · Distrib. · Endang. Sp. · Nest. Survey · TX
1631	**Winter Survey** · Distrib. · Nest. Survey · Reprod. Succ. · Status · TX
1632	**Winter Survey** · Distrib. · Habit. Use · Nest. Survey · Status · TX
1650	**Winter Survey** · Capture · Habit. Use · Hunt. Behav. · Intersp. Behav. · IL · Marking · Mississippi R · Prey · Techniques
1651	**Winter Survey** · Anat. · Behav. · Capture · Hunt. Behav. · IL · Marking · Plumage · Prey · Techniques · Telemetry
1671	**Winter Survey** · Cont. B.E. Proj. · Migration · Nest. Survey · NAS · Status
1672	**Winter Survey** · Cont. B.E. Proj. · Hurricane · Nest. Survey · NAS · Status
1673	**Winter Survey** · Cont. B.E. Proj. · Manage. · Migration · Nest. Survey · NAS · Status

Master No.	Keywords
1674	Winter Survey · Cont. B.E. Proj. · Manage. · Nest. Survey · NAS · Refuge · Status
1675	Winter Survey · Cont. B.E. Proj. · Nest. Survey · NAS · Status
1676	Winter Survey · Cont. B.E. Proj. · Nest. Survey · NAS · Status
1678	Winter Survey · Cont. B.E. Proj. · Manage. · Nest. Survey · NAS · Status
1686	Winter Survey · Autopsy · Cont. B.E. Proj. · Nest. Survey · NAS
1689	Winter Survey · CO · Status
1691	Winter Survey · Cont. B.E. Proj. · KY
1692	Winter Survey · Illinois R · KY · Mississippi R · Ohio R
1693	Winter Survey · KY · Mississippi R · Ohio R
1695	Winter Survey · Behav. · Ft. Randall D · Habit. Use · Hunt. Behav. · Karl Mundt NWR · L Andes NWR · SD
1696	Winter Survey · Climatology · Ft. Randall D · Habit. Use · Hunt. Behav. · Karl Mundt NWR · L Andes NWR · Manage. · Prey · SD
1697	Winter Survey · Ft. Randall D · Habit. Loss · Habit. Use · Hunt. Behav. · Migration · Prey · SD
1698	Winter Survey · Climatology · Disturb. · Electro. · Habit. Use · Manage. · Prey
1699	Winter Survey · Behav. · Disturb. · Ft. Randall D · Habit. Use · Manage. · Missouri R · SD
1713	Winter Survey · Nest. Survey · NB · NS · PE · Reprod. Succ.
1769	Winter Survey · Band. · Nest. Survey · Reprod. Succ. · Techniques · TX
1772	Winter Survey · Habit. Prot. · IL
1791	Winter Survey · AZ · Electro. · Nest. Survey
1794	Winter Survey · AZ · Techniques
1796	Winter Survey · Ches. Bay · Nest. Survey
1802	Winter Survey · NE · Platte R
1803	Winter Survey · BC · Gulf Is. · Nest. Survey
1820	Winter Survey · Habit. Prot. · Manage. · Nest. · USFS
1878	Winter Survey · Karl Mundt NWR · SD

Master No.	Keywords
1879	Winter Survey · Behav. · Hunt. Behav. · Intersp. Behav. · ID · L Couer D' Alene · Manage.
1893	Winter Survey · Mississippi R · MO · Nest. · Squaw Creek NWR
1895	Winter Survey · Behav. · Habit. Use · Hunt. Behav. · Intrasp. Behav. · Migration · NE · Platte R
1915	Winter Survey · Behav. · Migration · NE · Platte R · Prey
1931	Winter Survey · Amchitka Is. · AK · Egg. Thin. · Habit. Use · Nest. Survey · Prey
1967	Winter Survey · CA · Disturb. · Habit. Use · Lower Klamath Lake NWR · Modoc NWR · Tule Lake NWR
1983	Winter Survey · WY
1984	Winter Survey · Habit. Use · Platte R · Snake R · WY
1985	Winter Survey · Habit. Use · Platte R · Snake R · WY
1991	Winter Survey · Pub. Ed. · TN
31	Winter. Pop. · Distrib. · Nest. · NH
32	Winter. Pop. · MA · NH
38	Winter. Pop. · IA · Mississippi R · Nest.
42	Winter. Pop. · Nest. · OH · Status
53	Winter. Pop. · Distrib. · IA · Nest. · Status
54	Winter. Pop. · Art · Skagit R · WA
126	Winter. Pop. · NE
133	Winter. Pop. · Life History · Nest. · NJ · Pub. Ed.
142	Winter. Pop. · Poison. · Shooting · WY
153	Winter. Pop. · Habit. Prot. · Missouri R · NWF · SD
168	Winter. Pop. · Habit. Prot. · Manage. · Nat. Conserv. · Skagit R · Wash. Dept. Game · WA
169	Winter. Pop. · Acct. · NJ
177	Winter. Pop. · Nest. Survey · TX · Winter Survey
178	Winter. Pop. · AR · Field ID · Winter Survey
181	Winter. Pop. · ME · Nest. · Prey
185	Winter. Pop. · Acct. · AZ · Nest. · Pub. Ed.
186	Winter. Pop. · Acct. · AZ · Endang. Sp. · Nest. · Pub. Ed.
193	Winter. Pop. · NV
199	Winter. Pop. · MA · Nest.
204	Winter. Pop. · Gulf of Mex. · LA
207	Winter. Pop. · CO · Distrib. · Nest.

Master No.	Keywords
208	**Winter. Pop.** · IA · Nest. · Prey
211	**Winter. Pop.** · Anat. · Distrib. · Nest. · NM · Plumage · Prey
219	**Winter. Pop.** · Nest. · Yellowstone NP
220	**Winter. Pop.** · Hunt. Behav. · OH
225	**Winter. Pop.** · Boulder D · NV
231	**Winter. Pop.** · KY · Nest.
248	**Winter. Pop.** · Mississippi R · MN
251	**Winter. Pop.** · WI
252	**Winter. Pop.** · WI
253	**Winter. Pop.** · Migration · WI
256	**Winter. Pop.** · NY · Shooting
258	**Winter. Pop.** · Anat. · Nest. · NY · Prey · Status
268	**Winter. Pop.** · BC · CA · Nest. · OR · Status · WA
276	**Winter. Pop.** · IA · Mississippi R
286	**Winter. Pop.** · Mortality · NE
296	**Winter. Pop.** · IL
297	**Winter. Pop.** · IL · Pub. Ed.
298	**Winter. Pop.** · IL
301	**Winter. Pop.** · Disturb. · Habit. Use · IL · Nest. · Ohio R · Rehab. · Shooting · Techniques
302	**Winter. Pop.** · MA · Photo.
303	**Winter. Pop.** · Behav. · Illinois R
309	**Winter. Pop.** · Hunt. Behav. · Prey · Shooting · VA
310	**Winter. Pop.** · Disturb. · Migration · ME · Nest. · Shooting
343	**Winter. Pop.** · Captivity · Depred. · Trapping · WV
373	**Winter. Pop.** · Nest. · NY · Status · Taxonomy
374	**Winter. Pop.** · Nest. · ON
375	**Winter. Pop.** · WI
376	**Winter. Pop.** · Habit. Use · LA · Nest.
389	**Winter. Pop.** · Aleutian Is. · AK · Nest.
392	**Winter. Pop.** · Shooting · TN
402	**Winter. Pop.** · BC · Nest.
409	**Winter. Pop.** · AZ · Grand Canyon · Nest. · Status
411	**Winter. Pop.** · Captivity · Hunt. Behav. · NY
412	**Winter. Pop.** · Nest. · TX
420	**Winter. Pop.** · Nest. · NC · SC
422	**Winter. Pop.** · MI · Nest.
423	**Winter. Pop.** · Mississippi R · Nest. · Pub. Ed. · Reelfoot L · Shooting · Status · TN
447	**Winter. Pop.** · Behav. · CA · Disturb. · Hunt. Behav. · Manage. · Natl. For. · Prey · San Bernardino Mts. · USFS
456	**Winter. Pop.** · MI · Nest. · Status · Trapping
473	**Winter. Pop.** · CO · Disturb. · Field ID · Habit. Loss · Manage. · Nest. · Pest. · Pub. Ed.
475	**Winter. Pop.** · NH
478	**Winter. Pop.** · Hunt. Behav. · Prey · WI
510	**Winter. Pop.** · MO · Squaw Creek NWR
543	**Winter. Pop.** · Anat. · IA · Migration · Nest. · Taxonomy
544	**Winter. Pop.** · IA · Migration · Nest. · Shooting
554	**Winter. Pop.** · Band. · Behav. · Cedar Glen Roost · IL · Migration · Mississippi R · MN · Refuge · Techniques · Telemetry · TX
557	**Winter. Pop.** · Chippewa NF · Disturb. · Life History · Migration · Nest. · Photo. · Pub. Ed. · Status · Techniques · Telemetry
563	**Winter. Pop.** · CA · Nest. · OR
564	**Winter. Pop.** · Prey · RI
573	**Winter. Pop.** · Habit. Prot. · Marking · Nest. · Pub. Ed. · Techniques
584	**Winter. Pop.** · NY
600	**Winter. Pop.** · CO · Road. Census · Techniques
601	**Winter. Pop.** · CO · Prey
604	**Winter. Pop.** · Intersp. Behav. · NS · Prey
607	**Winter. Pop.** · IN · Nest.
608	**Winter. Pop.** · Distrib. · Electro. · Field ID · Life History · Prey · UT
611	**Winter. Pop.** · TX
623	**Winter. Pop.** · Mississippi R
629	**Winter. Pop.** · IL
630	**Winter. Pop.** · IL
640	**Winter. Pop.** · IL
642	**Winter. Pop.** · IL
658	**Winter. Pop.** · LA · Nest.
682	**Winter. Pop.** · CA · Disturb. · Klamath NF · Manage. · Nest. · Prey · Status
683	**Winter. Pop.** · Behav. · CA · Distrib. · Disturb. · Field ID · Flight · Hunt. Behav. · Life History · Manage. · Mortality · Nest.
686	**Winter. Pop.** · IL · Nest. · Terminology

Master No.	Keywords
690	**Winter. Pop.** · AK · Nest.
692	**Winter. Pop.** · AK · Nest.
702	**Winter. Pop.** · Habit. Prot. · Karl Mundt NWR · L Andes NWR · Manage. · Missouri R · NWF · Refuge · SD
703	**Winter. Pop.** · Habit. Prot. · Karl Mundt NWR · Missouri R · Refuge · SD
706	**Winter. Pop.** · Hunt. Behav. · MN · Prey
707	**Winter. Pop.** · KY · Nest.
714	**Winter. Pop.** · Distrib. · Habit. Use · Nest. · Plumage · Shooting · Taxonomy · TN
718	**Winter. Pop.** · Nest. · Prey · TN
747	**Winter. Pop.** · KS · Nest.
752	**Winter. Pop.** · IL · Migration · Nest. · Status
755	**Winter. Pop.** · Disturb. · Manage. · ME · Nest. Survey · Pub. Ed. · Shooting
758	**Winter. Pop.** · IA · Mortality
760	**Winter. Pop.** · UT
762	**Winter. Pop.** · IL · Pub. Ed.
771	**Winter. Pop.** · Nest. · VA
785	**Winter. Pop.** · IL · Mississippi R
788	**Winter. Pop.** · Nest. · Pymatuning · PA
792	**Winter. Pop.** · Behav. · CA · Habit. Use · Intersp. Behav. · Nest.
794	**Winter. Pop.** · CA · Distrib. · Habit. Use
795	**Winter. Pop.** · Nest. · NY
796	**Winter. Pop.** · Hunt. Behav. · MA · Nest. · Prey
799	**Winter. Pop.** · Hunt. Behav. · Intersp. Behav. · WI
803	**Winter. Pop.** · Habit. Use · Life History · Nest. · Photo. · Pub. Ed. · WA
804	**Winter. Pop.** · Art. Nest Site · AZ · Egg. Thin. · Habit. Use · Life History · Manage. · Marking · Nest. · Pest. · Research · Techniques · Telemetry
812	**Winter. Pop.** · NC
819	**Winter. Pop.** · Nest. · NY
823	**Winter. Pop.** · Field ID · WI
835	**Winter. Pop.** · ID · Nest.
838	**Winter. Pop.** · Hunt. Behav. · IA · Mississippi R · Prey
845	**Winter. Pop.** · KS · Missouri R · Nest. · Prey
858	**Winter. Pop.** · CO · Nest. · UT
892	**Winter. Pop.** · Hunt. Behav. · IA · Mississippi R · Prey
898	**Winter. Pop.** · MA · Nest. · Status
902	**Winter. Pop.** · Intersp. Behav. · NY
929	**Winter. Pop.** · MA · Nest.
933	**Winter. Pop.** · AR · Habit. Use · Shooting
934	**Winter. Pop.** · AL · Nest. · Prey · Shooting · TN
958	**Winter. Pop.** · MN
963	**Winter. Pop.** · MN
973	**Winter. Pop.** · AL · Nest. · Prey
974	**Winter. Pop.** · Captivity · KS · Prey
975	**Winter. Pop.** · KS · Prey
979	**Winter. Pop.** · IA · IL · Mississippi R
983	**Winter. Pop.** · Egg Trans. · Habit. Prot. · Nest. · Pub. Ed.
989	**Winter. Pop.** · AK · Habit. Use · Migration · Nest.
995	**Winter. Pop.** · Behav. · Fledging · VA
997	**Winter. Pop.** · Life History · Nest. · ON
998	**Winter. Pop.** · Habit. Prot. · Refuge · Skagit R Nat. Area · WA
1005	**Winter. Pop.** · CO · Road. Census · Techniques
1007	**Winter. Pop.** · OK
1010	**Winter. Pop.** · CO · Intersp. Behav.
1015	**Winter. Pop.** · Hunt. Behav. · Nest. · OH
1026	**Winter. Pop.** · Endang. Sp. · KS
1028	**Winter. Pop.** · MI
1033	**Winter. Pop.** · IL · Migration · Nest.
1047	**Winter. Pop.** · NE · Platte R
1055	**Winter. Pop.** · Migration · Nest. · WA
1059	**Winter. Pop.** · Nest. · Pub. Ed. · WA
1061	**Winter. Pop.** · ID
1067	**Winter. Pop.** · Art · Broley · Catesby · FL · Hudson R
1082	**Winter. Pop.** · Nest. · ND
1087	**Winter. Pop.** · Habit. Prot. · Manage. · NWF · Pub. Ed. · SD · Techniques · Young Trans.
1089	**Winter. Pop.** · Nest. · NWF · Pub. Ed. · Status
1098	**Winter. Pop.** · NE
1101	**Winter. Pop.** · Nest. · NM · Status
1114	**Winter. Pop.** · Arkansas R · Band. · Capture · Habit. Use · Intersp. Behav. · OK · Salt Plains NWR · Sequoyah NWR · Techniques · Wichita Mts. NWR · Winter Survey
1116	**Winter. Pop.** · Acct. · Disturb. · Nest. · OK · Status
1120	**Winter. Pop.** · IL

Master No.	Keywords
1122	**Winter. Pop.** · Acct. · NE · Road. Census · Techniques
1123	**Winter. Pop.** · NE · Road. Census · Techniques
1125	**Winter. Pop.** · Nest. · NE
1131	**Winter. Pop.** · Nest. · WI
1138	**Winter. Pop.** · MN
1155	**Winter. Pop.** · IA
1160	**Winter. Pop.** · CA · Distrib. · Life History · Nest. · Prey · Pub. Ed.
1183	**Winter. Pop.** · Reelfoot L · TN
1185	**Winter. Pop.** · Electro. · ID · Manage.
1196	**Winter. Pop.** · Band. · Chippewa NF · IL · MN · Nest. Survey · Techniques · USFS
1235	**Winter. Pop.** · Hunt. Behav. · Intrasp. Behav. · LA · Nest. · Prey
1237	**Winter. Pop.** · Distrib. · Endang. Sp. · Habit. Use · Migration · Nest. · ND · Status
1238	**Winter. Pop.** · Acct. · WV
1248	**Winter. Pop.** · KY · Nest.
1273	**Winter. Pop.** · Endang. Sp. · MO · Nest.
1282	**Winter. Pop.** · Acct. · OK
1283	**Winter. Pop.** · NE
1289	**Winter. Pop.** · IA · Mississippi R
1301	**Winter. Pop.** · Migration · Nest. · Status
1305	**Winter. Pop.** · IL · Mississippi R
1306	**Winter. Pop.** · IL · Mississippi R
1310	**Winter. Pop.** · CA · Migration
1313	**Winter. Pop.** · Glacier NP · MT · WA
1330	**Winter. Pop.** · Ferry Bluff Sanct. · Habit. Prot. · NWF · Refuge · Wisconsin R · WI
1337	**Winter. Pop.** · NE · Road. Census · Techniques
1355	**Winter. Pop.** · Hunt. Behav. · Prey · Territory
1372	**Winter. Pop.** · Anat. · Distrib. · Habit. Use · Nest. · Plumage · Taxonomy · TX
1382	**Winter. Pop.** · TN · TVA
1388	**Winter. Pop.** · History · Nest. · Pub. Ed. · SD
1389	**Winter. Pop.** · Nest. · Pub. Ed. · SD
1392	**Winter. Pop.** · WI
1397	**Winter. Pop.** · CO · Field ID
1402	**Winter. Pop.** · Pub. Ed. · Reelfoot L · TN
1432	**Winter. Pop.** · IA · IL · Mississippi R
1434	**Winter. Pop.** · CA
1437	**Winter. Pop.** · IN · Nest.
1444	**Winter. Pop.** · KY · Land Between the Lakes · Pub. Ed. · TVA
1446	**Winter. Pop.** · Cape May · Migration · NJ · Pymatuning · PA
1453	**Winter. Pop.** · Hunt. Behav. · IA · IL · Mississippi R
1459	**Winter. Pop.** · AZ · Nest.
1460	**Winter. Pop.** · IN · Nest.
1463	**Winter. Pop.** · Nest. · Reelfoot L · TN
1492	**Winter. Pop.** · DE · Nest.
1499	**Winter. Pop.** · Capture · OH · Techniques · Trapping
1505	**Winter. Pop.** · Habit. Use · Nest. · WA
1526	**Winter. Pop.** · IL · Nest.
1537	**Winter. Pop.** · Hunt. Behav. · Life History · Migration · MN · Nest. · Prey · Shooting · Status
1539	**Winter. Pop.** · Hudson R · NY
1545	**Winter. Pop.** · CA · Fowl Cholera
1546	**Winter. Pop.** · Intersp. Behav. · NF · Terra Nova NP
1559	**Winter. Pop.** · CT · Migration · Nest. · Shooting · Taxonomy
1566	**Winter. Pop.** · Migration · MT · Nest.
1582	**Winter. Pop.** · CO · Life History · Nest. · Status
1583	**Winter. Pop.** · Hunt. Behav. · Intrasp. Behav. · MA · Prey
1603	**Winter. Pop.** · Anat. · NH · Taxonomy
1609	**Winter. Pop.** · NM · Pub. Ed.
1620	**Winter. Pop.** · WY · Yellowstone NP
1638	**Winter. Pop.** · Nest. Survey · NM
1646	**Winter. Pop.** · Nest. · WI
1648	**Winter. Pop.** · Nest.
1649	**Winter. Pop.** · Band. · Capture · IL · Techniques
1652	**Winter. Pop.** · IL · Mississippi R · Prey
1655	**Winter. Pop.** · Christmas Count · Lower 48 · Migration · Prey · Refuge
1656	**Winter. Pop.** · Band. · Migration · Pub. Ed. · Techniques
1658	**Winter. Pop.** · Christmas Count · IL
1659	**Winter. Pop.** · Christmas Count · IL
1660	**Winter. Pop.** · Christmas Count · IL
1662	**Winter. Pop.** · ND
1664	**Winter. Pop.** · Nest. · NY
1666	**Winter. Pop.** · Dispersal · Nest. Survey · NY
1687	**Winter. Pop.** · IA · Nest.
1690	**Winter. Pop.** · Behav. · Disturb. · Manage. · WA
1701	**Winter. Pop.** · KS · Nest.

Master No.	Keywords
1705	**Winter. Pop.** · Band. · DC · Migration · MD · Nest. · Techniques
1715	**Winter. Pop.** · Nest. · NJ
1729	**Winter. Pop.** · Acct. · NC · TN
1734	**Winter. Pop.** · Habit. Use · Nest. · OK · Prey
1737	**Winter. Pop.** · AZ · Nest.
1739	**Winter. Pop.** · History · MA · Photo.
1740	**Winter. Pop.** · MA · Photo.
1743	**Winter. Pop.** · Habit. Use · Prey · UT
1754	**Winter. Pop.** · IL · Shooting
1756	**Winter. Pop.** · GA · Nest.
1765	**Winter. Pop.** · Nest. · NC · SC
1788	**Winter. Pop.** · AZ
1790	**Winter. Pop.** · AZ · Nest.
1801	**Winter. Pop.** · Intersp. Behav. · OH
1859	**Winter. Pop.** · IA · KS · Missouri R · MO · Nest. Survey · ND · NE · Rocky Mt. Region · SD · USFWS
1860	**Winter. Pop.** · Missouri R · Nest. Survey · NE · SD · USFWS
1880	**Winter. Pop.** · Missouri R · SD
1881	**Winter. Pop.** · Hunt. Behav. · Manage. · Nest. · OR · WA
1887	**Winter. Pop.** · UT
1888	**Winter. Pop.** · OK
1894	**Winter. Pop.** · Hunt. Behav. · IL
1898	**Winter. Pop.** · SD
1913	**Winter. Pop.** · NE · Platte R
1951	**Winter. Pop.** · AL · Wheeler NWR
1952	**Winter. Pop.** · FL · Nest.
1961	**Winter. Pop.** · KY
1963	**Winter. Pop.** · Missouri R
1975	**Winter. Pop.** · Migration · MI · Nest.
1993	**Winter. Pop.** · Chautauqua NWR · Hunt. Behav. · IL
1999	**Winter. Pop.** · MI · Nest.
518	**Wisconsin R** · Acct. · WI
635	**Wisconsin R** · Illinois R · IA · IL · KY · Mississippi R · Missouri R · MO · NE · Winter Survey
636	**Wisconsin R** · Illinois R · IA · IL · KY · Mississippi R · Missouri R · MO · NE · Winter Survey
637	**Wisconsin R** · Illinois R · IA · IL · KY · Mississippi R · Missouri R · MO · NE · Winter Survey
693	**Wisconsin R** · Winter Survey · WI
1330	**Wisconsin R** · Ferry Bluff Sanct. · Habit. Prot. · NWF · Refuge · Winter. Pop. · WI

Master No.	Keywords
1109	**Wolf Lodge Bay** · Behav. · Habit. Loss · Habit. Use · Intersp. Behav. · Intrasp. Behav. · ID · Manage. · Prey · Winter Survey
23	**WA** · Nest. Survey · Reprod. Succ. · San Juan Is.
24	**WA** · Capture · Manage. · Marking · Skagit R · Techniques
26	**WA** · AK · Depred. · Endang. Sp. · Life History · OR
54	**WA** · Art · Skagit R · Winter. Pop.
168	**WA** · Habit. Prot. · Manage. · Nat. Conserv. · Skagit R · Wash. Dept. Game · Winter. Pop.
174	**WA** · B.E. Nat. Area · Marking · Pub. Ed. · Skagit R · Techniques
268	**WA** · BC · CA · Nest. · OR · Status · Winter. Pop.
503	**WA** · Habit. Prot. · Nat. Conserv. · Prey · Refuge · Skagit R Nat. Area
505	**WA** · Acct.
507	**WA** · Anat. · Behav. · Captivity · Distrib. · Nest.
583	**WA** · Habit. Use · Manage. · Nest. Survey · OR · Poison. · Prey · San Juan Is. · Shooting · Status · Winter Survey
587	**WA** · San Juan Is. · Status
602	**WA** · Acct.
750	**WA** · San Juan Is.
801	**WA** · Disturb. · Nest. · Nest. Survey · Reprod. Succ. · Statistics · Territory
803	**WA** · Habit. Use · Life History · Nest. · Photo. · Pub. Ed. · Winter. Pop.
805	**WA** · Habit. Use · Nest. Survey · Reprod. Succ. · San Juan Is.
817	**WA** · Acct. · History
818	**WA** · Acct. · History · Shooting
826	**WA** · BC · Gulf Is. · Habit. Use · Migration · Nest. Survey · Prey · San Juan Is. · Techniques · Winter Survey
836	**WA** · Behav. · Disturb. · Habit. Loss · Habit. Use · Hunt. Behav. · Logging · Manage. · Prey · Winter Survey
859	**WA** · Hunt. Behav. · Intersp. Behav. · Prey
998	**WA** · Habit. Prot. · Refuge · Skagit R Nat. Area · Winter. Pop.
1003	**WA** · Life History · Nest.

Master No.	Keywords
1043	WA · Acct.
1053	WA · Acct.
1054	WA · Mt. Ranier NP · Nest. · Status
1055	WA · Migration · Nest. · Winter. Pop.
1059	WA · Nest. · Pub. Ed. · Winter. Pop.
1178	WA · Disturb. · Pub. Ed. · Skagit R
1187	WA · Habit. Use · Life History · Nest. Survey · Prey · Winter Survey
1262	WA · Nest. · San Juan Is.
1295	WA · Habit. Prot. · Manage. · Nat. Conserv.
1313	WA · Glacier NP · MT · Winter. Pop.
1334	WA · Habit. Prot. · Manage. · Nat. Conserv. · Refuge · Skagit R Nat. Area · Winter Survey
1354	WA · Disturb. · Nest. Survey · San Juan Is. · Status
1505	WA · Habit. Use · Nest. · Winter. Pop.
1510	WA · Nest.
1520	WA · Nest. · San Juan Is.
1521	WA · Aggress. · Behav. · Disturb. · Habit. Loss · Hunt. Behav. · Nest. · Prey · San Juan Is. · Shooting · Status · Vocal.
1522	WA · Prey · San Juan Is.
1572	WA · Habit. Loss · OR · USFWS
1591	WA · Behav. · Climatology · Disturb. · Habit. Use · Intrasp. Behav. · Plumage · Prey · Skagit R · Winter Survey
1593	WA · Behav. · Migration
1594	WA · Rehab. · Techniques
1690	WA · Behav. · Disturb. · Manage. · Winter. Pop.
1797	WA · Anat. · Taxonomy
1839	WA · CA · ID · MT · Nest. Survey · NV · OR · USFWS
1843	WA · ID · Nest. Survey · OR · USFWS
1844	WA · CA · ID · Nest. Survey · NV · OR · USFWS
1853	WA · CA · ID · Nest. Survey · NV · OR · USFWS
1881	WA · Hunt. Behav. · Manage. · Nest. · OR · Winter. Pop.
1940	WA · Nest.
35	WI · Egg Coll. · LA · MN · MS · Status
72	WI · Captivity · History · Old Abe
128	WI · Habit. Prot. · Indian Culture · Manage. · MN · Refuge · St. Croix R
140	WI · AK · DDT · FL · ME · Pest. · Reprod. Succ.
145	WI · Manage. · NWF · Reward · Shooting
234	WI · Nest.
251	WI · Winter. Pop.
252	WI · Winter. Pop.
253	WI · Migration · Winter. Pop.
257	WI · Apostle Is. · Nest.
281	WI · Nest. · Status
295	WI · History · Old Abe
375	WI · Winter. Pop.
387	WI · Hacking · Manage. · Montezuma NWR · NY · Techniques · Young Trans.
388	WI · Nest.
417	WI · History · Old Abe
445	WI · Great Lakes · Manage. · MI · MN · Natl. For. · Nest. Survey · USFS
478	WI · Hunt. Behav. · Prey · Winter. Pop.
518	WI · Acct. · Wisconsin R
520	WI · Distrib. · Habit. Use · Migration · Nest. Survey · Status · Winter Survey
547	WI · Band. · IL · MN · Techniques · TX
614	WI · IA · IL · Mississippi R · NE · Winter Survey
620	WI · Illinois R · IA · IL · Mississippi R · Winter Survey
641	WI · IL · Winter Survey
645	WI · IA · IL · Mississippi R · MN · MO · NE
670	WI · Fla. B.E. Sur. Comm. · FL · Great Lakes · Rehab. · Reprod. Succ. · Status · Techniques
693	WI · Winter Survey · Wisconsin R
787	WI · MI · MO · Rehab. · Reintroduction · Shooting · Swan Lake NWR
799	WI · Hunt. Behav. · Intersp. Behav. · Winter. Pop.
823	WI · Field ID · Winter. Pop.
978	WI · Capture · Intrasp. Behav. · IA · Mississippi R · Techniques · Upper Miss. NWR · Winter Survey
991	WI · Nest.
1064	WI · FL · Heavy Metals · ME · Nest. · Pest. · PCB · Reprod. Succ.
1068	WI · Habit. Loss · Habit. Use · Nest.
1069	WI · Habit. Loss · Habit. Use · Nest.
1131	WI · Nest. · Winter. Pop.
1132	WI · Nest.
1133	WI · Nest.
1134	WI · Nest.
1277	WI · Intersp. Behav.

Master No.	Keywords
1291	WI · Cedar Grove · Migration
1322	WI · Ferry Bluff Sanct. · NWF · Refuge
1325	WI · Ferry Bluff Sanct. · NWF · Refuge
1330	WI · Ferry Bluff Sanct. · Habit. Prot. · NWF · Refuge · Winter. Pop. · Wisconsin R
1362	WI · Manage. · Pub. Ed.
1363	WI · Habit. Use · Nest. Survey
1392	WI · Winter. Pop.
1431	WI · Ferry Bluff Sanct. · Habit. Prot. · Refuge
1486	WI · Great Lakes · Migration · MI
1524	WI · Egg Coll. · Migration · Nest.
1525	WI · Nest.
1534	WI · Nest.
1552	WI · Research
1580	WI · Nest.
1610	WI · Band. · Behav. · Dispersal · MN · Techniques
1646	WI · Nest. · Winter. Pop.
1647	WI · Nest.
1728	WI · Band. · MN · Techniques
1825	WI · Aircraft · Chippewa NF · Great Lakes · MI · MN · Nest. Survey · Reprod. Succ. · Status · USFS
1855	WI · IL · IN · MI · MN · Nest. Survey · OH · Terminology · USFWS
1861	WI · Egg Trans. · Manage. · ME · MN · USFWS
1868	WI · MI · MN · Nest. Survey · OH · USFWS
1871	WI · Egg Trans. · Hacking · Manage. · ME · MN · NY · Pest. · PCB · Techniques · Young Trans.
343	WV · Captivity · Depred. · Trapping · Winter. Pop.
344	WV · Acct.
455	WV · Depred. · Ohio R · Shooting
487	WV · Depred. · Plumage · Shooting
523	WV · Acct.
590	WV · Acct. · MD
1238	WV · Acct. · Winter. Pop.
1281	WV · Shooting
141	WY · Jackson's Canyon · Poison.
142	WY · Poison. · Shooting · Winter. Pop.
179	WY · Jackson's Canyon · Winter Survey
180	WY · Jackson's Canyon · Winter Survey
397	WY · Jackson's Canyon · Law · NAS · Poison.
398	WY · Jackson's Canyon · Law · Poison. · Shooting
736	WY · Habit. Use · Marking · Migration · MO · ND · SD · SK · Techniques
897	WY · Techniques · Winter Survey
972	WY · Behav. · Disturb. · Habit. Use · Nest. · Snake R
1035	WY · Nest. · Yellowstone NP
1136	WY · Band. · Jackson's Canyon · Techniques · Winter Survey
1137	WY · Band. · Poison. · Prey · Pub. Ed. · Techniques · Winter Survey
1182	WY · Acct. · Nest. · Yellowstone NP
1232	WY · Field ID · Life History · Nest. · Yellowstone NP
1298	WY · Aggress. · Yellowstone NP
1543	WY · Depred. · Law · Poison. · Shooting
1573	WY · CO · Poison. · Pub. Ed. · Shooting
1574	WY · CO · Poison. · Pub. Ed. · Shooting
1575	WY · CO · Law · Shooting
1577	WY · Law · Pub. Ed. · Shooting
1618	WY · Pub. Ed. · Trapping · Yellowstone NP
1619	WY · Nest. · Yellowstone NP
1620	WY · Winter. Pop. · Yellowstone NP
1694	WY · Autopsy · Poison.
1838	WY · AZ · CO · KS · Nest. Survey · NM · OK · Salt Fork R · TX · USFWS · UT · Verde R
1846	WY · CO · IA · KS · MO · MT · Nest. Survey · ND · NE · SD · USFWS · UT
1849	WY · CO · IA · KS · MO · MT · Nest. Survey · ND · NE · SD · USFWS · UT
1858	WY · MT · Nest. Survey · USFWS
1954	WY · AK · Hunt. Behav. · Law · Migration · Nest. · Pub. Ed. · Yellowstone NP
1955	WY · AK · Hunt. Behav. · Law · Migration · Nest. · Pub. Ed. · Yellowstone NP
1959	WY · Shooting
1981	WY · CO · Electro. · ID · Manage. · NV · UT
1983	WY · Winter Survey
1984	WY · Habit. Use · Platte R · Snake R · Winter Survey
1985	WY · Habit. Use · Platte R · Snake R · Winter Survey
219	Yellowstone NP · Nest. · Winter. Pop.
293	Yellowstone NP · Hunt. Behav. · Intersp. Behav.

Master No.	Keywords
1035	**Yellowstone NP** · Nest. · WY
1182	**Yellowstone NP** · Acct. · Nest. · WY
1232	**Yellowstone NP** · Field ID · Life History · Nest. · WY
1298	**Yellowstone NP** · Aggress. · WY
1299	**Yellowstone NP** · Habit. Use · Intersp. Behav. · Nest. Survey · Territory
1618	**Yellowstone NP** · Pub. Ed. · Trapping · WY
1619	**Yellowstone NP** · Nest. · WY
1620	**Yellowstone NP** · Winter. Pop. · WY
1741	**Yellowstone NP** · Disturb. · Habit. Use · Manage. · MT · Nest. Survey · Pop. Turnover · Reprod. Succ. · Status · Territory
1954	**Yellowstone NP** · AK · Hunt. Behav. · Law · Migration · Nest. · Pub. Ed. · WY
1955	**Yellowstone NP** · AK · Hunt. Behav. · Law · Migration · Nest. · Pub. Ed. · WY
163	**Young Trans.** · Manage. · NY · Techniques
166	**Young Trans.** · Hacking · Manage. · NY · Techniques
387	**Young Trans.** · Hacking · Manage. · Montezuma NWR · NY · Techniques · WI
414	**Young Trans.** · Hacking · Montezuma NWR · NY · Techniques · Telemetry
559	**Young Trans.** · Art. Nest Site · Behav. · Habit. Use · Manage. · MN · Nest. · Techniques
824	**Young Trans.** · Egg Trans. · Techniques
984	**Young Trans.** · Captivity · Egg Trans. · Heavy Metals · Law · Manage. · Migration · Nest. Survey · Pest. · Pub. Ed. · Status · Techniques · Territory
1087	**Young Trans.** · Habit. Prot. · Manage. · NWF · Pub. Ed. · SD · Techniques · Winter. Pop.
1253	**Young Trans.** · Behav. · Hacking · Heavy Metals · Intrasp. Behav. · Marking · Montezuma NWR · MI · MN · NY · Pest. · Techniques · Telemetry
1254	**Young Trans.** · Hacking · NY · Pub. Ed. · Techniques
1255	**Young Trans.** · Hacking · Manage. · NY · Techniques
1256	**Young Trans.** · Behav. · Hacking · Manage. · NY · Pest. · Prey · PCB · Techniques
1271	**Young Trans.** · ME · Pub. Ed.
1274	**Young Trans.** · Manage. · NY · Techniques
1275	**Young Trans.** · Dispersal · NY · Techniques
1488	**Young Trans.** · AR · Band. · FL · GA · Manage. · Migration · MI · Techniques · TN
1490	**Young Trans.** · Manage. · MI · Techniques
1732	**Young Trans.** · Egg. Thin. · Hacking · NY · Techniques · Telemetry
1871	**Young Trans.** · Egg Trans. · Hacking · Manage. · ME · MN · NY · Pest. · PCB · Techniques · WI
904	**YT** · Kluane Game Sanct. · Nest.
1074	**YT** · Acct. · AB · AK · NWT
1076	**YT** · Acct. · AB · AK · NWT
1930	**YT** · AK · Nest.

APPENDIX A.

DICTIONARY OF KEYWORDS

The following alphabetized and annotated list of Keywords is presented so the users of this bibliography can more quickly and easily
identify needed bald eagle references.

All of the keywords used in Chapter 4 are listed. In some cases, we
include synonyms to the keywords used. For those words, we point back
to the keyword actually used in Chapter 4 by stating: ("See....").

The keywords as they appear in Chapter 4 are listed in the lefthand
column. For clarification, some keywords are spelled out in the
adjacent column. Synonyms are also listed under this heading. The
third column reports the number of occurrences of that keyword in
Chapter 4 and the last column gives a definition for those keywords
whose meaning is not clear. Rivers, National Wildlife Refuges,
National Forests and the like are further identified geographically
by including their state or province.

KEYWORD	FULL WORD	NO. OCCUR-RENCES	DEFINITION OR LOCATION
Acct.	Account	87	Observation made under conditions which did not readily identify the bird(s) as wintering, nesting or migrating.
Agassiz NWR		1	Minnesota.
Aggress.	Aggression	30	Used mainly when aggressive be-havior was directed towards humans. (See "Intersp. Behav." and "Intrasp. Behav.")
Aging		4	Standards of physical appearance which can be used to determine the age of the bird.
Aircraft		5	Fixed-wing and helicopters.
Aircraft Coll.	Aircraft Collision	1	Colliding of bald eagle and aircraft.
AB	Alberta	5	
AK	Alaska	121	

KEYWORD	FULL WORD	NO. OCCUR- RENCES	DEFINITION OR LOCATION
AL	Alabama	5	
Aleutian Is.		13	Alaska.
Aleutian Is. NWR		1	Alaska.
Allegan SF	Allegan State Forest	1	Michigan.
Amchitka Is.		5	Alaska.
Anacapa Is.		5	California.
Anal. Tech.	Analytical Technique	3	Detailed or specific approaches to analyses or problem-solving in general.
Anat.	Anatomy	49	Body structure. (See "Museum Specimen")
Animal Dam.	Animal Damage	1	Depredation on species valuable from an economic or recreational standpoint.
Anthro.	Anthropology	2	Science of man; his distribution, origin, classification, physical character, environmental and social relations and culture. (This was not used unless the emphasis was on the role of the bald eagle in man's culture.)
AOU	American Orni- thologist's Union	5	
Apostle Is.		1	Wisconsin.
Archaeology		1	Study of material remains (as fossil relics, artifacts, monu- ments) of past human life and activities.
AR	Arkansas	10	
Arkansas R		1	

KEYWORD	FULL WORD	NO. OCCUR-RENCES	DEFINITION OR LOCATION
Art		15	Role of bald eagle in art, per se, or available sources of art involving this species.
Art. Nest Site	Artificial Nest Site	3	Nest site provided for by man.
Asper.	Aspergillosis	3	An avian respiratory disease.
Audubon	John James Audubon	4	Famous wildlife artist, collector and naturalist.
Autopsy		12	Used when document indicated the causes of mortality.
Autumn Conc.	Autumn Concentration	5	Large grouping of bald eagles in the fall of the year, as occurs in Glacier National Park.
AZ	Arizona	37	
Baja		2	California.
Bake Oven Knob		3	Pennsylvania.
Band.	Banding	49	Activities and techniques. Includes band-return information and sighting of marked birds. (See "Migration")
Barkley Sound		2	British Columbia.
BC	British Columbia	23	
Bear Valley NWR		1	Oregon.
Behav.	Behavior	124	(See "Intersp. Behav.", "Intrasp. Behav.", "Parent. Behav.", "Hunt. Behav.", "Aggress.")
B.E. Nat. Area	Bald Eagle Natural Area	1	Washington.
B.E. Prot. Act	Bald Eagle Protection Act	2	Federal Act protecting bald eagles.
Big Cypress Swamp		1	Florida.

KEYWORD	FULL WORD	NO. OCCUR- RENCES	DEFINITION OR LOCATION
Biochem.	Biochemistry	3	Chemistry that deals with the chemical compounds and processes occurring in organisms.
Biopsy		1	Relates to analysis of tissues or organs from living bird or techniques involved in this procedure.
-	Bird Strikes	-	(See "Aircraft Coll.")
BLM	Bureau of Land Management	3	U.S. Department of the Interior.
Blood		3	Deals with aspects of blood (e.g., chemistry, toxins).
Bombay Hook NWR		1	Delaware.
Boulder D	Boulder Dam	1	Nevada.
Bounty		42	Money paid in return for proof of bald eagle being killed. (See Shooting")
Breed. Behav.	Breeding Behavior	5	Any of several types of behavior relating to nesting, copulation, or pair bond formation.
Broley	Charles Broley	10	Also known as "Eagle Man" for his extensive efforts to band eaglets in Florida, other states, and Canada.
CA	California	91	
Caledon SP	Caledon State Park	3	Virginia.
Cannibal.	Cannibalism	1	Activity of young eagles eating others in nest. Does not necessarily indicate the cause of death.
CAP	Central Arizona Project	8	Hydrologic project proposed to be carried out by U.S. Army Corps of Engineers.

KEYWORD	FULL WORD	NO. OCCUR-RENCES	DEFINITION OR LOCATION
Cape May		9	New Jersey.
Captive Breed.	Captive Breeding	20	Efforts or guidelines to breed bald eagles in captivity.
Captivity		27	Bald eagles held by man.
Capture		21	Discussion of trapping techniques associated with the capturing of wild birds. (See "Trapping")
-	Carbamates	-	(See "Pest.")
CAS	Canadian Audubon Society	1	
Catesby	Mark Catesby	1	Naturalist and artist.
Cedar Glen Roost		2	Illinois.
Cedar Grove		1	Wisconsin.
Channel Is.		5	California.
Chautauqua NWR		1	Illinois.
Ches. Bay	Chesapeake Bay	40	Delaware, District of Columbia, Maryland, and Virginia.
Child. Eagle Area	Children's Eagle Nesting Area	2	Minnesota.
Children's Story		1	
Chilkat R		2	Alaska.
Chippewa NF	Chippewa National Forest	56	Minnesota.
Christmas Count	Christmas Bird Count	11	An organized bird count conducted around Christmas.
Churchill R	Churchill River	1	Saskatchewan.

KEYWORD	FULL WORD	NO. OCCUR-RENCES	DEFINITION OR LOCATION
Climatology		10	Study of weather.
CN	Canada	26	
CO	Colorado	28	
Comm. Bird Prot.	Committee on Bird Protection	2	National committee formed to protect birdlife.
Comm. Conserv.	Committee on Conservation	3	National committee formed to provide overview on conservation.
Cont. B.E. Proj.	Continental Bald Eagle Project	14	Survey which was initiated and organized by the National Audubon Society.
Cont. U.S.	Continental United States	1	
Corps	Corps of Engineers	1	
CT	Connecticut	8	
CU	Cuba	1	
Data Coll.	Data Collection	1	Primarily refers to data collection techniques, especially the forms used.
DC	District of Columbia	6	
DDT	Dichloro diphenyl trichloroethane	14	(See "Pest.")
DE	Delaware	13	
Depred.	Depredation	30	Predation on species of economic and/or recreational value. (See "Econ. Import." and "Prey")
Derby Hill		1	New York.
Dieldrin		4	One of several long-lasting cyclodien pesticides.

KEYWORD	FULL WORD	NO. OCCUR-RENCES	DEFINITION OR LOCATION
Digest.	Digestion	2	Avian gastric and pellet-forming mechanisms.
Dimorphism		1	Differentiation of sexes by color, size, etc.
Dioxins		1	A group of biologically active chemicals which are found as contaminants in pesticides and other compounds.
Disease		15	Biological impairment of vital functions. (See "Mortality")
Dispersal		10	Long-distance movement of individuals or groups of birds which is not necessarily characterized as migration. (See "Migration")
Distrib.	Distribution	63	Range of bald eagles as a species. Could be specific to particular political boundaries.
Disturb.	Disturbance	102	Change in eagles behavior induced by human activities.
Douglas Pt. Nuc. Plant	Douglas Point Nuclear Plant	1	Maryland.
Duluth Fly.	Duluth Flyway	1	Minnesota.
Eagle Valley Refuge		1	Wisconsin.
Econ. Import.	Economic Importance	25	Refers to studies which attempt to quantify economic value of eagles and/or economic losses attributable to them. (See "Depred." and "Prey")
Educ. Mat.	Educational Material	9	Reference is of a general, usually non-scientific nature. Also used when reference discusses educational materials which are available.
Egg		14	Bird egg.
Egg Coll.	Egg Collecting	64	Former widespread hobby of egg collecting.

KEYWORD	FULL WORD	NO. OCCUR-RENCES	DEFINITION OR LOCATION
Egg Trans.	Egg Transfer	10	Management practice involving the transfer of viable eggs into nests that are experiencing low hatching success.
Egg. Thin.	Eggshell Thinning	17	Used in reference to documented changes in eggshell thickness.
Electro.	Electrocution	16	Death and/or injuries sustained from making contact with electric wires, usually while attempting to perch.
Endang. Sp.	Endangered Species	55	Reference discusses the bald eagle in the context of a recognized endangered species program. Also used when document discusses endangered status. (See "Status")
England		1	
Everglades NP		1	Florida.
Evolution		6	Documented or suspected changes which have taken place through natural selection. May refer to paleontological data.
Eye		1	Anatomy of eye and/or visual acuity.
Falconry		15	Bald eagles used for falconry or kept using classical falconry techniques. (See "Hacking")
-	Fall Concentration	-	(See "Autumn Conc.")
FAS	Florida Audubon Society	1	
Feather War		1	Historic case of 14 Indians breaking 1918 law by selling feathers of migratory birds.
Ferry Bluff Sanct.	Ferry Bluff Eagle Sanctuary	4	Wisconsin.

KEYWORD	FULL WORD	NO. OCCUR-RENCES	DEFINITION OR LOCATION
Field ID	Field Identification	48	Description of gross features to be used in field to identify species.
Finger Lakes		2	New York.
FL	Florida	132	
Fla. B.E. Sur. Comm.	Florida Bald Eagle Survey Committee	2	
Fledging		16	Used to denote period after leaving the nest while young are still dependent on adults.
Flight		10	Characteristics of flight, including wing-loading, and other physical characteristics.
Folklore		25	Includes, but not limited to, stories and often unfounded tales.
Forestry		1	Management of forest lands; includes logging and silvicultural practices in general. (See "Logging")
Forrester Is.		1	Alaska.
Fowl Cholera		23	Disease in birds.
Ft. Randall D		4	South Dakota.
GA	Georgia	15	
Glacier NP		8	Montana.
Grand Canyon		2	Arizona.
Great Lakes	Great Lakes Region	26	Includes Wisconsin, Michigan, and Minnesota.
Great Slave L.	Great Slave Lake	12	Northwest Territories.

KEYWORD	FULL WORD	NO. OCCUR-RENCES	DEFINITION OR LOCATION
Ground Nest.	Ground Nesting	5	Restricted to nesting on the ground _per se_ and does not include nesting on cliffs, seastacks, etc.
Growth		13	Generally covers development but not restricted to it.
Gulf Is.		4	British Columbia.
Gulf of Mex.	Gulf of Mexico	3	
Habit. Loss	Habitat Loss	50	Specific instances of changes in land-use or natural catastrophies resulting in loss of bald eagle habitat.
Habit. Prot.	Habitat Protection	35	Incidences of protecting habitat through land purchase and/or other protective devices. (See "Refuge")
Habit. Use	Habitat Use	137	Description of habitat type, species of vegetation in relation to use by bald eagle (i.e., wintering and nesting primarily).
Hacking		11	Falconry technique utilized to release captive-raised, rehabili-tated, or young wild birds under controlled conditions. (See "Falconry" and "Reintroduction")
Hawk Mt.		12	Pennsylvania.
Heavy Metals		19	Includes copper, lead, cadmium, and other heavy metals.
Helicop.	Helicopter	6	Utilization of helicopter and/or its effects on observed birds.
Histology		3	Study dealing with tissue(s).
History		67	Role played by the bald eagle and other eagles in the history of man's civilization. (See "Anthro.")
Hook Mt.		1	New York.

KEYWORD	FULL WORD	NO. OCCUR-RENCES	DEFINITION OR LOCATION
Hudson Bay		1	Canada.
Hudson R		2	New York.
Hunt. Behav.	Hunting Behavior	121	Techniques and behavioral patterns used by bald eagles to catch prey. (See "Prey")
Hunt-Wesson		4	Food Corporation.
Hurricane		6	Tropical storm, accompanied by rain, lightning.
IA	Iowa	45	
ID	Idaho	19	
IL	Illinois	87	
Illinois R.		23	Illinois.
-	Immature	-	(See "Aging")
IN	Indiana	9	
Indian Culture		11	Role played by eagle and/or feathers in ceremonial and other practices of the American Indian.
Intersp. Behav.	Interspecific Behavior	77	Interaction between bald eagles and other species, including man.
Intrasp. Behav.	Intraspecific Behavior	23	Interaction between bald eagles.
Ireland		1	
Itasca SP		4	Minnesota.
IUCN	International Union for the Conservation of Nature and Natural Resources	1	
Jackson's Canyon		6	Wyoming.

KEYWORD	FULL WORD	NO. OCCUR-RENCES	DEFINITION OR LOCATION
Kalamazoo R		1	Michigan.
Karl Mundt NWR		7	South Dakota.
Karyotype		1	Sum of the characteristics of the chromosomes of a cell.
Kentucky Wood. NWR	Kentucky Wood-lands NWR	3	Kentucky.
Kepone		1	Organochlorine pesticide. (See "Pest.")
Kings Canyon NP		1	California.
Kissimee B.E. Sanct.	Kissimee Bald Eagle Sanctuary	2	Florida.
Klamath		2	Oregon/California.
Klamath NF		1	California.
Klamath R		1	Oregon/California.
Kluane Game Sanct.	Kluane Game Sanctuary	1	Yukon Territory.
Kodiak Is.		1	Alaska.
Kodiak NWR		4	Alaska.
KS	Kansas	10	
KY	Kentucky	37	
LA	Louisiana	21	
Lake of the Woods		1	Ontario.
L Andes NWR		4	South Dakota.
Land Between the Lakes		3	Kentucky.
L Apopka		2	Florida.

KEYWORD	FULL WORD	NO. OCCUR- RENCES	DEFINITION OR LOCATION
L Athabasca		1	Saskatchewan.
Lava Bed NM		1	California.
Law		84	Refers to various Acts and other legislation that involve the bald eagle; both protective and destructive.
LB	Labrador	2	
L Couer D'Alene		1	Idaho.
Lead Poison.	Lead Poisoning	4	Used when part or total cause of death or illness is shown to be lead. (See "Poison.")
L Erie		2	New York.
Life History		141	Covers, but not limited to, descriptive material concerning eggs, nest, plumage, range, prey and habitat.
Literature		2	Relates to broad-based coverage of previous literature; includes reviews.
L Ocklawaha		1	Florida.
Logging		8	Removal of trees from forest for economic gain. (See "Forestry")
-	Longevity	-	(See "Mortality" and "Pop. Turnover")
Lower 48	Lower 48 states	14	Used when more than 10 states are named specifically, such as in large-scale surveys.
Lower Klamath Lake NWR		2	California.
L Superior		1	Minnesota.
MA	Massachusetts	10	

KEYWORD	FULL WORD	NO. OCCUR-RENCES	DEFINITION OR LOCATION
Manage.	Management	175	Broad and general management techniques which can often be applied to a variety of raptor species; many references have been included which do not contain specific data on bald eagles.
Maritime Prov.	Maritime Provinces	1	Eastern Canada.
Marking		27	Includes activities such as the application of patagial wing markers, tarsal flags, coloring feathers, etc.
Mason Neck NWR		5	Virginia.
Mass. Spectro.	Mass Spectrometry	1	Analysis technique utilizing chromatograms.
Mattamuskett NWR		1	North Carolina.
MB	Manitoba	9	
McHarghian Overlay		1	Architectual or land-planning graphic technique used to indicate geographic areas of varying sensitivity to changes in land-use.
MD	Maryland	31	
ME	Maine	40	
Merritt Is. NWR		2	Florida.
MI	Michigan	62	
Midwest Region		1	Michigan, Wisconsin, Minnesota, Iowa, Illinois, Indiana.
Migration		113	To periodically move from one locality or climate to another for breeding, wintering and/or feeding purposes. (See "Band." and "Dispersal")
Mississippi R		7	

A14

KEYWORD	FULL WORD	NO. OCCUR-RENCES	DEFINITION OR LOCATION
Missouri R		20	
MN	Minnesota	125	
MO	Missouri	35	
Model		2	Statistical or computerized approach to analysis (and possibly prediction) of data, trends, etc.
Modoc NWR		1	California.
Molt.	Molting	3	Timing, or sequence of, feather loss and replacement. (See "Plumage")
Montezuma NWR		8	New York.
Mortality		20	Characterization of one or more cases of bald eagle death with causative factors usually identified. Also includes mortality rates. (See "Disease", "Trapping", "Shooting", "Poison." and other specific causative factors.)
MS	Mississippi	7	
MT	Montana	18	
Mt. Johnson Is. Sanct.	Mt. Johnson Is. Eagle Sanctuary	5	Pennsylvania.
Mt. Ranier NP		1	Washington.
Mud Lake NWR		1	Minnesota.
Museum Specimen		2	Reference to where one or more specimens are stored or details of specimen characteristics. (See "Anat.")
NAS	National Audubon Society	24	

KEYWORD	FULL WORD	NO. OCCUR-RENCES	DEFINITION OR LOCATION
Natl. For.	National Forest	2	
Nat. Conserv.	Nature Conservancy	4	
NB	New Brunswick	3	
NC	North Carolina	22	
ND	North Dakota	14	
NE	Nebraska	53	
Neosho R		1	Oklahoma.
Nest.	Nesting	534	Articles indicating casual accounts or bird lists usually not associated with an organized nesting survey. (See "Egg Coll.", "Reprod. Succ.", "Nest. Survey", and "Status")
Nest. Fail.	Nesting Failure	19	Documentation of unsuccessful nest(s) and/or discussion of reason(s) for this.
Nest. Survey	Nesting Survey	248	A regular, reasonably well organized survey by qualified professional investigators. (See "Reprod. Succ.", "Nest.", and "Status")
Nestling		12	Bird still in the nest.
New England		5	
NF	Newfoundland	3	
NH	New Hampshire	6	
NJ	New Jersey	40	
NM	New Mexico	12	
Nocturnal Behav.	Nocturnal Behavior	1	Characterization of behavior during the night.

KEYWORD	FULL WORD	NO. OCCUR-RENCES	DEFINITION OR LOCATION
Nongame Sp.	Nongame Species	1	References that deal with the bald eagle as part of a nongame program.
NS	Nova Scotia	4	
NV	Nevada	12	
NWF	National Wild-life Federation	30	
NWT	Northwest Territories	9	
NY	New York	44	
Oak V. Eagle Sanc.	Oak Valley Eagle Sanctuary	1	Illinois.
Ocala NF		2	Florida.
OH	Ohio	40	
Ohio R		4	
Okefinokee Swamp		2	Georgia.
OK	Oklahoma	16	
Old Abe		8	Historic bald eagle named after Abraham Lincoln: the mascot of the 8th Wisconsin Regiment during the mid 1800's.
ON	Ontario	35	
Oneida L		1	New York
OR	Oregon	28	
Orme D		9	Arizona
Ottawa NF		2	Michigan.
PA	Pennsylvania	41	

KEYWORD	FULL WORD	NO. OCCUR-RENCES	DEFINITION OR LOCATION
Paleontology		11	Science dealing with the life of past geological periods as known from fossil remains.
Parasites		5	Organisms that feed on a host.
Parent. Behav.	Parental Behavior	6	Behavior relating to raising of the young.
PCB	Polychlorinated biphenyls	24	Chemicals used as plasticizers or extenders in a variety of products; also used in several electrical devices such as transformers.
Pellets		1	Undigestible material from prey, which is regurgitated.
Pest.	Pesticides	74	Primarily organochlorine pesticides, but could include organophosphates and carbamates.
PE	Prince Edwards Is.	1	
Pest. Residues	Pesticide Residues	3	Residues of pesticides found in bald eagles, their eggs, or prey.
Photo.	Photography	31	Refers to photographic techniques including blinds, etc., and opportunities for photography.
Phys.	Physiology	1	Science dealing with functions and activities of living matter.
Platte R		13	Nebraska.
Plumage		36	Description of feather structure or color.
Poetry		13	Poems about bald eagles and other unidentifiable eagle species.
Poison.	Poisoning	23	Resulting from poisoned bait or secondary poisoning by consuming animals that have become contaminated with lead, strychnine, thallium sulfate, etc. (See "Pred. Cont.", "Lead Poison.", and "Mortality")

A18

KEYWORD	FULL WORD	NO. OCCUR-RENCES	DEFINITION OR LOCATION
-	Polychlorinated biphenyls	-	(See "PCB").
Pop. Turnover	Population Turnover	2	Data and/or discussion of rate at which population is replaced. (See "Mortality")
Pred. Cont.	Predator Control	3	Efforts to kill eagles and other predators, usually for economic gain. (See "Poison.")
Prey		190	Reference which documents prey species taken by bald eagles. Also used when unique prey was taken. (See "Econ. Import." and "Depred.")
Pub. Ed.	Public Education	212	Denotes general articles and/or those that were oriented toward the public; not used with a "scientific" article.
Pymatuning		3	Pennsylvania.
QU	Quebec	1	
Raccoon Ridge		1	New Jersey.
Recovery Team		1	Official group of bald eagle experts designated by the U.S. Dept. of the Interior to determine the status of specific regional populations and recommend management and research.
Red Tide		1	A discoloration in the water caused by high concentrations of microorganisms; can have deleterious effects on fish populations.
Reelfoot L		10	Tennessee.
Refuge		38	Used to denote any sanctuary where the major emphasis is on the protection of bald eagles. (See "Habit. Prot.")

KEYWORD	FULL WORD	NO. OCCUR- RENCES	DEFINITION OR LOCATION
Rehab.	Rehabilitation	26	Organized efforts to systematically rehabilitate bald eagles; also used with references that deal with a specific raptor rehabilitation technique which could be applicable to the bald eagle.
Reintro- duction		1	Release into the wild which does not involve hacking. (See "Hacking")
Reprod. Succ.	Reproductive Success	58	Data provided on the number of successful nesting attempts relative to total attempts; also used when relative data are provided on number of young successfully produced. (See "Nest.", "Nest. Survey", and "Status")
Research		6	Used sparingly with references that specifically address research needs.
Residues		3	Chemical residues of environmental pollutants found in bald eagles. (See "Pest.", "PCB", and "Heavy Metals")
Reward		6	Used in conjunction with management programs which provide a reward for information on bald eagle killers.
RI	Rhode Island	2	
RIC	Raptor Infor- mation Center	9	National Wildlife Federation.
Road Plan.	Road Planning	1	Planning techniques which can be used to lay out road systems so as to minimize the impact on bald eagle habitat.
Road. Census	Roadside Census	9	Survey which involves primarily counting birds which can be seen from the road (usually from a vehicle).
Rocky Mt. Region		1	

KEYWORD	FULL WORD	NO. OCCUR-RENCES	DEFINITION OR LOCATION
Rodman Reservoir		1	Florida.
-	Roosting	-	(See "Winter. Pop." and "Winter Survey")
Salt R		3	Arizona.
Salt Fork R		4	Oklahoma.
Salt Plains NWR		3	Oklahoma.
San Bernardino Mts.		2	California.
San Clemente Is.		3	California.
-	Sanctuary	-	(See "Refuge")
Sandy Hook		1	New Jersey.
San Juan Is.		11	Washington.
San Luis Valley		3	Colorado.
Santa Barbara Is.		4	California.
Santa Cruz		1	California.
Sapelo Is.		2	Georgia.
Savanna NWR		1	Georgia.
SC	South Carolina	17	
SD	South Dakota	29	
Seney NWR		1	Michigan.
Sequoia NP		1	California.
Sequoyah NWR		2	Oklahoma.
-	Seven-Eleven	-	(See "Southland")
Sexing		2	Technique(s) used to determine the sex of a bald eagle.

KEYWORD	FULL WORD	NO. OCCUR-RENCES	DEFINITION OR LOCATION
Shasta-Trinity NF		1	California.
Shooting		125	Refers to the shooting of bald eagles. (See "Bounty" and "Mortality")
SK	Saskatchewan	23	
Skagit R		6	Washington.
Skagit R Nat. Area	Skagit River Bald Eagle Natural Area	3	Washington.
Snake R		3	Idaho.
Southland		1	Parent corporation of Seven-Eleven stores, which has been involved in habitat protection. (See "Habit. Prot.")
Spermato.	Spermatogenesis	3	Formation of sperm.
Squaw Creek NWR		2	Missouri.
St. Croix R		1	Minnesota, Wisconsin.
Statistics		2	Mathematical technique for the analysis of data.
Status		266	Used in conjunction with references that emphasize a discussion on the status of the bald eagle; also used when several years of survey data are presented. (See "Reprod. Succ.", "Nest.", "Nest. Survey" and "Endang. Sp.")
Steroids		1	Biologically active enzymes which play an important role in reproduction.
Superior NF		5	Minnesota.
Susquehanna R		2	Pennsylvania.
Swan Lake NWR		2	Missouri.

KEYWORD	FULL WORD	NO. OCCUR-RENCES	DEFINITION OR LOCATION
Swimming		1	Swimming as a bald eagle behavior.
Symbolism		30	Using the bald eagle (and other eagle species) to express or represent the intangible.
Tamarac NWR		1	Minnesota.
Taxidermy		1	Art of preparing and mounting the skins of animals.
Taxonomy		57	Scientific classification of the bald eagle.
Techniques		185	Methods of problem-solving which meet specific research needs.
Telemetry		20	Use of radio sending and tracking equipment.
Tennessee NWR		1	Tennessee.
Terminology		11	Discussion of the use or misuse of terms; efforts to try to establish standard terminology.
Terra Nova NP		1	Newfoundland.
Territory		25	Geographic area which is defended.
Three Lakes Ranch		2	Florida.
Three Sisters B.E. Pres.	Three Sisters Bald Eagle Preserve	2	California.
TN	Tennessee	30	
Toxicol.	Toxicology	13	Science dealing with poisons and their effects. (See "Poison.")
Trapping		18	Incidental and/or accidental trapping of bald eagles when traps were set for other species such as furbearers. Does not include capture techniques. (See "Capture" and "Mortality")

KEYWORD	FULL WORD	NO. OCCUR- RENCES	DEFINITION OR LOCATION
Tule Lake NWR		2	California.
TVA		3	Tennessee Valley Authority.
TX	Texas	30	
Upper Miss.	Upper Mississ- ippi River	1	Iowa, Minnesota.
Upper Miss. NWR	Upper Mississ- ippi River NWR	1	Wisconsin.
USFWS	United States Fish and Wild- life Service	55	U.S. Department of the Interior.
USFS	United States Forest Service	52	U.S. Department of Agriculture.
UT	Utah	14	
VA	Virginia	35	
Vancouver Is.		1	British Columbia.
Verde R		8	Arizona.
Vocal.	Vocalization	2	Instances of sounds made by bald eagles.
WA	Washington	53	
Wash. Dept. Game	Washington Dept. of Game	1	
Weight		2	Data on weight of bald eagle(s).
Wheeler NWR		1	Alabama.
WI	Wisconsin	63	
Wichita Mts. NWR		2	Kansas.
Wilson Ornithol. Soc.	Wilson Ornitho- logical Society	1	
Winter Survey		172	Used to describe regular and orga- nized efforts usually by qualified observers or organizations, to

A24

KEYWORD	FULL WORD	NO. OCCUR- RENCES	DEFINITION OR LOCATION
Winter Survey (continued)			document numbers of bald eagles on specific wintering grounds, often repeated each year in a systematic fashion.
Winter. Pop.	Wintering Population	258	Used with casual observations and/or accounts of bald eagles on their wintering grounds; numbers or other documentation often not provided.
Wisconsin R		6	Wisconsin.
Wolf Lodge Bay		1	Idaho.
WV	West Virginia	8	
WY	Wyoming	35	
Yellowstone NP		13	Wyoming.
Young Trans.	Young Transplant	19	Management technique that involves taking young from a usually healthy population and moving it to a less healthy one to be raised by foster parents.
YT	Yukon Territory	4	